Frank Leslie

The soldier in our Civil War

A pictorial history of the conflict, 1861-1865

Frank Leslie

The soldier in our Civil War
A pictorial history of the conflict, 1861-1865

ISBN/EAN: 9783337135515

Printed in Europe, USA, Canada, Australia, Japan

Cover: Foto ©ninafisch / pixelio.de

More available books at **www.hansebooks.com**

Frank Leslie's

ILLUSTRATIONS

THE SOLDIER IN OUR CIVIL WAR:

COLUMBIAN MEMORIAL EDITION.

A PICTORIAL HISTORY OF THE CONFLICT, 1861–1865,

ILLUSTRATING THE VALOR OF THE SOLDIER AS DISPLAYED ON THE BATTLE FIELD.

FROM SKETCHES DRAWN BY

FORBES, WAUD, TAYLOR, HILLEN, BECKER, LOVIE, SCHELL, CRANE, DAVIS,

And numerous other Eye-witnesses to the Strife.

EDITED BY

PAUL F. MOTTELAY and T. CAMPBELL-COPELAND.

ASSISTED BY THE MOST NOTABLE GENERALS AND COMMANDERS OF BOTH SIDES.

WITH AN INTRODUCTION BY

ROBERT B. BEATH,

PAST COMMANDER-IN-CHIEF GRAND ARMY OF THE REPUBLIC.

HISTORY OF THE GRAND ARMY OF THE REPUBLIC, BY PAUL VANDERVOORT, PAST COMMANDER-IN-CHIEF.

HISTORY OF THE CONFEDERATE VETERANS' ASSOCIATION, BY COL. I. W. AVERY, ATLANTA, GEORGIA.

HISTORY OF THE SONS OF VETERANS, BY A. P. DAVIS, ORIGINATOR, AND BY FRANK P. MERRILL, COMMANDER-IN-CHIEF.

Valuable information has been contributed and courtesies extended by Generals GRANT, HANCOCK, LOGAN, Brevet Maj.-Gen. (S. N. Y.), J. WATTS DE PEYSTER, Generals BEAUREGARD, FITZHUGH LEE, LONGSTREET, EARLY, Captain WADDELL, late of the C. S. Navy, War and Navy Departments, etc

VOL. I.

NEW YORK AND ATLANTA, GA.:

STANLEY BRADLEY PUBLISHING COMPANY,

1893.

SOLD ONLY BY SUBSCRIPTION.

This Book is Dedicated

To the Veteran Soldier—the Hero of these Volumes—and
To the Sons of Veterans who Keep Green the Memory of their
Fathers' Sacrifice on the Battle-Fields of
Our Civil War.

INTRODUCTION.

NEARLY a generation has passed since the armies and navies of citizen-soldiers who had survived the hardships of over four years of War were mustered out and returned to their homes to enjoy the full fruits of peace in a united Republic.

On one side had been gathered over two millions of men, on the other nearly every available man who could be put to service in the field, together forming an army numbering nearly four millions.

The survivors of the conflict are fast passing away, and a new generation is forming, to whom the great events of those years of bloodshed can be but a faint memory, or "as a tale that is told."

Yet, until deeds of daring, and patriotism, and suffering cease to enlist admiration and sympathy, will the services of our soldiers and sailors be the theme of song and story that will longest command the thought and attention of our people; for did not nearly every family contribute its quota to the War, and have not all shared in the accepted results?

The graves of the dead of North and South, marked each year by loving hands with flowers of spring-time, the sufferings of the thousands yet living, have evoked a broad bond of sympathy that, with the cheerful acceptance of the duties of citizenship by the men of all sections, has long ago wiped out personal animosities, if, indeed, such existed, and all good men, no matter how divided in opinion from 1861 to 1865, join in devotion to a common country that stood such fearful tests as the struggles of the armies of Grant and Lee.

Each participant in the stirring scenes of the War could carry with him but few of the details that contributed to the formation of a grand History that will, through all time, testify to a devotion and bravery never surpassed and never to be forgotten.

Herein are to be gathered facts and figures as demonstrated and proven by years of research. Herein will be placed in an enduring form, as a supplement to histories already written, the incidents of battle; and here will be pictured the heroes whose forms and faces gave inspiration to the artist's pencil on the scene of strife.

The old soldier by his quiet fireside, surrounded by family and friends, will turn these pages and be vividly reminded of a thousand incidents of army life, and all will here find inspiration for increased devotion to a country worthy of all the sacrifices made in its behalf.

ROBERT B. BEATH.

INDEXED LIST

OF

DOUBLE-PAGE ILLUSTRATIONS.

VOL. I.

	Pages
Alabama, Confederate Privateer, View of Prisoners in the hold of	402-403
Alexandria, Camp, Washington, D. C.	166-167
Antietam (Sharpsburg), Battle of	386-387
Arkansas, Confederate Ram, Naval Engagement of, with the U. S. Gunboat *Carondelet*	374-375
Battle of Antietam, September 17th, 1862	386-387
" Bull Run (the First), July 21st, 1861	106-107
" " (the Second), Aug. 30th, 1862	378-379
" Cross Keys, June 8th, 1862	330-331
" Fort Donelson, February 15th, 1862	238-239
" " " "	254-255
" Gaines's Mills, June 27th, 1862	358-359
" Malvern Hill, July 1st, 1862 346-347	370-371
" Mill Spring (Logan's Cross Roads)	222-223
" Pea Ridge, March 6th, 1862	186-187
" Pittsburg Landing, April 6th, 1862	266-267
" " " "	274-275
" Port Republic, June 9th, 1862	330-331
" Rich Mountain, July 12th, 1861	98-99
" Roanoke Island, February 8th, 1862	202-203
" Savage's Station, June 29th, 1862	362-363
" Secessionville, June 16th, 1862	334-335
" Slaughter's Mountain, Aug. 9th 1862	302-303
" White Oak Swamp, June 30th, 1862	342-343
" Willis Church, June 30th, 1862	338-339
" Wilson's Creek (Oak Hill)	114-115
" Winchester, March 23d, 1862	322-323
Battles Fought in the Chickahominy Valley, The Scene of	354-355
Bombardment of Fort Hatteras, Pamlico Sound, N. C.	122-123
Bombardment of Fort Sumter, Charleston Harbor	34-35
Bombardment of Fort Walker, by Federal Fleet	174-175
" Island No. 10	258-259
Bull Run, The First Battle of	106-107
" The Second Battle of	378-379
Burning of the Gosport Navy Yard, Norfolk, Va.	62-63
Camp Alexandria, at Washington, D. C.	166-167
Carondelet, U. S. Gunboat, Engagement with the Confederate Ram *Arkansas*	374-375
Castle Pinckney, Charleston Harbor	46-47
Charleston City and Harbor, View of	34-35
Chickahominy, Scene of the Six Battles Fought in the Valley of	354-355
Commissariat Depot of the United States Army of the Rappahannock, Manassas, Va.	354-355
Confederate Battery at Harper's Ferry, Va.	394-395
Confederate Garrison, Retreat of, From Fort Walker	174-175
Confederate Prisoners Brought into the Captured Camp, behind Fort Huger, Roanoke Island	210-211
Confederate Ram *Arkansas*—Engagement with U. S. Gunboat *Carondelet*	374-375
Corcoran, General Michael, Reception of, at New York City	374-375
Corinth, Miss., Scene at Lick Creek Bottom	282-283
Cotton Gathering, Packing and Shipping	182-183
Cross Keys, Battle of	330-331
Departure of Ellsworth's Zouaves from New York	74-75
Donelson, Fort, Charge of the Second Iowa Regiment	238-239
Donelson, Fort, Gallant Charge of the Seventeenth, Forty-eighth and Forty-ninth, Illinois Vols.	254-255
Edwards's Ferry, Va., Retreat of the Federal Troops	150-151
Ellsworth Zouaves, Encampment of the, Washington, D. C.	74-75
Engagement at Romney, Va.—The Eleventh Indiana Zouaves Crossing the Potomac	86-87
Evacuation of Fort Moultrie	26-27
Fort Donelson, 238-239	254-255
" Hatteras	122-123
" Henry	230-231
" Huger	210-211
" Moultrie, 26-27	30-31
" Pickens	46-47
" Pinckney (Castle)	46-47
" Pulaski	290-291
" Sumter	34-35
" Thompson	218-219
" Walker	174-175
Fortifications at Hilton Head	290-291
Forty-eighth and Forty-ninth Illinois Volunteers, Charge of, at Fort Donelson	254-255
Gaines's Mills, Battle of	358-359
Gosport Navy Yard, Burning of	62-63
Grafton, Va., View of McClellan's Headquarters at	86-87
Hampton Roads, Naval Engagement in	246-247
Harper's Ferry, Confederate Battery at	394-395
Harrisonburg to Port Republic, Battle on the Road from	330-331
Harrison's Landing, James River, Va.	350-351
Hawkins's Zouaves at the Battle of Antietam	386-387
Henry Fort, Bursting of a 42 pound Gun in	230-231
Hilton Head Island, Government Works at, 186-187	218-219
" " View of Fortifications	290-291
Hooker, General, Engaging the Confederate Army at Malvern Hill	370-371
Horse Depot, near Washington	158-159
Island No. 10, Bombardment and Night Attack on	258-259
Jackson (Stonewall), Commencing his Great Flank Movement	378-379
James Island, Repulse of the Confederate Troops	314-315
Lexington, Mo., Siege of	130-131
Lick Creek Bottom, Corinth, Miss., Scene at	282-283
Lincoln, President, Members of the First Cabinet of	14-15
Lincoln Reviewing Troops in Washington	146-147
Logan's Cross Roads, Battle of	222-223
Manassas, Va., Commissariat Depot of U. S. Army of the Rappahannock	354-355
Malvern Hill, Battle of	346-347
Malvern Hill, General Hooker Engages the Confederate Army at	370-371
McClellan's Headquarters at Grafton, Va.	86-87
Merrimack and *Monitor*, Engagement in Hampton Roads between the	246-247
Military Execution	104-105
Mill Spring, Battle of	222-223
Naval Battles in Hampton Roads, Va.	246-247
New Berne, North Carolina, from the Interior of Fort Thompson	218-219
New Orleans, Panoramic View of	298-299
Oak Hill, Battle of	114-115
Pamlico Sound—Bombardment of Fort Hatteras	122-123
Pea Ridge, Battle of	186-187
Pennsylvania Bucktails, Gallant Attack of, upon a Detachment of "Stonewall" Jackson's Army	314-315
Pickens, Fort, Relief of, by U. S. Fleet	46-47
Pinckney, Castle, Charleston Harbor	46-47
Pittsburg Landing, Battle of—General Lewis Wallace's Division on the Right Wing	266-267
Pittsburg Landing—Final Stand of Grant's Army	274-275
Pontooning, Experimental Practice in	166-167
Port Republic, Battle of	330-331
President Lincoln and his Cabinet Reviewing Troops	146-147
Privateer, *Alabama*, Prisoners in Hold of	402-403
Pulaski, Fort—Mortar Battery "Stanton" Throwing a 13 inch Shell	290-291
Retreat of Federal Troops from Edwards's Ferry	150-151
Retreat of Confederate Troops from Fort Walker	174-175
Review of South Carolina Volunteers in Fort Moultrie, Charleston Harbor	30-31
Rich Mountain, Battle of	98-99
Roanoke Island, Battle of	202-203
Romney, Va., Engagement at	86-87
Santa Rosa Island—Relief of Fort Pickens	46-47
Savage's Station, Battle of	362-363
Savannah, Ga., Flight of the Inhabitants of	286-287
Secessionville, Battle of	334-335
Second Iowa Regiment at Fort Donelson	238-239
Seventeenth Illinois Volunteers, Charge of, at Fort Donelson	254-255
Sharpsburg (Antietam), Battle of	386-387
Sharpshooters' Trial of Skill at Washington	138-139
Siege of Lexington, Mo.	130-131
Sixth Massachusetts Regiment Repelling Mob at Baltimore	58-59
Slaughter's Mountain, Battle of	302-303
South Carolina Volunteers Reviewed at Fort Moultrie	30-31
Star of the West, United States Steamer, Fired upon from Fort Moultrie	26-27
Tiptonville Tenn.—Surrender of the Confederate Forces, under Generals McCall and Gantt, to General Paine	306-307
View of Grafton, Va., on the Monongahela River, Headquarters of General McClellan	86-87
View of the City and Harbor of Charleston, S. C.	34-35
Walker, Fort, Retreat of the Confederate Garrison	174-175
Wallace, General Lewis, at the Battle of Pittsburg Landing	266-267
White House, Va., Burning of	350-351
Willis Church, Battle of	338-339
Wilson's Creek or Oak Hill, Battle of	114-115
Winchester, Va., Battle of	322-323
Zouaves, Ellsworth's, Departure of, from New York, and Encampment at Washington, D. C.	74-75
Zouaves, Hawkins's, Charge on Confederate Batteries at Antietam	386-387

PREFACE.

AFTER twenty years, the memory of our Civil War fails to carry in detail the events that ushered in that event. The actors, one by one, are disappearing from the stage. The echo of the first gun fired at Sumter, and which called to arms and to deadly strife two sections of one great country, has become so faint as to be scarce a memory. The bloody chasm that run with the best blood and embraced in its unrelenting arms the precious bodies of gallant men who gave up blood and life for country and fireside, each equally conscious of the righteousness of their cause, has long since been filled with the roses heaped so profusely by both the "Blue" and the "Gray" on the graves of their departed comrades. Each passing year discloses some new-found beauty in the wealth of experience gained amid these scenes of strife.

There were 4,000,000 active, efficient, hardy soldiers, who did service, not for honor, glory, or reward, but to defend their firesides. They fought from a consciousness of duty, and were equally patriotic whether they marched under the "stars" or under the "bars," and these are the subjects, the authors, the actors, the heroes of our Book. It took soldiers massed together, willing to obey the orders of their commanders, and to face death at every step, to make an army. We picture these soldier-heroes—their faces gave the artists the inspiration that enabled them to make these battle scenes true to life. These pictures were made amid the very scenes they so vividly illustrate, and are now first published in a form to be preserved and supplement the histories already written. We aim to record only facts as demonstrated and proven by twenty-five years' historical research. We give no cause, no excuse, no apology for defeat, and no reason for victory. "The War for Independence" and "The War of the Rebellion" has no place in our book. We only care to illustrate the valor, patriotism, and bravery of the soldier as developed by and illustrated in the war. We gather from both parties to the strife the incidents of battle, and seek only to perpetuate their memories, as they serve to show our children and our children's children that whether their father wore the "blue" or the "gray," he was equally brave and honest in his efforts to defeat the foe hurled against him and his standard on the battle-field.

Prejudice, hatred, animosity, and revenge are of the past. Let us bury each, and looking beyond the political questions of that day, behold the spectacle of THE WAR as witnessed by the world, and proclaim the sons of the eight hundred thousand veteran soldiers as ready and able to defend their common country against the combined armies of the earth.

THE SOLDIER IN OUR CIVIL WAR.

SUMMARY OF LEADING EVENTS.

NOVEMBER, 1860—*MARCH*, 1861.

ON the 6th day of November, 1860, a general election for President and Vice-President of the United States took place which resulted in the choice of Abraham Lincoln, of Illinois, as President, and Hannibal Hamlin, of Maine, as Vice-President. Mr. Lincoln, besides receiving the majority vote of the Electoral College, had a popular majority of 48[illegible] votes over Mr. Douglas, 1,000,057 over Mr. Breckinridge, and 1,266,979 over Mr. Bell.

At this time the inhabitants of the Slaveholder States numbered about 12,000,000, of which nearly 4,000,000 were held as slaves.

The ruling class—those who exercised and controlled the political power as voters numbered about 1,000,000; of these, the large land and slave holders held an almost supreme influence, and of this class there were barely 200,000. Less than 170,000 men in the whole Slaveholding States owned 2,800,000 of the slaves; the remaining 11,830,000 owned but 500,000 slaves, and were counted as exercising but little influence in the councils of the Government, and were classed in round numbers as follows: 6,800,000 small slaveholders, non-slaveholders, mechanics and laboring men; 1,000,000 known in these regions by the common name of "poor white trash," scattered over those States; 4,000,000 of slaves.

The production of the great staple of cotton, regarded by them as "King," was in the hands of less than 200,000 men.

President Lincoln, in his first annual Message to Congress assembled in extra session, July 5th, (1861) describes this condition of the body-politic of the Southern States, and the subtlety of the conspirators in leading the masses to support their plans, in these words (we quote from Raymond's "Life of Lincoln," page 193): "It might seem at first thought to be of little difference whether the present movement at the South be called 'secession' or 'rebellion.' The movers, however, well understood the difference. At the beginning they knew

RECEPTION AT CHARLESTON, S. C., OF THE NEWS OF THE ELECTION OF LINCOLN AND HAMLIN, NOVEMBER, 1860.

Hon. Simon Cameron, of Pennsylvania, Secretary of War.
Hon. Salmon P. Chase, of Ohio, Secretary of the Treasury.

Hon. Gideon Welles, of Connecticut, Secretary of the Navy.
Hon. William H. Seward, of New York, Secretary of State.
Hon. Montgomery Blair, of Maryland, Postmaster-general.

Hon. Caleb B. Smith, of Indiana, Secretary of the Interior.
Hon. Edward Bates, of Missouri, Attorney-general.

THE MEMBERS OF LINCOLN'S FIRST CABINET

THE MEMBERS OF LINCOLN'S [illegible] CABINET

they could never raise their treason to any respectable magnitude by any name which implies violation of law. They knew their people possessed as much of moral sense, as much of devotion to law and order, and as much pride in, and reverence for, the history and Government of their common country as any other civilized and patriotic people. They knew they could make no advancement directly in the teeth of these strong and noble sentiments. Accordingly, they commenced by an insidious debauching of the public mind. They invented an ingenious sophism, which, if conceded, was followed by perfectly logical steps, through all the incidents, to the complete destruction of the Union. The sophism itself is, that any State of the Union may, consistently with the national Constitution, and, therefore, lawfully and peacefully, withdraw from the Union without the consent of the Union, or of any other State. The little disguise that the supposed right is to be exercised for just cause, themselves to be the sole judges of its justice, is too thin to merit any notice.

"With rebellion thus sugar-coated,* they have been drugging the public mind of their section for more than thirty years, until at length they have brought many good men to a willingness to take up arms against the Government, the day after some assemblage of men have enacted the farcical pretense of taking their State out of the Union, who could have been brought to no such thing the day before." We find in this first Message of Mr. Lincoln so much of wisdom, moderation and justice, that we are tempted to quote it entire, but will in passing give from page 196 his tribute to the citizen-volunteer soldier, used as an argument against the sophistry of secession: "So large an army as the Government has now on foot (July 5th, 1861) was never before known without a soldier in it, but who had taken his place there of his own free choice. But more than this: there are many single regiments whose members, one and another, possess full practical knowledge of all the arts, sciences, professions, and whatever else, whether useful or elegant, is known in the world; and there is scarcely one from which there could not be selected a President, a Cabinet, a Congress, and perhaps a Court, abundantly capable to administer the Government itself. Nor do I say this is not true also in the army of our late friends, now adversaries in this contest; but, if it is so, so much better the reason why the Government which has conferred such benefits on both them and us should not be broken up."

On November 7th, 1860, the news of Lincoln's election reached the South, the Palmetto Flag was raised in Charleston, and indignation meetings were held in many leading Southern cities. In Charleston, the Governor and Council of South Carolina met in secret session, and cheers were given for the *Southern Confederacy*.

The same day, by order of the Secretary of War, Major Fitz John Porter, A. A. G., made an inspection of the forts and garrisons in Charleston Harbor, which led to the immediate assignment of Major Robert Anderson to the command of these defenses, with a policy confidentially defined by Lieutenant-general Scott. Colonel Gardner, then in command, undertook, after sundown, to draw surreptitiously from the Charleston Arsenal a supply of arms and ammunition absolutely needed for Fort Moultrie, but his attempt was discovered by the city authorities, and the officer in charge, Captain T. Seymour, was arrested, and the collected material was seized. Six days later, the State determined to raise and equip 10,000 volunteers, and a State Convention was called to decide the secession of South Carolina.

November, 1860.

The action of Georgia was no less prompt. The Governor of that State at once convened the Legislature, which on the 18th of November voted $1,000,000 to arm the State; a Bill was also passed ordering the election of delegates to a State Convention to assemble on the 9th of January following. The order was made, in the language of the Act, because "the present crisis in national affairs demands resistance."

The Governor of Mississippi issued his proclamation convening the State Legislature for the 26th of November, in which he set forth that "the recent election of Messrs. Lincoln and Hamlin demonstrates that those who neither reverence the Constitution, obey the laws, nor regard their oaths, have now the power to elect to the highest offices in the Confederacy men who sympathize with them in all their zeal to destroy the peace, property and prosperity of the Southern section, and who will use the powers of the Federal Government to defeat all the purposes for which it was formed."

The Governor of Louisiana convened the Legislature of that State on December 10th. The Florida Legislature ordered a State Convention for December 1st, and the Governor of Alabama, after proclaiming the right as well as the necessity of secession, and declaring that "if a State withdraws from the Union, the Federal Government has no power under the Constitution to use military force against her." Virginia, under the call of Governor Letcher, also took steps for a State Convention, her Legislature ordering the same for January 7th, 1861.

On December 26th, 1860, Major Anderson evacuated Fort Moultrie, and occupied Fort Sumter in Charleston Harbor.

At about the same time, Forts Pulaski and Jackson, in the harbor of Savannah; Forts Gaines and Morgan at Mobile; Forts St. Philip and Jackson

THE PALMETTO FLAG.

in the Mississippi, below New Orleans; Forts Barrancas and McRae at Pensacola; Fort Clinch at Fernandina, and Forts Caswell and Johnson at Macon in North Carolina; the Mint and Custom House at New Orleans; the arsenal at Little Rock, Arkansas, etc., etc., were all seized by the State authorities. The various forts in Texas, built and manned by the national troops, as defenses against Indian incursions, also fell into the hands of the State authorities, chiefly through the treachery of General Twiggs, of Georgia, who was next in rank to Lieutenant-general Scott in the United States Army. He so dispersed and arranged the forces under his command as to make them easily overcome. He was successful in making over all the valuable materials of war—guns, ammunition, and supplies of all sorts, amounting in value to several millions of dollars. He had been placed in command of the Department of Texas only a few weeks before, by the same influence exerted in the War Department that made the other Southern departments and fortifications an easy prey to the Confederacy. For forty years General Twiggs had acceptably served his Government, and had at all times been honored with its confidence. He, now that he had determined to desert his flag, tried to seduce his officers from their allegiance, by representing the Government as unable to maintain its authority over the Southern States, closing with the assertion, "The Union will be at an end in less than sixty days, and if you have any pay due you, you had better get it at once, for it is the last you will ever get."

Intimations of the disloyalty of General Twiggs had reached Secretary of War Holt on the 18th of January, and in a general order the veteran officer was relieved from the command of the Department of Texas. This order was one of the most decisive as well as inspiring acts of the administration. The Secretary of War gives in his order as the reason for this action, "his [Twiggs's] treachery to the flag of his country, in having surrendered the United military posts and other property of the States, in his department and under his charge."

It is not supposed that all these proceedings were carried out with the unanimous concurrence of the people of the South. In Georgia, Alexander H. Stephens, subsequently made Vice-President of the Southern Confederacy, with many others, sought to stem the current, and by counseling delay and moderation, to prevent the consummation of the scheme of "precipitating the Cotton States into revolution." But the revolutionary leaders well understood the danger of delay, and hesitated at no measure or expedient to coerce the calm and patriotic portion of the population into their measures, and they successfully undertook to overawe and silence all opposition to immediate disunion.

INAUGURATION OF PRESIDENT LINCOLN.

MR. LINCOLN'S trip from his home in Springfield, Illinois, to the National Capital, had been, in the Northern States, one continuous ovation and hearty God-speed from the people. The spirit of opposition first manifested itself in the determination of insurgents in Maryland to prevent the President-elect from passing through their State. This opposition was cheated of its purpose by strategy, and Mr. Lincoln safely arrived at the capital some hours before his presence was announced.

The ceremony of Inauguration took place, as usual, in front of the Capitol, and in presence of an immense multitude of spectators. The oath of office was administered by Chief-Justice Taney, and immediately Mr. Lincoln read his Inaugural Address. We quote from this State Paper some of the passages, as indicating the plans, purposes and intentions of the President, as affecting the discontented element now actively engaged in revolution. Time has long since shown the wisdom, forethought, and eminent patriotism of Mr. Lincoln, and his State Paper now reads like words of inspiration:

March, 1861.

INAUGURAL ADDRESS.

"*Fellow-Citizens of the United States:*

"In compliance with a custom as old as the Government itself, I appear before you to address you briefly, and to take in your presence the oath prescribed by the Constitution of the United States to be taken by the President 'before he enters on the execution of his office.'

"I do not consider it necessary at present for me to discuss those matters of administration about which there is no special anxiety or excitement.

"Apprehension seems to exist, among the people of the Southern States, that by the accession of a Republican Administration their property and their peace and personal security are to be endangered. There has never been any reasonable cause for such apprehension. Indeed, the most ample evidence to the contrary has all the while existed and been open to their inspection. It is found in nearly all the published speeches of him who now addresses you. I do but quote from one of those speeches when I declare that 'I have no purpose, directly or indirectly, to interfere with the institution of slavery in the States where it exists. I believe I have no lawful right to do so, and I have no inclination to do so.'

* * * * * * *

"I take the official oath to-day with no mental reservation, and with no purpose to construe the Constitution or laws by any hypercritical rules. And while I do not choose now to specify particular Acts of Congress as proper to be enforced, I do suggest that it will be much safer for all, both in official and private stations, to conform to and abide by all those Acts which stand unrepealed, than to violate any of them, trusting to find impunity in having them held to be unconstitutional.

"It is seventy-two years since the first inauguration of a President under our National Constitution. During that period, fifteen different and greatly distinguished citizens have, in succession, administered the Executive branch of the Government. They have conducted it through many perils, and generally with great success. Yet, with all this scope for precedent, I now enter upon the same task for the brief constitutional term of four years, under great and peculiar difficulty. A disruption of the Federal Union, heretofore only menaced, is now formidably attempted.

"I hold that, in contemplation of universal law, and of the Constitution, *the Union of these States is perpetual*. Perpetuity is implied, if not expressed, in the fundamental law of all National Governments. It is safe to assert that no government proper ever had a provision in its organic law for its own termination. Continue to execute all the express provisions of our National Government, and the Union will endure for ever—it being impossible to destroy it, except by some action not provided for in the instrument itself.

"Again, if the United States be not a Government proper,

* Mr. Carpenter, in his "Six Months in the White House," relates the following anecdote concerning this word in the Message: "Mr. Defrees, the Government Printer, told me that when the Message was being printed, he was a good deal disturbed by the use of the term 'sugar coated,' and finally went to the President about it. Their relations to each other being of the most intimate character, he told Mr. Lincoln, frankly, that he ought to remember that a Message to Congress was a different affair from a speech at a mass meeting in Illinois—that the Messages became a part of history, and should be written accordingly. 'What is the matter now?' inquired the President. 'Why,' said Mr. Defrees, 'you have used an undignified expression in your Message'; and then, reading the paragraph aloud, he added, 'I would alter the structure of that, if I were you.' 'Defrees,' replied Mr. Lincoln, 'that word expresses precisely my idea, and I am not going to change it. The time will never come in this country when the people won't know exactly what *sugar-coated* means!'"

. . . an association of States in the nature of contract merely, can it, as a contract, be peaceably unmade by less than all the parties who made it? One party to a contract may violate it—break it, so to speak; but does it not require all to lawfully rescind it?

"Descending from these general principles, we find the proposition that, in legal contemplation, the Union is perpetual, confirmed by the history of the Union itself. The Union is much older than the Constitution. It was formed, in fact, by the Articles of Association in 1774. It was matured and continued by the Declaration of Independence in 1776. It was further matured, and the faith of all the then Thirteen States expressly plighted and engaged that it should be perpetual, by the Articles of Confederation in 1778. And, finally, in 1787, one of the declared objects for ordaining and establishing the Constitution was 'to form a more perfect union.' But if the destruction of the Union, by one, or by a part only, of the States, be lawfully possible, the Union is less perfect than before, the Constitution having lost the vital element of perpetuity.

"It follows, from these views, that no State, upon its own mere motion, can lawfully get out of the Union; that resolves and ordinances to that effect are legally void; and that acts of violence within any State or States, against the authority of the United States, are insurrectionary or revolutionary, according to circumstances.

"I, therefore, consider that, in view of the Constitution and the laws, the Union is unbroken, and to the extent of my ability, I shall take care, as the Constitution itself expressly enjoins upon me, that the laws of the Union be faithfully executed in all the States. Doing this I deem to be only a simple duty on my part; and I shall perform it, so far as practicable, unless my rightful master, the American people, shall withhold the requisite means, or, in some authoritative manner, direct the contrary. I trust this will not be regarded as a menace, but only as the declared purpose of the Union that it will constitutionally defend and maintain itself.

"In doing this there need be no bloodshed or violence; and there shall be none, unless it be forced upon the National authority. The power confided to me will be used to hold, occupy, and possess the property and places belonging to the Government, and to collect the duties and imposts; but beyond what may be but necessary for these objects, there will be no invasion, no using of force against or among the people anywhere.

* * * * * * *

"All profess to be content in the Union, if all constitutional rights can be maintained. Is it true, then, that any right, plainly written in the Constitution, has been denied? I think not. Happily the human mind is so constituted that no party can reach to the audacity of doing this. Think, if you can, of a single instance in which a plainly written provision of the Constitution has ever been denied. If, by the mere force of numbers, a majority should deprive a minority of any clearly written constitutional right, it might, in a moral point of view, justify revolution—certainly would if such right were a vital one. But such is not our case. All the vital rights of minorities and of individuals are so plainly assured to them by affirmations and negations, guarantees and prohibitions in the Constitution, that controversies never arise concerning them. But no organic law can ever be framed with a provision specifically applicable to every question which may occur in practical administration. No foresight can anticipate, nor any document of reasonable length contain, express provisions for all possible questions. Shall fugitives from labor be surrendered by National or by State authority? The Constitution does not expressly say. May Congress prohibit slavery in the Territories? The Constitution does not expressly say. Must Congress protect slavery in the Territories? The Constitution does not expressly say.

"From questions of this class spring all our constitutional controversies, and we divide upon them into majorities and minorities. If the minority will not acquiesce, the majority must, or the Government must cease. There is no other alternative; for continuing the Government is acquiescence on one side or the other. If a minority in such case will secede rather than acquiesce, they make a precedent which, in turn, will divide and ruin them; for a minority of their own will secede from them whenever a majority refuses to be controlled by such minority. For instance, why may not any portion of a new Confederacy, a year or two hence, arbitrarily secede again, precisely as portions of the present Union now claim to secede from it? All who cherish disunion sentiments are now being educated to the exact temper of doing this.

"Is there such perfect identity of interests among the States to compose a new Union, as to produce harmony only, and prevent renewed secession?

"Plainly, the central idea of secession is the essence of anarchy. A majority held in restraint by constitutional checks and limitations, and always changing easily with deliberate changes of popular opinions and sentiments, is the only true sovereign of a free people. Whoever rejects it, does, of necessity, fly to anarchy or to despotism. Unanimity is impossible; the rule of a minority, as a permanent arrangement, is wholly inadmissible; so that, rejecting the majority principle, anarchy or despotism, in some form, is all that is left.

* * * * * * *

"Physically speaking, we cannot separate. We cannot remove our respective sections from each other, nor build an impassable wall between them. A husband and wife may be divorced, and go out of the presence and beyond the reach of each other; but the different parts of our country cannot do this. They cannot but remain face to face; and intercourse, either amicable or hostile, must continue between them. It is impossible, then, to make that intercourse more advantageous or more satisfactory after separation than before. Can aliens make treaties easier than friends can make laws? Suppose you go to war, you cannot fight always; and when, after much loss on both sides, and no gain on either, you cease fighting, the identical old questions, as to terms of intercourse, are again upon you.

"This country, with its institutions, belongs to the people who inhabit it. Whenever they shall grow weary of the existing Government, they can exercise their constitutional right of amending it, or their revolutionary right to dismember or overthrow it.

* * * * * * *

"The Chief Magistrate derives all his authority from the people, and they have conferred none upon him to fix terms for the separation of the States. The people themselves can do this also if they choose; but the Executive, as such, has nothing to do with it. His duty is to administer the present Government as it came to his hands, and to transmit it, unimpaired by him, to his successor.

"Why should there not be a patient confidence in the ultimate justice of the people? Is there any better or equal hope in the world? In our present differences, is either party without faith of being in the right? If the Almighty Ruler of Nations, with His eternal truth and justice, be on your side of the North, or on yours of the South, that truth and that justice will surely prevail by the judgment of this great tribunal of the American people. By the frame of the Government under which we live, the same people have wisely given their public servants but little power for mischief; and have, with equal wisdom, provided for the return of that little to their own hands at very short intervals. While the people retain their virtue and vigilance, no Administration, by any extreme of wickedness or folly, can very seriously injure the Government in the short space of four years.

"My countrymen, one and all, think calmly and well upon this whole subject. Nothing valuable can be lost by taking time. If there be an object to hurry any of you in hot haste to a step which you would never take deliberately, that object will be frustrated by taking time; but no good object can be frustrated by it. Such of you as are now dissatisfied still have the old Constitution unimpaired, and, on the sensitive point, the laws of your own framing under it; while the new Administration will have no immediate power, if it would, to change either. If it were admitted that you who are dissatisfied hold the right side in the dispute, there still is no single good reason for precipitating action. Intelligence, patriotism, Christianity, and a firm reliance on Him who has never yet forsaken this favored land, are still competent to adjust in the best way, all our present difficulty.

"In your hands, my dissatisfied fellow-countrymen, and not in mine, is the momentous issue of civil war. The Government will not assail you.

"You can have no conflict without being yourselves the aggressors. You have no oath registered in heaven to destroy the Government; while I shall have the most solemn one to 'preserve, protect, and defend' it.

"I am loath to close. We are not enemies, but friends. We must not be enemies. Though passion may have strained it must not break, our bonds of affection.

"The mystic chords of memory, stretching from every battlefield and patriot-grave to every living heart and hearthstone all over this broad land, will yet swell the chorus of the Union, when again touched, as surely they will be, by the better angels of our nature."

EXTERIOR OF FORT MOULTRIE, ON SULLIVAN'S ISLAND, CHARLESTON HARBOR.

Raymond, in his "Life of Abraham Lincoln," says: "It was under trying circumstances that Mr. Lincoln entered upon the duties of his office. The declarations of his inaugural, as a general thing, gave satisfaction to the loyal people of the whole country.

"It was seen, everywhere, that while President Lincoln felt constrained, by the most solemn obligations of duty, to maintain the authority of the Government of the United States over all territory within its jurisdiction, whenever that authority should be disputed by the actual exercise of armed force, he would nevertheless do nothing whatever to provoke such a demonstration, and would take no step which would look like violence or offensive warfare upon the seceded States. In the Border States its reception was in the main satisfactory. But as a matter of course, in these States, as elsewhere throughout the South, the secession leaders gave it the most hostile co ction."

The President's first act was to construct his Cabinet, which was formed by the appointment of William H. Seward, of New York, Secretary of State; Salmon P. Chase, of Ohio, Secretary of the Treasury; Simon Cameron, of Pennsylvania, Secretary of War; Gideon Welles, of Connecticut, Secretary of the Navy; Caleb B. Smith, of Indiana, Secretary of the Interior; Montgomery Blair, of Maryland, Postmaster-general; and Edward Bates, of Missouri, Attorney-general. These nominations were all confirmed by the Senate, and the Cabinet entered upon the discharge of their several duties.

A SOUTHERN COMMISSION.

On the 12th of March, Messrs. John Forsyth, of Alabama, Martin J. Crawford, of Georgia, and A. B. Roman, of Louisiana, requested an unofficial interview with the Secretary of State, which the latter declined. On the 15th they sent to him a communication, informing him that they were in Washington as Commissioners for a Government composed of seven States which had withdrawn from the Union, and that they desired to enter upon negotiations for the adjustment of all questions growing out of this separation. Mr. Seward, by direction of the President, declined to see them, because it "could not be admitted that the States referred to had, in law or fact, withdrawn from the Federal Union, or that they could do so in any other manner than with the consent and concert of the people of the United States, to be given through a National Convention, to be assembled in conformity with the provisions of the Constitution of the United States." This communication,

APRIL, 1861.

though written on the 15th of March, was withheld, with the consent of the Commissioners, until April 8th, when it was delivered. The fact of its receipt, and its character, were instantly telegraphed to Charleston, and it was made the occasion for precipitating the revolution by an act which, it was believed, would unite all the Southern States in support of the Confederacy.

A. B. Roman, of Louisiana. John Forsyth, of Alabama. Martin J. Crawford, of Georgia.

THE COMMISSIONERS TO WASHINGTON FROM THE SOUTHERN CONFEDERACY.

THE DATES OF THE SECESSION OF THE CONFEDERATE STATES.

States.	*Secession.*	*Ratification.*
South Carolina	December 20th, 1860	April 3d, 1861.
Louisiana	December 23d, 1860.	March 21st, 1861
Mississippi	January 9th, 1861	March 30th, 1861
Alabama	January 11th, 1861	March 13th, 1861
Florida	January 11th, 1861	April 22d, 1861.
Georgia	January 19th, 1861	March 16th, 1861
Texas	February 1st, 1861	March 25th, 1861.
Arkansas	March 4th, 1861	May 19th, 1861.
Virginia	April 17th, 1861	——
Tennessee	May 6th, 1861	June 24th, 1861.
North Carolina	May 20th, 1861	May 20th, 1861.

JEFFERSON DAVIS.

JEFFERSON DAVIS.

JEFFERSON DAVIS was born June 3d, 1808, in Christian County, Ky.; graduated at West Point, 1828; served as lieutenant of infantry at Western posts, and on frontier service, from 1828 to 1834; resigned, 1835, and became a cotton-planter; chosen presidential elector from Mississippi, 1844; member of the United States House of Representatives, 1845-46; colonel First Mississippi Rifle Volunteers in the Mexican War, 1846-47; engaged at Monterey, and severely wounded at Buena Vista; member of United States Senate, 1847-51; Secretary of War in President Pierce's Cabinet, 1853-57; member of the United States Senate and Chairman of the Committee on Military Affairs, 1857 to 1861; President of the Southern Confederacy, February 18th, 1861; captured by the Federal troops, May 10th, 1865, at Irwinville, Ga.; prisoner of war, 1865-67, at Fortress Monroe, Virginia.

After his release he visited Europe, and on his return he took up his residence at Memphis, and became President of the Carolina Life Insurance Company. He afterward retired to his country place at Beauvoir, Miss., were he wrote his interpretation of the Civil War, under the title "Rise and Fall of the Confederate States," published in 1882 in two large volumes. He is still (1884) living in seclusion, and his name as his personality is almost forgotten in the rapid progress toward prosperity enjoyed and entered into by the wiser and less bitter of his *confrères*.

INAUGURATION OF JEFFERSON DAVIS.

THE inauguration of Jefferson Davis, as Provisional President of the Confederate States, took place at Montgomery, Alabama, February 18th, 1861, at noon, upon a platform erected in front of the portico of the State House. Three days before, at his home in Vicksburg, Miss., he had been notified of his election, and hastened to Montgomery, taking in his route Jackson, Grand Junction, Chattanooga, West Point, Columbus and Opelika. At each railroad station he was met by thousands of citizens, and in the route made twenty-five speeches. At the new capital, which Mr. Davis reached at ten o'clock at night, the ovation culminated. He was welcomed by the citizens eight miles outside the city, and escorted thither with the booming of cannon and the shouts of voices.

Escorted to the Exchange Hotel, he made a speech from the balcony to the assembled throng, addressing them as "Brethren of the Confederated States of America." His appearance at this late hour did not afford an opportunity for the people to see his face until two negroes, each with a candle, flanked him on either side, and reflected the flickering lights against his pale and anxious countenance. After the ceremony of Inauguration, Mr. Davis commenced to pronounce his Inaugural Address. He defended the right of secession, expressed his anxiety to cultivate peace and commerce, and said he hoped to avoid war, or at least to be acquitted by posterity of having needlessly engaged in it; justified the course of the Confederation by the entire absence of wrong on their part, and by wanton aggression on the part of others, which fact, he claimed, doubly insured their success; he averred that the world must have their agricultural productions, and that mutual interest would invite goodwill and kind offices, especially from the manufacturing and navigating States of the Union; adding, however, that if passion or lust of dominion should cloud the judgment or inflame the ambition of those States, then they must prepare to meet the emergency, and maintain, by the final arbitrament of the sword, that position they that day assumed among the nations of the earth.

Mr. Davis selected as his Cabinet, Robert Toombs, of Georgia, as Secretary of State; Charles G. Memminger, of South Carolina, as Secretary of the Treasury; Leroy Pope Walker, of Alabama, as Secretary of War; Stephen R. Mallory, of Florida, as Secretary of the Navy; and John H. Reagan, of Texas, as Postmaster-general. Afterward, Judah P. Benjamin, of Louisiana, was appointed Attorney-general; William M. Brown, late of the *Washington Constitution*, Assistant-Secretary of State, and Philip Clayton, of Georgia Assistant-Secretary of the Treasury.

THE FLAG OF THE CONFEDERACY.

Three stripes—the upper and lower red, the central white. Union blue extending to the top of lower stripe, with seven white stars

EVACUATION OF FORT MOULTRIE.

DECEMBER, 1860

WHEN the movements in Charleston Harbor following the election of Mr. Lincoln commenced, Castle Pinckney and Fort Sumter were without garrisons. The latter, indeed, was unfinished; Fort Moultrie was much out of repair. Its garrison consisted of two incomplete companies of the regular artillery, numbering only seventy men, including a band; all under the command of Colonel Gardner, who was early relieved by the appointment of Major Robert Anderson, of Kentucky, to the command. With the promulgation of the Ordinance of Secession in South Carolina, open intimations, often taking the form of threats, were given out, that unless the forts were speedily surrendered to the State authorities, they would be occupied by force. It was declared that any attempt to reinforce them, on the part of the National Government, would be regarded as an overt act of hostility.

Generals Scott and Wool urged upon President Buchanan the duty of immediately placing a force in these works, sufficient to crush the first overt acts of treason. Under his own theories of the restricted powers of the Government, and with a divided Cabinet, Mr. Buchanan hesitated to follow the advice of the heads of the army.

Major Anderson asked for instructions and succor from the Government, representing the weakness of Fort Moultrie and the hopelessness of effective resistance to a concerted attack. A private letter from him, dated in December, gives the following view of the situation:

"When I inform you that my garrison consists of only sixty effective men, and that we are in a very indifferent work, the walls of which are only about fourteen feet high; and that we have, within one hundred and sixty yards of our walls, sand hills which command our works, and which afford admirable sites for batteries, and the finest covers for sharpshooters, and that, besides this, there are numerous houses, some of them within pistol-shot, you will at once see that, if attacked in force, headed by any one but a simpleton, there is scarce a possibility of our being able to hold out long enough to enable our friends to come to our succor. Trusting that God will not desert us in our hour of trial, I am, sincerely yours."

Major Anderson directed the force under his command, with such additional aid as he could control, to repairing and strengthening Fort Moultrie. His exertions in this respect were made the subject of loud and violent remonstrance on the part of the press and authorities of South Carolina. Still, the Government gave him neither counsel nor support, and it was not until December 11th that, in answer to his repeated solicitations he received the following verbal instructions, through special messenger Major Buell:

"You are aware of the great anxiety of the Secretary of War that a collision of troops with the people of this State shall be avoided, and of his studied determination to pursue a course with reference to

JEFFERSON DAVIS ADDRESSING THE CITIZENS OF MONTGOMERY, ALABAMA.

the military posts and forts of this harbor which shall guard against such collision. He has, therefore, carefully abstained from increasing the force at this point, or taking any measures which might add to the present excited state of the public mind, or which would throw any doubt on the confidence he feels that South Carolina will not attempt, by violence, to obtain possession of the public works, or interfere with their occupancy.

"But as the counsel and acts of rash and impulsive persons may possibly disappoint these expectations of the Government, he deems it proper that you should be prepared with instructions to meet so unhappy a contingency. He has, therefore, directed me verbally to give you such instructions.

"You are carefully to avoid every act which would needlessly tend to provoke aggression, and *for that reason* you are not, without necessity, to take up any position which could be construed into the assumption of a hostile attitude; but you *are to hold possession of the forts in the harbor, and, if attacked, you are to defend yourself to the last extremity.* The smallness of your force will not permit you, perhaps, to occupy more than one of the three forts, but an attack or attempt to take possession of either of them will be regarded as an act of hostility, and then you may put your command into either of them which you may deem most proper, to increase its power of resistance. *You are also authorized to take similar steps whenever you have tangible evidence of a design to proceed to a hostile act.*"

Toward the middle of December, it became evident, from the magnitude of military operations going on, and other indications, coupled with significant threats in the South Carolina Convention and out of it, that an occupation of Castle Pinckney and Fort Sumter was meditated, even if no open manifestations should be made against Fort Moultrie. The question of the latter, in event Fort Sumter was occupied, was one entirely subordinate, as it was completely commanded by Sumter. Major Anderson determined, therefore, to anticipate the South Carolinians in their contemplated manœuvre, believing that the contingency had arisen contemplated in the closing paragraph of his instructions. Accordingly, on the night of December 26th, at the very time that the South Carolina Commissioners had arrived in Washington to demand the surrender of the forts, he evacuated Fort Moultrie, after spiking the guns, and providing for the destruction of their carriages and other material by fire; and with the aid of three small vessels successfully transferred his little command, his flag and available munitions to Fort Sumter.

RAISING THE FLAG ON FORT SUMTER

The raising of the national flag, which Anderson had brought with him from Fort Moultrie, was one of those imposing scenes which lend a romantic and thrilling inspiration to the exigencies which history is forced to record.

December, 1860

The flag was raised precisely at noon on the 27th. A short time previous, Major Anderson had assembled his little force of soldiers and workmen around the flagstaff. The flag was attached to the cord, and Major Anderson, holding the end, reverently knelt down. Many of the group followed his example, and the chaplain offered an earnest prayer, an appeal for support on earth, and mercy in heaven. When his fervid, solemn words were ended, and the men with deep feeling had responded "Amen," Major Anderson drew the cord, and the starry flag rose slowly to the top of the staff, when the band rolled out the anthem of "Hail Columbia," and the group—officers, soldiers and laborers—broke into an exultant salute, cheer following cheer, to the national emblem.

PRESIDENT BUCHANAN AND THE SOUTH CAROLINA COMMISSIONERS.

R. W. BARNWELL, J. H. Adams and James L. Orr, prominent citizens of the State of South Carolina, arrived in Washington on the 26th of December, 1860, as Commissioners from that State, with communications to President Buchanan, setting forth that, as the State of South Carolina had resumed the powers which she had delegated to the Government of the United States and declared her perfect sovereignty and independence, it became their duty to open negotiations in reference to all questions growing out of this act of the State with a view to the amicable settlement of all questions between the sovereign State of South Carolina and the United States. That the action of Major Anderson had rendered the initiation of such arrangements impossible pending the previous withdrawal of the United States forces from Charleston Harbor—a withdrawal which they now formally demanded.

December, 1860.

They claimed that the movement of Major Anderson was in contravention of an understanding had some time previously between the Members of Congress for South Carolina and the President. The President replied that the understanding referred to was nothing more than the mutual expression of a desire that nothing should be done on either side in the way of attacks on the forts in Charleston Harbor, or of their reinforcement, that might lead to collisions, in order to gain time for reflection and deliberate action. He confessed that he might have ordered Major Anderson back to Fort Moultrie, if it had not been that South Carolina had already occupied the remaining fortifications without waiting for, or asking, explanations. He added that it was under such circumstances that he was called upon to withdraw the troops from the Harbor of Charleston, coupled with the threat that, without this being done negotiations would be impossible. Under these conditions he firmly refused in these words: "This I cannot do—this I will not do!"

The Commissioners thereupon sent the President a bitter and upbraiding note, charging him with bad faith, and setting forth that, after he had declared that the Government had no right to coerce a State, after having removed a former commandant of Fort Moultrie for having attempted to increase his supply of ammunition, and after having accepted the resignation of General Cass rather than permit the garrison to be reinforced, he had now resolved to hold by force the position he had obtained through the misplaced confidence of South Carolina, and to convert the violation of orders by Major Anderson into a legitimate act of executive authority. They concluded by asserting that by his course the President had probably 'rendered' civil war inevitable, and by appealing to "the God of Justice and the God of Hosts" to enable South Carolina to perform the work before her, "hopefully, bravely and thoroughly." This last document the President returned, declining to receive it.

FORTS SEIZED BY SOUTH CAROLINA.

UPON Major Anderson's transfer to Fort Sumter, the Convention at once requested Governor Pickens to take possession of Forts Moultrie, Johnson and Castle Pinckney. General R. G. M. Dunovant seized Fort Johnson, and Colonel J. J. Pettigrew, Castle Pinckney. Lieutenant R. K. Meade, the commandant at Pinckney, with his troops, fled to Sumter.

December, 1860.

His men barricaded the door of the Castle, spiked the guns, ruined their carriages, removed the ammunition and prostrated the flagstaff. Pettigrew unfurled the Palmetto Flag over the Castle, amid the cheers of thousands on the shore. It was the first flag raised by the insurgents over a national fortification. The Washington, the German, the Lafayette and the Marine Artilleries, under Colonel Wilmot G. De Saussure, occupied Fort Moultrie.

The people of Charleston looked on with anxiety, not knowing the moment Major Anderson might open fire on their friends. But his instructions from Washington did not permit him to fire a gun.

MAJOR ANDERSON RAISING THE UNION FLAG ON FORT SUMTER, DECEMBER 27TH, 1860.

THE "STAR OF THE WEST."

Public sentiment in the North demanded some action on the part of the Government toward the relief of Major Anderson and his little band locked up in Fort Sumter; and, in conformity with this demand, the steamer *Star of the West*, loaded with supplies, but unarmed, was dispatched from New York, and reached Charleston Bay January 9th, 1861. While proceeding up the harbor, and when opposite Morris Island, she was fired into from the batteries on the island, and compelled to return to New York. The *Star of the West* had on board 250 artillerists and marines; she sailed from New York January 5th, 1861, cleared for New Orleans and Havana. On the 8th of January, the Secretary of the Treasury resigned, on account of the disregard shown to the objections offered by himself and the Secretary of the Interior to fitting out the *Star of the West*.

to Governor Pickens, asking him if the firing upon an unarmed vessel carrying the flag of the Government was authorized by him. Governor Pickens replied: "The act is perfectly justified by me." Major Anderson then asked for, and received, permission to send a messenger to Washington with dispatches and for instructions. Lieutenant T. Talbot was selected for this mission.

Before an answer could be received, Governor Pickens, on the 11th of January, made a formal demand for the surrender of the fort, which was refused.

MRS. ANDERSON AT FORT SUMTER.

Major Anderson's conduct in evacuating Fort Moultrie, and concentrating the available loyal forces of the United States troops, then in Charleston Harbor, within the stronger walls of Sumter, was looked upon as a breach of an implied agreement made between the secessionists and the Gov-

but she had not seen him in seven years. His name was Peter Hart. She knew him to be a tried and trusty friend, on whom she could rely in any emergency, and she resolved to find him, and place him by the side of her husband within the walls of Fort Sumter.

For a day and a half she sought a clew by visiting the residences of the various Harts named in the City Directory. She was an invalid. Her physician protested against her project, as he believed its execution would imperil her life. She would listen to no protests, but found Hart, and the two

January, 1861.

started the next day for Charleston. They traveled without intermission, and reached Charleston at the end of forty-eight hours.

The cars were crowded with recruits hastening to join in the attack on Fort Sumter. She neither ate, drank, nor slept, and heard her husband threatened with instant death should he fall into their

SPIKING THE GUNS OF FORT MOULTRIE BY MAJOR ANDERSON, BEFORE ITS EVACUATION, DECEMBER 26TH, 1860.

John A. Dix, of New York, was appointed in his place, January 11th, and he immediately took vigorous measures to prevent the property of the Government, under the control of the Treasury, falling into the hands of the seceding States. On the 19th he sent William Hemphill Jones, a special agent from his department, to New Orleans, with instructions to take charge of the Government property. This messenger ordered Captain John G. Breshwood, the commander of the *McClelland*, to proceed with her to New York.

January, 1861.

On refusal from the commander, the messenger telegraphed to Mr. Dix for further instructions, and received for answer a dispatch directing him to put the mutinous officer under arrest, and concluded the message with the memorable injunction: "If any one attempts to haul down the American flag, shoot him on the spot!"

When Major Anderson witnessed the firing on the *Star of the West*, and saw her depart without being allowed to communicate with him, he wrote

ernment; but the new Secretary of War, Joseph Holt, assured Major Anderson of the approval of the Government, and that his action was in every way admirable, alike for its humanity and patriotism, as for its soldiership.

Before these words of approval reached Major Anderson, the Legislature of Nebraska sent greeting two thousand miles by telegraph. Indeed, every patriotic heart in the land beat responsive to the spontaneous praise of a grateful people for a deed which seemed a promise of safety to the republic.

The position of Major Anderson and his little band, composed of ten officers, fifteen musicians and fifty-five artillerists—eighty in all—was an extremely perilous one. His friends were uneasy; his wife, a daughter of the gallant soldier, General Clinch, of Georgia, was in New York city. She knew her husband was exposed to ferocious foes without, and possible traitors within, the fort.

In the emergency she remembered a faithful sergeant who had been with her husband in Mexico,

hands. Their language was very violent, especially respecting the destruction of the old flagstaff at Moultrie, which was considered such an insult to the South Carolinians as might not be forgiven. At the Mills House Mrs. Anderson met her brother. She found no difficulty in procuring a permit from Governor Pickens, who was her father's old friend, to go to Fort Sumter.

The Governor refused one for Hart, saying he could not allow a man to be added to the Sumter garrison. She scornfully asked if South Carolina, claiming to be a sovereign power among the nations of the earth, would be endangered by the addition of one man to a garrison of seventy or eighty, while thousands of armed hands were ready and willing to strike them!

The Governor, seeing the absurdity of his refusal, gave a pass for Hart, requiring from Major Anderson a pledge that he should not be enrolled as a soldier. A small boat carried them to Sumter. On every hand she saw strange banners and warlike preparations. Nearing Sumter, she turned and saw the national ensign floating over the fort, the only one in the whole bay. "The dear old flag!" she exclaimed, and burst into tears.

Reaching the fort, her husband caught her in his arms, whispering, "My glorious wife!"

"I have brought you Peter Hart," she said "The children are well. I return to-night."

In two hours Mrs. Anderson was placed in the boat by her husband, and rowed back to the city. The same evening she started for the national capital. Her mission ended, she was utterly prostrate. A bed was placed in the car for her comfort. She was insensible when she arrived at Willard's Hotel, Washington, and after forty-eight hours of suffering from exhaustion, she proceeded to New York and rejoined her children.

This brave woman had done what the Government failed to do—she had not sent, but had taken, reinforcement to Fort Sumter. How faithful and useful this reinforcement was, the next three months' history of Fort Sumter will, in a measure, reveal.

JOHN ADAMS DIX.

JOHN ADAMS DIX, OF NEW YORK.

Born in New Hampshire, July 24th, 1798, John Adams Dix entered the United States Army in 1812, as cadet, and was ordered to report to his father, Major Timothy Dix, Jr., commanding the Fourteenth Infantry, stationed at Baltimore. In March, 1813, he met, in Washington city, General Armstrong, the Secretary of War, who questioned the lad as to his studies; and, finding him far advanced, told him he could learn little at West Point, except military tactics, and suggested that he should go to the frontier.

Having gained the consent of his father, General Armstrong gave him an ensign's commission, assigning him to service in his father's regiment, which, in April, received orders to march to Sackett's Harbor, N. Y., to report to General Jacob Brown, afterward commander-in-chief of the United States Army. On their march, young Dix, then not fifteen years old, visited West Point in company with his father and several of the other officers of the regiment, and inspected the forts and Academy. They found but seventeen cadets at the Academy, and the forts were out of repair.

Arriving at Sackett's Harbor, Ensign Dix was appointed adjutant to Major Timothy Upham, of the Twenty-first Infantry, and served on his staff until relieved from duty, and called to the bedside of his father, Colonel Dix, who was stricken with pneumonia, and died while with the army on their way down the river to attack Montreal.

Early in 1814, Adjutant Dix was ordered to Fort Constitution, Portsmouth, N. H., and appointed on the staff of Colonel Walbach, where he served until 1818; thence to Fort Washington, opposite Mount Vernon, on the Potomac, where he had command. The next year (1819), he was appointed regimental quartermaster, and ordered to Fort Columbus, New York Harbor. He was soon after appointed aid-de-camp to Major-general Jacob Brown, then commanding the Northern Military Department of the United States. While Major Dix was on General Brown's staff, he had unusual facilities to visit all parts of the United States, and mingle much with the prominent statesmen and scholars of that day. In 1826 Major Dix was sent as a special messenger by the President to deliver the treaty just made between the United States and the kingdom of Denmark to our Minister at Copenhagen. On his return in the Autumn, he was ordered to Fortress Monroe. In July, 1828, after sixteen years of service, he resigned his commission as captain of the Third Regiment of Artillery. He settled at Cooperstown, N. Y., and practiced law. In 1830 he was appointed adjutant-general of the State of New York. In 1833 he was appointed Secretary of State. In 1841 he was elected to the State Assembly for Albany County, N. Y. In 1845 he was elected by the Legislature of the State of New York United States Senator. While in the Senate, he strongly urged upon Congress the vigorous prosecution of the war with Mexico until a peace was conquered and the question of the boundary line for ever settled.

Appointed by President Pierce Assistant United States Treasurer at New York in 1853, pending his confirmation by the Senate as United States Minister to France which appointment was prevented by the pressure brought to bear by Southern Senators, on the ground of the Free-soil proclivities of General Dix. John Y. Mason, of Virginia, finally secured the appointment.

In 1849 General Dix was elected a member of the Vestry of Trinity Church, New York city, and at once became active in reorganizing the financial department, and securing State legislation that made it possible to successfully defend the property of the church against the claimants representing the descendants of Anneke Jans, who held claim to the ownership of all the real estate in possession of the Trinity Parish. He afterward became comptroller of the Vestry.

In 1860 President Buchanan appointed General Dix Postmaster of New York city. On the resignation of Howell Cobb as Secretary of the Treasury, Philip T. Thomas was appointed by President Buchanan. He came to New York seeking to obtain funds for the depleted Treasury. The banks and financial agents in Wall Street did not respond, and the President made inquiry as to what would satisfy them. They asked to name a Cabinet officer, and, with singular unanimity, named John A. Dix, and the President offered him the portfolio of War. This General Dix declined, and frankly stated to the President that he could be of no service to him, except in the Treasury Department. The President asked for time, and the next day secured the resignation of Mr. Thomas, and at once sent General Dix's name to the Senate, where it was at once confirmed. The financial deadlock was broken, and the Government found itself in possession of all the money it needed.

General Dix, when Secretary of the Treasury under President Buchanan's reorganized Cabinet, was the first of his advisers to assert the authority of the Government in a manner to meet the expectations, stir the patriotism and call forth the sympathies of the Northern people. The revenue cutters were under his control and orders as Secretary of the Treasury. When he came into office the cutter *Lewis Cass* was at Mobile, and the *Robert McClelland* at New Orleans. He at once (January 18th, 1861) ordered their commanders, through special messenger, to return with their vessels to New York. On the refusal of the commander of the *McClelland*, the Secretary sent the following telegram to his special agent at New Orleans. The telegraph being in the hands of the insurgents at both Mobile and New Orleans, the order was intercepted, and did not reach the agent of the Treasury Department, and the cutters were both lost to the Government; but the publication of the order in the newspapers, a few days afterward, did a service in awakening the public sentiment to the danger that threatened their country's flag—worth more to the Government at that time than a score of revenue cutters. The historic order reads as follows

"TREASURY DEPARTMENT, January 29th, 1861.

"*W. Hemphill Jones, New Orleans:*

"Tell Lieutenant Caldwell to arrest Captain Breshwood; assume command of the cutter, and obey the order I gave through you. If Captain Breshwood, after arrest, undertakes to interfere with the command of the cutter, tell Lieutenant Caldwell to consider him as a mutineer, and treat him accordingly. If any one attempts to haul down the American flag, shoot him on the spot.*

"JOHN A. DIX, Secretary of the Treasury."

In May 1861 General Dix was appointed major-general of Volunteer forces called for from the State of New York, in compliance with the requisition of the President of the United States, and assigned to the command of the troops in and about the City of New York. These troops were promptly equipped and sent off to the defense of Washington. Soon after he was appointed major-general in the army of the United States and was, by General Scott, assigned to the command of the troops at Arlington and Alexandria, the department nearest the enemy. He arrived in Washington just as the public was shouting for an immediate advance. This he opposed, and would not yield to the popular clamor. The War Department then ordered him to Baltimore, and while he was sequestered within the walls of Fort McHenry, his ambitious juniors commenced their march on Richmond—by way of Bull Run. The disaster met in that field made General Dix's Department of Pennsylvania the key to the military situation, and the base of operations on the Potomac. He saved Maryland to the Union, and kept Baltimore quiet, even while Confederate flags were displayed and Confederate colors borne on the streets. May, 1862, General Dix was transferred from the Department of Pennsylvania to Fortress Monroe, where he was to assume command and report to Major-general McClellan. At this post he was of great assistance to the commanding-general in his attempt on Richmond.

While at Fortress Monroe he was unanimously nominated by the Federal Union Committee as candidate for Governor of the State of New York. Those were the black days for the Federal Army. Defeat and wild rumors of disasters with threatened invasion of the Northern States pervaded the land. The result of the election was adverse to General Dix, and he continued at his post at Fortress Monroe, holding the Confederate forces in that quarter in check. On the 14th of June General Dix was ordered to threaten Richmond and occupy the large force of the Confederate Army, during the

---

* The original draft was shown to General Scott and Attorney-general Edwin M. Stanton before it was transmitted, and received their cordial approval. The President did not see it until it was published in the newspapers.—"Memoirs of John Adams Dix, by his son, Morgan Dix." (Harper & Brothers, 1883), to which we are indebted for much valuable information.

absence of the main body in Pennsylvania. In conformity with these orders, General Dix went up the York River with about 18,000 men, burned the bridges, cut General Lee's line of communication, captured many prisoners, including General Fitz Hugh Lee, and marched within ten miles of Richmond. At this moment he was ordered, by General Halleck, to fall back, and send all the troops, not actually required to the defense of Washington, to reinforce General Meade. It was not the plan of General Dix to attempt the capture of Richmond, but he hoped, by holding his troops within a few miles of its streets, fortifications, to not only keep idle the [illegible] within the lines, but to draw back to its defense ten or twelve thousand troops that were under orders to reinforce General Lee.

On the 18th of July, 1863, General Dix was ordered to New York, to the command of the Department of the East, immediately after the draft riots. He called for a sufficient force from the Government to keep the peace, and in August was supplied with ten thousand infantry and three batteries of artillery. The President also called to his aid the State Militia, and the draft was successfully executed.

General Dix retained his command of the Department of the East until July 15th, 1865, when he was relieved by General Joseph Hooker, and found occupation in his duties as President of the Union Pacific Railroad Company. In 1866 General Dix was appointed Naval Officer of the Port of New York, which position he soon resigned to accept the Mission to France. He returned to New York on June 15th, 1869, and on the 5th of November, 1872, was elected Governor of the State of New York, and on January 1st, 1875, he retired to private life, after an almost continuous service of sixty-three years. He died in New York City, April 21st, 1879.

LIEUTENANT NORMAN J. HALL.

NORMAN J. HALL,

Lieutenant United States Army, and one of the eight commissioned officers in Fort Sumter at the time of its occupation by Major Robert Anderson. He furnished Assistant Secretary of War Gustavus V. Fox, who [illegible] information as to the condition of the defenses of the fort, with a memorandum of supplies. After the Fall of Sumter, Lieutenant Hall was commissioned a Brigadier-general, and served gallantly throughout the war.

THE LETTER BORNE BY LIEUTENANT HALL TO GOVERNOR PICKENS.

To His Excellency the Governor of South Carolina.

SIR: Two of your batteries fired this morning on an unarmed vessel bearing the flag of my Government. As I have not been notified that war has been declared by South Carolina against the Government of the United States, I cannot but think that this hostile act was committed without your sanction or authority. Under that hope I refrain from opening fire on your batteries. I have the honor, therefore, respectfully to ask whether the above-mentioned act, one I believe without a parallel in the history of our country or any other civilized government, was committed in obedience to your instructions, and notify you, if it is not disclaimed, that I regard it as an act of war, and that I shall not, after reasonable time for the return of my messenger, permit any vessel to pass within range of the guns of my fort. In order to save, as far as in my power, the shedding of blood, I beg that you will take due notification of this, my decision, for the good of all concerned. Hoping, however, that your answer may be such as will justify a further continuance of forbearance on my part, I have the honor to be, very respectfully,

Your obedient servant,

ROBERT ANDERSON,

Major, First Artillery, U. S. A., Commanding.

FORT SUMTER, January 9th, 1861.

To this the Governor responded in a long letter, the gist of which was contained in the words:

"THE ACT IS PERFECTLY JUSTIFIED BY ME.

"F. W. PICKENS."

LIEUTENANT HALL, WITH FLAG OF TRUCE AND LETTER FROM MAJOR ANDERSON TO GOVERNOR PICKENS,
AFTER THE FIRING ON THE "STAR OF THE WEST."

SOUTH CAROLINA'S DEMAND UPON PRESIDENT BUCHANAN.

GOVERNOR PICKENS dispatched his Attorney-general, Isaac W. Hayne, with a letter to President Buchanan, making demand for the surrender of Fort Sumter "to avoid the bloodshed which a persistence in your attempts to retain the possession of that fort will cause." Mr.

JANUARY, 1861. Hayne had an interview with the President on the 15th of January but the President declined to recognize him in an official character, and turned him over to the Secretary of War. A number of the secession Senators now interfered to prevent the delivery of Governor Pickens's demands either for the purpose of trying to heal the difficulties or to gain time, in order to perfect their plans before the knowledge of the nature of the demand could result in open rupture. In the meantime, the South Carolina troops were erecting their heavy works to operate against Fort Sumter, and perfecting their military preparations. On the 31st of January, Colonel Hayne made his demand, accompanied by the statement that the assertion of the right to reinforce Fort Sumter would be regarded by South Carolina as a "declaration of war." The demand was accompanied by a proposition to purchase the fort, coupled with the declaration that, if the proposition was not accepted, the fort should be seized by force of arms.

ISAAC W. HAYNE,

ATTORNEY-GENERAL OF SOUTH CAROLINA, MESSENGER TO WASHINGTON WITH SOUTH CAROLINA'S ULTIMATUM TO PRESIDENT BUCHANAN.

Mr. Holt, Secretary of War, replied that Fort Sumter was peacefully ceded to the United States by South Carolina herself, to be held for the protection of the city of Charleston and harbor, from which purpose there was no intention to divert it. He added that the Government of the United States would continue to hold the fort in that spirit, and that the responsibility of an assault that might disturb the beneficent purpose of the Government in holding its undoubted property would rest on South Carolina, and not on the general Government. Taking advantage of the delays incident to the formal demand of South Carolina for possession, by purchase or conquest, of the Government forts in Charleston Harbor, the other States, acting in apparent concert, seized Forts Pulaski and Jackson, in the harbor of Savannah; Fort Gaines and Morgan at Mobile; Forts St. Philip and Jackson below New Orleans; Forts Barancas and McRee at Pensacola; Fort Clinch at Fernandina, Forts Caswell, Johnson and Macon in North Carolina; the Mint and Custom House at New Orleans, the Arsenal at Little Rock, Ark., and other Government properties in the South.

LIGHTHOUSE AT THE ENTRANCE TO CHARLESTON HARBOR, S. C.

THE OLD STATE HOUSE AT COLUMBIA, WHERE THE SOUTH CAROLINA LEGISLATURE UNANIMOUSLY ADOPTED THE ORDINANCE OF SECESSION DECEMBER 20TH, 1860.

EVACUATION OF FORT MOULTRIE BY MAJOR

THE "STAR OF THE WEST," WITH SUPPLIES FOR MAJOR ANDERSON, APPROACHING FO

EVACUATION OF FORT MOULTRIE BY MAJOR ANDERSON, ON THE NIGHT OF DECEMBER 26, 1860.

THE STAR OF THE WEST, WITH SUPPLIES FOR MAJOR ANDERSON, APPROACHING FORT SUMTER—FIRED UPON FROM FORT MOULTRIE AND THE BATTERIES ON MORRIS ISLAND.

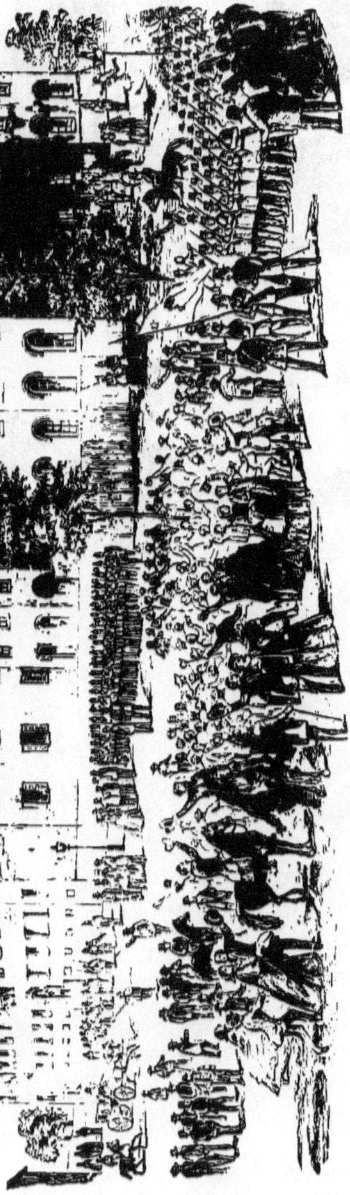

UNITED STATES ARSENAL AT CHARLESTON, S.C., SEIZED BY THE STATE AUTHORITIES, DECEMBER 28TH, 1860.

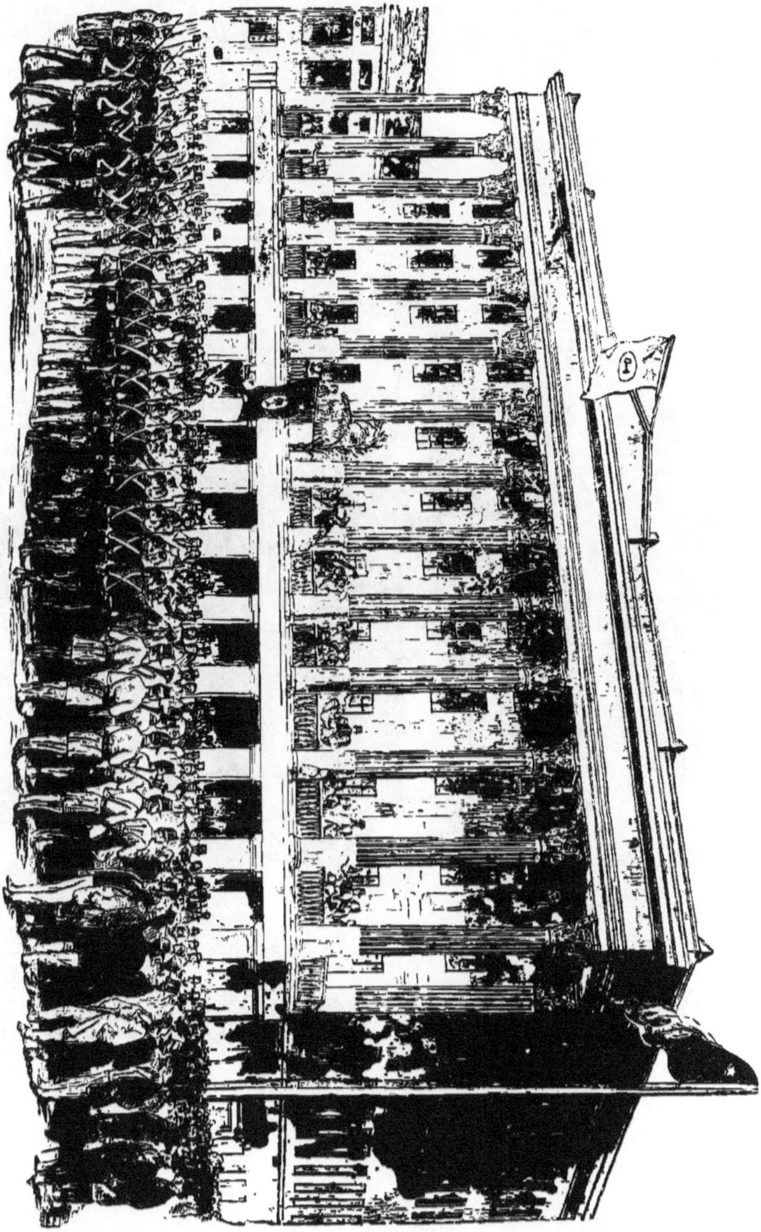

GENERAL McGOWEN ADDRESSING THE THIRTY-FIFTH ABBEVILLE (S. C.) VOLUNTEERS IN FRONT OF THE CHARLESTON HOTEL.

REVIEW OF SOUTH CAROLINA VOLUNTEER TROOPS IN FORT MOULTRIE, CHARLESTON

REVIEW OF THE CLINCH RIFLES ON THE PARADE-GROUND OF THE UNITED STATES ARSENAL AT AUGUSTA, GA., FEBRUARY, 1861.

THE SEIZURE OF THE UNITED STATES ARSENAL AT AUGUSTA, GA.

The following account of the seizure of the Arsenal at Augusta, Ga., we take from Avery's "History of Georgia." (New York: Brown & Derby, 1882):

"From the date of Georgia's secession, events went forward swiftly. Governor Brown, with characteristic promptitude, hastened to make practical the sovereignty of the State. The United States flag was still flying over the Augusta Arsenal. Captain Arnold Elzey was in charge of it, in command of eighty United States soldiers. During the heated public feeling before secession the people were in great excitement over Federal occupation of the arsenal. This excitement became almost uncontrollable when the Federal flag continued to float over the arsenal after secession, and it was the all-absorbing theme of talk. Governor Brown went promptly to Augusta, arriving there on the 22d of January, 1861.

January, 1861.

"WASHINGTON, January 23d, 1861.

"*Captain Arnold Elzey, Second Artillery, Commanding Augusta Arsenal, Ga.*:

"The Governor of Georgia has assumed against your post and the United States an attitude of war. His summons is harsh and peremptory. It is not expected that your defense should be desperate. If forced to surrender by violence or starvation you will stipulate for honorable terms and a free passage by water with your company to New York.

"J. HOLT,

"*Secretary of War.*"

During the day of the 23d, the volunteers of the city were ordered out, and some eight hundred troops responded. The refusal of Captain Elzey to surrender created the exciting prospect of a battle, and hence every man turned out that could raise a uniform and a gun. Troops came in from the country.

The companies out were the Augusta Battalion, companies A and B of the minutemen, and the militia, all under the immediate command of Lieutenant-colonel Cumming. Brigadier-general Harris had general direction, aided by Brigadier-general Williams, of Columbus. Colonel William Phillips was on the Governor's staff. Governor Brown determined to make no hostile demonstration on the 23d, but to allow Captain Elzey a day for consideration.

The troops were dismissed until the 24th, at nine o'clock A.M., when they reassembled, and were just about to march for the Arsenal, when Captain Elzey sent the following communication, which caused a countermanding of the order to march:

"HEADQUARTERS, AUGUSTA ARSENAL, GA.,
"January 24th, 1861.

"SIR: I have the honor to inform you that I am directed by Captain Elzey, commanding this post, to say, in reply to the demand of the Governor of the State of Georgia, made through you yesterday, requiring him to withdraw the command beyond the limits of the State: He begs to request an interview with His Excellency the Governor, for the purpose of negotiating honorable terms of surrender at as early an hour this morning as practicable. I have the honor to be, very respectfully, your obedient servant,

"J. C. JONES,

"*Lieutenant Second Artillery, Adj.*"

"To Colonel H. R. Jackson, *Aide-de-camp.*"

At ten o'clock Governor Brown, with Generals Williams and Harris and his staff, Colonel H. R. Jackson, Colonel William Phillips, Lieutenant-colonel M. C. Fulton, Lieutenant-colonel C. V. Walker and Lieutenant-colonel Henry Cleveland, rode to the Arsenal, where the terms of surrender were agreed upon:

1. The United States flag was to be lowered and saluted.
2. The company to march out with military honors.
3. A receipt to be given for the property with a view to future adjustment.
4. The company to retain its arms and property; to stay in its quarters until withdrawal from the State; and to have passage to New York by Savannah.

The State obtained a large quantity of valuable ordnance and munitions, among them a fine battery of two twelve-pound howitzers, two cannons, twenty-two thousand muskets and rifles, many of them of the best kind, and heavy stores of powder, grape and other ammunition.

A silent embrace was Captain Elzey's reply, and the incident filled with tears the eyes of those who witnessed the touching incident between these two old army friends, suddenly placed in hostile relations to each other. The two were at West Point together.

Colonel Walker was afterward made a Major-general in the Confederate Army. He was the possessor of the courage that bordered upon the desperate. He was peculiarly unfortunate, having been frightfully wounded on three different occasions in his service before the war, once being literally riddled by shot; he was finally killed in the battles around Atlanta.

The garrison was called out, and the four field-pieces used in firing the salute. Thirty-three guns were fired, one for each star on the old flag, Georgia included.

The flag descended from the staff between the thirty-second and thirty-third fire. All of the officers of the company, and some of those with the Governor, had seen active service under it, with Colonel Jackson, through the Mexican War.

Refreshments were ordered by Captain Elzey, and a number of toasts were pledged, several of them deserving preservation. Colonel Jackson offered this feeling and memorable sentiment: "The flag of stars and stripes, may it never be disgraced while it floats over a true Southern patriot." This toast was warmly appreciated by the officers of the Federal company who were Southern officers. Governor Brown, while not drinking wine, proposed a toast to Captain Elzey, in which he paid that officer a merited and generous compliment. Governor Brown returned immediately to Milledgeville.

THE ORDNANCE BUREAU AT CHARLESTON, S. C.

Colonel, afterward General H. R. Jackson, accompanied the Governor as his aid."

The following communication was addressed to Captain Elzey:

"AUGUSTA, GA., January 23d, 1861.

"*Captain Arnold Elzey, U. S. A., Commanding Augusta Arsenal*:

"SIR: I am instructed by His Excellency Governor Brown to say to you that Georgia, having seceded from the United States of America, and resumed exclusive sovereignty over her soil, it has become my duty to require you to withdraw the troops under your command at the earliest practicable moment from the limits of this State.

He proposes to take possession of the arsenal, and to receipt for all public property under your charge, which will be hereafter accounted for, on adjustment between the State of Georgia and the United States of America.

"He begs to refer you to the fact that the retention of foreign troops upon the soil of Georgia after remonstrance is, under the laws of nations, an act of hostility, and he claims that the State is not only at peace, but anxious to cultivate the most amicable relations, with the United States Government.

"I am further instructed to say that an answer will be expected by to-morrow morning at nine o'clock.

"I am, sir, very respectfully, your obedient servant,

"HENRY R. JACKSON,

"*Aide-de-camp.*"

Captain Elzey refused to give up the arsenal, and telegraphed the situation to the authorities at Washington, receiving at one o'clock at night this reply:

GENERAL VIEW OF THE CITY

GENERAL VIEW OF THE CITY AND HARBOR OF CHARLESTON, S. C.

THE BOMBARDMENT OF FORT SUMTER SKETCHED FROM MORRIS ISLAND, CHARLESTON HARBOR, S. C.

THE UNITED STATES REVENUE CUTTER "AIKEN," SEIZED IN CHARLESTON HARBOR BY THE SOUTH CAROLINA AUTHORITIES.

CHARLESTON HARBOR—FORTS AND DEFENSES.

CHARLESTON and Charleston Harbor were, before the War, defended by three fortifications—Castle Pinckney, a small, old-fashioned work on the main land; Fort Moultrie, near the entrance to the harbor, on Sullivan's Island; and Fort Sumter, a splendid work, on an artificial island, toward the mouth of the harbor.

Fort Moultrie was situated on Sullivan's Island, north side of Charleston Harbor, nearly opposite Fort Sumter, and distant from it about one and one-eighth miles. Correctly speaking, it was a huge water-battery, without any guns under cover. Its armament consisted of eleven guns of heavy calibre, and several mortars. The outer and inner walls were of brick, capped with stone and filled with earth, making a solid wall fifteen or sixteen feet in thickness. After its abandonment by Major Anderson, and before the attack on Fort Sumter, it was much strengthened, sand-bag covers having been built between the guns, so that the latter were protected from a transverse or raking fire. Fort Moultrie occupied the site of the old Palmetto Fort of the same name, where was fought one of the most brilliant and decisive battles of the Revolution, when a few hundred men, who had never before fired a gun, beat off and nearly destroyed a formidable British fleet, with a greater slaughter, in proportion to the numbers engaged, than that of the bloody fights of Trafalgar and the Nile.

Upon the plan of Charleston Harbor the relative

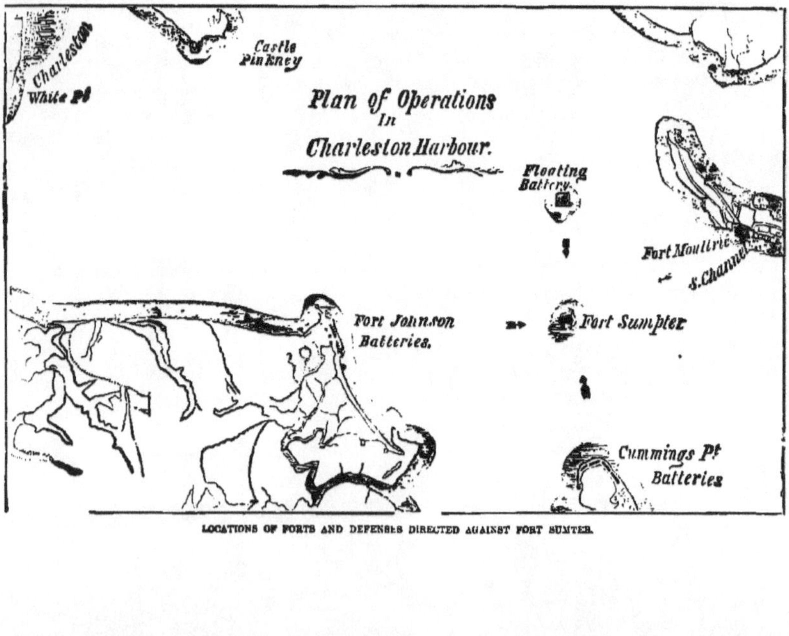

LOCATIONS OF FORTS AND DEFENSES DIRECTED AGAINST FORT SUMTER.

positions of Forts Sumter, Moultrie and Pinckney, the insurgent batteries on Morris Island, and the City of Charleston, are shown. The position taken by the floating battery, on the day preceding the attack on Fort Sumter, is also indicated in the plan. These illustrations present at a glance the belligerent operations against the Federal force in Fort Sumter, the immediate effect of which was so profound on the country at large.

THE FLOATING BATTERY.

THIS novel destructive, anchored off the southern extremity of Sullivan's Island, performed a leading part in the attack on Fort Sumter. It was constructed under a storm of ridicule, which was very effectually silenced by its practical test.

It may be taken, in connection with the iron battery on Cummings' Point, as demonstrating a new and important principle in the science of military defenses. The battery was about one hundred feet long by twenty-five wide, built of sawed pine timber twelve inches square, the bottom flat, the gun side presenting an angular front, the slope of which, upward and downward, was about forty degrees. This front was faced with two thicknesses of railway iron, running vertically, with four thicknesses additional of boiler iron, all bolted firmly to the wooden structure behind, and pierced for four guns of heavy calibre, requiring sixty men to work them properly. Behind the battery, at the time of the attack, was moored a floating hospital, completely protected from horizontal fire by the defenses in front, and only exposed to shell. The magazines were in the hold of the battery, protected by layers of sand-bags six feet in thickness, the weight of which served as a counterpoise to that of the guns.

EDMUND RUFFIN, OF VIRGINIA,
WHO BOASTED OF "THE HONOR OF FIRING THE FIRST SHOT AT FORT SUMTER."
In June, 1865, at eighty years of age, he committed suicide by blowing the top of his head off with a gun, saying: "I cannot survive the liberties of my country."

BOMBARDMENT OF FORT SUMTER.

MAJOR ANDERSON and his small garrison evacuated Fort Moultrie on the night of the 26th December, 1860, and the morning of the 27th broke, revealing to the astonished gaze of the people of Charleston the national flag floating defiantly over Sumter. They turned their eyes to Moultrie, only to see dense volumes of smoke rising from the burning carriages of the guns on its walls. An hour afterward, some workmen arriving from Sullivan's Island, explained to the excited citizens of Charleston what had occurred. The troops were immediately put in motion; the Convention hastily met in secret session, and the city was stirred to its centre. Governor Pickens sent a note to Major Anderson for an explanation of the movement, and demanding under what authority it had been made. That officer responded, assuming the responsibility of the act, and justifying it as one of defensive necessity.

DECEMBER, 1860.

On April 8th, over three months after Major Anderson occupied Fort Sumter, the Government decided on its line of policy in respect to Fort Sumter and the other menaced fortresses of the United States, and sent to Charleston two messengers, who reached that city on the 8th. One of these, Lieutenant Theodore Talbot, U. S. A., brought dispatches to Major Anderson; and the other, Mr. R. A. Chew, of the department of State, was directed to inform the authorities at Charleston that the Government had determined to send supplies to Major Anderson, peaceably if possible, but that no attempt would be made to reinforce that officer, unless the vessel carrying provisions should be assailed. The authorities at Charleston would not allow Lieutenant Talbot to proceed to Fort Sumter, and Major Anderson was consequently left in ignorance of the determination and plans of his Government. Mr. Chew, however, conveyed to Governor Pickens and General Beauregard the message with which he was intrusted, declining at the same time to receive a reply; the object of his mission being to so advise the local authorities that they might not interpret a peaceful and humane act into a menace, or hostile demonstration against themselves. General Beauregard immediately communicated by telegraph with the Provisional Government of the Confederate States at Montgomery.

APRIL, 1861.

On April 12th, 1861, 3:20 A.M., Major Anderson received the following communication:

"MAJOR ANDERSON, SIR: By authority of Brigadier-General Beauregard, commanding the provisional forces of the Confederate States, we have the honor to notify you that he will open the fire of his batteries on Fort Sumter in an hour from this time. We have the honor to be very respectfully, your obedient servants,

"JAMES CHESTNUT, JR., Aide-de-camp.
"STEPHEN D. LEE, Captain, C.S.A."

At 4:30 A. M. of the 12th of April fire was opened on Fort Sumter. Major Anderson resolved not to return the fire until broad daylight, not wishing to waste any of his ammunition. To the astonishment of Major Anderson, a masked battery of heavy columbiads, of the existence of which he had not the slightest intimation, opened fire from

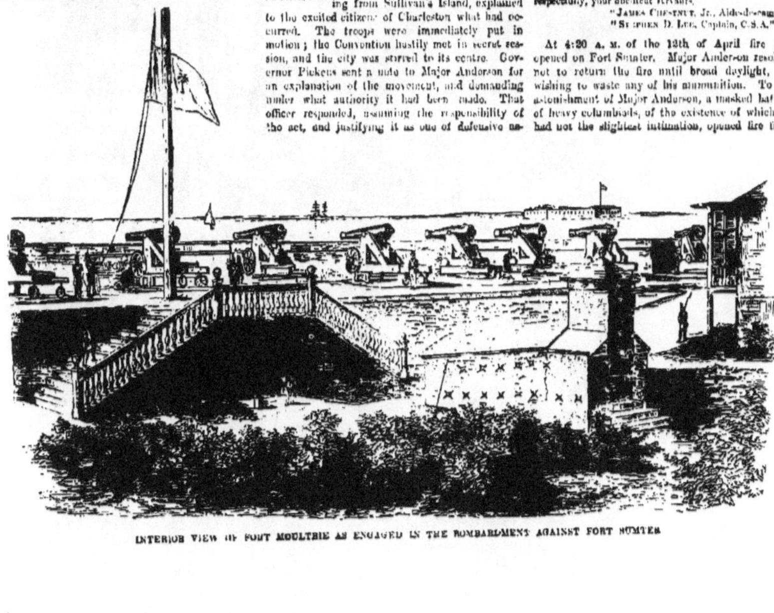

INTERIOR VIEW OF FORT MOULTRIE AS ENGAGED IN THE BOMBARDMENT AGAINST FORT SUMTER

SCENE ON THE FLOATING BATTERY IN CHARLESTON HARBOR DURING THE BOMBARDMENT OF FORT SUMTER

From a Drawing by a Confederate Officer

that part of Sullivan's Island near the floating battery. It was covered with brush and other material, which completely concealed it. It was skillfully constructed and well secured. Seventeen mortars, firing ten-inch shell, and thirty-three heavy guns, mostly columbiads, were engaged in the assault. The effect of the shot against the walls was terrific, and many of the shells took effect inside the fort.

Breakfast was had at half-past six o'clock, leisurely and calmly, after which the command was formed into three reliefs, equally dividing the officers and men. The first relief was under the command of Captain Doubleday, of the artillery, and Lieutenant Snyder, of the engineer, corps. This detatchment went to the guns, and opened fire upon the Cumming's Point Battery, Fort Moultrie, and Sullivan's Island. The iron battery was of immense strength, and most of the shot struck and glanced off again; the fire was so terrific on the parapet of Fort Sumter that Major Anderson refused to allow the guns to be manned. Had it been permitted, every one would have been sacrificed. Fort Moultrie was considerably damaged by the cannonading from Fort Sumter, many of the shot having taken effect on the embrasures. Several shot struck the floating battery, but very little damage was done. The reliefs were changed every four hours. The little garrison succeeded in dismounting two guns on Cumming's Point Battery. A new English rifled-gun, which was employed by the insurgents, was fired with great accuracy, several of the shot entering the embrasures of Fort Sumter, one of them slightly wounding four men. The full effect of the firing could not be known to those in the fort; it was impossible to see, and they had no reports from the other side. The men owed their safety to the extraordinary care exercised by the officers in command. A man was kept constantly on the lookout, who would cry "shot" or "shell" at every shot the enemy made, thus affording the men ample time to seek shelter. The workmen were at first rather reluctant to assist the soldiers in working the guns, but they gradually took hold, and rendered valuable assistance. But few shots were fired before every one of them became desperately engaged in the conflict. One gun had to be abandoned on account of the close fire made upon it. Hearing the firing renewed, Major Anderson went to the spot, and found a party of workmen engaged in serving the gun; one of these was seen stooping over it, with his hands on his knees, convulsed with joy.

"What are you doing here with that gun?" was asked.—"Hit it right in the centre!" was the reply; the man meaning that his shot had taken effect in the centre of the floating battery.

Peter Hart had been a most valuable assistant to Major Anderson and his little garrison, acting in the capacity of confidential mail agent and marketman before the actual siege began; and it was now found that Mrs. Anderson, in her estimate of this man's ability to aid and comfort her husband, had not been mistaken; for, since the day she gained for him admission in the fort, he, while keeping faithfully the promise exacted from Major Anderson by Governor Pickens "that he should not be enrolled as a soldier," had done such other service as no enlisted man or officer could have performed. During the bombardment he had successfully fought the fires constantly breaking out inside the fort from the hot shot of the besiegers' guns, until on the second day the barracks caught fire from a ten-inch shell, and the danger to be encountered in the attempt to extinguish it was so great that Major Anderson ordered him not to attempt it.

The effect of the fire was more disastrous than could have been supposed. The subsequent shots of the insurgents were more effective in consequence; the walls were weakened, and the men were more exposed. The main gates were destroyed by fire, thus leaving the garrison exposed from outside to assault. Five hundred men could have formed on the gorge, and marched into the fort without meeting much opposition. The fire spread around the fort on all sides. Fearful that the walls of the magazine might crack, and the shells pierce and prostrate them, the powder was taken out before the fire had fully enveloped it; ninety-six barrels of powder were taken out and thrown into the sea, leaving two hundred barrels still in the fort. Owing to a lack of cartridges, five men were kept inside the magazine, sewing them up as they were wanted; thus consuming sheets, blankets, shirts of the men, and all available material in the fort. When the magazine had finally to be closed, and the material for cartridges was exhausted, the garrison was left destitute of any means to continue the contest; the last biscuit had been eaten thirty-six hours before. The dense smoke from the burning buildings was stifling; the men lay prostrate on the ground, with wet handkerchiefs over their mouths and eyes, gasping for breath. It was a moment of imminent peril. If an eddy of wind had not ensued, all the men, probably, would have been suffocated. The crashing of the shot, the bursting of the shells, the falling of the walls, and the roar of the flames, made a pandemonium of the fort.

The aim of the insurgents had been principally directed at the flagstaff, from which waved proudly the Stars and Stripes. After two days' incessant firing, the flagstaff was finally shot away.

This was noticed only by the besiegers, and mistaken as a sign of surrender. No one in the fort had looked for, and missed, the Stars and Stripes, and, heeding not the fire or the shots of the

THE FLAG OF SUMTER

BROUGHT TO NEW YORK BY MAJOR ANDERSON, AND RAISED OVER THE EQUESTRIAN STATUE OF WASHINGTON AT THE "GREAT UNION MEETING" IN UNION SQUARE, APRIL 20TH, 1861.

enemy, Peter Hart gathered up the banner, and nailing it to a temporary staff, nailed this staff to the highest part of the remaining ruins: and when the besiegers soon after sought an interview with Major Anderson, they found "the flag was still there."

Roman, in his late book, "The Military Operations of General Beauregard" (Harper & Brothers, 1884), describes this scene in these words:

> "At about eight o'clock A.M., in the thickest of the bombardment, a thin smoke was observed curling up from Fort Sumter. It grew denser and denser as it steadily rose in the air, and it soon became apparent that the barracks of the fort had been set on fire by forty rounds of red-hot shot thrown from an eight-inch columbiad at Fort Moultrie, by a detachment of Company B, under Lieutenant Alfred Rhett. This sight increased the vigor of our attack, both officers and men feeling now that the garrison would soon be brought to terms. In spite, however, of this new and terrible element against which it had to contend, the fort still responded to the fire of our batteries, though at long and irregular intervals only.
>
> 'Appreciating the critical position of the enemy, and carried away by their own enthusiasm, our troops mounted the parapets in their front, and cheered Major Anderson at each successive discharge that came from the fort, deriding and hooting the while, what to them seemed the timorous inaction of the fleet outside the bar.
>
> "Matters had evidently reached a crisis for the men within the walls of Sumter. Fearing that some terrible calamity might befall them, and being informed that the United States flag no longer floated over the fort, General Beauregard immediately dispatched three of his aids, with offers of assistance to Major Anderson, who thanked him for his courtesy, but declined to accept aid. Before General Beauregard's aids could get to the fort, the United States flag, which had not been hauled down, as we supposed, but had fallen from the effects of a shot, was hoisted anew.'

Early in the afternoon of the 13th, ex-Senator Wigfall, of Texas, made his appearance at one of the embrasures, with a white handkerchief on the end of a sword, and begged for admittance. He asked to see Major Anderson. While Wigfall was in the act of crawling through the embrasure, Lieutenant Snyder called out to him, "Major Anderson is at the main gate." He passed through the embrasure in the casemate, paying no attention to what the lieutenant had said. Here he was met by Captain Foster, Lieutenants Meade and Davis. He said:

"I wish to see Major Anderson; I am General Wigfall, and come from General Beauregard." He then added, in an excited manner: "Let us stop this fighting; you are on fire, and your flag is down. Let us quit."

"No, sir," Lieutenant Davis replied, "our flag is not down. Step out here, and you will see it waving over the ramparts."

"Let us quit this," said Wigfall. "Here's a white flag; will anybody wave it out of the embrasure?"

"That is for you to do, if you choose," one of the officers replied.

"If there is no one else to do it," Wigfall responded, "I will." And, jumping into the embrasure, he waved the flag toward Moultrie and the batteries on Sullivan's Island.

In answer to his repeated request, one of the officers said that one of his men might hold the flag, and Corporal Binghurst jumped into the embrasure. The shot continuing to strike all around him, he leaped down again, after having waved the flag a few moments, and said: "They don't respect the flag; they are firing at it."

"If you will show a white flag from your ramparts, they will cease firing," Wigfall then said.

"If you request that a flag shall be shown there, while you hold a conference with Major Anderson, and for that purpose, it may be done," Lieutenant Davis replied.

At this point Major Anderson came up. Wigfall said:

"I am General Wigfall, and come from General Beauregard, who wishes to stop this."

Major Anderson, then rising to his full height, replied, "Well, sir!"

"Major Anderson," exclaimed Wigfall, "you have defended your flag nobly, sir. You have done all that it is possible for men to do, and General Beauregard wishes to stop the fight. On what terms will you evacuate this fort?"

Major Anderson's reply was: "General Beauregard is already acquainted with my only terms."

"Do I understand that you will evacuate upon the terms proposed the other day?"

"Yes, sir; and on those conditions only."

"Then sir," said Wigfall, "I understand, Major Anderson, that the fort is to be ours?"

"On those conditions only, I repeat."

"Very well," said Wigfall; and he retired.

A short time afterward, a deputation consisting of Senator Chesnut, Roger A. Pryor, Captain Lee, and W. Porcher Miles, came from General Beauregard, and had an interview with Major Anderson, when it came out that Wigfall had no authority to speak for General Beauregard, but acted on his own responsibility. "Then," said Lieutenant Davis, "we have been deceived." And Major Anderson, perceiving the state of the case, ordered the national flag to be raised to its place.

The deputation, however, requested him to keep the flag down until they could communicate with General Beauregard, as matters were liable to become complicated. They left, and between two and three hours afterward—the garrison meanwhile exerting themselves to extinguish the fire in the barracks—another deputation came from General Beauregard, agreeing to the terms of evacuation previously proposed. This was on Saturday evening. That night the garrison took what rest they could. Next day, the *Isabel* came down and anchored near the fort. The steamer *Clinch* was used as a transport to take the garrison to the *Isabel*, but the transfer was too late to allow the *Isabel* to go out with that tide.

The terms of the evacuation were, that the garrison should take their individual and company property, and that they should march out with their side and other arms, with the honors of war, in their own way and at their own time, and that they should salute their flag, and take it with them.

The insurgents agreed to furnish transports, as Major Anderson might select, to any part of the country, either by land or water. When the baggage of the garrison was all on board the transport, a portion of the soldiers remaining inside, under arms, were told off as gunners to serve in saluting the American flag.

When the last gun was fired, the flag was lowered amid the cheering of the men. At the fiftieth discharge there was a premature explosion, which killed one man instantly, seriously wounded another, and two more not so badly. The men were then formed and marched out, the band playing "Yankee Doodle" and "Hail to the Chief."

ROBERT ANDERSON,

THE DEFENDER OF FORT SUMTER.

Robert Anderson was born June 14th, 1805, in Kentucky. Entering the Military Academy at West Point, as a cadet, in 1821, he graduated July 1st, 1825; was breveted second lieutenant of the Second Artillery, and was almost immediately transferred to the Third Artillery. Steadily following his profession, he served as acting inspector-general of the Illinois Volunteers in the Black Hawk War, from May to October, 1832. In this connection, it is a striking coincidence that Abraham Lincoln and Jefferson Davis also served in that war. Abraham Lincoln was the captain of the Illinois Volunteers, of which Anderson was inspector-general; and Jefferson Davis, a second lieutenant in the regular army, won his first "spurs" at that period, having been detailed on special duties of an important character. Who could have foretold then that these three men would have been so peculiarly linked together, in the most important era of American history since the Declaration of Independence? that Anderson would in the future occupy so important and trying a position between the sectional allurements on the one side, and the national duties on the other, represented respectively by Davis and Lincoln?

Anderson was promoted to a first lieutenancy, June, 1833; was assistant-instructor of artillery in the Military Academy at West Point from September to December, 1835, when he was appointed instructor—in which position he remained until December, 1837. Lieutenant Anderson served as aide-de-camp to General Scott in 1838, and on the 2d of April of that year was breveted captain for gallant and successful conduct in the war against the Florida Indians; his next service was assistant adjutant-general, with the rank of captain, from July 7th, 1838, which office he relinquished in November, 1841, having been appointed captain in his own regiment in the October previous.

Captain Anderson served with conspicuous distinction throughout the Mexican War. From the siege of Vera Cruz, under General Scott, to the occupation of the capital of Mexico, he was noted for his calmness and efficiency as an artillery officer. At Vera Cruz, the battery under his command was unerring in its precision. El Molino del Rey was, as one of the historians of the Mexican War says, "proportionally the bloodiest battle of the war, long to be remembered as the scene of extraordinary actions, and long grieved over as that which made the graves of brave and noble men." Here Captain Anderson was severely wounded, and here he won, for gallant and meritorious conduct, his brevet as major, bearing date September 8th, 1847; a title which is so honorably linked with his name and national renown.

The conduct of Captain Anderson at El Molino del Rey is most favorably chronicled in the reports of the day. General Garland, in his dispatch, says: "Captain Robert Anderson (acting field-officer) behaved with great heroism on this occasion. Even after receiving a severe and painful wound, he continued at the head of the column, regardless of pain and self-preservation, and setting a handsome example to his men, of coolness, energy and courage." The effect of the heavy batteries which he directed at Chapultepec also commands the encomium of General Scott in his dispatches.

ROBERT ANDERSON.

In 1860 Major Anderson was appointed to the command of the forts in Charleston Harbor, and he took possession of Fort Sumter on the night of December 25th, 1860. The strategic course pursued by Major Anderson won the immediate applause of the country, and commanded even the respect of the secessionists. After the bombardment of Fort Sumter, on the 12th and 13th of April, and its evacuation on the 14th, Major Anderson with his command sailed for New York, where he arrived on the 18th of April. He was received with the utmost enthusiasm, and on the 23d was officially welcomed by the corporation, when the Mayor, Fernando Wood, presented him with the freedom of the city in a golden casket; after which he received the citizens at large in the Governor's Room of the City Hall.

By order of the President, the Secretary of War officially conveyed to Major Anderson the approbation of the Government; and, on repairing to Washington, he received in person a flattering acknowledgment of his services, and the offer of a lengthened furlough to recruit his health, considerably shattered by a long confinement in Fort Sumter, under a load of responsibilities. Breveted major-general, April 13th, 1861, he commanded the departments of Kentucky and of the Cumberland; and retired from active service October 27th, 1863. While endeavoring to seek a restoration to health abroad, he died, October 26th, 1871, at Nice, France, aged sixty-six. He translated "Instructions for Field Artillery, Horse and Foot," and "Evolutions of Field Batteries."

CORRESPONDENCE.

Headquarters Provisional Army, C. S. A.,
Charleston, S. C., April 11th—2 P.M.

To Major Robert Anderson, Commanding at Fort Sumter, Charleston Harbor, South Carolina.

Sir: The Government of the Confederate States has hitherto forborne from any hostile demonstration against Fort Sumter, in the hope that the Government of the United States, with a view to the amicable adjustment of all questions between the two Governments, and to avert the calamities of war, would voluntarily evacuate it. There was reason at one time to believe that such would be the course pursued by the Government of the United States; and, under that impression, my Government has refrained from making any demand for the surrender of the fort. But the Confederate States can no longer delay assuming actual possession of a fortification commanding the entrance of one of their harbors, and necessary to its defense and security. I am ordered by the Government of the Confederate States to demand the evacuation of Fort Sumter. My aids, Colonel Chestnut and Captain Lee, are authorized to make such demand of you. All proper facilities will be afforded for the removal of yourself and command, together with company arms and property, and all private property, to any port in the United States which you may select. The flag which you have upheld so long, and with so much fortitude, may be saluted by you on taking it down. Colonel Chestnut and Captain Lee will, for a reasonable time, await your answer. I am, sir, very respectfully, your obedient servant,

P. G. T. Beauregard,
Brigadier-general Commanding

Headquarters Fort Sumter, S. C.,
April 11th, 1861.

To Brigadier-general P. G. T. Beauregard, Commanding Provisional Army, C.S.A.

General: I have the honor to acknowledge the receipt of your communication demanding the evacuation of this fort, and to say in reply thereto that it is a demand with which I regret that my sense of honor, and of my obligation to my Government, prevent my compliance. Thanking you for the fair, manly and courteous terms proposed, and for the high compliment paid me, I remain, general, very respectfully, your obedient servant,

Robert Anderson,
Major United States Army, Commanding

Headquarters Provisional Army, C. S. A.,
Charleston, S. C., April 11th, 1861—11 P.M.

To Major Robert Anderson, Commanding at Fort Sumter, Charleston Harbor, S. C.

Major: In consequence of the verbal observations made by you to my aids, Messrs. Chestnut and Lee, in relation to the condition of your supplies, and that you would, in a few days, be starved out, if our guns did not batter you to pieces ir words to that effect, and desiring no useless effusion of blood, I communicated both the verbal observation and your written answer to my communication to my Government. If you will state the time you will evacuate Fort Sumter, and agree, in the meantime, you will not use your guns against us, unless ours shall be employed against Fort Sumter, we shall abstain from opening fire upon you. Colonel Chestnut and Captain Lee are authorized by me to enter into such an agreement with you. You are, therefore, requested to communicate to them an open answer. I remain, Major, very respectfully, your obedient servant.

P. G. T. BEAUREGARD,
Brigadier-general, Commanding.

HEADQUARTERS FORT SUMTER,
SOUTH CAROLINA,
2:30 A.M., April 12th, 1861.

To Brigadier-general P. G. T. Beauregard, Commanding Provisional Army, C. S. A.

GENERAL: I have the honor to acknowledge the receipt of your second communication of the 11th instant by Colonel Chestnut, and to state in reply that, cordially uniting with you in the desire to avoid the useless effusion of blood, I will, if provided with the necessary means of transportation, evacuate Fort Sumter by noon on the 15th instant, should I not receive, prior to that time, controlling instructions from my Government, or additional supplies, and that I will not, in the meantime, open my fire upon your forces unless compelled to do so by some hostile act against this fort or the flag of my Government, by the forces under your command, or by some portion of them, or by the perpetration of some act showing a hostile intention on your part against this fort or the flag it bears. I have the honor to be, General, very respectfully, your obedient servant,

ROBERT ANDERSON,
Major U. S. A., Commanding.

FORT SUMTER, S. C.,
April 12th, 1861—3.20 A.M.

Major Robert Anderson, U. S. A., Commanding Fort Sumter.

SIR: By authority of Brigadier-general Beauregard, commanding the provisional forces of the Confederate States, we have the honor to notify you that he will open the fire of his batteries on Fort Sumter in one hour from this time. We have the honor to be, very respectfully, your obedient servants,

JAMES CHESTNUT, JR.,
Aide-de-camp,
STEPHEN D. LEE,
Captain C. S. Army, etc.

P. G. T. BEAUREGARD,

THE BESIEGER OF FORT SUMTER.

PIERRE GUSTAVE TOUTANT BEAUREGARD, whose name is so widely known as the commander of the troops of the "Confederate States" in Charleston, S. C., was, previous to the resigning of his commission, a distinguished officer of engineers in the United States service, and in that capacity won the esteem of his superior officers on more than one occasion.

General Beauregard was born in the Parish of St. Bernard, near the City of New Orleans, in the State of Louisiana, on the 28th of May, 1818. He entered the United States Military Academy at West Point, as cadet, in 1834. Of Welsh and French stock, he early displayed those qualities which are strikingly characteristic of the Celtic and Gallic military minds. Young Beauregard graduated second in a class of forty-five, and on July 7th, 1838, he was appointed second lieutenant in the United States Engineers.

Lieutenant Beauregard was highly distinguished in the Mexican War. He was breveted captain, August 20th, 1847, "for gallant and meritorious conduct at the battles of Contreras and Churubusco," and won his brevet as major, September 13th, 1847, for "gallant and meritorious conduct at the battle of Chapultepec," in which he was twice wounded. General Totten, chief of the engineer department, added to the foregoing general orders: "It affords the department high satisfaction to communicate to you the well-earned record of your efforts on the fields of Mexico."

A lull in military affairs followed the close of the Mexican War, and Major Beauregard expressed a purpose to leave the service. General Scott and General Persifer F. Smith each wrote to Beauregard

P. G. T. BEAUREGARD.

to dissuade him, paying handsome tribute to his skill and gallantry, and the loss his resignation would be to the army and the country. He remained in the service in charge of "the Mississippi and Lake defenses of Louisiana."

On the 8th of November, 1860, he was appointed superintendent of the United States Military Academy at West Point by direction of the President. Major Beauregard, late in December, 1860, when *en route* for West Point, reported to General Totten at the War Department, Washington, and avowed his intention, should Louisiana secede from the Union, to resign his commission and go with his State. He also called on General Scott to express this determination to resign, but failed to find him in Washington. He then stopped in New York city. Several army friends, Captain Mansfield Lovell and Captain G. W. Smith, approved of his proposed course, and declared that, were they similarly situated, they would act in the same manner.

Major Beauregard had been but a few days in command at West Point, when the new Secretary of War, Mr. Holt, revoked the order appointing him, and ordered him to return to his former station at New Orleans. On his return he passed through New York, and there was informed of the secession of his State, and requested to immediately return. On reaching the dock to take passage for New Orleans, he witnessed the arrival of the *Star of the West* from off Charleston, with shot-holes in her hull and smokestacks. He went on board, and was entertained by her commander with a graphic account of his experiences in Charleston Harbor.

On reaching New Orleans, Governor Moore requested him to take charge of the defenses of the city, but declined until he had formally resigned his commission in the United States Army. This he did the same day, and joined as a private the battalion of New Orleans Guards, composed of the *élite* of the Creole population of New Orleans.

Major Beauregard advised the Military Board to arm Forts Jackson and St. Philip with the heaviest guns procurable, and transfer all the heavy guns from the four inferior works—concentrating the whole armament and force within the two forts. He also drew plans and made estimates for two river obstructions, consisting of heavy booms and river flat-boats, with chains, ropes, etc., to be worked from the shore, and raised or lowered at will, to allow free passage of friendly, and fully prevent the passage of the enemy's, boats. Had these plans been adopted the Federal flotilla, in April, 1862, would have found more difficulty in running the gantlet of the forts, and New Orleans would not have been so easily captured; but a Military Board did not approve of the plan.

Beauregard was summoned to Montgomery on the 22d of February, 1861, by L. P. Walker, Secretary of War, by request of President Davis. He arrived at the Confederate Capital on the 26th, and the same day suggested such a system of heads of bureaus in the War Department as would relieve the Secretary of detail work, and suggested friends in the old service competent to take charge of the several departments. Among these were Captains G. W. Smith and Mansfield Lovell, of New York, who accepted the positions, and arrived in Montgomery after the battle of Bull Run.

From cut, 1861

President Davis appointed Beauregard to take command at Charleston and to direct operations against Fort Sumter, and commissioned him first Brigadier-general in the provisional army of the Confederate States. His resignation from the United States Army had not yet, to his knowledge, been accepted, and he declined to take up arms against the United States flag until officially relieved from his fealty to it; and so expressed himself to President Davis, who urged his acceptance of the position. Telegraphic communication being yet open to Washington, he was informed the next day of the acceptance of his resignation by President

Buchanan, and he repaired to Charleston, to take command of the State troops, should the authorities of South Carolina so desire. Governor Pickens proposed to put General Beauregard in command without delay; but this offer was declined until he could thoroughly acquaint himself with the forces, various batteries, available resources in ordnance and progress of the works already begun.

March 1st, 1861.

General Beauregard's further military history will be found in the succeeding pages of this work, in connection with the battles and sieges in which he was an important factor and aggressive worker.

Beauregard was noted for prompt energy and as a brilliant strategist and a ready tactician, and his appointment to the command of Charleston was hailed with considerable favor by the advocates of the "Southern Confederacy." His command was soon in efficient order. He will hold a place in contemporaneous history as the assailant of Fort Sumter, and as the officer to whom Major Anderson and his gallant comrades were forced to yield their position. In chronicling "the victory," Jefferson Davis is said to have put the general's name into the following couplet:

> "With mortar, Paixhan, and petard,
> We sent the foe our *Beau-regard*."

SUMTER AFTER THE BOMBARDMENT.

The appearance of Fort Sumter after its evacuation by Major Anderson, was thus described by the Charleston *Mercury* of April 15th, 1861:

"Every point and every object in the interior of the fort, to which the eye was turned, except the outer walls and casemates, which are still strong, bore the impress of ruin. It was as if the Genius of Destruction had tasked his energies to make the thing complete; brooded over by the desolation of ages, it could scarce have been developed to a fuller maturity of ruin. The walls of the internal structure—roofless, bare, blackened and perforated by shot and shell—hung in fragments, and seemed in instant readiness to totter down. Near the centre of the parade-ground was the burried grave of one who had fallen from the recent casualty. To the left of the entrance was a man who seemed to be on the verge of death. In the ruins, to the right, there was another. The shattered flagstaff, marked by four balls, lay on the ground. At least four guns were dismounted on the ramparts, and at every step the way was impeded by portions of the broken structure. And so it was that the garrison, compelled to yield the fortress, had at least the satisfaction of leaving it in a condition calculated to inspire the least possible pleasure to its captors."

MOULTRIE AFTER THE BOMBARDMENT FROM SUMTER.

The Charleston *Courier* of April 20th, 1861, describing the appearance of Fort Moultrie after the bombardment, said: "The raking fire from Fort Sumter against Fort Moultrie was terribly destructive, and, viewed in connection with the fact that no lives were lost, is the most extraordinary case ever recorded in history. As you enter, the eye falls upon the battered walls of the archway, with openings, in some places, large enough for windows. In other places may be seen the hanging splinters of the rafters, large pieces of ceiling, seemingly about to drop, while the holes in the roof throw a clear light over the scene of destruction, which renders it painfully impressive. It would be an almost impossible task to count the number of balls discharged at this devastated fortress. The walls of the officers' quarters were battered with eight or ten balls, which had penetrated the whole depth of the building; the western wall on the upper balcony was entirely shot away. The barracks were almost entirely destroyed. The furnace for heating shot was struck four times; the flag of the Confederate States received three shots, and the Palmetto flag four—a rather singular and peculiar circumstance when viewed in connection with the seven Confederate States. The merlons of sand-bags, etc., remain unbroken.

"On the outside walls we counted over one hundred shots. Laborers were engaged in clearing away fallen brick, etc. It will be necessary to pull down the old walls, and rebuild them. Even the beds and bedding in the officers' quarters and the men's barracks were cut and torn into splinters and shreds. Had it not been for the bomb-proof shelter, the loss of life would, no doubt, have been appalling. One shell entered the brick wall of Major Ripley's bedroom, ran down the wall and burst on the bureau, immediately over the head of the bed. Our time prevented us from visiting the battery to the north of the fort. We learn, however, that though buildings surrounding it had been struck several times, and fences, trees, etc., cut away, the battery suffered no injury. Providentially no hot shot were thrown from Fort Sumter, probably from the fact that the garrison were without fuel."

It is a remarkable fact that not a single life was lost on either side during this fierce cannonading.

INTERIOR VIEW OF FORT SUMTER AFTER THE BOMBARDMENT.

THE DEFENDERS OF FORT SUMTER.

Major Robert Anderson, afterward commissioned a brevet major-general; Captains J. G. Foster and Abner Doubleday were both raised to full major-generals; First Lieutenants Jefferson C. Davis, Truman Seymour (then captain by brevet), and Norman J. Hall, were each commissioned brigadier-generals; First Lieutenants George W. Snyder and Theodore Talbot (assistant adjutant-general), both died in less than a year after the surrender; Second Lieutenant Richard K. Meade joined the Confederate Army, and Assistant-surgeon Samuel W. Crawford was promoted a brigadier-general.

The non-commissioned officers were: Sergeants William H. Hamner, John Renshaw, James E. Gallway, John Carmody, John Otto, John McMahon, Eugene Sheibner, William A. Harn, James Chester, Thomas Kiernan and John Kearney.

Corporals: Charles Bringhurst, Henry Ellerbrook Owen McGuire, Francis J. Oakes and Christopher Costolow.

Musicians: Robert Foster and Charles Hall

artificers: Henry Straudt, Philip Andermann and John E. Noack.

Mrs. Anderson's "*reinforcement*," Peter Hart, who acted as confidential mail and market messenger.

Privates: Peter Rice, Patrick Murphy, Tedeschi Ontdratto, Andrew Wickstrom, Henry Schmidt, John Urquhart, Edward Brady, Barney Cain, John Doran, Dennis Johnson, John Kehoe, John Lanagan, John Klein, Frederick Lintner, Frederick Meier, John Magill, James Moore, William Morter, Patrick Neilan, John Nixon, Michael O'Donald, William Walker, Robert Roe, Joseph Wall, Edmund Walsh, Henry R. Walter, Herman Will, Thomas Wishnowski, Casper Wutterpel, Cornelius Baker, Patrick Claney, Thomas Carroll, John Davis, James Digdam, George Fielding, James Gibbons, James Hays, Daniel Hough, John Irwin, James McDonald, Samuel Miller, John Newport, George Pinchard, Frank Rivers, Lewis Schroeder, Carl A. Sellman, John Thompson, Charles H. Tozer, William Witzmann, John Laroche, who deserted just after reaching New York, and Edward Gallway, who was killed by the premature discharge of his gun while saluting the flag, after the capitulation. He was buried by the Confederates with military honors.

REJOICINGS IN CHARLESTON.

General Beauregard, in orders issued after the surrender, congratulated his troops on "the brilliant success which had crowned their gallantry." Commenting on the terms offered to Major Anderson and his command, he said: "And to shew our magnanimity to the gallant defenders who where only executing the orders of their Government, they will be allowed to evacuate on the same terms which were offered to them before the bombardment commenced." He concluded as follow: "The general is highly gratified to state that the troops, in their labor, privations and endurance at the batteries, and at other posts, have exhibited the highest characteristic of tried soldiers."

April, 1861.

PAUL H. HAYNE

AID-DE-CAMP TO GOVERNOR PICKENS OF SOUTH CAROLINA, AND BEARER OF DISPATCHES FROM HIM TO MAJOR ANDERSON.

The day after the surrender being Sunday a *Te Deum* was sung, with great pomp, in the beautiful Cathedral of St. John and St. Finbar, and in the churches devout thanks were offered for the triumph of the army of South Carolina and the bloodless victory gained. The Right Rev. Thomas Frederick Davis, the venerable Bishop of the Diocese, who was totally blind and quite feeble, was led by the rector to the sacred desk in the old and historic St. Philip's Episcopal Church, where he addressed the congregation with a few impressive and stirring words. He said: "Your boys were there, and mine were there, and it was right that they should be there. They had laid their cause before God, and God had most signally blessed their dependence on him."

In less than three weeks the Confederates had entirely rebuilt, armed and garrisoned Fort Sumter.

DEMONSTRATIONS ON THE BATTERY AT CHARLESTON, S. C., DURING THE BOMBARDMENT OF FORT SUMTER.

THE CONFEDERATE SENATE IN OPEN SESSION AT THE CAPITOL, MONTGOMERY, ALA.—HOWELL COBB PRESIDING.

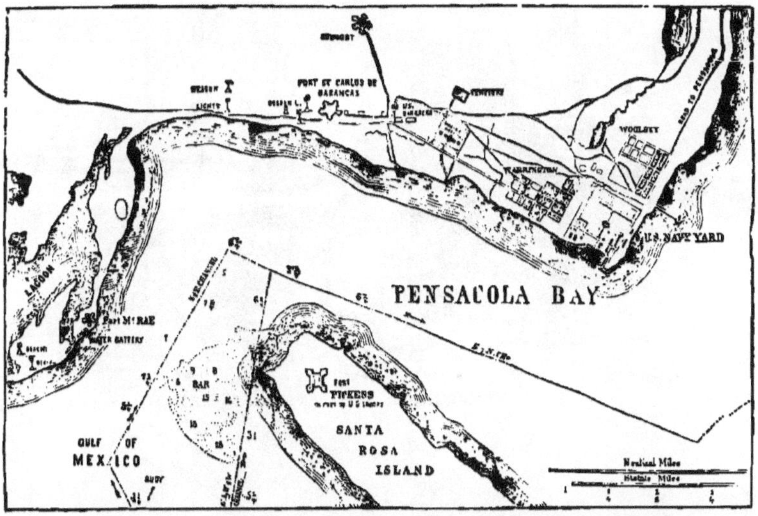

THE UNITED STATES NAVY YARD, PENSACOLA BAY, FLA.—SANTA ROSA ISLAND, AND THE GULF AND BAY FORTS.

PENSACOLA HARBOR.

The harbor of Pensacola is probably the largest and finest on the whole coast of the Mexican Gulf, for which reason it was selected by the Government of the United States as its principal southern naval station. It accordingly established there a navy-yard, an arsenal, and a marine hospital, and built several heavy fortifications for its defense.

The town of Pensacola, previously a miserable settlement, soon became of some importance, and now numbers several thousand inhabitants, chiefly workmen in the employ of the Government, or dependent on it. Pensacola is sixty-four miles to the eastward of Mobile, and one hundred and eighty from Tallahassee, Florida.

On the opposite side of the harbor from Pensacola is the long, low island of Santa Rosa, protecting it from the Gulf. At its extreme western point, and completely commanding the entrance to the harbor, as well as the harbor itself, is Fort Pickens. This is a bastioned work of the first class, built of New York granite. Its walls are forty-five feet in height, by twelve in thickness. It is embrasured for two tiers of guns, which are placed under bomb-proof casemates, besides having one tier of guns *en barbette*. The guns from the work radiate to every point of the horizon, with flank and enfilading fire, at every angle of approach. The work was commenced in 1828, and finished in 1853, at a cost of nearly one million of dollars. When on a war footing, its garrison consists of 1,260 soldiers. The total armament of the work, when complete, consists of 210 guns, 63 of which are iron forty-two-pounders, 17 thirty-two-pounders, 49 twenty-four-pounders, 5 eighteens, 13 twelves, 6 brass field pieces, 26 brass flank howitzers, 1 thirteen-inch mortar, 4 heavy ten-inch mortars, 4 light eight-inch mortars, 4 sixteen-inch stone-mortars, 5 Cohorn mortars.

President Buchanan, fearing to irritate the Southern Members of Congress, and desiring to find some peaceable solution to the question agitating the two sections, delayed reinforcing the forts. Learning that the State troops had seized the Navy Yard and Forts Barrancas and McRae, and threatened Fort Pickens, he consented to dispatch the war-steamer *Brooklyn* with provisions, military stores and ninety artillerymen from Fortress Monroe, to the relief of Pickens.

There were at this time three or four small steamers under Captain J. H. Ward, U.S.N., then in the Coast Survey service, which Captain Vogdes was also to employ. Under a promise from Senator Mallory, of Florida, that no attack would be made on Fort Pickens, the commander of the relief squadron was ordered by joint telegram from the War and Navy Departments not to land any troops at the fort unless it should be attacked. By this arrangement the garrison in

MAY, 1861.

FORT PICKENS, ON SANTA ROSA ISLAND, PENSACOLA BAY, FLA.

RELIEF OF FORT PICKENS, SANTA ROSA ISLAND, PENSACOLA

CASTLE PINCKNEY.

RELIEF OF FORT PICKENS, SANTA ROSA ISLAND, PENSACOLA BAY, FLA., BY THE UNITED STATES FLEET, APRIL 17th, 1861.

CASTLE PINCKNEY, CHARLESTON HARBOR, S. C.

Fort Pickens were left without reinforcements, while they saw their abandoned forts on shore being strengthened and strongly garrisoned by the State troops.

THE DEFENSE OF FORT PICKENS.

When Florida seceded, Governor Perry decided to seize this fort, and issued orders for its immediate possession by the State troops. Lieutenant A. J. Slemmer, the commander of the fort, had heard of this intention on the part of the Governor early in January, and soon after, when he learned that the Forts near Mobile had been surrendered to Alabama troops, he took immediate measures to save to his Government those under his command, if possible.

The Navy Yard was in charge of Commodore Armstrong, an old captain of the United States Navy. Lieutenant Slemmer, in company with Lieutenant Gilman, visited the Navy Yard, and sought the co-operation of Commodore Armstrong.

January, 1861.

As no special orders had been received from the Naval Department at Washington, the veteran commodore declined to join the young lieutenants in any action, unless under positive orders. Slemmer immediately took measures to secure the powder at Fort Barrancas, which fort he did not hope, with the small force at his command, to hold. He, however, caused the batteries to be put in order, strengthened the guard, and at sunset of January 8th raised the drawbridge that gave access to the fort.

The same evening a small force of armed State troops approached the fort. On their discovery by the sentinel an alarm was given; and, finding the draw up and their presence known, they withdrew. The next morning instructions were received by Lieutenant Slemmer to use all diligence and effort to protect the forts. The same orders, with instructions to co-operate with Lieutenant Slemmer, were received by Commodore Armstrong.

These commanders met, and agreed, in view of the smallness of the garrison, to make no effort to hold the less important fort, but to concentrate within the walls of Pickens, as the stronger and less liable to be attacked, and the most available to reinforcements that the Government might send.

Armstrong was to send the steamer *Wyandot*, Captain Berryman, to convey the garrison at Fort Barrancas to Fort Pickens, and add to the force such men as he could spare from the Navy Yard, and order the *Wyandot* and storeship *Supply*, Captain Walker, to anchor near the fort, under the protection of the guns.

Armstrong sent the *Wyandot*, but no men from the Yard, and a few provisions in place of the storeship. Slemmer went in person to the commodore, and demanded an explanation. He impulsively charged the veteran officer with deception and bad faith, and asked how he hoped to defend a fort that demanded a force of twelve hundred men to garrison, with only forty-six, the exact number of men he then had fit for garrison duty. The commodore had sent Lieutenants Farrand and Renshaw to see that the plans agreed on were carried out, and was greatly surprised to learn of the imperfect service, through disaffection and intrigue, against his wishes and orders. On the morning of the 10th of January the *Wyandot* carried over Slemmer's command. The day and night before, the men, the officers, and their wives and children, had worked incessantly preparing for the change of quarters.

The wives of Lieutenants Slemmer and Gilman were especially conspicuous in their good offices as helpers, and in their fortitude and zeal. About thirty ordinary seamen from the Navy Yard, without arms or equipments, were added to the little garrison. The powder in Fort Barrancas was secured, and by Lieutenant Slemmer's orders the guns were spiked

HORSES SWUNG OVERBOARD TO SWIM TO SANTA ROSA ISLAND.

in position, as he had neither time nor means to dismount them.

The *Wyandot* was ordered by Commodore Armstrong to the Southern shore of Cuba, and the *Supply* to her final destination, Vera Cruz. Slemmer remonstrated; but Armstrong acted on orders received from the Department at Washington as

ADAM J. SLEMMER,
THE COMMANDER OF FORT PICKENS.

to destination before the contingency arose. Captain Berryman, of the *Wyandot*, however, procured, with some difficulty, some muskets at the Navy Yard to arm the seamen, and delivered them to Lieutenant Slemmer. The same morning, five hundred troops from Florida, Alabama and Mississippi, commanded by Colonel Lennox, of Florida, demanded the surrender of the Navy Yard to the authorities of the State.

It was beyond the power of Commodore Armstrong* to resist, as he well knew that three-fourths of the officers and men under his command were in full sympathy with, and at least one of his lieutenants (Farrand) in the active service of, the State authorities.

Lieutenant Renshaw, the flag officer under Commodore Armstrong, openly deserted his flag, and ordered it to be pulled down. This was done with the greatest indignity, and the flag was allowed to fall to the ground amid derisive shouts by a greater portion of the men present, led by Lieutenant J. R. Eggleston, of the *Wyandot*.

The command of the Navy Yard was given to Captain V. M. Randolph, another naval officer who had determined to cast his fortune with the new occupants of the Yard, who gained possession of the post, with ordnance stores valued at over $150,000. Captain Randolph and Lieutenants Farrand, Renshaw and Eggleston, who had already sent their resignations to Washington, and had them accepted before the Government was aware of their purpose.

Lieutenant Slemmer learned through Commander Walker, of the *Supply*, that the Navy Yard was besieged, and at once sent a note to the commodore asking, in case he determined to capitulate, to send the marines to strengthen the command of Fort Pickens. He received no reply to his note, and a few hours afterward he saw the old flag go down at the Navy Yard.

This now placed Lieutenant Slemmer in a strong fort, with a garrison of eighty-one in all, officers and men. Fifty-four guns were in position ready for service, and he had five months' provisions. He at once set to work to put everything in working order, momentarily expecting an attack.

On the 12th of January a formal demand was made by Captain Randolph, Major Marks and Lieutenant Rutledge, all in military dress, and claiming to be citizens of Florida and Alabama, for the peaceable surrender of the fort in the name of their respective Governors.

Lieutenant Slemmer to this demand replied: "I am here under the orders of the President of the United States, and by direction of the General-in-Chief of the Army, and I recognize no right of any Governor to demand the surrender of United States property. My orders are distinct and explicit."

The Military Commissioners, apparently surprised at this determined opposition to their, so far, successful plans of occupation, withdrew. On the 15th, Colonel William H. Chase, late of the United States Army, but now in command of the entire force of the Sovereign State of Florida, although himself a native of Massachusetts, accompanied by Lieutenant Farrand, sought, and was allowed, an interview with Lieutenant Slemmer.

January, 1861.

Representing himself as having full power from the chief magistrate of Florida to take possession of the fort, the Massachusetts colonel, now the head and front of the army of the State of Florida, counseled the commander of the only United States force in Pensacola Bay to allow the

* The Observer, of Pensacola, Fla., January 15th, 1861, reported Commodore Armstrong as saying, when Colonel Lennox demanded the surrender of the Navy Yard: "I have served my country faithfully all my life. I love the old flag, and have protected it in sunshine and in storm. My heart is bleeding because of the destruction of my country. I am a native of Kentucky, which has seceded, and therefore I know not where to go to make a livelihood in my declining years. I have no adequate force to make resistance, and if I had, I would rather lose my own life than destroy the lives of my countrymen. In view of this condition of affairs, I relinquish my authority to the sovereignty of Florida."

LANDING REINFORCEMENTS ON SANTA ROSA ISLAND.

surrender of the fort without bloodshed; that he (Slemmer) could do so now without sacrificing his own honor, or that of his gallant officers and men; that he would consider the surrender of the fort as subject to any agreement that might be entered into between Commissioners Mallory and Yulee (now in Washington in the double capacity of United States Senators and Commissioners for the Sovereign State of Florida) and the National Government. Colonel Chase would not counsel Lieutenant Slemmer to do anything dishonorable, but if he consented to such an arrangement, he would secure for himself the commendation of all Christian gentlemen, and avoid making himself guilty of allowing fraternal blood to flow. He proposed that Lieutenant Slemmer and his garrison should be given comfortable quarters at Fort Barrancas, pending the negotiations in Washington, and in conclusion urged Slemmer to consider the situation, and take care not to act so as to have the fearful recollections of a tragedy that he could now avoid, but rather to make the present opportunity redound to his glory as the most Christian-like act of his life. Lieutenant Slemmer, first consulting with the commanders of the *Wyandot* and *Supply*, positively refused to surrender the fort.

ADAM J. SLEMMER.

Born in Montgomery County, Pennsylvania, in 1828; graduated at the United States Military Academy at West Point, July 1st, 1850; appointed brevet second lieutenant in the artillery—first lieutenant, 1854; served in Seminole War, Florida, 1850-1; in California, 1851-4; professor at West Point, 1855-9; rejoined his company of the First United States Artillery at Fort Moultrie, Charleston Harbor, in 1859; transferred to Fort Barrancas, Pensacola Harbor, 1860. On occupation of United States Navy Yard at Pensacola by the Florida State troops in January, 1861, he transferred his little force to Fort Pickens, on Santa Rosa Island, which he held until reinforced in April, 1861, when he was superseded by Colonel Harvey Brown. May 4th, 1861, he was promoted to the rank of major of the Sixteenth Infantry, and ordered to New York Harbor with his command, which had become broken down in health by reason of their long confinement inside the walls of Fort Pickens during the beleaguerment; was acting inspector-general of the Department of Ohio until November, 1861, when ill health compelled him to take a leave of absence. In May, 1862, he returned to duty, and was assigned to General Buell's army; participated in the siege of Corinth, Miss., and in the movement to Louisville, Ky., and Nashville, Tenn.; was commissioned brigadier general of volunteers November 29th, 1862, engaged in the battle of Murfreesboro, December 31st, where he was severely wounded, and incapacitated from further service in the field. From July, 1863, to the close of the war he served on an examining board as president. In August, 1865, he was mustered out of the volunteer service, and resumed his regular army commission of lieutenant-colonel of the Fourth Infantry, won for gallantry at Murfreesboro; he was further promoted, for gallant and meritorious conduct during the war, colonel and brigadier-general. He served on garrison duty until October, 1866, when, on account of increasing ill-health, he was assigned to board duty, and died at Fort Laramie, October 7th, 1868.

LANDING REINFORCEMENTS ON SANTA ROSA ISLAND.

APRIL, 1861.

THE Government decided to reinforce Fort Pickens on Santa Rosa Island. The steam-frigate *Powhatan*, of 11 guns and 275 men, and the steam-transports *Atlantic* and *Illinois*, were commissioned for that purpose. The *Atlantic* sailed from New York on the 7th of April, having on board 450 troops, including two companies of light artillery and a company of sappers and miners, under command of Colonel Harvey Brown, besides 69 horses, and a large quantity of munitions of war and supplies. She reached Key West on the 13th, when she took additional troops, and ordnance, shot, shell, etc., and sailed for Pensacola Bay on the 14th, and reaching the anchorage of the squadron lying off Fort Pickens at half-past six o'clock P. M. on the 16th, in advance of the *Powhatan* and *Illinois*. Immediate measures were taken, by aid of the boats of the squadron, for throwing reinforcements into Fort Pickens that night, with so much success that the larger portion of the officers and men were in the fort before midnight. The remainder of the troops were landed early on the morning of the 17th, the horses during the afternoon and night of the 18th, and the stores and munitions between that period and the 23d. The *Illinois* left New York on the night of April 8th with 300 troops, 500 cases of muskets, and a supply of munitions of war and provisions. On the night of the 19th she reached the anchorage off Fort Pickens, and at once landed her troops and cargo. The war-steamer *Powhatan*, Commander D. D. Porter, reached the rendezvous on the 17th. Previous to the arrival of the reinforcements sent from New York, viz., on the night of the 12th of April, reinforcements were thrown into Fort Pickens, consisting of Company A, First Artillery, 86 men and 115 marines. The garrison then stood, rank and file: The old garrison, 82; Company A, First Artillery, 86; United States Marines, 115. Total, 283.

The marines were only landed temporarily, and, after the arrival of the main body of reinforcements, were returned to their respective ships, so that on the 25th of April the garrison of Fort Pickens was as follows: Companies F and A, Third Infantry (old garrison), 121; Companies A and M, Second Artillery, 122; Sappers and Miners, 62; Company G, C, E, B, F, D, H and K, recruits, 574. Total, 879.

JUSTICE TO WILLIAM CONWAY.

In the testimony before the Naval General Court Martial, in the trial of Captain James Armstrong on charges growing out of the surrender of the Navy Yard on Pensacola Bay, an incident of devotion to the Government was made known and rewarded, as shown in the following communications:

WASHINGTON, D. C., April 8th, 1861.

The president, members, and judge advocate, of the court lately held in the City of Washington, D. C., for the trial of Commodore Armstrong, beg leave respectfully to submit to the Honorable Secretary of the Navy the propriety, justice and good policy of bestowing some appropriate mark of its approbation of the loyalty, spirit and good conduct of William Conway, a quartermaster of the navy, on duty in the Navy Yard at Warrington, Florida, when the same was surrendered on the 12th of January, 1861, who, with manly pride, and in a spirit of patriotic devotion, refused to obey the order to haul down the national flag on the occasion of said surrender. The evidence of this honorable devotion to the dignity and credit of the flag of his country is found in the record of the testimony in Commodore Armstrong's case.

Respectfully submitted by order of the Court,

A. B. MAGRUDER, *Judge Advocate*.

NAVY DEPARTMENT, April 24th, 1861.

It appears, from the testimony taken in Captain Armstrong's case, that William Conway, an aged seaman, doing duty as quartermaster in the Warrington Navy Yard, at the time of its surrender, when ordered by Lieutenant F. B. Renshaw to haul down the national flag, promptly and indignantly refused to obey the order. The love and reverence thus impulsively exhibited for his country's flag in the hour of its peril is not the less worthy of being called noble and chivalric because displayed by one in an humble station. It is the more deserving of commemoration, for subordinates in the service are not usually expected to set examples of patriotism and fidelity in their trusts, but to follow them. The Department deem it no more than strict justice to William Conway that this testimonial from the court in his behalf should be made known throughout the service. It therefore directs that this general order be publicly read as early as practicable after its receipt by the commanders of all naval stations and all vessels of the navy in commission, in the presence of the officers and men under their command.

GIDEON WELLES, *Secretary of the Navy*.

THE UPRISING OF THE PEOPLE.

The fall of Fort Sumter—the first success of the Confederates; the humiliation attending the lowering of the American Flag; and the giving to the breeze the banner of the Palmetto State, had a two-fold effect.

In the hands of the secessionists the news served as the lever with which they roused the martial spirit of their people, and made the leaders, leaders indeed. They had already organized in all the States considerable armies, and this success of their first effort multiplied recruits and stimulated the whole people, who magnified the exploit into a glorious victory, and from that moment cemented into one nation of revolutionists the radical and conservative elements, and taught all to believe that they could soon dictate terms of peace, or even, with the aid of the great Democratic party, conquer the abolition North.

The banks emptied their vaults into the Confederate Treasury. Planters gave their available fortunes, and themselves, with their sons, left for the tented field. The women sent to their State's Treasury their silver plate and jewelry, and at once set to work to make clothes for their husbands and sons in the army.

In the North the news acted at once on the people themselves, and they awoke to realize a terrible fact. The flag of their country had been assailed. It might soon be dishonored. The people must fight for that flag, or the nation's life would end.

A political contest had divided the people of the North. The firing on the flag of Fort Sumter made the people one. Union meetings were held all over the North, notably in New York City, where the South had hoped for the most help, and from which city they had so far received the greatest material aid.

While neither side expected actual war, the South had prepared for the worst, and was with an equipped army in the field, while the North, on the call of President Lincoln for 75,000 troops, had but the National Guard of citizen soldiers to draw from. Underrating the strength and determination of the enemy, both sides looked upon the struggle as to be of short duration, and President Lincoln called for the men for ninety days; while President Davis told his troops that in even less time they could conquer a peace and possess themselves of the national capital.

The South failed to make it, as they had hoped, a political war. It became, instead, a sectional strife, and the lines were drawn, with a few earnest Union men in Virginia and Tennessee, and a few secessionists in West Virginia, Maryland, Kentucky and Missouri—below, solid for secession, and above, as solid for maintaining the old flag on every foot of territory in the United States.

To her standard the defenders flocked, and State vied with State as to expedition and numbers. Rhode Island's millionaires enlisted in the ranks, and marched to defend Washington. New York's citizen soldiers left with a day's notice, and hastened to the front. Massachusetts, first in the field, had multiplied her volunteers. The great West asked to be alone allowed to whip the South, and her regiments were filled up with men long before the State or Federal Government could supply arms and equipments.

Private individuals equipped whole regiments, private contributions swelled the Treasury, and the workshops of the whole North were run night and day to provide equipments and clothing for this great army, the growth of a single fortnight.

Nothing like this great uprising of the people of the two sections had ever before been attained in the history of modern wars. Each seemed actuated by loyal and patriotic motives. Each appealed to the same God, and found in their cause reason for His help.

Men, women and children were alike fired with patriotic enthusiasm, and in the North, as if by concerted arrangement, the national flag was everywhere displayed, even from the spires of churches and cathedrals, and adorned the halls of justice and places of worship. In the South flags and rosettes as suddenly appeared, and the "strange device" soon won a place—if not of veneration, at least of hope and expectation.

In describing the uprising of the people in the State of Georgia, Avery, in his "History of Georgia," (New York: Brown & Derby), 1882, says: "During the year 1861, the military activity in the State of Georgia was incessant and ubiquitous. The commonwealth was one vast recruit camp. The roll of the drum and stirring notes of the fife resounded from mountain to seaboard. Hill and valley echoed to the tread of armed men gathering, organizing, and leaving home and comfort for the tented field and the soldier's life.

"It was a wild time—a continuous day of fevered enthusiasm. Men, women and children participated in the exaltation of patriotic spirit. There was no looking back. A brave people had turned their energies to war, and they went at it as a business. The war spirit boomed like a storm. The rivalry to enlist was universal.

"Letters poured in upon the Governor, seeking commissions for perilous service, until the burden became so heavy that he was forced to advertise in the papers that he did not have the clerical labor to even answer. For every requisition of troops there was a fifty-fold proffer of eager soldiers. Such a spirit of willing chivalry as was exhibited was never exceeded in the annals of warfare; and to show the character of the men and organizations, a cavalry company in Rome—the Floyd Cavalry—represented a money property of $730,000 among forty men; while another of thirty-five men in Milledgeville, the Governor's Horse Guards, stood for two and a half millions of wealth on the tax-book.

SHIPMENT OF GUNS AND AMMUNITION FROM THE WATERVLIET ARSENAL, WEST TROY, N. Y.

"All over the State citizens were offering pecuniary sacrifices for the cause. Governor Brown himself subscribed, and paid one thousand dollars toward the support of the Georgia troops in the service, and determined to appropriate the net income of his farm to the same great cause. His wife devoted her time, as did thousands upon thousands of other noble and delicate women, to making clothing for the soldiers.

"Miss Henrietta Keenan, of Milledgeville, a daughter of Colonel Augustus H. Keenan, a brilliant, queenly woman, tendered to Governor Brown, in behalf of herself and her mother, for the use of the State, their silver plate, of considerable value. The Governor said, if it became a necessity, he would accept it.

"A company was organized below Gaddistown, in Fannin County, and named 'Mrs. Joe Brown's Boys.' In recognition of the compliment, Mrs. Brown, the wife of the Governor, fitted this company with a suit of clothes, purchasing the cloth in Milledgeville, and making and sending one to each member.

"All over the State voluntary generous patriotism was shown. Some idea may be formed of how gloriously Georgia responded to the demands on her manhood, from the fact that, up to the 1st of

MOVEMENT OF TROOPS AND MUNITIONS OF WAR—COLLINS LINE DOCK, CANAL STREET, NEW YORK—OUTSIDE VIEW.

October, 1861, she had sent forty magnificent regiments to the battle-field. This makes a grand fact in her war record."

General Dix presided at the principal stand at the great mass-meeting at Union Square, New York City, April 20th, 1861. In his speech he said: "I regard the pending contest with the secessionists as a death-struggle for constitutional liberty and law—a contest which, if successful on their part, could only end in the establishment of a despotic government, and blot out, whenever they were in the ascendant, every vestige of national freedom. . . . We stand before the statue of the Father of our Country. The flag of the Union which floats over it hung above him when he presided over the convention by which the Constitution was framed. The great work of his life has been rejected, and the banner by which his labors were consummated has been trampled in the dust. If the inanimate bronze in which the sculptor has shaped his image could be changed from the living form which led the armies of the Revolution to victory, he would command us, in the name of the hosts of patriots and political martyrs who have gone before, to strike for the defense of the Union and the Constitution."

Daniel S. Dickinson, a venerable leader of the Democratic party, said: "We are called upon to act. There is no time for hesitation or indecision; no time for haste or excitement. It is a time when the people should rise in the majesty of their might, stretch forth their strong arm and silence the angry waves of tumult. It is a question between Union and anarchy—between law and disorder."

Senator Baker, of Oregon, a leading Democratic Senator, who afterward fell at Ball's Bluff, made an eloquent speech. "Young men of New York," he said—"young men of the United States—you are told this is not to be a war of aggression. In one sense that is true; in another, not. We have committed aggression upon no man. In all the broad land, in their rebel nest, in their traitor's camp, no truthful man can rise and say that he has ever been disturbed, though it be but for a single moment, in life, liberty, estate, character or honor.

"The day they began this unnatural, false, wicked, rebellious warfare, their lives were more secure, their property more secure by us—not by themselves, but by us—guarded far more securely than any people ever have had their lives and property secured from the beginning of the world. We have committed no oppression, have broken no compact, have exercised no unholy power—have been loyal, moderate, constitutional and just.

"We are a majority of the Union, and we will govern our own Union, with our own Constitution, in our own way. We are all Democrats. We are all Republicans. We acknowledge the sovereignty of the people within the rule of the Constitution, and, under that Constitution and beneath that flag, let traitors beware. . . . I propose that the people of this Union dictate to these rebels the terms of peace. It may take thirty millions; it may take three hundred millions. What then? We have it. Loyally, nobly, grandly, do the merchants of New York respond to the appeal of the Government. It may cost us seven thousand men; it may cost us seventy-five thousand men in battle; it may even cost us seven hundred and fifty thousand men. What then? We have them. The blood of every loyal citizen of this Government is dear to me. My sons, my kinsmen, the young men who have grown up beneath my eye and beneath my care, they are all dear to me; but if the country's destiny, glory, tradition, greatness, freedom government, written constitutional government—the only hope of a free people—demand it, let them all go. I am not here now to speak timorous words of peace, but to kindle the spirit of manly, determined war. . . .

"Upon the wings of the lightning it goes out throughout the world that New York, the very heart of a great city, with her crowded thoroughfares, her merchants, her manufacturers, her artists—that New York, by one hundred thousand of her people—declares to the country and to the world that she will sustain the Government to the last dollar in her Treasury—to the last drop of your blood. The national banners leaning from ten thousand windows in your city to-day proclaim your affection and reverence for the Union."

Robert J. Walker, of Mississippi, who was Secretary of the Treasury in the Democratic administration of President Polk, denounced secession as a crime, and said: "Much as I love my party, I love my country infinitely more, and must and will sustain it, at all hazards. Indeed, it is due to the great occasion here frankly to declare that, notwithstanding my opposition to the election of Mr. Lincoln and my disposition most closely to scrutinize all his acts, I see, thus far, nothing to condemn in his efforts to save the Union. . . . And now let me say, that this Union must, will and shall be perpetuated; that not a star shall be dimmed nor a stripe erased from our banner; that the integrity of the Government shall be preserved, and that from the Atlantic to the Pacific, from the Lakes of the North to the Gulf of Mexico, never shall be surrendered a single acre of our soil nor a drop of its waters."

David S. Coddington, an influential member of the Democratic party, gave a scathing review of the efforts of disunionists, and said:

"Shall I tell you what secession means? It means ambition in the Southern leaders and misapprehension in the Southern people. Its policy is to imperialize slavery, and to destroy and to degrade the only free republic in the world.

FORGING WORK FOR THE GUN CARRIAGES AT THE WATERVLIET ARSENAL, WEST TROY, N. Y.

Nothing so disappoints secession as the provoking fidelity of New York to the Constitution.

"From the vaults of Wall Street Jefferson Davis expected to pay his army, and riot in all the streets and in all the towns and cities of the North, to make their march a triumphant one. Fifty thousand men to-day tread on his fallacy."

Such was the response of some of the ablest representatives of the venerable Democratic party to the slanderers of that party, such as Sanders and his like in the South and the trading politicians in the North.

It was the unbiased sentiment of the great body of that organization then and throughout the war, who were truly loyal in sentiment, and formed a strong element of the powerful Union party that faithfully sustained the Government in spite of the machinations of demagogues.

That meeting relieved the citizens of the commercial metropolis of the nation from the false position of apparent selfish indifference to the fate of the republic, in which they had been placed before Europe by an able correspondent of the London *Times*, who had been utterly misled by a few men, among whom he unfortunately fell on his arrival in this country. It gave assurance of that

WASHINGTON, APRIL 18th, 1861.

heartfelt patriotism of the great body of the citizens of New York, who testified their devotion to the country by giving about one hundred thousand soldiers to the army; and making the sacrifice, it is estimated, in actual expenditures of money, the loss of the labor of their able-bodied men, private and public contributions, taxes, etc., of not less than three hundred million of dollars in the course of four years.

"That meeting dismayed and exasperated the conspirators, for they saw that they had been deceived, and observed that, unlike themselves, their political brethren in the Free-labor States loved their country more than their party—were more patriotic than selfish—and would boldly confront with war, if necessary, every enemy of the Union and of American nationality. It also amazingly encouraged and strengthened the President and his cabinet in their efforts to suppress the rising rebellion."

In that meeting the profound intellect, the science of the Free-labor States, was represented by Professor O. M. Mitchell, one of the brightest lights of the century who also gave his services and his life in defense of the Union. No speech on that occasion thrilled the vast multitude who heard his voice more than that of Professor Mitchell.

"I have been announced to you," he said, "as a citizen of Kentucky. Once I was, because I was born there. I love my native State as you love your native State. I love my adopted State of Ohio as you love your adopted State, if such you have; but, my friends, I am not a citizen now of any State. I owe allegiance to no State, and never did; and, God helping me, I never will. I owe allegiance to the Government of the United States." After referring to his own education at the Military Academy at West Point, he said: "My father and my mother were from old Virginia, and my brothers and my sisters from Kentucky. I love them all—I love them dearly. I have my brothers and friends down in the South now, united to me by the tenderest ties of love and affection. I would take them in my arms to-day with all the love that God has put into this heart; but if I found them in arms against my country I would be compelled to smite them down. You have found officers of the army who have been educated by the Government, who have drawn their support from the Government for long years, who, when called upon by their country to stand for the Constitution and for the right, have basely, ignominiously and traitorously either resigned their commissions or deserted to traitors and rebels and enemies. What means all this? How can it be possible that men should act in this way? There is no question but one. If we ever had a Government and a Constitution, or if we ever lived under such, have we ever recognized the supremacy of right? I say, in God's name, why not recognize it now? Why not to-day? Why not for ever? Suppose those friends of ours from old Ireland—suppose he who made himself one of us, when a war should break out against his own country—should say, 'I cannot fight against my own countrymen,' is he a citizen of the United States? They are countrymen no longer when war breaks out. The rebels and the traitors in the South we must set aside. They are not our friends. When they come to their senses, we will receive them with open arms; but, till that time, while they are trailing our glorious banner in the dust—when they scorn it, condemn it, curse it, and trample it under foot, then I must smite. In God's name I will smite, and as long as I have strength I will do it. Oh, listen to me! listen to me! I know these men; I know their courage; I have been among them; I have been with them; I have been reared with them. They have courage, and do you not pretend to think they have not. I tell you what it is, it is no child's play you are entering upon. They will fight, and with a determination and a power which is irresistible. Make up your mind to it. Let every man put his life in his hand, and say, 'There is the altar of my country; there I will sacrifice my life!'"

Representative men of the Democratic party in all the loyal States made speeches, and took substantially the same ground, contributing their influence, time and money to the National cause. The venerable General Cass, late Secretary of State, made a stirring speech at Detroit on the 24th of April. "He who is not for his country," he said, "is against her. There is no neutral position to be occupied. It is the duty of all zealously to support the Government in its efforts to bring this unhappy civil war to a speedy and satisfactory conclusion, by the restoration, in its integrity, of that great charter of freedom bequeathed to us by Washington and his compatriots."

The veteran General Wool, a Democrat of the Jefferson and Jackson school, and then commander of the Eastern Department, said, in response to the greetings of the citizens of Troy, who, at the close of an immense meeting on the 16th of April, went to his house in a body: "Will you permit that flag to be desecrated and trampled in the dust by traitors? Will you permit our noble Government to be destroyed by the rebels in order that they may advance their schemes of political ambition and extend the area of slavery? No, indeed; it cannot be done. The spirit of the age forbids it. My friends, that flag must be lifted up from the dust into which it has been trampled, placed in its proper position, and again set floating in triumph to the breeze. I pledge you my heart, my hand, all my energies to the cause. The Union shall be maintained. I am prepared to devote my life to the work, and to lead you in the struggle!"

Caleb Cushing, of Massachusetts, who presided at the Charleston Convention and at the Seceders' Convention at Baltimore, in 1860, made a soul-stirring speech at Newburyport, Mass., on the same day, in which he said that he cordially participated in the patriotic manifestations around him. He would yield to no man in faithfulness to the Union or in zeal for the maintenance of the laws and the constitutional authorities of the Union; and to that end he stood prepared, if occasion should call for it, to testify his sense of public duty by entering the field again, at the command of the Commonwealth or of the Union. Mr. Cushing did offer his services in the field to the Governor of Massachusetts, but they were not accepted.

At a public reception of Senator Douglas, Mr. Lincoln's opponent for the Presidency, at Chicago, Ill., on the 1st of May, that statesman, in a patriotic speech, said: "There are only two sides to this question. Every man must be for the United States or against it. There can be no neutrals in this war; only patriots or traitors. . . . I express it as my conviction before God that it is the duty of every American citizen to rally round the flag of his country."

Similar meetings were held simultaneously in the prominent cities of the North and West, and the people were so thoroughly aroused to the dangers that beset the Government, that purse and swords were placed in its hands with a faith and devotion unexampled in the history of the world.

Between the 15th of April and the 1st of May, 1861, $40,000,000 was voluntarily contributed for war purposes by the Northern States; 350,000 troops mustered from the North and West within the same fifteen days; Ohio, whose quota was 10,000, sent into the field over 80,000. Pennsylvania troops were the first to reach Washington. Five companies passed through Baltimore April 18th, hooted, but not attacked.

By the end of 1861, the State of New York had one hundred and seven volunteer regiments in the field. Michigan was asked for one regiment, and sent ten. All the States North and West were equally generous, and their measures were filled up and running over. During the whole of 1861 there was but one purpose on the part of the people of the North—to save the Government.

LIGHTER WITH SUPPLIES FOR SHIPMENT BY STEAMERS.

THE SIXTH MASSACHUSETTS REGIMENT IN NEW YORK.

THE Sixth Massachusetts Regiment, composed of nine companies from the towns of Lowell, Lawrence, Groton and Acton (a part of General Butler's old brigade), under the command of Colonel Edward F. Jones, which passed through the City of New York, on the 18th of April, 1861, was invested with peculiar interest, from the circumstance that it was the first regiment from the North to respond to the call of the President, issued on the 15th, but three days before. It was welcomed on its arrival by the citizens of the great metropolis

April, 1861.

with an enthusiasm unprecedented in that city of high excitement, and was sped on its way to Washington with the hearty well-wishes of more than one hundred thousand patriotic spectators of its departure. They reached the station of the New Haven Railway early in the morning; but, notwithstanding the early hour they were met by a body of upward of five thousand citizens and a detachment of police, by whom

THE SEVENTH REGIMENT, N. G. S. N. Y., LEAVING NEW YORK, APRIL 19th, 1861, FOR THE DEFENSE OF WASHINGTON.

ey were escorted to the various hotels for breakfast. Their march through the city was unexpected, but was, nevertheless, a complete ovation. At every step they were greeted with cheers for the "Bunker Hill Boys!" The enthusiasm, however, did not reach its height until about noon, when the regiment formed in City Hall Park, and proceeded down Courtlandt Street to the Jersey City Ferry. The streets were gay with flags, and it was with difficulty that the troops could penetrate the dense masses that had gathered to welcome them. Those who have witnessed all the great demonstrations of the city for a half a century back, remember none so spontaneously enthusiastic. As the regiment filed off to go up the ferry-boat, which was gayly decorated with flags, as was the ferry-house, there were loud cries of "God bless you! God bless you!" and unlimited cheers for the Old Bay State.

The ferry-boat reached Jersey City at half-past one o'clock P.M., where some thousands had already congregated to welcome the troops. The railroad depot was crowded with ladies, who filled the balconies which extend around the building, nearly every one bearing the Stars and Stripes. The depot was also beautifully decorated with flags, presenting a most imposing appearance. While the troops approached, a salute was fired from the Long Dock, and the Cunard steamer *Persia* dipped her colors several times. As soon as the boat had been made fast to the bridge, and the order given to forward, the band struck up the "Star Spangled Banner," which was accompanied by deafening cheers from the crowd in and about the depot. As they entered the railroad depot, cheer after cheer broke forth, the ladies waving handkerchiefs and flags, which lasted for nearly twenty minutes. The train, numbering eighteen cars, was covered with flags. A little delay was occasioned on account of the crowd in the building blocking the place; but while the troops were in waiting, the ladies amused themselves by throwing the soldiers their pocket-handkerchiefs and little flags. The order being given, the several companies were marched to their respective cars, and in about half an hour they were all safely on board the train.

At two o'clock Colonel Jones informed the superintendent that all was ready, and the signal was given for the train to start. The first movement of the locomotive brought out cheers, and as the train slowly glided out from the depot, the crowd kept up the cheers and waving of flags. Among the ladies could be seen several in tears, deeply affected at the scene, and one old gentleman wept like a child. When asked if he had any friends among the troops, he said no; but he felt as though every one who composed the little band were his own sons. Several companies of the New Jersey militia accompanied the troops as far as Trenton, the capital of the State, where their regiments were mustering for equipment and dispatch to Washington.

THE SEVENTH REGIMENT,

NATIONAL GUARD, STATE OF NEW YORK.

THIS regiment, the just pride of New York City, and widely noted for its perfect discipline and equipment as well as its promptitude in every emergency requiring the interposition of the strong military arm, was the first regiment from the Empire State to respond to the call of the President. The night after the call the members of the regiment, although many of them were engaged in responsible business requiring constant attention, met in their armory, and unanimously volunteered their services to the Governor of the State. They were accepted, and on Friday, April 19th, nine hundred and ninety-one strong, under the command of Colonel Marshall Lefferts, commenced their march to Washington. Forming on Lafayette Place, opposite the Astor Library, they marched through Fourth Street down Broadway and Courtlandt Street through a crowd so dense that it seemed to block up the way impassably; through walls of human beings, under a perfect canopy of flags, with cheers rolling along like enthusiastic thunders, past buildings whose fronts were covered with flags, and whose doors, windows, steps, and balconies, were jammed with people; past Major Anderson, who reviewed the regiment from a commanding balcony; past mottoes declaring that the "National Guard is for the Union," and that members imitate the "National Guard of 1776." With bayonets brightly gleaming in the sun, with step firm, with bearing proud and erect, as befitted the men and the occasion, the Seventh Regiment marched down Broadway. But one accustomed to see only the everyday Broadway can form no idea of it as it appeared on this occasion, flaunting with flags, and packed with tier upon tier of people, from sidewalk to house-roof.

The citizens had assembled along the line of the march, and while waiting for the passing of the Seventh, gave a greeting and a "godspeed" to

MARSHALL LEFFERTS.

the Massachusetts Eighth, under Colonel Timothy Monroe, accompanied by General Benj. F. Butler.

It was not until the Eighth reached Philadelphia that they learned of the attack that day in Baltimore upon their comrades of the Sixth. The news of the attack in Baltimore reached New York while the Seventh were in line ready to march, and each man was served with forty-eight rounds of ball cartridge.

The New York and Massachusetts regiments met at Philadelphia, but proceeded by different steamer routes toward Washington, to meet again, on the morning of the 22d, at the Naval Academy wharfs, in Annapolis, the old capital of Maryland.

By their united efforts the two commands had, ere long, fully repaired the bridges and railway line leading to Annapolis Junction, which had been seriously damaged and partly destroyed by the insurgents the previous day. The Junction was reached by the combined regiments early on the 25th, and the Eighth Massachusetts being left to guard the road just opened, the Seventh proceeded at once to Washington, where it arrived the same afternoon.

Without loss of time they were marched up Pennsylvania Avenue to the "White House," in order to report to the President, and were subsequently quartered at the Capitol, whence they were soon called to duty at Arlington Heights. This, the most threatening position, opposite the City of Washington, they soon placed in a condition to check, if not totally arrest, any advance likely to be made by the Confederate forces. They constructed an admirable line of earthworks, continuing in active duty there in accordance with orders from the Government, even after the period for which they had so promptly enlisted under the President's proclamation.

This regiment, which had everywhere deservedly won the highest plaudits for its fine military behavior and discipline, was, unfortunately, not destined to appear again as the same full body in the country's service. But the admirable training it had received secured at once for many of its men and officers such leading positions as would, by some, have been supposed then open only to graduates of the United States Military Academy, and few were the engagements of note thereafter occurring in which this far-famed organization had not one or more of its representatives.

Well may the North be proud of its achievements, and long may it continue in the justly prominent position it has already so long occupied. Two days after the departure of the Seventh from New York, on Sunday, April 21st, it was followed by the Sixth, Colonel Pinckney; the Twelfth, Colonel Butterfield; the Seventy-first, Colonel Vosburg, and within ten days after the call of the President for troops, over eight thousand of the National Guard of the State of New York, fully armed and equipped, had gone forward to Washington from the City of New York alone.

MARSHALL LEFFERTS.

THE subject of this sketch was born in Brooklyn, N. Y., in 1821. He was a descendant of one of the old Knickerbocker families of Long Island. During his active business life in New York City as a merchant, he took a lively interest in military matters, and early connected himself with the State Militia. He was also one of the first promoters of the telegraph business, and closely identified with the progress and success of its development, as well as with many leading manufacturing interests of the country. He furnished the first zinc-plated wire used for telegraphic purposes in the United States; was the first President of the New York and New England and of the New York State Telegraph Companies, and at the time of his death was President of the Gold and Stock Telegraph Company of New York, and of the Celluloid Manufacturing Company of Newark, N. J.

But it was as colonel of the famous Seventh Regiment of New York that he was more widely known to the country at large. Under his command the Seventh Regiment responded to the calls of President Lincoln, and in 1863 was stationed at Frederick, Md., of which place Colonel Lefferts was made Military Governor. At the close of the war he tendered his resignation as colonel, but the Governor demurred to accepting it, and offered him a commission as brigadier-general. Colonel Lefferts, however, wished to retire from his active life in the service, and his resignation was finally accepted.

He died suddenly, July 3d, 1876, while *en route*, with the Veteran Guard of his regiment, to the Centennial Exhibition.

ATTACK ON THE MASSACHUSETTS TROOPS IN BALTIMORE.

BALTIMORE was on the direct highway between the Northern States and Washington, and all troops marching to the defense of the National Capital were naturally to pass through it. The people of Maryland were divided in opinions and sentiments, and the indignity to the flag of the Government at Sumter had served to intensify the spirit of opposition to the defenders of the national life. The lawless class in the city, possibly incited by emissaries from the seceded States, determined to obstruct the Northern road, and thus retard, if not entirely prevent, the defense of the National Capital.

Learning of the approach of the Massachusetts and Pennsylvania troops, they gathered their clans, and on the approach of the train with the Sixth Massachusetts Regiment, representing a State regarded justly as the leader in the Anti-Slavery movement, it was an easy matter to incite the mob to lawless acts. The better class of the people of Maryland were in full

APRIL, 1861.

THE SIXTH MASSACHUSETTS REGIMENT REPELLING THE

THE SIXTH MASSACHUSETTS REGIMENT REPELLING THE ATTACK OF THE MOB IN PRATT STREET, BALTIMORE, APRIL 19th, 1861

sympathy with the Government, and deplored the acts and threats of the more active, violent and aggressive populace. This class had, but a month before, threatened the life of the President-elect should he pass through Baltimore, and but for the prudence of those who knew the temper of the threateners, and the strategy of the railroad officials, their threats would have led to serious consequences. On the approach of the train on the morning of the 19th of April, the threatening crowd gathered with all speed at the station.

The engine had to be left, and horses attached to each car, to be drawn through the city. This separated the train, and the first cars were in advance of the mob, and were greeted only by threats and curses. As car after car was dispatched, the soldiers remained quietly seated. The last of the cars were pelted with stones, and the horses were seized and stopped. The police repeatedly drove back the mob, only to have them rush up with increased strength.

Nine of the eleven cars passed safely. The last two were stopped, and the soldiers were ordered to alight and march to the other depot, where the train was made up, with its locomotive ready to speed on to Washington. They formed, amid furious shouts of derision and defiance from the mob. The staff officers were in advance, and the command of the remnant of the regiment devolved on Captain Follansbee, of Lowell. He called upon the police to lead the way, and keeping his little band in close ranks, they marched on, amid showers of bricks, stones and missiles of all kinds.

A bridge had been torn up, and the soldiers had to cross on the timbers. This broke their ranks, and caused some confusion, while many were severely hurt by the flying missiles. At this juncture a shot was fired into their ranks from the mob, and Captain Follansbee ordered his men to defend themselves. Their fire was answered by guns and pistols, as well as paving-stones. The Mayor of Baltimore placed himself at the head of the column, and tried to drive back the mob; but it had grown to a surging mass of infuriated men, who would listen to no appeal, even of their own municipal head. Here were about one hundred Massachusetts troops making their way through thousands of rioters. They kept in close ranks, and marched on, only stopping to wheel and fire when the attack became unbearable.

Thus they fought their way for one mile through the streets of Baltimore. On rejoining their regiment at the Washington depot, Captain Follansbee and his little band were quickly sheltered in the cars of the awaiting train; but the mob continued to obstruct the track with telegraph-poles, logs and iron anchors. The police force, now largely reinforced, removed these barriers, and the train moved out of the depot on toward Washington.

In the meantime, the companies of Pennsylvania militia, unarmed and ununiformed, were stopped in a train closely following the Sixth Massachusetts. These defenseless soldiers were unmercifully stoned, and after waiting two hours in the cars, they were obliged to return to Philadelphia.

The Baltimore *Sun* of April 20th, 1861, gave the following account of the riot: "Yesterday morning the excitement which had been gradually rising in this city for some days, with reference t the passage of Northern volunteer troops southward, reached its climax upon the arrival of the Massachusetts and other volunteers, some from Philadelphia. At President Street depot, at half-past ten o'clock, a large crowd had assembled, evidently to give them an unwelcome reception.

"Six of the cars had succeeded in passing before the crowd were able to accomplish their purpose of barricading the way, which they now began to effect by placing seven or eight large anchors lying in the vicinity across the track.

"Having accomplished this, the crowd commenced cheering for *Jefferson Davis*, South Carolina and secession, with groans for sundry obnoxious parties. The troops thus delayed, remained quietly in the cars until, tired of their inaction, and apprehending a more formidable demonstration, they came to the conclusion to face the music and march through the city.

"They accordingly abandoned the cars, and the word was given to march, and the head of the line had advanced some fifteen paces, when it was driven back upon the main body by the immense crowd, still further increased by a body of men, who marched down to the depot, bearing at their head a secession flag.

"Eight of the cars started, and six passed safely to the Camden Station. The other two returned, the track in the meantime having been obstructed at Pratt and Gay Street by anchors, paving-stones, sand, and other *débris* at hand.

"After considerable delay, it was determined to make the attempt to march the remaining troops through the city, only sixty of whom were supplied with arms. The remainder were recruits, and occupied second-class and baggage-cars. At the head of this column on foot Major Brown placed himself, walked in front, and exerted all his influence to preserve peace.

"At the corner of Fawn Street two of the soldiers were struck with stones and knocked down. One of them was taken by the police to the drug-store of T. J. Pitt, at Pratt and High Street, and the other to the Eastern Police Station.

"The stones flew thick and fast, and continued until the corner of Gay street was reached, when the troops fired. Several persons fell on the first round, and the crowd became furious.

"A number of revolvers were used by the crowd, and their shots took effect in the ranks. The firing continued from Frederick Street to South Street in quick succession. At Howard and Dover Street the troops in one of the cars fired into the crowd. The balls struck the brick walls of the dwelling-houses. Several soldiers were wounded here, but no citizens were struck by the bullets of the soldiers. The faces of many of the soldiers, as seen through the car-windows, were streaming with blood, from cuts received from the shattered glass of the car-windows, and from missiles hurled at them.

"At Gay Street the soldiers fired a number of shots th ugh without hitting any one, so far as ould b ascertained. After firing this volley, the soldiers broke into a run; but another shower of stones being hurled into their ranks at Commerce Street, with such force as to knock several of them down, the soldiers then wheeled, and fired some twenty shots, but from their stooping and dodging to avoid the stones, but four or five shots took effect; the marks of a greater portion of their balls being visible on the walls of the adjacent warehouses, even up to the second stories.

"Here four citizens fell. Two of them died in a few moments, and the other two were carried off, supposed to be mortally wounded. As soon as the troops had fired at this point, they again wheeled, and started off on a full run, when some three or four parties issued from the warehouses there, and fired into them, which brought down three more soldiers, one of whom died in a few moments. The others succeeded in regaining their feet, and proceeded on with their comrades, the whole running as fast as they could, and a running fire was kept up by the soldiers from this point to the depot; the crowd continuing to hurl stones and other missiles into the ranks throughout the whole line of march.

"The mob were kept posted between the depots by men on horseback, who rode back and forth. Finally, crowds rushing pell-mell from the lower streets toward the depot gave notice that the cars were coming, and they arrived one after the other, each drawn by four horses. The blinds of most of the cars were shut down, and in those not provided with blinds, the troops laid down flat, to avoid the bricks thrown at them. The car-windows were perfectly riddled, and their sides bore great indentations from the rocks and bricks hurled at them.

"The scene while the troops were changing cars was indescribably fearful. Taunts, clothed in the most fearful language, were hurled at them by the panting crowd, who, almost breathless with running, passed up to the car-windows, presenting knives and revolvers, and cursed up into the faces of the soldiers. The police were thrown in between the cars, and formed a barrier; the troops changed cars, many of them cocking their muskets as they stepped on the platform.

"After embarking, the assemblage expected to see the train moved; but it was delayed, in the vain hope that the crowd would disperse. But no, it swelled, and the troops expressed to the officers of the road their determination to go at once, or they would leave the cars, and make their way to Washington.

"A wild cry was raised on the platform, and a dense crowd ran down the long platform and out on the railroad track toward the Spring Gardens, until the track for a mile was black with an excited

BURNING OF GUNPOWDER BRIDGE, ON THE PHILADELPHIA AND WASHINGTON RAILROAD, APRIL 19TH, 1861.

rushing mass. Great logs, telegraph-poles, requiring a dozen or more men to move them, were laid across the rails.

"A body of police followed after the crowd, both on a full run, and removed obstructions as fast as they were put on the track. The police interfered on every occasion; but the crowd, growing larger and more excited, would dash off at a break neck run for another position further on, until the county line was reached. When the train went out, the mass of people had almost returned to the depot.

"The names of the killed in the attack are given in the following list, also the wounded. The names of some of the soldiers killed—A. O. Whitney, Luther C. Ladd. Soldiers wounded—Asa Needham, Michael Green, D. B. Tylor, Edward Colvin, H. W. Danforth, William Patch.

"Three unknown citizens killed—Robert W. Davis, Philip S. Mills, John McMahon, William R. Clark, John McCann, James Carr, Sebastian Giles, William Maloney, Michael Murphy.

"Citizens wounded—James Myers, mortally; —— Coaly, William Reed, and boy unknown."

As in the case of all riots, a great many of the wounded were carried off by their friends, thus not being reported.

BURNING OF THE GUNPOWDER BRIDGE

On the night of April 19th, 1861, Marshal Kane and ex-Governor Lowe, of Maryland, accompanied by Major Brown and his brother, hastened to the office of Charles Howard, the President of the Board of Police of the City of Baltimore, who was waiting for them, when that officer and the Mayor issued orders for the destruction of the railroad bridges, near Baltimore, furnishing highway between Philadelphia and Washington.

The work was soon accomplished. A gang of lawless men hastened out to the Canton Bridge, two or three miles from the City of Baltimore, on the Philadelphia, Wilmington, and Baltimore Railroad, and destroyed it. As the train from the north reached the station, it was stopped by the interference of a pistol fired at the engineer.

The passengers were at once turned out of the cars, and these were filled by the mob, who compelled the engineer to run his train back to the long bridges of the Gunpowder and Bush Creeks. These bridges were fired, and large portions of them were speedily consumed.

BURNING OF THE GOSPORT NAVY YARD.

IMMEDIATELY after the fall of Fort Sumter the attention of the Confederate Government was turned to the military stores, ships-of-war and heavy guns at the Navy Yard opposite Norfolk, Va. The day before the passage of the secession ordinance by Virginia (April 16th, 1861), boats were scuttled in the channel of the Elizabeth River to prevent the Federal Government from making use of the several ship-of-war anchored near the Navy Yard, the Secessionists intending thereby to possess themselves of the Yard and ships for the use of the Confederate Government.

It was one of the largest and best appointed naval stations in the United States, and had, besides its ship-houses, machine shops and granite dry dock, enormous quantities of arms and munitions of war, including two thousand pieces of heavy cannon fit for service, three hundred of which were new Dahlgren guns. The property of the Yard of all kinds was worth ten millions of dollars, and included the man-of-war *Pennsylvania*, a three-decker, one hundred and twenty guns; the ships-of-the-line *New York*, eighty-four guns; *Columbus*, eighty guns; *Delaware*, eighty-four guns, on the stocks; the frigates *United States*, *Columbia* and *Raritan*, each fifty guns; the sloops-of-war *Plymouth* and *Germantown*, each twenty-two guns; and the steam-frigate *Merrimac*, afterward so destructive to the Federal fleet in Hampton Roads, until silenced by the little *Monitor*.

April, 1861.

Commodore Charles S. McCauley, in command of the Gosport station, had been cautioned by the Government to take no unnecessary action, to give needless alarm, but to be ready to move if it became necessary. On the 14th of April, Engineer-in-chief B. F. Isherwood arrived at the Yard to put the *Merrimac* in order at once for sea; and Captain Paulding brought instructions from Washington to Commodore McCauley to proceed at once to arm the *Merrimac*, get the *Plymouth* and *Dolphin* beyond danger, prepare the *Germantown* to be towed out, and to put on board the ships the most valuable property, ordnance stores, etc., preparatory to being moved beyond danger, if necessary.

The orders of the Secretary of the Navy were, to defend the vessels and other property in his charge at all hazard, using force, if necessary, to prevent their seizure, either by mob violence, organized effort, or assumed authority. Captain Paulding advised and directed the frigate *Cumberland* to be moved in position to cover the harbor, the Navy Yard, the cities of Norfolk and Portsmouth, and the channel through which they were approached. With these arrangements of precaution completed, Captain Paulding left for Washington, April 17th.

Mr. Isherwood, the same day, had the *Merrimac* ready for sea, and proposed to Commodore McCauley that the fires be lighted and the frigate got under steam before other obstructions be placed in the river. McCauley said, "To-morrow will do." The fires were lighted the next morning, and every one ready for departure. The commodore again suggested delay. Mr. Isherwood reminded him that the orders were peremptory; but the vessel was not ordered off, the fires were put out and the *Merrimac* remained at anchor. Commodore McCauley afterward explained to the Naval Department that he was influenced by the advice of his junior officers, whom he believed to be true to their flag, but who, when they heard of the secession of Virginia, resigned to join the Confederates.

General Taliaferro, in command of the Confederate forces, occupied Norfolk, and on the 18th of April, with the aid of the naval officers lately resigned, and who had already arranged with the workmen in the Yard, determined to seize the station. They waited one day for reinforcements from Richmond and Petersburg with heavy rifled cannon and ammunition. McCauley sent word to Taliaferro that he would not move a vessel or fire a shot except in self-defense. This promise gave him time to scuttle the ships, sparing none except the *Cumberland*.

On the afternoon of the 20th, just as the ships had been sunk, Captain Paulding came up in the *Pawnee*, with orders from the Secretary of the Navy to relieve McCauley, take command of the ships and Yard, and save or destroy the public property. Paulding had added one hundred marines to his crew at Washington, and at Fortress Monroe he was reinforced by Colonel David W. Wardrop and three hundred and fifty Massachusetts volunteers who had arrived the same day. Captain Paulding saw that the scuttled ships could easily be raised and used by the Confederates, and that, with but two ships afloat and his small land force, he could not defend the Navy Yard. He at once decided to apply the torch and burn the property he could not rescue and carry off. Trusted and efficient officers and men, including Lieutenant J. H. Russell, Captain Charles Wilkes, Commodore Allen, Sands and Rogers, Captain Wright, and Lieutenant H. A. Wise, were each assigned to special duties, to make the destruction as thorough and speedy as possible, and the troops, marines, sailors, and workmen who had remained true to the flag of their Government, were taken on board the *Pawnee* and *Cumberland*, and the *Yankee*, Captain Gorman, fastened her hawser to the *Cumberland* ready to tow her out of danger.

Captain Paulding then sent up a rocket, and the incendiaries applied the match. The spectacle of the conflagration was a surprise to the inhabitants and to the Confederate troops. It lit up the whole country for miles, and the heavy loaded guns on the *Pennsylvania* discharging as the fire reached them added to the grandeur of the scene. With the elements of destruction in full possession, the *Pawnee*, and *Yankee* with the *Cumberland* in tow, steamed down the river, and the officers and men left on shore reached them in small boats, except Commodore Rogers and Captain Wright, who were unable to secure a boat, and were taken at day break prisoners of war by the Confederates.

STEAM-TUG "UNCLE BEN" SEIZED BY THE SECESSIONISTS AT WILMINGTON, N. C., APRIL 20TH, 1861.

The fire, as far as accomplishing the full destruction of the property, was ineffective. The ship-houses, barracks and lofts were destroyed, but the dry dock, the heavy ordnance, the machine shops, the ordnance buildings, foundries, sawmill, provisions and officers' quarters, were saved. The ships that were scuttled and fired were but partly destroyed, and the Confederates gained the use of the *Merrimac*, *Raritan* and *Plymouth*, by their raising and repairs, which were readily made in the Yard. On the 21st the Confederates seized Fort Norfolk, 300,000 pounds of powder, and large quantities of loaded shells.

Batteries were erected at Sewell's Point and Craney Island, and supplied with the heavy guns from the Navy Yard. This gave the Confederates the control of the harbor of Norfolk, as well as valuable materials of war. Within one week after the evacuation of Sumter the Confederates had possession of Harper's Ferry and Gosport Navy Yard—important preliminary movements looking to the seizure of the national capital.

"UNCLE BEN."

THE steam tug *Uncle Ben* was owned by Messrs. Johnson & Higgins, merchants of Wall Street, New York, and was commanded by Captain W. H. Dare. She sailed from New York on April 6th, 1861, and anchored in the harbor of Wilmington, N. C., on

BURNING OF THE GOSPORT NAVY

BURNING OF THE GOSPORT NAVY YARD, NORFOLK, VA. APRIL 21st 1861

BURNING OF THE UNITED STATES ARSENAL AT HARPER'S FERRY, VA., APRIL 18TH, 1861.

RECRUITING FOR THE HAWKINS NEW YORK ZOUAVES.

the 20th. In the afternoon of that day she was boarded and seized by a body of armed Secessionists, and her captain and pilot were imprisoned.

After eleven days' confinement they were released by the interposition of the Cape Fear Flying Artillery. They were conveyed by the *Alba*, a New York vessel, Captain Powell, to New York. The *Uncle Ben* was held by its captors.

BURNING OF THE U.S. ARSENAL AT HARPER'S FERRY.

The village of Harper's Ferry, Va., obtained a sad celebrity in the Autumn of 1859, through what is known as the "John Brown raid"; and was again, on April 18th, 1861, brought into prominent notice by the burning of the United States Arsenal at that place by the United States forces, to prevent its falling into the hands of the insurgent troops who endeavored to seize it. The Arsenal, containing a large quantity of machinery and arms, was garrisoned by a small detachment of United States Rifles, numbering about forty men, under command of Lieutenant Roger Jones.

April, 1861.

Having been apprised of the approach of an overwhelming force of insurgent troops, under instructions from the Governor of the State of Virginia, to seize on the Arsenal, Lieutenant Jones instantly set fire to trains of gunpowder that had been previously laid, and, three minutes afterward, both of the Arsenal buildings, containing the arms, together with the carpenter's shop, which was at the upper end of a large and connected series of workshops of the armory proper, were in a blaze.

Every window in the building had been thrown open, so as to increase the fury of the conflagration. When this work was accomplished, Lieutenant Jones and his little garrison crossed the Potomac, over the covered bridge, followed by an excited crowd of citizens, who threatened him with the direst vengeance. He wheeled his men at the bridge and threatened to fire upon the pursuers, when they fell back. He then fled up the canal, crossed the hills, and, wading streams and swamps, reached Hagerstown at about seven o'clock in the morning. There he procured vehicles to convey his command to Chambersburg, Pa., and thence he

THE NAVAL RECRUITING OFFICE IN CHERRY STREET, NEW YORK.

RHODE ISLAND REGIMENTS EMBARKING AT PROVIDENCE FOR NEW YORK AND WASHINGTON

went by railway to Carlisle Barracks, their destination, where they arrived on the afternoon of the 19th. The Government highly commended Lieutenant Jones for his judicious act and his officers and men for their good conduct; and the commander was immediately promoted to the office of Assistant Quartermaster-General, with the rank of Captain.

WILLIAM SPRAGUE

Born at Cranston, R. I., September 12th 1830; engaged in the print-works established by his grandfather; became a partner on the death of his father in 1844; was Governor of Rhode Island, 1860-3. In 1861 offered a regiment and battery to President Lincoln, with which he took the field, having a commission as brigadier-general; was present at the battle of Bull Run, where he had a horse shot under him; was in several other actions during the Peninsular Campaign in 1862. In 1862 was chosen United States Senator; re-elected in 1868, his term closing in 1875, and is now living retired at Providence, R. I.

WILLIAM SPRAGUE,
THE WAR GOVERNOR OF RHODE ISLAND.

RHODE ISLAND VOLUNTEERS.

WITHIN five days after the President's call for 75,000 troops, the Rhode Island Marine Artillery, with eight guns and one hundred and ten horses, commanded by Colonel Tompkins, passed through New York on their way to Washington, and the First Regiment of Infantry, 1,200 strong, under Colonel Ambrose E. Burnside, was ready to move. It was composed of many of the wealthier citizens of the State, and accompanied by the youthful and patriotic Democratic Governor, William Sprague, who had, from his private purse, armed and equipped the regiment, as well as contributed to the general war fund.

May, 1861.

The little State, by an Act of the Legislature, under a call of Governor Sprague for an extra session, held on the 18th of May, 1861, appropriated half a million dollars for equipping volunteers.

The New York *Tribune*, speaking of the prompt response of Rhode Island to the President's call for volunteers, said:

"Before the President had stirred the heart of the country with his proclamation, ringing in long reverberations, like a bugle blast, from coast to mountain range, a column of troops, perfect in discipline and equipment beyond any which had yet mustered to the national colors, rushed to the rescue of the menaced capital.

"Not only the officers of the regiment, but the Governor and Lieutenant-governor, led the van, bearing with them the sovereignty of the State. With the side-arms of the officers and the shouldered muskets of the privates, came, in the simple blouse of their uniform, the representatives of more than $30,000,000 of wealth. No such event has ever before been recorded in war, nor has there been seen, by the past or present generation, such an impersonation of the muscle and the material aid of a campaign upon its muster and within its roll-call. Its moral influence has been immense, and he who, hereafter, shall write the chronicle of what has been, and is yet to be, in this strife, will note this as the pivot upon which the divided North wheeled into a compact and solid form of resistance to rebellion."

RATE OF PAY TO VOLUNTEERS.

THE United States Government paid, per month, to volunteers who enlisted in response to the first call of the President as follows:

Colonel	$218 00
Lieutenant-colonel	194 00
Major	175 00
Captain	108 50
First Lieutenant	108 50
Second Lieutenant	103 50
Brevet Second Lieutenant	103 50
First, or Orderly Sergeant	29 00
Other Sergeants	27 00
Corporals	22 00
Privates	20 00
Musicians	21 00

Officers were required to provide their own uniforms and equipments, but the men received their clothing and arms from the Federal Government. This rate of pay was considerably changed when further calls were made during the progress of the war.

THE WINANS STEAM-GUN, CAPTURED BY GENERAL BUTLER'S COMMAND NEAR THE RELAY HOUSE, MD.

LANDING OF TROOPS AT THE WHARF OF THE NAVAL ACADEMY, ANNAPOLIS, MD.

THE U. S. NAVAL ACADEMY AT ANNAPOLIS.

On August 7th, 1845, George Bancroft, Secretary of the Navy under President Polk, issued orders for the establishment of a Naval School, and instructed Commander Franklin Buchanan (who subsequently commanded the Confederate ironclad *Merrimac*, and was afterward taken prisoner by Admiral Farragut in Mobile Harbor) to open a naval school in Fort Severn, Annapolis Harbor, Maryland.

October 10th, 1845, the school was formally opened, and the object of the enterprise, with course of instruction, was set forth as follows: "To collect the midshipmen, who, from time to time, are on shore, and give them occupation during their stay on land in the study of mathematics, nautical astronomy, theory of morals, international law, gunnery, the use of steam, the Spanish and French languages, and other branches essential in the present day to the accomplishment of a naval officer." There were present fifty-six midshipmen and eight instructors. The buildings in the fort were found sufficient for instruction-rooms, quarters and mess.

In 1846 Congress appropriated $28,200 to support the School, and a like sum in 1847. At the end of 1847 the School numbered ninety midshipmen in attendance. In 1849 the institution was reorganized by a special board of naval officers, who were instructed to make the course of instruction and the regulations conform to the system pursued at the Military Academy at West Point. The title of the institution was changed from Naval School to United States Naval Academy.

In 1851, the duration of the course of study was fixed at four years, the number of instructors was increased to eleven, and the sloop-of-war *Preble* was assigned to the Academy as a practice-ship, and for the Summer cruise of three and a half months each year. A board of visitors was also provided for each year to annually inspect the Academy, and report to Congress its condition.

During the first year of our Civil War, Annapolis became an important military depot, being occupied by General Butler as a rendezvous for troops *en route* to the defence of the capital. The Academy, with its apparatus, and such of its corps of instructors and cadets as did not join the Confederacy, was transferred to Newport, R. I., where it continued until the close of the war, when it returned, September, 1865, to its original home at Annapolis. The list of successive superintendents is as follows: Commander Franklin Buchanan, 1845–7; Commander George P. Upshur, 1847–50; Captain C. K. Stribbling, 1850–3; Captain L. M. Goldsborough, 1853–7; Commander George S. Blake, 1857–65; Vice-admiral D. D. Porter, 1865–9; Rear-admiral John L. Worden, 1869–74; Rear-admiral C. R. P. Rogers, 1874.

The departments of study are supplied with all the paraphernalia of actual naval warfare, including guns of the various calibre; ships, from the steam-launch to the steam-frigate and ironclad; a complete workshop and foundry. Steam engineering, gunnery, philosophy, chemistry, and astronomy, are illustrated by the latest and most approved apparatus; and the Summer cruise each year perfects the cadet midshipman in naval warfare.

ANNAPOLIS AND BALTIMORE OCCUPIED BY GENERAL BUTLER.

On the 19th of April, General Benjamin F. Butler, who had been placed by Governor Andrew in command of the first contingent of Massachusetts troops raised under President Lincoln's proclamation, left Boston with the Eighth Regiment, Colonel Timothy Munroe, reaching Philadelphia late the following day. There he heard of the attack which had been made that morning on the Sixth Massachusetts Regiment, while passing through Baltimore, and, after consultation with the commander of the recently-created "Department of Washington," Major-General Robert Patterson, as well as with Commodore Dupont, then in charge of the League Island Navy Yard, Philadelphia, it was decided to proceed to Washington by way of Annapolis.

April, 1861.

Before noon of the 20th, on arriving at Havre de Grace, and not meeting with the armed resistance which many had led him to expect, he rapidly embarked the regiment on the powerful ferry-boat *Maryland*, which latter yet remained in charge of her regular crew, and arrived at Annapolis shortly after midnight, fortunately in time to save the frigate *Constitution* ("Old Ironsides"), which some

BARRACK OF THE SEVENTH REGIMENT OF NEW YORK, AFTER A MARCH OF TWENTY MILES FROM ANNAPOLIS TO ANNAPOLIS JUNCTION.

insurgents were on the point of seizing. With the aid of the *Maryland*, the old vessel was towed to a place of safety, and left in charge of her late gallant commander, Captain Blake, who was directed to keep the guns trained upon the riverbanks.

In aiding the frigate, however, the ferryboat got aground, and forcibly remained so till the following day, adding to the already great discomforts of the troops on board, and naturally intensifying the anxiety of General Butler, who foresaw the serious complications which, in the then excited condition of affairs, every minute's delay might bring. Nor can it well be conjectured how much more compromising the position would have become had not the Seventh Regiment of New York City, in command of Colonel Marshall Lefferts, having sailed by steamer from Philadelphia, arrived on the scene, and not only thus aided the landing of the Eighth Massachusetts Regiment but strengthened materially the available military force placed within the general's immediate reach.

Both regiments were quartered at the United States Naval Academy, in opposition to Governor Thomas H. Hicks, whose recent protest, addressed to President Lincoln, against the landing of troops upon the soil of Maryland, had met with no sterner a rebuke at the hands of our then able Secretary of State, William H. Seward, than that administered by General Butler, who, besides taking decided umbrage at the Governor's unflattering designation of the force under his command, took occasion to remind the Governor that his troops were not "Northern troops," but "a part of the whole

THE BOUQUET BATTERY, COMMANDING THE VIADUCT OVER THE PATAPSCO RIVER, ON THE BALTIMORE AND OHIO RAILROAD NEAR THE RELAY HOUSE.

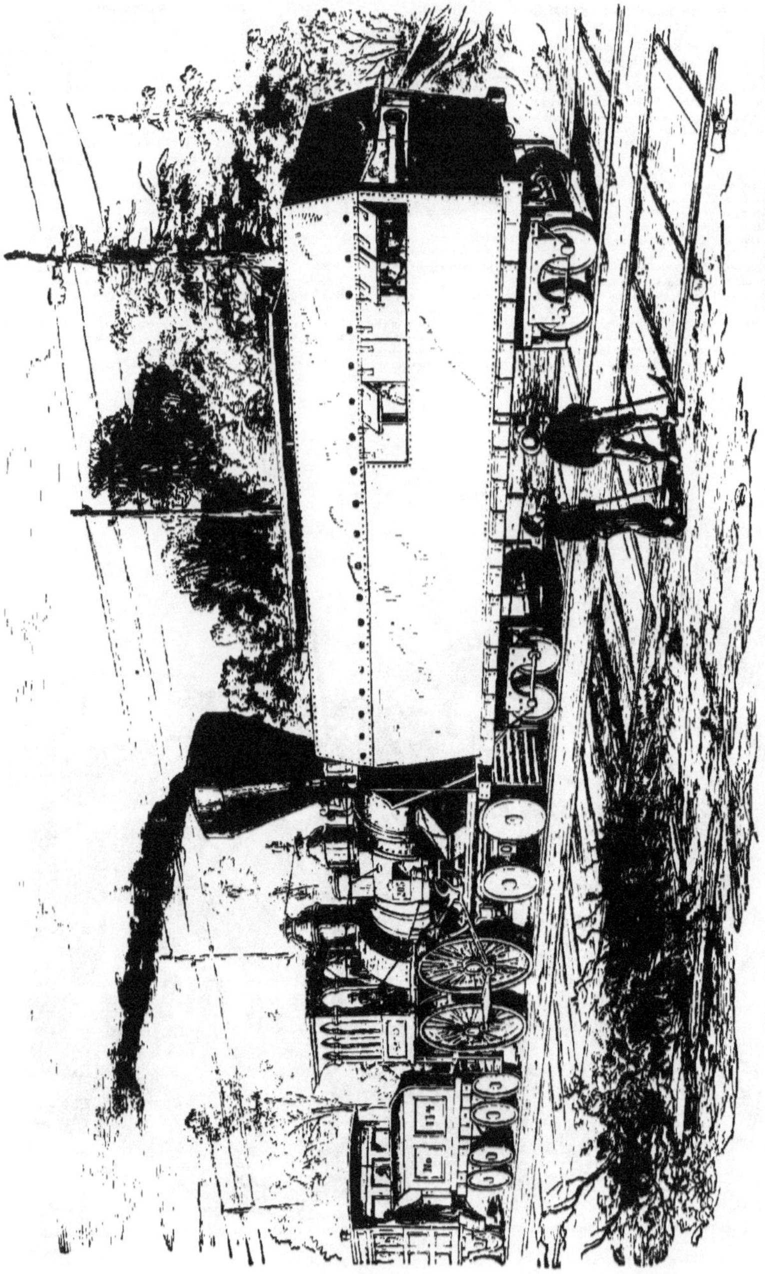

THE RAILROAD BATTERY BUILT TO PROTECT THE WORKMEN WHILE REBUILDING THE BURNED BRIDGES ON THE PHILADELPHIA, WILMINGTON AND BALTIMORE, AND THE BALTIMORE AND OHIO RAILROADS.

militia of the United States, obeying the call of the President."

The further progress of the troops was impeded by the tearing up of much of the line of the Annapolis and Elk Ridge Railway, as well as the destruction of all that company's rolling stock, which had taken place the previous day. It was, therefore, determined to rebuild the road at once, and place the disabled engines in running order, the more readily to procure long-needed supplies for the men, and in order to open a way for the additional troops which were expected soon to follow. The work, though difficult under the circumstances, was completed on the 24th of April, with the help of skilled workmen, now volunteer soldiers, and the two regiments then left Annapolis for the Junction, which they reached the following day. It was then decided that the Eighth Massachusetts would remain to hold the road just opened, while the Seventh New York should proceed to Washington.

The Seventh reached its destination the same evening, and with the Sixth Massachusetts, as well as a few companies of Pennsylvania troops, already

TROOPS REPAIRING THE MILLERSVILLE BRIDGE, ON THE RAILROAD FROM ANNAPOLIS TO WASHINGTON.

Mills, the justly celebrated Winans steam-gun, which had just been finished by its inventor, Dickinson, and was expected to revolutionize the then existing system of warfare.

Late on the 13th of May, the first small detachment

BATTERY ON ELK RIDGE, NEAR THE RELAY HOUSE, COMMANDING THE WASHINGTON BRANCH OF THE BALTIMORE AND OHIO RAILROAD

in the city, and which were the first volunteers that reached Washington, constituted, strange though it may appear, *a total military force of about two thousand men available for the defense of the capital.* The "Department of Annapolis," including the country for twenty miles on either side of the railway leading to Washington, was then created by Lieutenant-general Scott, who placed General Butler at its head, with full discretionary powers. By the end of April there had assembled at Annapolis, which was then practically the key to the only open road to Washington, a force of ten thousand men.

On the 4th of May, General Butler issued orders for the dispatching from Washington of the Eighth New York, under the command of Colonel Lyons; Major A. M. Cook's Boston Light Artillery, and the already famous Sixth Massachusetts, and, with this force, he proceeded the following day to within a few miles of Baltimore, seizing the Relay House, which was then, as now, a very important station at the junction of the railway lines leading to Washington and to Harper's Ferry. It was while General Butler was at the Relay House perfecting his plans that the Eighth New York and Major Cook's artillery force captured, at Ellicott

May, 1861.

ment of troops was sent toward Baltimore. On the following evening, during the prevalence of a frightful rainstorm, General Butler, with the Sixth Massachusetts and the Eighth New York Regiment, entered the city, and, without meeting any resistance, established his headquarters on Federal Hill, an eminence commanding the city proper, as well as Fort McHenry in the near distance. His arrival was followed by the issuing of a proclamation setting forth his mission, which was

FRANK PIERCE, OF LYNN, A MEMBER OF THE EIGHTH MASSACHUSETTS, DIVING FOR A MISSING RAIL.

chiefly to aid in the maintenance of the laws, and appealing to the good faith of the people. From it we extract the following:

". . . . A detachment of the forces of the Federal Government under my command have occupied the City of Baltimore for the purpose, among other things, of enforcing respect and obedience to the laws as well of the State, if requested thereto by the civil authorities, as of the United States laws, which are being violated within its limits by some malignant and traitorous men, and in order to testify the acceptance by the Federal Government of the fact that the city and all the well-intentioned portion of its inhabitants are loyal to the Union and the Constitution, and are to be so regarded and treated by all. To the end, therefore, that all misunderstanding of the purpose of the Government may be prevented, and to set at rest all unfounded, false and seditious rumors; to relieve all apprehensions, if any are felt, by the well-disposed portion of the community, and to make it thoroughly understood by all traitors, their aiders and abettors, that rebellious acts must cease, I hereby, by the authority vested in me as commander of the Department of Annapolis, of which Baltimore forms a part, do now command and make known that no loyal or well-disposed citizen will be disturbed in his lawful occupation or business; that private property will not be interfered with by the men under my command, or allowed to be interfered with by others, except in so far as it may be used to afford aid and comfort to those in rebellion against the Government, whether here or elsewhere. . . .

"The ordinary operations of the corporate Government of the City of Baltimore, and of the civil authorities, will not be interfered with, but, on the contrary, will be aided by all the power at the command of the general, upon proper call being made, and all such authorities are cordially invited to co-operate with the general in command to carry out the purposes set forth in the proclamation, so that the City of Baltimore may be shown to the country to be, what she is, in fact, patriotic and loyal to the Union, the Constitution and the laws.

* * * * * * * *

"To make it more apparent that the Government of the United States by far more relies upon the loyalty, patriotism and zeal of the good citizens of Baltimore and vicinity than upon any exhibition of force calculated to intimidate them into that obedience to the laws which the Government doubts not will be paid from inherent respect and love of order, the commanding general has brought to the city with him, of the many thousand troops in the immediate neighborhood which might be at once concentrated here, scarcely more than an ordinary guard, and, until it fails him, he will continue to rely upon that loyalty and patriotism of the citizens of Maryland which have never yet been found wanting to the Government in time of need. The general in command desires to greet and treat in this part of his department all the citizens thereof as friends and brothers, having a common purpose, a common loyalty and a common country."

GROUP OF ELLSWORTH'S CHICAGO ZOUAVE CADETS, OF [illegible] IN [illegible]

"The general believes that, if the suggestions and requests contained in this proclamation are faithfully carried out by the co-operation of all good and Union-loving citizens, and peace and quiet, and certainty of future peace and quiet, are thus restored, business will resume its accustomed channels, trade take the place of dullness and inactivity, efficient labor displace idleness, and Baltimore will be, in fact, what she is entitled to be, in the front rank of the commercial cities of the nation." . . .

General Butler's proclamation was followed by one from Governor Hicks, calling for the State quota of four regiments, in response to the call of the President. These troops were to serve only within the State of Maryland, or, if need be, for the defense of the capital. Almost simultaneously, likewise, came the reproof administered by the Lieutenant-general of the Army at what he was pleased to term the "hazardous occupation of Baltimore." The result was General Butler's recall to Washington, where, however, he was promoted to be a major-general of volunteers, and was given the command of a new and more extended military district, which included Virginia, North Carolina and South Carolina, with headquarters at Fortress Monroe. General Butler was succeeded in command at Baltimore by General George Cadwallader, U. S. A., and the troops were temporarily withdrawn from the city, in accordance with a previous understanding between President Lincoln and the Governor of Maryland.

BENJAMIN F. BUTLER.

BENJAMIN F. BUTLER.

Born in Deerfield, N. H., November 5th, 1818; graduated at Waterville College, Me.; admitted to the bar at Lowell, Mass., in 1840; served in the State Militia through all grades, from private to brigadier-general; represented Lowell, Mass., in the Legislature; member of the Constitutional Convention, and in 1859 member of the Senate of Massachusetts; member of the National Democratic Convention held at Charleston, S. C., April 23d, and adjourned to Baltimore, June 18th, 1860; shortly withdrew therefrom, announcing: "I will not sit in a convention where the African slave trade—which is piracy by the law of my country—is approvingly advocated." Headed the Breckinridge electoral ticket in the Presidential election of 1860.

On April 15th, 1861, upon a call for troops to hasten to the defence of Washington and Fortress Monroe, Brigadier-general Butler, of the Massachusetts State Militia, issued the necessary orders for mustering the regiments of his brigade, and at the head of the Eighth Regiment, took his departure for Washington. Prevented from reaching the capital by way of Baltimore in consequence of the burning of the bridges, he took his command to Havre de Grace, where he seized the *Maryland* for the transport of his men to Annapolis. There he prevented the frigate *Constitution* (the renowned "Old Ironsides") falling into the hands of the insurgents, and landed his command; and, with the New York Seventh, Colonel Marshall Lefferts, occupied the Naval Academy grounds, against the opposition of the Governor of Maryland; repaired the railroad to Annapolis Junction, thus securing a clear road for the transportation of Northern troops to the capital; seized the Relay House, captured the Winans steam-gun, and, May 13th, 1861, occupied Fort Federal Hill, Baltimore, in command of the city, with a body of less than one thousand men. These, in a letter issued to Governor Hicks, he terms "*Not Northern troops,*" but "*a part of the whole militia of the United States, obeying the call of the President.*" Promoted to be a major-general of volunteers, May, 1861, and placed in command of the "Department of Virginia," with headquarters at Fortress Monroe.

In conjunction with Admiral Farragut, took possession of New Orleans, May 1st, 1862, carrying out many administrative reforms which remain to this day; captured City Point and Bermuda Hundred, dug the Dutch Gap Canal, aided the movement of General Grant upon Petersburg, and performed other valuable services. In 1866 was elected to Congress from the Essex District, and served several terms; was elected Governor of Massachusetts in 1882, served one term, and is now (1884) practicing law in Lowell.

HEADQUARTERS OF GENERAL BUTLER ON FEDERAL HILL, BALTIMORE.

THE ZOUAVES

The dashing exploits of the French Zouaves in the Crimean War, and the report made to the United States Government by its Military Commission sent to Europe during that war, attracted the emulative attention of all the light infantry tacticians of our country.

Our young men were fascinated with the stories of the agile, impulsive, effective and somewhat dramatic movements of the French Zouaves; and when young Ellsworth made a tour of the East with his Chicago Cadets, in the several cities upon their route their exhibitions inspired many similar organizations. Immediately a number of companies were formed, which, at the beginning of the War of Secession, were at once recruited and extended into regiments, some of them being organized and commanded by men who had seen active service as officers in the war of the United States with Mexico.

No military organization was more brilliant than these "Chicago Zouave Cadets"—with their striking and gay uniforms, with their flowing red pants, their jaunty crimson caps, their peculiar drab gaiters and leggings, and the loose open blue jackets, with rows of small thickly set sparkling buttons, and the light blue shirt beneath.

They were armed with the Minié rifle, and their manual was founded on Hardee's Light Infantry Tactics, much modified and improved by Colonel Ellsworth. In all their evolutions they displayed great precision.

FEDERAL HILL, BALTIMORE (TAKEN FROM THE NORTH SIDE BASIN), OCCUPIED BY THE TROOPS OF GENERAL BUTLER'S COMMAND.

DEPARTURE OF THE ELLSWORTH FIRE ZOUAVES FROM NEW YOR

ENCAMPMENT OF THE ELLSWORTH NEW YORK F

DEPARTURE OF THE ELLSWORTH FIRE ZOUAVES FROM NEW YORK, APRIL 29TH, 1861—ESCORTED BY THE NEW YORK FIRE DEPARTMENT

ENCAMPMENT OF THE ELLSWORTH NEW YORK FIRE ZOUAVES, OPPOSITE THE NAVY YARD, WASHINGTON

EPHRAIM E. ELLSWORTH.

Born in Saratoga County, New York, April 23d, 1837, he was killed at Alexandria, Va., May 24th, 1861. He early displayed a taste for a military life, and sought to enter West Point as a cadet. Lacking political influence, he entered a store in Troy, and afterward in New York City.

In 1855 he removed to Chicago, entered a law office as student, and soon achieved an honorable position. His martial tendencies being still strong, he connected himself with a military company. He soon became its captain, and infused new life in it by adopting the dress, drill and practices of the French Zouaves, as illustrated by that arm of the service in the Crimean War. His company, known as the Chicago Zouave Cadets, were sworn to total abstinence from liquor, tobacco and all excesses. Profanity was made a ground for dismissal, and chivalrous courtesy at all times exacted.

About this time he entered the law office of Abraham Lincoln, then practicing law in Springfield, Illinois.

The reputation won by his company of Zouave Cadets, and the desire of the public to witness the peculiar drill, led to invitations to visit the Eastern cities, and in 1860 he complied with their request.

In New York, he gave an exhibition drill in the City Hall Park before

EPHRAIM ELMORE ELLSWORTH.

eight thousand spectators. He was commissioned Second Lieutenant in the army early in 1861, and, when volunteers were called for, he resigned his commission in the army, went to New York, and from the firemen of that city organized a regiment of one thousand men, who, accustomed to exposure, hard work and extreme vigilance, proved excellent material for active service, especially under the peculiar drill and discipline adopted by Colonel Ellsworth.

This regiment was known as the New York Fire Zouaves, and on the 29th of April, 1861, sailed for Washington, and on the 24th of May occupied Alexandria, Virginia.

Before going into camp, and while engaged in destroying means of communication southward by railroad and telegraph, Colonel Ellsworth, accompanied by a small guard, caught sight of a Confederate flag flying from the Marshall House.

ARMY, 1861.

Determined to capture it, he entered the house, mounted to the roof, tore down and secured the flag, and on his way to the street was shot down by J. W. Jackson, the proprietor of the hotel. Private Francis E. Brownell, one of his guards, immediately raised his rifle, shot Jackson through the head, and by the next movement thrust his bayonet through the body before it had fallen from the step.

Colonel Ellsworth's body was carried

THE ELLSWORTH (FIRE) ZOUAVES FIGHTING THEIR OLD NEW YORK ENEMY IN THEIR USUAL WAY—ADJOINING WILLARD'S HOTEL, WASHINGTON.

DEATH OF COLONEL EPHRIAM E. ELLSWORTH AT THE HANDS OF JAS. JACKSON, OF THE MARSHALL HOUSE—SHOOTING OF JACKSON BY PRIVATE FRANCIS E. BROWNELL

to the White House in Washington, where the funeral service was performed, and thence, with impressive ceremonies, through New York City, to the home of his parents at Mechanicsville, N. Y., where a company of his devoted regiment fired a volley over his grave.

THE FIRE ZOUAVES.

On the morning of May 9th, 1861, it was announced at Washington that fire was in a liquor establishment next door to Willard's Hotel. Immediately General Mansfield, Colonel McDowell, and others, were in attendance. In a short time the fire was extinguished, and all was pronounced safe.

Two hours after, another fire announcement was made, and this time fierce flames were seen rushing from the same building. The flames spread with fearful rapidity toward the hotel, which was filled with dense volumes of smoke and panic-stricken guests. After interminable delay, one or two inefficient fire companies appeared, against whose feeble efforts the fire made continuous progress. At this juncture General Mansfield dispatched an aid to Colonel Ellsworth, asking for a detachment.

"Fire! fire!" rang through the quarters; and in a moment ten men from each company, headed by their colonel, were running swiftly and in order down the avenue. On reaching the engine-house, they found it so fastened as for a long time to defy their entrance; but they broke in the door, and rushed the engine to the fire. Here they were joined by several hundreds of their companions. Some of their acts were frightful to behold: Two of them held each a leg of the third, they standing on the roof enveloped in flames, while he, head downward, was suspended over the burning building, until he succeeded in reaching a hose pipe which was extended from a short ladder. Colonel Ellsworth seized the trumpet from a fireman who remonstrated, insisting upon his right to command.

"Well," said the colonel, "if you have more men here than I have, you can take it."

After two hours' hard work, they subdued the fire. General Mansfield addressed them, thanking and praising them, and repeating several times, "I am proud of you, very proud of you." After breakfasting with Mr. Willard, they gave three cheers, sang "Dixie," and marched to their quarters.

New Yorkers took great delight in them. Abraham Wakeman, Thurlow Weed, Simeon Draper, and Farmer Abel, praised the boys, who stood metaphorically on their heads with delight.

THE MARSHALL HOUSE, ALEXANDRIA, VA., FROM WHICH COLONEL ELLSWORTH REMOVED THE CONFEDERATE FLAG

THE FUNERAL CORTEGE AT BOSTON OF THE MASSACHUSETTS SOLDIERS KILLED AT BALTIMORE.

THE FUNERAL OF THE MASSACHUSETTS SOLDIERS KILLED AT BALTIMORE.

Luther C. Ladd, a young mechanic of Lowell, a little more than seventeen years of age; Addison O. Whitney, another young mechanic, of Lowell, twenty-one years of age; Charles A. Taylor, a decorative painter of Boston—who were killed outright—and Sumner H. Needham, of Lawrence, a plasterer by trade, who was mortally wounded, were the slain of the Sixth Massachusetts in Baltimore, on the 19th of April, 1861.

Private Merrill S. Wright, of the Richardson Light Infantry of Lowell, was detached by Colonel Jones to receive the bodies from Marshal Kane of Baltimore, and to convey them to their former homes. The bodies were received in Boston on the 1st of May by a military escort under Governor Andrew and Adjutant-general Schouler, accompanied by a large concourse of citizens, and were which Lieutenant-colonel Thomas J. Morris, of the staff of Governor Bradford of Maryland, presented a beautiful national flag, made of silk, and wrought by the loyal women of Baltimore for the purpose. On the polished black walnut staff was a silver plate, bearing an engraving of the arms of Maryland and of Massachusetts, and the words:

MARYLAND TO MASSACHUSETTS,
APRIL 19TH, 1865.
MAY THE UNION AND FRIENDSHIP OF THE FUTURE
OBLITERATE THE ANGUISH OF THE PAST.

This was the crowning evidence of the sorrow of true Marylanders for the wrongs inflicted on citizens of Massachusetts. Only a few months after the occurrence, the Legislature of Maryland took steps to "wipe out," as they expressed it, the foul blot of the Baltimore riot, and on the 5th of March, 1862, the Assembly appropriated seven thousand dollars, to be dispensed, under the direction of the Governor of Massachusetts, for the relief of the families of those who were then injured. To-day, Massachusetts and Maryland cordially embrace each other as loving sisters in the great family of the nation.

THE BODIES OF THE SIXTH MASSACHUSETTS SOLDIERS KILLED AT BALTIMORE RECEIVED BY THE CITIZENS OF LOWELL.

temporarily deposited in the vaults of King's Chapel. On the 6th of May, those of Ladd and Whitney were removed to Lowell. The day was dark and stormy. All the mills were stopped running, the stores were closed, and all business was suspended. The bodies were received by a great concourse of citizens and six military companies just organized for the war, and escorted to Huntingdon Hall, which was draped in black.

The funeral services were held in the Hall. The Rev. W. R. Clark, of the Methodist Church, preached an impressive sermon before the authorities of the city and the people, and then the two bodies were placed in a vault in the Lowell Cemetery. A little more than four years afterward the remains of these "first martyrs" were deposited beneath a beautiful monument erected by a popular subscription.

It was dedicated on the 17th of June, 1865, in the presence of nearly 20,000 people, with imposing ceremonies, by the Masonic fraternity, and a large number of military organizations.

Governor Andrew delivered an oration, after

GENERAL JOHN E. WOOL
AND
THE NEW YORK UNION DEFENSE COMMITTEE.

During the time the national capital was cut off from communication with the North, five companies of Pennsylvania troops, who had preceded the Sixth Massachusetts, had succeeded in passing through Baltimore before the mob had organized, and were assailed with threats and oaths instead of paving-stones and shotguns. These, with the Sixth Massachusetts, constituted the national guard protecting the seat of government.*

Major-general John E. Wool, second in command to Lieutenant-general Winfield Scott, General-in-chief, United States Army, was at Troy, N. Y. He at once, as Commander of the Eastern Department, which included the territory east of the Mississippi River, took the active control of the troops being raised and poured into the City of New York, and, making his headquarters at the St. Nicholas Hotel, issued orders to have all troops forwarded. He, likewise, made requisitions for arms, subsistence and transportation, and actively co-operated with the Union Defense Committee of New York City, of which General John A. Dix was chairman.

April, 1861.

The crisis demanded immediate action, and General Wool assumed extraordinary authority, justified only by the exigency in view of the impossibility of communication with Washington. New Jersey was asking for transportation for her regiments, now equipped by voluntary contributions. General Wool sent them on to Philadelphia, and thence by transports across the Chesapeake to Annapolis. He early looked to the safety of the Gosport Navy Yard, to Hampton Roads and Fortress Monroe, and sent by transports, accompanied by armed steamers, provisions, ammunition and reinforcements, as he well knew the importance of these strategic points and the value of the armament at Gosport to the enemy, should they fall into their hands.

The Governors of the various States in his department, as they were cut off from communicating with Washington, applied to him for counsel as well as for munitions of war, and for arms and for equipments for the volunteers waiting to be sent to the defense of the capital. Governor Yates appealed for arms and ammunition for five thousand waiting Illinois volunteers, and was directed, in conjunction with Frank P. Blair, of Missouri, to take possession of the United States Arsenal at St. Louis and use the 21,000 stand of arms and 110,000 rounds of ammunition there stored.

General Wool ordered the Ellsworth Zouaves

* These five companies were the Washington Artillery, Captain James Wren, of Pottsville; the National Light Infantry, Captain E. McDonald, of Pottsville; the Ringgold Light Artillery, Captain James McKnight, of Reading; the Logan Guards, Captain J. Selheimer, of Lewistown, and the Allen Infantry, Captain Thomas B. Yeager, of Allentown.

THE ("BILLY") WILSON ZOUAVES, AT TAMMANY HALL, TAKING THE OATH OF FIDELITY TO THE FLAG AND SWEARING TO "GO THROUGH BALTIMORE OR DIE," APRIL 23RD, 1861.

SIXTEEN TRANSPORTS CROSSING CHESAPEAKE BAY WITH NEW YORK TROOPS FOR WASHINGTON, VIA ANNAPOLIS, MAY 4th, 1861.

forward, in opposition to the technical objections of Governor Morgan of New York, who delayed them until they should reduce their overflowing ranks to the number authorized by law. He furnished the Pennsylvania troops with 16,000 muskets and 500,000 cartridges. To six Ohio regiments he issued 3,000 muskets and 118,000 cartridges. To other Ohio troops, 16,000 muskets and 400,000 cartridges. Five thousand muskets and 200,000 cartridges were issued to Indiana troops. Illinois drew 200,000 cartridges; Massachusetts, 4,000 stand of arms; New Hampshire, 2,000 muskets and 20,000 cartridges; New Jersey, 3,000 muskets; and 10,000 muskets and 400,000 cartridges were issued to General Patterson, in command in Pennsylvania, and 10,000 muskets to Major-general Sandford, of New York. He made Fortress Monroe secure, saved the capital from seizure, and by his prompt action kept alive the fires of patriotism, and sent forward, organized and armed, volunteers who, without such prompt encouragement, might have, in waiting for an order for arms and equipments from the seat of Government, been called to repulse from the soil of New York and Massachusetts and Illinois an invading army possessed of the capital of the nation, and armed with the prestige of successful invasion.

SLEEPING QUARTERS OF THE RHODE ISLAND REGIMENT IN THE PATENT OFFICE, WASHINGTON.

The reward for this fidelity was an order from the General-in-chief, in the first mail from Washington received after its investment (April 30th, 1861), directing General Wool to return to his headquarters at Troy, and there await the recovery of his health, known to be feeble. The Union Defense Committee, who appreciated his services, as did the whole people north, unanimously adopted resolutions of congratulation and thanks, and conveyed a request to the War Department to ratify and approve the conduct and action of General Wool, and to continue him in command of the city and department. These resolutions were furnished to the President of the United States, to Lieutenant-general Scott, and to Major-general Wool April 30th, 1861, and on August 17th, 1861, General Wool was called from his retirement, and placed in command of the Department of South-eastern Virginia, to succeed General Butler at Fortress Monroe.

THE ("BILLY") WILSON ZOUAVES.

In June 16th, 1861, Santa Rosa Island, on which stands Fort Pickens, was made lively by the encampment there of the Sixth New York Regiment of Volunteers, known as "Billy" Wilson's Zouaves.

They left New York, June 13th, on which day they were presented with a beautiful silk flag by the Ladies' Soldiers' Relief Association. Colonel William Wilson had been one of the very first to offer his services to the Government on the breaking out of the war. He recruited a regiment of nearly twelve hundred men from the rowdy and crimina

FIRST DIVISION OF PENNSYLVANIA VOLUNTEERS, UNDER GENERAL CALWALLADER, ENTERING BALTIMORE HARBOR, MAY 15th, 1861.

THE GERMAN REGIMENT, "STEUBEN" VOLUNTEERS, [illegible] RECEIVING THEIR FLAGS AT THE CITY HALL, NEW YORK, MAY 24TH, 18[illegible]

THE ATTACK UPON THE CONFEDERATE BATTERIES, AT THE ENTRANCE OF AQUIA CREEK, POTOMAC RIVER, BY THE UNITED STATES VESSELS "PAWNEE," "YANKEE," "THOMAS FREEBORN," "ANACOSTA" AND "RESOLUTE," JUNE 1st, 1861.

THE FIGHT AT PHILIPPI, VA., JUNE 3D, 1861.—THE UNITED STATES TROOPS UNDER COMMAND OF COLONEL DUMONT, SUPPORTED BY COLONELS KELLEY AND LANDER; THE CONFEDERATES UNDER COLONEL PORTERFIELD.

classes … New York city, who were drawn together by the avenging cry, "Death to the Plug Uglies of Baltimore!" and the popular clamor of the infuriated mob elements to punish summarily the perpetrators of the Baltimore attack on the Sixth Massachusetts Regiment.

June, 1861.

Colonel Wilson formally mustered his regiment in the old Tammany Hall, and there, on April 25th, with the men arranged around the room, with the officers in the centre, the Colonel, with a sword in one hand and the American flag in the other, knelt on one knee, and all present knelt with him, and repeated after him the oath: "To support the flag, and never flinch from its path through blood or death." He then denounced the Plug Uglies of Baltimore, and declared that Wilson's Zouaves would leave but a monument of their bones in the streets.

Amid yells of "Death to the Plug Uglies!" he said: "Though I may be the first man slain, I have but one request to make: Let each of you, my followers, select his man and avenge my death." The regiment was transported the same day to Staten Island, where they went into camp until they were, on the 13th of June, embarked, as they supposed, for Baltimore, but really for Santa Rosa Island.

They encamped about a mile eastward of Fort Pickens. The Confederates had despaired of ever capturing the fort, but they used every effort to break up the Zouave camp, and looked upon "Billy Wilson" as the foremost man on the island.

On the 6th of October, 1861, a Confederate force of between twelve hundred and two thousand men, under command of Brigadier-general Anderson, effected a landing on the island four miles above the camp.

Sickness and desertion had so depleted the regiment that Colonel Wilson had but two hundred men able to take the field. The Zouaves were surprised, and had so often given false alarms, and played practical jokes on the garrison in the fort, that the firing of the pickets did not alarm them, and not until the engagement became general did the regulars become aware of the serious nature of the attack.

In the meantime, Colonel Wilson and Lieutenant-colonel Creighton encountered the centre column of the enemy, but could not prevent a flank movement by which the Confederates gained possession of their camp, and after completely plundering it of clothing, money and baggage, set the camp on fire.

The Confederates finally retreated to their boats, under a terrible fire from the Zouaves and regulars, and, under the cover of the darkness, escaped with a considerable loss. This was the first battle of the Zouaves, and very little precaution had been taken against an attack. They lost 10 killed, 16 wounded, and 9 prisoners. The rebel loss was as high as 410 killed, wounded and missing. Among the prisoners were three officers.

ATTACK ON THE CONFEDERATES AT AQUIA CREEK.

Aquia Creek enters the Potomac River from the left or Virginia side, forty miles below Washington. The point of junction is the eastern terminus of the Fredericksburg and Potomac Railway, seventy-five miles southwest of Richmond, Va., and here, in the early part of May, several batteries and other obstructions had been erected by the Confederates to interfere with the free navigation of the river, and to prevent vessels carrying supplies to the capital.

Captain J. H. Ward, who was in command of the Potomac flotilla, had frequently to contend with these batteries erected at different points, his flagship, the *Thomas Freeborn*, usually bearing the brunt of the attacks. It was with the latter that he succeeded in silencing the heavy guns mounted on Craney Island and at Sewall's Point, which commanded the passage through Hampton Roads. The batteries at and on the heights above Aquia Creek landing were, however, reported to be of a more formidable nature than any yet encountered, and after conferring with Commodore Stringham, it was decided to destroy them if possible.

On the 31st of May, Captain Ward, in command on board the *Thomas Freeborn*, and assisted by two more of his gunboats, the *Resolute* and the *Anacosta*, began the attack, and, after a two-hours' fight, succeeded in silencing the batteries at the landing, but, for want of long-range ammunition, could not effectually respond to the heavy fire from the heights, and so had to withdraw.

May, 1861.

The following day, however, with additional aid from the sloops-of-war *Pawnee* and *Yankee*, the attack was resumed, and during an almost continuous bombardment on both sides the batteries were twice silenced, and the wharf and railway depot burned; but whether they were fired by shells from the ships, or by the Confederates in their retreat, is unknown.

During the engagement the *Freeborn* fired 160 rounds, 60 of which were shell; the *Pawnee*, 350 rounds; the *Anacosta*, about 100; and the *Yankee*, 11. The *Anacosta*, which was chiefly manned by volunteers from the Seventy-first Regiment, New York, did effective service. The *Freeborn* received several shots from the batteries, but was not seriously injured. The *Pawnee* was struck nine times, and yet no one on the side of the flotilla was found to have sustained serious injury.

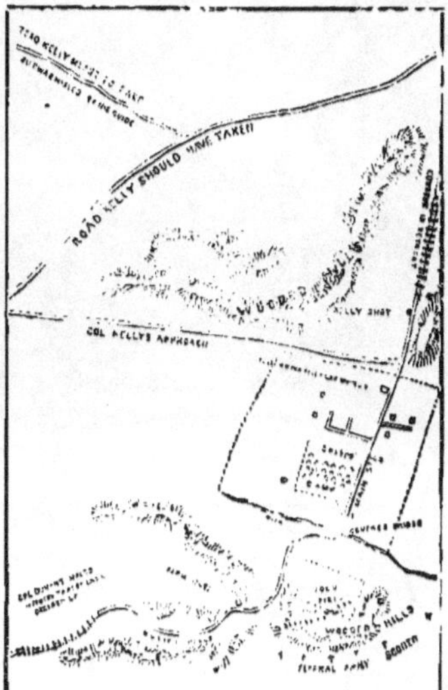

PLAN OF THE FIGHT AT PHILIPPI, JUNE 3d, 1861.

SURPRISE AND ROUT AT PHILIPPI.

Philippi is a little town in Western Virginia, twenty-two miles southward of Grafton, where the Baltimore and Ohio and the Northwestern Railways make an important connection, and has become noted as the scene of the surprise and rout of the Confederate forces which were concentrated there June 3d, 1861, under Colonel Porterfield.

Acting under instructions from Brigadier-general T. A. Morris, the Federal troops were arranged in two columns: one commanded by Colonel B. F. Kelley, whose force consisted of his own regiment, the First Virginia, the Ninth Indiana, Colonel Milroy, and a portion of the Sixteenth Ohio, under Colonel Irwin; while the other column was commanded by Colonel E. Dumont, who had with him eight companies of his own regiment, the Seventh Indiana, four companies of the Sixth Indiana, Colonel Crittenden, a portion of Barnett's Ohio Artillery, under Lieutenant-colonel Sturges, and four companies of the Fourteenth Ohio, under Lieutenant-colonel Steadman.

It was agreed that Colonel Kelley's command should proceed along the Beverly Turnpike above Philippi, a distance of about twenty-two miles, with the view of engaging Colonel Porterfield's rear at four o'clock on the morning of the 3d, when Colonel Dumont's column would simultaneously open fire from the heights overlooking the village of Philippi.

June, 1861.

Colonel Dumont's column, accompanied by Colonel F. W. Lander, of General McClellan's staff, reached its destination at the appointed time, after a very wearisome march of nearly thirteen miles in a drenching rainstorm, and was about taking its position, when Colonel Porterfield's pickets engaged it in consequence of the alarm caused by a pistol-shot, which was fired by a woman at Colonel Lander, while he was reconnoitring ahead of the column. There being, up to that time, no signs of Kelley's troops, contrary to their preconcerted arrangement, and fearing Colonel Porterfield might escape, Colonel Dumont opened fire upon the Confederates with both of his guns, and, under their cover, made a dash upon the enemy's pickets, carrying consternation in their ranks, and capturing the barricaded bridge across the river.

Meanwhile, Kelley's command, which had been delayed by being treacherously led at the side instead of in the rear of Colonel Porterfield's position, advanced rapidly upon the fugitives, and pursued them through the streets of Philippi, compelling them to abandon everything in their flight. It was while thus engaged, gallantly leading his troops, that Colonel Kelley was shot by a retreating Confederate through the left breast, and believed to be mortally injured.

In this emergency, Colonel Dumont was assigned to the command of the two operating columns, and continued the pursuit until, under the instructions of General Morris, he brought the troops back to Grafton, which, for a while, became the headquarters of the national troops in Western Virginia. Colonel Kelley finally recovered his health, and received the well-merited promotion of brigadier-general, his commission being dated May 17th, 1861, sixteen days earlier than the date of the battle in which he so brilliantly distinguished himself.

ENGAGEMENT AT ROMNEY.

On the 10th of June, 1861, news was brought to Colonel Lewis Wallace, of the Eleventh Indiana Volunteers, a Zouave regiment, that a large Confederate force had been concentrated at the town of Romney, the county seat of Hampshire County, Va., about fifty miles to the southeast of Cumberland. Colonel Wallace left Cumberland of the 11th inst., proceeding by railroad, twenty-eight miles to New Creek Bridge, which he reached at eleven o'clock the same evening. His command at once commenced their march for Romney, twenty-two miles distant, reaching there at eight o'clock on the following morning. He at once charged the Confederates, who had been advised by their mounted scouts, whom Colonel Wallace's advance had driven in, of the approach of the Zouaves.

June, 1861.

Although numbering 1,200 men, the Confederates made but feeble resistance, and fled in wild disorder. In the rough-and-ready language of a letter-writer among the assailants: "The Zouaves advanced at the 'double-quick.' The Confederates went 'about face,' and invited the Eleventh to a foot-race, taking a long start. The mounted officers, not being very expert in fence-leaping, dismounted, and joined the 'field race.'

"Some stragglers, whose running was not so good as their boasting, lagged behind, and were taken prisoners. The Zouaves entered Romney at half-past eight o'clock A.M., in time to partake of the breakfast which had been prepared for the Confederates.

"They captured one major, ten horses, tents,

THE ENGAGEMENT AT ROMNEY, VA., JUNE 11th, 1861.—THE ELEVENTH INDIANA ZOUAVES.

VIEW OF GRAFTON, VA., ON THE MONONGAHELA RIVER.

ENCAMPMENT AT ROMNEY, VA., JUNE 1861, OF THE ELEVENTH INDIANA ZOUAVES, COLONEL LEWIS WALLACE, CROSSING, ON THE DOUBLE QUICK, THE BRIDGE OVER THE POTOMAC

VIEW OF GRAFTON, VA., ON THE MONONGAHELA RIVER, HEADQUARTERS OF GENERAL GEORGE B. McCLELLAN, JUNE, 1861

THE FIRST BATTLE OF THE WAR, FOUGHT AT BIG BETHEL, JUNE 10TH, 1861.—FEDERALS UNDER GENERAL PIERCE; CONFEDERATES UNDER GENERAL MAGRUDER.

medical chests, camp utensils, two flags several rifles and a number of uniforms. They occupied the place until eleven o'clock, spending the time in missionary efforts by convincing the women (fifty of whom were found locked in one house) that Federal soldiers were civilized beings.

"After partaking of dinner they commenced their return, and reached New Creek at twelve o'clock at night, and were conveyed back by railroad, reaching camp by daybreak; having ridden upward of fifty miles by rail, marched forty-five on foot, and fought a battle, all without sleep, and in a little over twenty-four hours."

The effect of this dashing exploit was to encourage the Federal Army, who had so repeatedly been defeated, inspire the North with new courage, alarm Johnston by its boldness, and threaten his line of communication with Richmond and Manassas, forcing him to evacuate Harper's Ferry, and move up the valley to near Winchester.

THE DAY AFTER "ROMNEY."—THE ELEVENTH INDIANA ZOUAVES, COLONEL LEWIS WALLACE, IN CAMP McGINNIS, JUNE 12TH, 1861.

GRAFTON, W. VA.

This beautiful little town is situated on the banks of the Monongahela River. It is ninety-six miles below Wheeling, one hundred and ninety from Pittsburgh, and two hundred and seventy-nine miles from Baltimore. In June, 1861, General McClellan, while operating in West Virginia, established his headquarters at Grafton.

Our sketch was made at the time of Lieutenant Tompkins's return there with his gallant Company B, U. S. Dragoons, after their dashing raid into Fairfax Court House, on June 1st, 1861, in the face of fifteen hundred Confederate troops.

BATTLE OF BIG BETHEL.

The first serious reverse which the national forces met in the campaign of 1861 was on the 10th of June, at a point named Bethel Church, about twelve miles from Fortress Monroe, on the road from Hampton to Yorktown, on the James River.

June, 1861

The original purpose of the expedition was the capture of a considerable body of Confederates established at Little Bethel, eight miles north of Newport News, whence they were accustomed to annoy the outposts of the Federal troops. Accordingly, on the night of Sunday, June 9th, General Butler dispatched from Fortress Monroe the regiment of New York Zouaves under Colonel Duryee, and the Albany (N.Y.) regiment, under Colonel Townsend, while the New York Steuben (German) Regiment, under Colonel Bendix, and detachments from the First Vermont and Third Massachusetts Regiments, were ordered forward from Newport News.

Accompanying the division from the fort was a small detachment of United States Artillery, under Lieutenant Greble, with three pieces of light artillery. The command of the whole expedition was given to Brigadier-general Pierce of Massachusetts.

Colonel Duryee's Zouaves were sent forward from Camp Hamilton an hour in advance of the other regiments, in order to reach the rear of the Confederates, and cut off their retreat, while the Massachusetts and Vermont detachments, under Lieutenant-colonel Washburn, advanced at the same time to attack them in front.

The German and Albany regiments, designed to act as reserves, were to effect a junction at the intersection of the roads leading to Little Bethel from Hampton and Newport News, and move to the support of Colonel Washburn. All these movements were carried out accurately.

In the darkness, however, and by some strange fatuity or unexplained blunder, when Colonel Townsend's command came marching up, they were mistaken by the German regiment for the Confederates, and fired on with fatal effect, both by musketry and artillery.

Overwhelmed with surprise, his men returned a straggling and ineffectual fire, and fell back to a defensible position in the full belief that they had encountered a column of the Confederates, of the strength of which they could form no estimate.

The detachment under Lieutenant-colonel Washburn, hearing the firing in their rear, and naturally supposing that the Confederates had got between them and the reserves, immediately faced about, and also the Zouaves, and both hastened at double quick time to what they regarded as the scene of action. They reached the spot, only to find out the cruel and fatal mistake that occurred, while the Confederates, thoroughly alarmed by the firing, retired on the main body intrenched at Big Bethel.

After explanations and a consultation of officers the Federal force hastily resolved to move on Big Bethel, of the strength of which they knew nothing, and the position of which they were ignorant. General Pierce then gave the order for advance. Little Bethel was taken and burned by the troops. Big Bethel was reached. Skirmishers were thrown out by the Federal advance, and they were first made aware of the Confederate position by a heavy fire of artillery from a masked battery immediately in their line of march, and which swept the road by which they were proceeding. Unable to return it effectively with musketry, the Federal forces were deployed—the German regiment and the Massachusetts and Vermont Volunteers into a forest to the right of the road, and the Zouaves and Colonel Townsend's regiment across some open fields into an apple orchard to the left of the road, with a view to flank the operations; while Lieutenant Greble, with his howitzers, and supported only by the ordinary complement of gunners, opened fire on the battery. The guns were worked with great rapidity and effect, keeping the Confederates within their works.

The Confederate forces were on the left bank of the Black River, with the stream directly in front. They had erected earthworks on each side of the road commanding the bridge, as well as a line of intrenchments along the wooded swamp to their right. This line was concealed by green boughs. The Confederate force was about eighteen hundred strong, many of them Virginian cavalry, under Colonel Magruder, and a North Carolina regiment under Colonel D. H. Hill, supported by a battery of twenty pieces of heavy cannon, and the Richmond Howitzer Battalion, commanded by Major Randolph. The storm of shot and shell showered upon the Federal troops from their masked batteries continued incessant for two hours, and about noon

GENERAL ROBERT C. SCHENCK, WITH THE [illegible] OHIO [illegible], FIRED INTO BY A MASKED BATTERY, NEAR VIENNA, VA., JUNE 17TH, 1861.

General Pierce ordered a charge, with instructions to dash across the morass, flank the works, and drive the Confederates out at the point of the bayonet. Colonel Duryee's Zouaves' attack was on the left, Colonel Townsend's on the right; and Colonel Bendix's German regiment, and Colonels Allen and Carr, with the First and Second New York Regiments, were to assail the left flank and rear. A number of charges were made, under a murderous fire from the invisible Confederates. But it was found that the works were protected in front by a morass and a deep stream, and by a ditch which could only be passed by aid of ladders.

In several instances the Zouaves, as well as the German regiment, charged up to the very edge of the obstructions, and were gradually, but with great exposure and uncertainty, making their way to the rear of the works, when the command was given by General Pierce to retire, after Colonel Duryee assured him that his ammunition was exhausted, and Colonel Townsend had fallen back, mistaking a detachment of his own men for Confederates.

Among the killed in this charge was Major Theodore Winthrop, of New Haven, Conn., Military Secretary of General Butler, and previously attached to the Seventh Regiment, National Guard, State of New York, who was shot by a Confederate drummer-boy while within thirty yards of the battery.

During this time Lieutenant Greble and his men were entirely exposed, but never for a moment slackened their fire. That gallant officer was struck in the head by a cannon-ball, and instantly killed. The gunners having now exhausted their ammunition, and the larger number having been killed or disabled, they, together with their guns, were withdrawn, under protection of a part of Colonel Washburn's men, the body of Lieutenant Greble being carried off the field under the guard of Co. E, 2nd N. Y. Vols., and amidst the fire of the Confederates.

The retreat was made with great order and deliberation, and all the dead and wounded were brought off the field, except Major Winthrop and two Zouaves of Duryee's Regiment.

The number of Federal troops actually engaged in the affair at Big Bethel was about 3,000. The Federal loss was sixteen killed, fifty-three wounded, and five missing. General Butler was greatly censured by the people of the North, as was General Pierce and the commanders of the several regiments, while the soldiers were everywhere extolled for their bravery. The Confederate loss was trifling, and they counted another to their succession of victories—Sumter, Harper's Ferry, Norfolk, and now the first success in the field in the first battle of the war, Big Bethel.

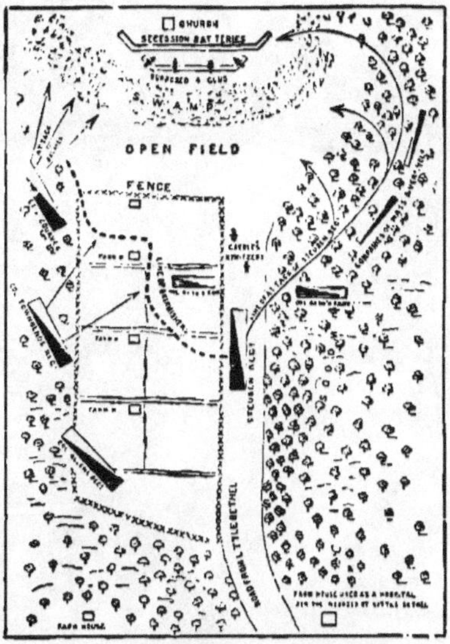

PLAN OF THE BATTLE OF BIG BETHEL.

In the National Senate, the confirmation of General Butler's nomination as major-general was secured just after this battle by only two votes, and these through the exertions of Senator Baker of Oregon.

THE FIRST OHIO REGIMENT SURPRISED BY A MASKED BATTERY.

Four companies of the First Ohio Regiment, commanded by Colonel McD. McCook, accompanied by Brigadier-general Robert C. Schenck, were ordered to guard the railroad between Alexandria and Leesburg.

They left their encampment at Alexandria on the 17th of June, 1861, and proceeded cautiously in cars and on trucks pushed ahead of a locomotive in the direction of Vienna. McCook and about three hundred of his men had just entered a deep cut, entirely exposed on platform cars, when the cars were swept from front to rear by grape and canister shot fired from a masked battery of the Confederates—a South Carolina regiment, commanded by Colonel Maxcy Gregg—a detachment of General Beauregard's army.

June, 1861.

The shot went high, and most of the soldiers were sitting. The frightened engineer, instead of drawing the whole train out of the peril, uncoupled the engine and one passenger-car, and fled with all possible speed toward Alexandria. The troops leaped from the remaining cars, and rallied in a grove, maintaining so bold a front, that the Confederates retired to Fairfax Court House, leaving the handful of Ohio troops, whom they might have captured with ease, to make their way leisurely back, carrying their dead and wounded companions on litters and in blankets. The Union loss was five killed, six wounded, and thirteen missing.

GENERAL PATTERSON

IN MARYLAND AND NORTHERN VIRGINIA.

On the 3d of June General Robert Patterson took command of the United States Volunteer forces gathered at Chambersburg, Pa. On the 4th, the General-in-chief instructed him to add to his army of three-months' men a battery of artillery and some companies of regular infantry. On the 8th of June a letter of instructions was sent him, in which he was told that there must be no reverse—that a check or drawn battle would be a victory to the Confederates, and therefore to act circumspectly and attempt nothing without a clear prospect of success.

On Friday, the 13th, he was informed that, on a supposition that he would cross the river into Virginia the next Monday or Tuesday, General McDowell would be instructed to make a demonstration on Manassas Junction, where Beauregard was intrenched. In obedience to this understanding, Patterson marched to

June, 1861.

CAPT. GEO. W. WILLSON'S CO. (E, 2ND REGT. N. Y. VOLS.) CARRYING THE BODY OF LIEUTENANT GREBLE FROM THE FIELD, AT BIG BETHEL, AMIDST THE FIRE OF THE CONFEDERATE FORCES

THE SIXTEENTH REGIMENT, OHIO VOLUNTEERS (COLONEL IRWINE), CROSSING THE TRAY RUN VIADUCT, NEAR CHEAT RIVER ON THE BALTIMORE AND OHIO RAILROAD

Hagerstown, reaching there on the 15th, and on the 16th, a large part of his army moved south of the Potomac, on Virginia soil. His design was to turn Johnston's left, and take Harper's Ferry in rear, thus to cut off Johnston's retreat and compel him to give battle at great disadvantage. But on the 15th, General Johnston, who kept himself well advised of Patterson's movements, and had been sending his supplies to the rear, suddenly abandoned Harper's Ferry, and took a fortified position at Winchester, thirty-two miles to the south.

Johnston thus approached Manassas, whither, largely by rail, he could repair, should Beauregard require aid either to resist McDowell or to attack Washington, or from whence he could quickly strengthen his own forces in order to resist Patterson, or to crush him in case the latter should pursue him or make any other serious false movement.

The demonstration promised by the General-in-chief on Manassas Junction by General McDowell was not made, and on the 16th, three days after he had been told he was expected to cross the river into Virginia, he received a telegram from the General-in-chief to send at once to Washington all the regular troops, horse and foot, and the Rhode Island Regiment and Battery, and to keep within the limits of Maryland with his remaining forces until satisfied it was safe to go beyond them.

The inquiry of the General-in-chief, "Why pursue Johnston? You are only driving him toward Manassas," showed plainly the non-aggressive policy desired at Washington of Patterson. But General Scott had become alarmed for the safety of Washington. This demand, if persisted in for horse, foot and artillery of Patterson, would deprive the latter of the power to longer remain south of the Potomac, and force him to assume a defensive, though threatening, attitude on the Maryland bank of that river.

On the 17th, another telegram was received from General Scott demanding the troops "already twice called for." This imperative order General Patterson at once obeyed, and having no alternative, recalled his army from Virginia.

On the 20th, General Scott asked for a plan of operations from General Patterson. On the 21st, the plan to abandon the present line of operations (the movement upon Winchester, through Martinsburg), move all supplies to Frederick, occupy Maryland Heights with Doubleday's heavy guns and a brigade of infantry to support him, and with everything else to cross the river at Point of Rocks and unite with Colonel Charles P. Stone's forces at Leesburg, from which point he could operate as circumstances would demand or general order require, was proposed by Patterson. No reply was received by him, but on the 28th General Scott, under great pressure for active operations, telegraphed him that he supposed he was that day crossing the river in pursuit of the enemy. On that day General Johnston, at Winchester, had 15,000 men and 24 guns, and was intrenched. General Patterson had 10,000 men, 6 guns, and the latter immovable for want of harness.

On the 28th, General Patterson informed the General-in-chief of the relative forces of each army, and that he would not risk an attack without explicit orders to do so. No order was given. On the 29th, he received harness for his single battery of six smoothbore guns, and on the 30th gave the order to cross the river into Virginia. On the 2d of July he crossed, met the enemy, whipped them, and moved on and occupied Martinsburg.

At Martinsburg, Patterson was greatly crippled by want of transportation for provision and grain, one day's extra supply of which he could not maintain. He was in advance of the contemplated movements of McDowell from Washington upon the enemy at Manassas. By moving eastward to Charlestown, he could avail himself of railroad transportation from Harper's Ferry, where he could establish his depots. From Charlestown he could advance at any moment upon the enemy at Winchester, or if the enemy retired to join Beauregard, he could cross the mountains, and almost as quickly reinforce McDowell at Manassas.

The three-months volunteers began to get restless, and were clamoring to be sent home by the expiration of their term. Many were without shoes, clothes were worn out, provisions were scarce, and a desire for battle did not prevail.

On the 9th of July, at Martinsburg, a council was held, at which commanders of divisions, brigades, and chiefs of staff, were present. Colonel Stone advised against an advance, and advocated a direct movement to Charlestown. All spoke against an advance, and all voted against one. The same day Patterson informed the General-in-chief of the condition of affairs, and of the situation in the Valley, proposed that he should go to Charlestown, establish depots at Harper's Ferry, and asked to be informed when the attack would be made on Manassas.

On the 12th he was instructed to go to Charlestown, and was informed that Manassas would be attacked on Tuesday, the 16th. In the meantime he had to await the arrival of troops under General Sandford, sent from Washington to join him. These came without transportation and provisions. They added to his incumbrances, and still further rendered essential the establishment of a depot at Harper's Ferry, the reopening of railroad communication, and the movement to Charlestown to protect it.

On the 13th he was ordered by telegram: "If not strong enough to beat the enemy early next week, make a demonstration so as to detain him in the Valley, or at Winchester." On that day he telegraphed to General Scott that Johnston was in position at Winchester to have his strength doubled just as he could reach him, and asked to be instructed. No instructions came. He made the required demonstration by moving to Bunker Hill on the road to Winchester. This he did on the 15th, the day General Scott said he would attack Manassas. He drove in the enemy's picket.

MAJOR TAYLOR, OF THE CONFEDERATE ARMY, ESCORTED BACK THROUGH THE LINES, AFTER HIS DELIVERY, UNDER A FLAG OF TRUCE, OF LETTERS FROM GENERAL BEAUREGARD TO GENERAL SCOTT, AND FROM JEFFERSON DAVIS TO PRESIDENT LINCOLN, JULY 6TH 1861.

THE ENGAGEMENT AT BEALINGTON, VA., BETWEEN OHIO AND INDIANA REGIMENTS AND A DETACHMENT OF GEORGIA TROOPS

m, and General Johnston intrenched at Winchester, and on the 17th General Patterson marched to Charlestown.

On the 17th General Scott telegraphed: "McDowell's first day's work has driven the enemy beyond Fairfax Court House; to-morrow, the Junction will probably be carried." By this, General Patterson supposed that he had fully carried out his own part of the programme, as Johnston was still at Winchester, and on the 18th, at half-past one in the morning, he telegraphed General Scott the condition of the enemy's forces and his own, referred to his letter of the 16th, and closed his dispatch with the inquiry: "Shall I attack?" He received no answer. At this time he expected to be attacked where he was, and was acting on the defensive, at the same time keeping General Johnston in check. On the 20th, he telegraphed General Scott that General Johnston had moved his troops, thirty-five thousand strong, and a large artillery force, in a southeasterly direction. This dispatch General Scott received the same day. In accordance with instructions, Patterson occupied Harper's Ferry on the 21st, and held that place until relieved by General Banks.

GEORGE B. McCLELLAN.

BEALINGTON, CARRICK'S FORD AND RICH MOUNTAIN.

JULY, 1861.

THE troops which had so greatly distinguished themselves at Philippi were not destined long to remain idle at Grafton, for, three days later, July 6th, we find them all—the First Virginia, the Sixth, Seventh and Ninth Indiana, the Fourteenth and Sixteenth Ohio, and Barnett's Cleveland Artillery, together with the Sixth Ohio, the Eighth, Tenth and Thirteenth Indiana, and Burdsall's Cavalry—in the neighborhood of their former scene of victory, and about to add greatly to their already brilliant record.

General McClellan, who had, two weeks previous, taken command of the troops at and near Grafton, now controlled an available force of about twenty thousand men, and decided upon an immediate advance, in order to offset any movement likely to be made by General R. S. Garnett, who had succeeded Porterfield, and was at the time in command of the Confederate troops in Northwestern Virginia. Garnett's headquarters were then at Beverly, in Randolph County, on the eastern base of a long ridge parallel to the Alleghanies, and known as Laurel Hill.

A detachment of Federal troops, under General T. A. Morris was sent toward Beverly; while another, under General J. D. Cox, entered the Kanawha Valley, where it was likely to meet General Henry A. Wise, and could keep him in check; and a third force, under General Hill, was dispatched toward Western Union, in Tucker County, and eastward of Philippi, to prevent the passage of the Confederates by that way over the Alleghany Mountains. The main body, consisting of about ten thousand men, under McClellan's command, then marched in the direction of Buckhannon, which was reached on the 7th of July.

JULY, 1861.

General Morris's force encamped at Bealington, a village at the foot of Laurel Hill, and in close proximity to Garnett's position. Morris had been ordered to engage Garnett in a series of feints which would lead to the belief that the main Federal assault might be expected from that quarter, thus giving McClellan a chance to attack the rear of Garnett's forces. These were estimated at fully eleven thousand men, including three thousand under Colonel John Pegram, at Rich Mountain.

So eager were the troops for active work, that skirmishes were incessantly kept up, and one of

SCOUTING PARTY OF THE NINTH INDIANA VOLUNTEERS. COLONEL MILROY—CALLED "THE TIGER" OF THE BLOODY NINTH."

Colonel Steedman's Fourteenth Ohio Regiment on the Bank of the Cheat River — General Garnett's Position on the Cliff. — Dumont's Men Crossing the River and Climbing the Cliff to Turn the Enemy's Position

THE BATTLE AT CARRICK'S FORD, VA., BETWEEN THE TROOPS OF GENERAL McCLELLAN'S COMMAND, LED BY GENERAL MORRIS,
AND THE CON[illegible]ERATE ARMY, UN[illegible]ER GENERAL [illegible] JULY [illegible]

these, which took place on the 8th of July, has by many been dignified by even a higher name. Early in the afternoon of that day, while observations were going on near Bealington, two large bodies of Confederate troops were seen emerging from the woods, and detachments from the Ninth Indiana and the Fourteenth Ohio at once pushed forward to meet them. This they soon did, and a lively engagement began between the two parties. This had not held by the Ninth Indiana, who, by their daring and the fierceness of their attacks, had already been dubbed by the insurgents "Swamp Devils," and had likewise become known as "The Tigers of the Bloody Ninth."

General McClellan's force has, meanwhile, been engaged in some brilliant skirmishes at Buckhannon, but it was not till July 10th that any large body of Confederate troops was met with. This over, accidentally discovered through the capture of a courier whom McClellan had sent after Rosecrans, and, after a wearisome, and in many respects quite dangerous, march in a heavy rain through the mountains, he found the enemy prepared to meet him.* The engagement commenced at once, and was made with such impetuosity that, notwithstanding the fact of Rosecrans being without cannon, and opposed to the enemy's

JULY, 1861.

ADVANCE OF GENERAL ROSECRANS'S DIVISION THROUGH THE FORESTS, TO ATTACK THE CONFEDERATES AT RICH MOUNTAIN.

continued long, however, before a strong body of Confederate cavalry appeared on the scene, and would doubtless soon have made the position untenable to the Federal troops but for the timely arrival of Barnett's Cleveland Battery.

The latter's admirable shelling of the woods alone prevented the further rallying of the opposite force, and soon compelled its flight. The Federal loss in this engagement was two killed and six wounded, whilst that of the Confederates was reported to be fully twenty killed and twice as many *hors de combat.* General Morris's force was afterward advanced close to the western base of Laurel Hill, the woods being was a part of the force under Colonel Pegram, found to be in a strongly intrenched position on Rich Mountain, which commanded the road to Staunton, the principal highway to Southern Virginia. McClellan immediately divided his force, sending the Sixteenth Ohio, and the Eighth, Tenth and Thirteenth Indiana Regiments, as well as Burdsall's Cavalry, the whole under command of Colonel W. S. Rosecrans, who was accompanied by Colonel F. W. Lander, to attack Pegram's position, while he himself would advance on the Confederate camp at Laurel Hill.

The movement of Colonel Rosecrans was, however, masked battery, the fight lasted scarcely an hour, and resulted in the total rout of the Confederates, who, in that short time, lost about four hundred in killed and wounded, besides their guns and all their ammunition, tents and camp equipage.

* This circuitous march through the dense forests of Laurel Hill, over a wild and broken country, was guided by a woodsman named David L. Hart, who [illegible] the march as follows: "We started at day[illegible] [illegible] through a path[illegible] [illegible] [illegible] our circuit was about [illegible] and it was very cold. [illegible] Confederate pickets, and after [illegible] immediately opened the action."

BATTLE OF RICH MOUNTAIN BEVERLY PIKE, VA. BETWEEN A DIVISION OF

BATTLE OF RICH MOUNTAIN BEVERLY PIKE, VA. BETWEEN A DIVISION OF GENERAL McCLELLAN'S COMMAND LED BY GENERAL ROSECRANS, AND THE CONFEDERATES UNDER GENERAL PEGRAM JULY 12th 1861

General McClellan discovering, meanwhile, that Garnett had evacuated Laurel Hill, which General Morris afterward took possession of, occupied Beverly, and advanced his position in front of Pegram's camp, with the intention of assaulting it the next morning. It was found, however, that Pegram had abandoned it during the night, and that he was then endeavoring to join Garnett's forces. This was, however, impossible, as McClellan was already at Beverly, and, finding resistance useless, Pegram offered to surrender to General McClellan, which he did on Sunday, July 14th.

On learning of Garnett's flight, General Lander had been sent with a force of Ohio men after the fugitives, with whom he had several skirmishes, in one of which he had a horse shot under him, and the result of which was the capture of many prisoners, with a loss of but two men.

McClellan had likewise dispatched Captain H. W. Benham, United States Engineers, with eighteen hundred men, to the assistance of General Morris, who had actively pursued the enemy one or two miles beyond Leedsville, where they had halted for the night. Captain Benham effected the desired junction with General Morris, and the combined forces continued the pursuit, notwithstanding the rain, all the following day, finally overtaking the enemy at a place called Carrick's Ford, eight miles south of St. George. There the Confederates made a stand, and, with cannon planted on an elevation, disputed the advance; but Captain Benham's men dashed into the river, halting under the bluff until their artillery came up, and then attacked the enemy's flank, forcing him to disperse.

JULY, 1861.

The pursuit was continued until another ford was reached, when General Garnett again attempted to rally his forces. Colonel James Barrett Steedman, of the Fourteenth Ohio, was close upon them, and bore the brunt of the heavy fire directly upon his men by Colonel Taliaferro, of the Twenty-third Virginia Regiment. He stood his ground well until joined by Burnett's Battery and the Seventh and Ninth Indiana Regiments.

The Seventh Indiana, under Colonel Dumont, was then ordered to cross the river between the two fires, and to engage the Confederates in front. This was promptly done, but by the time the men had reached the summit of the opposite bank, the Confederates had dispersed. Garnett endeavored to make one more stand, at a ford a quarter of a mile further on, and, while doing so, was mortally wounded, his men flying in wild confusion to the mountains.

Further pursuit was abandoned. The Federals, who had by this time made a forced march of twenty miles, bivouacked that night at the Ford, having lost in all not over twelve killed and wounded. It was expected that General Hill, who was then at Rowlesburg, on the line of the Baltimore and Ohio Railroad, would intercept the remnant of Garnett's army before it could cross the mountains, and would capture it at either St. George or Western Union, but for some unexplained reason this was not done. The entire body was allowed to escape into the Shenandoah Valley, and to join the forces gathered there under General T. J. ("Stonewall") Jackson, at Monterey.

While all this was going on, General Cox had successfully held his own in the Kanawha Valley. He had captured Barboursville, repulsed Wise's forces at Scarytown, and forced their retreat to Charleston, then to Gauley Bridge, and as far as Lewisburg, the capital of Greenbrier County.

The immediate result of the above brilliant series of victories under Generals McClellan, Rosecrans, Morris, and Cox, was the evacuation of Harper's Ferry and the abandonment by the Confederates of all of Western Virginia.

On the 24th of July, Colonel Rosecrans was promoted to be a brigadier-general, and was placed in command of the "Department of the Ohio," just vacated by General McClellan, who was ordered to Washington, to take personal command of the

THE BATTLE OF RICH MOUNTAIN, VA.—THE UNITED STATES TROOPS UNDER GENERAL ROSECRANS, OF GENERAL McCLELLAN'S COMMAND; THE CONFEDERATES UNDER GENERAL PEGRAM—THE THIRTEENTH INDIANA CAPTURE A GUN.

THE BURIAL OF THE INDIANA VOLUNTEERS WHO FELL IN THE BATTLE OF RICH MOUNTAIN.

Army of the Potomac. General Garnett was succeeded by General Robert E. Lee, who, on the 20th of April, resigned his commission in the United States Army, and was appointed, by Governor Letcher, to the command of all the forces of the State of Virginia.

FIRING ON A FLAG OF TRUCE.

COMMODORE STRINGHAM, in a dispatch dated July 8th, 1861, gave the following account of the firing upon a flag of truce off Sewell's Point: "A small steamer was sent with a flag, Commander Case in command, for the purpose of taking away a daughter of Colonel Segar, in compliance with instructions from the Navy Department, notice having been given to Brigadier-general Benjamin Huger. After passing the batteries at Sewell's Point and Bush Point, a shot was fired at the steamer from Craney Island, which passed directly across her bow, and struck within twenty feet. 'Had not the engine been stopped,' says Commander Case in his report, 'at the flash, and the boat turned a little to starboard, the shot must, I think, have struck her.' Commander Case then took to his barge, and had not proceeded more than three or four boat's lengths from the steamer toward Craney Island, where the flags were usually communicated, when a second shot was fired at the barge, which passed directly over, and struck about thirty yards from her. Two officers came off in a boat, and to the question of Commander Case, 'Who commanded at Craney Island?' they answered: 'Colonel Richardson.' To the question, 'Whether they intended to fire upon a flag of truce?' the senior officer replied: 'It was the result of ignorance. The commanding officer gave the word to fire the shot and stop the steamer.'"

Commodore Stringham's letter, stating that Commander Case was ready to receive Miss Segar, was forwarded to General Huger, and, receiving no answer after four hours waiting, the Commander returned. Commodore Stringham closed his dispatch as follows: "I can but express very great surprise at such treatment, considering the courtesy with which flags of truce from Norfolk have been received by me. I feel unwilling to hold further communication until a full explanation is offered by Brigadier-general Huger or the commanding officer at Norfolk."

THE "ADRIATIC," OF PHILADELPHIA, BEARING A FLAG OF TRUCE, FIRED UPON BY THE CONFEDERATE BATTERY ON CRANEY ISLAND, NEAR NORFOLK, VA.

AT ARLINGTON, VA., THE HEADQUARTERS OF GENERAL RUNYON'S NEW JERSEY BRIGADE

THE BATTLE OF BULL RUN, OR MANASSAS.

The battle of Bull Run, which the Confederates called the battle of Manassas, was the first really important action of the Civil War.

July, 1861

The scene lay a few miles to the north-west of Manassas Junction, about twenty-nine miles south of Washington, on the banks of the Bull Run, a small stream which rises in the range of hills bearing the same name, and which runs nearly west to east, emptying in the Occoquan River.

General Irvin McDowell, who since his appointment, May 27th, to the command of the newly-created "Department of Washington," had been steadily organizing the troops which, under President Lincoln's proclamations of April 15th and May 3d, kept pouring into the capital, found himself, early in July, with an available *force* of about thirty-five thousand men. Nearly one-third of these, however, were then about completing the three-months term for which they had enlisted.

An advance upon the daily increasing Confederate forces opposing, and threatening the seat of government, had been decided upon by the War Department, though, it must justly be said, contrary to the better judgment of Lieutenant-general Scott and General McDowell.

The "On to Richmond" popular cry had long resounded throughout the North, and, sharing in the general belief that an advance in *force* would not only prevent the meeting of the First Confederate Congress, to be held July 20th, but substantially end the war, pressure was exerted to the utmost, lest even the Government be charged with something more than actual indifference.

Arrangements for an aggressive movement were finally completed, July 15th

McDowell had organized his forces into five divisions, as follows:

First Division, embracing four brigades, under General Daniel Tyler. The First Brigade, commanded by Colonel Erasmus D. Keyes, included the First, Second and Third Connecticut, and the Fourth Maine Regiments, with Captain Varian's New York Battery, and Company B of the Second United States Cavalry. The Second Brigade, commanded by Brigadier-general R. C. Schenck, included the Second New York, and the First and Second Ohio Regiments and a light battery, with a part of Company E, Third United States Artillery. The Third Brigade, commanded by Colonel William T. Sherman, included the New York Thirteenth, Sixty-ninth and Seventy-ninth, and the Second Wisconsin Regiments, and a light battery, with part of Company E, Third United States Artillery. The Fourth Brigade, commanded by Colonel J. B. Richardson, included the Second and Third Michigan, the Twelfth New York, and the First Massachusetts Regiments.

Second Division, embracing two brigades, under Colonel David Hunter. The First Brigade, commanded by Colonel Andrew Porter, included the the Eighth and Fourteenth New York Regiments, a battalion of regular infantry, a squadron of the Second United States Cavalry, and a battery of the Fifth United States Artillery. The Second Brigade, commanded by Colonel Ambrose E. Burnside, included the First and Second Rhode Island, the Second New Hampshire and the Seventy-first New York Regiments, with a battery of the Second Rhode Island Artillery.

Third Division, embracing three brigades, under Colonel Samuel P. Heintzelman. The First Brigade, commanded by Colonel W. B. Franklin, included the First Minnesota, the Fourth Pennsylvania and the Fifth Massachusetts Regiments, Company E, Second United States Cavalry, and a light battery, with Company I, of the First United States Artillery. The Second Brigade, commanded by Colonel O. B. Wilcox, included the Eleventh New York and the First Michigan Regiments, and a light battery, with Company D, of the Second United States Artillery. The Third Brigade, commanded by Colonel O. O. Howard, included the Second Vermont and the Second, Fourth and Fifth Maine Regiments.

Fourth Division, constituting the reserve, under General Theodore Runyon, included the First, Second, Third and Fourth New Jersey three-months militia, and the First, Second and Third New Jersey three-years volunteer regiments.

Fifth Division, embracing two brigades, under Colonel Dixon S. Miles. The First Brigade, commanded by Colonel Louis Blenker included the Eighth and Twenty-ninth New York, the New York Garibaldi Guard, and the Twenty-fourth Pennsylvania Regiments. The Second Brigade, commanded by Colonel Thomas A. Davies, included the Sixteenth, Eighteenth, Thirty-first and Thirty-second New York Regiments, and a light battery, with Company G, of the Second United States Artillery.

All the divisions left camp on the afternoon of the 16th of July, the main body advancing early the following day toward Fairfax Court House, where it was expected the Confederates would make a stand.

July, 1861

General Tyler's division, forming the extreme right wing, took the Leesburg Road, and occupied Vienna that evening. The central column, under General Hunter, entered the direct turnpike road leading to Fairfax Court House. Heintzelman's division went out from near Alexandria, along the Little River Turnpike, and Miles's force entered

THE FIRST MICHIGAN REGIMENT AND THE ELLSWORTH ZOUAVES IN THE ENTRENCHMENTS AT ALEXANDRIA, VA.

the old Braddock Road, occupying the extreme left of the Federal advance.

General Patterson's troops, numbering about 16,000 men, were opposing at Martinsburg the force of General Joseph E. Johnston, who occupied Winchester. In accordance with instructions, Patterson reached Charlestown on July 17th, and remained there, holding in check, but not daring to attack, what he supposed to be a much superior force, well intrenched, and believing that Johnston could not elude him in time to meet McDowell's attack, promised by General Scott on the 16th or 17th. This Johnston did, however, on the morning of the 18th, and, as will be seen later, succeeded in joining and co-operating effectually with Beauregard's forces at Bull Run, which were not attacked until the 21st.

Upon arriving at Fairfax Court House, about noon of the 17th, it was found that the enemy had abandoned the place and retired to Centreville. General McDowell, with Tyler's division, then marched on to Georgetown, a small village about two miles farther on the Warrenton Turnpike, where they encamped for the night, and from which place they made a reconnoissance early the following morning, which resulted in their marching through Centreville, at about nine o'clock. They halted in a valley close by, where the Confederates had erected strong earthworks, then held by a brigade of South Carolina troops, under General M. L. Bonham.

These, however, retired, at Tyler's approach, to Mitchell's Ford, in accordance with previous instructions. These instructions, which likewise affected the Confederate troops then at Fairfax Court House, as well as at Fairfax Station, had, strange as it may appear, been issued by General Beauregard, as far back as the 20th of June. In saying this, we bear full tribute to what Mr. Roman calls "one of the most remarkable instances in military history, of an order providing fully and precisely, nearly a month in advance, for all the exigencies of a strategic movement remotely contingent upon the operations of an enemy."

Another reconnoissance, with four regiments of Richardson's brigade, Ayres's battery and a squadron of cavalry, was made toward noon in the direction of Blackburn's Ford, where General Beauregard then was, and where General James Longstreet had been posted with the First, Eleventh and Seventeenth Virginia Regiments and two guns. Most of these troops lay concealed in the woods. The Confederate line extended some five miles, and embraced, besides Longstreet's troops, the brigade of General Bonham, with Colonel Radford's cavalry and Kemper's and Shields's batteries, at Mitchell's Ford, and a part of Evans's brigade, with four guns and two companies of cavalry, at the Stone Bridge.

On Longstreet's right stood General D. R. Jones's brigade, with cavalry and artillery, at McLean's Ford, and Ewell's brigade was at the Union Mills Ford, with some Virginia cavalry and four guns, supported by Early's brigade, with seven guns in the rear.

Ayres's battery opened on the Confederates, and the Second Michigan Regiment went forward as skirmishers. These, however, soon being engaged in a severe contest, the Third Michigan, Twelfth New York, First Massachusetts, and the Second United States Cavalry, were sent to support them, and were met by a strong fire from hidden artillery and infantry which compelled them to fall back.

Reinforced at once by Sherman's brigade, in front of which stood Corcoran's New York Sixty-ninth Regiment, they again advanced on Longstreet's position, which had, meanwhile, received the assistance of Early's brigade.

The fight continued fiercely till after four o'clock, when General McDowell ordered a retreat to Centreville, having found, by an extended reconnoissance, that his intended movement on the enemy's left would be impracticable.

The total Confederate loss was reported at seventy; that of the Federals being eighty-three killed, wounded and missing.

The time was fast approaching when the term of enlistment of many of McDowell's troops would expire, and he felt, besides, the necessity for a vigorous and a prospective final attack, which, he thought, could be most successfully carried out by isolating Beauregard's forces through the seizure of the Manassas Gap Railway. He concentrated all his troops about Centreville, and kept up reconnoissances all the 19th, with the view of renewing the attack the day following, but was not then in a position to advance, by reason of the needed supplies not reaching him as expected.

JULY, 1861.

McDowell's forces on the evening of July 20th, not counting the 5,000 reserve of New Jersey regiments under General Runyon, stationed back of Centreville, was about 28,000 men, with forty-nine cannon, the Fourth Pennsylvania and Varian's battery having completed their time of service, and returned to Washington on their way home.

The advance took place at two o'clock Sunday morning, the 21st. Tyler's division, with Ayres's and Carlisle's batteries, moved along the Warrenton

IRVIN McDOWELL.

Turnpike, and was to be in position at four o'clock to open fire on the Confederates at the Stone Bridge, whilst the real attack was to be made by the combined forces under Hunter and Heintzelman, who should, by about that time, have completed their circuit through the forest road and across the Cub Run, near Sudley Church, and been ready to fall on the Confederate rear.

Miles's division, reinforced by Richardson's brigade, was to act as a reserve on the extreme left at Centreville, the brigade under Keyes remaining to watch the road leading to Manassas. McDowell now felt certain of success, as he believed in his superiority of numbers, being ignorant of the fact that Johnston's force, instead of being held back by Patterson at Winchester, had, as we have seen, been allowed to escape, and had already by that time added six thousand men to the Confederate force under General Beauregard, then representing 30,888 men and fifty-five guns.

By a singular coincidence, Beauregard had contemplated an attack upon the Federals at the same time, his order for an advance upon the latter at Centreville, though for a later hour, bearing the same date as that of McDowell.

The Confederate line was much the same as on July 18th. Longstreet had additional support in Barksdale's Mississippi regiment, and in both Bee's and Bartow's brigades, taken from the recently arrived portion of the force under Johnston, whose other brigade, under General T. J. ("Stonewall") Jackson, was given to General Bonham. Jones had received Early's brigade, and that under General Holmes, as well as the First Arkansas and the Second Tennessee, was given a place in Ewell's rear.

The Island, Bull and Lewis Fords were protected by ten companies of infantry, two of cavalry and four guns, and Hampton's Legion was sent to the Lewis House, to aid there in case of need. The reserves were at Camp Pickens, and Evans's brigade still held the Stone Bridge.

The fire was opened by Edwards's Fifth Artillery, then attached to Carlisle's, under Lieutenant Haines, and was kept up both directly in front and by a brigade which Tyler had sent down toward the ford to carry out the original plan.

Colonel Evans, believing that a real attack had been begun upon his forces, so advised General Beauregard, and reinforcements were sent forward, especially with the object of engaging the Federal left wing at Centreville. The possibility of such a move had, however, been anticipated by McDowell, who had ordered Howard's brigade to be ready there to assist Miles and Richardson if necessary.

It was not long before Evans became satisfied that the real assault would be on his flank, and at half-past eight he determined to change his position. Leaving only four companies of Sloan's Fourth South Carolina Regiment at the Stone Bridge, which he had been ordered to hold at all hazards, he took the remainder of Sloan's regiment and five companies of Wheat's Louisiana regiment, also two guns from Latham's battery, and, with them, occupied a position on the Brentsville Road.

There, Burnside's brigade, which had been long delayed by the difficult road it had to encounter, came up at ten o'clock, led by the Second Rhode Island, under Colonel Slocum, which, with the New York Seventy-first, Colonel Martin, the Second New Hampshire, Colonel Marston, and Griffin's and Reynolds's artillery, at once opened fire.

This was kept up fiercely for over an hour, and told severely on the smaller Confederate force, until the latter was reinforced by additional guns and by detachments under Generals Bee and Bartow. This enabled the Confederates the better to maintain their position, and might have turned the tide but for the timely arrival of Sherman's brigade, led by the New York Sixty-ninth, Colonel Corcoran, as well as of detachments from Porter's brigade, then coming down the Sudley Springs Road, and of the much-delayed Third Division, under General Heintzelman. This additional force soon broke the Confederate lines, compelling them to fall back upon a plateau south of the Stone Bridge.

It was now high noon. The first real engagement had resulted in favor of the Federals, leaving them in an excellent position to follow up the vantage gained. No time was to be lost, however, in order to reap, if possible, more substantial results before the enemy could be reinforced.

The position of Howard's brigade was unchanged. Burnside's brigade, after exhausting its ammunition, had been ordered to the rear, but the brigades under Keyes and Sherman had joined the forces commanded by Hunter and Heintzelman, and, as the Confederates had been forced beyond the Stone Bridge, the latter might be crossed by the remainder of Tyler's division.

The plateau could only be successfully commanded from where stood the Henry House, and this was the Confederates' strongest position, defended by thirteen guns admirably distributed, and supported by the brigades under Evans, Bee and Bartow.

In a southwesterly direction from the Henry House was a hill which, in turn, commanded the plateau. Both Griffith's and Ricketts's batteries, supported by the New York Eleventh (Ellsworth's Fire Zouaves), were ordered to take and hold it. Before this was done, however, the Zouaves, who had

BATTLE OF BULL RUN, VA, FOUGHT JULY 21st, 1861, BETWEEN THE FEDERAL ARMY, COMMANDED BY

BATTLE OF BULL RUN, VA., FOUGHT [illegible] BETWEEN THE FEDERAL ARMY, COMMANDED BY GENERAL McDOWELL AND THE CONFEDERATE ARMY COMMANDED BY GENERALS BEAUREGARD AND JOHNSTON

advanced boldly, had been confronted by an Alabama regiment, which attacked them on the flank, while two companies of the Black Horse Cavalry dashed upon their rear, dispersing the entire body. Then Heintzelman ordered successively the Fourteenth New York, the First Minnesota and the First Michigan to the support of the batteries, but the force every time opposed to them was too great, and they also had finally to retire, leaving behind them the batteries, the men and horses attached to which had become disabled at the very first volley.

"Stonewall" Jackson subsequently attempted at three different times to take these batteries away from the field; but he was every time driven back by the Zouaves and by the Thirty-eighth New York Regiment, who finally bore them away beyond the enemy's reach.

The Second Maine, Colonel Jamieson, and the Third Connecticut, Colonel Chatfield had, meanwhile, been ordered to silence a battery of eight guns, which was at Robinson's buildings, and had been doing considerable damage. Their efforts were, however, unsuccessful. They found themselves exposed to a galling fire on all sides and they, likewise, had to fall back.

While this was going on, Sherman's brigade, occupying the central position, had been ordered to charge upon the Confederate batteries still on the plateau. It crossed the Warrenton Turnpike, and dashed up the hill in face of a terrific fire, alternately advancing and retreating in front of the masses hurled against it until, repulsed for the third time, it fell back, leaving Colonel James Cameron (brother of the Secretary of War), of the New York Seventy-ninth, dead upon the field, and Colonel Corcoran, of the Sixty-ninth New York, a prisoner.

It was now after three o'clock. The Confederates had succeeded in holding their position on the plateau, and had been meanwhile reinforced, mainly by the remainder of Johnston's army, under General Kirby Smith, as well as by Fisher's North Carolina regiment and by part of Elzey's brigade, with Lieutenant Beckham's battery from the reserves at Camp Pickens.

The slaughter on both sides had been frightful, the loss of the Confederates including Generals Bee and Bartow, who were killed while respectively at the head of the Fourth Alabama and Seventh Georgia regiments. Generals Beauregard, Jackson and Hampton had, besides, been wounded, but remained on the field, determined to make a final, united effort with the entire force at their command, now swollen to double its former proportions.

JAMES CAMERON.

McDowell had then in advanced position only thirteen thousand men, no reinforcements whatever having crossed Bull Run after noon. Burnside's brigade, it is true, stood within call at a point leading down from Sudley's Springs to Groveton, having rested since twelve o'clock, and the brigade under Schenck remained at the Stone Bridge. Neither of them, however, were now called into requisition.

Beauregard concentrated his forces upon McDowell's right and rear. The rear was at once fiercely attacked by Early's brigade, while upon the flanks dashed the fresh brigade led by General Elzey, with the Tenth, Thirteenth and Twenty-eighth Virginia, the First Maryland, Second and Eighth South Carolina, and the Third Tennessee Regiments. Under this resolute and combined attack that part of the plateau which the Federal troops had just occupied was soon abandoned.

The overpowering blow seemed instantaneous on all sides. The repeated efforts to rally the troops were fruitless. In a short time the entire Federal line seemed to have broken in disorder, the force under General Sykes apparently alone making an effort to withstand the tide. His eight companies of regular troops not only held the enemy in check, but maintained a bold front while covering the retreat, until, last to leave the field, they were finally compelled to yield to the masses against them.

Heintzelman endeavored to make a stand with detachments of United States Cavalry and Arnold's battery, but to no purpose. A panic had apparently seized the Federals, who, abandoning everything, were now flying on all sides toward the passages leading to Centreville. The route was complete.

Early's brigade was sent in pursuit with flying artillery, likewise detachments under Stuart and Beckham, whilst other forces under Cash, Kershaw,

THE UNITED STATES GENERAL HOSPITAL AT GEORGETOWN, D. C., FORMERLY THE UNION HOTEL.

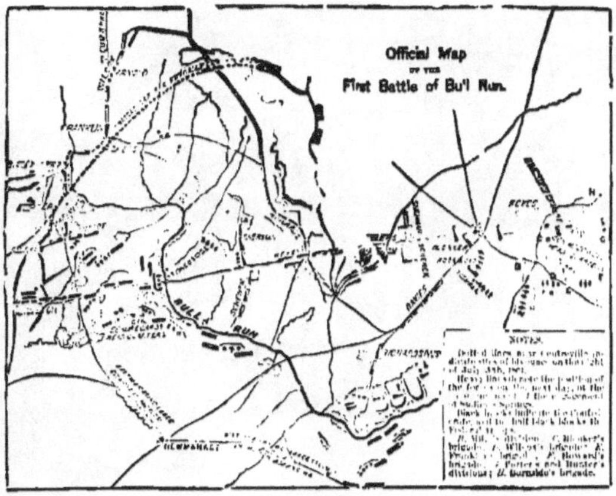

Preston and Withers, Hampton's Legion and Kemper's battery, followed by the Warrenton Road across the Stone Bridge, which Schenck had cleared away for the passage of troops forward when the rout began.

The Confederates continued the pursuit until the last of the Federals had found refuge beyond the Centreville ridge.*

To protect the retreat, McDowell had ordered a brigade placed at the Cub Run, on the Warrenton Road, as well as detachments under Colonels Porter and Blenker, both of whom admirably fulfilled the difficult task assigned them.

By nine o'clock that evening the last of the Federal fugitives had reached Centreville. A council was then held, at which it was decided best to continue the retreat to the defenses of Washington, and with Richardson's brigade acting as a rear guard, the army commenced its march homeward before midnight, reaching Arlington Heights early in the morning.

The Confederate loss was reported to be 378 killed, 1,489 wounded and 30 missing—total, 1,887; that of the Federals being 481 killed, 1,011 wounded and 1,460 missing—total, 3,051, besides 27 guns, 9 flags, 4,000 muskets, ammunition, tents, etc., etc.

In recognition of the services rendered at the battle of Manassas by General Beauregard, he was promoted to be "General" of the army of the Confederate States, to take rank from July 21st, 1861.

* Roman, in his "Military Operations of General Beauregard," Vol. I., page 116, says: "Another obstacle of no minor importance intervened, which was sufficient of itself to cut short all idea of then following the routed Federal army. On the evening of the 21st, at about nine o'clock, the heavens began to assume a threatening appearance, and, a few hours later, a heavy rain fell, which lasted unremittingly throughout the whole of the succeeding day."

JAMES CAMERON.

Born at Maytown, Pa., March 1st, 1801; at an early age entered a printing-office, and subsequently became editor, He studied law, in the practice of which latter his high moral qualities, energy and dignified bearing soon won him great popularity.

At the beginning of the Civil War he was induced to take command of the Seventy-ninth New York Highland Regiment by many who appreciated his dauntless energy and the executive ability he had displayed while at the head of a regiment of Pennsylvania militia some years before. His distinguished brother, Simon Cameron, was then Secretary of War, a post which he held until appointed Minister to Russia in 1862.

The Seventy-ninth Regiment, of which James Cameron was the colonel, formed part of the Third Brigade, under Colonel (afterward General) William Tecumseh Sherman, belonging to General Daniel Tyler's division. At the battle of Bull Run, it was one of the regiments ordered from the centre to carry the heavy Confederate batteries located on the hills across the Warrenton Turnpike. Their behavior on that occasion was truly memorable. Time and time again did they assault the hills against a murderous fire, spurred on by their brave officers, but to no purpose. Regiment after regiment was hurled back, until, in the final rally, Cameron fell at the head of his men, mortally wounded.

A popular historian describes his fall as follows: "No mortal man could stand the fearful storm that swept them as they fell back. Cameron again and again led them up, his 'Scots' following, ringing above the din of battle, till at last Wade Hampton, who had marked his gallant bearing and fired rifle after rifle at him as his men handed them up, accomplished his murderous purpose."*

The day following Cameron's death, July 22d, 1861, a letter was addressed by Mr. Arnold Harris to General Beauregard for leave to pass the Confederate lines to search of the body, an exceptional course which the general was forced to decline. Not anticipating such a result, Mr. Harris had proceeded to the field, in company with Mr. N. S McGraw, and both were arrested and sent to Richmond. The body of Colonel Cameron was afterward found buried near the junction of the Warrenton Turnpike with the Sudley Springs Road.

THE PROVOST MARSHAL EXAMINING PASSES

The human race is notoriously fond of following its inclinations, and when the inactivity of an army becomes monotonous, every regiment has a floating proportion willing to escape for a brief interval on any pretense. A gallant volunteer wishes to take a short furlough, in order to show his *fiancée* the wonders of the capital city. The provost marshal, or his representative, is scrutinizing the presented document with interest, as though he had some doubts of its genuineness.

THE EXPRESS COMPANIES.

Only those who are in camp can tell the feverish anxiety of the troops to hear from their loved ones at home, from

* We sent this quotation to Senator Hampton for explanation, and received the following:

"Washington, April 11th, 1884.

"My Dear Sir: There is not one word of truth in the inclosed quotation sent to me. It is utterly untrue in every particular.

"Respectfully, yours, Wade Hampton."

"P. F. Mottelay, Esq., Editor, etc."

A SALUTE OF ONE HUNDRED GUNS FIRED IN FRONT OF THE STATE HOUSE, RICHMOND, VA., AFTER THE BATTLE OF BULL RUN

MILITARY AUTHORITIES AT WASHINGTON.—THE PROVOST MARSHAL EXAMINING PASSES.

whom a few months since, they had fondly hoped only death could tear them away. At last duty, a principle as inexorable as death to the honorable mind, stepped in, and demanded the sacrifice of separation from those most held so dear—a separation which might be only for a season, but, alas! might also be for all time. We need scarcely describe a scene which so thoroughly explains itself. The name of the Adams and other Expresses became household words, both to the donor and receiver of good things sent to the absent soldier.

THE "QUAKER CITY."

The *Quaker City*, Commander Carr, one of the United States flotilla of the Potomac, while cruising in Lynn Haven Bay, near Cape Henry, picked up a refugee from North Carolina, who represented that the master plumber of the Norfolk Navy Yard was ashore, and wished to be taken off. An armed boat, which was sent for the purpose, was fired upon when near the shore, mortally wounding Mr. Lloyd, a seaman, of Charlestown, Mass. A few thirty-pound shells dispersed the Confederates.

THE ADAMS EXPRESS COMPANY'S OFFICE RECEIVING SOLDIERS' LETTERS AND PACKAGES FROM HOME.

THE "QUAKER CITY" IN LYNN HAVEN BAY, NEAR CAPE HENRY, VA.

AN ENGINE OF DESTRUCTION.

A MACHINE designed to blow up the *Pawnee* and other vessels of the Potomac flotilla was set adrift near Aquia Creek. It was picked up while floating toward the *Pawnee*. It was constituted of two large eighty-gallon oil-casks, perfectly watertight, acting as buoys, connected by twenty-five fathoms of three-and-a-half-inch rope, buoyed with large squares of cork, every two feet secured to casks by iron handles. A heavy bomb of boiler-iron, fitted with a brass top, and filled with powder, was suspended to the casks six feet under water. On top of the cask was a wooden box, with fuse in a gutta-percha tube. In the centre of the cork was a platform with a great length of fuse coiled away, occupying the middle of the cask. It was intended by the contrivers of this weapon of warfare that the shock of a collision should light the fuse, explode the charge, and blow up any craft with which it came in contact.

MACHINE DESIGNED TO DESTROY THE UNITED STATES FLOTILLA IN THE POTOMAC.

THE CHARGE OF THE FIRST IOWA REGIMENT, WITH GENERAL LYON AT ITS HEAD, AT THE BATTLE OF WILSON'S CREEK

BATTLE OF WILSON'S CREEK (OAK HILL).

THE battle of Wilson's Creek or, as the Confederates called it, the battle of Oak Hill—was, next to that of Bull Run, the most important engagement of the year. It took place August 10th, at a point on Wilson's Creek, distant about nine miles south of Springfield, Mo.

August, 1861.

General Nathaniel Lyon, who had already achieved signal victories over the confederate forces which were under Colonel J. S. Marmaduke, at Booneville, June 18th, and under General G. J. Rains, at Dug Springs, August 2d, had been stationed at Springfield since the 6th of August. The principal commands under him were then in charge of General T. W. Sweeney, Colonel Franz Sigel and Major S. D. Sturgis, all of whom had already figured in engagements that had practically helped to narrow down the Confederate hold in Southern Missouri.

Lyon's position at Springfield was one of imminent peril, since he had but 5,300 men all told, and re-inforcements could not be spared him by General Fremont from St. Louis, whilst the threatening Confederate force, just united at and near Wilson's Creek, under Generals Ben McCulloch, Sterling Price and Gabriel James Rains, was actually four times larger than his own. Nothing but a bold forward movement could help him stay the possible advance of the enemy and maintain his position.

With this view he marched, on the 9th of August, at the head of his small army to Wilson's Creek, and at about dawn the following day was in a position to engage both the front and the right wing of the Confederate forces.

His own column, which was to attack the front, had been divided into three brigades. One brigade, commanded by Major Sturgis, embraced a battalion of regular infantry under Captain Plummer, a battalion of Missouri volunteers under Major Osterhaus, a company of mounted Kansas volunteers under Captain Wood, a company of regular cavalry under Lieutenant Canfield, and Captain Totten's light battery of six pieces. Another brigade, commanded by Lieutenant-colonel Andrews, embraced the First Missouri Volunteers, Captain Steele's battalion of regulars, and Lieutenant Du Bois's battery of four pieces. The third brigade, commanded by Col. Deitzler, included the First Iowa, the First and Second Kansas Volunteers and two hundred mounted Missouri Home Guards.

Sigel's column, intended for the attack on the Confederate rear, embraced the Third and Fifth Missouri Volunteer Regiments, a company of recruits, with a battery of six guns, under Lieutenant Lothrop, one company of dragoons under Lieutenant Farrand, and a company of cavalry under Captain Carr.

General Sweeney, who had alone strongly opposed the advance, was not in the engagement.

Lyon had expected to surprise the enemy, but found him prepared, as an attack on the Federal forces was then about being planned, to be made within the next twenty-four hours.

The fire was opened on the Confederates at five o'clock on the morning of the 10th. The batteries under Captain Totten and Lieutenant Du Bois, supported by strong reserves, did splendid work, following the main column until met by bodies of Missouri Guards under Generals J. B. Clark, J. H. MacBride, W. Y. Slack and M. M. Parsons, which were soon engaged by the infantry, the mounted Home Guards

August, 1861.

STERLING PRICE.

and part of Totten's battery, in charge of Lieutenant Sokalski, the remainder of the battery being on an elevation.

The enemy was soon driven beyond the hill, which were immediately occupied by the First Kansas, First Iowa and the First Missouri Regiments. Totten's cannon being advanced to another elevation, while Du Bois's guns stood in the rear facing a masked battery of the Confederates. The Federals pushed on, the First Missouri engaging the enemy's right, and, with the aid of Totten's guns, doing them great damage.

The severest punishment inflicted upon them, however, proved to be by the combined efforts of Totten's and Du Bois's men, who, during the engagement, had been approached closely by a body of Confederates, waving the Federal flag, with the intention to capture some of the guns. It was owing also to the excellent fire from the batteries

BEN McCULLOCH.

that Captain Plummer's troops were saved from being crushed by an overwhelming force of over two thousand Confederates, which unexpectedly opened on him while at the bend of the stream, and sought ineffectually to turn the Federal left flank.

Colonel Sigel had, in the meantime, engaged the Confederate rear, with the 1,200 men and six guns under his command, and had so well directed them as to successively compel the retirement of Colonel Churchill's regiment, and bodies of Missourians and Texas Rangers under Colonel Brown, the fire from his guns finally driving them into the woods.

Sigel then continued his way along the Fayetteville Road as far as Sharp's Farm. By the time he had reached it, the fire from Lyon's heavy guns was being heard only at intervals, leading him to suppose that a victory had already been won at the front. He then, the more actively, set about for an immediate demonstration, and had already planted his battery, when he was informed that a strong body of Federals was approaching.

Preparations for an advance at once, therefore, came to a standstill. When, however, the advancing column, which in dress presented much the same appearance as Sigel's men, had reached within gunshot, Confederate flags were substituted for the United States standards, and a murderous fire from two hidden batteries opened on the Federals. The result to them proved fatal.

The Confederates dashed forward, killed the artillery-horses, and turning the Federal flank, soon compelled Sigel's men to fly in the greatest disorder. Of his 1,200 men and six guns, Sigel took away about 300 men and but one gun, which latter Captain Flagg had compelled some Confederate prisoners to draw from the field.

Under General Lyon, Du Bois's battery still held the enemy in check, but on the left of Totten's battery the Federals had by this time commenced to yield to the ever-renewing lines. Seeing this, General Lyon transferred Steele's force from Du Bois to Totten's battery, and went forward to rally the troops. His entire line was engaged, and for nearly an hour the fight was terrific, neither side yielding. Lyon appeared everywhere, encouraging the men, who had become well nigh demoralized at the repeated attacks made by the enemy in every direction. His horse was killed under him, and he was wounded, being shot through the leg and afterward in the head; but, assisted to another horse, he once more came forward, this time leading a bayonet-charge at the head of Kansas and Iowa regiments, which had just lost their officers.

While in the act, however, he was fatally wounded in the side, and had to be taken from the field. It was now about nine o'clock. Although opposed four entire hours to much superior numbers, the Federals had succeeded in maintaining their ground, and had then compelled the enemy to fall back once more.

The command at the front now devolved upon Major Sturgis, who, not knowing whether Sigel had carried out his part of the undertaking, remained in doubt as to what had best be done. While in this suspense, the Federal troops were, for the third time, deceived by the approach of a Confederate force under the Union flag, and, although naturally suffering again greatly from the unexpected attack that followed, stood their position manfully till the artillery, well supported by a detachment under Captain Gordon Granger, of General Lyon's staff, compelled the enemy to again leave the field. The lull was however, but temporary. Reinforcements

BATTLE OF WILSONS CREEK, OR OAK HILL, NEAR SPRINGFIELD, MO., AUGUS
CONFEDERATES UNDER GENE

BATTLE OF WILSON'S CREEK, OR OAK HILL, NEAR SPRINGFIELD, MO., AUGUST 10, 1861. UNITED STATES TROOPS UNDER GENERAL LYON AND GENERAL SIGEL; CONFEDERATES UNDER GENERAL McCULLOCH AND GENERAL PRICE.

filled up the Confederate ranks, which again poured upon the Federal lines till further resistance seemed impossible. They yielded forcibly, and in turn had to fall back. After six hours of unavailing slaughter, Sturgis gave orders to retreat.

The army was joined by the remnant of Sigel's detachment, while on the way back to Springfield, which latter place was reached at about five o'clock that afternoon, the enemy having suffered too much to interfere with the Federal retreat.

The Federal loss was 223 killed, 721 wounded, and 292 missing, a total of 1,236; that of the Confederates was reported to be 265 killed, 800 wounded and 30 missing, although General McCulloch had

DEATH OF GENERAL NATHANIEL LYON AT THE BATTLE OF WILSON'S CREEK, SPRINGFIELD, MO., AUGUST 10TH, 1861.

said that the Confederate losses much exceeded those on the Federal side, and General Price, in his report of August 12th, 1861, states that he lost nearly one-fifth of his entire force.

BEN McCULLOCH.

Born in Rutherford County, Tenn., in 1811; received but little schooling, his early days being passed in hunting; proceeded to Texas with the view of joining the expedition of Davy Crockett, reaching there, however, after the latter's death; served as a private at the battle of San Jacinto in 1836; entered the Mexican war at the head of a body of Texas Rangers, and greatly distinguished himself at the battles of Monterey, Buena Vista, and at the capture of the City of Mexico; was appointed a United States marshal in 1853, and made Commissioner to Utah in 1857. On the outbreak of the Civil War he espoused the Southern cause. He, while stationed at Seguin, Tex., during the month of February, 1861, made the famous raid on the Federal position at San Antonio, which resulted in the surrender of Major-general David E. Twiggs, who offered no resistance to the attack, notwithstanding his high rank in the United States Army.

By the terms of the surrender McCulloch was to receive about 2,500 men, and all the forts, arsenals and posts within the limits of Twiggs's command, as well as arms and ammunition valued at fully a million and a half of dollars. Twiggs was immediately "dismissed from the army of the United States for treachery to the flag of his country." McCulloch was soon made a brigadier-general in the Confederate Army, and in the following June entered the Arkansas border at the head of about eight hundred men, on their way to Springfield, Mo., near which place, on the 14th of July, they, as well as General Price's detachment, effected a junction with the forces under General Claiborne F. Jackson, ex-Governor of Missouri. July 18th, 1861, McCulloch was defeated by General Lyon at the battle of Dug Springs, and, August 10th, he took part in the battle of Wilson's Creek, which ended in the rout of the Federal troops. February 20th, 1862, he joined the forces of General Sterling Price which were defeated at Sugar Creek, and March 7th, 1862, was fatally wounded, while gallantly leading his division, at the battle of Elkhorn, called by the Federals the battle of Pea Ridge.

STERLING PRICE.

Born in Prince Edward County, Va., September, 1809; served in the Missouri Legislature, member of Congress, 1845-7; entered the Mexican War as colonel of cavalry volunteers; commanded, and was wounded, at the battle of Canada, N. M., January 24th, 1847; appointed brigadier-general, July 20th, 1847, and made military governor of Chihuahua; won the battle of Santa Cruz de Rosales, March 16th, 1848; Governor of Missouri, 1853-7; was made Major-general of the Missouri State forces by Governor Claiborne F. Jackson, who, with General Price, went afterward on the Confederate side.

On June 18th, 1861, the forces under Price and Jackson were defeated by General Lyon at Booneville. He recruited a large army, and with General McCulloch, joined the forces under General Jackson near Springfield, July 14th, 1861, and in turn, defeated General Lyon at Wilson's Creek, August 10th, 1861. He was likewise successful at Lexington, September 20th, 1861, capturing the place with its entire force of about 2,200 men, a large quantity of war material and $900,000 in money, after an eight days siege. For this he received the thanks of the Confederate Congress, leading to a Major-general's commission. He abandoned Lexington, September 30th, 1861, and retreated toward Arkansas. Joined anew by Ben McCulloch, he was defeated at Sugar Creek, February 20th, 1862. On March 7th, 1862, he took a prominent though unsuccessful part in the battle of Elk Horn, called by the Federals the battle of Pea Ridge; and was again defeated at Iuka, September 19th, 1862, and at Corinth, October 5th, 1862. While in command of the Department of Arkansas, 1863-4, he founded and commanded the secret organization of "the Knights of the Golden Circle," and advanced with 20,000 men, in September, 1864, on Pilot Knob, Mo., but was forced back by General Rosecrans, then commander of the Department of Missouri.

On October 7th, 1864, he appeared with a large body of men opposite Jefferson City but, by the beginning of the following month, had been compelled to retreat again into Arkansas by the forces under Generals Curtis and Pleasonton. When peace was declared, he obtained from Maximilian a grant of land in Mexico, upon which he established a colony of ex-Confederate officers. This colony, at Icheme, was a failure. In 1867 he returned to Missouri, and died in great poverty at St. Louis, September 27th, 1867.

NATHANIEL LYON.

Born at Ashford, Windham County, Conn., July 14th, 1819; after graduating at West Point, entered the army in July, 1841, as second lieutenant of infantry; made first lieutenant in 1847; took part in a short Indian campaign in Florida, and was sent out to Mexico at the commencement of the war; figured in many important battles; was wounded at the Belen Gate, and afterward made brevet captain for gallantry; was appointed captain in 1851; served in Kansas, and remained on active frontier duty until, in April, 1861, he was placed in charge of the important United States Arsenal at St. Louis, then garrisoned by about 500 United States troops, and afterward appointed commandant of the post, in place of Major W. H. Bell, who had joined the Southern Confederacy. By the prompt erection of suitable earthworks, and through constant vigilance, succeeded in protecting the Arsenal from seizure; and, April 26th, with the aid of Colonel Frank P. Blair, removed during the night, first by steamboat to Alton, and thence by railway to Springfield, Ill., 21,000 stand of arms, 2 cannon, and 110,000 rounds of ammunition.

In May, 1861, under President Lincoln's order of April 30th, he enrolled a large number of volunteers, giving them headquarters at and close by the Arsenal ground, and later on, with about 6,000 men and heavy guns, under Colonels Blair, Boernstein, Schüttner and Sigel, and Lieutenants Lathrop and Saxton, surrounded the insurgent Camp Jackson, compelling its prompt surrender with a large quantity of small arms, cannon and ammunition, that had been taken from the Baton Rouge Arsenal. May 17th was made a brigadier-general. May 29th succeeded General W. S. Harney, who was relieved of his command of the Department of the West, now called the Department of Missouri.

June 11th, refused to comply with the demand of Governor Jackson of Missouri for the disbandment of all Home Guards. June 9th secured Cairo against General Pillow's intended attack, by fortifying Bird's Point, on the opposite side of the Mississippi River, with the aid of Captain Henry W. Benham, United States Engineers, and Colonel Nicholas Schüttner. Also dispatched the Second Missouri Regiment, under Colonel Franz Sigel, for the protection of the Pacific Railway. June 13th, left St. Louis by steamboat with some 2,000 men, under Colonels Blair and Boernstein and Captain Lathrop, also Captain James Totten's battery, and reached Jefferson City two days later, preparatory to his successful attack, June 18th, on the Confederates at Booneville, under Colonel J. S. Marmaduke.

NATHANIEL LYON.

August 2d, was victorious at Dug Springs against the Confederate forces under General G. J. Rains. August 10th, forced a battle at Wilson's Creek with the Confederate army, four times larger than his own. In this engagement, certainly one of the most desperate of the entire civil war, he was three times wounded, the last shot cutting open the back of his head to the skull, covering him with blood. In this condition he was assisted to another horse, and, riding between the Kansas and Iowa regiments, he led them to the charge, and received a fatal shot from a Minié ball through the heart. He fell in the arms of his servant, saying: "Lehman, I am killed; take care of my body!" During the retreat which caused that eventful day, General Lyon's body was left on the field, whence the Confederate general Sterling Price sent it in his own conveyance to Springfield. When the Federal troops under Colonel Sigel retreated to Rolla, early the next morning, the body was again left behind, at Springfield. It was, however, carefully prepared for burial by members of the staff of the Confederate general J. B. Clark, and delivered to Mrs. J. S. Phelps, who had it properly interred. It was shortly after taken up and sent to its final resting-place at East Hartford, Conn., receiving great military honors there, as well as in all the cities through which it passed. The ceremonies at his funeral were participated in by over 20,000 people. By will he had left almost his entire property, upward of $30,000, to the Government, to aid in preserving the Union. Congress ordered, by resolution, that in recognition of his "eminent and patriotic services" be entered upon its records.

EVACUATION OF HAMPTON, VA.

The village of Hampton, situated on the left bank of the James River, about two miles from its entrance into Chesapeake Bay, is a very old town, of much historic interest, having been settled as early as 1705. It derives its principal importance from its proximity to Fortress Monroe and Old Point Comfort. It contains several churches, a large number of stores and many fine private dwellings.

On the 27th of July, 1861, it was deemed necessary by Major-general Butler to evacuate the village, destroy some of the most prominent buildings, and retire the forces there within the Federal lines. It was reported that the Confederates were advancing in force, and prudence demanded the concentration of Butler's forces round his entrenched position at Newport News. Odd-fellows' Hall, the Jail, and several other buildings, were unavoidably destroyed, and also a portion of Hampton Bridge. On August 7th, General Magruder, with a force of seven thousand Confederates, advanced upon Hampton, destroying by fire all but five of its five hundred houses, with its picturesque Episcopal church, one of the oldest in the State.

EVACUATION OF THE VILLAGE OF HAMPTON, VA., ON THE JAMES RIVER, BY THE FEDERAL TROOPS UNDER GENERAL BUTLER IN ANTICIPATION OF THE ADVANCE OF THE CONFEDERATES IN FORCE.

GENERAL VIEW OF FORTS HATTERAS AND CLARK, N. C., CAPTURED ON THE 29TH OF AUGUST, 1861, BY THE UNITED STATES NAVAL AND MILITARY FORCES, UNDER THE COMMAND OF COMMODORE STRINGHAM AND MAJOR-GENERAL BUTLER.

OPERATIONS ALONG THE COAST OF NORTH CAROLINA.

In the early part of August, 1861, Commodore Silas H. Stringham, United States Navy, then commanding at Hampton Roads, was informed that supplies for the Confederate troops
August, 1861.
were being continually carried through Hatteras Inlet, the entrance to Pamlico Sound, on the coast of North Carolina, and that the Inlet was defended by Forts Clark and Hatteras, both in command of Major W. S. G. Andrews.

It was at once decided to fit up a joint military and naval expedition to capture the forts, and, on the 26th of August, it left Hampton Roads. The squadron was under the command of Commodore Stringham, and the military force in charge of General B. F. Butler, who had been succeeded at Fortress Monroe by Major-general John E. Wool, who had volunteered to lead the troops.

This squadron, the first sent out, was composed of the frigate *Minnesota*, flagship, Captain G. A. Van Brunt; the frigate *Wabash*, Captain Samuel Mercer; the gunboats *Monticello*, Commander John P. Gillis; the *Pawnee*, Commander S. C. Rowan; and the *Harriet Lane*, Captain John Faunce; the steam transports *George Peabody*, Lieutenant R. B. Lowry, and *Adelaide*, Commander H. S. Stellwagen; and the tug *Fanny*, Lieutenant Pierce Crosby.

SILAS H. STRINGHAM

The troops on board the transports consisted of 220 men from the Ninth New York Regiment, Colonel Rush C. Hawkins; 500 men from the Twentieth New York Regiment, Colonel Max Weber; 100 men of the Union Coast Guard, Captain Nixon; and 60 men from the Second United States Artillery, under Lieutenant Larned.

The sailing frigate *Cumberland*, Captain John Marston, and the steam frigate *Susquehanna*, Captain J. Chauncey, had been ordered to follow the squadron. The expedition arrived off of Hatteras Inlet about five o'clock the next afternoon, and at once made preparations for an advance early the following morning.

At five o'clock, A.M., on Wednesday, the 28th, the troops were being landed on the beach, two and a half miles north of the forts, under cover of the guns from the *Monticello*, *Pawnee* and *Harriet Lane*, and later on the forts were attacked from the front by the *Wabash* and the *Cumberland*, which latter had just joined the squadron. These were soon followed by the flagship *Minnesota* and the *Susquehanna*.

The fire was kept up incessantly until about nine o'clock, when it ceased on both sides, the flags of the forts having been hauled down, and the garrison of Fort Clark having evacuated it. The latter was at once occupied by the Coast Guard and men under Colonel Weber, and the *Monticello*, steamed toward the Inlet, it being supposed that Fort Hatteras, which occupied the point, had likewise been abandoned. But she had only advanced to within six hundred yards of the fort, followed closely by

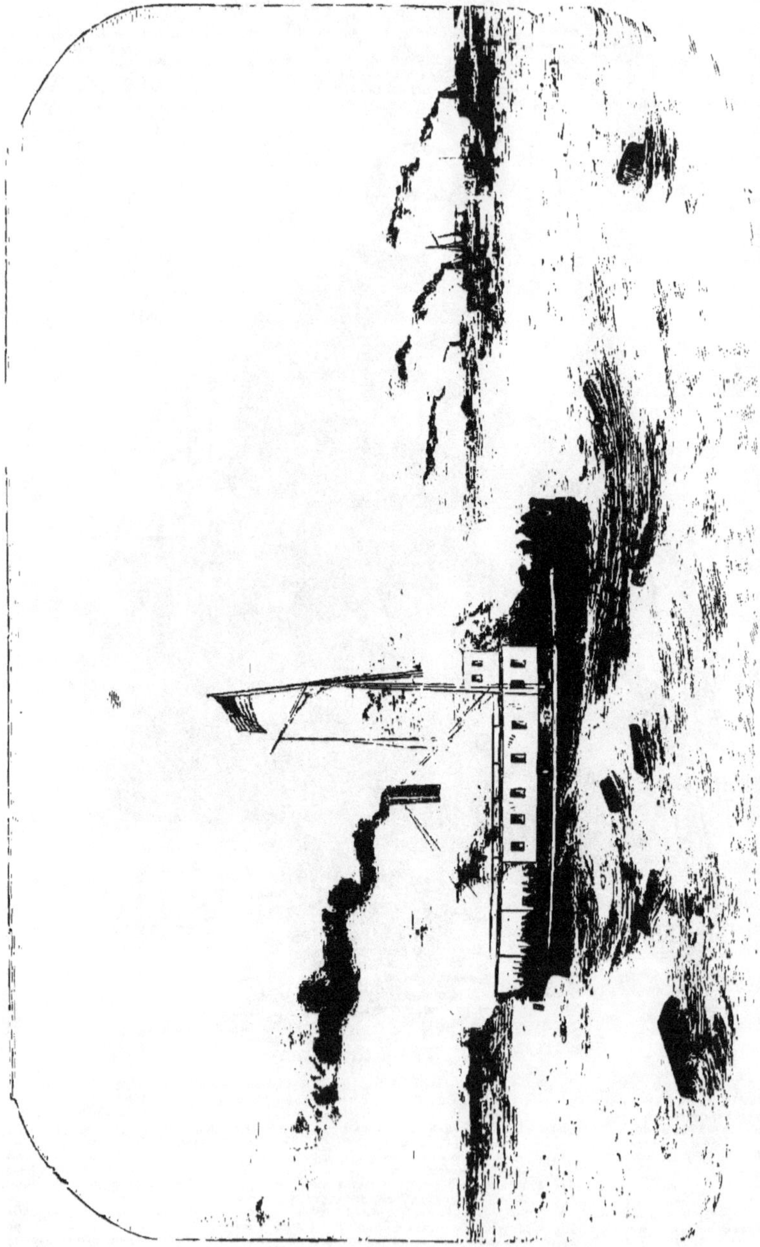

CAPTURE, BY CONFEDERATE STEAMERS, OF THE PROPELLER "FANNY," IN PAMLICO SOUND, ON THE 1st OF OCTOBER, 1861, WHILE CONVEYING MEN AND STORES TO THE TWENTIETH INDIANA REGIMENT, ENCAMPED AT CHICAMACOMICO, N. C., FORTY MILES FROM HATTERAS INLET.

the *Harriet Lane*, when the heavy guns opened such a scathing fire on her as to endanger her safety. Though considerably damaged, she escaped, making room for the *Minnesota*, the *Pawnee*, and the *Susquehanna*, which engaged the fort until dark, when the *Harriet Lane* and the *Pawnee* were left alone for the night in the immediate front.

Early the following morning the *Susquehanna* opened fire, and was followed by the *Minnesota*, the *Wabash*, the *Harriet Lane* and the *Cumberland*. Fort Hatteras had been ably defended the previous day by Colonel William F. Martin, whom night found completely prostrated by fatigue, and who had, in consequence, to give way to Flag-Officer Samuel Barron, then in command of the few Confederate vessels lying in Pamlico Sound. Barron, who was then Assistant Secretary of the Confederate Navy, had come up during the night with reinforcements, in company with Major Andrews, who was absent in the interior at the commencement of the engagement.

August, 1861.

Heavy guns had been mounted in the direction of Fort Clark, which the Federals had occupied the day previous; but no damage was done by their fire, as Colonel Weber had judiciously vacated it, and employed his men during the night in the erection of a battery of three guns. These, in charge of Lieutenant Johnson, of the Coast Guard, did signal service on that morning in beating off Confederate vessels conveying troops to the relief of Fort Hatteras.

The fire from the squadron continued almost incessantly, scarcely stopping even to be caught again by Barron's tricky lowering of his flag and apparent submission, until, at about half-past ten o'clock, a white flag was displayed above the fort, and an offer made to surrender with all the honors of war. This was refused by Commodore Stringham and General Butler, and, shortly after, the capitulation was signed on board the *Minnesota*, giving to the Federals 715 prisoners, 1,000 stand of arms, 31 cannon, 5 stand of colors, a large quantity of ammunition, and several vessels laden with stores, cotton and other merchandise.

While the capitulation was being signed, the *Harriet Lane*, *Adelaide* and *Fanny* had entered the Inlet, the two first grounding near the fort while attempting to cross the bar. The Confederates had thus within their grasp the three vessels and the troops they carried; but the surrender having been accepted, they were not molested, and the two grounded vessels were soon hauled off.

The Confederates lost 49 killed and about as many wounded. Their officers, Major W. S. G. Andrews, Flag Officer Samuel Barron, and Colonel William F. Martin, Seventh Light Infantry, North Carolina Volunteers, were sent to Fort Hamilton, in New York Harbor, and afterward exchanged.

Upon hearing of the victory, Secretary Welles issued an order thanking Commodore Stringham and his men "for the brilliant achievement accomplished without the loss of a man on the Union side." General Wool likewise congratulated the troops.

HATTERAS ISLAND AND CHICAMACOMICO, N. C.

Especial mention should here be made of the fact that upon the abandonment of Fort Clark by the Confederates, an acting aide-de-camp of General Butler, Mr. Fiske, swam from one of the vessels to the shore, through a very heavy sea, carrying orders to Colonel Weber, and afterward entered the fort, collecting therein many valuable books and papers. Of these he made a package, which he strapped to his shoulders, and with which he swam back to the vessel, delivering it to General Butler, who found the documents to be of very great service.

RUSH C. HAWKINS

The forts commanding the Inlet remained in charge of detachments under Colonels Weber and Hawkins, and General Butler at once proceeded to Washington in order to lay before General Scott and the Secretary of War his reasons for holding the forts, instead of destroying them, as he had been ordered to do. His views were carried out, and he was commissioned to proceed to New England and to raise a large force, which, as we shall see later on, was destined to make a brilliant record in many Southern localities.

The troops at Hatteras Inlet were reinforced late in September by the Twentieth Indiana Regiment, under Colonel Brown, in order to complete operations along the coast.

An important entrance to Pamlico Sound was still open, south of Fort Hatteras. It was called Ocracoke Inlet, and was defended by a fort bearing the same name and by another called Fort Morgan.

On the 16th of September, Commander S. C. Rowan sent an expedition to capture them. It was under the command of Lieutenant James Y. Maxwell, who started in the tug *Fanny*, having on board sixty-seven of the Naval Brigade, under Lieutenants Rowe and Tillotson. The *Fanny* had in tow a launch belonging to the gunboat *Pawnee*, carrying the latter's howitzer and twenty-eight of her men, in charge of Lieutenant Eastman.

September, 1861.

The frigate *Susquehanna* and the *Tempest* had joined the expedition, but finding their draft of water too great, were compelled to return to their former anchorage.

Ocracoke Inlet was reached by the *Fanny* at eleven o'clock in the morning, and a detachment was immediately landed, expecting to draw an attack from the forts. Their progress met with no opposition, however, and on reaching the forts they found them to have been deserted and partly burned. As it was not intended to occupy the Inlet, orders were given to complete the work of destruction as thoroughly as possible. Not only were the guns broken in pieces, and much of the masonry and other work laid low, but the torch was everywhere applied, and in a short time it was in ashes.

The expedition having completed its purpose, returned to Fort Hatteras early on the 18th.

There remained still two other entrances north of Cape Hatteras, called Loggerhead (New) Inlet and Oregon Inlet, the last being in close proximity to Roanoke Island, which the Confederates were said to be then fortifying.

In order to make a reconnoissance of the island south of Loggerhead Inlet, Colonel Hawkins ordered Colonel Brown and his regiment to proceed in that direction, and on the 29th of September they sailed by the steamers *Ceres* and *Putnam* with the intention of landing at a small place between Chicamacomico and Keneckut. The shallowness of the water necessitated the landing of the men by small boats. They encamped, awaiting the arrival of the tug *Fanny*, which was to have followed them on the 30th with stores of all descriptions. It was,

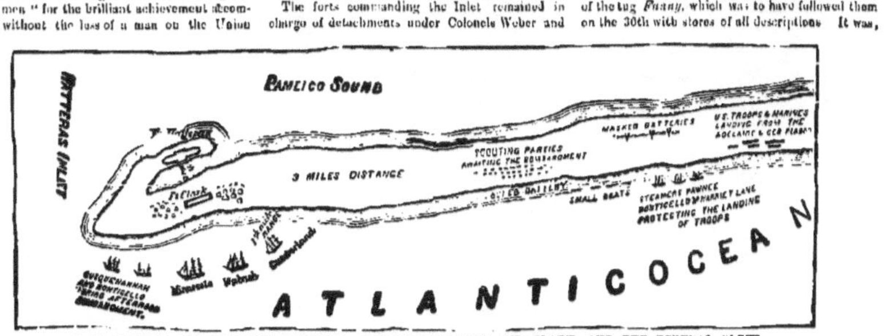

PLAN SHOWING THE RELATIVE POSITIONS OF FORTS HATTERAS AND CLARK, AND THE FEDERAL FLEET UNDER COMMODORE STRINGHAM.

BOMBARDMENT OF FORT HATTERAS PAMLICO SOUND, N.C. AUGUST 2[illegible] 1861 BY THE FEDERAL FLEET UNDER COMMODORE STRINGHAM.

VIEW OF THE CAMP OF THE TWENTIETH INDIANA REGIMENT, ALSO OF FORT HATTERAS AND THE ANCHORAGE AT HATTERAS INLET, N. C., TAKEN FROM THE RAMPARTS OF FORT CLARK.

DISCOVERY OF A CONFEDERATE BATTERY AT MESSECH'S POINT, ON THE POTOMAC, NEAR THE MOUTH OF BACK RIVER, BY A SCOUTING PARTY OF THE TENTH REGIMENT OF NEW YORK ZOUAVES.

however, only on the afternoon of the 1st of October that the tug appeared near Chicamacomico, when she was captured by Confederate vessels just coming down Pamlico Sound, with a loss to the Federals of thirty-one prisoners, and the cargo, valued at about $150,000.

October, 1861.

The seizure of the *Fanny*, and the disadvantageous position of the Federals on the island, induced the Confederates to send an expedition against them. Six vessels, carrying about 2,500 men, were accordingly fitted out at Roanoke Island, and on the 4th of October arrived opposite the Federal position, which they began shelling, whil at the same time landing large bodies of troops above and below the camp.

Colonel Brown's force met the attack boldly though at a frightful disadvantage, until night admitted of his cutting his way through the forc

SEARCHING VIRGINIAN FARMERS' WAGONS, AT THE GATE OF FORT RUNYON, BEFORE ALLOWING THEM TO PASS THE LONG BRIDGE INTO WASHINGTON

RESCUE OF MAJOR REYNOLDS'S BATTALION OF MARINES FROM THE FOUNDERING STEAMER "GOVERNOR," BY THE U. S. FRIGATE "SABINE," NOVEMBER 4th, 1861, OFF CAPE HATTERAS, N. C.

EXPLOSION OF A SHELL IN THE CUTTER OF THE U. S. STEAMER "NIAGARA," FROM THE CONFEDERATE "IVY," NOVEMBER 8th, 1861

FROM A SKETCH BY A SAILOR

TAKING AWAY THE COLORS OF THE SEVENTY-NINTH NEW YORK REGIMENT, FOR MUTINY, WASHINGTON, AUGUST 14TH, 1861.

on his left at Chicamacomico, and making his retreat toward Hatteras Lighthouse. He reached the latter early the following morning, and there met a detachment of 500 men, whom Colonel Hawkins had brought up to his relief, in conjunction with the frigate *Susquehanna* and the gunboat *Monticello*. With the aid of the gunboat, proceeding abreast along the shore, the Federals marched northward to dispute the advance which it was supposed the Confederates had commenced in the morning. The *Monticello* first came upon the enemy, when about fifteen miles from Hatteras Lighthouse, and began shelling them with terrible effect, compelling them to hide in the woods, and afterward to run toward their former position, near

DRUMMING OUT THIEVES FROM FORTRESS MONROE.

MONUMENT SQUARE, BALTIMORE, MD.—SECTION OF COOK'S BOSTON LIGHT INFANTRY, WITH ARTILLERY IN POSITION, BY ORDER OF MAJOR-GENERAL BANKS, TO QUELL AN ANTICIPATED RIOT ON ACCOUNT OF THE ARREST OF MARSHAL KANE AND THE POLICE COMMISSIONERS.

which lay the vessels into which they had been brought to the island. These were, in turn, engaged by the gunboat as they advanced to re-one the fast retreating Confederates, the shelling being continued until night brought it to a close. The *Monticello* then came down toward Hatteras Lighthouse, covering the encampment of the Federals.

SILAS HORTON STRINGHAM.

Born at Middletown, Orange County, N. Y., November 7th, 1798; entered the United States Navy 1809 as midshipman on board the frigate *President*, then commanded by Commodore Rodgers. He became lieutenant in 1811, and served in Decatur's squadron in the Algerine War. In 1830 he was placed in command of the *Falmouth*, of the West India squadron, and in 1835 took charge of the *John Adams*, belonging to the Mediterranean squadron.

Shortly after his return to this country, in 1837, he was ordered to proceed on board the *Porpoise*, in search of pirates that had been troubling merchant vessels along the coast. This was followed by a period of comparative quiet, in which he was in command of the *Independence*, then attached to the Home squadron.

In 1841 he was made a captain, and sent, with the *Ohio*, to Brazil upon a special mission. He was placed in charge of the Brooklyn Navy Yard afterward, and upon the declaration of war with Mexico, he returned to his former command of the *Ohio*, which latter led the United States fleet at the capture of Vera Cruz and of San Juan of Ulloa. He was appointed to the command of the Mediterranean squadron in 1852, and remained in constant service on sea or home duty until 1861.

When at the breaking out of the Civil War, President Lincoln decided to blockade the Southern ports, Stringham was ordered to take charge of the squadron on the Atlantic station, whose operations lay between Key West on the south and Cape Charles, at the mouth of the Chesapeake Bay, on the north. He was given for the purpose the forty gun steam frigate *Minnesota* for a flagship, and a fleet of twenty-five vessels, manned by some three thousand five hundred sailors and marines. With these he did active service, although not meeting with any encounter worth mentioning until the end of August, 1861.

On the 26th of the latter month he left Hampton Roads, in accordance with instructions from Washington, with the *Minnesota*, *Monticello*, *Pawnee*, *Wabash*, *Harriet Lane*, and some steam transports and tugs carrying troops under General Butler, arriving off Hatteras Inlet the following afternoon. The squadron was joined at the latter place by the *Susquehanna* and the *Cumberland*, both of which took part in the engagement, which resulted, after two days' hard fighting, in the surrender, August 29th, of Forts Clark and Hatteras. These commanded an important inlet to Pamlico Sound, by which the Confederates had been receiving supplies. Commodore Stringham was promoted rear admiral on the retired list in 1862. From 1864 to 1866 he was in charge of the Charleston Navy Yard as commandant, was appointed port admiral of New York in 1867, and died in Brooklyn, N. Y., February 7th, 1876.

THE SEVENTY NINTH NEW YORK.

This regiment carried their flag with honor at Bull Run, but they discredited it by open mutiny at Washington, and by order of General McClellan their colors were taken from them. The scene during the reading of the order was exceedingly impressive. The sun was just going down, and in the hazy, uncertain twilight the features and forms of officers and men could scarcely be distinguished. Immediately behind his aid was General Porter, firm and self-possessed. Colonel Stevens was in front of the regiment, endeavoring to quiet his rather nervous horse. In the rear of the regulars, and a little distant apart, General Sickles sat carelessly on horseback, coolly smoking a cigar, and conversing with some friends.

At one time during the reading a murmur passed through the line of the mutineers and when that portion of the order directing the regiment to surrender its colors was read, a private in one of the rear lines cried out in broad Scotch tones, "Let's keep the colors, boys!" But no response was made by any man of the regiment. Major Sykes at once rode up the line to where the voice was heard. It would have been all that the soldier's life was worth had he been recognized at the moment in pistol-range of any of the officers.

SIEGE AND BATTLE OF LEXINGTON.

After the battle of Wilson's Creek, General Sterling Price kept on recruiting the Confederate ranks so actively, that, by the end of August, he felt in the position to assume the offensive. He then began his march toward the northern section of Missouri, meeting on the way with no opposition until the 7th of September, when some skirmishing was had, at a place near the Kansas border, called Dry Wood Creek, with a detachment of Federals under General James H. Lane. These he drove across the line beyond Fort Scott, and leaving a force there, continued on his way, reaching Warrensburg on Wednesday, the 11th of September. His advance upon the latter place was the more hotly pressed since learning that Federal troops had been sent there by General Fremont's orders to take away in safety the money belonging to its loyal inhabitants, and at the same time protect them if possible from the threatening Confederate invasion.

September, 1861.

The Federals had, however, anticipated Price, who felt not only injured on learning that the money had been by them carried to Lexington, but insulted, besides, at having the fact illustrated in broad German caricatures on the walls throughout the city.

Price lost but little time in Warrensburg, and after a rainstorm that raged furiously for a while, he pushed on toward Lexington, where he encamped the same night. The Federal force at Lexington, consisting of only half a regiment of Home Guards, had been strengthened only two days before by the

JAMES H. LANE.

Thirteenth Missouri Regiment under Colonel Peabody, just returned from Warrensburg, and by the detachment sent from Jefferson City. This last embraced five hundred Home Guards, as well as the Twenty-third Illinois Regiment of the "Irish Brigade" under Colonel James A. Mulligan, a portion of the Eighth Missouri under Colonel White, and the First Regiment of Illinois Cavalry under Colonel T. M. Marshall.

Colonel Mulligan, who had assumed command by reason of his seniority, felt that an attack from Price must take place in the near future, and he, therefore, had meanwhile availed himself of every chance to strenghten his position, pending the arrival of reinforcements.

Lexington the capital of Lafayette County, Mo., is situated on the south bank of the Missouri River, about three hundred miles from St. Louis, and nearly one hundred and twenty miles west of Jefferson City, at a point commanding the most important route to Kansas. Not on the latter account alone was Lexington now about to be so eagerly contested for, however. Its position, it is true, was a controlling one, but in addition to the money brought back from Warrensburg, the vaults there held $800,000 in gold coin and the State seals, which ex-Governor Claiborne Jackson and his legislature had been suddenly compelled to abandon upon Mulligan's approach.

The new portion of the City of Lexington is built upon an elevation close by the river, Old Lexington, as the other section is called, lying further back on the hills.

Colonel Mulligan's force of 2,640 men was continually at work making entrenchments, his extreme outer line being in front of the college building on Masonic Hill, where he had his headquarters. The inner line of breastworks circled around a building, to the right of the college, used as a boarding-house. In addition to the earthworks, faced by a ditch eight feet wide, were pits surrounded by mines fully supplied with gunpowder. Of the latter article Mulligan had a fair supply, but he had no shells for his two mortars, only six small cannon and but little ready ammunition; the cavalry, too, being without guns or rifles.

On Thursday, the 12th of September, the Confederate General Gabriel James Rains opened fire, with nine guns, under Captains Churchill, Clark and Emmett McDonald, upon that portion of the earthworks which had forcibly been left the weakest, on the New Lexington side. In the rear stood Colonel Congreve Jackson's detachment, whilst on the extreme left the forces under General Parsons, with Captain Guibor's battery and General Steen, faced Colonel Anderson's house, then used as a hospital, leaving Pierce's main body directly in the centre.

September 12, 1861.

The Confederate attack was soon directed from four different points, and continued the rest of the day. At sunset, when the fire ceased, the hospital was found to have suffered most of all. Dr. Winer, surgeon of the brigade, and the Rev. Father Butler, had been taken prisoners during an attack repelled by the men under Captain Gleason, some outworks had been taken, and the Federals had been forced into an interior line.

Mulligan set to work during the ensuing night, everywhere strengthening his position, which was likely to become more and more isolated. Active preparations, in fact, continued on both sides from the 12th to the 17th, amid occasional firing, the Federals having succeeded in putting up additional earthworks by that time, while the reinforced Confederates had closed in their line of batteries around the besieged under cover of movable breastworks made of large wet bales of hemp.

Price had also in the meantime set a large number of soldiers to scour the country around, in order to prevent the looked-for Federal aid. His men had intercepted, forty miles below the city, the steamer *Sunshine*, having on board Lieutenant Rains and ten men of the "Irish Brigade," sent by Mulligan to Jefferson City for reinforcements. They had also captured a Federal vessel loaded with provisions, clothing, and the much needed ammunition, and had either forced back, defeated or captured several Federal detachments likely to come to Mulligan's relief. The supply of water was likewise cut off from the city.

At a given signal, fired at precisely eight o'clock on the morning of the 17th, from the headquarters of General Price, then at the Court House of the New Town, General Rains again opened on the Federals.

September, 1861.

The fire continued, it may be said, almost unremittingly night and day, and throughout some heavy rain, until the morning of the 20th. By this time General Harris, who had just joined Price with his 2,700 men—thus swelling the Confederate force to 24,000—had, with General MacBride's assistance, attacked and carried the hills north of the town, as well as Colonel Anderson's house. The latter had once been retaken by Captain Gleason at the head of only eighty men of the Irish Montgomery Guards, who, after losing thirty of their number, and having their captain wounded, were, however, forced to retire.

Price asked for an unconditional surrender

SIEGE OF LEXINGTON, MO., SEPTEMBER 17TH, 18TH, 19TH AND
TO GENERAL S7

SIEGE OF LEXINGTON, MO., SEPTEMBER 17TH, 18TH, 19TH AND 20TH, 1861, RESULTING IN THE SURRENDER OF THE FEDERAL FORCES, [illegible] STRONG, UNDER COLONEL JAMES A. MULLIGAN, TO GENERAL STERLING PRICE, WHO COMMANDED THE CONFEDERATE FORCES, 24,000 STRONG

It seemed idle for the Federals to count any longer upon outside aid. They were down to near the last of their carefully nursed provisions and ammunition. The position, on this account, as well as from the scarcity of water, seemed untenable; but Mulligan's determined answer, "If you want us, you must take us," came, nevertheless.

The Home Guards, who had long before become discouraged, raised a white flag upon hearing this; but Mulligan immediately ordered Captain McDermott to proceed with the Detroit Jackson Guard to take it down.

The fight went on more fiercely than ever on the part of the Confederates, until, by two o'clock, their lines were within a few rods of the Federal works. Further resistance was deemed impossible. For his heroic defense Colonel Mulligan received the thanks of the United States Congress and the commission of brigadier-general. He refused the promotion, preferring to remain colonel of the Twenty-third Illinois, which was given the right to use the name of "Lexington" upon its colors.

General Sterling Price, on the other hand, received the thanks of the Confederate Congress, which led afterward to his being given the commission of major-general.

JAMES HENRY LANE.

Born June 22d, 1814, at Lawrenceburg, Ind. His father was Hon. Amos Lane, an able politician and lawyer. The son was admitted to the Bar in 1840, and practiced his profession until 1846, when he enlisted as a private in the Third and continued in the office until attacked by a paralytic stroke, which incapacitated him from further legislative service, and so affected his mind, that, on July 11th, 1866, he took his own life at his home in Leavenworth, Kan.

ATTEMPTED DESERTION OF FEDERAL RECRUITS.

The system of recruiting had not, up to the month of September, 1861, been freed of many of its defects. Safeguards had to be established, particularly against desertion. While all officers were striving for rapid organization and consequent promotion, all kinds of subterfuge were resorted to for procuring men. The high bounties which were afterward paid, were not then yet spoken of, and desertions were, therefore, more the result of the favoritism of recruiting-agents than the bounties then current.

Many of the camps had been seriously depleted by wholesale disappearances, and a more severe *regime* was adopted

A DETACHMENT OF THE NEW YORK RIFLES FIRING UPON CAPTAIN CRESTO'S COMPANY OF THE SAME REGIMENT, SEPTEMBER 9TH, 1861.

A council of officers decided upon surrender. The white flag was hoisted and firing ceased.

At four o'clock on Saturday afternoon, the 21st, the actual surrender took place. It embraced Colonels Mulligan, Peabody, Marshall and Grover, Majors Becker and Van Horn, and 118 other commissioned officers, about 2,100 men; 6 cannon, 2 mortars, over 3,000 stand of arms, 750 horses, and a large quantity of equipments, etc. The Confederates also became possessed of the money, about $100,000, brought from Warrensburg, as well as of the additional $800,000, the State records and the seals hitherto in ex-Governor Jackson's hands.

The Confederate losses were heavy—between two and three thousand—mainly owing to the judicious explosion by the Federals of six mines during the siege. The Federals lost between three and five hundred killed and wounded. In the last day's fight, Colonel Mulligan was wounded in the leg and in the right arm, Colonel Marshall received a wound in the cheek, and Colonel White was shot through the lungs, dying Saturday morning.

Indiana Volunteers, in the war with Mexico. Rapid promotion followed his service in Mexico, and at Buena Vista he commanded a brigade, and displayed conspicuous bravery.

In 1848 he was elected Lieutenant-governor of Indiana; represented the State in the United States Congress in 1853–5, voting for the Nebraska Bill. In 1855 he removed to the Territory of Kansas, then the battle-ground of the Pro-Slavery and Anti-Slavery parties, each party maintaining a form of State government. Colonel Lane was a prominent member of the first Free State government; was president of both the Topeka and Leavenworth Constitutional Conventions, and commanded the Free State forces, with the rank of major-general. In 1856 he was chosen United States Senator by the Free State Legislature, and proceeded to Washington, but was not allowed to take his seat. The same year he was indicted for high treason by the opponents of the Free State government, and was compelled to flee from the State. In 1858, in an affray, he shot and killed a neighbor, for which offense he was tried, but acquitted. The Legislature of the State of Kansas elected General Lane to the United States Senate in 1861 and 1865.

At the breaking out of the Civil War he actively engaged in organizing the Kansas troops, and took a conspicuous part in the battle of Lexington as a brigadier-general of volunteers. On the meeting of the United States Congress, in December, 1861, he took his seat as United States Senator

in consequence. Amongst these recruiting camps was the one located at Willett's Point, N. Y.

Colonel Le Gendre was raising a regiment to be called the New York Rifles, and Colonel Fardella was likewise close by raising a regiment mostly composed of his countrymen. Recruiting had been actively carried on by both parties, creating jealousy, yet nothing occurred to seriously mar the relations existing between the two commands until Colonel Le Gendre learned that a company of his men were about to be turned over by their captain, Cresto, to Colonel Fardella's command.

The captain had his company on guard the night the desertion was to take place, September 9th, 1861, but ere the plan could be carried out, Colonel Le Gendre ordered Captain Gosamer and Lieutenant George of his command to take charge of the camp, and to order every man to his quarters.

While Captain Cresto was parleying about the matter a pistol was accidentally discharged by one of his guard, creating much excitement. Colonel Le Gendre's detachment, fancying it was attacked, at once fired a volley into Captain Cresto's men. Two of the latter, Dominick Sassi and Ferdinand Marker, were killed, while several were wounded.

The company was at once placed under arrest and severely disciplined. The act was not one of disloyalty so much as an expression of preference for a particular command, and the men were soon sent to the front.

REVIEW OF CONFEDERATE TROOPS EN ROUTE TO VIRGINIA, AS THEY PASS THE PULASKI MONUMENT, SAVANNAH, GA., AUGUST 7TH, 186[illegible]

ENCAMPMENT OF FEDERAL TROOPS ON THE BATTERY AT ANNAPOLIS, MD.

BATTLE OF CARNIFEX FERRY.

CARNIFEX FERRY is located at a point on the Gauley River, below Meadow Creek, near Summersville, the capital of Nicholas County, in Western Virginia.

General W. S. Rosecrans, who, since he succeeded General George B. McClellan on July 22d, had been organizing a large army, learned early in the month of September that the Confederate forces under General John B. Floyd, late United States Secretary of War, were stationed at Carnifex Ferry.

SEPTEMBER, 1861.

General Henry A. Wise's forces had been left at Pickett's Mills to guard against a possible rear attack by General J. D. Cox, then at Hawk's Nest, while the Confederate division under General Robert E. Lee was at Cheat Mountain opposing the force which General Rosecrans had placed under General Joseph J. Reynolds.

Rosecrans determined to attack Floyd without delay, lest the Confederates soon become in a still better position to menace the Federals in Western Virginia, as well as in Pennsylvania and Ohio. In order to reach Floyd's strongly entrenched position on the heights overlooking the *ferry*, Rosecrans had to cross both the Kreitz and the Powell Mountains, the last named being the loftiest in Western Virginia. This was a very difficult undertaking, as most of the passes were very rugged and narrow, it being in many places necessary for the men to go in single file and to crawl upon their hands and knees.

The summit of the last range was reached by Rosecrans at about noon of the 9th of September, and, although the troops were then wellnigh exhausted after their very wearisome march of nearly seventeen miles, no time was lost in making reconnoissances by the Federals. These led to an exchange of fire between pickets, nothing of much moment occurring, however, until after General Henry W. Benham's brigade had come up early the following day.

The latter's force made the total Federal army there under Rosecrans about 4,000, as against 2,000 under General Floyd, the latter having the advantage in position.

General Benham had asked, and was ordered, to advance, which he did, with his entire brigade, composed of the Tenth Ohio, Colonel William Haines Lytle, the Twelfth Ohio, under Colonel Lowe, and the Thirteenth Ohio, Colonel W. S. Smith, with two batteries under Captains McMullen and Schneider.

FRANCIS H. PIERPONT,

GOVERNOR OF VIRGINIA 1863 TO 1865, WITH STATE GOVERNMENT AT ALEXANDRIA.
PROVISIONAL GOVERNOR, APPOINTED BY PRESIDENT JOHNSON, 1865 TO 1868.

The Tenth Ohio, known as the Irish Regiment, which was in the lead, soon came upon and engaged a Confederate parapet battery located near the main road. This at once drew a concentrated fire from the enemy's large supporting force, which would have completely swept Colonel Lytle's men but for the timely assistance given by Captain McMullen's and Captain Schneider's guns. These played successfully upon the enemy and enabled Lytle to attack the central Confederate position on the neighboring hill.

Under a scathing fire the four companies attempted to carry it, Colonel Lytle's rallying-cry of "Follow, Tenth!" leading them on to renewed efforts which, however, proved unavailing. The entrenched force was too strong. In the last attempt, directly in the centre, Lytle had been severely wounded in the leg, and had, besides, been thrown to the ground by his horse, which, through a wound, had become unmanageable.

The Colonel had to be taken from the field, after ordering his men to fall back beyond the range of the galling fire to which they were being exposed. Color sergeant Fitzgibbons, who was close by Lytle when he fell, had his right hand shattered, but immediately caught up and waved the standard with his left hand until killed by a round-shot. The colors were then taken by Sergeant O'Connor, and held up until, exhausted by a wound he had received, he fell by the roadside. His place was filled by Captain Stephen McGroarty, who bore the flag aloft till his company had nearly reached cover, when he, too, yielded up his life to a ball that pierced his right breast.

The "Bloody Tenth," as it was called, had signalized itself to a man. Its lieutenant-colonel, Korff, Major Burke, and Captains Annis and Moore, were ever spurring them on; their much-beloved chaplain, Father O'Higgins, likewise taking an active and often too risky a share in the duties of the moment.

The enemy's right flank had in the meantime been engaged by Colonel Lowe's Twelfth Ohio, led by Adjutant-general Hartsuff, and by the Thirteenth Ohio, under Colonel Smith, which latter stood at the extreme right close by the river. Schneider's battery remained in nearly its former position, but McMullen's guns had been brought to bear on the main Confederate battery.

There stood at the same time, on the extreme Confederate left, the brigade which had been given to Colonel Robert L. McCook, and which was composed of his own German regiment, the Ninth Ohio, as well as of the Third Ohio, and the Twenty-eighth Ohio under Colonel Mohr. Scammon's detachment acted as a reserve.

McCook had displayed much annoyance at not being allowed to engage the enemy at an earlier period, and as soon as he was given a brigade, became almost wild with joy.

Standing in the saddle, he harangued his men excitedly, drawing from them repeated cheers of approval, and waving his slouched hat, cried: "Forward, my bully Dutch! We will go over the entrenchments if every man dies on the other side!" The entire regiment seemed electrified, and, accompanied by Hartsuff, at once plunged ahead through the woods, all eager for the fray.

The assault from McCook's men, as well as along the whole line, continued actively for quite a while, in face of serious losses. These included Colonel Lowe who was killed by a musket-ball piercing his head while he was in the advance. By the time evening came most of Floyd's guns had been silenced, and the Thirteenth Ohio was making ready to enter the works at Floyd's right.

Rosecrans, however, deemed best to fall back for the night, preparatory to a renewed attack the following day. The men lay on their arms until the next morning, when, to their surprise, they found the works to have been silently evacuated.

Either through fear of a more serious engagement or by reason of Wise refusing to send him reinforcements, Floyd had taken his men across the Gauley River, leaving behind a large quantity of arms, stores and ammunition. The losses of the Confederates the previous day had been one killed and ten wounded, the latter including General Floyd, whilst the Federals were reported to have lost fully eighty-five in killed and wounded.

Floyd's army first fled to Dogwood Gap, the junction of the Summersville and Charleston roads, thence to Meadow Bluff (or Bridge), where he was joined by General Lee, nine days later.

Rosecrans encamped at Cross Roads (or Lanes), leaving McCook's brigade for a while to pursue Floyd, the Federal forces finally resting on New River, directly facing the position then held by General Lee on the Big Sewell Mountain.

OPERATIONS AT AND NEAR SANTA ROSA ISLAND.

WE have already seen how Fort Pickens, located on Santa Rosa Island, was, in January, 1861, saved from the insurgent grasp through the foresightedness and active energy displayed by Lieutenant Adam J. Slemmer.

The little force garrisoning the place had been strengthened, April 12th, by marines and artillery carried during the night, under the guns of Forts McRae and Barrancas, by the sailing frigate *Sabine*, Captain Adams; the steam sloop-of-war *Brooklyn*, Captain Walker; the gunboats *Crusader* and *Wyandot*, and the storeships *Supply* and *St. Louis*. Additional reinforcements and stores had reached it a few days later by the steam transports *Atlantic* and *Illinois*, raising the entire force to about nine hundred men.

Colonel Harvey Brown, who had charge of the last expedition, took command of the post on the 17th of April, in place of Lieutenant Slemmer, who was ordered with his little band of men to Fort Hamilton, in New York Harbor, to recruit. While here, Lieutenant Slemmer was, on May 4th, commissioned major of the Sixteenth Regiment of United States Infantry.

In June, as we have seen, Fort Pickens was further strengthened by the arrival of the Sixth New York (Billy Wilson's) Zouaves.

Until October, nothing of moment occurred between the Federals, occupying the fortress as well as two shore batteries, and the Confederates, located at Forts McRae and Barrancas, on the other side of the channel leading to Pensacola Bay, except the burning of the Warrington Navy Yard dry dock, September 2d, by a force under Lieutenant Shipley, and the daring attack on the schooner *Judah* while fitting out as a privateer at the Navy Yard.

During the night of the 13th of September, a force of one hundred men, under Lieutenant John H. Russell, of the *Colorado*, but recently arrived, had manned some boats, and with muffled oars managed to reach the *Judah* unperceived. To board the vessel, spike her ten-inch columbiad, and set her on fire, was the work of but a few moments. All was done as had been planned by Captain Bailey of the *Colorado*, and with a Federal loss of only three killed and ten wounded.

Early on the 9th of October a force of about 1,400 Confederates, under Generals Anderson and Ruggles, landed on Santa Rosa Island, about *four miles* from the encampment of Wilson's Zouaves, and advanced upon the latter, in three columns, before daylight.

OCTOBER, 1861.

The Zouaves, then numbering about 200, endeavored to made a stand, but only for a moment, and were forced to retreat to the cover of the Lincoln and Totten batteries, which had been erected beyond Fort Pickens, leaving their camp in the hands of the enemy. Reinforced, however, by detachments under Majors Arnold and Vogdes, Captains Hildt and Robinson, and Lieutenants D'Orville, Shipley and Zeeley, they returned and attacked the Confederates, compelling them, after a lively fire, to

RETURN OF FEDERAL FORAGING PARTIES INTO CAMP, NEAR ANNANDALE CHAPEL, VA.

fall back beyond the burning camp to their boats. These were fired upon on leaving the island, one of them being so riddled with shot that it sank with all on board. This night skirmish, which has by some been called the battle of Santa Rosa Island, resulted in a total loss to the Confederates of about 150, the Federals losing 64 in killed, wounded and prisoners. The latter included Major Vogdes, who was succeeded in command by Captain Hildt of the Third Infantry.

After this engagement, both sides kept reinforcing and strengthening their position, until by the middle of the following November the garrison at Fort Pickens had increased to 1,300 men, still under Colonel Brown, and that of the opposing forces to as many as 6,500 men, under General Braxton Bragg. The latter were distributed in works extending from the Navy Yard to Fort McRae, in all about three and a half miles, and possessed as many as fourteen batteries of long and short range artillery.

With the co-operation of Flag-officer McKean, who commanded the blockading squadron, then composed of the *Niagara*, *Richmond* and *Montgomery*, Colonel Brown determined to attack the Confederates, and by sunrise on

November, 1861.

the 22d of November they were in readiness to commence operations.

At about ten o'clock that morning, Fort Pickens opened fire upon the enemy's transports lying off the Navy Yard, and afterward, with the assistance of the shore battery, and of the *Niagara* and *Richmond*, engaged Forts McRae and Barrancas. The fight lasted all the remainder of the day, and when evening came, the guns in the direction of the Navy Yard had all been silenced as well as most of those in both the Confederate forts.

The following day operations were resumed by Fort Pickens alone, as the water proved too shallow to admit of the *Niagara* and *Richmond* coming within range of the Confederate positions. At three o'clock in the afternoon, part of the Warrington village and Navy Yard had been set on fire by shells from the fort, causing much destruction.

No further operations disturbed the comparative quiet of Santa Rosa Island until the morning of January 1st, 1862, when Fort Pickens engaged a Confederate steamer making her way to the Navy Yard. This attack was answered by a Confederate fire that led to a general engagement lasting in all twenty-four hours, without much loss, except the burning of buildings in the Pensacola Navy Yard, and the greater part of the village of Woolsey.

BRAXTON BRAGG.

BRAXTON BRAGG.

Born in Warren County, N. C., in 1817, he entered West Point Military Academy, and graduated with high honors in 1837. He was immediately appointed lieutenant of artillery, and served mainly in Florida until 1838, when he engaged in conveying the remnant of the Cherokee tribe of Indians to their new reservation in the Indian Territory. From 1843 to 1845 he had command at Fort Moultrie, in Charleston Harbor, and in 1846 joined in the military occupation of Texas. He was, in May, 1846, made captain by brevet for gallant conduct in the defense of Fort Brown, Texas, and in June was made captain of artillery in the army of occupation, which, under General Taylor, had crossed the Rio Grande, occupied Matamoras and advanced on Monterey, September 21st, 1846, where Bragg displayed conspicuous bravery, and arrested the attention of the commanding general, whose brief order, "A little more grape, Captain Bragg," became a rallying-cry in storming the Mexican strongholds. Here he was promoted major by brevet. At the battle of Buena Vista, fought February 22d-23d, 1847, Bragg was again promoted brevet lieutenant-colonel. He was engaged in frontier duty from 1848 to 1855. He resigned his commission in the army in 1856, and became a planter in Louisiana; was Commissioner of Public Works for the State of Louisiana from 1859 to 1861; was commissioned brigadier-general and took command of the forces operating against Fort Pickens in 1861; was made major-general in 1862, and joined the Army of the Mississippi. At the battle of Shiloh, April 6th and 7th, 1862, he commanded the Second Corps, succeeding Albert Sydney Johnston, who was killed on that battlefield. He was promoted to the rank of General, and after the evacuation of Corinth succeeded General Beauregard in command of the Department of the Mississippi. He took active measures against General Buell in Kentucky, but was obliged to retire before superior forces at Perryville. For this failure he was removed from command and placed under arrest. He was, however, soon restored, and in 1863 opposed Rosecrans. He was defeated at Murfreesboro, December 20th, 1862. At Chickamauga, one of the most desperate conflicts of the war, he totally routed Rosecrans, and met Grant at Mission Ridge and Chattanooga, where he was badly defeated; he was again relieved of his command, and ordered to Richmond, where he acted as military adviser to President Davis, with whom he was a great favorite. In 1864 he led a small force from North Carolina to Georgia to operate against Sherman in his march to the sea, but met with no success.

After the surrender he settled in Mobile, and became chief engineer of the State of Alabama in improving Mobile Harbor. He died in Galveston, Texas, on September 27th, 1876.

THE FEDERAL WAR STEAMER "SOUTH CAROLINA" SHELLING THE BATTERIES AT GALVESTON, TEXAS AUGUST 3TH, 1861.

SHARPSHOOTING.—TRIAL OF SKILL OF BERDAN'S RIFLEMEN BEFORE

SHARPSHOOTING—TRIAL OF SKILL OF BERDAN'S RIFLEMEN BEFORE GENERAL McCLELLAN AND STAFF AT WASHINGTON, SEPTEMBER 20TH, 1861.

UNITED STATES CAVALRY SCOUTING IN THE NEIGHBORHOOD OF FAIRFAX COURT HOUSE, VA.

THE POPULAR LOANS

At the North and South.

In order to provide all the means that were likely to be needed for a thorough prosecution of the Civil War, the United States Congress acted upon the suggestion of Salmon P. Chase, then Secretary of the Treasury, and authorized a loan of $250,000,000. For this there were to be issued bonds bearing seven per cent. annual interest, and redeemable in twenty years; also Treasury notes payable in three years, and bearing seven and three-tenths per cent. annual interest. An Act was also passed by Congress on the 5th of August, 1861, for the increase of revenues from imports and by taxes, in order to provide for the interest to accrue on the new loan.

ENTRANCE TO ASSAY OFFICE, TREASURY BUILDING, BLOCKED BY ANXIOUS PURCHASERS.

The combined banks of New York, Philadelphia and Boston, seeing the obvious advantages of the loan, at once agreed to take it; but Mr. Chase preferred to place it within the reach of all, and, during the month of Sep-

SCENE IN THE UNITED STATES TREASURY, WALL STREET, NEW YORK CITY.—BUYING GOVERNMENT BONDS.

tember, 1861, he publicly invited subscriptions at par for $150,000,000 of the seven and three-tenths interest-bearing notes.

We give an illustration of one of these notes with the interest coupons attached. It is of the denomination of $100 dollars, bearing a half-yearly coupon representing $3.65 of interest, which equals two cents per day, and is convertible into United States six per cent. bonds, redeemable twenty years after their date, if so desired by the holder.

The eagerness of the people throughout the Northern States to respond to Mr. Chase's appeal was so great, that crowds gathered continually at the appointed subscription agencies, depositing their savings, large and small, and soliciting information with regard to subsequent investments. Our cuts represent the street entrance and the main room of the largest of these agencies, the Assay Office, connected with the Sub-Treasury, located in Wall Street, New York City. In a very short time the full amount of the loan had been absorbed, it being afterward satisfactorily shown that a call for over three times the sum named would have been equally well disposed of at that period.

The subsequent loans authorized by the United States Congress have, as is well known, met with even a greater degree of favor, if that can be possible, from American as well as foreign investors. From 1861 to the beginning of the present year (1884) there have been several loans called for, and the success that all have met with, and are still enjoying, is evidenced by the fact that the existing issues now command a very high premium both here and abroad.

ROOM OF ASSISTANT UNITED STATES TREASURER, JOHN J. CISCO.

The first loan at the South was authorized by the Confederate Congress, at the session held in July, 1861, and issued through Charles G. Memminger, Secretary of the Treasury.

It was for $200,000,000, of which one-half was to be in bonds bearing eight per cent. interest per annum, and running twenty years, and the other half in Treasury notes, payable in six months after the ratification of peace.

The loan in its entirety was soon absorbed in the South, and by the Southern sympathizers residing in Europe. The success which the Confederate army had just met with at Bull Run (Manassas), and which was naturally much exaggerated by public report, had inspired the Southern people with great confidence in the near and permanent realization of their plans, and, under the circumstances, a much heavier loan would, no doubt, have then met with equal favor.

As time grew on, however, and the effects of the first great victory were offset by repeated defeats, which, in face of the more strongly recuperative powers of the Northern people, greatly narrowed down the chances for a speedy termination of the conflict, the calls from the Confederate Treasurer were but feebly responded to at home, and could not, likewise, toward the last, attract attention abroad except at a very high, not to say extortionate and ruinous premium.

In addition to the issues above

THE NAVAL PRACTICE B[illegible]Y AT THE NAVY YARD WASHINGTON

alluded to, there were others emanating from the General Government, as well as the State Governments at the South. We give an illustration of a ten-dollar note issued by the Confederate States of America, payable two years after date, and fundable in Confederate States stock bearing eight per cent. interest. There were also several fractional currency notes, issued in the same month of July, 1861, by the State of South Carolina.

These and other similar tokens of value issued the South during the progress of the Civil War, gradually depreciating in value, until, at its termination, their specie representation, if any, was what may be called infinitesimal. Their creator having, with the end of the war, ceased to exist, without leaving any means for redemption, they virtually disappeared from public view. Nor would any of them have been ever heard from but for an unexplained and short-lived demand for some particular denominations of bonds issued by the Southern Confederacy, which were asked for at a small premium through the newspapers of the country during the years 1882 and 1883.

FAC-SIMILE OF TREASURY NOTE ISSUED BY THE CONFEDERATE STATES GOVERNMENT, 1861.

THE NATIONAL FINANCES.*

At the beginning of the year 1861, the United States Government found itself with a debt of $90,580,873, and with but limited resources to meet its accruing interest. But with the breaking out of the Civil War a new era began, and the necessity of creating means for suppressing the rebellion in the Southern States led to the establishment of a stable foundation upon which the past as well as the large prospective indebtedness was to be satisfactorily cared for.

The foundation lay in the issue of bonds and of a legal-tender paper currency, in the creation of the National Banking system through which the Government loans might find a ready market, and in the return to internal revenue taxes.

By the efforts of the Government brokers the bonds were greatly popularized throughout the country, and by using the facilities of the National Banking system the inhabitants of the remotest town were given the opportunity to buy them.

The bonds of the Government were bought because it was patriotic to lend to the Government in its time of urgent need.

From the maximum of $90,580,873 in 1861, the debt of the United States steadily increased until its maximum was reached on the 31st of August, 1865, the year of the cessation of hostilities, when its total stood at $2,844,649,626, with an annual charge for interest of $150,977,697.

Since then it has been reduced, chiefly by the payment of bonds, and the annual interest charge has been reduced in far greater proportion by refunding the loans, as opportunity offered, at lower rates.

The largest amount of legal tenders ever in circulation was $432,687,966 in 1863, and the greatest extent of the depreciation was in July, 1864, when it required $285 in notes to equal $100 in gold.

In 1879 specie payments were resumed, and at present the Government is performing the functions of a bank. The notes are redeemable in specie whenever presented, and are paid out again in the course of business. Under existing laws their cancellation and entire withdrawal is prohibited. Since resumption, a specie (gold) reserve has been held in the Treasury, amounting to about 40 per cent. of the $346,681,016 of notes outstanding.

The United States Government has maintained a high and constantly increasing credit for financial integrity, and to-day deservedly stands in the front rank. The example of the General Government has had a salutary effect, and the credit of most of the States is only second to that of the United States. The list of States which have been among the delinquents is daily growing smaller, their people realizing the value of public honesty as a means of promoting their material wealth and securing recognition by the commercial nations of the world.

FAC-SIMILE OF TREASURY NOTE, WITH COUPONS, ISSUED BY THE UNITED STATES GOVERNMENT IN 1861.

COUPON BONDS.

These bonds called into circulation a large amount in small savings of gold and silver previously lying idle in old bureaus, hidden boxes, and stockings, where the careful housewife had fore gone the interest for the sake of *safety*. The seven-thirty coupons were a new source of revenue to many.

THE SAWYER GUN.

This rifled cannon was the one which General B. F. Butler adopted, in conjunction with the Hotchkiss shell, as the most effective for use against the Confederate batteries erected at Sewall's Point. Several trials had been made of it, in presence of distinguished army and navy officers and foreign representatives, by all of whom it was pronounced as singularly remarkable in its execution. It was adopted almost exclusively at Fort Calhoun, which had been erected at the Rip-Raps, near Fortress Monroe, especially for active work against the enemy's batteries. This gun did more effective work, and more serious damage, than all the other heavy guns used against the Confederate forces while located across the water at Sewall's Point, during the year 1861. This was due to the precision with which the gun carried its shot to points beyond the range looked for by the Confederates

* For much of the data herein contained, we are indebted to the valuable "Memoranda Concerning Government Bonds" issued by Fisk & Hatch, of New York City.

MORNING MUSTERING OF THE [illegible] ON THEIR WAY TO THEIR DAY'S WORK

INDIGNITIES SHOWN A MASSACHUSETTS EDITOR FOR PUBLISHING EXPRESSIONS OF SYMPATHY WITH THE SOUTH.

PRACTICING WITH THE CELEBRATED SAWYER GUN, ON THE CONFEDERATE BATTERIES AT SEWALL'S POINT NEAR NORFOLK, VA.
FROM FORT CALHOUN, ON THE RIP-RAPS, IN FRONT OF FORTRESS MONROE

REVIEW IN WASHINGTON, UNDER GENERAL McCLELLAN, OF EIGHT BATTERIES OF ARTILLER

REVIEW IN WASHINGTON UNDER GENERAL McCLELLAN OF EIGHT BATTERIES OF ARTILLERY AND THREE REGIMENTS OF CAVALRY, BY PRESIDENT LINCOLN AND MEMBERS OF HIS CABINET.

THE BATTLE OF BALL'S BLUFF—THE BATTLE OF LEESBURG.

AFTER the battle of Bull Run, the entire Maryland bank of the Potomac River, from Washington to Harper's Ferry, had been carefully guarded against a possible advance on the capital by the Confederates, occupying the other side.

By the middle of October, General N. P. Banks, who had superseded General Patterson, held the line from Darnestown to Williamsport, near Edwards's Ferry; the forces under Generals William F. Smith and George A. McCall were at and near the Chain Bridge; General Charles P. Stone's brigade stood between Edwards' Ferry and Conrad's Ferry, with headquarters at Poolesville; and the remaining section to Harper's Ferry was in charge of detachments mainly under Colonels John W. Geary and Frederick W. Lander.

Oct., 1861.

General Stone's force commanded the road leading to Leesburg, the capital of Loudon County, Va., about forty miles from Harper's Ferry, where the Confederates, under General N. G. Evans, were reported stationed, and faced Harrison's (Swan's) Island, located exactly in the centre of the river.

On the 18th of October, General McClellan had ordered McCall to move and occupy Dranesville, in order to ascertain if possible, from there, the exact position and strength of the opposing forces, which were said to have just left Leesburg. In the execution of this order no resistance was met with. A line of skirmishers was subsequently deployed as far as Goose Creek, a small place just north of Aldie, and about four miles distant from Leesburg; but up to the 20th all reconnoissances strengthened the belief that Leesburg had been evacuated, and McCall so reported.

The latter report being followed by one from General Banks to the same effect, communicated by the signal station at Sugar Loaf Mountain, McClellan at once advised General Stone of McCall's movement, and of the fact that "heavy reconnoissances" would be immediately sent out "in all directions." Stone was likewise ordered to keep "a good lookout on Leesburg," where the Confederates might at any time put in an appearance, McClellan adding: "Perhaps a slight demonstration on your part would have the effect to move them."

This reached Stone at about noon of the 20th, and he lost no time in acting accordingly. Part of Colonel Charles Devens's Fifteenth Massachusetts Regiment was stationed on Harrison's Island. To Conrad's Ferry, where already stood part of Rickett's battery, there was sent a detachment from Colonel W. Raymond Lee's Twentieth Massachusetts Regiment, Colonel Milton Cogswell's Tammany Regiment, and a section of Vaughan's battery, whilst General Willis A. Gorman was placed at Edwards' Ferry with the Seventh Michigan Regiment, the First Minnesota Regiment, the Putnam Rangers, two troops of the Van Alen Cavalry, and a section of Bunting's Rhode Island Battery. A force of about three thousand men, under Edward D. Baker, who had just received his commission of brigadier-general, was held in reserve near the two ferries.

General Gorman was ordered to make a feint of crossing from Edwards's Ferry, and to disperse a party of Confederates that had been seen on the opposite hill. This he did, with a few shells fired from the flatboats in the river. Captain Philbrick was at the same time directed to advance from Harrison's Island, with about twenty men taken from Devens's Fifteenth Massachusetts Regiment, and to make a reconnoissance toward Leesburg. They crossed the river, and ascended the steep and slippery bank opposite, called Ball's Bluff, which rises about one hundred and fifty feet above the river, but had not proceeded far when they came upon what they thought to be a Confederate camp.

General Stone was advised of the fact, and, believing that McCall was within helping distance, he made all his arrangements for a more important demonstration the next day, after telegraphing McClellan what he had done, and notifying the latter that he possessed the means of crossing one

CAPTURE OF LIEUTENANT H. L. SEGAL, OF THE CONFEDERATE ARMY, NEAR FALLS CHURCH, VA., BY LIEUTENANT-COLONEL WINSLOW AND CAPTAIN SHATTUCK, OF THE NEW YORK THIRTY-SEVENTH.

hundred and twenty-five men once in ten minutes at each of two points.

Colonel Devens was ordered to be in readiness to leave Harrison's Island with part of his force, to attack the camp, early the next morning. Two howitzers were placed on the island in position to command the Virginia shore, and four companies of the Twentieth Massachusetts were to occupy the island upon Colonel Devens's departure, while another of Colonel Lee's companies was to remain on the bluff to cover Devens's return. Colonel Baker was instructed to have the First California Regiment, under Lieutenant-colonel Wistar, at Conrad's Ferry, and the remainder of the reserves within easy call.

No further advices were received from McClellan, who, it afterward appeared, had ordered McCall back to the Chain Bridge, and General Stone's orders were carried out early on the 21st. The supposed camp could not, however, be found by Devens, nor did he come upon any of the enemy. He therefore sent for further orders, and was told to remain, pending the arrival of reinforcements. These soon followed under Lieutenant-colonel Ward, increasing his force to six hundred and twenty men.

October, 1861.

Colonel Dana was ordered to cross Edwards's Ferry, with two companies of the First Minnesota Regiment, under cover of guns from Ricketts's battery, and to search the country around as well as protect a detachment of Van Alen's cavalry sent ahead for the same purpose. The skirmishers came upon a Confederate regiment and exchanged fire, without, however, much damage to either side.

Devens's force had had a slight skirmish while in the woods, and had afterward crossed to the open space on the right, where they halted, and where, shortly after twelve o'clock, they were set upon suddenly by the Confederates. These consisted of the Eighteenth Mississippi and the Eighth Virginia Regiments, as well as of a small body of cavalry, and soon forced the Federals to fall back toward the position occupied by Colonel Lee.

Upon hearing the sound of battle, the two howitzers had been sent from Harrison's Island, and followed by the First California Regiment with one gun of Bunting's battery under Lieutenant Bramhall.

Baker reached the bluff as Colonel Cogswell's regiment came up the winding path, and at once took command of the assembled force, then numbering nineteen hundred men.

General Evans had, in the meantime, prepared to assume the offensive and at about three o'clock commenced a vigorous attack upon three sides, with the Seventeenth Mississippi, under Colonel Featherston, the Eighteenth Mississippi, under Colonel Burt, some cavalry, and the Thirteenth Mississippi and Eighth Virginia Regiments, under Colonels Jenifer, Barksdale and Hunton.

The fight became general, and the strong force on the Federal front and flanks was soon telling severely upon the latter. General Baker had been foremost in the fray, encouraging his men in every possible way.

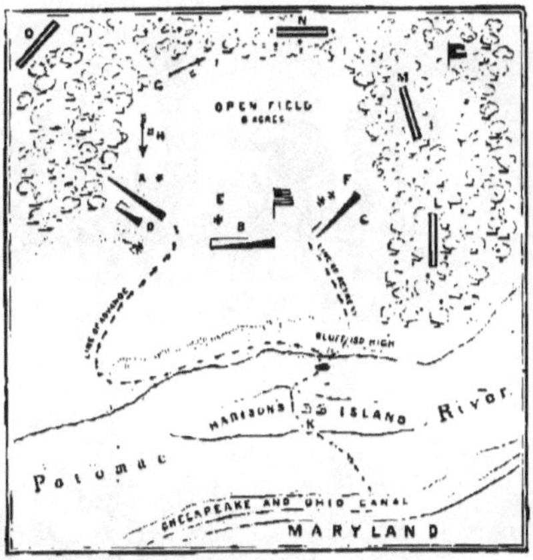

PLAN OF THE BATTLE OF BALL'S BLUFF.

The Federals advanced, in face of a terrific fire pouring in upon them from all quarters; but, at the very outset, their commanding general fell dead, pierced by bullets in the head, side and arm.*

* General Baker had been wounded a week or two previous in the field [illegible] It was said that [illegible] at the same time that [illegible] struck him [illegible] and that [illegible] his arm and side. The Confederate who shot him was in the act of taking [illegible] Colonel [illegible] Francis G. Young, by whose care it was taken across the river.

EDWARD DICKINSON BAKER.

Colonel Coggswell took Baker's place, and the fight went on for a while; but the additional losses, including both Lieutenant Bramhall and Lieutenant French, who had been serving the guns, and both of whom were wounded, seemed to render useless a continuation of the conflict.

Colonel Cogswell first thought of falling back, but the strong current of the river seemed to preclude the possibility of retiring, without great loss, by the bluff, and, as evening was coming on, it was decided best to endeavor to cut their way through to Edwards's Ferry, in the hope of reaching a part of Gorman's forces. As this was about being done, the ammunition gave out on the left of the line, which would have wavered, and perhaps broken in disorder, but for the help extended it by the right and centre.

An order was then given to carry out the first idea of reaching Harrison's Island, and the retreat was made under cover of the Fifteenth Massachusetts Regiment. But, as well may be imagined, under pressure of the victorious Confederates, the retreat soon became a rout, and the Federal loss in killed, wounded and prisoners proved very great. This was especially the case when, arriving at the foot of the bluff, it was found that no suitable means of transport had been provided. But one large scow was there, which, becoming filled by a surging mass, and being riddled with bullets, soon sank with all on board. The fugitives had then to resort to the water and swim to Harrison's Island, or escape in the darkness through the woods in hopes of reaching Gorman's camp.

More than one-fourth of Cogswell's force was lost, he himself and Colonel Lee being made prisoners. Colonel Devens had escaped on his horse, swimming across the river. The Confederates lost many wounded, and about 150 killed, the latter including Colonel E. R. Burt, of the Eighteenth Mississippi Regiment.

Although General Stone had not been made aware of the disadvantages under which Colonel Baker was laboring, he had become anxious at the apparent fierceness and the duration of the conflict on the other side of the river, and, ignorant still of McCall's position, he had telegraphed General Banks for a brigade to be immediately sent him. He was finally on the point of ordering Gorman ahead, when news of Baker's death reached him. Stone at once crossed the river, followed by 2,500 of Gorman's brigade, but was soon met by some fugitives, who reported the Confederates as advancing in great force.

Nothing was then to be done but to insure the safety of Gorman's men, and to hold Harrison's Island, pending the expected reinforcements. The last of Gorman's force reached Edwards's Ferry early on the morning of the 22d, just at the time General Banks arrived and took chief command.

October, 1861.

After the battle of Ball's Bluff, the House of Representatives, yielding to the great clamor that naturally arose in consequence of the serious disaster to the Federal arms, suggested an inquiry, which was satisfactorily

ENGAGEMENT BETWEEN FEDERAL AND CONFEDERATE TROOPS ON THE VIRGINIA SIDE OF THE

[illegible] CONFEDERATE [illegible] ON THE VIRGINIA SIDE OF THE POTOMAC [illegible] EDWARDS FERRY [illegible] BATTERY OF PARROTT GUNS ON THE MARYLAND [illegible]

RETREAT OF THE FEDERAL [illegible] FROM THE VIRGINIA SHORE ACROSS [illegible] EDWARDS FERRY ON THE NIGHT OF [illegible]

met, for the time, by the commanding general's statement that General Stone was without blame, a conclusion McClellan had arrived at when at Poolesville on Tuesday, the 23d.

Many were not, however, satisfied with this disposition of the matter, and Congress was for a long time agitated by warm discussions on the subject. This led, February 8th, 1862, to the arrest and incarceration in Fort Lafayette of General Stone, by order of the Secretary of War, although he had in the meantime been placed by General McClellan in command of an increased force of twelve thousand men, and had had no charges preferred against him.

General Stone was shortly afterward transferred from Fort Lafayette to better quarters at Fort Hamilton, also located in New York Harbor, and was finally released unconditionally, August 16th, taking command again under General Banks in May of the following year.

EDWARD DICKINSON BAKER.

Born in London, Eng., of Quaker parents February 24th, 1811, emigrated to the United States in his youth, remaining but a short time in the City of Philadelphia, Pa., and finally settling in what was at that time called the Far West (the State of Illinois); studied law, and, notably at the Springfield (Ill.) Bar, attained a very high degree of eminence. His fine address, sympathetic manner, and great eloquence, gained for him in after years such a popularity, that he was elected to the United States Senate from Illinois in 1848, and from Oregon in 1860. He had, meanwhile, volunteered in the Mexican War, and on the field had won the admiration of all by a rigid and conscientious attention to the arduous duties of the camp, as well as by his singular fortitude through the trying ordeals of the march and battle. He had afterward visited California, and there also had strengthened his already great reputation as an orator and debater, the truly brilliant oration he delivered over the remains of his friend Broderick, killed in a duel, being of itself sufficient to merit him a national fame.

When the civil war broke out, he aided materially the popular movement in behalf of the North by his frequent, well-timed and powerful speeches made at Union meetings in New York City and elsewhere. He then also began recruiting a regiment for the war, and was soon offered a general's commission, but preferred to remain colonel of the regiment he had himself raised. Though composed largely of Pennsylvanians, his command was given the name of First California Volunteers, and formed part of General Stone's brigade, acting as a special corps of observation on the right flank of the Army of the Potomac just before the battle of Ball's Bluff.

It was at the latter engagement that Colonel Baker, who had, just before he entered the battle, been notified of his appointment as brigadier-general, was killed, October 21st, 1861, while at the head of his command. He had been foremost in the fight, and it was while making a final desperate effort to rally against numbers far greater than his own that he fell, pierced by bullets. His death must have been instantaneous, for it was found that he had been shot in the head, body, arm and side. He seemed to have a presentiment of death, and had directed his men to take his body off the field in case he was killed, as he justly feared. This request was carried out by Captain Beirel, of the First California Regiment, who was near, and shot the Confederate soldier whom he had seen emptying his revolver at General Baker.

General McClellan's report of the battle alluded to the loss of Baker "in the fullness of his power as a statesman, and in the course of a brilliant career as a soldier distinguished in two wars;" and Congress subsequently named a day for the consideration of his death. In presence of the President, the Cabinet, the Judiciary and Congress, fitting eulogies were accordingly pronounced in the House of Representatives, Washington, on the 11th of December, 1861, a day on which almost the entire nation likewise joined in expression of grief over the country's loss in the death of the eminent Senator and noble soldier.

DEATH OF COLONEL EDWARD DICKINSON BAKER, WHILE LEADING HIS REGIMENT AT THE BATTLE OF BALL'S BLUFF, OCTOBER 21st, 1861.

THE UNITED STATES MILITARY TELEGRAPH.

The illustration represents a station of the Military Telegraph. As the army advanced, it was accompanied by a corps of men belonging exclusively to the Telegraph Bureau, who made all the necessary wire connections for the prompt transmission of orders between the General Commanding and the War Department. The operator is here seen at his right work, receiving dispatches, while a mounted orderly is awaiting in order to convey them to the division generals.

The Military Telegraph played an important part in the conduct of the several campaigns, and was perfected so as to become indispensable to the War Department in directing operations, although some of the Federal generals who gained success in the West claimed that their success was due to the fact that they were not in telegraphic communication with Washington, and the only use of the line was to announce their victory.

SKIRMISHING BETWEEN THE PICKETS OF THE TWO ARMIES IN VIRGINIA.

UNITED STATES MILITARY TELEGRAPH STATION IN VIRGINIA.

RETURN OF FIFTY-SEVEN WOUNDED SOLDIERS OF THE NATIONAL ARMY, CAPTURED AT BULL RUN—SCENE ON BOARD THE UNITED STATES STEAMER "LOUISIANA," TO WHICH THEY WERE TRANSFERRED UNDER A FLAG [illegible]

CHARLES WILKES.

Born in New York City, 1801. When eighteen years old he was appointed to the United States Navy as midshipman; in 1826 he was promoted to a lieutenant's commission, reached the rank of commander in 1843, was made captain in 1855, commodore in 1862, and rear admiral in 1866. He conducted the celebrated "Wilkes Exploring Expedition" in the Southern and Pacific Oceans from 1838 to 1842, and published the narrative, which was of great interest and value.

In 1861, in command of the frigate *San Jacinto*, he sailed for the West Indies, in search of the Confederate cruiser *Sumter*. His plans of operation were changed on learning of the embarkation of the Confederate commissioners, Mason and Slidell, for Europe, and he intercepted the British mail-steamer *Trent* in mid-ocean, and took from her the commissioners, who, together with the captain of the *Trent*, claimed the protection of the British flag, under which they were sailing. He, however, carried them to Boston. This act was loudly applauded by all the people of the North, and received the approbation of the Navy Department and of Congress, and these commissioners were for nearly two months held as prisoners-of-war.

In spite of the apparent approval of the whole North, and in the face of the willingness of the people to [illegible] war with [illegible], [illegible] the State department determined to release them, and Mr. Seward, the Secretary of State, received the denunciation of the people who were [illegible] conversant with the [illegible] of international law, while expression of disapproval ran so high as to actually endanger his position in the Cabinet. [illegible] showed his wisdom, and it is one of the many instances in which the able Secretary of State avoided complications with foreign governments, all of which, [illegible], perhaps, [illegible], were ready and anxious to seize any pretext to acknowledge the Southern Confederacy as a nation. In 1862, Commodore Wilkes was placed in command of the flotilla cooperating with the Army of the Potomac on the Peninsula.

On the withdrawal of McClellan's army from the Virginia Peninsula, Commodore Wilkes organized a flying squadron for the purpose of breaking up blockade-running between the Southern States and the West Indies. He took many important captures. In July, 1866, he was promoted rear-admiral, and soon after placed on the retired list. He died in Washington, D. C., February 8th, 1877.

CHARLES WILKES.

JAMES MURRAY MASON.

Grandson of George Mason, a celebrated Virginian patriot of the American Revolution, an intimate friend and neighbor of George Washington. The subject of this sketch was born in Fairfax County, Va., on November 3d, 1798; graduated in 1818 at the University of Pennsylvania; studied law at the celebrated College of William and Mary at Virginia; practiced law, was elected to the State Legislature, and in 1837 to the United States Congress of Representatives from Virginia; served as United States Senator from 1847 to 1861. Senator Mason was the author of the Fugitive Slave Law.

At the time of the secession of Virginia he resigned his seat in Congress, was elected to the Confederate Congress, and sent, with John Slidell, as a commissioner from the Confederate States to England and France; was captured by Captain Wilkes of the United States Navy, while [illegible] on board the British [illegible] *Trent*, November 8th, 1861. The Confederate commissioners were carried to Boston, and incarcerated in Fort Warren, Boston Harbor. On demand of the British government they were released, January 2d, 1862, and proceeded on their mission to Europe. At the close of the war Senator Mason returned to his old home, near Alexandria, Va., [illegible] He died, April 28th, 1871, at the age of 73 years.

JOHN SLIDELL.

Born in New York City about 1793. He attended Columbia College, where he graduated in 1810, and settled in New Orleans. In his new Southern home he became very popular, and soon won for himself an enviable reputation as a lawyer and statesman. From 1829 to 1833 he was United States District-attorney, and was elected to the United States [illegible] 1843-5. President Polk appointed him Minister to Mexico in 1845, but by reason of the war with the United States he was not received by the Mexican government. Was elected United States Senator, and served from 1853 to 1861 when, in consequence of the secession of Louisiana, in which [illegible] he resigned, and joined the fortunes of the Confederacy. President Davis appointed him commissioner to France, and he sailed with James M. Mason, commissioner to England, on the British steamer *Trent*, from which he was taken, November 8th, 1861, by Captain Wilkes, who [illegible] both were carried to Fort Warren, Boston Harbor, and imprisoned until released, by demand of the British Government, January 2d, 1862. He resided in England until his death at London, July 29th, 1871.

SECRETARY SEWARD'S POSITION.

The main point of the note addressed by Mr. W. H. Seward, Secretary of State, to Lord Lyons, the British Minister at Washington, under date November 30th, 1861, [illegible] of Mason and Slidell was vitiated merely by reason Captain Wilkes, of the steamer *San Jacinto*, did not at the same time seize the *Trent* and send her before a prize court.

Mr. Seward added: "In coming to my conclusion, I have not forgotten that, if the safety of the Union required the detention of the captured persons it would be the right and duty of this Government to detain them; but the effectual check and waning proportions of the existing insurrection, as well as the comparative unimportance of the captured persons themselves, when dispassionately weighed, happily forbid me from resorting to that defence. [illegible] Only the captured persons, however, or others interested in them, could justly raise a question on that ground."

JAMES MURRAY MASON

JOHN SLIDELL

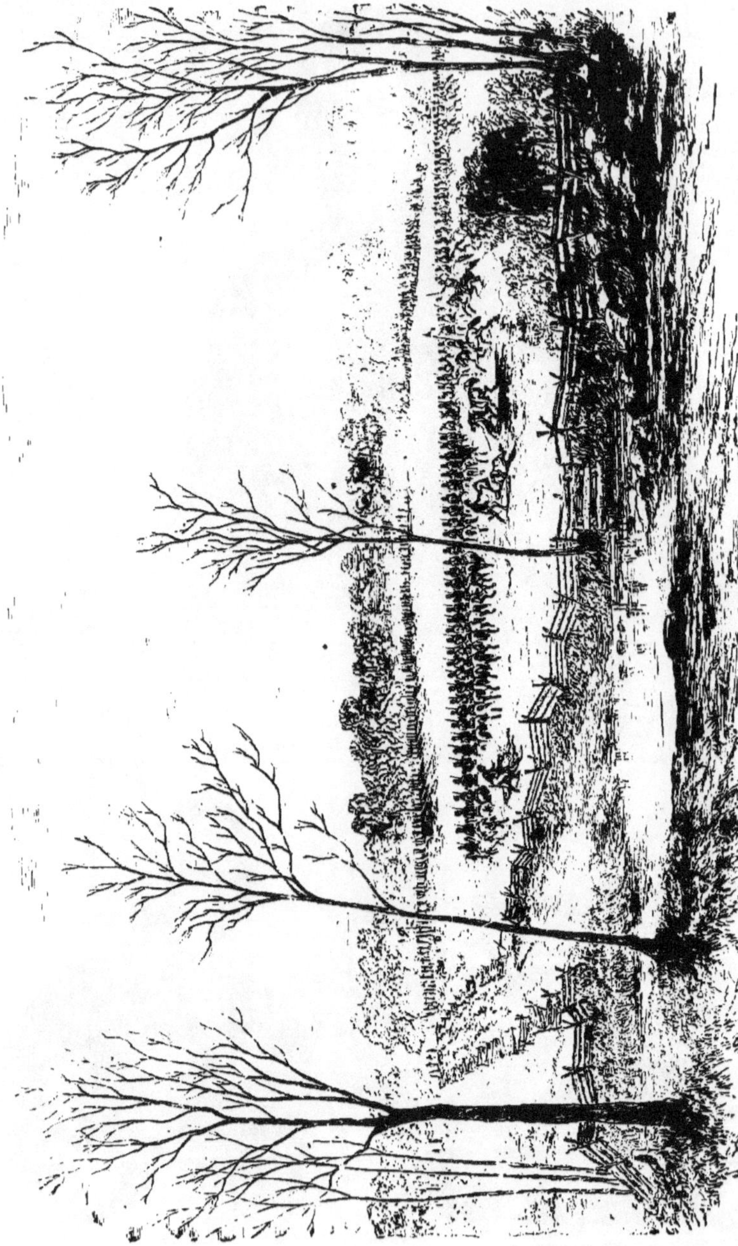

FIRST CHARGE OF FREMONT'S BODYGUARD, [illegible] ON [illegible] SPRINGFIELD, MO., OCTOBER [illegible], 1861.

OPERATIONS OF FREMONT IN MISSOURI.

As soon as General Fremont had succeeded in re-establishing order in the Department of the West, providing for the recruiting of his forces and for the defense of the Upper Mississippi as well as an offensive movement against the Confederates below Cairo, he seized the Sub-Treasury in St. Louis, and set about fortifying the latter city.

After providing for the security of St. Louis, Fremont turned his attention to the strengthening of the City of Cairo, which, from its situation at the confluence of the Ohio and the Mississippi rivers, offered, in conjunction with Bird's Point, great strategic advantages.

General Lyon had already ordered its occupation on the 28th of May, 1861, by Colonel Schuttner's Fourth Regiment of St. Louis Volunteers, and, later on, fortified camps had been established there under the command of General B. M. Prentiss, which, with those at Bird's Point, on the opposite side of the river, held at one time as many as six thousand men. These had been sent in all directions, until by the end of July there remained not more than twelve hundred men at the two places.

Cairo was reinforced by about four thousand men, whom Fremont conducted on board the steamers *City of Alton*, *Empress*, *January*, *Jeannie Dean*, *Graham*, *Louisiana*, *War Eagle* and *Warsaw* on the 30th of July, 1861, in face of a threatened attack by Generals Pillow and Thompson. Shortly after, when the Southern sympathizers became emboldened and troublesome, in consequence of news of the Federal retreat from Wilson's Creek and Springfield, martial law was declared and observed with such severity, that disturbances with the Home Guards frequently occurred especially in the St. Louis suburbs. One of the most severe of these encounters occurred at a place called Charleston, August 19th, and another at Commerce. Both resulted in favor of the Federals, who, at the latter place, captured one of Thompson's batteries.

JOHN CHARLES FREMONT.

On the 31st of August, Fremont issued a proclamation declaring martial law throughout Missouri, and that the property of all persons in the State proven to have taken an active part in the field with the enemies of the Government, should be confiscated to the public use, and that their slaves, if they had any, should be thereafter free men.

August, 1861.

The emancipation feature of this proclamation was, however, modified, eleven days later, by order of the President, and made to apply only to such slaves as were employed in the military service of the Confederates.

The occupation of Cairo and of its immediate vicinity arrested the threatened advance of the Confederates under Generals Pillow and Thompson.

Next in immediate importance to Cairo, at that time, was Cape Girardeau, situated on the Mississippi River, about forty-five miles to the northward, and the possession of which would almost insure that of Cairo itself, as it was in reality the landing-point for troops and supplies going from the latter city to Central Missouri.

General Prentiss was sent to occupy the Cape, as well as Ironton and Pilot Knob, both somewhat important localities to the westward, and on the possession of which it was supposed the Confederates laid great value. Reinforcements of artillery, cavalry and infantry were dispatched him from Bird's Point, and with these he, in time, took quiet possession of all three places. This was done just as it was found the Confederates were about advancing closely upon them, under General Hardee, and who could, at a great distance off, see the Federal ensign which had been placed on the summit of Pilot Knob.

The army of occupation thrived on the product:

CAMP LILLIE, HEADQUARTERS OF FREMONT AT JEFFERSON CITY. 140

HAY & STRAW DEPT COR. OF F & 18TH ST
COCCORAN'S PRIVATE

GRAND CORRAL OR HORSE DEPOT NEAR WASHINGTON, D. C., FOR THE REQUIREMENTS OF THE ARMY OF THE POTOMAC

SECOND CHARGE UPON THE CONFEDERATES, BY GENERAL FREMONT'S BODY-GUARD, UNDER MAJOR ZAGONYI, NEAR SPRINGFIELD, MO., ON OCTOBER 25TH, 1861

of the country through which it advanced, and became especially rich in the supply of oats and straw, of which a large quantity was secured while on its way from Ironton to Cape Girardean.

Toward the end of September, Fremont set out to prevent the contemplated junction with Price of the forces raised by McCulloch in Arkansas. He took with him an army of about 15,000 infantry, nearly 5,000 cavalry, and as many as 86 pieces of artillery, under the command of Generals David Hunter, John Pope, Franz Sigel, H. Asboth, and J. A. McKinstry, arriving at Jefferson City, the State capital, on the 28th of the month. There he established Camp Lillie, and carefully made his preparations for the intended movement against Price, who, on the 30th of September, had abandoned Lexington in a retreat toward Arkansas.

On the 11th of October, Fremont had reached Tipton, where his force was encamped on the Fairgrounds, and on the 15th, after a two-days march over the dusty prairies to Haw Creek, he arrived at a place called Warsaw, situated on the Osage River. Here he was soon joined by a squadron of cavalry, called the "Prairie Scouts," who, under the bold leadership of Major Frank J. White, had succeeded in releasing the Federal captives whom Price had left at Lexington in charge of five hundred of his men, many of which latter White had made prisoners, and brought along with the released Federal soldiers.

From Warsaw, Fremont's force proceeded in the direction of Springfield by way of Bolivar, the heavily-swollen streams compelling the army and its guns to make use of a flatboat and of a temporary bridge, whilst Fremont's Hussars and the rest of the cavalry had to cross the Osage River by fording it at different points.

FRANK J. WHITE

Fremont continued in pursuit of Price, and on the 22d of October had reached Pomme de Terre, a small town located about fifty miles north of Springfield, Mo., where he encamped. Learning that a Confederate force had just been established at the latter place, he ordered Major Charles Zagonyi, commanding his Bodyguard of cavalry, to take it, with Major White's "Prairie Scouts," on a reconnoissance, and to capture the Confederate camp if deemed practicable.

October, 1861.

The Bodyguard and "Scouts," numbering together 300 men, advanced, October 25th, to within a few miles of Springfield, where they were informed by some foragers that the Confederate force in that city was nearly 2,000 strong. Zagonyi had then with him only 150 men, for Major White had been unable to march his little band as rapidly as the others; but, rather than delay and await their arrival, Zagonyi determined to meet the disparity in forces, and to make an immediate attack. Turning around to his men, he exclaimed: "Follow me and do like me! Comrades, the hour of danger has come. Your first battle is before you. The enemy is two thousand strong, and we are but one hundred and fifty. It is possible no man will come back. If any of you would turn back, you can do so now!" Cheers were the only response that came from the men, so eager were they for the encounter. Then Zagonyi shouted: "I will lead you! Let the watchword be, '*The Union and Fremont!*' Draw sabres! By the right flank—quick trot—march!" and away they dashed, down a narrow lane, into the open, across a small brook, and over a rail-fence, to meet the fire of a strong line of infantry, flanked on the left by a body of cavalry. On they go, notwithstanding that many have fallen

COOKING IN CAMP-KITCHEN OF THE FREMONT DRAGOONS

GENERAL FREMONT'S ARMY ON ITS MARCH FROM TIPTON TO WARSAW OCTOBER 13TH, 1861.

FREMONT'S HUSSARS [illegible] THE OSAGE RIVER [illegible]

FEDERAL TROOPS OF FREMONT'S ARMY FORAGING IN MISSOURI.

under the heavy fire pouring in upon them, until, at a given signal, Lieutenant Majthenyi and thirty men engage the Confederate cavalry, and Zagonyi's command, "In open order — charge!" is executed. Then the engagement is at its height.

The horsemen dash fiercely into the force against them, cutting to the right and left, and in a few moments the enemy is forced to break away in wild disorder, both in the immediate front and in the direction where Majthenyi had first engaged them. Just as this takes place, Captain McNaughton reaches the [illegible] with fifty men of Major White's force. The order to follow is given, and all dash ahead for a second charge through the woods, overtaking many of the fugitives there, as well as in the streets of Springfield and in the forest beyond the city, returning only when further pursuit appeared useless.

Zagonyi's brave followers suffered a loss of eighty-four dead and wounded in this engagement, which, for the boldness of its undertaking and the rapidity of its execution under the singularly great disparity of numbers, certainly has but few parallels in any history.

Upon hearing of this truly brilliant achievement, the army was wild with enthusiasm, and when Zagonyi's men reached camp, they met with the ovation they richly deserved on all sides, besides receiving due mention in general orders from the commanding general.

The troops behaved admirably during their repeated marches, through good and bad weather, and notwithstanding the fact that "hard tack" alone had, for quite a while, necessarily to be put up with.

Only once, while passing through Berryville, were they successful in foraging on a large scale. Quite an ext[illegible] poultry yard belonging to Southern sympathizers was the scene of the attack, whence, after a spirited, somewhat humorous and prolonged contest, all the innocents were captured, the living as well as the dead, and borne away in triumph.

On the 1st of November, 1861, part of Fremont's army lay on the Ozark Hills around Springfield, and lost no time in arranging for the long-anticipated attack on Price; but on the following day an order was received directing him to turn over his command to General David Hunter. The latter being then some distance in the rear, did not arrive until midnight of the 3d, while renewed preparations were again being made for the attack. These, however, were subsequently countermanded. Fremont and his staff returned to St. Louis early on the 4th of November, and by the middle of the latter month the Federal army was ordered to retreat from Springfield in the same direction

JUSTUS McKINSTRY.

JOHN CHARLES FREMONT.

Born in Savannah, Ga., January 21st, 1813. His father, who had emigrated to Georgia from France, died when he was four years old, providing to give him a good education. He graduated from the Charleston (S. C.) College in 1830; taught mathematics and acquainted himself thoroughly with the science of engineering. In this he acquired distinction, and was recommended for service in the Mississippi survey. The Government

FEDERAL TROOPS LANDING ON THE KENTUCKY SHORE OPPOSITE CAIRO, ILL., FOR THE [illegible] OF [illegible] COL. HOLT.

appreciating his services, made him second lieutenant of engineers in 1838 in which capacity he was sent to make a survey of the Des Moines River.

In October, 1841, he eloped with and married Jessie, the daughter of United States Senator Thomas H. Benton, and [illegible] month of May [illegible] he was sent to [illegible] [illegible] explorations through the Rocky Mountains, which were completed in October in the same year, and [illegible] attracted a great deal of attention. These were [illegible], in 1843, by explorations through Oregon and along [illegible] Coast, during which he [illegible] the [illegible] geographical position of many important points in the [illegible] unknown.

In 1845 he was appointed captain by brevet, and again [illegible] to the Pacific Coast on a more extended exploration than any of the previous ones. During the last [illegible], he encountered many severe hardships, and was once [illegible] in his advance by the Mexican General [illegible], whom he defeated, after quite a prolong resistance.

He was elected Governor of California by the settlers in 1847 and received promotion to lieutenant-colonel in the army on the 14th of January, 1847. During his occupation of the executive chair [illegible] the treaty [illegible] the Mexican [illegible] by which the California Territory became a part of the United States.

On the breaking out of the Mexican War he was on the [illegible] the army; but a chance of mutiny [illegible] preferred against him, he was court-martialed, and [illegible] to be dismissed from the service, a sentence which the President, however, refused to enforce. Fremont, nevertheless, resigned his position in the army, and, toward the end of the year 1848, he made another exploration, during which he surveyed a new road from the Mississippi to San Francisco, and successfully traversed the country of the Apaches, Comanches and other tribes, arriving at Sacramento on the Pacific Coast, in one hundred days from Santa Fe, January, 1849.

He served as United States Senator from California, 1849 [illegible], and in 1853 made another exploration of the Pacific. In 1856 he was a nominated for President as the first candidate of the newly formed Republican party, but was defeated by the election of James Buchanan. He returned to [illegible] in 1858, and remained on the Coast until the early part of 1861, when he made another trip to Europe in order to effect the sale of the large property he had acquired many years before in Mariposa, Cal., in which tract the celebrated Yosemite Valley and Big Trees are located.

While abroad, he was notified of his appointment as a major-general of volunteers, and immediately returned to the United States, receiving [illegible], July [illegible], 1861, the assignment of the Department of the West, with headquarters at St. Louis.

On his arrival at St. Louis, November 8th, he was given an enthusiastic reception, receiving an address of welcome from the citizens, who had organized for him a large torchlight procession, and had united in the public presentation to him of a [illegible] costing $1,000, inscribed:

TO THE PATHFINDER,
FROM THE [illegible] THE WEST.

On the 11th of March, 1862, he was placed in charge of the Mountain Department. He was [illegible] nominated for President by the Cleveland Convention in 1864, but soon withdrew his name from the candidacy.

He was made Governor of Arizona in 1878 and is now (1884) living in retirement on Staten Island.

GENERAL PRENTISS'S DIVISION ON ITS MARCH FROM IRONTON TO CAPE GIRARDEAU GATHERING SECESH OATS.

JUSTUS McKINSTRY.

Born in New York, from which State he was appointed a cadet in the Military Academy at West Point in 1833; entered the army, on his graduation, as second lieutenant of the First Infantry, made [illegible] commissary of subsistence in September, 1838; promoted to a first lieutenancy in April, 1841, and to an assistant quartermastership, with the rank of captain, in March 1847; was placed in command of a company of volunteers during the Mexican War, and promoted to be a brevet-major "for gallant and meritorious conduct in the battles of Contreras and Churubusco."

When at the breaking out of the Civil War, General Fremont was placed in command of the Department of the West, with headquarters at St. Louis and when by reason of the continued serious disturbances on the part of Southern sympathizers, it was found necessary to place St. Louis under martial law, McKinstry was [illegible] to the post of provost marshal. During his term of office he was made a brigadier-general. He fulfilled admirably the requirements of the position at a time when the execution of the laws, and of all official acts was attended with no small degree of danger. By his [illegible], some of the most noted Southern [illegible] and [illegible] of the peace were arrested, thus preventing the possibility of serious outbreaks. He also caused the suspension of the *Evening Missourian*, *Morning Herald*, and *War Bulletin*, charged with the publication of disloyal articles; his most important act, however, while holding office being the execution of a deed of emancipation to two slaves belonging to Thomas L. Snead, of St. Louis, the latter having, in the words of Fremont's proclamation of August 31st, 1861, "taken an active part with the enemies of the country."

EXPERIMENTAL PRACTICE IN PONTONING—CONSTRUCTING ROPE SUSPENSION

A PONTON.
ROPE BRIDGE.
CAMP ALEXANDER. WASHINGTON D.C.

CAPE GIRARDEAU, OCCUPIED BY THE FEDERAL TROOPS, UNDER GENERAL U. S. GRANT, SEPTEMBER 8TH, 1861.

EARTHWORKS ERECTED BY THE FEDERAL TROOPS TO DEFEND PADUCAH.
FROM A SKETCH BY W. R. McCOMAS.

CAPTURE OF PADUCAH.

THE seizure, by the Confederate General Polk, of Columbus and Hickman, Ky., on the 4th of September, and the consequent threatening of Paducah, made it necessary for the Federals to at once occupy the latter place, situated about forty-seven miles east of Cairo, and occupying an important strategic position at the confluence of the Ohio and Tennessee Rivers.

September, 1861.

The City of Cairo had been reinforced and taken possession of by General Fremont on the first of the previous month, and was then the centre of a district lately placed in command of General Grant, who, on Thursday, the 5th of September, was in readiness for the advance.

He had ordered the embarkation, on the transports *G. W. Graham* and *W. H. B.*, of both the Ninth and the Twelfth Illinois Infantry Regiments, then commanded respectively by Major Phillips and Colonel McArthur, with four guns belonging to Smith's Chicago Artillery, under Lieutenant Willard, and on the evening of the last-named date he left Cairo, preceded and followed by the gunboats *Tyler*, Commodore Rodgers, and the *Conestoga*, Captain Phelps, reaching Paducah early the following day.

The troops were immediately landed, and marched throughout the city, the Ninth Regiment finally locating in the depot at the northern terminus of the Mobile and Ohio Railway, and the Twelfth Regiment being quartered at the Marine Hospital. There was found at the depot a large quantity of military stores of all kinds, valued at about $20,000, and much important mail matter at the post-office, all of which was seized.

Major Phillips then took five companies of the infantry and Lieutenant Willard's guns to a point nearly seven miles distant on the railroad track, where a large bridge and trestlework were burned, and meeting no opposition on the line, returned to the depot.

In the meantime, Commodore Rodgers had seized the telegraph-office, and hearing that some Confederate vessels were expected down the Tennessee River, he had ordered Captain Phelps to take the *Conestoga* on a reconnoissance. The latter had proceeded but a short distance when a Confederate steamer was seen endeavoring to escape. Chase was immediately given, and the steamer was soon run ashore and captured, being found to contain a very valuable cargo of tobacco. The following day, the *Conestoga* captured two more vessels, making three in all, which were afterward taken to Cairo.

OCCUPATION OF PADUCAH BY GENERAL GRANT, SEPTEMBER 6TH, 1861.

ACCIDENT ON THE OHIO AND MISSISSIPPI RAILROAD, SEPTEMBER 17TH, [illegible]. THE NINETEENTH ILLINOIS LOSING ONE HUNDRED MEN KILLED AND WOUNDED.

With the view to making Paducah a permanent centre, the troops began, very shortly after their arrival, to strengthen the approaches to the town, and with the aid of the Eighth and the Forty-first Illinois, as well as the American Zouave, Regiments, which arrived on the 7th, constructed earthworks and other defences in every direction. On the 19th of September they commenced building a pontoon bridge across the Ohio River, by strongly anchoring together a number of coal-barges sent from Cincinnati. The bridge had a total length of nearly 6,000 feet; was made in two sections, connected at Low Island, also called the Tow Head; and was put together so rapidly, that it required but four days for its completion.

Grant followed the capture of Paducah by that of the town of Smithland, situated close by the mouth of the Cumberland River, and, having left General Charles F. Smith in command of Paducah, soon completed preparations which led to a successful encounter at Belmont, on the Mississippi River.

THE BATTLE OF BELMONT.

Ulysses S. Grant, while in command of the district around Cairo, had taken military possession of Paducah, at the mouth of the Tennessee River, and of Smithland, located higher up near the mouth of the Cumberland River, thus closing two important points of supply to the Confederates from the Ohio River.

Upon hearing, early in November, 1861, that the Confederate General Polk was about sending reinforcements to General Price from Columbus, Grant thought it might be well merely to threaten the latter place by an attack on Belmont, situated on the opposite side of the Mississippi River, since, with his comparatively small force, it seemed useless for him to attempt the capture of so strongly garrisoned a post as Columbus, or even to take Belmont alone, as it practically lay under the guns of the former place. He ordered General Charles F. Smith to move from Paducah southward on Mayfield with one column, and to within a few miles of Columbus with a second column, while a small force was sent to Ellicott's Mills, twelve miles north of Columbus, and he himself started from Cairo late on Wednesday, the 6th, with 2,850 men, taken from General John A. McClernand's brigade. This force embraced the Seventh Iowa, Colonel Lamon; the Twenty-second Illinois, Colonel H. Dougherty; the Twenty-seventh Illinois, Colonel N. B. Buford; the Thirtieth Illinois, Colonel Philip B. Fouke; the Thirty-first Illinois, Colonel John A. Logan; Captain Ezra Taylor's Chicago battery of six guns, and the three companies of cavalry under Captain Delano, Captain J. J. Dollin and Lieutenant J. R. Catlin.

November, 1861.

They had been taken by the steam-transports *Belle, Memphis, Montgomery* and *Scott*, conveyed by the gunboats *Lexington*, Captain Stembel, and *Tyler*, Captain Walke, and lay all night at Island Number One, toward the Kentucky shore, about eleven miles south of Cairo, thus leading the Confederates to believe that Columbus was their intended destination.

A. Landing of Federal troops. *B*. Route taken by General Grant. *C*. First line of battle. *D*. Second line of battle. *E*. Cornfield. *F*. Lakes. *G*. Fallen timber. *H*. Drill-ground and Belmont. *I*. Columbus. *J*. Hills. *K*. Battery. *L*. Cavalry route. *M*. Colonel Buford's route. *N*. Colonel Logan's regiment. *O*. Thirtieth Illinois. *P*. Seventh Iowa. *Q*. Twenty-second Illinois. *R*. Twenty-seventh Illinois. *S*. Captain Delano's cavalry. *T*. Taylor's battery. *U*. Confederate tents. *X*. Landing of Confederate reinforcements. (Distance from *A* to *I*, three miles and a half.)

PLAN OF THE BATTLE OF BELMONT, MO.

Early the next morning, the troops were landed across the river at Hunter's Point, three miles above Belmont, and just out of range of the Columbus batteries. Two companies of the Seventh Iowa, and three companies of the Twenty-second Illinois, under Captain Detrick, were left to guard the transports, while the remainder marched on in two brigades toward Belmont, and the gunboats proceeded in the same direction.

The first brigade, under General McClernand, consisted of the Twenty-seventh, Thirtieth and Thirty-first Illinois Regiments, Taylor's battery and Dollin's cavalry.

The second brigade, under Colonel H. Dougherty, embraced seven companies of his own regiment, the Twenty-second Illinois, eight companies of the Seventh Iowa Regiment, and the other two companies of cavalry.

The centre of the attacking column was given to Colonel Fouke, while its right lay in charge of Colonel Buford, and Colonel Logan led its left.

Upon discovering the real design of the Federal commander, General Polk had sent over three regiments under General Pillow to reinforce those holding Belmont. The Confederates had marched out of their camp and attacked the advancing columns, but had soon to fall back before the entire force which Grant had thrown out as skirmishers. They were driven inside their encampment, after a series of hand-to-hand encounters, and especially a sharp cavalry engagement on the right of the Federal line.

The Confederate force, under General Pillow, now facing Grant, was composed of the Thirteenth Arkansas, and the Twelfth, Thirteenth, Twenty-first and Twenty-second Tennessee Regiments, under Colonels Tappen, Russell, Wright, Pickett and Freeman, supported by Beltzhoover's battery, in charge of Captain Watson, and a battalion of cavalry under Lieutenant-colonel Miller.

These troops now lay under cover of the Columbus guns, and could receive reinforcements by transports; but, nothing daunted, the Federals moved on with determination, and in face of the terrific storm of shot and shell that soon followed from the other side of the river, as well as the steady fire directed from behind a range of several hundred yards of strong *abatis* made of lumber and slashed trees, they dashed forward, crowding fast ahead, until, in a final effort, the obstructions were scaled, the seven-gun battery was captured after a determined bayonet-charge, and the Confederates were forced to run under the river-bank.

Colonel Buford's force was the first inside the camp, where the Twenty-seventh Illinois Regiment immediately raised the stars and stripes, saluting the flag with round after round of cheers. The Federals could not, however, long remain exposed to the galling fire directed upon them from Columbus, and after burning the camp, as well as all that, from the want of wagons, they could not well carry away, they marched back toward the place at which they had landed in the morning.

The gunboats had, in the meantime, attacked the Confederate battery of twenty heavy guns, located on the Iron Banks, near Columbus, and two hundred feet above the river, and it was under the fire of this same battery that Grant's force pushed on. It was likewise subjected to attacks from several thousand fresh troops which Polk had meanwhile sent over under General Cheatham to a place between the camp and the transports; but after beating back some of Cheatham's troops on his flank, and a still more active detachment led by Colonel Mark on the rear, he reached the transports, and embarked under the protection of the gunboats.

At five o'clock that afternoon, the entire force was on its way to Cairo, where it arrived at ten o'clock in the evening, carrying with it two of Beltzhoover's heavy guns, some horses, arms, ammunition, and about two hundred prisoners.

The fight had lasted six hours, and resulted in a Confederate loss of 632, the killed including Colonel John V. Wright, of the Thirteenth Tennessee and Major Butler, of the Eleventh Louisiana Regiment. Their bodies were sent over to General Cheatham.

The Federals lost 607 men, the Seventh Iowa losing more than any other regiment. Major

EARTHWORK BATTERIES SURROUNDING PADUCAH, BUILT BY THE FEDERAL TROOPS

EXPLANATION: 1 Brigadier-general Grant and Staff directing the movements of the troops. 2. Brigadier-general McClernand leading the charge at the head of the Thirty-first Illinois. 3. Thirty-first Illinois, Colonel Logan. 4. Body of Lieutenant-colonel Wentz, Seventh Iowa. 5. Body of Captain Pulaski, Aide-de-Camp to McClernand, killed while leading the charge. 6. Caisson ordered to the field from the rear. 7. Twenty-seventh Illinois, Colonel Buford, taking the camp [illegible] of the Confederates. 8. Thirtieth Illinois, Colonel Fouke. [illegible] Twenty-second Illinois, Colonel Dougherty. 9. Light artillery, Captain Taylor. 10. Seventh Iowa, Colonel Lauman. 11. Captain Schwartz, Acting Chief of Artillery, taking the Confederate battery. 12. Watson's Louisiana field battery. 13. Confederate artillery-horses. 14. Battery [illegible] Columbus. 15. [illegible] 16. Confederate [illegible]

BATTLE OF BELMONT, MO., OPPOSITE COLUMBUS, KY., NOVEMBER 7TH, 1861.—FEDERAL FORCES COMMANDED BY U. S. GRANT; CONFEDERATE FORCES, BY LEONIDAS POLK

VIEW OF FORT LAFAYETTE, NEW YORK HARBOR, IN WHICH STATE PRISONERS WERE INCARCERATED.

McCherie, of the latter, and Colonel Dougherty, of the Twenty-second Illinois, were both very severely wounded, and taken prisoners. General Grant and General McClernand each had a horse shot under him. A second horse taken by McClernand being wounded and unmanageable, he mounted a gun that had just been captured, and from it rallied his men, displaying coolness and judgment that called forth admiration from all, and received public notice in the general order of the day following. General Grant said; "It has been my fortune to have been in all the battles fought in Mexico by Generals Scott and Taylor, save Buena Vista, and I never saw one more hotly contested, or where troops behaved with more gallantry."

FORT LAFAYETTE.

At the commencement of the Civil War, Fort Lafayette was designated by the State Department of the Federal Government as the place of detention for political prisoners.

It is situated at what is called the Narrows, which is the entrance proper to the Bay of New York; and, in conjunction with Fort Hamilton, situated on the bluff at its rear on the Long Island shore, as well as Fort Richmond on the opposite or Staten Island shore, formed at that period the main defense to New York Harbor.

Fort Lafayette was built on a shoal entirely surrounded by water, and about 350 yards from the mainland. Its armament consisted of two rows of heavy guns in bombproof casemates, besides a few guns *en barbette*. Owing to its peculiar quadrangular shape, it originally bore the name of Fort Diamond, being afterward changed as above in honour of the Marquis de Lafayette, who rendered such signal services to this country during the Revolution, and revisited this country in 1844.

During the progress of the Civil War, Fort Lafayette held a large number of prominent persons as political prisoners, many of whom, however, remained only until they were willing to take the oath of allegiance to the United States Government. Like in all arrests for political offenses, many innocent persons suffered.

From the list before us we give a few names:

James G. Berrett, Mayor of the City of Washington, D. C.; Pierce Butler, prominent citizen of Philadelphia, Pa.; Captain De Lagnel, Confederate States Navy, Alexandria, Va.; Joseph Howard, journalist, New York City; Algernon S. Sullivan, counselor-at-law, New York City; Marcus Cicero Stanley, journalist, New York City; Charles J. Faulkner, ex United States Minister to France; S. Barron, flag-officer in Confederate States Navy; W. S. G. Andrews, commanding Forts Hatteras and Clark; W. F. Martin, colonel Seventh Infantry, North Carolina Volunteers (prisoners at the capture of Hatteras Inlet); Charles P. Stone, brigadier-general in command of the Federal troops defeated at the battle of Ball's Bluff; A. D. Wharton, United States Navy, Tennessee; Robert Tansill, captain United States Marine Corps, Virginia; Thomas S. Wilson, lieutenant United States Marine Corps, Missouri; H. B. Claiborn and Hillary Cenas, midshipmen of the United States Marine Corps, New Orleans; and the crew and passengers of the schooner *Colonel Long*, captured by the *Jamestown*

LANDING STATE PRISONERS AT FORT LAFAYETTE.

RETREAT OF THE CONFEDERATE GARRISON, COMMANDED BY GENERAL DRAYTON.

RETREAT OF THE CONFEDERATE GARRISON, COMMANDED BY GENERAL DRAYTON, FROM FORT WALKER, DURING THE BOMBARDMENT BY THE FEDERAL FLEET, NOVEMBER 7th, 1861.

[illegible]

FORT WALKER, HILTON HEAD, PORT ROYAL HARBOR, S.C., UNDER BOMBARDMENT BY THE UNITED STATES FLEET, NOVEMBER 7TH, 1861.

SAMUEL FRANCIS DUPONT

BORN in 1803, at Bergen Point, N. J., four years after his parents had emigrated from France; appointed midshipman in the United States Navy by President Madison, December 19th, 1815; made his first cruise in the *Franklin*, under Commodore Stewart and Captain Ballard, in 1817; cruised in the West Indies with the *Warren*, 1836, and the *Perry*, 1848, and, two years later, commanded the *Congress*, belonging to the Pacific squadron. He was a member of the board which organized the naval school at Annapolis, in 1845, and was for many years actively connected with its Board of Examination. He was also one of the organizers of the present lighthouse system, and has been always closely identified with all the reforms established at various times in the navy.

When, at San Francisco, in 1846, he was ordered to the *Cyane*, which figured prominently on the California and Mexican coasts during the war with Mexico. It was on this vessel that he took General Fremont and his followers to San Diego, being the first to enter that harbor, and his conduct during the entire war was such as to call forth an eloquent panegyric by Senator Clayton, in the United States Senate chamber at Washington. He remained on shore duty until 1857, when he was ordered to China in the *Minnesota*, and not long after his return was appointed commandant of the Philadelphia Navy Yard. This post he held during the trying period of 1860-1, when he ably exerted his powerful influence in every possible way for the benefit of the Northern cause. He was a member of the board of navy and army officers convened at Washington, in July, 1861, for the purpose of establishing a naval rendezvous in the South, and when the very extensive expedition to Port Royal was decided upon, he was placed at its head. This, it will be remembered, consisted of seventy-seven vessels of all descriptions, and carried a land force of about 15,000 men, under General T. W. Sherman. The services of the latter were not, however, called into requisition.

The expedition left Hampton Roads on the 29th of October following, and after experiencing very severe weather and some losses, reached its destination on the 4th of November. On Thursday, the 7th, the fleet engaged Forts Walker and Beauregard, commanding the Port Royal entrance, and after a vigorous exchange of fire silenced both earthworks, and occupied them the same afternoon, thus establishing the first foothold on South Carolina soil held by Northern troops since the fall of Fort Sumter. This was followed by the occupation of Beaufort and of Big Tybee Island before the end of the year, as well as by the capture of Port Royal Ferry, January 1st, and the occupation of Fort Clinch, and of Fernandina, Brunswick, Jacksonville, Fort Marion, St. Augustine, and other localities in Florida. By this means Commodore Dupont established a rigid blockade of the Southern coast, pushing his vessels into the many bays, inlets and rivers of the States of South Carolina, Georgia and Florida, and stopping a source of supply that promised speedy recognition from foreign powers.

On the 7th of April, 1863, Rear-admiral Dupont engaged Fort Sumter with nine ironclads for one hour and a half, during which time he fully tested the defensive powers of the fort; and, with the loss of the monitor *Keokuk*, sunk in the action, he withdrew, convinced that Fort Sumter and the defenses of Charleston could not be taken by a purely naval attack, unsupported by the co-operation of a land force.

In July, 1863, Dupont was relieved from the command of the South Atlantic fleet; he returned to his home at Bergen Point, N. J. where he died, on the 23d of June, 1865.

SAMUEL FRANCIS DUPONT.

PORT ROYAL.

CAPTURE OF PORT ROYAL ENTRANCE, BEAUFORT, BIG TYBEE ISLAND, AND PORT ROYAL FERRY.

ON the very day, and at about the same hour, that General Grant was advancing on Belmont, the most powerful naval expedition that had ever been organized in this country was forcing its way into the entrance to Port Royal, on the coast of South Carolina.

NOVEMBER, 1861.

A joint board of navy and army officers, held in Washington, had decided that the above locality answered best the existing requirements for a naval rendezvous, where vessels on the way to or from blockading squadrons could coal, and take refuge in case of need. After several months' preparation the expedition was fitted out under the auspices of both the navy and the army departments, and on the 21st of October, 1861, sailed from Annapolis, Md., for Hampton Roads, whence it departed, under sealed orders, eight days later.

The fleet, including the transports, coal, and other vessels, consisted of seventy-seven all told. It was under the command of Commodore Samuel F. Dupont, and embraced the steam frigate *Wabash*, flag-ship, Commander C. R. P. Rogers; and the gunboats *Augusta*, Commander E. G. Parrott; *Bienville*, Commander Charles Steedman; *Curlew*, Lieutenant Commanding P. G. Watmough; *Florida*, Captain J. R. Goldsborough; *Isaac P. Smith*, Captain J. W. A. Nicholson; *Mohican*, Commander L. W. Godon; *Ottawa*, Lieutenant Commanding R. H. Wyman; *Pawnee*, Lieutenant Commanding T. H. Stevens; *Pocahontas*, Captain Percival Drayton; *Penguin*, Lieutenant Commanding F. A. Budd; *Pembina*, Lieutenant Commanding J. P. Bankhead; *R. B. Forbes*, Captain H. S. Newcomb; *Seminole*, Commander J. P. Gillis; *Seneca*, Lieutenant Commanding Daniel Ammen; *Unadilla*, Lieutenant Commanding N. Collins; besides twenty-three transports, two steam tugs, twenty-six sailing vessels, and some steamboats, ferryboats, etc.

To these were added the *Susquehanna*, Captain J. L. Lardner, which Commodore Dupont sent for as the fleet was passing Charleston; and the *Vandalia*, Lieutenant Commanding J. W. A. Nicholson, which joined the fleet from the blockading squadron off Savannah.

The land forces were under the command of Brigadier-general T. W. Sherman, and was divided into three brigades. The first brigade, under General Egbert L. Viele, comprised the Forty-sixth, Forty-seventh and Forth-eighth New York Regiments, Colonels Rudolph Rosa, Henry Moore and James H. Perry, the Third New Hampshire Regiment, Colonel E. W. Fellows, and the Eighth Maine Regiment, Colonel Lee Strickland. The second brigade, under General Isaac I. Stevens, comprised the Eighth Michigan Regiment, Colonel William M. Fenton; the Fiftieth Pennsylvania and the Pennsylvania "Roundhead" Volunteers, Colonels B. C. Christ and David Leasure; and the Seventy-ninth New York Regiment, Lieutenant-colonel William H. Noble. The third brigade, under General Horatio Gates Wright, comprised the Fourth New Hampshire, Sixth and Seventh Connecticut, and the Ninth Maine Regiment, Colonels Thomas J. Whipple, James L. Chatfield, A. H. Terry, and Richworth Rich.

In addition to the above were the Third Rhode Island and Twenty-first Massachusetts Regiments, as well as the New York volunteer engineer battalion, to which no place had as yet been assigned.

The fleet had very fine weather and a calm sea until after it had passed the much dreaded Cape Hatteras, when an unusually severe storm set in, and so completely scattered the vessels, that, on the morning of Saturday, the 2d of November, but one of them could be seen from the flagship.

NOVEMBER, 1861.

It was afterward found that four of the transports had been lost, and that two gunboats had saved themselves by throwing some of their guns overboard, whilst one of the steamers and two of the ferry-boats had been compelled to go

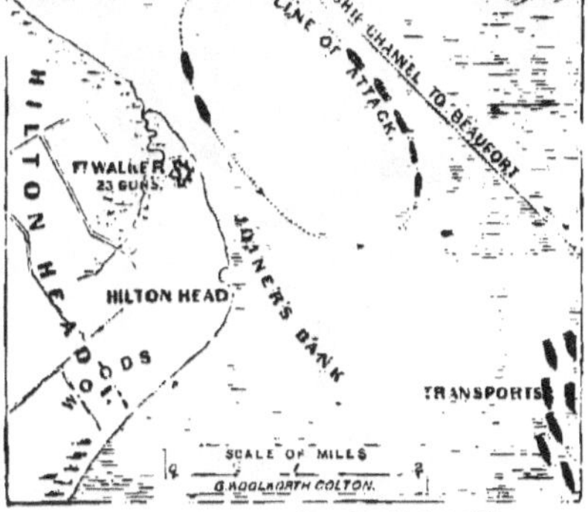

PLAN OF THE NAVAL BATTLE, PORT ROYAL HARBOR.

LANDING OF UNITED STATES TROOPS AT FORT WALKER, AFTER THE BOMBARDMENT, NOVEMBER 7th, 1861.

back to Fortress Monroe. The four lost transports were the *Peerless*, which sank after colliding with the *Star of the South*, sent to her assistance, and whose crew was saved by the gunboat *Mohican*; the *Osceola* and the *Union*, both of which went ashore, and had all on board made prisoners; and the *Governor*, whose 350 marines, under Major John George Reynolds, with the exception of a corporal and six men, were saved by the frigate *Sabine*, Captain Ringgold, which happened to be [illegible] in view of its signals of distress.

The sealed orders which had been [illegible] each vessel of the expedition directed it to the rendezvous off Port Royal, where the *Wabash* and many others anchored on the morning of November 4th.

Additional arrivals followed in time. [illegible] were made under the united direction of Mr. Boutelle, of the Coast Survey, and of Commander Charles Davis, fleet captain and chief of [illegible] commander's staff, and on the 5th November a reconnoissance of the Confederate works was made in force by Commander John Rodgers, of the [illegible], and by General Wright, with the gunboats *Curlew*, *R. B. Forbes*, *Ottawa* and *Seneca*.

These had not proceeded far up the channel when they were met by four Confederate steamers, with which a lively exchange of fire soon took place, they retreating as the Federal gunboats advanced toward the batteries on Hilton Head and at Bay Point opposite.

When within range, the batteries opened on the Federals, as was naturally expected, and another engagement of nearly an hour ensued, when the object of the reconnoissance having been accomplished, the gunboats hauled off.

It was decided to attack the forts the following day, but a high wind having come up, this was found impossible, and it was not until the 7th

Nov. 7, 1861.

that it could be properly made. The forced delay in commencing operations had enabled the Confederates to strengthen their defenses. Earthworks had been put up wherever practicable.

The largest of all, named Fort Walker, stood on Hilton Head, contained twenty-four guns, and was commanded by General T. F. Drayton, the brother of Captain Percival Drayton,

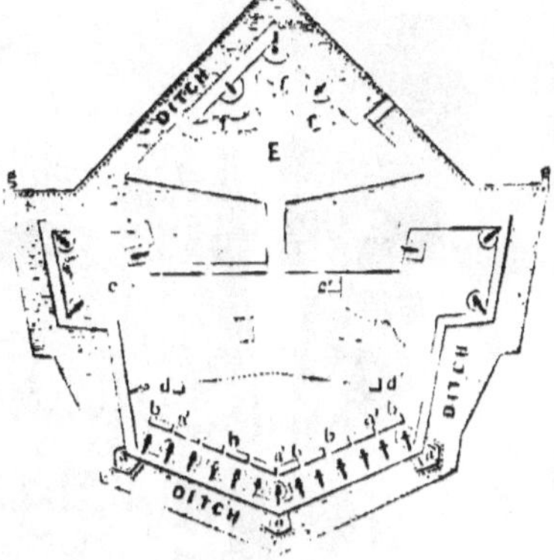

PLAN OF FORT WALKER.

DESTRUCTION OF GUNS AT THE CONFEDERATE ARSENAL, BEAUFORT, S. C., BY CAPTAIN AMMAN, OF THE U. S. GUNBOAT "SENECA."

VIEW OF THE INTERIOR OF FORT BEAUREGARD, ON BAY POINT, OPPOSITE FORT WALKER

of the gunboat *Pocahontas*. General Drayton had under him Colonel De Saussure's Fifteenth South Carolina Regiment, three companies of Hayward's Ninth South Carolina Regiment, four companies of Colonel Dunovant's Twelfth South Carolina Regiment, under Major Jones, Captain Berry's Georgia Volunteers, Captain Reed's battery, and two companies of Wagner's South Carolina Artillery.

The second largest earthwork was called Fort Beauregard, and stood at Bay Point. It was under the command of Colonel R. G. M. Dunovant, and held twenty guns, with 640 men belonging to Dunovant's regiment and to the Beaufort Volunteer Artillery. The other earthworks held six guns. The Confederates had, besides, a small squadron of eight steamers, under command of Commodore Josiah Tatnall.

Early on the 7th of November the fleet advanced in battle order, the *Wabash* at the head. Dupont's plan of attack was to pass up between Forts Beauregard and Walker, receiving and returning the fire of both; then to turn around, and, with a flanking squadron provided against an attack in

EFFECT OF THE SHELLS ON THE FLEEING CONFEDERATE FORCES IN THE WOODS.

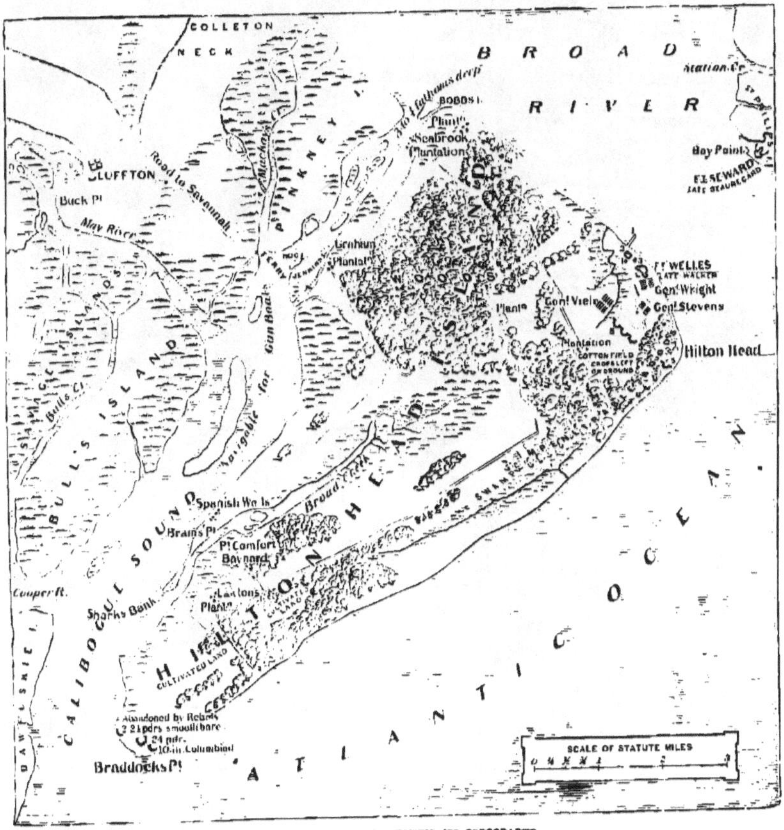

MAP OF HILTON HEAD, SHOWING ITS TOPOGRAPHY.

GATHERING PACKING AND SHIPPING THE COTTON CROP CAPT

GATHERING PACKING AND SHIPPING THE COTTON CROP CAPTURED BY THE FEDERAL ARMY ON THE SEA ISLANDS, AT PORT ROYAL S.C

GENERAL STEVENS'S BRIGADE TAKING POSSESSION OF BEAUFORT, S. C., ON THE EVENING OF DECEMBER 5TH, 1861.

SUNKEN HULKS TO PREVENT THE ENTRANCE OF FEDERAL VESSELS INTO SOUTHERN HARBORS.

SKIRMISH, NEAR BEAUFORT, S. C., BETWEEN CONFEDERATE CAVALRY AND FEDERAL PICKETS.

GOVERNMENT WORKS ERECTED ON HILTON HEAD I

BATTLE OF PEA RIDGE, MARCH 6TH, 1862.—FEDERAL FORCES UNDER GENERALS CURTIS, SIGEL

FROM A SKETCH BY A

GOVERNMENT WORKS ERECTED ON HILTON HEAD [illegible] BY THE [illegible] FORCES UNDER T. W. SHERMAN.

BATTLE OF PEA RIDGE, MARCH 8th, [illegible]—FEDERAL FORCES UNDER GENERALS CURTIS, SIGEL [illegible] CONFEDERATE ARMY COMMANDED BY GENERALS VAN DORN, PRICE AND McCULLOCH.
[illegible]

SCENE IN THE MILITARY MARKET AT BEAUFORT, S. C.

From a Sketch by W. T. Crane.

COLLISION BETWEEN THE STEAM TRANSPORTS "STAR OF THE SOUTH" AND THE "PEERLESS," IN THE GREAT STORM OF NOVEMBER 2D, 1861.

rear from Tatnall's steamers, to engage Fort Walker in front, after having enfiladed its water-faces. This was carried out to the letter. The firing began a little before ten o'clock, and continued incessantly, until, at half-past one, signal was given that both forts had been abandoned.

The firing of the fleet had been made at very close quarters since noon, and evidences of its terrible effect were manifest when the forts were afterward taken possession of. Numbers of dead and dying lay amidst dismounted and shattered guns in all directions, the hospital building at Fort Walker being shot through and through in many places.

General Drayton's force, as was afterward shown, had been obliged to abandon everything, and retreat hastily across an open space that lay for a distance of nearly a mile between the fort and some woods in the direction of Bluffton, whilst the men at Fort Beauregard had retreated to St. Helena, Cat and Port Royal Islands.

The transfer on shore of all the troops, who had unwillingly remained merely spectators of the engagement, was completed the same evening.

The loss of the fleet was eight killed and twenty-three wounded. None of the vessels were permanently damaged, though the *Pawnee* received ... shots, the *Bienville* five, and the *Wabash* was struck as many as thirty-four times, and made to leak badly.

The reoccupation of South Carolina soil was cause for great rejoicing throughout the North, and celebrations were rendered the more extensive when, by a general order thanking the commanders of the expedition, the Secretaries of the Navy and Army directed that a salute be fired from each navy yard in honor of the event.

General Sherman set about fortifying Hilton Head and Bay Point, Fort Walker being called Fort Welles, and Fort Beauregard named Fort Seward, while Commodore Dupont organized armed expeditions throughout the islands, which proved everywhere successful.

On the 9th of November, the City of Beaufort was captured, and its arsenal subsequently destroyed by the crew of the *Seneca*, and on the 25th of the same month Big Tybee Island, at the entrance to the Savannah River, was also taken possession of, and held in aid of the blockading squadron. All this was done without meeting any resistance whatever, the only stand made, in fact, by the Confederates being at Port Royal Ferry, when, as late as the 31st of December, 1861, an expedition was dispatched to destroy their earthworks at that place.

It was understood that they had some 8,000 men there under Generals Gregg and Pope. Commander C. R. P. Rogers took with him the *Ellen*, *Ottawa*, *Pembina*, *Seneca*, one ferryboat, and four of the large boats belonging to the *Wabash*, each carrying a twelve-pounder, and was joined by General Stevens, with the Forty-seventh, Forty-eighth and Seventy-ninth New York, the Eighth Michigan, and the Fifteenth and One Hundredth Pennsylvania Regiments.

While some of the vessels ascended Broad River and entered Whale Creek, the land force was carried on the other side through the Coosaw River, meeting near the Ferry, where, early the next morning, they attacked the enemy, doing quick work.

The Eighth Michigan Regiment was deployed as skirmishers, and soon came upon a masked battery, which, after a very bitter contest, was silenced with the aid of the Seventy-ninth New York and of the gunboats. These kept pouring a hot fire into the woods, which soon caused the Confederates to fall back, while another determined attack on the part of the Fiftieth Pennsylvania Regiment, and the howitzers in the *Wabash* boats, completed the task.

The abandoned works were at once taken possession of by the Federals, who returned to Beaufort, after having burned and demolished everything of any importance in the vicinity.

GRAVES OF THE OFFICERS AND MEN OF THE FEDERAL FORCES KILLED AT PORT ROYAL.

MORNING DETAIL—THE FOURTH NEW HAMPSHIRE VOLUNTEERS GOING TO THEIR WORK ON THE FORTIFICATIONS AT HILTON HEAD.
FROM A SKETCH BY W. T. CHASE.

RECONNOITERING DETACHMENTS OF BANKS'S DIVISION — HYATTSTOWN, MD., IN THE DISTANCE.

GENERAL BANKS IN MARYLAND AND THE SHENANDOAH VALLEY.

On the 27th of July, 1861, General N. P. Banks was succeeded by General John A. Dix in the command of the Department of Pennsylvania, with headquarters at Baltimore, and was appointed to the command of the Department of the Shenandoah, relieving General Robert Patterson, who had just been honorably discharged from the service.

General Banks set about organizing the forces under his command, and at the time of the battle of Ball's Bluff had them well stationed on the line of the Maryland side of the Potomac River, extending between Darnestown and Williamsport. Here they remained, successfully doing their share in guarding the Capital and State against all possible incursions from the neighboring Confederates.

One of the positions held by some of the forces under General Banks lay at Hyattstown, a beautiful little village situated in Montgomery County, Md., about thirty-five miles west of Washington. Here took place the great review of General Thomas's large force by the commanding general and his full staff, and from this locality date many notable reconnoissances, especially by the cavalry detachments, which proved of great value in the subsequent advance upon Harper's Ferry.

The latter was effected under great difficulties and hardships, but fortunately without the loss of life that might well have occurred had not the roads and the positions of the opposing forces been studiously looked into, especially while encamped

IMPROMPTU FIELD-OVENS OF THE NINETEENTH NEW YORK VOLUNTEERS, BANKS'S DIVISION.

GRAND REVIEW OF GENERAL THOMAS'S BRIGADE, IN WESTERN MARYLAND, BY GENERAL BANKS AND STAFF.

BIVOUAC OF THE FIELD AND STAFF OFFICERS OF THE TWELFTH MASSACHUSETTS, NEAR HYATTSTOWN, MD.

at Hyattstown. Added to the unusually heavy roads was the severity of the weather, to encounter which the troops were not suitably prepared. Their march through the thick woods was made under a chilling rainstorm, which made the narrow roads so slippery that horses were, in many instances, unable to pull the wagons after experiencing a number of falls. The men of the Twelfth Massachusetts Infantry Regiment, among others, were for that reason compelled to haul their own baggage-train through much of the way, and, greatly wearisome in consequence, were glad enough to rest for the night in the open wherever chance led them, the officers rejoicing, after the heavy march, in the unusual and comparatively fine, though not very roomy, quarters afforded by a few haystacks. In the excitement of the moment, even the necessarily limited rations were forgotten; content were they to

GENERAL NATHANIEL P. BANKS AND STAFF

MILITARY EXECUTION OF A PRIVATE OF THE LINCOLN CAVALRY FOR DESI

MILITARY EXECUTION OF A PRIVATE OF THE LINCOLN CAVALRY, FOR DESERTION AND ATTEMPTED COMMUNICATION WITH THE ENEMY, DECEMBER 13th, 1861

NORTH BATTERY OF THE CONFEDERATES, AT SHIPPING POINT, LOOKING UP THE POTOMAC RIVER

UNSUCCESSFUL ATTEMPT OF THE CONFEDERATE TROOPS TO DESTROY DAM NO. 5, NEAR WILLIAMSPORT, MD.
From a Sketch by Captain Harry Bacon.

look forward to the time when, encamped anew, their impromptu field-ovens would give them the wished-for "fresh bread," which proved to them a staff indeed.

It was in February, 1862, that Banks's forces occupied the heights near Harper's Ferry. Later on, he took possession more particularly of Charleston, Leesburg and Winchester, his command being attacked at the last-named place on the 22d of March, 1862, as will be seen hereafter, by the forces under General "Stonewall" Jackson, which were repulsed, after a heavy loss.

BATTLE OF DRANESVILLE.

After the battle of Ball's Bluff, the town of Dranesville, from which General McCall had been ordered to retire, was occupied by Confederate troops, who sorely troubled the Federals and the loyal inhabitants throughout that section of the country by their frequent incursions on both the Maryland and Virginia borders. They had grown so bold in their demonstrations, and, by the middle of December, had pushed their picket lines so close

December, 1861.

to those of the Federals, that McCall obtained General McClellan's leave to attack them, and narrow their field of operations.

SHELLING THE CONFEDERATE CAVALRY FROM THE HEIGHTS OF GREAT FALLS, MD.

BATTLE OF DRANESVILLE, VA., DECEMBER [illegible] 1861.—FEDERALS [illegible] GENERAL M[illegible]; CONFEDERATES COMMANDED BY GENERAL J. E. B. STUART

A suitable opportunity for striking the intended blow did not, however, present itself until the 20th of that month, when Brigadier-general E. O. C. Ord was ordered to march on Dranesville, while the brigades of Generals J. F. Reynolds and George G. Meade were to support him at Difficult Creek.

General Ord's brigade, which, as it happened, was the only one engaged, consisted of the Sixth, Ninth, Tenth and Twelfth Pennsylvania Infantry, besides the Bucktail Rifles, two companies of the First Pennsylvania Cavalry, and Captain H. Easton's battery of four guns.

It had advanced to within two miles of Dranesville, with Lieutenant-colonel T. L. Kane's Bucktail Rifles, Colonel Bayard's cavalry and the artillery in the lead, when it was attacked by the Confederate force under General J. E. B. Stuart.

The latter's force embraced the First Kentucky, Sixth South Carolina, Tenth Alabama and Eleventh Virginia Infantry, under Colonels Taylor, Secrest, Forney and Garland, the Captain Cutts's four pieces of artillery, and Major Gordon's [illegible] of North Carolina Cavalry. [illegible] force had that morning set out from Dranesville with two hundred wagons on a foraging expedition.

The Eleventh Virginia and the Sixth South Carolina came suddenly upon the head of the line, and a regiment forced it back; but the Sixth and Ninth Pennsylvania coming up to its support, and Captain Easton's battery being placed upon a slight eminence that commanded Captain Cutts's artillery, the lost ground was fully made up, and the Confederates in turn gave way.

General McCall, who, with his staff, now reached the scene of action, found the enemy about making an effort to turn the Federal left, and immediately notified Colonel McCalmont of the danger threatening his men.

When the Confederate infantry and cavalry debouched from the woods, they were met by a combined fire from the Federal infantry and artillery, which compelled them to retire to their former position. They were at the same time repulsed by the right and centre, and under an enfilading fire directed by General Ord upon their right and rear, the entire Confederate line soon broke in disorder, and finally disappeared in a complete rout.

Upon reaching the position which had been occupied by the Confederate artillery, evidences were patent of the effective work done by Captain Easton's twelve and twenty-four pounders. The road was strewed with the dead and wounded men, as well as horses, many broken wagons, and the remains of one of the caissons that had been exploded by a shell.

The Confederates lost 43 killed and 143 wounded, besides some prisoners, the arms, ammunition and clothing abandoned in the flight, and full 16 wagon-loads of hay and 22 loads of corn, which General McCall collected and took away.

SOLDIERS OF THE TWELFTH MASSACHUSETTS DRAGGING THEIR BAGGAGE-TRAIN DURING A STORM.

A small part of the Confederate loss was due to the error committed by their First Kentucky Regiment firing upon the advancing Sixth South Carolina Regiment, supposing the latter to be Federals. Colonel Thomas Taylor, of the First Kentucky, soon afterward came upon another regiment, without marked distinguishing signs, and to guard against the possibility of another mistake, called out: "Who are you?"

"The colonel of the Ninth," was the reply.

"Of what Ninth?"

"The Ninth Pennsylvania," answered its colonel, S. F. Jackson, at the same time ordering a fire that did terrible execution.

Near the exploded caisson lay a wounded Confederate, who, while being carried to a neighboring house by Colonel J. H. Taggart's orders, exclaimed: "We whipped you at Manassas, but you have the best of us today."

Although severely wounded, he appeared in good spirits, and attracted much sympathy; but notwithstanding the care given him by those surrounding him, he passed away, after being placed on a mattress, and asking for one more cup of water to allay the great thirst that seemed to be devouring him.

The Federals lost 7 killed and 60 wounded. They pursued the enemy for nearly a mile, but unavailingly, and came back to the scene of conflict, whence General McCall ordered them to proceed on their return march the same evening. To have tried to maintain the position gained would have been useless, since but little ammunition remained, and the Confederates could, besides, at any moment, throw from Centreville immense bodies of troops between Dranesville and McCall's camp.

INCIDENT IN THE MARCH OF GENERAL BANKS'S DIVISION IN WESTERN MARYLAND

THE CAPTURE OF ROANOKE ISLAND.

ELIZABETH CITY, EDENTON, WINTON, PLYMOUTH.

The naval expeditions which had been dispatched from Hampton Roads had proved so successful that the Government decided upon organizing another one, in order to secure Roanoke Island, which was the key to two sounds protecting a large portion of North Carolina, as well as an important section of Virginia.

General Ambrose E. Burnside was appointed Commander-in-chief of the entire expedition. The naval portion embraced twenty light-draught vessels, carrying about fifty guns, viz.: the *Stars and Stripes*, *Louisiana*, *Hetzel*, *Underwriter*, *Delaware* and *Valley City*, under Lieutenants Commanding Worden, Murray, Davenport, Leffers, Quackenbush and Chaplin; the *Southfield* and *Hunchback*,

THE NAVAL BRIGADE, UNDER LIEUTENANT PERKINS, CONSTRUCTING THE MARINE BATTERY ON SHUTTER'S HILL, TO GUARD ALEXANDRIA, VA. AND TO COMMAND THE FAIRFAX ROAD.

under Acting Volunteer Lieutenants Commanding Behm and Colhoun; and the *Morse*, *Whitehead*, *Seymour*, *Shawsheen*, *Lockwood*, *Ceres*, *General Putnam*, *Brinker*, *Granite*, *Commodore Perry*, *Commodore Barney* and *Whitehall*, under Acting Masters Hayes, French, Wells, Woodward, Graves, McDiarmid, Hotchkiss, Giddings, Boomer, Flusser, Renshaw, and West. This part of the expedition was placed in charge of Flag-officer Louis M. Goldsborough, then the commander of the North Atlantic Squadron.

The military division comprised about 16,000 men, carried by about 40 transports, and was divided into three brigades. The First Brigade, under General John G. Foster, included the Tenth Connecticut and the Twenty-third, Twenty-fourth, Twenty-fifth and Twenty-sixth Massachusetts Regiment. The Second Brigade, under General Jesse L. Reno, included the Sixth New Hampshire, Ninth New Jersey, Twenty-first Massachusetts, Fifty-first New York and Fifty-first Pennsylvania Regiments. The Third Brigade, under General John G. Parke, included the Fourth and a battalion of the Fifth Rhode Island, the Eighth and Eleventh Connecticut, and the Fifty-third and Eighty-ninth New York Regiments of Infantry, besides Belger's Rhode Island Battery of 6 guns, which was served by 104 men and 120 horses.

The following gunboats also formed part of the military division, viz.: The *Picket*, Burnside's flagship, *Pioneer*, *Hussar*, *Chasseur*, *Ranger*, *Lancer* and *Vidette*, commanded by Captains and Acting Captains Ives, Baker, Crocker, West, Childs and Morley.

This force of gunboats was divided into two columns, and placed in charge of Commanders Samuel F. Hazard and Stephen C. Rowan.

The active expedition left Hampton Roads on the evening of Sunday, the 11th of January, 1862, many of the vessels reaching Hatteras Inlet the following day, although having been detained on the way by quite a heavy fog. Such as had not, however, reached the Inlet on Monday evening were smitten by one of the severest northwestern

LOUIS M. GOLDSBOROUGH.

gales known in that locality. The tempest was so violent that it was impossible for one vessel to communicate with another during the two following days and nights.

Many of the vessels were driven out to sea, while others, by reason of the peculiar nature of their cargo or otherwise became unmanageable, and went ashore. Among the latter was the transport *City of New York*, Captain Nye, which broke to pieces in sight of many others that could render it no assistance. Only a portion of her crew was saved, although during the whole of the 14th of January nearly all had been lashed to the rigging, in order to prevent their being swept overboard. The steamers *Louisiana*, *Zouave* and *Pocahontas*, as well as the floating battery *Grapeshot*, which was in tow of the *New Brunswick*, were also wrecked, though all on board were saved. A collision also occurred during the storm between the *Cossack* and the *Hope*, without, however, causing any permanent damage or any loss of life. The only losses were those already mentioned and that of Colonel J. W. Allen and Surgeon Weller, belonging to the Ninth New Jersey Regiment, who, in company with Second Officer Taylor, of the transport *Ann E. Thompson*, tried to render assistance to those on shore, and who were all three drowned by the swamping of their boat.

During the continuance of the terrible storm all the officers exhibited the greatest heroism, General Burnside notably distinguishing himself by his continued efforts to assist in all directions. His little flagship *Picket* was seen running to and fro where danger seemed the greatest, the general often giving orders while standing on the rail and holding on to the ropes.

It was not until January 28th that all the surviving vessels had passed through Hatteras Inlet, and it afterward took several days to complete preparations for the intended attack on Roanoke Island.

The latter place was then under the command of Colonel Shaw, of the Eighth North Carolina Regiment, as General Henry A. Wise happened to be lying ill at Nag's Head, and his forces consisted of the Eighth and Thirty-first, as well as of three companies of the Seventeenth, North Carolina Regiments, under Colonels H. M. Shaw, J. N. Jordan, Major G. H. Hill, besides 450 men under Colonel Anderson. The fortifications on the island and in its immediate vicinity contained over forty guns.

Obstructions of piles and sunken vessels had been placed in Croatan Sound, and behind these lay a flotilla of eight vessels with eleven guns under Lieutenant W. F. Lynch.

GUARDHOUSE AT LANGLEY, VA., WITH CONFEDERATE PRISONERS, AFTER THE BATTLE OF DRANESVILLE.

BATTLE OF ROANOKE ISLAND, FEBRUARY 8TH, 1862.—DECISIVE BAYONET CHARG[E]

FROM A

BATTLE OF ROANOKE ISLAND, FEBRUARY 8th, 1862—DECISIVE BAYONET CHARGE OF THE NINTH NEW YORK VOLUNTEERS ON THE CONFEDERATE THREE-GUN BATTERY.

DEATH OF COLONEL J. W. ALLEN, SURGEON WELLER, AND THE SECOND MATE OF THE "ANN E. THOMPSON,"
NEAR HATTERAS INLET, JANUARY 15TH, 1862.

THE UNITED STATES FLEET AND TRANSPORTS OFF HATTERAS DURING A STORM.—GENERAL BURNSIDE GIVING ORDERS

From a Sketch by H. Schell.

On the 4th of February, the little steamer *Putuxent* was sent to all the vessels of the fleet, with orders to advance, and on the following morning they proceeded, with gunboats in the lead, under Commander Rowan. Reconnoissances were made on the 6th, and at ten o'clock of the 7th, Flag-officer Goldsborough, having hoisted on the *Southfield* or the *Philadelphia* the signal, "*This day our country expects every man to do his duty,*" ordered the gunboats ahead in three columns. These were led respectively by the *Stars and Stripes*, the *Louisiana* and the *Hetzel*, all of whom, one hour later, were engaged in the bombardment of Fort Bartow, situated off Pork Point, and mounting nine guns.

February, 1862.

The fire was soon directed on all the batteries, as well as on Lynch's flotilla, which had come forward and joined in the fray, diverting much of the fleet's attention. The little Confederate fleet was, before long, compelled to retire, with its largest steamer, the *Curlew*, so badly disabled as to compel its being beached under cover of Fort Forrest, situated on the main land. The whole attention of the fleet was then centred on Fort Bartow, and at about one o'clock its flagstaff had been shot away, its barracks were in flames, and two hours later it had entirely ceased firing.

The transports had meanwhile come up to Ashby's Harbor, and effected a landing, after the gunboats had dispersed a body of 2,000 Confederates, who had been stationed there in anticipation of their arrival.

By midnight nearly eleven thousand troops had reached shore, most of them after wading several hundred feet through mud fully knee-deep, and in the midst of a cold rainstorm, but very few of the small-boats could proceed far enough through the shallow water.

At seven o'clock the next morning the troops advanced in three columns, under Generals Foster, Reno and Parke, toward the entrenchments located in the interior of the island, where nearly all the Confederates had repaired from the redoubts. There, also, General Wise—who, notwithstanding his illness, directed all the Confederate movements—had sent ten companies of the Wise Legion, under command of his son, Captain O. Jennings Wise, and of Lieutenant-colonel Frank Anderson.

The advance was a dangerous as well as a difficult one, by reason of an intervening swamp, which extended almost across the island, and was either covered by water or brushwood nearly its entire distance. At night the troops remained under arms in a heavy rainstorm, without shelter or suitable food, and early on the 9th resumed their march, which soon brought them face to face with the Confederate skirmishers, whom they drove into their earthworks.

Foster opened fire upon these with six howitzers, under Midshipman B. F. Porter, and with the Twenty-third and Twenty-fifth Massachusetts Regiments, on which the excellent firing of the Confederate sharpshooters was telling heavily until dispersed by the Twenty-fourth Massachusetts, who succeeded in dislodging them from the woods where they had lain hidden. The Tenth Connecticut and Twenty-sixth Massachusetts were also ordered up, and stood their ground well under the well-directed fire from the earthworks, while Reno's and Parke's brigades were coming up to turn the Confederate left flank.

Reno's force plowed ahead on Foster's right, and was soon confronted by the Wise Legion, with whom it had a fierce encounter, but which it finally drove back, with heavy losses on both sides, including the wounding of young Wise. The fire had, in the meantime, continued actively at the right, the artillery doing a great deal of havoc in all directions. Finally the ammunition began to give out. Nothing was left but to charge the earthworks and this was speedily decided upon.

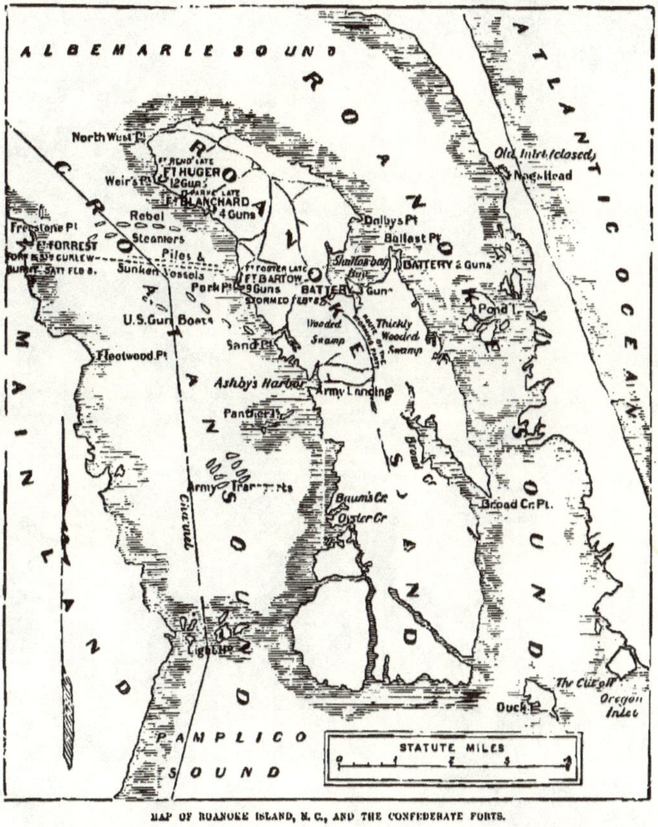

MAP OF ROANOKE ISLAND, N. C., AND THE CONFEDERATE FORTS.

HEADQUARTERS OF VINCENT COLLYER, SUPERINTENDENT OF THE POOR AT NEW BERNE, N.C.—DISTRIBUTING CAPTURED CLOTHING TO THE NEEDY

Major E. A. Kimball, of Hawkins's Ninth New York Zouaves, offered to lead the bayonet-charge, and while Reno's brigade was advancing toward the Confederate left, and Parke stood on its right, the *Zouaves* rushed forward, crying: "*Zou, zou, zou, zou!*" accompanied by Colonel Hawkins, and followed by the Tenth Connecticut. The earthworks were soon enfiladed from both sides in such a way as to necessitate the flight of its occupants. The Federals climbed over the parapets of the three-gun battery to find that the guns had even been left unspiked, and that all the enemy's dead and wounded had been hurriedly abandoned in a retreat toward Nag's Head, on the other side of Roanoke Sound. The Twenty-first Massachusetts and the Fifty-first New York, who had come up on the Confederate right, were the first to plant their flags on the battery, and they afterward followed the fast-retreating troops to the river, where about 200 Confederates, including Captain Wise, who proved to have been fatally wounded, were taken prisoners. At the same time Reno had received the surrender of Colonel Jordan's force, and Foster, while pushing toward the northern portion of the island, had been met by a flag-of-truce asking what terms of capitulation would be granted. Foster demanded the unconditional surrender of Shaw's troops, which was acceded to, and about 2,000 more prisoners laid down their arms.

J. H. ALLEN

Attention was now given to Fort Bartow, which, with a small force, had resumed a desultory fire with the gunboats. It was soon occupied, and from it the signal, "The fort is ours!" given to the fleet.

The Federal loss was reported at 235 killed and wounded, that of the Confederates being much greater. The latter lost nearly 3,000 in prisoners, besides over 3,000 stand of arms and 42 heavy guns.

Colonel Charles S. Russell, of the Tenth Connecticut, and Lieutenant-colonel Vigier de Monteuil, of the Ninth New York, were among the killed on the Federal side. The Federal fleet lost 6 killed and 19 wounded.

The Confederate fleet had gone quite a distance up Albemarle Sound to Elizabeth City, after setting fire to the *Curlew* and to the barracks at Redstone Point. Commander Rowan was ordered to pursue it, and at the same time to destroy part of the Albemarle and Chesapeake Canal.

February, 1862.

Early on the 10th, Rowan started ahead with fourteen vessels, and in the river near Elizabeth City he met Lynch's eight vessels, close by a battery of four guns, that had been erected on shore. The engagement lasted but forty-five minutes. Deeming the case hopeless, Lynch signaled to abandon the vessels, and they were accordingly run ashore and set fire to. Only

AMBROSE E. BURNSIDE

E. A. KIMBALL

SWORD PRESENTED TO GENERAL BURNSIDE BY THE STATE OF RHODE ISLAND.

VIEW OF THE CITY OF NEW BERNE, N. C., FROM THE OPPOSITE BANK OF THE NEUCES RIVER.—THE TENTH CONNECTICUT REGIMENT AWAITING TRANSPORTATION BY THE FLAGSHIP "DELAWARE," COMMODORE ROWAN.

one, the *Ellis*, escaped total destruction, and was afterward added to the Federal fleet, whose loss in the encounter was two killed and six wounded.

An instance of extraordinary bravery was reported in connection with the last named engagement. A Confederate shell had entered close by the magazine of the *Valley City*, and had set fire to some of the woodwork. One of the gunners, named John Davis, seated himself upon, and otherwise protected, an open barrel of gunpowder, from which he had been serving his gun, until the fire had been extinguished, and thus prevented the fearful loss which would have resulted from an explosion. For this the Secretary of the Navy soon after made him acting gunner, and raised his salary from $300 to $1,000 a year, and Congress ordered the presentation to him of a medal of honor, bearing the words: "PERSONAL VALOR—JOHN DAVIS, GUNNER'S MATE, U. S. S. *Valley City*, Albemarle Sound, February 10th, 1862."

The Confederates, in their flight, set fire to Elizabeth City; but the flames were extinguished by the troops, assisted by the colored people who would not desert their old homes.

The following day Rowan sent out Lieutenant Maury to take possession of Edenton, which he did, without opposition. He destroyed a schooner on the stocks and eight cannons, and captured two schooners, with 4,000 bushels of corn.

On the 13th of February some of the vessels were ordered to proceed under Lieutenant Jeffers to the Albemarle and Chesapeake Canal, in order to destroy it, but they found that the Confederates were engaged in the same work. The latter fled before the Federals, who returned, after destroying two vessels in the river.

On the 19th of February an extended reconnoissance was sent from Edenton, up the Chowan River, to Winton, which place was taken on the 20th, after the vessels had been subjected to a sharp fire from a North Carolina battery. Another reconnoissance was made to Plymouth, on Albemarle Sound, on approaching which the vessels were fired upon from the river banks. Commander Rowan ordered the town to be shelled, and it was soon destroyed.

GENERAL BURNSIDE ON THE ROAD FROM NEW BERNE TO BEAUFORT, N. C.

BATTLE OF NEW BERNE, N. C

OCCUPATION OF WASHINGTON, MOREHEAD CITY, AND BEAUFORT, N. C.

March, 1862.

ON the 12th of March, an expedition consisting of nearly the full brigades of Generals Foster, Parke and Reno, numbering altogether about 8,000 men, besides a detachment of the Union Coast Guard, three companies of marines, and McCook's battery, took passage at Hatteras Inlet, with General Burnside and staff, in the steamers *Alice Price*, *New Brunswick*, *Patuxent* and *Pilot Boy*. These were preceded by the naval force under Commander Rowan, which embraced the seven gunboats, *Delaware*, flagship, *Stars and Stripes*, *Hetzel*, *Decatur*, *Ohio*, *Perry*, and *St. Lawrence*.

They arrived off Slocum's Creek in the evening, disembarked the following day, and on the 14th advanced upon New Berne.

General Branch was in charge of the Confederate forces at the latter place, consisting of eight regiments of infantry, 500 cavalry, and 18 pieces of artillery, nearly all distributed in five fortifications along the river.

LIEUTENANT TILLOTSON'S NAVAL BATTERY, CENTRAL DIVISION, UNDER LIEUTENANT McCOOK AT THE BATTLE OF NEW BERNE, N. C

The fight lasted all day with varying successes, until the Federals carried the earthworks by assault, and forced the Confederates to flight. The gunboats afterward cleared the obstructions and came up to New Berne, which was taken possession of, as well as the forts.

The Federal loss was 547; the Confederates losing 578 in killed, wounded and prisoners, besides 2 steamboats, 52 guns, ammunition, etc., etc.

On the 20th of March, Colonel Stevenson took a force, under convoy of three gunboats, to operate against Washington, on the Pamlico River, where they landed without opposition.

On Sunday the 23d, another expedition, consisting of gunboats and of the brigade under General Parke, had reached and taken possession of Morehead City, at the terminus of the Atlantic and North Carolina Railway, and two days later, Beaufort was occupied without opposition, and left in charge of the Fourth Rhode Island and Eighth Connecticut Regiments, the other troops being engaged in preparations for the attack on Fort Macon.

Major John H. Allen, of the Fourth Rhode Island, was appointed Provost Marshal of Beaufort, and succeeded in making himself very popular while in the exercise of his difficult duties.

HEADQUARTERS OF GENERAL BURNSIDE AT NEW BERNE, N. C.

BRINGING CONFEDERATE PRISONERS INTO THE CAPTURED CAMP [illegible] ROANOKE ISLAND, AFTER THE BATTLE

[illegible]

PASSAGE DOWN THE OHIO RIVER, OF GENERAL JAMES S. NEGLEY'S PENNSYLVANIA BRIGADE, THE SEVENTY-SEVENTH, SEVENTY-EIGHTH AND SEVENTY-NINTH REGIMENTS. PENNSYLVANIA VOLUNTEERS, UNDER COLONELS HAMBRIGHT, STAMBAUGH AND SEWALL.

JAMES S. NEGLEY.

Born in Allegheny County, Pa., in 1830; served throughout the Mexican War as a private soldier, although against the wishes of his parents, he being a minor; received a complimentary discharge from the Secretary of War on account of his age, which he refused, and remained with his company until the close of the war. At [illegible] call for volunteers in 1861, [illegible] was appointed third brigadier-general, commanding the [illegible] western portion of the [illegible] of Pennsylvania. He was [illegible] ly efficient as an organizer. His brigade, consisting [illegible] the Seventy-seventh, Seventy-eighth and Seventy-ninth Pennsylvania Volunteers, was [illegible] to Louisville to join the Federal army operating there, and he dispatched [illegible] down the Ohio on six [illegible] steamers.

FASCINES AND GABIONS.

The making of these forms [illegible] of the instruction given [illegible] soldier in establishing [illegible] of defense. Fascines [illegible] made by securing together [illegible] of sticks or branches [illegible] are used for raising [illegible], filling ditches and making [illegible] Gabions are [illegible] cylinders of wickerwork [illegible] with earth, which serve [illegible] soldiers from the [illegible] fire.

A DARING EXPLOIT.

While Lieutenant A. D. [illegible] was in command of [illegible] steamer *Union*, of the Potomac flotilla, he learned that [illegible] Confederates had collected [illegible] Quantico or Dumfries Creek quite a body of troops which they intended sending in a large schooner across the Potomac. He determined to destroy the vessel, and early one morning he pulled off with a boat and two launches, commanded by Acting Master Amos Foster, of the *Resolute*, and Midshipman W. F. Stewart, of the *Re*[illegible], taking with him, also, Master E. L. Haynes of the last named vessel, Acting Surgeon W. R. Bersall, and the pilot of the *Lewis* [illegible]. They entered the narrow creek within pistol [illegible] of the enemy on either side, and followed it until they reached the schooner, which lay close by the shore in charge of a sentry. The latter fired on their approach, and alarmed the camp, while the schooner was boarded and set afire. The destruction of the newly-fitted vessel was complete, but the conflagration revealed the position of the escaping boats, which had to run the gantlet before reaching a place of safety, though, fortunately, without any serious injury.

J. S. NEGLEY.

BURNING OF THE "HARVEY BIRCH."

The *Harvey Birch*, an American merchantman of 1,480 tons, while on her way from Havre to New York, in command of Captain Nelson, with a crew of twenty-nine men, was brought to, on the 17th of November, 1861, by a shot from the Confederate privateer *Nashville*, Captain Pegram, in latitude 49 deg. 6 min. north, and longitude 9 deg. and 52 min. west. She was then boarded by a Confederate officer and a boat's crew, who took Captain Nelson and his men as prisoners, carried away all that was valuable from the *Harvey Birch*, and then set fire to her, causing the entire destruction of a vessel valued at fully $150,000.

The *Nashville* then steamed into Southampton, where she landed her prisoners, as well as Colonel and Mrs. Peyton, of North Carolina, whom she had brought as passengers, by order of the Confederate Secretary of the Navy.

The *Nashville* was of 1,100 tons burden and 800-horse power, carried two 12-pound rifled guns, and was officered by Lieutenants Pegram, Fauntleroy, Bennett, and other well known naval experts who had already seen active service at Bull Run and in the defenses at Charleston and along the coasts.

CAPTAIN MULLER'S BATTERY, SEVENTY-SEVENTH PENNSYLVANIA REGIMENT, MAKING FASCINES AND GABIONS FOR BREASTWO[illegible]

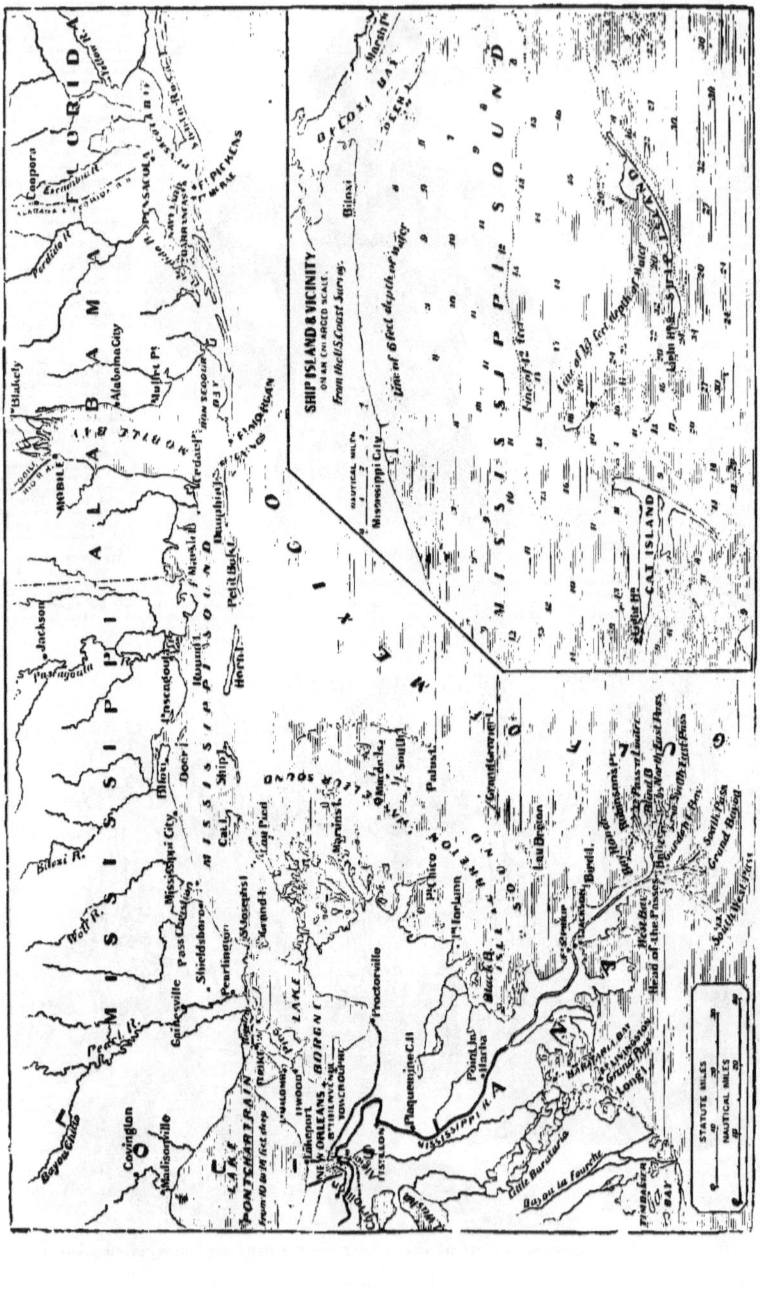

SOUTHERN COAST OF THE UNITED STATES, FROM PENSACOLA TO THE MOUTH OF THE MISSISSIPPI, SHOWING THE STRATEGIC POSITION OF SHIP ISLAND.
WITH APPROACHES TO NEW ORLEANS.

BURNING OF THE AMERICAN MERCHANTMAN "HARVEY BIRCH," OF NEW YORK, IN THE BRITISH CHANNEL, BY THE CONFEDERATE STEAMER "NASHVILLE," NOVEMBER 17TH, 1861.

SHIP ISLAND.—UNITED STATES STEAMER "MISSISSIPPI" FIRING ON A CONFEDERATE STEAMER

CONSTRUCTION OF FLOATING MORTAR BATTERIES BY THE FEDERAL GOVERNMENT, AT THE UPPER FERRY, ST. LOUIS, MO.

THE BATTLE OF PRESTONBURG.

The year 1862 opened with active military operations in Eastern Kentucky, which latter was about the only field in which anything of moment transpired during the entire month of January.

The first battle fought in the new year took place at Prestonburg, a town situated on the west fork of the Big Sandy River.

The Confederate General Humphrey Marshall had, early in the year, entrenched his force at Paintville, in Johnson County, for the purpose of interfering with the movements of General Don Carlos Buell, one of whose divisions, under General George H. Thomas, was advancing toward the Cumberland River.

Colonel James A. Garfield, who had been ordered to dislodge Marshall, had, on the 7th of January, broken up his camp on Middle Creek, and with the Fourteenth Kentucky and the Forty-second Ohio Infantry Regiments, besides 300 of the Second Virginia Cavalry, had marched upon Paintville, only to find that Marshall had evacuated the place on hearing of his approach, and that he had fled up the river. Garfield had ordered the cavalry to pursue the retreating force, with which an encounter had taken place the same day at the mouth of Jennie's Creek, three miles west of Paintville, resulting in a small loss on both sides, but it was not until the 9th that he had succeeded in overtaking the main body of the Confederates.

January, 1862.

Garfield had, in the meantime, been reinforced by the Fortieth Ohio Infantry and Wolford's detachment of cavalry, bringing his force up to nearly 2,400 men, as against the 3,000 which Marshall then had on the heights overlooking the forks of Middle Creek. The latter comprised two Kentucky and two Virginia regiments, two detachments of cavalry and four pieces of artillery.

The Federals slept on their arms that night, and early on the 10th moved up Abbot's Creek and reached Prestonburg at about eight o'clock the following morning. It was not, however, until after twelve that Garfield had completed his arrangements for the attack. Then, sending a small force of cavalry to discover the exact position of the enemy, he followed with another along the brow of the hill, after placing his artillery in a position to sweep all approach from the creek. The right of the advancing column soon

January, 1862.

JAMES A. GARFIELD.

came upon Colonel Trigg's Fifty-fourth Virginia Regiment, supporting the artillery near the Cross Roads, and a lively fight ensued, the Confederate guns being, however, too badly served to effect much damage. Reinforcements having reached both sides, the fighting continued from one crest to another, along the line, until toward four o'clock, when, Colonel Sheldon's force of 700 men having arrived from Paintville, Garfield pressed still further the advantage gained, and ordered the entire reserve to advance and silence the enemy's guns. By dark the enemy had been driven from all his positions, and Marshall had begun a retreat which continued as far as Abingdon, across the Clinch River, into Virginia. Such stores as had not been burned by Marshall were taken possession of and carried away, when a few days later the Federals returned to Paintville.

The Confederate loss was reported at 60 killed besides about 100 wounded and made prisoners, while that of the Federals was said to be only 2 killed and 25 wounded.

For his services on the occasion, Colonel Garfield was made a brigadier-general the day following the engagement at Prestonburg.

JAMES A. GARFIELD.

Born at Orange, Cuyahoga County, O., November 19th, 1831; lost his father at a very early age, and became a driver of tow-horses on one of the Western canals, until able to enter the Ohio Western Reserve Eclectic Institute; afterward continued his studies at Williams College, Mass., whence he graduated in 1856, with the very highest honors; returned to his native State, where he became a clergyman, and later on was appointed to the presidency of the Institute where he had made his first studies. A few years later he studied law, and was admitted to practice, giving at the same time some little attention to politics. His great urbanity, and an unusually strict observance of all the duties which he was called upon to perform, soon won for him great popularity, and in 1859-60, he was called to a seat in the Ohio Senate.

When the Civil War broke out in 1861, he tendered his services to the United States Government, and set about actively recruiting in his native State, soon entering the service at the head of the Forty-second Regiment of Ohio Volunteers. On the 11th of January, 1862, he was promoted to a brigadier-generalship, for having, with less than 1,000 men of his Eighteenth Brigade, defeated nearly twice that number of Confederates under General Humphrey Marshall, at Middle Creek, near Prestonburg, Ky. During April, 1862, he took part in the battle of Shiloh, commanding the Twentieth Brigade of the Army of the Ohio under General Buell, composed of the Thirteenth Michigan, Fifty-first Indiana, and the Sixty-fourth and Sixty-fifth Ohio Regiments. He likewise served at Corinth, which the Federals took possession of on the 29th of May, 1862. On the 19th of September, 1863, he was made a major-general of volunteers for gallantry at the battle of Chickamauga, where, as chief of staff to General Rosecrans, he so aided General Thomas as to insure the safety of the Federal army. He continued to serve under Rosecrans until the commencement of the following December, when he resigned his position in the army to take his seat as a member of the Thirty-eighth Congress, to which he had just been elected. He was re-elected at every successive term, and thus continued to represent his native State, until called by it to the United States Senate, in January, 1880.

In the Fall of the latter year he was elected President of the United States, and was duly inaugurated as such on the 4th of March, 1881. On the 2d of July following he was shot by Guiteau, in the City of Washington, D. C., and died of his wounds at Elberon, N. J., on the 19th of September of the same year.

The grief of the nation at the loss of their Chief Magistrate was universal, the South vying with the North in its expression of sorrow.

FEDERAL TROOPS REBUILDING THE BRIDGE OVER BACON'S CREEK, KY

VIEW OF NEW BERNE, N. C., FROM THE INTERIOR OF FORT THOMPSON, AFTER THE CAPTU

FROM A SKI

VIEW OF NEW BERNE, N. C., FROM THE INTERIOR OF FORT THOMPSON, AFTER THE CAPTURE BY THE FEDERAL FORCES—BURNING ROSIN WORKS, RAILWAY BRIDGE, AND NAVAL STORES.

HILTON HEAD, S. C.—GOVERNMENT WORKS ERECTED FOR THE COMFORT OF THE FEDERAL ARMY OF OCCUPATION.

From a Sketch by [illegible]

EMBARKING TROOPS AT BIRD'S POINT, MO., TO REINFORCE THE FEDERAL ARMY UNDER GENERAL PRENTISS.
From a Sketch by Henry Lovie.

THE BATTLE OF MILL SPRING.

To the second important engagement of the year 1862, the names of Beech Grove, Fishing Creek, Somerset, and Logan's Cross Roads, have been given, although it was actually fought at the last mentioned place, about midway between Mill Spring and Somerset. Like the battle of Prestonburg, it proved to be a victory for the Federals.

The Confederate General Felix K. Zollicoffer had strongly entrenched his force both at Beech Grove and at Mill Spring, on the opposite side of the Cumberland River, early in January, and had meet the advancing force under General Thomas. Zollicoffer's brigade comprised one Mississippi and three Tennessee regiments, with Captain Rutledge's battery of four guns; and Carroll's brigade embraced three Tennessee regiments, with Captain McClung's battery of two guns, the reserve consisting of one Alabama regiment and two battalions of cavalry, making a total of nearly 5,000 men.

General Thomas's force consisted of the Second Minnesota, Fourth and Twelfth Kentucky, Ninth Ohio and Tenth Indiana Regiments of Infantry, a detachment of Wolford's Kentucky Cavalry, and three batteries of artillery under Captains Kinney, field, in order to separate the Federal positions, but General Thomas, who happened near, and saw the likelihood of a flanking movement, ordered up the Ninth Ohio, Colonel R. L. McCook, and the Second Minnesota, Colonel H. P. Van Cleve. The Confederates' advance, which had likewise been strengthened by Carroll's brigade, then opened a most galling fire upon the Federals. This was barely withstood by the latter until Colonel W. A. Hoskins's Twelfth Kentucky Regiment had come up to their aid.

The contest now became more severe than ever, and although the Confederate artillery occupied a

DEATH OF GENERAL ZOLLICOFFER, ON THE BATTLEFIELD OF MILL SPRING, KY., JANUARY 19TH, 1862.

been joined by the troops under General Carroll, as well as by Major-general George B. Crittenden, who had then taken the chief command. It was known to them that General George H. Thomas had divided his forces, leaving the smaller portion with General Schoepf at Somerset, and taking the remainder with him for a flank movement southwestward by way of Jamestown, it having been intended that they should co-operate in an attack on Zollicoffer, to be made by them on Sunday, the 19th. As the latter's force was not such as to successfully withstand the contemplated attack, Crittenden decided to take the offensive before the two sections could unite, and shortly after midnight of the 18th the two Confederate brigades led by Zollicoffer left camp to

Jan. 19, 1862.

[illegible] Standart and Wetmore, representing in all about 3,000 men.

After a heavy march, through a drizzling rain, the Confederates came upon the pickets of Wolford's cavalry, driving them back upon Colonel M. D. Manson's Tenth Indiana and the Fourth Kentucky under Colonel S. S. Fry, then at the junction of the Mill Spring and Somerset Roads. The attack upon these began at six o'clock on the morning of the 19th, and was bravely withstood, but the heavy opposing force was too much for the Federals. They lost their position on the hill, and were being driven up the slope of another, when, their ammunition giving out, they took shelter in the wood.

The Confederates rushed forward across the open less favorable position than that of the Federals, the latter had difficulty in maintaining their ground, so fierce was the attack of the opposing force, and they had finally to fall back while contesting the possession of a commanding hill. Just then Zollicoffer appeared in the advance of his line, attended by his staff, and directing the movements of his troops.

Colonel Fry, noticing the group, advanced and fired, and in return was shot at by one of Zollicoffer's aids, who unhorsed him. Fry arose, and with another more deliberate shot killed Zollicoffer who fell off his horse, and was left by his attendants, while the maddened Confederates rushed wildly ahead, causing a hand-to-hand encounter which lasted until a final bayonet-charge of the

BATTLE OF MILL SPRING, OR LOGAN'S CROSS ROADS, KY., BETWEEN A CONFEDERATE FORCE UNDER

BATTLE OF MILL SPRING, OR LOGAN'S CROSS ROADS, KY., BETWEEN A CONFEDERATE FORCE UNDER GENERAL ZOLLICOFFER, AND THE FEDERAL TROOPS COMMANDED BY GENERAL THOMAS, JANUARY 19TH, 1862

[illegible]

MAJOR BOWEN, OCCUPYING SALEM, MO., WITH A FEDERAL FORCE ATTACKED BY THE CONFEDERATES UNDER COLONEL FREEMAN. REPULSE OF THE ATTACKING PARTY, DECEMBER 3D, 1861.

Ninth Ohio on the Confederate flank forced the latter to give way.

General Crittenden, who had taken Zollicoffer's place, tried to rally his troops, but unavailingly, and before night they had been driven back into their entrenchments at Beech Grove. This left Moulden's Hill in possession of the Federals, who, with their batteries, were enabled, until dark, to shell the camp of the Confederates, and to prevent their escape across the river.

Late in the evening, General Thomas's force was strengthened by the brigade of General Schoepf—which had been long delayed by the almost impassable condition of streams that had been swollen by heavy rains—and by the Tenth Kentucky and the Fourteenth Ohio Regiments. With these he intended renewing the contest the following morning, but early on the 20th it was found that the Confederate position had been abandoned in the night.

January, 1862.

To the Ninth Ohio belongs the credit of first causing the Confederate retreat and subsequent rout. Its bayonet-charge was certainly the most stirring incident of the engagement. Colonel McCook had had a horse shot under him in the charge, and as he had been wounded in the leg, the surgeon had urged him to retire from the field, but he would not leave his command, and when he saw some of the troops faltering, he boldly went ahead on another charger, and quickly ran along the front with pistol in hand, shouting: "Take courage anew! Bayonets out! Charge! Charge!" This led to a furious attack on the part of his men, who, with a yell, dashed forward, and carrying everything before them.

The Confederate earthworks were taken possession of on the 20th, and were found to contain guns, nearly 1,000 stand of arms, 100 wagons, and a large quantity of ammunition and stores. This capture was increased by six guns and additional stores, found afterward across the river, at White Oak Creek.

The body of General Zollicoffer lay for some time before one of the tents of the Minnesota Regiment. It bore a wound in the breast, besides slighter ones at the hip and on the right arm. The men tenderly cared for it, washing off the thick mud which covered it almost entirely, and afterward placed it in a wagon, which took it to Mumfordsville, whence it was sent by flag-of-truce to Confederate General Buckner, after being honored with a Federal military salute.

The Confederate lost, besides 191 killed, 62 wounded and 89 prisoners.

The Federal loss was 39 killed and 208 wounded.

FELIX K. ZOLLICOFFER.

Born in Maury County, Tenn., May 19th, 1812; received an academic education; entered a printing office at a very early age, and in 1828 was placed in charge of a small newspaper published in the town of Paris, in his native State. He was editor of the Columbia *Observer* one year and was the State Printer during the years ... taking the editorship of the Nashville ... in 1842. He was a man of great energy, and the conduct of his several editorial enterprises displayed so much ability as to win for himself a prominent reputation in the political field, where his great usefulness chiefly lay. He became the State Comptroller at three different periods between 1843 and 1847, and in 1849 he entered the State Senate, being subsequently elected a Representative in the United States Congress, serving ... 1853-9. In Congress he was a pronounced Southern man and advocated extreme measures, but was a delegate to the Peace Congress of February, 1861.

When the Civil War broke out he espoused the Southern cause, was made a brigadier general, and placed in command of quite a large body of men in East Tennessee. Thence he invaded Kentucky, occupying Barboursville on the 19th of September, 1861, and attacking Camp Wild Cat, or Crab Orchard, in Rockcastle County, on October 21st of the same year. The latter place was the scene of two attacks, in both of which Zollicoffer was repulsed, with quite a heavy loss, by the troops under Colonels Garrard, Coburn, Connell and Woolford, of which General Schoepf had taken the chief command. He subsequently entrenched himself on the banks of the Cumberland River, both at Mill Spring and at Beech Grove, where he advanced, on the 19th of January, 1862, to prevent the junction of General Thomas's forces with those led by General Schoepf.

An engagement took place early the following day at Logan's Cross Roads, between his force and that of General Thomas, which lasted till night had set in, and resulted in his defeat as well as in the evacuation of the Confederate camps, which were taken possession of, with a large amount of war material, by the Federal troops. His death was a great loss to the Confederates. He was killed while in the advance, directing the movement of his troops, being wounded in the breast and arm, and at the hip. His last words were: "Bring my men inside the breastworks."

Zollicoffer's body was, by orders of General Thomas, embalmed and placed in a metallic coffin, and afterward delivered under a flag of truce to General Buckner. The remains were honored with a military salute when carried over Green River and were interred at Nashville, Tenn., with great honors.

S. B. BRITTAN, JR.

ANDREW H. FOOTE.

Born at New Haven, Conn., May 4th, 1806; entered the United States Navy as midshipman in the year 1822, making his first cruise under Commodore Gregory in an expedition to the West Indies, which had been organized against the pirates operating in the Malayan Archipelago. He distinguished himself in this undertaking, and becoming one of the officers of the *John Adams*, was directly instrumental in causing the complete destruction of the pirate rendezvous in those quarters. He then went on a cruise upon the coast of Africa, where he was stationed during three years, operating against the slavers, and thence proceeded to China, where he remained during the troublesome period when that empire was at war with the united forces of England and France. While stationed here his vessel was once fired upon, either accidentally or otherwise, by one of the Chinese forts and he at once operated against the latter, and finally succeeded in capturing it. This won him the admiration of all, and hastened his promotion to a lieutenancy.

When the Mexican War broke out, he was placed in charge of the Charlestown Navy Yard, and superintended the fitting-out of vessels then intended to co-operate with the United States Army. In the year 1852 he was made a commander, rising to a captaincy in 1861, the year of the commencement of the Civil War, which found him in charge of the Brooklyn Navy Yard. Here he was engaged in superintending the fitting-out of vessels destined for the blockade of Southern ports. He was thence transferred to the Department of the West, and given the command of a flotilla to open the navigation of the Mississippi and other rivers.

On the 6th of February, 1862, he aided in the capture of Fort Henry, receiving the surrender of its garrison before the forces under General Grant were able to gain the place, and a few days later attacked Fort Donelson, which likewise soon fell into the hands of the Federal forces, and in the attack against which he was injured seriously in the foot. After a hard-fought engagement he received the surrender of Island No. 10, on the 7th of April, 1862, and was about engaging in another important movement, when his long neglected wound compelled him to relinquish all active duty. He resigned his command in the navy, and returned home. On the 10th of the following June he received the thanks of Congress, and this was followed, six days later, by his promotion to the rank of rear-admiral, and his appointment to the superintendency of the Bureau of Equipment and Recruiting. He was ordered, on the 4th of June, 1863, to relieve Rear-admiral Dupont, who was stationed off Charleston Harbor; but on his way he was taken ill, and died in New York City, on the 26th of the same month.

A. H. FOOTE.

CAPTURE OF FORT HENRY, TENN.

RECONNOISSANCES made in January, 1862, by order of General Grant, having satisfied him that Fort Henry could easily be taken, if attacked promptly from the Tennessee River, he proposed to General Halleck that an advance be at once made in that direction, and on the 30th of the month he received permission to make the intended movement.

On Monday, the 2d of February, General Grant's army, preceded by a flotilla of seven gunboats, left Cairo for Paducah, reaching the latter place the same evening.

February, 1862.

The army comprised the divisions of Generals John A. McClernand and C. F. Smith, including the Seventh, Eighth, Ninth, Eleventh, Twelfth, Eighteenth, Twentieth, Twenty-seventh, Twenty-eighth, Twenty-ninth, Thirtieth, Thirty-first, Forty-first, Forty-fifth and Forty-eighth Illinois, the Seventh and Twelfth Iowa, the Eighth and Thirtieth Missouri and the Eleventh Indiana Regiments, besides a large force of cavalry and artillery.

The gunboats were the newly armored *Cincinnati* (flagship), *Carondelet*, *Essex* and *St. Louis*, in charge of Commanders Stembel, Walke, Porter and Paulding, and the wooden *Conestoga*, *Lexington* and *Tyler*, in charge of Lieutenants Commanding Phelps, Shirk and Gwin, the whole commanded by Flag-officer Andrew H. Foote.

Fort Henry was at the time garrisoned by about 3,000 men under Brigadier-general Lloyd Tilghman. This force was divided into two brigades: one under Colonel A. Heiman, comprising his own regiment, the Tenth Tennessee, Lieutenant-colonel McGavock; the Forty-eighth Tennessee, Colonel Voorhies; the Twenty-seventh Alabama, Colonel Hughes; a battalion of cavalry under Lieutenant-colonel Gantt, and four guns in charge of Captain Culberson; while the other brigade was under the command of Colonel Joseph Drake, and embraced his own regiment, the Fourth Mississippi, then in charge of Major Adair; the Fifteenth Arkansas, Colonel Gee; the Fifty-first Tennessee, Colonel Browder; a battalion of Alabama troops under Major Garvin, a detachment of Rangers under Captain Melton, two companies of cavalry under Captains Milner and Padgett, and three guns in charge of Captain Clare. The fort was armed with seventeen heavy guns in charge of Captain Jesse Taylor.

RECONNOISSANCE IN FORCE BY GENERAL GRANT TOWARD COLUMBUS, KY.—GENERAL GRANT'S BODYGUARD PASSING OVER MAYFIELD BRIDGE

From a Sketch by Henry Lovie

Early on the 3d of February, the gunboats had advanced to a point about nine miles below Fort Henry, and the troops had been landed by the transports at Bailey's Ferry, subsequently encamping on a high ridge close by the river. Reconnoissances were duly made, both on land and by water, and on the 5th all was in readiness for the attack. The advance was to be made simultaneously the following morning by the troops and the gunboats, and the engagement was to commence at eleven o'clock. But an unusually heavy rainstorm came up during the night, and while the rising river benefited the flotilla, the muddy roads and swollen streams before long, render his position untenable, and while there remained a chance to save his force by a retreat to Fort Donelson, he availed of it, remaining himself in Fort Henry until all but seven of the heavy guns had been dismantled by the incessant shelling of the fleet. He then forcibly surrendered to Commander Foote, who sent Commander Stembel, of his flagship, and Lieutenant Commander Phelps, to hoist the Union flag over Fort Henry.

General Grant's force came up afterward, and a pursuit was ordered, but it resulted only in the capture by the Fourth Illinois Cavalry of a few prisoners and some light artillery.

forty-two pound shot struck the lad in the head, causing his instant death.

This tragic termination to a life so full of youth and hope was universally regretted.

The Confederate loss was reported at ten killed and fifteen wounded, many being injured by the bursting of one of the twelve thirty-two pound guns in the fort, besides about 100 prisoners, including General Tilghman, Captain Jesse Taylor and ten other commissioned officers. The fort contained, besides its regular armament, many small-arms and equipments a large quantity of stores, and a sufficient number of tents for 8,000 men.

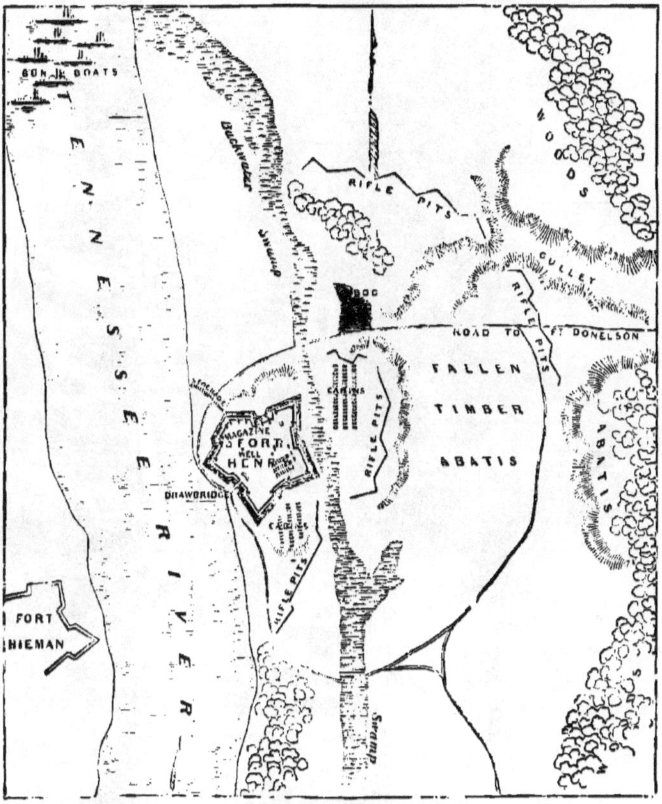

PLAN OF FORT HENRY AND ITS APPROACHES.

proved a serious obstacle to the march of the troops.

The armored gunboats, with the wooden ones in the rear, had succeeded in escaping the long-range fire of the fort by taking cover of Panther Island, in the western channel, and had opened on the batteries, finally, at a distance of about 600 yards, while Grant's force was slowly advancing through the woods and mud; General Smith's column in the direction of Fort Hieman, and that of General McClernand toward a point on the Dover Road, between Forts Henry and Donelson.

The bombardment continued until near two o'clock, and was warmly responded to by Captain Taylor's guns; but it soon became evident to General Tilghman that the enemy's movements would,

Colonel Lewis Wallace, of the Eleventh Indiana Regiment, was placed in command of Fort Henry, while Grant commenced his preparations for the advance on Fort Donelson.

The Federals lost two killed and thirty-eight wounded, twenty-nine of the latter being on board the *Essex*, whose boiler was pierced by a thirty-two pound shot from the fort.

Among the killed was Lieutenant S. B. Brittan, Jr., son of Dr. S. B. Brittan, of New York City. He had enlisted in the navy at the early age of seventeen, and had made himself a favorite, especially on board of the *Essex*, where he acted as Captain Porter's aide and private secretary. While Captain Porter and young Brittan were watching the effect of the firing upon the Confederate position, a

RECEPTION AT NEW YORK OF THE SIXTY-NINTH REGIMENT.

This regiment, composed entirely of Irish citizens, upon its return to New York City, after a three-months service in the field, were met by their fellow-citizens and the Seventh Regiment and given a reception that any organization might envy. The Sixty-ninth had rendered good service at Arlington Heights by its erection of admirable and extensive earthworks in defense of the national capital, and had especially distinguished itself at the battle of Bull Run, where it unfortunately met with serious losses. Its Colonel, Michael Corcoran, was taken prisoner, and held as a hostage for a year, when he was exchanged.

ARRIVAL AND DEPARTURE OF FEDERAL SOLDIERS, ON THEIR WAY TO "THE FRONT," AT THE UNION VOLUNTEER REFRESHMENT SALOON, PHILADELPHIA.

From a Sketch by F. B. Schell.

COLONEL LEWIS WALLACE AND STAFF.—ZOUAVE REGIMENT, ELEVENTH INDIANA VOLUNTEERS

BURSTING OF A RIFLED 42-POUND

BURSTING OF A RIFLED 42-POUND GUN IN FORT HENRY DURING THE BOMBARDMENT

RECEPTION BY THE PEOPLE OF THE CITY OF NEW YORK OF THE SIXTY-NINTH REGIMENT ON THEIR RETURN FROM VIRGINIA ESCORTED ON THEIR ARRIVAL BY THE NEW YORK SEVENTH REGIMENT.

BURNING A CONFEDERATE SCHOONER IN QUANTICO CREEK, BY A DETACHMENT OF THE POTOMAC FLOTILLA UNDER LIEUTENANT HARRELL.

From a sketch by a Flotilla officer.

STATIONHOUSE CELL IN WASHINGTON.

At the time General Porter was appointed Provost-marshal of Washington, D.C., he found existing there so much demoralization and dissipation among the officers and soldiers, who had abused the leniency extended them, when either passing through or quartered at the national capital, that the *morale* of the army was fast declining. General Porter established a rigid supervision, causing the arrest and imprisonment of all offenders, and the city resumed its usual quiet.

SCENE IN A STATION-HOUSE CELL, WASHINGTON, D. C., AFTER THE APPOINTMENT OF GENERAL PORTER AS PROVOST-MARSHAL.

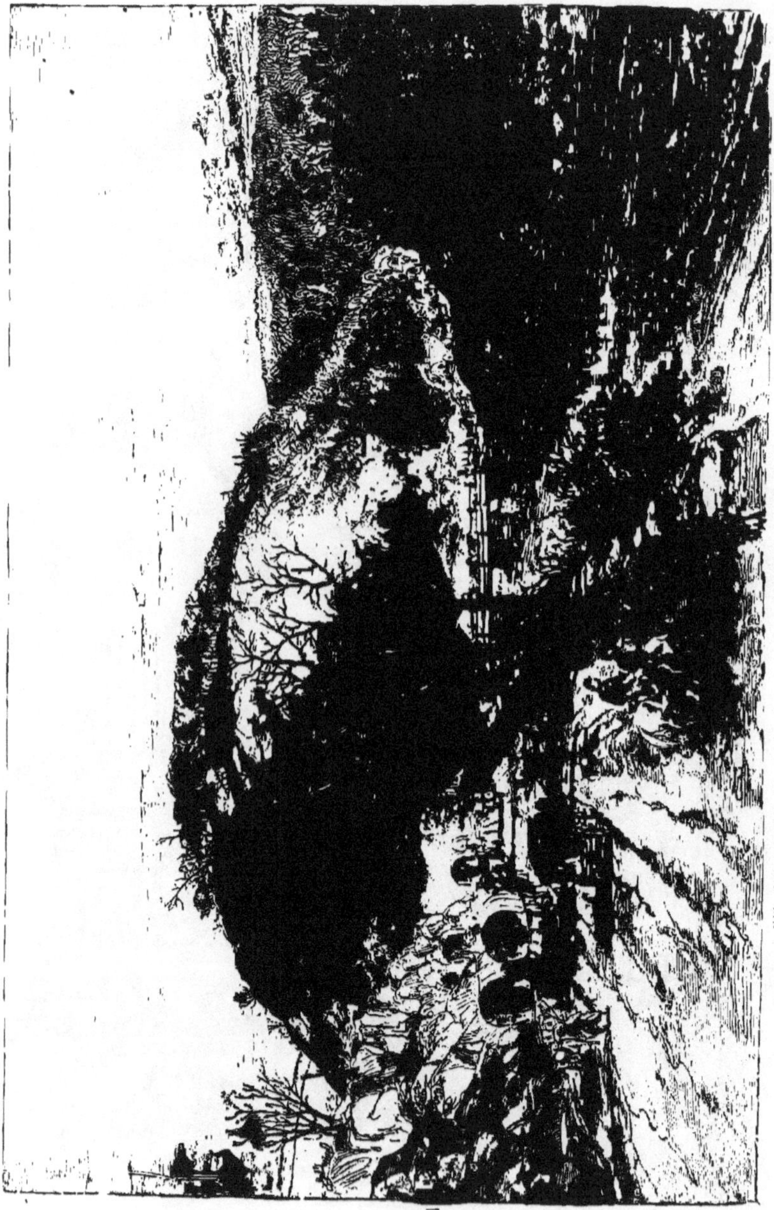

NEW MILITARY ROAD ... NEAR THE CHAIN BRIDGE, ABOVE WASHINGTON, D.C.

LOUIS BLENKER.

Born in Germany, at Worms, on the Rhine, in 1812, died October 31st, 1863; entered the army of Greece, wherein he served several years, leaving it after he had been made a first lieutenant, to return to his native city, where he commenced business as a wine merchant. He was elected colonel of the Worms Militia, after the revolution of 1848, and joined the revolutionary movement in Baden, where he was placed at the head of a body of 8,000 men. These figured in many engagements with the Royalists, in all of which Blenker and his heroic wife bravely contended side by side, until they were attacked by a force of Prussians nearly seven times greater than their own. Unable to withstand such odds, they passed into Switzerland with the remnant of their brave followers, and remained there until the end of September, 1849, when Blenker was expelled by a special order of the President of the Helvetian Confederacy. Colonel Blenker and his wife then took refuge in the United States, settling in Rockland Co., N. Y., on a farm which they had purchased. Here Blenker remained until the Civil War broke out. He then came to New York City, where he was given the command of the First German Rifle Regiment, Eighth New York State Volunteers, which was one of the first that went to the seat of war. At the battle of Bull Run, Blenker was placed at the head of the First Brigade of the Fifth Division, commanded by Colonel Dixon S. Miles, and, aided by Colonel [illegible], covered the retreat of the Federal army. He was afterward made a brigadier-general, and given the command of the German division of the Army of the Potomac.

SIMON BOLIVAR BUCKNER.

Born in Kentucky in 1823; entered the Military Academy at West Point in 1840; brevetted second lieutenant of infantry July 1st, 1844; served at frontier posts 1844-5; assistant professor of ethics at the Military Academy from August, 1845, to May, 1846; entered the Mexican War, and was brevetted first lieutenant of the Sixth Infantry for his bravery in the battles of Contreras and Churubusco, where he was wounded. His gallant conduct at the battle of El Molino del Rey, in September, 1847, won him the grade of captain. He was afterward made quartermaster of the Sixth Infantry, and became assistant instructor of infantry tactics at West Point, 1848-50, and commissioner of subsistence at New York City, 1852-5. Resigned from the army March 26th, 1855. At the breaking out of the Civil War he joined the Southern Confederacy, was made a general, placed in command at Bowling Green, which he evacuated on the fall of Fort Henry, taking his troops to Fort Donelson, where he surrendered with his forces to General Grant on the 16th of February, 1862. Was confined in Fort Warren till August, 1862, then exchanged and placed in command of a division of Hardee's corps in Bragg's army, in Tennessee, and, as major-general, assigned to the Third Grand Division engaged at Murfreesboro' and at Chickamauga, being included, May 26th, 1865, in Kirby Smith's surrender to General Canby.

ORMSBY McKNIGHT MITCHELL.

Born in Union County, Ky., August 28th, 1810; was quite young moved to Lebanon, O., and at twelve years of age became clerk in a store at Miami, O.; cadet at the Military Academy at West Point in 1825, and four years later graduated in the Class including Robert E. Lee and Joseph E. Johnston; entered the artillery corps with the rank of brevet second lieutenant, was assistant professor of mathematics at the Academy until 1831, resigned his position in the army to study law and practiced in Cincinnati, O., till 1834, when he was elected professor of mathematics and of astronomy in the Ohio University. This position he retained ten years. On the 19th of April, 1845, he founded the Cincinnati Observatory, and became its director. In 1848-9 he held the office of adjutant-general of the State of Ohio, and in 1853-4 made two voyages to Europe as chief engineer of the Ohio and Mississippi Railway. In 1859 he became director of the Dudley Observatory at Albany N.Y.

Upon the breaking out of the Civil War he tendered his services to the Federal Government, was made a brigadier-general, and ordered to the Department of the Ohio. He distinguished himself by the seizure of the railway running between Corinth and Chattanooga, was made a major-general in April, 1862, and given the command of the Department of the South in September of the same year. While at Beaufort, S. C., he was, however, taken sick with yellow fever, and died from its effects on the 30th of October, 1862.

The course of lectures which Professor Mitchell commenced delivering in 1842 gave such a stimulus to astronomy, that observatories were the more promptly established in different parts of the country. He invented the chronograph for measuring automatically right ascensions by electro-magnetic mechanism, as well as two declinometers, with which many important observations were made, and an apparatus for personal equation. He established the *Sidereal Messenger*, and was besides, the author of a great many popular works, notably, "The Astronomy of the Bible," "Popular Astronomy," "The Planetary and Stellar Worlds," and "The Orbs of Heaven."

DON CARLOS BUELL.

Born near Marietta, O., March 23d, 1818; entered the Military Academy at West Point in 1837, and graduated in 1841 as brevet second lieutenant of infantry; served in the Florida War, 1841-2; on frontier duty, 1842-5; and in the military occupation of Texas, 1845-6, made first lieutenant in June 1846, and captain in the following September for gallantry at the battle of Monterey. At the battle of Churubusco he was wounded in the chest, and made a brevet major. In 1848 he became assistant adjutant-general, with the full rank of captain. In 1861-62 he was made a brigadier-general, and placed at the head of the Department of the Ohio, succeeding General William T. Sherman. He set about organizing an efficient army and planned several movements which won for him an excellent reputation. He became subordinate to Halleck, when the latter was placed in command of the Department of the Southwest, and was at the same time promoted to be a major-general. He took command of the Army of the Ohio, and at its head succeeded, with Grant, in gaining for the Federals at the battle of Shiloh, or Pittsburg Landing, a victory which would otherwise undoubtedly have fallen to the Confederates under the successive leadership of Generals Johnston and Beauregard. He took part in the siege of Corinth, in the operations carried on in Northern Alabama, and the retreat to Louisville, in order to cut off Bragg's army, which he drove from Kentucky. He resigned from the army June 1st, 1864, and since 1865 has been president of the Green River (Ky.) Iron Works.

COL. MURPHY'S REGIMENT.

The Fifteenth N. Y. Regiment, Colonel J. McLeod Murphy, originally enlisted as a corps of sappers and miners, was selected by McClellan to be trained as pontoniers, and placed in a school of instruction near the Navy Yard, Washington, D. C. Our illustration on pages 166-167 represents the regiment, after less than a month's drill, engaged in throwing a bridge over the Anacostia River. At the word of command one hundred trained men seized the India-rubber floats, launched them, mooring them stem and stern; one hundred men, each handling his proper beam and plank, the lashers lashed the framework to the floats, placed the timbers in position and thus, as by magic, in the brief space of twenty minutes was built a broad, substantial bridge, three hundred feet in length, and capable of sustaining three companies of infantry, artillery, horsemen and loaded wagons.

LOUIS BLENKER.

POSITION OF FORT DONELSON.

This fort was situated at Dover, Tenn., twelve miles east of Fort Henry, on the west bank of the Cumberland River. The fort was built in the Summer of 1861, about the same time that Fort Henry was constructed. Its location was selected as a rear defense to Bowling Green, and also as a defense against the approach of the Federal troops on Nashville by way of the Cumberland River. The Confederates designed that this fort should be an effectual barrier to the progress of the enemy into Tennessee. The railroad from Bowling Green to Memphis passed four miles south of it

CHARGE OF THE EIGHTH MISSOURI AND THE ELEVENTH INDIANA REGIMENTS, LED BY GENERAL LEWIS WALLACE, AT FORT DONELSON, FEBRUARY 15TH, 1[illegible]

CAPTURE OF FORT DONELSON.

After the surrender of Fort Henry, General Grant ordered reconnoissances to be made immediately up the Tennessee River, while he located his troops on the roads leading to Fort Donelson, and while Commander Foote proceeded to Cairo to repair damages and to complete arrangements for the next expedition.

Foote, having taken with him the gunboats *Cincinnati*, *Essex* and *St. Louis*, there remained the *Carondelet* at Fort Henry, and the three wooden gunboats *Conestoga*, *Lexington* and *Tyler*, which were placed in charge of Lieutenant-commander S. L. Phelps. With these he soon reached the bridge of the Memphis and Ohio Valley Railway, which crosses the Tennessee River at a point about twelve miles south of Fort Henry. Its draw was closed and its machinery disabled, but in about an hour the draw was opened, and the *Tyler*, being left to destroy the railroad and part of the bridge, the *Conestoga* and *Lexington* gave chase to some Confederate transports, which had been seen attempting to escape up the river. These were so closely pursued, that they were set on fire and abandoned.

The gunboats continued on their way, capturing a steamer at Cerro Gordo, two more at Eastport, and compelling the flight of a number of Confederates at Savannah, which place Phelps had contemplated attacking. After proceeding as far as Florence, Ala., where he captured a portion of the supplies on board of three steamers, which had been set afire on his approach, and where he found most of the citizens kindly disposed, he returned to his place of departure.

On Tuesday, the 11th of February, Grant called a council of war, at which it was decided to move immediately on Fort Donelson rather than wait for additional reinforcements. Part of McClernand's division advanced the same afternoon, but the main column did not get into motion until the following day.

February, 1862.

Grant had organized his forces, as before, into

S. B. BUCKNER.

two divisions, commanded by Generals McClernand and Smith, and had arranged for another division to be brought by Commander Foote, and to be placed in charge of Lewis Wallace, who had been made a brigadier-general on the day of the capture of Fort Henry. Part of McClernand's force advanced by the Telegraph Road, and halted within two miles of Fort Donelson, while the remainder marched by the Dover Road, in the same direction, with orders to unite and form the right investing wing. The other troops were to follow likewise by the Dover Road, Smith being ordered to prevent the possible retreat of the Confederates by the occupation of Dover, if practicable. General Wallace remained at Fort Henry.

Fort Donelson was situated on the left bank of the Cumberland River, at an elevation of about 100 feet, and mounted eight guns. Below it, at an elevation of about 30 feet, were two water batteries, containing together twelve guns.

The position was defended by 15,000 men, under the command of General John B. Floyd, who had, on the 13th, superseded General A. Sidney Johnston. This force consisted of the Third, Tenth, Eighteenth, Twenty-sixth, Thirtieth, Thirty-second, Forty-first, Forty-second, Forty-eighth, Forty-ninth, Fiftieth, Fifty-first and Fifty-third Tennessee; the First, Third, Fourth, Fourteenth, Twentieth and Twenty-sixth Mississippi; the Thirty-sixth, Fiftieth, Fifty-first and Fifty-sixth Virginia; the Second and Eighth Kentucky; the Seventh Texas; the Fifteenth Arkansas and the Twenty-seventh Alabama Regiments of Infantry; besides Colms's and Gowan's battalions of Infantry, Forrest's, Gantt's and Milton's battalions of Cavalry, and nearly 700 artillerists.

The Federal troops met with no opposition on the way, and early in the afternoon of the 12th occupied the positions which had been assigned them, after some skirmishing, during which the Confederate pickets were driven in.

On Thursday, the 13th, Colonel Berge's Sixty-sixth Regiment of Illinois Sharpshooters engaged the enemy's pickets, and kept up, at a distance of about two hundred yards, an incessant fire, which told severely on the Confederate gunners serving one of the land batteries, and during which arrangements were completed for more important work. Major Cavender's heavy guns were placed on the spurs opposing the lines of defense; Oglesby's brigade held the extreme right, McClernand's division came next, and Smith's force took the extreme left, the entire line occupying nearly four miles in length.

At about midday, Colonel Wallace was ordered

GROUP OF CONFEDERATE PRISONERS CAPTURED AT FORT DONELSON.

From a Sketch by H. Lovie.

DECISIVE BAYONET-CHARGE OF THE SECOND IOWA REGIMENT ON THE

FROM A SKET

DECISIVE BAYONET-CHARGE OF THE SECOND IOWA REGIMENT ON THE CONFEDERATE INTRENCHMENTS AT FORT DONELSON, FEBRUARY 15th, 1862.

[illegible]

GHT EXPEDITION TO ISLAND NO. 10, BY COLONEL ROBERTS, WITH FORTY PICKED MEN OF THE FORTY-SECOND ILLINOIS—SPIKING THE GUNS OF THE UPPER BATTERY

From a Sketch by H. Lovie

to capture a battery called the Middle Redoubt, and taking with him the Seventeenth Illinois, under Major Smith, the Forty-eighth Illinois, Colonel Hayne, and the Forty-ninth Illinois, Colonel Morrison, besides McAllister's battery, he advanced rapidly up the hill until within forty rods of the battery, when a terrible fire from the entire line of infantry, as well as from the artillery, compelled them for a moment to fall back. They were reinforced by Colonel Smith's Forty-fifth Illinois Regiment, then supported by Schwartz's and Taylor's batteries, and made rally after rally, but to no purpose, in face of the superior numbers against them, and after suffering great losses during the full hour they held their ground, they fell back to their original position.

Further to the left, the Fourteenth Iowa and the Twenty-fifth Indiana Regiments had been ordered to assault another position commanded by Carondet's heavy guns, with the Seventh Iowa and the Sixty-sixth Illinois Regiments as a reserve. They had met with a heavy fire, and had suffered greatly, while ascending a hill amid brushwood and fallen timber, but they had succeeded, nevertheless, in gaining ground, and had maintained till night a favorable position whence Carender's guns were enabled to inflict serious damage. These troops were likewise called back to the positions held in the morning, though the artillery kept up a fire nearly all the ensuing night.

The water batteries had, in the meantime, been engaged by the *Carondelet*, which had come around from Fort Henry, and had kept up a brisk fire until struck by a 128-pound shot, which broke her steam heater and burst in the engine-room, though, strange as it may appear, without injuring any one.

At about midnight, Commander Foote's flotilla of six gunboats and fourteen transports arrived with, and landed, three miles below Fort Donelson, about 10,000 men, comprising the third division, given General Wallace. This consisted of two brigades, one commanded by Colonel Craft, embracing the Thirty-first Indiana, Forty-fourth Indiana, Seventeenth Kentucky, and Twenty-fifth Kentucky Regiments, Colonels Osborn, Reed, McHenry and Shackleford; while the other brigade, under Colonel John M. Thayer, included the First Nebraska, Fifty-eighth Ohio and Seventy-sixth Ohio, Colonels McCord, Steadman and Woods; and subsequently received the Forty-sixth, Fifty-seventh and Fifty-eighth Illinois Regiments, Colonels Davis, Baldwin, and Lynch. General Wallace arrived late on the 14th, with the Eighth Missouri and the Eleventh Indiana Regiments, as well as the Chicago Battery, which General Grant had sent specially for, and at once took command of his division, which was placed between the positions occupied by McClernand and by Smith.

The delay forcibly experienced by the third division reaching its position, through a necessarily circuitous route in order to avoid the forts, rendered it impossible for the land forces to cooperate with the gunboats in an attack Friday afternoon, as Grant had contemplated. The gunboats, therefore, acted alone, aided simply by a continued desultory fire from the artillery, as well as from the Federal sharpshooters.

At three o'clock in the afternoon of Friday, the 14th, the *Carondelet* opened fire on the water batteries, and was soon joined by the armored gunboats *St. Louis*, flagship, *Louisville* and *Pittsburg*, supported by the wooden gunboats *Conestoga*, *Lexington* and *Tyler*. The object of the fleet was to pass beyond the batteries so as to enfilade them with broadsides.

FEBRUARY, 1862.

Only twelve of Foote's guns could at one time be trained against the hail that met his first attack. The Confederates were serving their pieces with singular precision, and their shots were

DON CARLOS BUELL.

telling severely upon the armored boats gradually approaching them, yet Foote reserved his fire until within about three hundred yards. Then the heavy guns of the fleet responded to those on shore, the fight raged fiercely, and before long the men in the upper battery were observed abandoning it, and Foote saw the wished-for opportunity to pass them. Just then, however, the *Louisville* was seen drifting helplessly, having had her tiller-chains cut away, and in a few moments the *St. Louis* herself was almost as helpless, by reason of a shot having entered her wheelhouse, destroying one of the wheels and mortally wounding her pilot.

Seeing the plight of the fleet, the Confederate gunners had returned to their batteries, and, serving them with renewed energy, they soon compelled the *Carondelet* and the *Pittsburg* to retire from the scene as the two others had done. The wooden gunboats were ordered to follow, and the engagement came to an end. It was found that the *St. Louis*, *Louisville*, *Pittsburg* and *Carondelet* had

ORMSBY M. MITCHELL.

received respectively fifty-nine, thirty-six, twenty and twenty-six shots, and that the total loss to the fleet was nine killed and forty-five wounded, including six killed by the bursting of a gun on the *Carondelet*.

Commander Foote, later on, took four of his vessels back to Cairo, in order to repair damages, and to organize a still more formidable fleet, two of the gunboats being left to cover the transports, while Grant continued the investiture of Fort Donelson, and the *Tyler* was sent to complete the destruction of the railroad bridge above Fort Henry, in order to prevent all Confederate reinforcements in that direction.

On the evening of the 14th, Floyd called a council of war, whereat he submitted the fact that Fort Donelson could not be successfully held with less than 50,000 men, and that it were doubtless better to make a sortie in force rather than wait longer the possibility of additional troops strengthening the enemy, and consequently preventing all possible escape. It was unanimously decided, therefore, to take the offensive, and at about five o'clock on Saturday morning, the 15th, Generals Gideon J. Pillow and Bushrod R. Johnston left the fort at the head of some 10,000 men, with Colonel Baldwin's brigade in the advance.

FEBRUARY, 1862.

McClernand's force was the objective, and its pickets were soon reached and forced back upon the actually unsuspecting camp, whose safety was for a while endangered, so still and quietly conducted had been the Confederate advance. Oglesby's brigade, which held the road, and had but little artillery support, withstood the first attack, fortunately thwarting a cavalry advance on his extreme right, until its ammunition began to give way, when the whole line fell back, with exception of the extreme left, where stood the Thirty-first Illinois under Colonel John A. Logan. So firmly did the latter force hold the ground, that what might have at one time proved a panic was averted. To the support of Oglesby's line came the Eleventh and the Twentieth Illinois, belonging to W. H. L. Wallace's brigade, which were followed by nearly 3,500 more men of the same command, as well as by the light batteries under Dresser, McAllister and Taylor. Column after column of fresh Confederate troops kept pouring in upon the Federals, notwithstanding the terrible fire of grape and canister directed against them. Position after position was gained and lost on both sides, until, by nearly eight o'clock, it looked as if no advantage had been gained on either hand.

The steadiness and apparent regularity with which fresh Confederate troops were being brought forward began, however, to alarm McClernand, and he finally decided to send for assistance to General Lewis Wallace. As the latter had been ordered to hold the centre at all hazards, he sent to headquarters for instructions. Not hearing from him, McClernand asked again for immediate aid, stating that his flank had been turned, when, in the absence of General Grant, who was then in conference with Commander Foote, Wallace took the responsibility of ordering ahead the brigade under Colonel Craft.

Craft was, unfortunately, guided too far to the right of the line, where he came upon a greatly superior force, which had just left a ravine in Oglesby's rear. This force he engaged deliberately, but could not overcome. He was soon forced back, as well as were the forces under W. H. L. Wallace, McArthur and Oglesby, when Thayer's brigade came up, with General Wallace himself in the advance. This brigade was placed between the retiring troops and the advancing Confederates, with its light artillery, under Lieutenant Wood, in position to sweep the road along which the enemy was approaching

WOMAN'S MEETING AT COOPER UNION HALL, COOPER INSTITUTE, NEW YORK CITY, TO ORGANIZE THE "WOMAN'S CENTRAL ASSOCIATION OF RELIEF" FOR THE ARMY

The attack soon followed upon the Federals, the First Nebraska Regiment bearing its brunt for a time; but after an active encounter, the Confederates were compelled to retire.

Soon after, General Grant ordered an advance upon the retiring force, which was done, with Colonel Morgan L. Smith's Eighth Missouri and Colonel George McGinnis's Eleventh Indiana in the lead, and Colonel Ross's two Ohio regiments in reserve.

While these regiments were marching toward the ridge occupied earlier in the day, Cruft's brigade was being taken around the base of the hill to engage the enemy's left flank, which it did successfully by the time the ridge had been reached. The fight upon the latter was especially severe, but the position was finally gained and held during the ensuing night while the enemy remained in its earthworks.

The Confederate right had at the same time been engaged by Smith's forces. The assault there was led by the Second and Seventh Iowa and the Twenty-fifth Indiana Regiments, under cover of Stone's Missouri Battery, supported by the Fifty-sixth Indiana, Fourteenth Iowa and Berge's Sharpshooters. They had marched with General Smith in the immediate advance, receiving the galling fire of the Confederates unflinchingly, and when within proper distance had, without firing a gun, carried the rifle-pits with the bayonet. Night coming on, they had been unable to follow up the advantage gained, and had merely kept their position in anticipation of another forward movement the day following.

That same night, however, the Confederate generals held another council of war, at which, after a long and very bitter consultation, it was decided to give up all further contest. Floyd escaped with some of his men on board a steamer at Dover, on the way to Nashville, and was followed by General Pillow, who fled to Columbia, in Middle Tennessee, while General Buckner was left to arrange the terms of capitulation.

On Sunday morning, the 16th of February, as the Federals were preparing to follow up the successes of the previous day, while flags were seen floating over the enemy's works, and soon after the unconditional surrender of the Confederates was accepted.

The fort was immediately occupied by the forces in the advance, the water batteries being taken possession of by troops landed from the Cumberland River. The capitulation embraced 13,500 men as prisoners, including Generals Buckner and Johnson, 20,000 muskets, 3,000 horses, 17 heavy guns, 48 field-pieces, and a large quantity of military stores.

The Federals had lost 446 killed, 1,745 wounded, and a few prisoners, who had already been taken across the Cumberland. The additional losses of the Confederates were 237 killed and 1,007 wounded.

Generals Grant, McClernand and Wallace were each promoted to a major-generalship in recognition of the services rendered by them at Fort Donelson.

HENRY WAGER HALLECK.

Born at Waterville, Oneida County, N. Y., January 16th, 1815; entered the Military Academy at West Point, graduating July 1st, 1839, as second lieutenant of engineers; became assistant-professor of engineering at the Academy until June 1840, and for nearly a year afterward was assistant to a board of engineers at Washington, D. C. From 1841 to 1846 he was made assistant in charge of the construction of fortifications in New York Harbor, being absent only a short time in 1845, when he was sent on a tour of examination of the public works in Europe. At the time of the Mexican War he took an active part in the military and civil operations of the Government on the Pacific Coast, remaining there until nearly the close of the year 1854. He was then made director-general of the New Almaden Quicksilver Mine, and in 1854 resigned from the army, devoting himself mainly to the practice of law in San Francisco.

At the beginning of the Civil War he was made a major-general of the regular army, and assigned to the command of the Department of Missouri, which latter was made to embrace other States early in 1862, and then called the Department of the Mississippi. He took personal command after the battle of Shiloh, occupied Corinth, and soon after was called to Washington as General-in-chief. When U. S. Grant was made Lieutenant-general, Halleck assumed command of the Department of the James, April, 1865. In August of that year he was transferred to the Pacific Coast, and in 1869 to the Department of the South. He died at Louisville, Ky., January 9th, 1872.

WOMAN'S PART IN THE WAR.

And what can gentle woman do
 In this dark hour of strife,
When men, with hearts so brave and true,
 Are staking limb and life?

The soldier's flag to give is well,
 The martial scarf to tie—
To twine with wreaths the fond farewell,
 To bid "to do, or die!"

Yet these are but the bright array
 Of war's portentous form;
The lightning's distant fitful play,
 Before the coming storm.

A better still is woman's part,
 Her zeal her power to prove,
Her truthful, her religious heart,
 Her self-denying love.

Put every idle good aside;
 Of luxury, all thought;
The vain expense, the selfish pride,
 Prosperity has brought.

Be earnest, patient, just and brave,
 To woman's instinct true;
Give freely of the best you have
 For those who die for you.

HENRY WAGER HALLECK.

Your wealth, your time, your wonted ease,
 Your fervent secret prayers;
The thoughtless joys that once might please,
 Reject for nobler cares.

Our suffering men like angels tend
 The soothing draught to give,
While accents from your lips descend,
 That bid the wounded "live!"

And, oh, let woman's kindly speech
 Sweet words of healing find,
Our Marah's bitter waves to reach,
 Our country's wounds to bind!

—*Boston Transcript.*

RE-OCCUPATION OF BOWLING GREEN, CLARKSVILLE, NASHVILLE AND COLUMBUS.

The successive evacuation of Bowling Green, Clarksville, Nashville and Columbus by the Confederates was the natural result of the surrender of Forts Henry and Donelson to the Federals.

General Ormsby M. Mitchell, commanding the Third Division of General Don Carlos Buell's army, had broken camp on Tuesday, February 11th, and marched from Bacon's Creek, across the Green River, at Munfordsville, in the direction of Bowling Green, Ky., resting at Camp Madison on the 13th. He reached Bowling Green on the 15th, after making the last forty-two miles in as little as thirty-two hours, and found the city deserted, and both of the bridges over the Big Barren River destroyed. Nearly half a million dollars worth of property had been burned by the Rangers belonging to Johnston's retreating force, while all the stores and provisions that could be removed had been taken away to Nashville.

February, 1862.

On the eventful Sunday, the 16th of February, Commodore Foote had caused the destruction, by the *St. Louis*, of the Tennessee Iron Works, situated nearly seven miles above Dover, and although suffering greatly from the wound received while engaging Fort Donelson, he had, on the day following, himself proceeded from Cairo for another advance up the Cumberland River with the two gunboats *Cairo* and *Conestoga*. On the 19th he had reached Clarksville, Tenn., fifty miles to the northwest of Nashville, and had made preparations to attack Forts Lavier and Clark, defending the town.

These had been abandoned, however, and Foote entered Clarksville the following day. The retreating force had set fire to the railroad bridge across the Cumberland. General Charles F. Smith soon after occupied Clarksville with a strong force, and Foote returned to Cairo to arrange for another expedition against Nashville, the capital of Tennessee.

The last named place was entered on Sunday, the 23d of February, by the Fourth Ohio Cavalry, under Colonel Kenner, and belonging to General O. M. Mitchell's division, the remainder of which latter soon after encamped at Edgefield, opposite the City of Nashville, pending the arrival of General Buell. He arrived on the 25th, the same day that Commodore Foote reached it with the gunboat *Conestoga*. The latter had been taken up at Clarksville to convoy the transports on which were the troops commanded by General Nelson.

On the 26th, Major R. B. Cheatham came over to Buell's headquarters at Edgefield, where he made a formal surrender of the City of Nashville, and on the 28th, the Federal banner once more floated over both the City Hall and the State Capitol.

Before abandoning Nashville, the Confederate General Floyd had ordered the destruction of its two bridges and of two unfinished gunboats, as well as the dispersion by the mob of such stores and other property as he could not well carry away.

As the Governor and the State Legislature had likewise gone, it was determined with General Grant, who arrived on the 27th, to appoint a military governor, who should administer the affairs of the State under martial law, with the rank of brigadier-general. Andrew Johnson, who subsequently became President of the United States at the death of Lincoln, was appointed to fill the place.

Immediately on the return of Foote from Nashville to Cairo, he organized an expedition to capture the town of Columbus, Ky., situated opposite Belmont, against which General Grant had marched in November, 1861.

The expedition consisted of four mortar-boats, under Lieutenant Commanding Phelps, and the gunboats *Cincinnati*, *St. Louis*, *Carondelet*, *Louisville*, *Pittsburg* and *Lexington*, commanded by Captains Davis, Walke and Stembel, and Lieutenants Commanding Paulding, Kirk and Thompson, besides three transports, *Aleck Scott*, *Illinois* and *T. L. McGill*, with about 2,000 men under General W. T. Sherman. The latter's force comprised the Twenty-seventh Illinois and part of the Fifty-fourth Ohio, Seventy-fourth Ohio, and of the Fifty-fifth Illinois Regiments. General George W. Cullum, of General Halleck's staff, accompanied the expedition.

It left Cairo very early on the 4th of March, and at sunrise it was close by its destination, ready for the attack, although information had been received to the effect that Columbus was abandoned. The Federal flag was seen floating over the fort, but to make sure that no deception was being practiced, Colonel Buford was ordered to take a detachment of the Twenty-seventh Illinois Regiment and reconnoitre. They landed, and on reaching the fort, found it occupied by some 250 men of the Second Illinois Cavalry under Lieutenant Hogg, which had been sent out as scouts by General Sherman from Paducah, and who, on finding the place vacated, had occupied it the previous afternoon.

March, 1862.

Upon the levee was found a very large number of torpedoes, anchors, weights, and a portion of the chain which had been stretched across the river, whilst near the railway that had been built to raise articles up the bill stood a quantity of ordnance and stores ready for transportation.

After leaving a garrison of nearly 2,000 infantry and 400 cavalry, the flotilla returned to its place of departure.

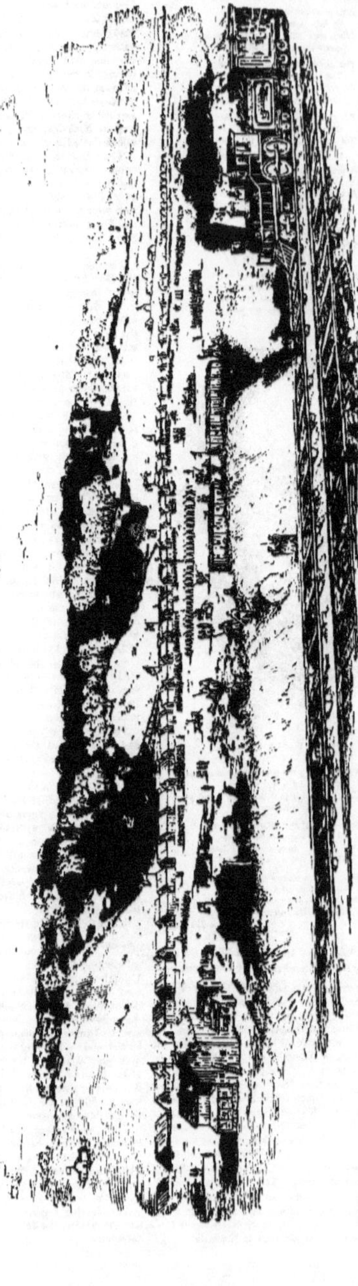

CAMP DENISON, ABOVE CINCINNATI, O., ON THE BANKS OF THE MIAMI RIVER, FIRST USED BY GENERAL COX AS A RECRUITING CAMP, AND LATER IN THE WAR AS A PERMANENT CAMP OF INSTRUCTION IN THE WEST.

DARING EXPLOIT OF COLORED MEN IN CHARLESTON HARBOR.

ROBERT SMALLS, pilot; John Smalls and Alfred Gradine, engineers; and Abraham Jackson, Gabriel Turny, William Morrison, Samuel Chisholm, Abram Allston, and David Jones, of the crew of the steamer *Planter*, taking advantage of a night in which the white officers were on shore, quietly got up steam, and slipped down the harbor, immediately under the frowning guns of Sumter. As they passed the fort, day had just dawned, and they gave the usual signals, and were allowed to pass. When out of range of the guns they hoisted a white flag, and steered straight for the United States steamer *Augusta*, on blockade duty, and gave up their prize to the United States officers. The *Planter* was a large vessel of light draught, and had already proved, with her armament of six guns of heavy calibre, a troublesome visitor among the blockading squadron. Commander Parrott, of the *Augusta*, forwarded the prize to Port Royal, with late papers from Charleston to Commander Dupont, and on receipt of the vessel and information, Dupont made a report to the Navy Department recounting the exploit and its importance to the United States Government, and recommended that the captors be suitably rewarded, either under the

William Morrison. Robert Smalls. A. Gradine.
John Smalls.

FOUR OF THE NINE COLORED MEN WHO CAPTURED THE CONFEDERATE STEAMER "PLANTER."

claim of the steamer as a prize, or in some other way.

On Monday, May 19th, 1862, in the United States Senate, a Bill was introduced for the relief of Robert Smalls and others (colored), who had recently delivered the steamer *Planter* to Commodore Dupont's squadron. The Bill provided that the steamer, with her armament, cargo, etc., be appraised by a competent board of officers, and that one-half the value thereof should go to Robert Smalls and his associates, who ran the *Planter* out of the Harbor of Charleston, and providing that the Secretary of the Navy should invest the sum in United States stocks, the interest to be paid to Smalls and his associates or heirs. The Bill was promptly passed.

The pilot, Robert Smalls, at once joined the Federal Army, and became a prominent organizer of the colored troops at Hilton Head. He attained the rank of colonel in the Volunteer Army, and at the close of the war took an active part in politics, becoming a leader of the freedmen, and represented them both in the Legislature of the State of South Carolina and in the Congress of the United States. On June 3d, 1884, he was the most prominent delegate from South Carolina in the National Republican Convention assembled at Chicago, and his vote and voice helped to elevate another of his own race, John R. Lynch, of Mississippi, to the honorable position of Chairman of the Convention.

BATTLE BETWEEN THE "MERRIMACK" AND THE "MONITOR."

WHAT proves to have been a most extraordinary and a decidedly unique naval encounter, took place in Hampton Roads, on the 8th and 9th of March.

March, 1862.

At that time, the only Federal men-of-war lying in the Roads were the steam-frigate *Roanoke*, flag-ship, 40 guns, and *Minnesota*, 40 guns, besides the sailing-frigates *Congress*, 50 guns; the *St. Lawrence*, 50 guns; and the *Cumberland*, 24 guns. In their immediate vicinity stood a number of steam-tugs and transports.

At about noon on Saturday, the 8th of March, there suddenly appeared, coming down the Elizabeth River, three Confederate vessels, which afterward proved to be the *Patrick Henry*, 6 guns, and the *Jamestown*, 4 guns, slightly in advance of an iron ram called by the Confederates the *Virginia*, although the stranger was the result of a transformation of the old United States frigate *Merrimack*, which had been fired and sunk in April, 1861, and was afterward raised, at the Norfolk Navy Yard.

It had been long known and often bruited that the Confederates were fashioning a novel and formidable engine of war, which, it was intended, should possess the requisite appliances for overcoming and destroying any known vessel afloat. After repeated delays, the transformed *Merrimack* now appeared in the shape of a huge floating battery, with a long projecting ram, and heavily ironplated throughout. She was propelled by two engines, had large furnaces for heating shot besides an apparatus for throwing hot water, and carried eight 80-pound rifled guns, besides two guns capable of throwing a 120-pound shell or a 100-pound solid shot.

The *Merrimack* first attacked the *Cumberland*, while the gunboats engaged the *Congress*, and when within an eighth of a mile, fired a broadside into her, which met with an earnest response from the frigate, though with but little real damage to the battery, as nearly all the balls glanced off the *Merrimack's* armor-plates.

The *Cumberland* was again approached, and at a distance of about twenty yards given another broadside, which killed over 60 of her men. The *Merrimack* then retired a short distance, and, under a full head of steam, drove her long ram into the side of the frigate, making a large opening under the water-line. She then backed again and repeated the operation in the waist of the *Cumberland*, causing the latter to sink in a very short time. Such as remained of her officers and crew, about 150 out of 211, sought escape by jumping into the water, and by using a few boats, until taken by the propeller *Whilden*, which General Mansfield had sent from Newport News to their rescue.

After disposing of the *Cumberland*, the *Merrimack* engaged the water battery on shore, shelling the Federal camp from under the bluff in such a way that the guns in the battery could not be used effectively against her. She then approached the *Congress*, which the gunboats had been engaging, and poured into her such a destructive fire as to soon compel the hoisting of a white flag by Lieutenant Pendergast. The latter was then in command, by reason of the death of Lieutenant Joseph B. Smith, which was followed by that of Acting Master Moore and of Pilot Rhodes. The *Jamestown* came alongside to take off the prisoners from the *Congress*, which was set on fire the same evening, and finally destroyed.

While all this was going on, the other Federal vessels had been ordered forward. The *Roanoke*, which had long been lying off Fortress Monroe with a broken shaft, had two steam-tugs to assist her getting into position, and was followed by the *Minnesota* and the *St. Lawrence*. While passing Sewall's Point, however, the *Minnesota* was fired into by the shore batteries, one of the shots damaging the mainmast seriously, and soon got aground on the Horseshoe Bar, about a mile and a half from Newport News. There she was attacked by the *Merrimack*, and by a few gunboats that had just come up from the James River.

The *Merrimack* could not approach the *Minnesota* nearer than a mile, owing to the shallowness of the water, but the gunboats kept up a fire at close quarters, and, while they caused some damage on board the frigate, they likewise sustained injury from its heavy guns, one of them having finally to be towed off.

The fight lasted till dark, when the Confederate vessels retired again to the mouth of the Elizabeth River.

The *St. Lawrence* had approached the *Minnesota* during the fight, and had likewise got aground. She had joined in the fray, nevertheless; but, unfortunately for her, a shell had passed through her

JOHN ERICSSON.

side, just above the water-line, and had damaged her so seriously, that tugs had to be called to tow her to Fortress Monroe.

The *Roanoke* did not participate in the engagement, as she grounded at a point half way between Fortress Monroe and Newport News, whence she could not be gotten off until about ten o'clock in the evening. Efforts were, at the same time, made to get off the *Minnesota*, but unavailingly.

The loss of the Federals was 244 killed, drowned and wounded, as against a total of only 17 on the side of the Confederates.

Anxiety was naturally great on all sides regarding the immediate future, and many were the conjectures indulged in as to what the *Merrimack* and her consorts would succeed in doing the following day. Despondency, which was fast giving way to despair, at the prospects of no outside aid possibly reaching the Federal vessels, was, however, relieved at about nine o'clock in the evening, when John Ericsson's floating battery was seen approaching Fortress Monroe.

This battery, named the *Monitor*, was of an entirely original design, and had been constructed, by order of the Federal Government, at the Greenpoint (N. Y.) "Continental Works." Her flush deck lay but a few inches above the water, and bore nothing upon it but the wheelhouse, the low covering to the telescopic-slided smokestack, and a round revolving tower twenty feet in diameter. The whole was protected by a thick armor of iron, and was made bombproof. In the tower, or turret as it is called, were placed two eleven-inch Dahlgren guns, the heaviest that had, up to that time, been mounted upon any vessel.

The *Monitor* was ordered, on the 6th of March, to proceed on its trial trip to Fortress Monroe, and, as we have seen, reached the latter place three days later, being towed by the *Seth Low*, and having encountered rather boisterous weather. She was in command of Lieutenant John L. Worden, United States Navy, who, on reporting to Flag-officer Marston and to General Wool, was ordered to proceed to Newport News immediately upon receiving an additional supply of ammunition. Shortly after midnight the *Monitor* lay close by the *Minnesota*.

March, 1862.

Before sunrise, on Sunday, the 9th of March, the *Merrimack* and her consorts appeared, and advanced in the direction of the grounded *Minnesota*, but when she had come within about three miles of the latter, the *Monitor* placed herself between the two, compelling the stoppage of the Confederate battery.

The *Merrimack* then commenced firing at the *Monitor*, upon whose armor but one of her many heavy shots made any impression. She also occasionally fired a gun at the *Minnesota*, the two batteries all the while manœuvring for position.

The fight continued in this way for nearly two hours, the *Monitor* in that time having had her turret penetrated half way through by a 100-pound Armstrong solid shot, and having meanwhile hurled her heavy bolts against the *Merrimack*, without any apparent damage, even while the latter was temporarily aground.

The Confederate battery, not having succeeded in disabling the *Monitor*, turned her whole attention to the *Minnesota*, which had received a heavy shot near the water-line. As she approached, the frigate sent a full broadside into her, though with little effect, and received in return two heavy shells in quick succession. One of the shells penetrated through four rooms, exploding two charges of powder in its passage, and setting the vessel temporarily on fire. The other shell barely struck the frigate, but passed through and exploded the boiler of the steam-tug *Dragon*, which lay alongside, trying to pull the *Minnesota* off.

As the *Merrimack* was about sending a third shell in the same direction, the *Monitor* approached her, compelling a change of position in the engagement that was again renewed between the two batteries, and warding off repeated attempts made to run down the *Minnesota*. During the manœuvres that followed, the *Merrimack* once more got aground, and afforded the *Monitor*, for a while, a good opportunity to give her some well-directed shots, which doubtless told severely, as, when again afloat, she only made one unsuccessful and harmless attempt to run down the Federal battery, and at once started off for Norfolk. She was followed in this direction by her consorts, which had remained passive spectators of the whole encounter.

The engagement had come to an end with a loss on the Confederate side of 7 killed and 17 wounded, including among the latter, Captain Buchanan and Lieutenant Minor, of the *Merrimack*; the Federals having lost on board the *Minnesota* 3 killed and 16 wounded, besides a number on the *Dragon*.

There were no casualties on board the *Monitor*, with the exception of three men stunned by concussion, when the turret was once fairly struck, and the injury to the eyes of Lieutenant Worden, who was for a while blinded from the effects of cement or powder having entered his eyes while watching at the peephole in the pilot-house.

NAVAL BATTLE BETWEEN THE CONFEDERATE VESSELS "MERRIMACK," "YORKTOWN" AND "JAMESTOW
AND VICTORY FOR TH

FIGHT BETWEEN THE "MONITOR" (TWO GUNS) AND THE CONFEDERATE RAM "MERRIMACK" AND GUNBOATS
AND RESCUE OF THE UNITED

NAVAL BATTLE BETWEEN THE CONFEDERATE VESSELS "MERRIMACK," "YORKTOWN" AND "JAMESTOWN," AND THE FEDERAL [illegible] "CUMBERLAND" AND "CONGRESS" — SINKING [illegible] "CUMBERLAND," AND VICTORY FOR THE CONFEDERATE NAVY, MARCH 8th, [illegible]

FIGHT BETWEEN THE "MONITOR" (TWO GUNS) AND THE CONFEDERATE RAM "MERRIMACK" AND GUNBOATS "[illegible]" AND "JAMESTOWN," CARRYING TWENTY-FOUR GUNS — DEFEAT OF THE CONFEDERATE RAM AND GUNBOATS AND RESCUE OF THE UNITED STATES STEAMER "MINNESOTA," HAMPTON ROADS, VA., MARCH 9th, 1862.

DESTRUCTION OF THE CONFEDERATE IRONCLAD "MERRIMACK," BLOWN UP BY HER COMMANDER, MAY 11TH, 1862.
From a Sketch taken from Craney Island.

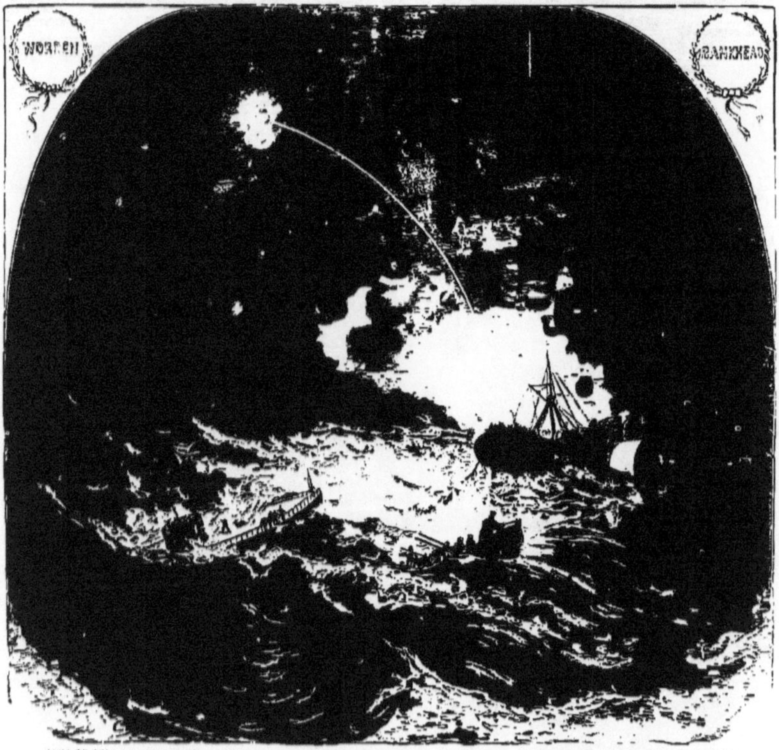

LOSS OF THE "MONITOR" IN A STORM OFF CAPE HATTERAS, DECEMBER 30TH, 1862.—GALLANT EFFORTS TO RESCUE THE CREW BY THE "RHODE ISLAND."

During the two-days fight, the *Minnesota* used 282 shells and 247 solid shot, while the *Monitor* fired 41 shots from her two guns, and was struck twenty-two times. The injuries to the *Merrimack* could not be ascertained.

The *Minnesota* was got afloat at about two o'clock Monday morning, with the aid of several tugs and after throwing all but eleven of her serviceable guns overboard. She was at once taken to Fortress Monroe.

The *Monitor* remained in Hampton Roads, watching for the reappearance of the *Merrimack* from the Elizabeth River. Only once, however, on the 11th of April, 1862, did she appear, and succeeded in capturing three temporarily unguarded Federal transports before the *Monitor* could reach her. The subsequent forced abandonment of Norfolk compelled the evacuation of the Confederate positions at Sewall's Point and at Craney Island, and on the 11th of May, 1862, the *Merrimack* was blown up, to prevent her falling into the hands of the Federals.

On the 15th of May, the *Monitor* was one of five vessels taken by Commander Rogers up the James River, with the view of attacking Richmond, and which were compelled to fall back by the obstructions placed in the channel at Drewry's Bluff, under protection of Fort Darling, whose full fire they encountered. She was then in command of Lieutenant William N. Jeffers, who had succeeded Lieutenant Worden when the latter was disabled, and who had seen active service in the Pacific and during the Mexican War, besides taking part in the Japan expedition. The *Monitor* then remained at and near Hampton Roads for its additional protection, until the end of the year, when she was ordered to proceed to Beaufort, S. C., and left on the 29th of December, 1862, in tow of the steamer *Rhode Island*.

On the 31st of December a heavy gale sprang up, and soon increased in such intensity that it was deemed best to take off the crew in the boats of the *Rhode Island*. Nearly all the men were taken off with the greatest difficulty, Commander Bankhead being the last to leave the battery. The latter was last seen at midnight, when she must have foundered, carrying down with her twelve men, who from excessive fear, could not be induced to make the hazardous attempt of leaving the turret to enter the boats.

JOHN ERICSSON.

Born at Wermeland, Sweden, July 31st, 1803. As a boy he showed genius for invention. At eleven years of age he was appointed a cadet in the Swedish Engineer Corps, where he soon rose to a lieutenancy. He was engaged on several public works in his own country, and in 1820 entered the Swedish army as ensign. While in the service, in 1826, he invented a "flame-engine," which he was given leave to take to England, in order to try and introduce it there. In this enterprise he did not succeed, and encountered heavy expenditures, which induced him to retire from the service and to devote his time exclusively to mechanical pursuits. One of the successful results of his efforts was the application of artificial draft to steam boilers, introduced on the Liverpool and Manchester Railway, in England, and the use of which has since become universal. He invented the screw as a means of propulsion in steamers, and made that new arrangement in ships-of-war which places the machinery below the water-line, thus revolutionizing the navies of the world. The invention he offered to the British Admiralty, but not succeeding in having it adopted in England, he came to the United States in 1839, through the influence of Captain R. F. Stockton, U.S.N. Two years after his arrival, he commenced in New York the construction of the screw-steamer *Princeton* on the principle rejected by the British Admiralty. She was the first ship-of-war built with the propelling machinery below the water line. In 1852, he so perfected the caloric engine which he had invented nineteen years before, that he succeeded in propelling with it the steamer *Ericsson*, which made her first trip in 1853. In 1861, he proposed to the United States Government the building of an iron steam floating battery upon an entirely novel and unprecedented plan, and obtained the contract for one to be launched in a hundred days. The battery was to be built entirely at Ericsson's expense, and to be accepted only after proof of its efficiency. It was built accordingly, with the aid of public-spirited men in Troy and New Haven, and on the 9th of March, 1862, it appeared in Hampton Roads, succeeding in a few hours, under the command of Lieutenant J. L. Worden, in disabling and forcing back the Confederate ram *Merrimack*, which was five times her size, and had an armament four times greater than her own. Ericsson named the battery, *Monitor*, for reasons explained in the following letter to the Assistant Secretary of the Navy:

New York, January 20th, 1862.

Sir: In accordance with your request, I now submit for your approbation a name for the floating battery at Greenpoint. The impregnability and aggressive character of this structure will admonish the leaders of the Southern rebellion that the batteries on the banks of their rivers will no longer present barriers to the entrance of the Union forces. The ironclad intruder will thus prove a severe Monitor to those leaders. But there are other leaders who will also be startled and admonished by the booming of the guns from the impregnable iron turret. Downing Street will hardly view with indifference this last Yankee notion—this Monitor. To the lords of the admiralty the new craft will be a Monitor, suggesting doubts as to the propriety of completing those four steel-clad ships at three and a half millions a piece. On these and many similar grounds I propose to name the new battery, *Monitor*.

I am, sir, respectfully, your obedient servant,

J. Ericsson.

Gustavus V. Fox, *Assistant Secretary of the Navy, Washington*.

JOHN LORIMER WORDEN.

In recognition of his services, Ericsson received resolutions of thanks from the New York Chamber of Commerce, who sent a copy of the same to the President of the United States.

JOHN LORIMER WORDEN.

Born March 12th, 1818, in New York City; entered the navy as a midshipman January 10th, 1834, and became a lieutenant in 1840, commander in 1862, commodore in 1868, and rear-admiral in 1872. He was in command of the sloop-of-war *Savannah*, in blockading service, during November, 1860, and, after a brief leave of absence, was sent as special messenger to Fort Pickens with dispatches advising Captain Adams of the *Sabine* how he was to be reinforced. He took the land route, and fearing arrest, destroyed the dispatches. When he reached Montgomery, he was stopped and searched, but no papers being found upon him, he was given by General Bragg a pass allowing him to visit Captain Adams, to whom he gave from memory the contents of the dispatches. The reinforcements reached their destination, and upon his return to Pensacola he was arrested and confined as a prisoner of war until exchanged in November, 1862.

WILLIAM N. JEFFERS.

In March, 1862, he was given the command of the *Monitor*, in which his heroic and skillful conduct during her notable engagement with the Confederate ram *Merrimack* gained him a world-wide reputation. Toward the close of the action his eyes were seriously injured by the explosion of a shell against the pilot-house of the *Monitor*, causing nearly total blindness for a long period afterward.

A few days after the engagement President Lincoln called upon Commander Worden in Washington, and found him lying in bed attended by Mrs. Worden, and with his eyes closely bandaged. As Lincoln sat beside Worden, the latter exclaimed: "Mr. President, you do me great honor!" to which Lincoln replied: "No, sir, no, sir; it is you who do me honor, and confer honor on the country."

For his services he received the thanks of the United States Congress and of the New York Chamber of Commerce.

THE BATTLE OF PEA RIDGE—ELK HORN

While the forces under General Grant and Commander Foote were operating against Fort Henry and Fort Donelson, the army which had been placed in charge of General Samuel R. Curtis was actively on its way southward from Springfield, Mo., which had been again occupied by the Federals late on the 13th of February, in hopes of meeting Price's forces.

Curtis had had running fights with the enemy and captured on the way a large number of recruits intended for Price's army, among these being the latter's son, Edward Price, who had recently been promoted to a brigadier-generalship.

On the 20th of February, Curtis had ordered forward two regiments of infantry under Lieutenant-colonels Herron and Phelps, Captain Hayden's battery of artillery, and four detachments of cavalry under Colonel Ellis and Majors Bolivar McConnell and Wright, to attack a brigade of Confederate troops at Cross Hollows under the command of Colonel Hubert, which he defeated, after losing nineteen killed and wounded. He had subsequently pushed on as far as Fayetteville, which the Confederates had left burning before crossing over the Boston Mountains, and there remained subsisting all along on the enemy, until the 1st of March, when, learning that Price was being strongly reinforced, he first fell back to Sugar Creek, close by Bentonville, and, later on, to a place near Mottsville, south of Pea Ridge.

March, 1862.

General Curtis's army then consisted of four divisions. The First and Second Divisions, under General Franz Sigel, embraced three brigades in the First Division, commanded by Colonels Peter J. Osterhaus, Nicholas Greuse, and Coler; and two brigades in the Second Division, commanded by Colonel A. Asboth, who had under him Colonels Frederick Schaeffer and Joliet. These two divisions included part of the Third Missouri and the Second, Twelfth, Fifteenth and Seventeenth Missouri; the Twenty-fifth, Thirty-sixth and Forty-fourth Illinois Infantry Regiments; the Sixth Missouri, and part of the Third and Fourth Missouri Cavalry; the Benton and the Fremont Hussars; part of the Thirty-ninth Illinois Cavalry, and twenty-four pieces of artillery. The Third Division, under Colonel Jefferson C. Davis, embraced two brigades, commanded by Colonels Benton and Julius White, and included the Eighth, Eighteenth and Twenty-second Indiana, the Ninth Missouri and the Thirty-seventh Illinois Regiments of Infantry, the First Missouri Cavalry and the First Indiana and Second Illinois Batteries of Artillery, ten guns. The Fourth Division, under Colonel Eugene A. Carr, embraced two brigades, commanded by Colonels Grenville M. Dodge and William Vandever, and included the Fourth and Ninth Iowa, Thirty-fifth Illinois, and the Twenty-fifth Missouri Regiments of Infantry, the Third Illinois Cavalry, and the First and Third Iowa Batteries of Artillery, ten guns. Besides the above, were the following not brigaded: The Twenty-fourth and part of the Third Missouri Infantry, the Third Iowa Cavalry, Bowen's battalion of Missouri Cavalry, and Captain Stevens' battery of four guns.

General Price's army had been strengthened by General Ben McCulloch's force, of both of which the chief command was taken by General Earl Van Dorn, who, on the 29th of January, had been appointed Commander of the Trans-Mississippi Department, comprising the States of Arkansas, Missouri and Louisiana as far south as the Red River and the Indian Territory west of Arkansas. To these forces were afterward added the large bodies of Indians under General Albert Pike.

REFUGEES FROM SOUTHERN MISSOURI DRIVEN FROM THEIR HOMES BY THE CONFEDERATE TROOPS UNDER GENERAL VAN DORN

From a Sketch by Henry Lovie

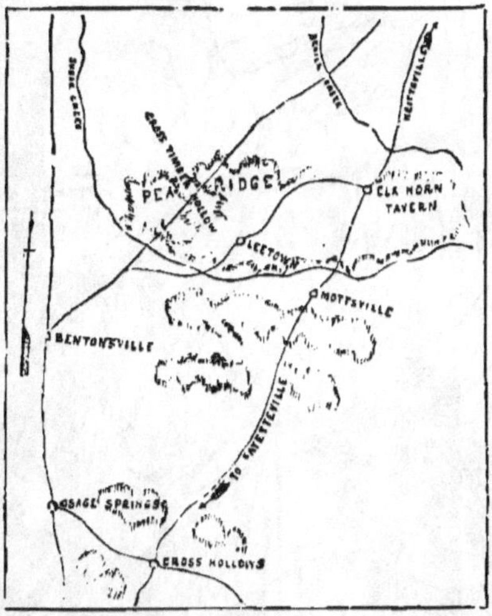

MAP OF THE COUNTRY AROUND PEA RIDGE.

The total Confederate force was about 25,000, and that of the Federals nearly 11,000 men.

General Van Dorn, accompanied by Generals Price, McCulloch, Pike and McIntosh, began his advance on the morning of the 5th of March toward the position held by Sigel's divisions, then near Bentonville, halting that night at Cross Hollows, about twelve miles from Sugar Creek. When Sigel became aware of the perilous condition of his force, both by scouts and by a message from General Curtis, he sent his cavalry to Osage Springs, in order to cover his right flank, and, having the Thirty-sixth Illinois and part of the Second Missouri at Bentonville as a rear guard, he dispatched his train forward to join the main army at Sugar Creek.

The misunderstanding of an order by Colonel Schaeffer came near, however, proving disastrous to the Federals. He had also marched forward, leaving behind some 600 men and five pieces of artillery, which were shortly after surrounded by a battalion of Louisiana infantry and some cavalry, by whom they would have been captured, had it not been that Sigel was within easy reach, and at once so skillfully handled the rear guard, as to repel the attacks made upon it, both from the rear and on its two flanks. Sigel's force cut its way through finally, and bravely fell back, contesting every inch of the road, until joined by a detachment sent out by General Curtis, when the pursuit ended. The Federal loss was 28 killed and wounded, and nearly 50 prisoners, General Sigel himself at one time having barely escaped capture.

The battle of Pea Ridge, or Elk Horn, as it was called by the Confederates, commenced on Friday evening, the 7th of March. Price's force was then found to be on the main road, near Elk Horn Tavern, north of Curtis's camp; McCulloch and McIntosh were confronting Sigel and Osterhaus, on Curtis's right, Van Dorn's headquarters facing the divisions under Asboth, Carr and Davis; and General Pike's force had been sent further to the right, mainly to divert attention from the intended attack in Curtis's rear.

General Curtis was thus forced to change his line of battle. He placed Sigel and Asboth on the left, Carr and Osterhaus on the right, and Davis in the centre, the line extending about three and a half miles from Sugar Creek to Elk Horn Tavern, and leaving between the contending forces a deep ravine called Cross Timber Hollow.

The Twenty-fourth Missouri was the first attacked, near Elk Horn Tavern, and Colonel Carr immediately went to its relief, bringing on a general engagement. Osterhaus was sent with part of the Third Iowa Cavalry, the Twenty-second Indiana Infantry, the First Missouri Cavalry, and Davidson's Peoria Battery of three guns, to attack what was believed to be a small body of Confederates in the direction of Leetown.

The cavalry and the battery were sent ahead, and had apparently dispersed them, but when the remainder of the Federals had come up, the woods were found to be full of Confederates, who fell upon the advancing force, and made such a fierce onslaught upon it, that it was broken asunder and almost swept from the field, with the loss of two of its guns.

Its total rout must, under the circumstances, have been the result of the admirable trap set for it but for the timely succor given it by General Davis, who, with White's brigade, came up, and engaged the forces under McCulloch, McIntosh and Pike. Here the battle raged fiercely, each side alternately advancing and retreating, until, finally, it seemed impossible for the Federals longer to withstand the fresh reinforcements continually reaching the Confederates.

The Eighteenth Indiana Regiment, however, coming up and engaging both the Indians and Texans with the bayonet, inspired the Federals with renewed courage. They made another advance, and forced back the opposing force, recapturing the two guns which they had previously lost, and which they trained once more upon the enemy, at last compelling its flight, with quite a severe loss, including Generals McCulloch and McIntosh, and Colonel Hebert, who were left on the field, mortally wounded.

The Confederates tried to reform, but by the time they were ready for an advance they were met by a force under Sigel, which had arrived with two batteries, and these, being well posted, did such effective work as to compel the enemy to once more fall back in dismay toward the position held by General Price.

Here the engagement had been going on steadily, Price being determined, apparently, to carry the ground at all cost. Regiment after regiment was hurled against Carr's force, until it had to yield, losing one of its guns. Reinforcements had been asked for, but did not come up. Carr was wounded in three places, and ammunition was running short. Discouragement was becoming apparent. Finally Curtis sent, under Major Bowen, his bodyguard of cavalry and a small howitzer, all he could spare.

Carr felt that a supreme effort must now be made, and advancing along the line, bareheaded, covered with blood, and one arm in a sling, cried out: "One more struggle, boys, and the day is ours! Sigel is coming up to reinforce you." At this the men advanced with the bayonet, and pressed ahead quickly, soon recovering the field they had abandoned, and maintaining it, under cover of Asboth's guns, although the latter shortly became useless for want of ammunition.

Night put an end to any further active work, and the wearied troops slept on their arms, in anticipation of perhaps a still more serious engagement the following day.

Saturday morning found the lines changed once more. General Davis had the right, Sigel the left, and Carr the centre. The battle was opened by Davis's brigades, well supported by artillery, and at once became very active on both sides. In addition, there was concentrated upon the Confederates the fire of two Iowa batteries, while Sigel was preparing to carry out the most important part of the intended operations.

At last, after the artillery had done its allotted work, the left wing advanced up the hills, while Davis pushed on also vigorously, and turning the Confederate left, exposed it to an enfilading fire from the artillery, which seemed to carry all before it. Both of the Confederate flanks were soon enveloped, and a charge with the bayonet was ordered.

Position after position was taken, the Twelfth Missouri and the Thirty-sixth Illinois Regiments especially distinguishing themselves, and within two hours the Confederates were in flight along the whole line, Van Dorn's army taking a southern direction, while Price's made its way toward Keitsville, followed closely by Sigel's forces.

The Federal loss in killed, wounded and missing was 1,384, of which 1,026 belonged to Davis's and Carr's divisions. The Confederates lost 2,000 in killed, wounded and prisoners.

Among the missing Federals was Lieutenant-colonel F. J. Herron, who commanded the Ninth Iowa while its Colonel, William Vandever, headed one of Carr's brigades. During the second day's fight, while leading a charge, his horse was shot under him by a cannon-ball, which at the same

FRANZ SIGEL.

UNITED STATES TRANSPORT "W B TERRY" PUSHING HER WAY THROUGH THE SWAMPS AT ISLAND NO. 10 TO THE ASSISTANCE OF GENERAL POPE AT NEW MADRID

From a Sketch by H. Lovie

and broke one of his ankles. He remained, nevertheless, at the front, and while in the act of cheering his men, suddenly found himself attacked by a large Confederate force by which he was made a prisoner.

FRANZ SIGEL.

Born at Sinsheim, in Bavaria, November 18th, 1824; received his education at the military school of Carlsruhe; entered the army of the Grand Duke of Baden, in which his promotion was so rapid, that in 1847 he had attained the rank of chief adjutant; resigned from the army, and took part in the revolutionary movement of 1848, being soon appointed to the chief command of one of the armies of the Liberals, and becoming Minister of War on the 1st of June of the last-named year. He took part in the unsuccessful campaign against the Prussians, and greatly distinguished himself in many engagements, having, in one instance, but 30,000 troops opposed to nearly 80,000, and succeeding in effecting a retreat without the loss of men or artillery. He withdrew to Switzerland, and remained there until expelled by the Swiss Government, when he came to the United States. He was for a few years teacher of mathematics in a New York academy, and became major of the Fifth New York Militia.

In 1858 he was chosen professor in a St. Louis college, where he gave instruction in military art, as well as in other branches. In 1861 he abandoned academic life, and took command of the Germans in St. Louis who had tendered their services to the Federal Government, being then made colonel of the Third Missouri Volunteers. He took part in the capture of Camp Jackson, and in the battles of Carthage and Wilson's Creek; conducted the retreat from Springfield to Rolla, and was commissioned a brigadier general to date from May 17th, 1861. He commanded a division under Fremont in Southern Missouri, and took prominent part at the battle of Pea Ridge, in March, 1862. He resigned from the army two months later, in consequence of unpleasant relations with Major-general Halleck, but was afterward summoned to Washington, made a major-general to date from March 21st, 1862, and placed in charge of the troops at Harper's Ferry, June 2d, 1862. He succeeded to the command of General Fremont's army corps, June 26th; served under Pope in Virginia; took part in the second battle of Bull

F. J. HERRON.

Run; was placed at the head of the Eleventh Army Corps, September 14th, 1862, and in command of the Department of West Virginia, March, 1864; defeated by Breckinridge at Newmarket, May 15th, he was shortly after relieved of his command by General Hunter. Since the war he has resided in New York City, being elected as Register in 1871, giving its attention exclusively to business pursuits.

CAPTURE OF NEW MADRID AND OF ISLAND NO. 10.

General Halleck's plans for the unobstructed passage of the Mississippi River could not, of course, be carried out, so long as the Confederates were allowed a stand at New Madrid and at Island No. 10.

The garrison at New Madrid had been strengthened by the force previously guarding Columbus, and was in charge of General J. P. McCown, while that at Island No. 10 was commanded by General Beauregard, who had just been placed at the head of the Department of the Mississippi.

In accordance with Halleck's orders, General Pope had left St. Louis, with a large force, on the 22d of February, 1862, reaching Commerce two days later, and after defeating the guerrilla chief Jeff Thompson in a cavalry skirmish, and capturing three guns as well as a number of prisoners, he had arrived before New Madrid on the 3d of March. There he found not only the Confederate troops that he had been led to expect, but likewise a flotilla of the enemy's gunboats, under Commodore Hollins. He encamped at a safe distance, sent to Cairo for heavier artillery than he had brought with him, and on the 12th of March he received three eighty-two-pound guns and an eight-inch mortar, which were set up during the night, and with which he commenced bombarding the town and the gunboats early the following morning.

March, 1862.

His fire was vigorously replied to, but was kept up, nevertheless, very steadily all day, and when night came on the Federals had succeeded in silencing three of the heavy guns in Fort Thompson, as well as disabling several of Hollins's gunboats, besides driving in the Confederate pickets

GENERAL ASBOTH AND STAFF AT THE BATTLE OF PEA RIDGE, ARK.

GALLANT CHARGE OF THE SEVENTEENTH, FORTY-EIGHTH AND FORTY-NINTH ILLINO

GALLANT CHARGE OF THE SEVENTEENTH, FORTY-EIGHTH AND FORTY-NINTH ILLINOIS REGIMENTS, LED BY COLONEL MORRISON, ON THE OUTWORKS OF FORT DONELSON, FEBRUARY 13th, 1862

with the forces under Generals E. A. Paine and J. M. Palmer.

Perceiving that their position had become untenable, both by the gradual advance of Pope's lines and his facilities for reinforcements, as well as by the occupation of Point Pleasant, which had meanwhile been fortified by General J. B. Plummer, the Confederates decided to abandon New Madrid. They took advantage of an unusually heavy thunderstorm in the middle of the night, and, leaving everything behind them, fled to Island No. 10, situated a few miles above New Madrid, and nearly seventy miles below Cairo.

On the morning of the 14th, a flag of truce brought the information that the place had been abandoned, and Captain Joseph C. Mower was at once sent by General Schuyler Hamilton to take possession of the fort. With it the Federals captured thirty-three cannon, several thousand stand of arms, a large quantity of ammunition, and many tents, tools, horses, mules and wagons.

The Federals had lost in the engagement a total of 51 killed and wounded. The losses of the Confederates could not be ascertained.

While Pope's forces were taking possession of New Madrid, Commodore Foote was on his way from Cairo with a fleet of eight gunboats, ten mortar-boats, several transports, and six small tugs.

The gunboats were the *Benton* (flagship), Lieutenant Phelps; *Cincinnati*, Commander Stembel; *Carondelet*, Commander Walke; *Conestoga*, Lieutenant Blodgett; *Louisville*, Commander Dove; *Mound City*, Commander Kelley; *Pittsburg*, Lieutenant Thompson; and *St. Louis*, Lieutenant Paulding. At Columbus, this force was joined by the Twenty-seventh Illinois and the Fifteenth Wisconsin Regiments under Colonels Buford and Heck.

On the way down the river, the town of Hickman was quietly taken possession of, and, on the 15th, the fleet anchored within five miles of Island No. 10, where it was joined by two steam-transports conveying the Sixteenth and the Forty-second Illinois Regiments and two batteries of light artillery.

Reconnoissances were immediately made in all directions, and on Sunday, the 16th of March, Commodore Foote was ready to open fire on the Confederate works.

These had been rendered almost impregnable to assault by one series of batteries supported by another, and in all of which were mounted guns of the heaviest calibre which bore in every direction whence an advance was likely to be attempted. The great engineering skill of the commanding general was everywhere apparent. In addition to the seventy-five guns, distributed throughout eleven different earthworks, there were sixteen guns mounted *en barbette* upon an ironclad floating battery, and quite a number upon the Confederate gunboats located in the Mississippi, between New Madrid and Island No. 10.

The bombardment was commenced at half-past eight o'clock on the morning of the 16th by the flag-ship *Benton*, and was soon after joined in by the mortar-boats and the gunboats. Their united fire was kept up incessantly, and one might say fiercely, until about half-past four o'clock in the afternoon, without eliciting any reply from the Confederates, and without creating any apparent damage.

Just before five o'clock, Lieutenant Kerth's Second Illinois Battery was landed on the Missouri shore, and opened on the Confederate gunboats, driving them away before dark, after sustaining a loss of three men.

On the 17th, the fleet could not well get into position for a renewal of the attack, by reason of a thickly-settled fog, until near eleven o'clock. At this time, a somewhat novel and formidable floating battery had been contrived by the Federals, who had lashed together the gunboats *Benton*, *Cincinnati* and *St. Louis*, and advanced them close to the

SIEGE OF ISLAND NO. 10.—NIGHT BOMBARDMENT BY THE FEDERAL MORTAR-BOATS, MARCH 18TH, 1862.

FROM A SKETCH BY HENRY LOVIE

Confederate batteries. This battery was supported by the gunboats *Carondelet, Mound City* and *Pittsburg*, and, under their combined fire, two of the enemy's guns were dismounted, and some of their earthworks and buildings seriously damaged. The engagement lasted until near seven o'clock, when the gunboats and the battery withdrew. The firing of the Confederates had been steadily served, mainly from their 64-pounders and from a very powerful rifled gun.

The *Benton* received three shots and the *Cincinnati* one; but, strange as it may appear, no one on board the boats was injured by the guns from the island. On board the *St. Louis*, however, two men were killed outright, and two others were very seriously wounded by the bursting of her rifled 22-pound port-bow gun, which occurred early in the afternoon.

With the exception of the firing of a few shots by the *Benton*, the mortar-boats alone attacked the island on the 18th. The latter continued throwing shells all through the night, at intervals of only fifteen minutes, and were reinforced before morning by six additional boats sent from Cairo. All of these did the main part of the work throughout the following day, the *Benton* and the *Mound City* sending only a few shots. The firing was only continued till about one o'clock, owing to the very stormy and windy weather which naturally prevented the desired manœuvres.

There was only occasional firing on both sides during the three following days; but on the 23d the *Mound City* fired for quite a while, and the mortar-boats kept up the attack throughout the day, succeeding in silencing the upper Confederate battery placed along the Kentucky shore.

The siege continued, without any remarkable occurrence, until the night of

April, 1862.

April 1st, when the upper battery of Island No. 10 was permanently silenced in a most daring manner.

While a violent hurricane was raging around the island, Colonel Roberts, of the Forty-second Illinois Regiment, with forty picked men belonging to the latter, embarked in yawls given by the gunboats, which had likewise furnished selected crews, and proceeded with muffled oars along the bank. As they approached, a flash of lightning revealed them to the sentinels, who fired wildly in the darkness over them, and then ran back of the battery. The Federals made no reply, but in a few moments afterward they had jumped ashore, spiked every one of the heavy guns constituting the battery, and returned in their yawls to the gunboats *Benton, Pittsburg, St. Louis, Cincinnati* and *Mound City*, which had stood off as reserves.

On the 2d of April, nothing of any moment occurred, but on the following night another daring feat was performed by the Federals. It had been found conclusive that the Confederate works could not be captured by the fleet alone, and that a land force should be in a position to co-operate effectively by attacking the rear of the batteries on the Kentucky side. General Pope had frequently asked that one of Foote's gunboats should be sent him, and it was finally decided, in response to Commander Walke's request, that the *Carondelet* should make the attempt of passing the Confederate batteries and gunboats, and thus reach New Madrid.

Another unusually heavy rain and thunderstorm set in early on the evening of the 3d, and at midnight the *Carondelet* set out on her perilous undertaking. She had entertained hopes of passing the batteries in the intense darkness that sometimes followed the flashes of lightning, but the latter became almost continuous after she had got beyond the upper fort, and, revealed as she was to the Confederates, she had to encounter their fire at all points. On she sped, however, as fast as she could, making no reply whatever, and finally reached New Madrid without the loss of a man or injury to herself.

Commander Walke and his crew were received with the wildest enthusiasm by Pope's soldiers, and the gallant feat was praised in all directions. The Secretary of the Navy duly thanked the officers and men for their courageous act, and for the important service they had rendered the Federal cause.

Long before the arrival of the *Carondelet*, General Pope had come to a like conclusion relative to the co-operation of a land force, but he had found no means of assisting Foote until General Schuyler Hamilton suggested the construction of a canal that should admit of the transportation of troops to the desired point. Hamilton's plans were fully indorsed, and, with the able assistance of Colonel J. W. Bissell and Lieutenant Henry D. Gaw, of the Engineers, the work was proceeded with.

The steamboats *W. B. Terry, Emma* and *Gilmore*, and several gun-barges, were ordered from Cairo, and the undertaking was pushed with so much interest and energy, that, by the 5th of April, a canal fully twelve miles long and about fifty feet in width most of the way had been constructed from opposite Island No. 8 across the swamps to a point opposite New Madrid. This was done by cutting through irregular bayous and thick timber, a great deal of which had to be sawed three, and often as much as four, feet under the water. Simultaneously with the completion of the canal several floating batteries which Pope had ordered made by lashing

JOHN POPE.

and otherwise fastening coal-barges together, and with which he intended attacking the Confederate batteries while landing his troops, were ready to co-operate.

At about noon on the 6th of April General Pope sent the *Carondelet* on a reconnoissance as far as Point Pleasant, with General Granger, Colonel Smith, of the Forty-third Ohio Regiment, and Captain Marshall, belonging to his staff. They found the shore lined with earthworks, from which a fire was opened upon the *Carondelet*, which did not, however, respond to it very earnestly until after returning from the conference held with General Plummer at Point Pleasant. Just above the latter place she silenced a battery, of which the guns were afterward spiked by Captain Marshall and a few men who were sent ashore for the purpose.

After her return to New Madrid, the *Carondelet* was joined by the *Pittsburg*, which had succeeded in running safely past the Confederate boats and batteries, and both the gunboats were ordered to proceed on a reconnoissance and clear the way beyond Tiptonville, where Pope intended to land his own troops, as well as those arriving by the canal. They succeeded, after a steady and systematic cannonading, in silencing all the batteries on the shore, Commander Walke spiking many of the guns below Watson's Landing. **Thus was a passage cleared for Pope's advance, which took place as soon as he observed the signal that no obstructions remained.**

As Pope's forces were crossing the river, however, they learned that the Confederates were abandoning their works and fleeing in the direction of Tiptonville, the only avenue through which they could escape.

The troops were therefore hurried forward as soon as landed at Watson's Landing, and Hamilton's force bivouacked that night at Tiptonville. Early the next morning, Hamilton's men were ordered to skirt the shore of Reelfoot Lake, while General D. S. Stanley moved along the Mississippi shore and General Paine continued up the road. The Confederates were thus driven back toward the swamps, and nothing was left them but to surrender.

A flag of truce was at the same time being dispatched from Island No. 10 to Commodore Foote, with an offer to surrender, which was accepted, and Colonel Buford was immediately sent with the Twenty-seventh Illinois Regiment to occupy the island and neighboring batteries.

General Beauregard had become satisfied that his position could not be held as soon as the blockade had been successfully run and the canal was finished. He had then determined to evacuate Island No. 10, and after sinking the gunboat *Grampus* and six steamboats so as to obstruct the channel, had turned over the command of the island to General V. D. McCall, left the other forces in charge of General McCown, and taken the best portion of the army with him to Corinth.

The surrendered troops numbered 7,273, and included Generals McCall, Walker and Gantt. The Federals captured, besides, 123 cannon and mortars, nearly 10,000 stand of arms, a floating-battery, several steamboats, many horses and mules, and a large quantity of ammunition and stores of all descriptions.

The casualties on either side prove to have been very few during the entire siege.

JOHN POPE.

Born in Louisville, Ky., March 16th, 1823; entered the Military Academy at West Point in 1838, and graduated in 1842, receiving the rank of brevet second lieutenant of Topographical Engineers on the 1st of the following July. He took part in the survey of the Northeast boundary-line between the United States and the British Possessions in North America; entered the Mexican War, and distinguished himself therein, more particularly at the battles of Monterey and Buena Vista, where he was given the brevets of first lieutenant and captain. He afterward served as an Engineer officer in New Mexico and in Minnesota Territory. Between 1853 and 1859 he explored the route for a Pacific railway from the Rio Grande to the Red River, having meanwhile, in 1856, been made a captain in the Regular Army. He was placed on lighthouse duty until the breaking out of the Civil War, when he was commissioned a brigadier-general of Volunteers. His operations in Missouri were carried on with great judgment, and it was mainly through his able management of the campaign that Price was forced to the southeastern portion of the State, and that New Madrid was taken (March 14th, 1862). One week later he was commissioned a major-general, and on the 8th of April, Island No. 10 was captured by him, with the assistance of Commodore Foote. At the head of 25,000 men he joined the combined armies under General Halleck on the 22d of April, and participated in the advance on Corinth. On the 26th of June he was ordered East, and two days later he took command of the Army of Virginia, comprising the forces under Banks, McDowell and Fremont. Satisfied that no effective co-operation could exist between his army and that of the Potomac without a general-in-chief, he suggested that Halleck be called from the West and appointed to the chief command. On the 14th of the same month Pope was promoted to be a brigadier-general in the Regular Army, and issued an address wherein he stated that he had left at the West an army whose policy had been "attack and not defense," and who had "always seen the backs of their enemies." He had heard a great deal of "taking strong positions and holding them," as well as of "lines of retreat and bases of supplies"; what he wanted was to find positions from which his men could "most easily advance against the enemy, study the probable lines of retreat of their opponents, and leave their own to take care of themselves"; they should all, in fact, "look before and not behind." Pope took the field on the 29th of July, and one month later fought the unsuccessful second battle of Bull Run. He took part also in the engagement at Chantilly, which was fought on the 1st of September, 1862, and ended his military career in the East. He afterward bitterly complained of the lack of co-operation shown him throughout by McClellan and some of his subordinates. On the day after the last-named battle he was granted his request to be relieved from command of the Army of Virginia, which latter became part of the Army of the Potomac, and he resumed command of the Department of the Northwest.

BOMBARDMENT OF ISLAND NO. 10 AND THE CONFEDERATE FORTI

FROM A SKETC

NIGHT ATTACK ON ISLAND No. 10 BY THE FEDERA

BOMBARDMENT OF ISLAND No. 10 AND THE CONFEDERATE [illegible] ON THE KENTUCKY SHORE, OPPOSITE, MARCH 17th, 1862.

[illegible]

NIGHT ATTACK ON ISLAND No. 10 BY THE FEDERAL [illegible] AND MORTAR FLEET, MARCH [illegible], 1862.

FROM A [illegible]

CAPTAIN MORRIS'S BATTERY OF 30-POUND PARROTT GUNS FIRING ON FORT MACON, APRIL 20TH, 1862.
FROM A SKETCH BY J. H. SCHELL.

CAPTURE OF SOUTH MILLS AND OF FORT MACON.

SHORTLY after the occupation of Beaufort, N. C., a force under General Reno, consisting of the Sixth New Hampshire, Ninth and Eighty-ninth New York, Twenty-first Massachusetts and Fifty-first Pennsylvania Regiments, had advanced up the Pasquotank River to intercept a body of Confederates about leaving for Norfolk.

By an oversight the Confederates were informed of the movement, and when the Federals had come within about a mile and a half of South Mills, they were unexpectedly met by a fire of grape and canister from a force concealed in the woods. This attack was bravely withstood and responded to, and in a short time the opposing force was compelled to fall back in the woods, whence they were afterward rapidly driven by one of the transports in charge of Captain Flusser.

The Federal loss was 113. That of the Confederates could not be ascertained.

A few hours after the battle, General Reno's force returned to its starting-point.

In the meantime, General Parke had made a reconnoissance on Bogue Spit, and, with the aid of the Fourth and Fifth Rhode Island and the Eighth Connecticut Regiments, had driven in the Confederate pickets, and secured a favorable location for the batteries intended to operate against Fort Macon. These batteries

MORTAR PRACTICE—PUTTING IN THE SHELL.

THE 10-INCH MORTAR BATTERY, LIEUTENANT FLAGLER, IN ACTION AT FORT MACON, APRIL 20TH, 1862.
FROM A SKETCH BY J. H. SCHELL.

TRANSFER OF RELEASED PRISONERS FROM THE "PILOT BOY" TO THE "COSSACK," IN PAMLICO SOUND, N. C.

FROM A SKETCH BY J. H. SCHELL.

consisted of four 10-inch mortars, four 8-inch mortars and three 30-pound Parrott guns, under the respective commands of Lieutenants Flagler and Prouty, Third New York Artillery, and of Captain Morris, First Regular Artillery.

Preparations were completed on the 24th of April, when General Burnside arrived, and early the following morning the bombardment began with the 10-inch mortars, which were soon followed by the other batteries, as well as by a steady fire from the gunboats *Daylight*, *Gemsbok*, *Chippewa* and *State of Georgia*. These, however,

SHELLING FORT MACON—SIGHTING THE MORTAR

could not well hold their own to advantage in the rough sea, and after fighting a little over an hour, were withdrawn.

The bombardment was continued by the batteries until four o'clock in the afternoon, when a white flag was displayed over Fort Macon, followed shortly with an offer to surrender.

The following morning, April 26th, Fort Macon was taken possession of, with about 500 prisoners, 20,000 pounds of powder, 400 stand of arms, and a quantity of ammunition.

The Confederates had lost 7 killed and 18 wounded, and the Federals only 1 killed and 3 wounded.

SURRENDER OF FORT MACON—LOWERING THE CONFEDERATE FLAG, APRIL 26TH, 1862.

FROM A SKETCH BY J. H. SCHELL.

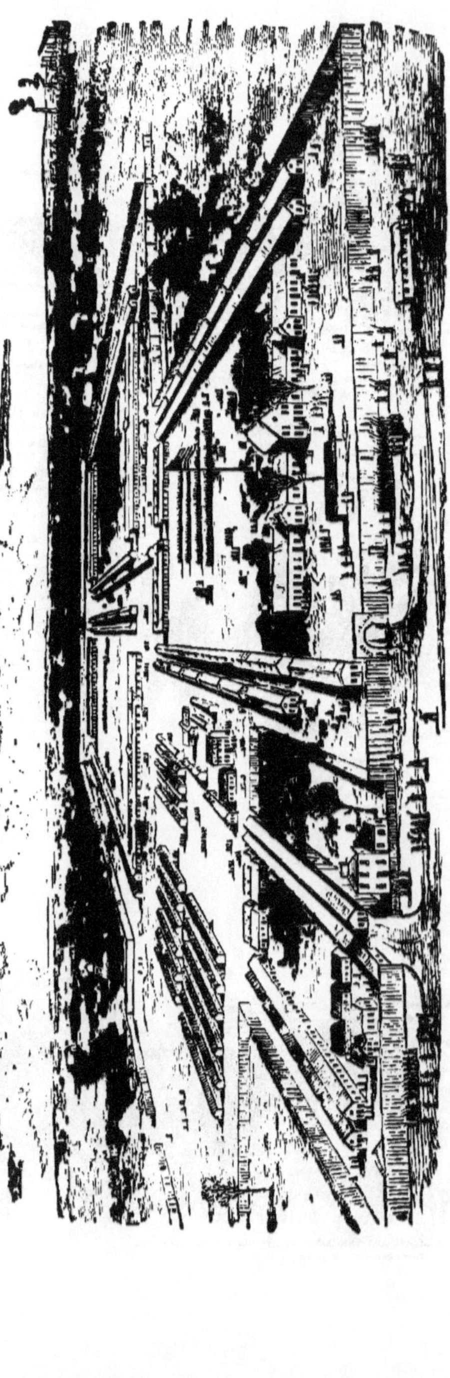

CAMP DOUGLAS, CHICAGO, ILL., USED FOR THE DETENTION OF CONFEDERATE PRISONERS OF WAR.

From a sketch by F. [illegible]

ALBERT SIDNEY JOHNSTON.

Born in Kentucky in 1803; appointed to the Military Academy at West Point, and entered the army, July 1st, 1826, as second lieutenant of the Sixth Infantry. He served in the Black Hawk War, and afterward left the army until 1836, when he emigrated to Texas, and once more entered the service as a private. His promotion was so rapid that he soon took the place of General Felix Houston, who held the chief command. This led to a duel between the two, in which Johnston was wounded. He remained senior-brigadier-general until 1838, when he was made Secretary of War of Texas, and during the following year organized an expedition against the troublesome Cherokees, who were totally routed in an engagement on the Neches.

In 1840 he settled upon a plantation, and in 1846 entered the Mexican War, at the head of a Texan volunteer rifle regiment. He served as inspector-general on the staff of General W. O. Butler, and distinguished himself notably at the battle of Monterey. In 1849 he was appointed paymaster in the army, with the rank of major, by President Taylor, and served as such until 1855, when he was made colonel of the Second United States Cavalry. Two years later he commanded the forces which were sent to Utah to force the Mormons into obedience to the Federal laws, became commander of the Department of Utah, and for the zeal he displayed while so engaged, received a brevet-brigadier-generalship. In 1860, he was removed to the command of the Department of the Pacific. He resigned his position in the army at the commencement of the Civil War, and traveled overland to reach the seat of the Confederate Government which immediately appointed him a general, and placed him at the head of the Department of the Mississippi.

At the battle of Shiloh, or Pittsburg Landing, he was in chief command, with General Beauregard second, and displayed on that occasion great ability in the handling of his troops, which at one time bid fair securing for them the fruits of a very important victory. On the afternoon of the first day's battle, however, he received a wound in the thigh, which severed the femoral artery, and caused his death ten minutes later. He had been held in such high esteem as a man and as a soldier, that his loss was at first concealed from the troops, and no public mention was made of the fact until the Confederate army reached Corinth. General Worth once said: "I consider Sidney Johnston the best soldier I ever knew." Johnston's body was left on the field of Shiloh just outside of General McClernand's original encampment, when the Confederates fled from it, on the 7th of April, 1862. It was afterward buried there, by the Federals, and reinterred at Austin, Tex., in January, 1867.

FREDERIC WEST LANDER.

Born at Salem, Mass., December 17th, 1821; studied at the Military Academy at Norwich, Vt. In the years 1858 and 1859 he served as superintendent of the Overland Wagon Road to California. In this service he distinguished himself in repeated encounters with the Indians, who threw serious obstacles in his way. In his second expedition, surveying for a railroad, he was the only survivor of his party.

At the breaking out of the Civil War he rendered many important services to the Federal Government. He joined the staff of General McClellan, in Western Virginia, as a volunteer, and participated in the successful battle of Philippi, having there been given the command of the Ninth Indiana and Fourteenth Ohio Regiments. He was afterward assigned to General Rosecrans's command, and distinguished himself at the battle of Rich Mountain, July 11th, 1861. It is said that when his horse was shot under him, at the last-named engagement, he fought on foot, and advanced to the attack of one of the enemy's guns. He shot all the men serving it, excepting three, who had fled, and a lieutenant, who had remained alone, and who continued to discharge it. Lander called out to him: "If you fire that gun again, you are a dead man!" to which the lieutenant replied: "Sir, I shall fire the gun as long as I have life in my body!" Lander then turned around to his men, exclaiming: "I cannot shoot so brave a man. You must do it!" and the next moment the young lieutenant fell, pierced by many bullets. After the battle Lander sought the body, and had it conveyed, under an escort, across the mountain, and caused it to be delivered to the Confederates. Lander, who had been made a brigadier-general, figured subsequently in a skirmish at Edward's Ferry, a few days after the battle of Ball's Bluff, where he received a very painful wound in the leg. Though still suffering greatly from the latter, he took command, in January, 1862, of a force of some 4,000 men, destined for the protection of the Baltimore and Ohio Railroad. With these he successfully repelled and made several attacks, the most daring being that of February 14th, 1862, when, with but 400 cavalry, he advanced in the night upon a Confederate camp at Blooming Gap, capturing 75 men, including 17 commissioned officers. For his valuable services in Western Virginia, Secretary of War Stanton publicly thanked him, February 17th, 1862.

Constant work and exposure, however, aggravated his wound, and after a while led to a fatal congestion of the brain, from which he died, on the 2d of March, 1862, while at Paw-Paw, Va., on the Upper Potomac. His wife, Jean Margaret Davenport, was a distinguished actress previous to her marriage in 1860. She served as hospital nurse all through the war, and in 1865, returned to the stage.

Upon General Lander's death, McClellan issued a general order commending his many qualities. His body was taken to Washington and embalmed, and lay in state at the residence of Salmon P. Chase, Secretary of the Treasury, being afterward removed to New York, and thence to Salem, where imposing ceremonies were held at his last resting-place.

BATTLE OF SHILOH OR PITTSBURG LANDING.

OCCUPATION OF CORINTH, MISS.

IMMEDIATELY after the surrender of Fort Donelson, General Grant was assigned by General Halleck to the command of the new West Tennessee District, "limits not defined," and set about actively making preparations for the capture of Corinth, which was a point of great strategic value, at the junction of the Mobile and Ohio and the Charleston and Memphis Railways.

Grant's plans were being extensively and rapidly carried out, when, to the great astonishment of all around him, he was ordered, on the 4th of March, 1862, to turn over his forces to General Charles Ferguson Smith, and to await further instructions at Fort Henry. No reason being assigned for this sudden outranking, General Grant immediately courted an inquiry and asked, meanwhile, to be at once fully relieved from duty. This was not done, however, for Halleck looked into the groundless charges, mainly of neglect, which a jealous fellow-officer had raised, and satisfying himself that nothing attached to Grant but what was highly commendable, the latter was once more placed in chief command of the district on the 14th of the same month.

Grant set about more vigorously than ever to complete his original plans, and to make up for the delays forcibly incurred, and at the commencement of April his army, as well as the two unarmored gunboats *Tyler* and *Lexington*, had arrived at Pittsburg Landing, on the Tennessee River. The latter place was a little over twenty miles to the northeast of Corinth, where lay the forces commanded by General Albert Sidney Johnston, and which had just been strengthened by those brought from Island No. 10.

APRIL, 1862.

LEWIS WALLACE.

General Beauregard had generously declined the offer made him by General Johnston to turn over to him the command of the united forces, having, he said, come to the West to assist Johnston, and not to supersede him.

The army under General Grant consisted, first, of five divisions, led by Generals John A. McClernand, Lewis Wallace, William T. Sherman, Stephen A. Hurlbut and W. H. L. Wallace, the latter being given the division heretofore led by General Charles F. Smith, who had but just died at Savannah. A sixth division was afterward made up of the forces constantly arriving, and given to General B. M. Prentiss. The divisions and the subdivisions were as follows:

First Division.

Major-general John A. McClernand.

First Brigade—(1.) Colonel A. M. Hare; (2.) Colonel M. M. Crocker—Eighth and Eighteenth Illinois, Eleventh and Thirteenth Iowa, Second Illinois Light Artillery (Battery D).

Second Brigade—Colonel C. C. Marsh—Eleventh, Twentieth, Forty-fifth and Forty-eighth Illinois.

Third Brigade—(1.) Colonel Julius Raith; (2.) Lieutenant-colonel E. P. Wood—Seventeenth, Twenty-ninth, Forty-third and Forty-ninth Illinois, Carmichael's Illinois Cavalry.

Not Brigaded—Stewart's Illinois Cavalry, First Illinois Light Artillery (Battery D), Second Illinois Light Artillery (Battery E), Fourteenth Ohio Battery.

Second Division.

(1.) Brigadier-general W. H. L. Wallace;
(2.) Colonel James M. Tuttle.

First Brigade—Colonel James M. Tuttle—Second, Seventh, Twelfth and Fourteenth Iowa.

Second Brigade—(1.) Brigadier-general John McArthur; (2.) Colonel Thomas Morton—Ninth and Twelfth Illinois, Eighty-first Ohio, Thirteenth Missouri, Birge's Sharpshooters (Fourteenth Missouri).

Third Brigade—(1.) Colonel T. W. Sweeny; (2.) Colonel S. D. Baldwin—Eighth Iowa, Seventh, Fiftieth, Fifty-second, Fifty-seventh and Fifty-eighth Illinois.

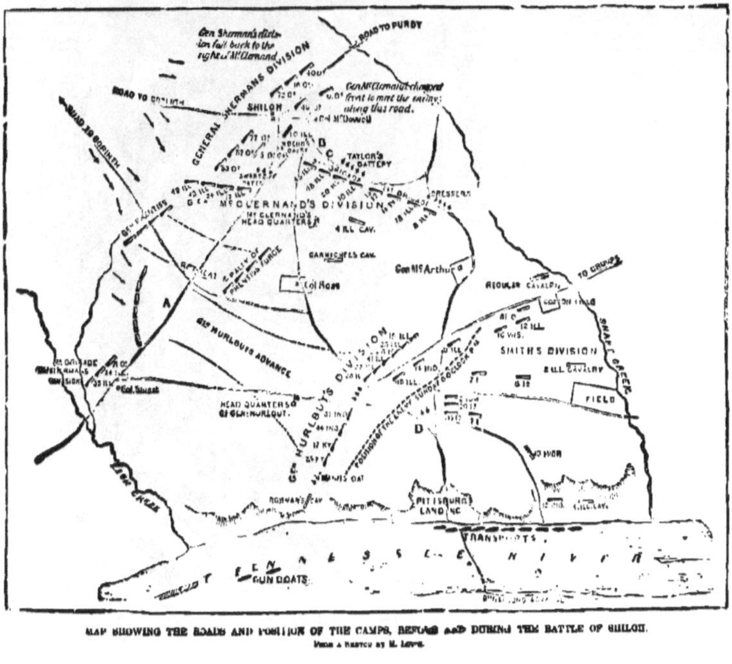

MAP SHOWING THE ROADS AND POSITION OF THE CAMPS, BEFORE AND DURING THE BATTLE OF SHILOH.

FROM A SKETCH BY H. LOVIE.

BATTLE OF PITTSBURG LANDING, SUNDAY, APRIL 6th, 1862.—DESPERATE DEFENSE OF GENERAL McCLERNAND'S SECOND LINE BY THE FEDERAL TROOPS.

From a Sketch by Henry Lovie.

Not Brigaded—Second United States Cavalry (Company C), Fourth United States Cavalry (Company I), Second Illinois Cavalry (Companies A and B) First Illinois Light Artillery (Battery A) First Missouri Light Artillery (Batteries D, H and K).

Third Division.

Major-general Lewis Wallace.

First Brigade—Colonel Morgan L. Smith—Eighth Missouri, Eleventh and Twenty-fourth Indiana.

Second Brigade—Colonel John M. Thayer—First Nebraska, Twenty-third Indiana, Fifty-sixth and Fifty-eighth Ohio.

Third Brigade—Colonel Charles Whittlesey—Twentieth, Sixty-eighth, Seventy-sixth and Seventy-eighth Ohio.

Not Brigaded—Thurber's First Missouri Light Artillery (Battery I), Thompson's Ninth Indiana Battery, Fifth Ohio Cavalry (Third Battalion), Eleventh Illinois Cavalry (Third Battalion).

Fourth Division.

Brigadier-general Stephen A. Hurlbut.

First Brigade—(1) Colonel N. G. Williams; (2) Colonel Isaac C. Pugh—Third Iowa, Twenty-eighth, Thirty-second and Forty-first Illinois.

Second Brigade—Colonel James C. Veatch—Twenty-fifth Indiana, Fourteenth, Fifteenth and Forty-sixth Illinois.

Third Brigade—Brigadier-general J. G. Lauman—Thirty-first and Forty-fourth Indiana, Seventeenth and Twenty-fifth Kentucky.

Not Brigaded—Fifth Ohio Cavalry (First and Second Battalions), Thirteenth Ohio Battery, Missouri Light Artillery (Mann's Battery), and Second Michigan Battery.

Fifth Division.

Brigadier-general W. T. Sherman.

First Brigade—Colonel J. A. McDowell—Sixth Iowa, Forty-sixth Ohio, Fortieth Illinois, and Sixth Indiana Battery.

Second Brigade—(1) Colonel David Stuart; (2) Colonel T. Kilby Smith—Fifty-fifth Illinois, Fifty-fourth Zouaves, and Seventy-first Ohio.

Third Brigade—Colonel J. [illegible] —Fifty-third, Forty-ninth and Seventy-seventh Ohio.

Fourth Brigade—Colonel R. P. Buckland—Forty-eighth, Seventieth and Seventy-second Ohio.

Not Brigaded—Fourth Illinois Cavalry (First and Second Battalions), First Illinois Light Artillery (Battery E), First Illinois Light Artillery (Battery B).

Sixth Division.

Brigadier-general B. M. Prentiss.

First Brigade—Colonel Everett Peabody—Twenty-first and Twenty-fifth Missouri, Sixteenth Wisconsin and Twelfth Michigan.

Second Brigade—Colonel Madison Miller—Eighteenth Missouri, Sixty-first Illinois and Sixteenth Iowa.

Not Brigaded—Eleventh Illinois Cavalry (eight companies), Fifth Ohio Battery, First Minnesota Battery, Eighteenth Wisconsin, Twenty-third Missouri and Fifteenth Iowa.

Unassigned Troops—Fifteenth Michigan, Fourteenth Wisconsin, Eighth Ohio Battery, First Illinois Light Artillery (Battery H), First Illinois Light Artillery (Battery I), Second Illinois Light Artillery (Battery B), Second Illinois Light Artillery (Battery F).

Grant's army, which represented a total of nearly 45,000 men, lay at Pittsburg Landing awaiting the arrival of the forces under General Buell, which had left Nashville on the 28th of March and Columbia on the 2d of April. His intention was to march at once upon Corinth with Buell's reinforcements, and, pending their early arrival, he did not deem it necessary to construct any earthworks or other temporary means of defense.

Upon learning of the intended junction of the two armies, however, General Beauregard decided to move immediately from Corinth, and not only prevent their union, but, if possible, to first attack and defeat Grant's force, and then to likewise successfully engage Buell's army, which, it was thought, could not reach the ground before the 7th of April.

Orders were accordingly given at one o'clock on the morning of the 3d, under the supposition that the entire Confederate force could be in the vicinity of Shiloh Church very early on the 5th, when the battle would be opened. But the delays incident to the movement of an army of nearly 40,000 men, coupled with the difficulties arising from a very heavy rain-storm on the 4th, prevented the concentration of the advancing forces at the intended point until late on the afternoon of the following day. On the same evening, Buell's army of nearly 23,000 men had, by steady marching through bad roads, succeeded in reaching Savannah, only eight miles away on the opposite side of the river. There it encamped, for no suitable transports were yet in readiness to convey it across.

WILLIAM J. HARDEE

The Confederate army now opposing Grant's forces, and under General Albert Sidney Johnston, with General P. G. T. Beauregard second in command, was subdivided in the following manner:

FIRST CORPS.

Major-general Leonidas Polk.

First Division.

Brigadier-general Charles Clark.

First Brigade—Colonel R. M. Russell.

Second Brigade—Brigadier-general A. P. Stewart.

Second Division.

Major-general B. F. Cheatham.

First Brigade—Brigadier-general Bushrod R. Johnson.

Second Brigade—Colonel W. H. Stephens.

Total First Corps, present for duty, 9,136.

SECOND CORPS.

Major-general Braxton Bragg.

First Division.

Brigadier-general Daniel Ruggles.

First Brigade—Colonel R. L. Gibson.

Second Brigade—Brigadier-general Patton Anderson.

Third Brigade—Colonel Preston Pond.

Second Division.

Brigadier-general J. M. Withers.

First Brigade—Brigadier-general A. H. Gladden.

Second Brigade—Brigadier-general J. R. Chalmers.

Third Brigade—Brigadier-general J. K. Jackson.

Total Second Corps, present for duty 16,279.

THIRD CORPS.

Major-general William J. Hardee.

First Brigade—Brigadier-general T. C. Hindman.*

Second Brigade—Brigadier-general Patrick R. Cleburne.

Third Brigade—Brigadier-general S. A. M. Wood.

Total Third Corps, present for duty, 6,789.

RESERVE CORPS.

Major-general J. C. Breckinridge.

First (Kentucky) Brigade—Colonel R. P. Trabue.

Second Brigade—Brigadier-general J. S. Bowen.

Third Brigade—Colonel W. S. Statham.

Total Reserve Corps, present for duty 7,211.

Total infantry and artillery, 37,398; Cavalry, 2,000. Grand total, 39,398.

Several regiments joined the army on the march to Corinth, increasing the effective force present on the field to 40,335. Colonel Hill's Tennessee regiment joined during the engagement on Sunday.

At about three o'clock on Sunday morning, April 6th, the Confederate army moved forward very quietly in three lines of battle, General Hardee's being in the lead across the Corinth Road, while Polk's forces were deployed on his left toward Owl Creek, and Bragg's division stood on his right opposite Ridge Road, with Breckinridge's reserves extending behind Bragg's right wing toward Lick Creek. At about five o'clock all was in readiness for the attack. General Hardee's pickets drove in those of General Prentiss, and a few minutes later the active Confederate line followed. Almost simultaneously the Confederate brigades of Anderson and Pond attacked the left of Sherman's division, posted a little beyond the Shiloh Church, and fell upon Prentiss's force, which lay below, and almost in a line with Sherman's, across the Ridge Road.

April, 1862.

The attack proved a complete

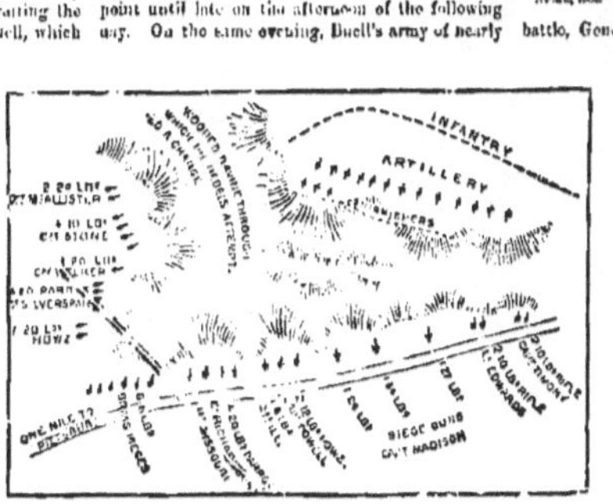

PLAN SHOWING THE POSITION OF THE FORCES DURING THE GREAT ARTILLERY FIGHT JT PITTSBURG LANDING.

* Hindman commanded two brigades when the troops were aligned, leaving his brigade under command of Colonel R. G. Shaver, Seventh Arkansas Infantry.

GENERAL HURLBUT'S DIVISION RECEIVING THE COMBINED ATTACK OF JOHNSTON, CHEATHAM, WITHERS AND BRECKINRIDGE, AT THE BATTLE OF SHILOH APRIL 6TH, 1862.
REPULSE OF THE CONFEDERATES AT THE PEACH ORCHARD.

From a Sketch by Henry Lovie.

surprise, although the Federals should have been warned of the danger threatening them by an injudicious reconnoissance which some of the cavalry of Bragg's division had previously made in force, and during which they had captured one officer and several men.

The Confederate onslaught was so fiercely made, that Colonel Hildebrandt's brigade, which was largely composed of raw troops, fled back in dismay. The First and the Fourth Brigades, under Colonels McDowell and Buckland, which had just about completed a new line, were likewise rapidly forced back, with the loss of a battery, upon McClernand's division. The latter lay in the rear of Prentiss's force, and had been called up to assist Sherman on the left, while Hurlbut was asked to come to the aid of Prentiss.

By seven o'clock the whole of Sherman's line and McClernand's left were engaged. With the aid of Taylor's Chicago Battery of heavy guns, which did admirable execution, the troops now held their ground well, encouraged as they were by General Sherman himself, who was seen exposed in the very thickest of the fight, although he had been shot through the hand very early in the action.

Two hours later, Hardee's full column and part of Bragg's force had emerged from the woods opposite Sherman's extreme left, and engaged the latter while Polk was moving toward Sherman's rear. The Federal columns had been hurriedly reorganized by General Grant, who had joined Sherman without delay upon hearing the sound of battle. Grant had sent orders to General Lewis Wallace to come up from Crump's Landing, and a new line had been formed upon a ridge in advance of Snake Creek, where the Confederates were ably held in check, but the remainder of Bragg's division had in the meantime thrown nearly its whole weight upon Prentiss's First Brigade under Colonel Peabody threatening to overcome it, and make an opening to the river.

Hurlbut had, at the first attack, sent only his Second Brigade, under Colonel Veatch; but these not proving sufficient, the First and the Third Brigades, under Colonels Williams and Lauman, had followed, too late, however, to do much, if any, good. Nor did Prentiss's Second Brigade or General McArthur's brigade of W. H. L. Wallace's division help matters. McArthur had been sent to help Stuart's brigade of Sherman's division, which had injudiciously been placed beyond a large intervening gap on the Hamburg Road, and was then in danger of being cut off. Mistaking the road, however, he had, like Colonel Miller, come upon a large force of Confederates, which had compelled both brigades to fall back.

An overwhelming force had, meanwhile, been opposed to Prentiss's First Brigade, which had become entirely separated from the rest, and had to fight its way unaided. With his few regiments, Prentiss maintained his ground for several hours, fighting steadily all the while, until his rear being gained by the Confederates, the force was completely surrounded, and he was compelled to surrender.

Colonel Everett Peabody was killed early in the action. He had gone forward with the Twenty-fifth Missouri Regiment, and by the steadiness with which they met the Confederate fire, had prevented what might well have proved a total surprise to the Federals.

After the division of Prentiss's force, Stuart's brigade was compelled to fall back from ridge to ridge until almost entirely

LOVELL H. ROUSSEAU.

SAVED BY HIS WIT.

EVERETT PEABODY.

out of the field, the main attack of the successful Confederates being, however, directed against the remainder of McClernand's forces, then well stationed along the Corinth and Pittsburg Landing roads.

Fresh Confederate regiments were so ably directed at this point, that McClernand soon had to give way to the superior numbers, and by eleven o'clock his army was on a line with that of General Hurlbut.

At noon, the Confederates held possession of the camps which McClernand, Prentiss, Sherman, and Stuart had occupied in the morning, and in addition to the capture already mentioned, had taken many prisoners, nearly half of both McAllister's and Schwartz's artillery, besides several of Dresser's cannons, some caissons, and a large number of horses.

There remained almost intact, and within reach, but two divisions, those of General Hurlbut and W. H. L. Wallace, which, with the remnants of Prentiss's army, covered the depots of stores and ammunition, as well as the transports. Wallace had closed up the gap on Hurlbut's left, and was strongly stationed with the batteries of Richardson, Stone and Webber, under Major Cavender.

The object of the Confederates was to turn the left of the Federals, and to drive them down to the river after capturing their base at the Landing. Opposite Hurlbut stood Johnston, with the divisions of Generals Cheatham, Withers and Breckinridge. These were hurled against the Federal line, and the battle commenced anew, raging fiercely all the afternoon. The chief objective appeared to be Hurlbut's artillery, which, admirably located and served, was doing great damage.

An assault was made upon the latter, but was repulsed with great loss. The attack was renewed again and again, but unavailingly, as the Federals were unflinching. For a long while they maintained a successful resistance, and with the signal aid afforded them by Mann's Ohio Battery of light guns, especially while deployed at the Peach Orchard, they held their ground doggedly. Superior numbers of Confederates, which had forced back the right of the line, soon commenced an attack upon their flanks, however, and after battling through burning woods and across several heavy ridges, pressed them further toward the river. Here the remnants of McClernand's and of Sherman's armies soon had to follow them.

By five o'clock the Federals, after their persistent fighting across all the ridges and roads, and losing nearly 4,000 in killed, wounded and prisoners, were huddled together in a confused mass upon a plateau near the high banks of the Landing, as well as under the banks along the river close by the transports.

For a while all efforts to reform the troops proved unavailing. There was no time to lose, however, as the Confederates could not but soon follow up the advantages gained. A stand must be made at all cost, pending the arrival of some of Buell's forces, of which the vanguard was already in sight. The remnants of the army were finally crowded inside a semi-circle, hurriedly formed, with some heavy artillery that had been parked at the Landing, as well as with the guns that had been brought in from the field, and under the direction of Colonel J. D. Webster, Grant's chief of staff, the guns were mounted upon a line of earthworks thrown up while the Confederates were completing arrangements

CAPTURE OF McCLERNAND'S HEADQUARTERS, McALLISTER'S AND SCHWARTZ'S ARTILLERY, AND DRESSER'S BATTERY, BY THE CONFEDERATES, AT PITTSBURG LANDING, SUNDAY, [illegible]

for a final assault. These guns had scarcely been placed in position when the Confederates again appeared in force, and opened a vigorous fire upon the Federals, which the latter promptly met.

Just then the gunboats *Tyler* and *Lexington*, under command of Lieutenant William Gwin, were afforded the opportunity they had been all day looking for. They, too, responded to the Confederate fire, and by unexpectedly hurling their eight-inch shell and sixty-four-pound shot up the hill, created dismay throughout the ranks in which they were rapidly falling.

Toward evening the head of Nelson's Fourth Division of Buell's army came upon the scene. It had hurried along the overflowed roads on the opposite side of the river, and after dropping the artillery, which they found they could not drag along quickly enough, the men were ferried across in time to aid the wellnigh disconcerted Federals.

As Ammen's brigade rushed quickly to the front, new life seemed to spring through the huddled troops. The Confederates attempted time and time again to assault the Federal position across the wooded ravine that now separated them, and had once nearly succeeded in turning the Federal right, but with the aid of Ammen's three regiments they were beaten back, retiring altogether at about nine o'clock, when the fire ceased.

Lewis Wallace, whom Grant had ordered in the morning to come up from Crump's Landing and form on the right, reached the Landing at nightfall, and was then severely censured for his apparent failure to carry out orders. He explained, however, that after leaving two of his regiments at Crump's Landing, he had put his entire division in motion immediately upon receiving Grant's order, the roar of battle quickening his steps toward what he believed was the nearest point to the right of the Federal army.

After marching about six miles, Captain John A. Rawlins, Grant's adjutant-general, had overtaken him, and stated that, by reason of the successful advance of the Confederates, the Federal right had become the Confederate rear, in the direction of which he was advancing. He had then retraced his steps, crossed Snake Creek by the river road, and reached the Landing without loss of time.

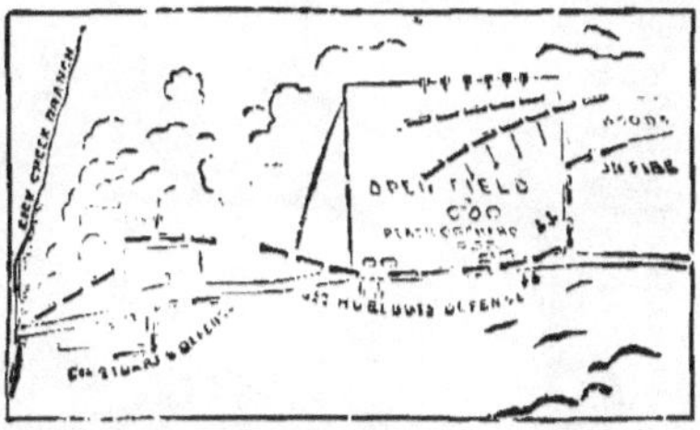

PLAN OF DEFENSE AT THE PEACH ORCHARD—LEFT WING.

The night closed with the Confederates occupying the former Federal camps, upon which the gunboats kept a running fire till the next morning. The Confederate losses had been very great, indeed, the most important being that of their commander-in-chief. General A. S. Johnston had been killed during the afternoon, while almost recklessly exposing himself, directing the movements of his troops. The chief command had then devolved upon General Beauregard, whose headquarters were established at the Shiloh Church.

On the Federal side, General W. H. L. Wallace had been mortally wounded, while endeavoring to stem the advance of Generals Polk and Hardee's forces upon his own and those of General Sherman, his place being taken by Colonel J. M. Tuttle, who had previously headed the First Brigade.

April, 1862.

Monday, April 7th, found the contending armies established upon new lines, arranged with great difficulty during the dark and very stormy night that had followed the previous day's battle.

The incessant firing of the gunboats had compelled the Confederates to abandon fully one-half the ground they had previously gained, and they were now stationed a little in advance of the camps originally occupied by Sherman, McClernand and Prentiss. General Hardee held the right of the line with his own division, having on the extreme right of the latter both Chalmers's and Jackson's brigades belonging to Withers's division, and next to these came Breckinridge's and Polk's forces, the last named being reduced by Clark's division, which, with the remainder of Bragg's troops, occupied the extreme left.

The remainder of Buell's forces had been arriving by land and water during the entire night, and at break of day the Federals had the Fourth Brigade of McCook's division, and the comparatively fresh divisions of Generals Nelson and Crittenden of Buell's army, as well as Lewis Wallace's division of Grant's army, in position for a renewal of the conflict. The Fifth and Sixth Brigades of McCook's division could not be brought up until about eight o'clock in the morning. The First Division of Buell's army, commanded by General George H. Thomas, was too far in the rear to take part in Monday's engagement, and but one brigade, Colonel

FORTY-FOURTH REGIMENT, INDIANA VOLUNTEERS, ENGAGED AT PITTSBURG LANDING, APRIL 6th, 1862 — THE WOODS ON FIRE.

From a Sketch by H. Lovie

RECAPTURE OF ARTILLERY, AT PITTSBURG LANDING, BY THE FIRST OHIO REGIMENT, UNDER GENERAL ROUSSEAU, MONDAY, APRIL 7TH, 1862

G. D. Wagner's, of General T. J. Wood's division, arrived in time to participate actively in the pursuit of the Confederates at the close of the action.

The following constituted that portion of the Army of the Ohio which reached the field of Shiloh:

Second Division.

Brigadier-general Alexander McDowell McCook.

Fourth Brigade—Brigadier-general Lovell H. Rousseau—Battalions of the Fifteenth, Sixteenth and Nineteenth United States Infantry, First Ohio, Sixth Indiana and Third Kentucky.

Fifth Brigade—Colonel E. N. Kirk—Seventy-first Pennsylvania, Twenty-ninth and Thirtieth Indiana, and Thirty-fourth Illinois.

Sixth Brigade—Colonel W. H. Gibson—Fifteenth and Forty-ninth Ohio, Thirty-second and Thirty-ninth Indiana, Fifth United States Artillery (Battery H).

Fourth Division.

Brigadier-general William Nelson.

Tenth Brigade—Colonel Jacob Ammen—Sixth and Twenty-fourth Ohio, and Thirty-sixth Indiana.

Nineteenth Brigade—Colonel William B. Hazen—Sixth Kentucky, Ninth Indiana, and Forty-first Ohio.

Twenty-second Brigade—Colonel S. D. Bruce—First, Second and Twentieth Kentucky.

Fifth Division.

Brigadier-general Thomas T. Crittenden.

Eleventh Brigade—Brigadier-general J. T. Boyle—Nineteenth and Fifty-ninth Ohio, Ninth and Thirteenth Kentucky.

nessee and Alabama regiments, well supported by artillery. These assailed Nelson, and finally compelled him to fall back until his force came up with the advance of Crittenden's troops. Then the whole line assumed the offensive, with the support of Mendenhall's and Bartlett's batteries, and in turn compelled the retirement of the Confederates, with the temporary loss of a battery, captured by the brigade under Colonel Hazen.

The Confederates were quickly reinforced, however, and by eight o'clock were engaging the two Federal divisions, as well as Rousseau's brigade, which had just reached the ground on Crittenden's right, accompanied by General Buell himself. Cheatham's division was ordered up from Shiloh Church and thrown on Breckinridge's line, and the contest soon raged fiercely on both sides. The Confederate attack became so severe that Hazen's force was completely thrown across the open field into the woods on Crittenden's left, and subjected to a cross fire of artillery which caused a heavy loss. Ammen's brigade, posted on Nelson's left, was meanwhile heavily pressed by superior numbers, and was in imminent danger of being turned, when Terrell's battery of twenty-four-pound howitzers, which belonged to McCook's division, and had just arrived from Savannah, came dashing along, and, with Ammen's aid, silenced the Confederate pieces.

McCook's left. Seeing this, Colonel Willich's regiment was ordered up, and resorting mainly to a bayonet-charge, prevented the movement. Willich was followed by Kirk's brigade, which entered the position held by Rousseau while the latter retired for a fresh supply of ammunition. The Confederates in the meantime renewed their efforts to separate McCook from Crittenden, and fell on Gibson's brigade so heavily, that the Forty-ninth Ohio Regiment, occupying the left of the line, had to change its front twice in order to prevent the turning of the position.

It was close on two o'clock when Rousseau's brigade was ready to reoccupy the front. It was then supported by McClernand on the right, and by the two regiments of Hurlbut's brigade on the left. This force, aided by the fire from both McAllister's and Wood's remaining batteries, moved steadily on, meeting with comparatively little resistance until it neared the thick woods, when a general advance was ordered, and the Federals overcame the last decided stand made by the Confederates. These Beauregard commanded in person, with the assistance of Generals Polk, Bragg and Breckinridge.

On the extreme Federal right, Wallace had begun the attack before sunrise by shelling, with Thurber's and Thompson's batteries, the Confederate position,

SOLDIERS BURNING THE DEAD HORSES AFTER THE BATTLE OF PITTSBURG LANDING, NEAR THE PEACH ORCHARD.

FROM A SKETCH BY H. LOVIE.

Fourteenth Brigade—Colonel William L. Smith—Thirteenth Ohio, Eleventh and Twenty-sixth Kentucky, Mendenhall's Regular Battery and Bartlett's Ohio Battery.

Not Brigaded—Third Kentucky Cavalry, First Ohio Light Artillery (Battery G), Fourth United States Artillery (Batteries H and M), and Second Indiana Cavalry.

Sixth Division.

Brigadier-general T. J. Wood.

Twentieth Brigade—Brigadier-general J. A. Garfield—Sixty-fourth and Sixty-fifth Ohio, Thirteenth Michigan and Fifty-first Indiana.

Twenty-first Brigade—Colonel G. D. Wagner—Fifteenth, Fortieth, and Fifty-seventh Indiana, and Twenty-fourth Kentucky.

The Federal line was almost perpendicular to the river, and extended from the Hamburg and Purdy Road to near Owl Creek. Buell held the extreme left of the advance, while the forces of Nelson, Crittenden and McCook were extended, in the order named, toward the corps of Lewis Wallace, which occupied the extreme right. Between the forces of Buell and of Wallace lay the remnants of the divisions engaged in the first day's battle, McClernand being in the centre, and having Sherman and Hurlbut respectively on his right and left.

At about half-past five o'clock, Nelson's division moved forward through the open woods and fields, and was quickly followed by Crittenden's division and Rousseau's Fourth Brigade. Nelson soon came upon some of Forrest's cavalry pickets, which he drove in, and shortly after stood face to face with Chalmers's brigade, part of Gladden's and of Jackson's brigades, and several independent Ten-

The Federal success was only assured, however, when Boyle's brigade came on Nelson's left, and, aided by a concentric fire from Terrell's, Mendenhall's, and Bartlett's batteries, drove the Confederates beyond their second and third batteries, capturing several of their guns.

While all this was going on, McCook had been strengthened by his Fifth Brigade, under Colonel Kirk, and by part of the Sixth, led by Colonel Gibson. These had been quickly ferried across from Savannah, and placed on Rousseau's right and rear, and were supported by Colonel August Willich's Thirty-second Indiana Regiment, as well as two regiments belonging to Hurlbut's division. Rousseau had, from the first, taken an advanced position, repulsed a heavy Confederate charge, and in turn attacked the enemy, which he had forced back, capturing one of its batteries.

The giving way of the Confederate right allowed Rousseau to push along more freely until he met the troops that had been withdrawn from Nelson's front, and were being massed in McClernand's camp of the previous day. There an obstinate contest took place; but the camp was at last yielded to Rousseau's troops, who, in addition, captured one of the batteries which the Confederates had taken on Sunday, and from whose fire Rousseau had suffered greatly.

The direction which Rousseau had been compelled to take left a gap between the forces of McCook and Crittenden, which the Confederates were about entering for the purpose of turning

situated in a deep, wooded ravine opposite. He had soon silenced one of the enemy's guns, and followed up the first attack by an advance upon the Confederate left, commanded by General Bragg, whose position on the hill he shortly after occupied.

There he remained, waiting for Sherman's division to come up, and by changing his front, made an attempt to turn the Confederate left, in expectation that Sherman would quickly close up the intervening gap. But the Confederates were too quick for him, and made a counter move, endangering his right. The Federal batteries, ably served, checked this, however, and, aided notably by part of the Eighth Missouri Regiment, succeeded also in driving back a detachment of cavalry which attempted to capture Thurber's six-gun battery. Colonel Smith's First Brigade had also, meanwhile, repelled an attack made by a strong infantry force supported by Watson's powerful Louisiana Battery.

When Sherman finally came up, both divisions advanced steadily, not meeting with any marked resistance until close by Shiloh Church, where they encountered such a fierce infantry and artillery fire, that Sherman's force was compelled to fall back rapidly. This left Wallace's flank exposed. Upon it a squadron of Confederate cavalry immediately advanced, but it was met and promptly driven back by the Twenty-third Indiana and the First Nebraska Regiments. Before Sherman's lines could be re-formed, Wallace's left had again been seriously endangered by the obstinate attacks made upon it; but the arrival of McGinnis's Eleventh Indiana

THE FINAL STAND OF THE ARMY OF GENERAL GRANT APRIL 6th. 1862, NEAR PITTSBURG

BURNING RAILWAY STATIONS, WAREHOUSES, AND SUPPLIES, AT CORINTH, MISS.—RETREAT OF THE CONFEDERATE AND ENTRY OF THE FEDERAL ARMY

From a Sketch by Henry Lovie.

Wood's Seventy-eighth Ohio, and part of McClernand's force, afforded timely aid, and enabled Wallace to hold his ground until a brilliant dash, made by Colonel Willich's regiment, which McCook had sent forward, compelled the Confederates to give way.

When Sherman's force again advanced, it moved abreast of Rousseau's brigade, thus completing an unbroken Federal line which, with Wallace's force ahead in the wood, pressed steadily forward, until the enemy was found retreating in all directions, and the Federals came to a stand not far from Shiloh Church.

The Confederates had been ordered to withdraw from the field, when Beauregard saw that further resistance was useless without additional reinforcements. He had sent couriers to hurry forward Van Dorn's army of nearly 20,000 men, with which he had contemplated renewing the attack.

Failing, however, to ascertain its exact whereabouts at that time, he had asked Colonel Chisholm to superintend the clearing of the roads, and leaving Colonel Thomas Jordan, adjutant-general of the army, to protect the retreat, he had caused the retirement of his forces, which was begun at about half-past two, and continued in perfect order and precision, in the direction of Corinth.

Beauregard's reserve of nearly 12,000 men, in charge of Breckinridge, was posted on a commanding ridge, and remained there for nearly half an hour awaiting attack. It is said that, in the expectation of a vigorous pursuit, Beauregard had told Breckinridge: "This retreat must not be a rout! You hold the enemy back, if it requires the loss of your last man," and that the reply was: "Your orders shall be executed to the letter."

Breckinridge's forces were not attacked at their first stand, and were therefore withdrawn, and at last encamped some two miles from the battle-field, where they remained for the night, having been finally pursued, in the cold, drizzly rain and hail, only as far as the bluffs of Lick Creek by the advance of General Wood's division, which had just reached the battle-ground.

At four o'clock firing had entirely ceased. The reported losses in the two days' battle were, 1,673 killed, 7,495 wounded, and 3,022 missing, a total of 12,190, on the side of the Federals; and 1,728 killed, 8,012 wounded, and 959 missing, a total of 10,699, on the side of the Confederates.

Among the additional casualties on the Confederate side were George W. Johnson, the Provisional Governor of Kentucky, killed on Monday; General Gladden, who died from wounds previously received; General Cheatham, who had three horses shot under him, and who was also wounded; and Generals Bowen, Clark, Johnston, and Hindman, who were wounded on the first day.

On the Federal side, General Sherman was again wounded, and had three horses shot under him, during Monday's battle; Colonel Stuart was wounded severely early the same morning, but kept the field till weakness compelled him to give way to Colonel T. Kilby Smith; Colonel Hicks and Lieutenant-colonels Kyle and E. F. W. Ellis were mortally wounded on Sunday, and Lieutenant-colonel Walcutt, of the Forty-sixth Ohio, was severely wounded the same day.

For sanitary reasons, the Confederate and Federal dead were buried and the horses burned immediately after the second day's battle.

On Tuesday, the 8th, General Sherman took two brigades and some cavalry on a reconnoissance along the lower Corinth Road, while General Wood advanced with two brigades on the upper road for the same purpose.

April, 1862.

They encountered some cavalry at General Breckinridge's encampment of the previous night, and pursued it until meeting with Colonel Forrest's force, who had with him detachments of Texas and Kentucky troops, and a company of Wirt Adams's regiment. These engaged the Federals, and forced them back, only retiring again toward General Breckinridge's camp after the severe wounding of Colonel Forrest.

On the 9th of April, Major-general H. W. Halleck left St. Louis, and proceeded to Pittsburg Landing, where he arrived, and took the field on the 12th. He reorganized the armies by giving the right wing to General George A. Thomas, the centre to General Buell, and the left to General Pope's Army of the Missouri, nearly 25,000 strong. This whole force, of about 108,000 men, was given the name of *The Grand Army of the Tennessee*, with General Grant second in command. The reserves were placed in charge of General McClernand.

No movement of any importance was again made toward Corinth until the 3d of May, when the Federal troops took possession of Monterey, located about six miles from Beauregard's new lines.

On the 30th of April, Colonel Morgan L. Smith was sent out by General Lewis Wallace with a brigade of infantry and three battalions of cavalry, and, after a short engagement in the woods with a body of Confederates, successfully tore up the track of the Mobile and Ohio Railway, near Purdy. They likewise destroyed an important bridge close by, thus cutting off the supplies and reinforcements likely to reach Beauregard's army from Jackson, Tenn. While the bridge was burning, the Federals captured and destroyed a locomotive that had been dispatched from Corinth to help through some trains filled with troops from Memphis.

SCENE IN CAMP LIFE BEFORE CORINTH.—MESS OF THE THIRTEENTH ILLINOIS VOLUNTEERS.

From a Sketch by H. Lovie.

On the 3d of May, Pope ordered Generals Paine and Palmer to proceed on a reconnoissance toward an important Confederate outpost commanded by General J. S. Marmaduke.

May, 1862.

They took with them the Tenth and Sixteenth Michigan, and the Tenth, Sixteenth, Twenty-second, Twenty-seventh, Forty-second, and Fifty-first Illinois Regiments, Yates's Illinois Battalion of Sharpshooters, Hezcock's Ohio and Houghtaling's Illinois Batteries, and the Second Michigan Cavalry, and met the Confederates at a small place called Farmington, situated about five miles to the northwest of Corinth.

A short though sanguinary engagement took place, with a Federal loss of 2 killed and 21 wounded, the Confederates having lost nearly 150 killed and wounded, besides their camp, supplies and 200 prisoners.

EVACUATION OF CORINTH, MISS., MAY 30TH, 1862.—DESERTED CONFEDERATE FORTIFICATIONS—PURSUIT OF THE RETREATING ARMY BY THE FEDERAL CAVALRY.

From a Sketch by H. Lovie.

Marmaduke returned to Corinth, and the Federals continued on with cavalry and artillery to Glendale, east of Corinth, where they tore up the railway-track, and destroyed two very important trestle-bridges.

On the 9th of May, the Confederates attacked the force which Pope had left to hold Farmington, intending to cut off the Federal line of retreat. Generals Van Dorn, Hardee, Polk, Bragg and Breckinridge co-operated in the attack, but, mainly through the inefficiency of the principal guide, the advance was delayed, and the Federals discovered the intended flanking movement in time to partly effect it.

The capture of the entire Federal force was, in fact, only prevented by its prompt retreat behind Seven Miles Creek. This was effected after losing nearly 200 in killed and wounded, besides a number of prisoners and a large quantity of arms and equipments.

Pope returned, however, on the 18th of May, toward Farmington, and not meeting any resistance, occupied the place with his whole army, while Sherman's force was advancing toward the Confederate left, in front of which latter he succeeded in planting his heavy guns a few days later.

General Halleck had steadily advanced the Federal army, after cutting Beauregard's railway communications to the north and east of Corinth, and sending Colonel Elliott to cut off the Mobile and Ohio Railway in the rear, and by May 28th he had, through strong reconnoissances, compelled the abandonment of the Confederate advance batteries, and enabled the Federals to place their siege-guns in position within about 1,300 yards of Beauregard's works.

Halleck expected to give battle early on the 30th, and all was in readiness for the attack, but it was then found that the Confederates had completed the evacuation of Corinth during the night, after firing the town at all important points and blowing up the magazines.

Beauregard had, for several days, been removing his sick and wounded, as well as all the valuable stores that he could easily carry away, destroying all the rest, and when the Federals entered the town, they found on nearly all sides but smouldering ruins.

The Confederates first halted behind the Tuscumbia River, at a point about six miles from Corinth, in the anticipation of pursuit, but none being made, aside from that instituted by Gordon Granger in the direction of Guntown, on the Mobile and Ohio Railway, where a few stragglers were captured, they continued their retreat to Baldwin, some twenty-four miles further. There they remained until the 7th of June, when they resumed their march southward to a place called Tupelo, the capital of Lee County, Miss., about fifty-two miles from Corinth.

While General Halleck remained in personal command, no other military movement of note took place. On the 11th of July he was called to Washington, and twelve days later given the chief command of all the Federal armies. General Thomas was left in charge of that portion of the Grand Army of the Tennessee remaining at Corinth, and General Grant resumed the command of his old army, with a more extended jurisdiction.

WILLIAM J. HARDEE.

Born in Savannah, Ga., 1818, died at Wytheville, Va., November 6th, 1873; was admitted to the United States Military Academy at West Point, and graduated from it with General Beauregard in 1838, entering the army as second lieutenant of dragoons. He displayed great aptitude throughout his studies, and soon evinced an extraordinary liking for, and remarkable proficiency in, all pertaining to the arts of war. His strict observance of military discipline soon won the admiration of all around him, and his advancement was very rapid. One year after his graduation he was made a first lieutenant, and promoted to a captaincy in 1844,

E. F. W. ELLIS.

receiving the commission of brevet-major, and of lieutenant-colonel not long after, in recognition of his gallant conduct in the Mexican War. He was promoted to be major of the Second Regular Cavalry in 1855, and one year later was appointed to the command of the cadets at the West Point Academy, with the rank of lieutenant-colonel. While at the Academy, he gave courses of instruction in artillery, cavalry and infantry tactics, his book upon the latter becoming afterward the standard for use by the militia and in the Regular Army. In 1860 he was made a lieutenant-colonel of cavalry, and during January of the following year resigned his commission in the Federal Army to enter that of the Confederates, wherein he was appointed a brigadier-general, and soon attained a major-generalship.

At the battle of Shiloh, or Pittsburg Landing, April 6–7, 1862, Hardee was given command of the Third Corps, comprising the brigades of Patrick R. Cleburne, S. A. M. Wood, and T. C. Hindman, and at the battle of Chaplin's Hills, or Perryville, October 8th, 1862, he commanded the left wing of General Bragg's army. His services, especially at the last named engagement, won for him the rank of lieutenant-general. He was also in command of one of Bragg's *corps d'armée* at the battle of Stone River, or Murfreesboro, December 31st, 1862–January 2d, 1863; and had charge of Bragg's right wing at the battle of Chattanooga, November 23d–25th, 1863. General Hardee was assigned to command in South Carolina and in Georgia, evacuating Savannah December 20th, 1864, and Charleston, February 17th, 1865. He took part in the battle of Bentonville, N. C., March 19th–21st, 1865, and surrendered to General W. T. Sherman with Joseph E. Johnston's army, at Durham Station, N. C., on the 26th of April, 1865.

LOVELL H. ROUSSEAU.

Born in Lincoln County, Ky., August 4th, 1818; studied law in his native State, as well as in Indiana, and was admitted to practice at the early age of twenty-three; entered the political field immediately thereafter, and was elected to the Indiana State Assembly, 1844–5, and to the Indiana State Senate in 1847. He entered the Mexican War as captain of the Second Indiana Regiment of Volunteers, receiving special mention, more particularly for his gallantry at Buena Vista, February 22d–23d, 1847.

In 1849 he resumed his legal practice at Louisville, Ky., where he soon attained great prominence in the criminal branch of the law. He was elected to the Kentucky State Senate in 1860, and at the breaking out of the Civil War was mainly instrumental in establishing "Camp Joe Holt," quite a large military rendezvous near Louisville. He also raised the Fifth Regiment of Kentucky Volunteers, of which he became colonel in September, 1861, being made a brigadier-general on the 1st of the following month. In command of the Fourth Brigade of McCook's corps, belonging to Buell's army, at the second day's battle of Pittsburg Landing, or Shiloh, he greatly distinguished himself, retaking the headquarters previously occupied and abandoned by General McClernand, and contributing greatly to the Federal victory. His gallantry was again manifested so strongly at the battle of Perryville, or Chaplin's Hill, Ky., fought October 8th, 1862, that he was afterward made a major-general of volunteers. He also took part at the battle of Murfreesboro, or Stone River, December 31st, 1862; and from November, 1863, to the close of the war, remained at the head of the District of the Tennessee.

On the 30th of November, 1865, he resigned his command in the army to take a seat in the United States Congress, and two years later was commissioned a brigadier-general and brevet major-general in the Regular Army, being appointed to the command of the Department of Louisiana July 28th, 1868. While in charge of the latter department, he died at New Orleans, on the 7th of January, 1869.

LEWIS WALLACE.

Born in Fountain County, Ind., about the year 1828; practiced law until the breaking out of the Mexican War, when he entered the field as second lieutenant of the First Indiana Volunteers. Upon leaving the army, he resumed the practice of law, and gave some attention to politics, which led to his election as a member of the Indiana State Senate.

At the time of the breaking out of the Civil War, he was a resident of Crawfordsville, Ind., whence he was called to Indianapolis by Governor Oliver P. Morton, who offered him, April 16th, 1861, the position of adjutant-general, and commissioned him to immediately raise the State quota of six regiments of volunteers called for by the President. So actively and judiciously did Wallace set about his work, that in three days he notified the Governor of his having organized not only the desired number of regiments, of which the sixty companies were already at Camp Morton, near Indianapolis, but likewise nearly eighty other companies, which were also ready for service. He then tendered his resignation, which was reluctantly accepted, and within twenty-four hours had completed the organization of the Eleventh Indiana (Zouave) Volunteer Regiment, of which he took the command.

With the latter he succeeded in effecting the capture of Romney, June 11th, 1861, and likewise carried on many important operations throughout Western Virginia and Kentucky, which won him the rank of brigadier-general, on the day of the capture of Fort Henry.

At the battle of Fort Donelson he was given command of the Third Division, and assigned to the centre of the advancing column, displaying so much ability and gallantry, that he was rewarded with the commission of major-general, March 21st, 1862. He did not take part in the first day's engagement at Pittsburg Landing, or Shiloh, fought during the following month, but he figured conspicuously on the second day, April 7th, at the head of the forces assigned to the extreme Federal right, and subsequently formed part of the advance on Corinth. He was president of the court of inquiry called to investigate the conduct of General Buell, and subsequently

HOISTING THE STARS AND STRIPES, BY THE FEDERAL TROOPS, ON THE CORONA FEMALE COLLEGE, CORINTH, MISS.

FROM A SKETCH BY H. LOVIE.

SHILOH LOG CHAPEL, WHERE THE BATTLE OF SHILOH COMMENCED, APRIL 6TH, 1862.

From a Sketch by B. Lovie.

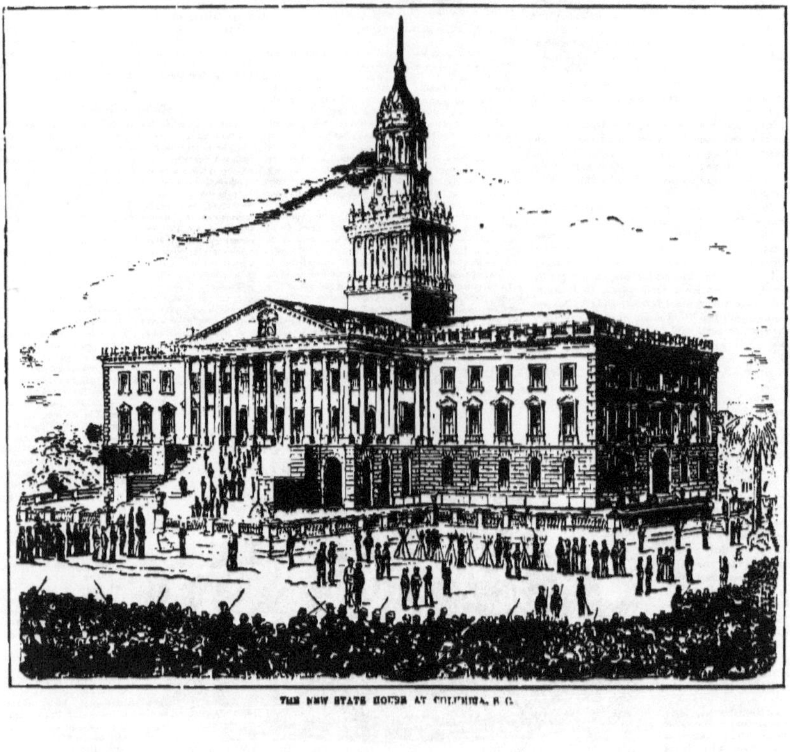

THE NEW STATE HOUSE AT COLUMBIA, S. C.

placed as the head of the Middle Department embracing the State of Delaware and a portion of Maryland.

At the battle of the Monocacy, July 9th, 1864, he so checked the advance of the Confederates as to prevent their capture of the national capital. For this he received the thanks of the Secretary of War and of Lieutenant-general Grant, the latter referring as follows to the part which Wallace was left to take in the battle at the head of a comparatively small number of men: "His force was not sufficient to insure success; but he fought the enemy, nevertheless, and although it resulted in a defeat to our arms yet it detained the enemy, and thereby served to enable General Wright to reach Washington, with two divisions of the Sixth and the advance of the Nineteenth Corps, before him."

General Wallace was a member of the commission appointed, in 1865, for the trial of persons implicated in the fatal shooting of President Lincoln, and in the attempted assassination of Secretary Seward and the other heads of departments. He has since filled many important official positions, and is now (1884) the United States Minister to Turkey.

THE STONE FLEET.

The United States Government, in order to blockade the Southern harbors without the presence of a large force of armed vessels, determined to purchase a fleet of old vessels of large tonnage, load them with stones, sail them to the mouths of the harbors of Charleston and Savannah, and then sink them in the channels. They would thus seal the cities to future commerce, and, by the presence of a small fleet, prevent any effort on the part of the Confederates to raise the sunken hulks.

On the 20th of November, 1861, there sailed from the harbor of New Bedford, Mass., a fleet of twenty-five vessels for this purpose. The experience of a similar blockade of the harbor of Sebastopol had proven the value of thus closing a harbor, and the skill and time it required to raise such a submarine blockade. The fleet cost the Government about $50,000, and arrived off Charleston on the 19th of December, 1861, and fifteen of the vessels of the first were quickly got into position, as indicated on the map, the plugs previously prepared knocked out, and the ships with sails set and flags flying gradually sank out of sight, leaving but the upper rigging in view. The remaining ten vessels and their convoys, taking the crews on board, proceeded to the mouth of the Savannah River, and were consigned to the shifting sands of that channel, to stop the passage to the harbor. The English merchants denounced this system of blockade, and protested against the permanent destruction of the entrances to those harbors. The Confederates had before this used the same means of blockade. At the time the Federal forces took possession of Tybee Island, they scuttled and sank several hulks in the channel to prevent the ingress of the Federal fleet.

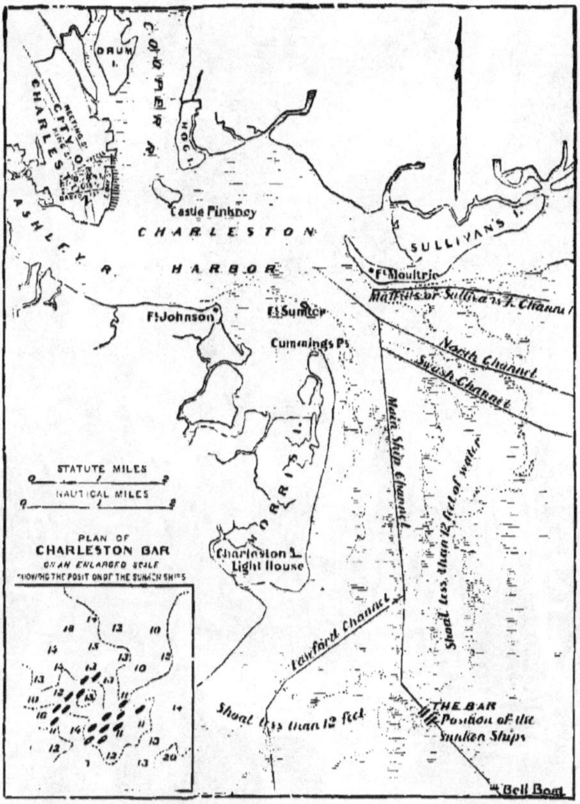

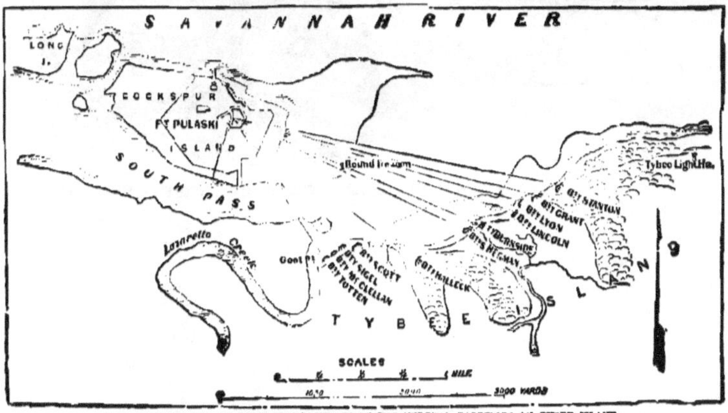

MAP OF FORT PULASKI, WITH THE POSITIONS OF THE FEDERAL BATTERIES ON TYBEE ISLAND.

ADVANCE OF THE FEDERAL TROOPS ON CORINTH.—SCENE AT L

ADVANCE OF THE FEDERAL TROOPS ON CORINTH.—SCENE AT LICK CREEK BOTTOM, [illegible] 1862—GENERAL HURLBUT'S DIVISION FORCING THEIR WAY THROUGH THE MUD.

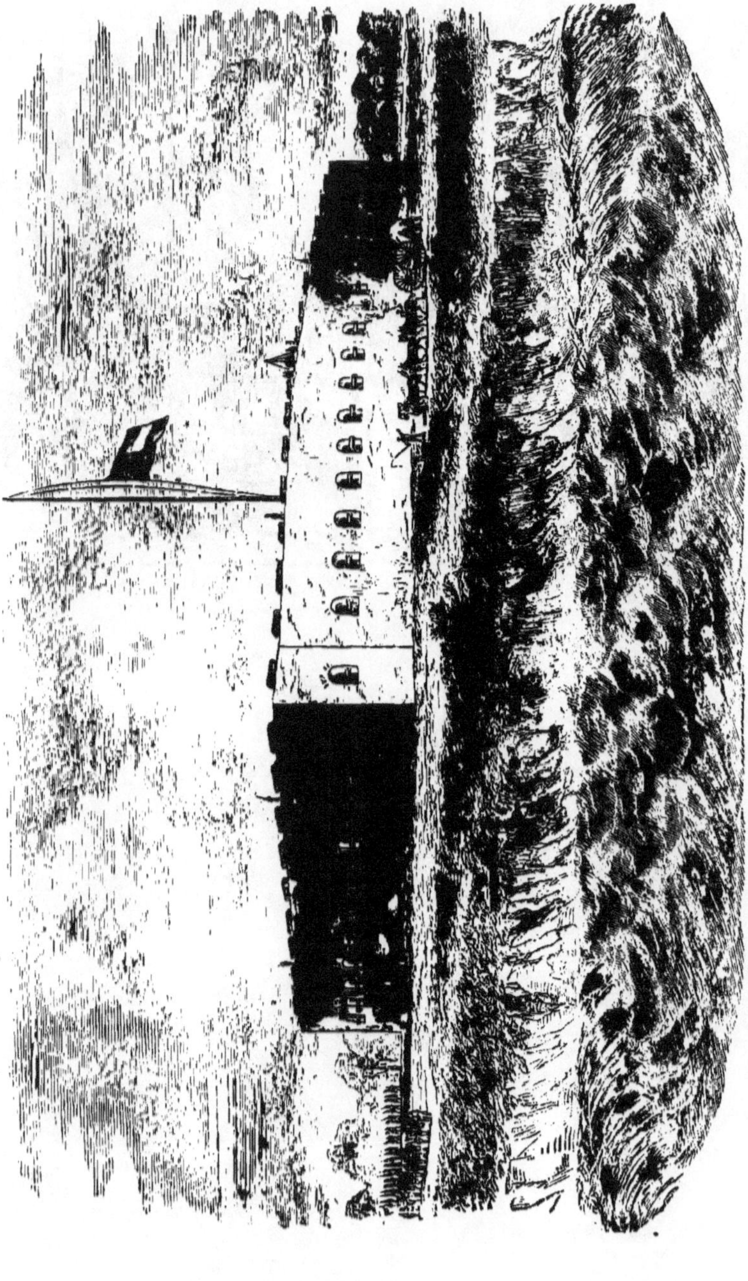

FORT PULASKI, ON COCKSPUR ISLAND, COMMANDING THE ENTRANCE TO THE SAVANNAH RIVER AND CITY OF SAVANNAH GA.

SIEGE AND CAPTURE OF FORT PULASKI

Fort Pulaski, on Cockspur Island, was built by the United States Government in 1829-31, for the defense of Tybee Roads and the Savannah River approach to the City of Savannah, Ga. In January, 1861, it was seized and occupied by the military authorities of the State of Georgia, and held by them until transferred to the Confederate Government, by whom it was strongly armed and garrisoned. The lighthouse, known by all coast-wise sailors as Tybee Light, 108 feet in height, and to be seen at a distance of twelve miles, was extinguished, together with all the other lighthouses in the hands of the Confederates, and, shortly before the Federal troops took possession of the island, was set on fire, and the woodwork and reflectors destroyed.

The capture of Fort Pulaski had been determined upon shortly after the taking of Port Royal, and Tybee Island was occupied on the 24th of November, 1861, for the purpose of erecting batteries, and to enable the making of reconnoissances with gunboats and land forces.

One of these reconnoissances was made by General H. G. Wright, with the co-operation of Commander C. H. Davis, and of the Fourth New Hampshire, Sixth Connecticut, and Ninety-seventh Pennsylvania Regiments, under Colonels Whipple, Chatfield and Guess. It entered the Savannah River, in the rear of Fort Pulaski, through Warsaw Sound, Wilmington Narrows and St. Augustine Creek. Another reconnoissance was made at the same time by Captain John Rogers, aided by General E. L. Viele and the Forty-eighth New York Regiment, Colonel Perry, as well as two companies of New York Engineers, and two companies, with twenty guns, of the Rhode Island Artillery. This last expedition went to the north of the Savannah River, by way of Wall's Cut and the Wright and Mud Rivers.

These two expeditions were able to co-operate on the 28th of January, 1862, in an attack on Commodore Tatnall's Confederate flotilla of five gunboats, which were driven back.

The reconnoissances satisfied the Federals that the Savannah River could not well be reached at that time by their gunboats. An effective blockade of the river was then made, and a fortification, named Fort Vulcan, erected at Venus Point, on Jones's island, while a second fort, called Fort Hamilton, was erected at the western head of Bird Island, opposite Fort Vulcan, and a battery placed upon a hulk anchored in Lazaretto Creek.

General Quincy A. Gillmore took personal command of Tybee Island on the 20th of February, and at once began the construction of earthworks for a series of eleven distinct bomb-proof batteries upon that part of Tybee Island called Goat Point. As all this section lay within range of Fort Pulaski, the earthworks could only be put up during the night.

The building of these, as well as of the accompanying magazines and trenches, occupied six entire weeks, and was chiefly performed by the Forty-fifth New York Regiment, Colonel Ross; the Seventh Connecticut Regiment, Colonel Alfred Howe Terry; and a detachment of Volunteer Engineers under Lieutenant-colonel Hall. The transportation and mounting of the thirty-seven guns upon the earthworks, and the landing and storing of the ammunition, were completed under the supervision of Lieutenant Horace Porter, United States Army, who received further assistance from detachments of the Eighth Maine Infantry and of the Third Rhode Island Artillery Regiments.

The names, commanders and armaments of the different batteries were as follows:

Totten, Captain Rodman, four 10-inch mortars; McClellan, Captain Rogers, two 84-pound and two 64-pound James; Sigel, Captain Seldeneck, five 30-pound Parrott and one 48-pound James; Scott, Captain Mason, four 10 and 8-inch columbiads; Halleck, Captain Sanford, two 13-inch mortars; Sherman, Captain Francis, three 13-inch mortars; Burnside, Sergeant Wilson, one 13-inch mortar; Lincoln, Captain Pelouze, three 8-inch columbiads; Lyon, Captain Pelouze, four ten-inch columbiads; Grant, Captain Palmer, three 10-inch mortars; and Stanton, Captain Skinner, three 10-inch mortars.

On the 9th of April everything was in readiness for the bombardment, and early on the following

TYBEE ISLAND, SAVANNAH RIVER, GA.—VIEW OF THE LIGHTHOUSE AND BARRACKS—DESTRUCTION OF THE LIGHTHOUSE BY THE CONFEDERATES, ON ITS EVACUATION.

SCENE IN SAVANNAH, GA., ON THE RECEIPT OF THE NEWS OF THE OCCUPATION OF

From a S

SCENE IN SAVANNAH, GA., ON THE RECEIPT OF THE NEWS OF THE OCCUPATION OF [illegible] ISLAND BY THE [illegible] — [illegible] OF THE INHABITANTS.

[illegible]

FORT PULASKI DURING THE SECOND DAY'S BOMBARDMENT, FRIDAY, APRIL 11th, 1862.

From a Sketch by W. T. Crane.

morning a summons for the surrender of Fort Pulaski was sent, through Lieutenant J. H. Wilson, to its commander, Colonel Charles H. Olmstead, of the First Georgia Volunteer Regiment, by General David Hunter, who had just superseded General Sherman in the command of the land forces at Hilton Head.

April, 1862.

The surrender having been refused, order was given to immediately open fire. This was done, at about eight o'clock on the morning of the 10th, from the two 13-inch mortars in charge of Captain Sanford. The remaining ten batteries joined in, and their united fire thundered all day, and was steadily responded to from the fort.

At about one o'clock in the afternoon, the main flagstaff of Fort Pulaski was shot away, and later on five guns were dismounted, and a large breach was made in the direction of the magazine, at the south-eastern portion of the fort.

The bombardment of the fort was kept up until the next morning, shells being thrown from three batteries at intervals of fifteen minutes, and at daybreak of the 11th the firing again commenced on both sides. The Federals had then the co-operative fire of an additional battery, which General Viele had just finished upon the southern extremity of Long Island, about two miles distant from the fort, and were somewhat aided also by the fire of the gunboat *Norwich*, lying near the bulk in Lazaretto Creek.

Captain Seldeneck was relieved in the morning by a portion of the crew of the frigate *Wabash*, under Captain C. R. P. Rogers, who did very effective work with the powerful columbiads at Battery Sigel.

The Federal fire was mainly directed against the south-eastern portion of the fort, and by two o'clock in the afternoon the breach had become so wide, that the arches of the casemate were laid bare, and there was every likelihood of the powder magazine being soon reached. By that time, also, two batteries that had been erected on Cockspur Island were silenced.

The propriety of landing a storming party was then discussed, but the loss of life which it would necessarily entail caused the plan to be abandoned, and General Benham was just about sending a messenger to ask for the surrender of the fort when its flag was seen being lowered. This was followed by the hoisting of a white flag, when firing ceased.

Generals Gillmore and Benham immediately went to Goat Point, whence they put off, with their aids and Mr Badeau, for the fort. Mr. Badeau landed with a white flag, and met the Confederate bearer, Colonel Sims after which the whole party went to the fort, where they were soon after joined by a messenger sent by General Hunter, who had witnessed the whole engagement from the deck of the *McClellan*.

The immediate and unconditional surrender of the fort was agreed on, and Major Halpine, assistant adjutant-general, received the officers' swords as the representative of General Hunter, and the Federals withdrew before dark, after raising their flag upon the ramparts.

With the fort were surrendered 360 prisoners, 47 guns, and a large supply of stores and ammunition. Colonel Terry was left in charge with the Seventh Connecticut Regiment, two companies of the Third Rhode Island Artillery, and one company of New York Volunteer Engineers.

Fort Pulaski was visited the following day by Generals Hunter, Gillmore and Benham, and on Sunday, the 13th, the Confederate officers and men were taken on board the *Honduras* and the *Ben de Ford* to Bay Point, and thence transferred by the *McClellan* and *Star of the South* to Fort Columbus, in New York Harbor.

DAVID HUNTER

HOSPITAL BUILDING ON TYBEE ISLAND.

CHARLES HENRY DAVIS

DAVID HUNTER

Born in Washington, D. C., July 21st, 1802; entered the United States Military Academy, September, 1818, and upon graduating, July 1st, 1822, was commissioned second lieutenant of the Fifth Artillery, and in June, 1828, was made first lieutenant; in March, 1833, he was appointed captain in the First Dragoons, and remained on frontier duty until 1836, when he resigned from the army, and settled in Illinois. Six years later he re-entered the service as paymaster with the rank of major, serving in that capacity until May 14th, 1861, when he was appointed colonel of the Sixth United States Regular Cavalry, a new regiment just recruited. On the 17th of May, 1861, he was made a brigadier-general of volunteers, and at the first battle of Bull Run, where he was wounded, he commanded the Second Division of the Federal army, which included the brigades of Colonels Andrew, Porter and Ambrose E. Burnside. Among the soldiers he bore the sobriquet of "Black Dave." He was promoted to be a major-general of volunteers in August, 1861, and ordered to report to General Fremont, and in the following month of November assumed the command *pro tem.* of the Western Department. He was afterward placed at the head of the Department of the Southeast, and in May, 1862, issued an order declaring slavery abolished in his department. This order created so much feeling at the time, that President Lincoln promptly issued a proclamation annulling it.* Hunter was transferred to the Department of West Virginia, replacing General Sigel in May, 1864, and subsequently took part in the battle of Piedmont, as well as in the operations against Lynchburg. He was relieved of command, at his own request, by General Sheridan on the 7th of August, 1864. In the following year, Hunter was made a member of the military commission appointed to try those engaged in the shooting of President Lincoln and in the attempted assassination of Secretary Seward and others. He retired from active service in 1866.

CHARLES HENRY DAVIS.

Born in Boston, Mass., January 16th, 1807; entered the navy as midshipman, August 12th, 1823, and became passed midshipman in 1829, lieutenant in 1834, and commander in 1854. In the year 1849 he was appointed superintendent of the American publication called the *Nautical Almanac*, and at the time of the breaking out of the Civil War he was a member of the board of officers which met in Washington to report upon the condition of the Southern coast preparatory to active operations against the Confederate forces. He was Dupont's chief of staff and fleet captain with the Port Royal expedition, had the superintendence of the sinking of the stone fleet in Charleston Harbor, and for the untiring energy he displayed in the execution of orders throughout the most trying periods of that expedition, he was rewarded with the grade of captain, which was rapidly followed by that of commodore, while in command of the flotilla operating against the fleet of the Confederate Commodore Tatnall, in the Savannah River, January 28th, 1862. On the 9th of May, 1862, he relieved Foote of the command of the Western fleet off Fort Pillow, and on one occasion, with but seven vessels, he succeeded in beating off eight Confederate iron-clads.

Three days after the abandonment of Fort Pillow, Davis attacked the Confederate ironclads and rams, nearly opposite the City of Memphis, and after a bitter contest captured all but one of the Confederate fleet, and secured the surrender of Memphis. For his gallant services he received the thanks of Congress and the commission of rear-admiral. In 1865 he was placed at the head of the Bureau of Navigation and made superintendent of the Naval Observatory at Washington, and two years later he was appointed commander-in-chief of the United States squadron off the coast of Brazil. There he remained two years, and upon his return, was ordered to Washington on special duty, and subsequently appointed to command the Navy Yard at Norfolk, Va.

---

* HEADQUARTERS DEPARTMENT OF THE SOUTH,
HILTON HEAD, S. C., May 9th, 1862.

GENERAL ORDERS No. 11.

The three States of Georgia, Florida and South Carolina, comprising the Military Department of the South, having deliberately declared themselves no longer under the protection of the United States of America, and having taken up arms against the said United States, it becomes a military necessity to declare them under martial law. This was accordingly done on the 25th day of April 1862. Slavery and martial law in a free country are altogether incompatible. The persons in these three States—Georgia, Florida and South Carolina—heretofore held as slaves, are therefore declared forever free.

DAVID HUNTER,
Major General Commanding.
ED. W. SMITH, A. A. Adjutant General.

EXTERIOR VIEW OF FORTIFICATIONS ERECTED BY TH

FROM

INTERIOR OF THE MORTAR BATTERY "STANTON," TYBEE ISLAND, SHOWING THE OPERAT

EXTERIOR VIEW OF FORTIFICATIONS ERECTED BY THE FEDERAL TROOPS AT HILTON HEAD, PORT ROYAL HARBOR, S. C.

[illegible]

INTERIOR OF THE MORTAR BATTERY "STANTON," TYBEE ISLAND, SHOWING THE OPERATION OF [illegible] THIRTEEN-INCH MORTAR DURING THE BOMBARDMENT OF FORT PULASKI, APRIL [illegible], 1862

From a sketch [illegible]

Jackson. Pensacola. Confederate Ram. Mississippi. Confederate Boat. Confederate Boat.

PASSAGE OF THE SECOND DIVISION OF THE FEDERAL SQUADRON PAST FORTS JACKSON AND ST. PHILIP, APRIL 24TH, 1862.

FROM A SKETCH BY WM. WAUD

CAPTURE OF NEW ORLEANS.

As soon as General Butler had carried out the orders which the Secretary of War had given him after the surrender of Fort Hatteras, "to raise, arm, uniform and equip a volunteer force" especially for service in Southern waters, he was asked to suggest the best place of rendezvous for an expedition against Mobile. He named Ship Island, located off the Mississippi coast, between Lake Borgne and Mobile Bay, and his suggestion was adopted, as Ship Island proved to be within striking distance of every important locality of the Gulf of Mexico.

In the month of December, 1861, General J. W. Phelps was sent to the island in the steamship *Constitution*, with the advance of Butler's troops, which were duly landed. The *Constitution* then returned to embark the remainder, and had already taken 2,000 more men, who were to be accompanied by General Butler himself, when the latter received a Government message directing him to disembark the men, and not to sail until further instructions.

General Butler immediately sought and obtained an interview with Secretary of War Edwin M. Stanton, who had superseded Simon Cameron on the 13th of January, 1862, and learned that the complications likely to arise with Great Britain from the Mason and Slidell capture, necessitated a change in the contemplated movements. The result of their conference was the selection of New Orleans as the first most important objective point in lieu of Mobile, and when the decision was laid before President Lincoln, it met with his immediate approval.

The Department of the Gulf was created, and General Butler placed at its head. On the 25th of February, 1862, Butler embarked at Hampton Roads, aboard the steamship *Mississippi*, with his wife and staff, and reached Ship Island on the 25th of March, after a protracted and dangerous passage, especially along the coast of North Carolina, where the *Mississippi* was twice wrecked, and after experiencing further delay at Port Royal, where the injuries to the vessel had to be repaired.

Captain David Glasgow Farragut had, meanwhile, reached Ship Island on the 20th of February, after a voyage of eighteen days from Hampton Roads. He had, on the 20th of the previous month, been instructed by the Secretary of the Navy to proceed without delay to the Gulf of Mexico and there receive from Flag-officer McKean the command of the Western Gulf Squadron. This done, he was to take with him a fleet of mortar-boats, which were to rendezvous at Key West, under Commander David D. Porter, and, with such of the blockading vessels as could be spared, proceed to attack New Orleans, and hold the city or its approaches until Federal troops could be sent to his assistance.

It was likewise decided that, in the event of Farragut not silencing the Confederate guns, he should make an attempt to run by the forts, and take all the defenses in the rear, while the land forces under General Butler would make an attempt to carry the forts by assault.

The last of Farragut's fleet could not successfully be got over the bar until the 8th of April, nor was it till the 17th of the same month that the combined naval and land forces were ready for action.

April, 1862.

During that long interval, the entire course of the river had been surveyed up to the two forts commanding the approaches to the city. These were Fort Jackson, on the western side, containing seventy-four guns, with a supplemental battery of six guns, and Fort St. Philip, on the opposite side of the Mississippi, mounting forty guns. The fortifications were under the command of Lieutenant-colonel Edward Higgins, while all the river defenses were in charge of General J. K. Duncan.

In addition to the forts and the battery before alluded to, the entrance to the city was defended by a fleet of thirteen Confederate gunboats, the ironclad floating battery *Louisiana*, the ironclad ram *Manassas*, and several fire-rafts. All these lay under the guns of the forts and behind a heavy iron chain, with but one opening, which was stretched over eight hulks, and extended from Fort Jackson to the battery opposite.

BURNING OF CONFEDERATE GUNBOATS, RAMS AND VESSELS, AT NEW ORLEANS AND ALGIERS, ON THE APPROACH OF THE FEDERAL FLEET.

FROM A SKETCH BY WM. WAUD.

The *Louisiana* had 16 guns and the *Manassas* only 1. The Confederate gunboats were: The *Governor Moore*, 3; *General Quitman*, 2; *Stonewall Jackson*, 2; *Warrior*, 2; *Resolute*, 2; *Defiance*, 2; *McRae*, 8; *Galveston*, 2; *Anglo-Norman*, 2; *Breckinridge*, 1; *Lovell*, 1; and *Star*, 1. The first six gunboats had iron prows attached to them, and were made shot-proof by cotton-bale bulkheads. They were commanded respectively by Captains Kennon, Grant, Philips, Stephenson, Hooper and McCoy.

Early on the 17th, all the Federal vessels were drawn together about four miles below the forts. These consisted of the steamships *Hartford* (flagship), 28, Captain Wainright; *Pensacola*, 24, Captain Morris; *Brooklyn*, 26, Captain Craven; *Richmond*, 26, Captain Alden, and the *Mississippi*, 12, Captain M. Smith, besides the gunboats and armed tugs, *Iroquois*, 9, Commander De Camp; *Oneida*, 10, Commander S. P. Lee; *Portsmouth*, 17, Commander Rogers; *Varuna*, 12, Captain Boggs; *Cayuga*, 5, Lieutenant Harrison; *Winona*, 4, Lieutenant Nichols; *Katahdin*, 6, Lieutenant Preble; *Itasca*, 5, Lieutenant Caldwell; *Kineo*, 5, Lieutenant Ransom; *Wissahickon*, 5, Lieutenant A. N. Smith; *Pinola*, 5, Lieutenant Crosby; *Kennebec*, 5, Lieutenant Russell; *Sciota*, 6, Lieutenant Donelson; *Kittatinny*, 9, Lieutenant Lamson; *Westfield*, 6, Captain Renshaw; the *Clinton*, *Jackson*, *Saxon*, and the *Miami*, 6, Lieutenant Harrell.

The mortar-boats were made up in three divisions, commanded respectively by Lieutenants Watson, Smith, Queen and White. They consisted of the *Norfolk Packet*, *T. A. Ward*, *Horace Beales*, *Oliver H. Lee*, *C. P. Williams*, *William Bacon*, *Para*, *Orletta*, *Sidney C. Jones*, *M. Vassar, Jr.*, *M. J. Carleton*, *Adolph Hugel*, *Orvetta*, *George Mangham*, *John Griffith*, *Sarah Bruin*, *Henry James*, *Dan Smith*, *Racer*, and the *Sea Foam*.

Commander Porter's flagship was the steamer *Harriet Lane*, 4, which was accompanied by the gunboat *Owasco*, 5, Lieutenant Guest.

The land forces, embracing about 9,000 men, were on the following transports:

Mississippi, with General Butler and staff, the Twenty-sixth and Thirty-first Massachusetts Regiments, under Colonels Jones and Gooding, and Everett's Sixth Massachusetts Battery.

Great Republic, General Williams, with the Fourth Wisconsin, Sixth Michigan, and Twenty-first Indiana Regiments, under Colonels Paine, Cortines and McMillen.

North America, the Thirtieth Massachusetts Regiment, Colonel Dudley, and a company each of Durivage's and Reed's Cavalry.

Matanzas, General Phelps, with the Ninth Connecticut Regiment, Colonel Cahill, and Holcomb's Second Vermont Battery.

Will Farley, the Twelfth Connecticut, Colonel Deming.

The Confederates sent down several of their fire-rafts during the afternoon and night of the 17th, but they were dragged out of harm's way by boats from the *Iroquois* and the gunboat *Westfield*, and allowed to burn out along the shore without causing any damage whatever.

On the morning of the 18th, Fort Jackson opened fire, which was at once responded to by the *Owasco* and the mortar-boats, six of which were in full view of the fort, while the remaining fourteen lay concealed by the woods along the shore. The better to hide his schooner mortar-boats from view, Porter had covered their sides with Mississippi mud, and attached branches of trees to their rigging and masts.

April, 1862.

All day long fire was exchanged between the fort and mortar-boats, the gunboats occasionally taking part in the engagement, and when the firing ceased at dark, the Federals had but two of their vessels struck, and had sustained a loss of one killed and three wounded.

The bombardment was resumed the day following, when the Federals had one man killed and two wounded, and had, besides, one mortar-boat (*M. J. Carleton*) sunk and another temporarily disabled by Confederate shells.

The firing was thus exchanged with the forts, and without much damage on the Federal side, until the 20th of the month, when a council of captains was called by Farragut on board of the flagship *Hartford*, as it was apparent that other and more effective means must be employed to reduce the forts.

It was decided that the forts should be run, and that, preparatory thereto, the chain and hulk

FIRST DAY'S BOMBARDMENT OF FORTS JACKSON AND ST. PHILIP BY FEDERAL SCHOONER FIRST DIVISION OF THE SQUADRON PREPARING FOR ACTION.

obstruction should be removed. The latter work was assigned to Fleet-captain Bell, who took with him that very night the gunboats *Itasca* and *Pinola*, supported by the *Iroquois*, *Winona* and *Kennebec*.

The *Itasca* and *Pinola* crept up to the barricade in face of the fire from both Fort Jackson and the battery, but under cover of darkness. The *Pinola* had been given a petard to throw on board one of the hulks, and to be ignited by an electric spark. But after throwing it, the *Pinola* was caught by the strong current thrown down stream, and her connecting wire broken before the spark could be transmitted.

The *Itasca* had, meanwhile, lashed herself to one of the hulks, upon which her men had jumped, soon severing the heavy chain with hammer, saw and chisel. When the chain parted, the *Itasca* had been forced back toward the shore against the lowered hulk, and was for a while in imminent danger of being swamped; but with the aid of the *Pinola*, she was, after many efforts, successfully removed, and both returned, with the three supporting vessels, to their former anchorage.

On the evening of the 23d, Farragut was ready for the advance, and all precautions were taken to guard the fleet against the dangers to which it might necessarily be exposed.

The most important safeguard was devised by the engineer of the *Richmond*, and was adopted by the whole fleet. It consisted in hanging over the sides of vessels loops of iron chain cables, to arrest the progress of shot and prevent damage more particularly to the machinery. Farragut's general order seemed to provide for every possible contingency. In it he says: "You will be called upon to meet the enemy in the worst form for our profession. Hot and cold shot will, no doubt, be freely dealt to us, and there must be stout hearts and quick hands to extinguish the one and stop the holes of the other." Among other things, the commanders were ordered to "trice up the topmast stays, or land the whiskers, and bring all the rigging into the bowsprit, so that there be no [illegible] in the range of the direct fire ahead. Mount one or two guns on the poop and topgallant forecastle, bearing in mind that you will always have to run head to the current, and can only avail yourself of the sheer of the helm to point a broadside gun more than three points forward of the beam. [illegible] a kedge in the mizzen-chains; a hawser [illegible] through the stern-chock; also grapnels to tow off fire-ships. Have light Jacob-ladders made to throw over the side for the use of carpenters in stopping shot-holes. See that pumps and hose are in good order for extinguishing fire. Have many tubs of water about the decks, for the purpose of extinguishing fire and for drinking. Have heavy kedge in the port main-chains, and whip on the main-yard, ready to run it up and let fall on the deck of any vessel you may run alongside of, in order to secure her for boarding. . . . . ."

April, 1862.

The night of the 23d of April was very dark, owing to a heavy fog, which caused the smoke from the steamers to settle upon the water.

The *Itasca* ran up at about eleven o'clock to where the chain had been extended, and signaled the channel clear of all obstructions except the hulks. Shortly after one o'clock on the morning of the 24th everybody was called to action, and about an hour later two small red lights were shown as a signal for the advance. At about half past three the entire fleet was well under way.

The *Hartford*, with Farragut perched in the foretrigging, sightglass in hand, led the left column, including the *Richmond* and *Brooklyn*, and Captain Theodorus Bailey, in the *Cayuga*, led the right division, embracing the *Pensacola*, *Portsmouth*, *Mississippi*, *Oneida*, *Katahdin*, *Varuna*, *Kineo*, *Wissahickon*, and *J. P. Jackson*. The third division, under Captain Henry H. Bell included the *Sciota*, *Iroquois*, *Pinola*, *Itasca*, *Winona*, and *Kennebec*. As soon as the fleet had

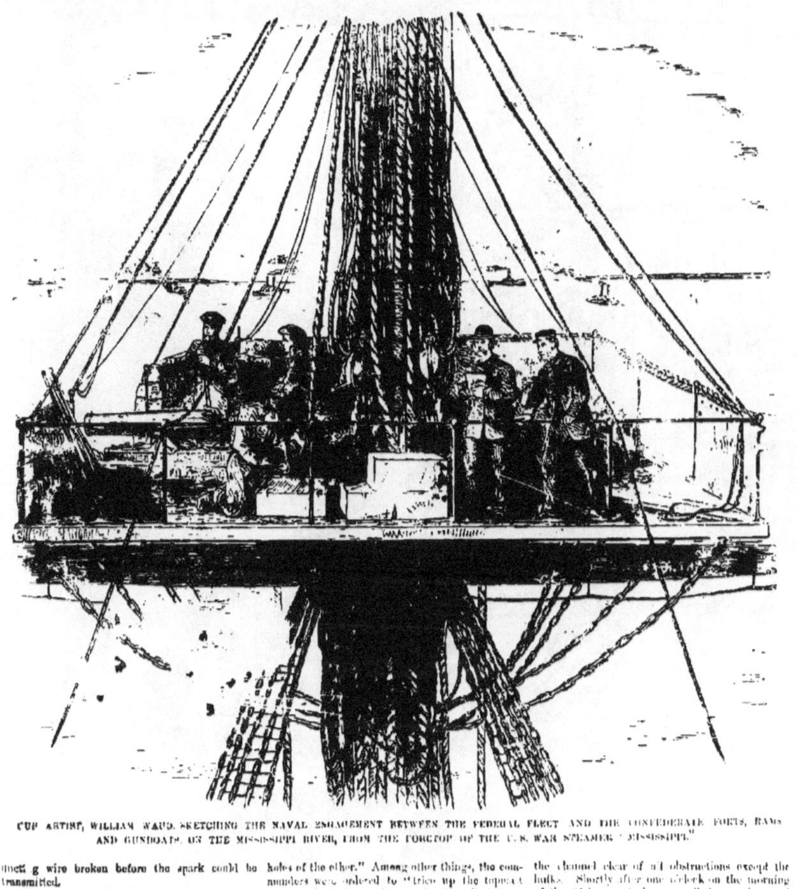

OUR ARTIST, WILLIAM WAUD, SKETCHING THE NAVAL ENGAGEMENT BETWEEN THE FEDERAL FLEET AND THE CONFEDERATE FORTS, RAMS AND GUNBOATS ON THE MISSISSIPPI RIVER, FROM THE FORETOP OF THE U. S. WAR STEAMER "MISSISSIPPI."

LANDING OF CAPTAIN BAILEY AND LIEUTENANT PERKINS ON THE LEVEE, NEW ORLEANS, WITH A FLAG OF TRUCE TO DEMAND THE SURRENDER OF THE CITY TO THE FEDERAL FORCES

LAST BROADSIDE OF THE "VARUNA."—COMMANDER BOGGS FIRES THREE GUNS OF THE FEDERAL GUNBOAT BEFORE SHE SINKS.
From a Sketch by W. Waud.

fairly started, the mortar-boats opened a terrible storm upon Fort Jackson, as well as upon the battery, the latter being also engaged by the *Harriet Lane*, *Owasco*, *Westfield*, *Clinton* and *Miami*.

Fort Jackson did not reply until the *Cayuga* came nearly on a line with the battery, when a heavy Confederate fire was opened on all sides. Nor did the *Cayuga* respond until close upon Fort St. Philip, when she opened upon the latter heavy broadsides of grape and canister. Captain Bailey's other vessel in turn followed suit, and with the exception of the *Portsmouth*, which lost her tow, the *Jackson*, and drifted down the river, all passed by without experiencing much damage. As the *Cayuga* got beyond Fort St. Philip, she was attacked by the Confederate flotilla, under command of Captain Mitchell of the *Louisiana*. With no supporting vessel then within easy reach, she would have succumbed to the combined attack had not Captain Bailey rapidly exercised the utmost caution in warding off attempts to ram and board his vessel, and used his guns to the best advantage. Before the *Varuna* had come up to his rescue, Bailey had compelled the surrender of three of the Confederate gunboats, and caused the grounding of another.

As the now badly crippled *Cayuga* continued her way up the river, in accordance with Farragut's instructions, the *Varuna* found herself nearly hemmed in by Confederate vessels. Captain Boggs, however, rushed in their midst, delivering broadsides in every direction, and before long had completely disabled one of the vessels, apparently crowded with troops, as well as driven ashore and forced the blowing up of three others.

The *Varuna* was about moving ahead, when she was fiercely assailed by the *Governor Moore*, which, under the command of Beverley Kennon, succeeded in ramming her simultaneously with the delivery of a raking fire that killed four and wounded nine of the *Varuna's* crew. Captain Boggs managed, however, to get some 3-inch shells and rifle shots abaft the *Moore's* armor, compelling her to drop out in a disabled condition. He was then attacked by another vessel having a concealed iron prow, which was driven twice into the *Varuna*, the second time crushing in her side to such an extent that she sank some fifteen minutes later. Before the *Varuna* settled, however, the Confederate vessel had become entangled, and was so drawn around as to expose her unarmored side, into which latter Captain Boggs was enabled to fire some of his 8-inch shells. After this, the Confederate vessel went ashore, where she was burned by her commander.

The *Oneida* had come up in the meantime to aid the *Varuna*, but Captain Boggs had motioned him off to the *Moore*, which Kennon had caused to be set afire before abandoning her. The flames were extinguished, and the second officer and crew surrendered to the *Oneida*, which took off afterward part of the crew of the *Varuna*, the remainder being rescued by Captain Bailey's vessels, which had by that time come up.

While battling with the forts, a large raft, all ablaze, had been suddenly pushed against the *Hartford* by the *Manassas*, and had set fire to the flagship; but the flames had been speedily extinguished, and the *Hartford* had proceeded on her way, after again pouring full broadsides into both forts.

The *Hartford* had become engaged with Fort Jackson when within a mile and a quarter of it, giving it first the benefit of the two guns which Farragut had ordered placed upon her forecastle, and afterward full broadsides of grape and canister that seemed for the while to thoroughly clear all the barbette guns of the fort.

The *Pensacola* suffered greater loss than any of the other vessels. She had deliberately engaged Fort St. Philip, frequently returning its heavy fire, and her men had successfully avoided the first discharges by laying flat on the decks, but the subsequent fire had proved quite destructive, and her loss in wounded was very large indeed.

The *Richmond*, which was the slowest of the three vessels, also fired on both forts, without suffering damage, while on her way up; but the *Brooklyn* was less fortunate. She had become entangled in the hulks, and, while in this situation, had been attacked by the *Manassas*, in charge of Captain Warley. The latter sent into the *Brooklyn*, at a distance of only ten feet, some heavy shots that injured her somewhat, and would doubtless have disabled her completely but for the sandbags that had been judiciously heaped around her steam drum, and at all important quarters. The *Manassas* tried twice to ram her, but ineffectually, as she lay too close to get up sufficient speed for overcoming the chain cable armor that had been swung around her.

The *Brooklyn* had, besides, been exposed, meanwhile, to a raking fire from Fort Jackson, and had just managed to disentangle herself and escape the *Manassas* in the darkness, when she was attacked by a large Confederate steamer, which she, however, soon disabled and set afire. She then proceeded as best she could in the dark, and soon found herself in only thirteen feet of water, just abreast of Fort St. Philip, which she so effectively engaged as to completely silence for a while all the Confederate guns. She subsequently met on the way several of the Confederate gunboats, into which she also poured a destructive fire before joining the other vessels.

The third division was the least fortunate of all. The *Scioto*, *Iroquois* and *Pinola* successfully passed the forts, but the *Winona* and *Kennebec* had got entangled among the hulks, and were somewhat damaged by a severe fire from both forts, before

ENGAGEMENT BETWEEN THE U. S. GUNBOAT "VARUNA" AND THE CONFEDERATE RAM "BRECKINRIDGE" AND GUNBOAT "GOVERNOR MOORE."
From a Sketch by Wm. Waud.

PANORAMIC VIEW OF NEW ORLEANS.—THE FEDERA

PANORAMIC VIEW OF NEW ORLEANS—THE FEDERAL FLEET AT ANCHOR IN THE RIVER, APRIL [illegible] 1862

[illegible]

A DISCHARGE OF GRAPE FROM FORT JACKSON STRIKES THE DECK OF THE UNITED STATES GUNBOAT "IROQUOIS," KILLING EIGHT AND WOUNDING SEVEN OF A GUN'S CREW OF TWENTY-FIVE MEN MANNING A DAHLGREN GUN.

From a Sketch by Wm. Waud.

they could release themselves and return to their moorings. The *Itasca* had advanced bravely, but had at the outset been pierced by several shots, one of which had entered her boiler, and caused such an escape of steam as to drive every one from below. Other shots had struck her below the water-line, and she was almost in a sinking condition, when Captain Caldwell reluctantly gave orders to withdraw.

Thirteen vessels were thus placed within Farragut's immediate reach above the forts, and close by the Quarantine grounds, where the crippled *Cayuga* had stopped, after silencing a battery on the west side of the river and capturing the companies of Chalmette (Louisiana) Sharpshooters which were guarding it under Colonel Szymanski.

As soon as the last of the fleet had passed the forts, at the dawn of day, the ram *Manassas*, which was then practically the only effective remnant of the Confederate flotilla, was seen advancing toward the Federal vessels. The *Mississippi* was ordered to engage her, and Captain Smith at once dashed at full speed, expecting to run her down; but the ram dodged the blow, and in doing so got aground, where she was at once abandoned by her officers and crew. The *Mississippi* then poured two broadsides into the ram, and boarded her, but as she was not deemed worth saving, she was set afire and sent adrift. The burning craft was soon amidst the mortar-boats, some of which opened fire on her, but she settled before long, and, after a faint explosion on board, went to the bottom.

The time had now come when the land forces could be availed of. The mortar-boats were yet below the forts, close by which General Butler and his staff had, in the midst of serious danger, been reconnoitring on board the *Saxon*. As Captain Boggs was without a vessel, he volunteered to take a boat and make his way through the shallow bayous in the rear of Fort St. Philip, in order to convey Farragut's messages to General Butler and to Commander Porter. This was done without delay, and while Porter remained to attend to the forts, pending their possible surrender, Butler's troops were taken to Sable Island, situated a little over eleven miles from Fort St. Philip. From here they were piloted, mainly by Lieutenant Weitzel, across the bayou in small boats, as well as on foot through the muddy creeks, until they finally reached the Quarantine grounds on the following Saturday night.

Early on the morning of Friday, the 25th, Farragut moved up the river with nine of his vessels, headed by the *Cayuga*. (April, 1862.) The latter had not observed the signal for close order, and was quite far in the advance, when she came upon General Smith's Chalmette batteries, which had been erected just below the city, and whose united fire of twenty guns she had to withstand until the other vessels came up and aided in silencing both batteries.

The fleet encountered burning cotton-ships and floating timber as it advanced, and when it rounded the bend at about noon, came in full view of New Orleans, casting anchor an hour later while a violent rain and thunder storm was prevailing. The scene here was one long to be remembered. For a distance of five miles along the levees, some fifteen thousand bales of cotton, and many thousands of barrels of sugar and other staples, were burning, while in the stream and at the docks lay many large ships, steamboats and other craft, which had been set afire upon learning that the Federals were about reaching the city.

Both the Governor of Louisiana and General Mansfield Lovell, in command of the Confederate Department of the South as the successor of General Twiggs, had thus ordered the general destruction of property as soon as they knew of Farragut's advance. They had, besides, not only directed the firing of the Algiers shipyard, opposite New Orleans, as well as of the immense, though yet unfinished, ironclad ram *Mississippi*, and of all the dry-docks, warehouses, wood and coal yards, but they had sent down-stream burning cotton-ships, which the Federals had encountered, in hope that they might destroy some of Farragut's vessels. All of these, however, escaped injury.

The panic which had set in when the above named occurrences took place would have been still greater but for the aid given by the European brigade, whose prompt efforts in suppressing the tumult was very effective and fully appreciated. The Governor of the State had fled up the river, scattering proclamations which directed the burning of all cotton and other valuable property likely to fall into the hands of the Federals, and General Lovell had, with the concurrence of the city

DAVID G. FARRAGUT.

authorities, sent away nearly all of his troops and a large portion of the militia.

In the midst of the rain, Captain Bailey, bearing a flag of truce, put off in a boat, accompanied by Lieutenant George H. Perkins, with a demand for the surrender of the city, as well as for the immediate substitution of the Federal for the Confederate ensigns. They stepped ashore, and made their way to the City Hall through a motley crowd, which kept cheering for the South and for Jefferson Davis, and uttering groans and hisses for President Lincoln and the Yankee fleet. General

THEODORUS BAILEY.

Lovell, on his part, returned an unqualified refusal, besides advising John T. Monroe, the Mayor of New Orleans, not to surrender the city, and not to allow the taking down of the Confederate flags. While Captain Bailey was on his way back, some marines had landed from the *Pensacola*, and had hoisted the Federal ensign over the Mint. As they had left no guard, the ensign was hauled down after their departure by one William B. Mumford and three men belonging to the Pinckney Battalion. The occurrence was observed by the watch in the top of the *Pensacola*, whence a howitzer was fired in the direction of the Mint, without, however, doing any damage.

On the following day, Captain Bell was sent, with about one hundred marines, to the Mint and the Custom House, upon which the Federal flag was raised, and remained undisturbed. The peaceful Federal occupation of the city was delayed by the city authorities from day to day, upon the plea of want of authority, until the 30th of April, when Farragut determined that he would not resort to force, but simply maintain his ground, and he informed the authorities that he would hold no further intercourse with them, and would await the arrival of General Butler, who would be given the entire charge of the city.

Commander Porter had, in the meantime, kept up the fire upon Fort Jackson, and he had, on the 26th, demanded its surrender, stating that New Orleans was already held by Farragut; but Lieutenant-colonel Higgins had replied that, without positive knowledge as to the latter fact, he could not entertain any proposition. The next day, however, he accepted Porter's terms, upon learning that Farragut had actual possession of the city, and finding that the troops had not only mutinied at Fort Jackson, but that many had already spiked some of the guns and surrendered to the pickets of Butler's troops, which had just been stationed on the western side of the river.

The capitulation was signed on the 28th by Commanders D. D. Porter and W. B. Renshaw, as well as Lieutenant W. W. Wainwright, commanding the *Harriet Lane*, on the part of the Federals, and by General J. K. Duncan and Lieutenant-colonel Edward Higgins for the Confederates. By the terms of the capitulation, the Confederate officers and men were allowed to go on parole, the officers alone retaining their arms.

Everything was surrendered as it stood when the white flag was raised. Although several thousand shells had fallen into the forts and the battery, in addition to the shots poured into them by the fleet, Fort Jackson alone was found to be damaged to any extent. Its drawbridge had been broken down, some of the causeways and casemates were in fragments, and the citadel had been completely destroyed by fire.

While the capitulation was being signed on board the *Harriet Lane*, Captain Mitchell towed out the *Louisiana* battery, which had been left above the forts, and after shotting all her guns and setting fire to her, he abandoned her into the strong current, believing she would blow up in the midst of the mortar-boats. She did not, however, go beyond Fort St. Philip, in front of which she exploded, killing one of its garrison, and afterward sank to the bottom of the river. Mitchell and his aids were put under arrest by Porter for thus continuing hostilities while the white flag was flying on the ramparts.

After sending a small force on the western side of the river, just above Fort Jackson, and placing another force under cover of the guns of the *Mississippi* and *Kineo*, close by Fort St. Philip, Butler had reported to Farragut on board the *Hartford*, and returned to bring up the remainder of his troops by the river. He embarked with his wife and staff on the same steamship (*Mississippi*) that had brought them from Hampton Roads, and at about noon of the 1st of May all the transports lay along the New Orleans levees. (May, 1862.) Butler determined to take immediate possession of the city. At four o'clock he sent some troops to occupy Algiers and landed the Thirty-first Massachusetts and Tenth Wisconsin Regiments, as well as Everett's battery of heavy guns, all of which acted as an escort for Generals Butler and Williams and their respective staffs.

To the tune of the "Star Spangled Banner," and under the guidance of Lieutenant Weigel, they marched up to Canal Street, took possession of the Custom House, which was left in charge of the Thirty-first Massachusetts, and, after posting Everett's battery around the building, they returned to the *Mississippi*, in which they spent the night, the Twelfth Connecticut Regiment standing guard over it upon the levee.

On the following day Colonel Deming encamped in Lafayette Square, and General Butler occupied General Lovell's former headquarters at the

INGENIOUS METHOD OF DISGUISING THE HULLS AND MASTS OF COMMODORE PORTER'S MORTAR FLOTILLA, TO GAIN A POSITION IN RANGE OF FORTS ST. PHILIP AND JACKSON.

From a Sketch by Wm. Waud.

St. Charles Hotel, where he invited the city authorities to meet him for a conference. The Mayor peremptorily refused, adding that his place of business was the City Hall. General Butler then informed him that the reply was totally unsatisfactory, and the Mayor, taking counsel of prudence, called at the appointed hour, with Pierre Soulé and several friends.

While the conference was being held, a dense, hooting crowd assembled in the open space around the hotel, and threatened to make an open rupture with the troops. General Williams sent an aid to General Butler informing him that he feared he could not much longer control the mob. Butler replied calmly: "Give my compliments to General Williams, and tell him, if he finds he cannot control the mob, to open upon them with artillery." "Do not do that!" shouted the Mayor. "Why not, gentlemen?" said Butler. "The mob must be controlled: we can't have a disturbance in the street." As cannon had been planted at each corner of the hotel, and were then in charge of a force of soldiers only too eager to avenge the insults which the crowd had been heaping upon them, the result of conveying such an order as Butler's can well be conjectured. But the Mayor and his friends prevented for the time all further disturbance and possible outbreak, by going out on the balcony and addressing the crowd, which slowly dispersed.

The rage of the mob broke out anew, however, upon seeing Lieutenant Kinsman and a detachment of fifty men escorting Judge Summers to a place of safety. The instructions given the troops upon entering the city had been very stringent. They were to march in silence, not to take any offense at threats or insults, and, if fired upon, should endeavor to arrest the guilty parties, but they were on no account to fire upon the crowd unless it proved absolutely necessary for self-defense, and not even then except by orders.

Judge Summers's escort had not proceeded much beyond the St. Charles Hotel when they encountered an individual creating a disturbance, and who was ordered to desist. As he refused and became more abusive, the lieutenant directed the sergeant to lower his bayonet and to run him through if he did not cease. This had the desired effect, and no more trouble was experienced.

At the adjourned conference held the same evening at the St. Charles Hotel, Butler read the proclamation which he had addressed to the inhabitants of New Orleans, and which he had caused to be printed by some of his own soldiers at the office of the *True Delta* newspaper, upon being told that its proprietor would not allow his types to be used for the purpose.

In his proclamation, all who had taken up arms against the Government of the United States were called to lay them down; all flags and devices of the Confederate Government were to disappear, and the national flag to remain undisturbed, and in all cases to be treated with respect. He promised protection to the person and property of all well disposed citizens, and enjoined the inhabitants to continue at their peaceful avocations, in which they would be fully protected. He directed that all shops and all places of amusement should be kept open as usual, and the services in all churches and religious meeting-places be continued and maintained the same as in times of peace. He proclaimed martial law the governing force, and required all keepers of drinking-saloons and public houses to obtain a license from the provost-marshal. He assured the inhabitants that the soldiers were able to and would preserve order in the city, and that the killing of any Federal soldier would be punished as murder. Civil cases would be referred to civil tribunals, but all interference with the forces and laws of the United States would be referred to a military court. The use of Confederate bonds, money, or obligations, was prohibited. Seditious publications would be suppressed. A military censor would pass upon all newspaper articles and telegrams. Outrages committed by Federal soldiers upon the persons or property of the citizens would be severely dealt with by the provost-martial, and were to be reported to the provost-guard at once; and the citizens were assured that all the requirements of the proclamation would be vigorously and firmly administered.

The proclamation was issued on May 6th, 1862, contrary to the advice of Soulé and others who thought it would create renewed trouble. But he not only maintained his ground, but declared that he meant to avail of and would certainly use all the power at his command in such manner that in a short time he would be able to ride through the entire city free from insult and danger, or else, he added, "this metropolis of the South shall be a desert from the plains of Chalmette to the outskirts of Carrollton."

General Butler at last found it necessary to exercise a rigid administration of public affairs, and appointed Major Joseph W. Bell and Colonel Jonas H. French respectively provost judge and provost marshal. Actuated then by a desire to remove all possible causes for irritation and to conciliate the people, he moved his headquarters from the St. Charles Hotel to the late residence of General Twiggs, and gradually removed all the Federal camps from the city.

Additional troops were sent to Algiers, others garrisoned the forts, and a permanent encampment was established at Carrollton, while a force under General Williams proceeded up the river, with Farragut, and captured Baton Rouge, the capital of Louisiana, without any resistance, on May 7th.

General Butler did all he could to alleviate the long-prevailing distress, and to restore the city to its wonted prosperity, resorting to unusual and extraordinary means in order also to ward off the threatened Spring pestilence. The men and boys in the community had been brought to reason through fear of the soldiery, but there yet remained an element that battled against the quiet restoration of order, and threatened to endanger all substantial reforms—the women.

Insults offered on every possible occasion to Federal officers and soldiers had been borne patiently, and, not being openly taken notice of, had failed to create any open rupture, but when a woman deliberately spat in the face of two officers who were quietly walking along the street, Butler resolved to immediately stop the growing evil, and, on the 15th of May, startled the community by issuing the celebrated order No. 28.

It read as follows:

HEADQUARTERS, DEPARTMENT OF THE GULF,
NEW ORLEANS, May 15th, 1862.

General Order No. 28:

As the officers and soldiers of the United States have been subject to repeated insults from the women (calling themselves ladies) of New Orleans, in return for the most scrupulous non-interference and courtesy on our part, it is ordered that hereafter, when any female shall, by word, gesture, or movement, insult or show contempt for any officer or soldier of the United States, she shall be regarded and held liable to be treated as a woman of the town plying her avocation.

By command of MAJOR-GENERAL BUTLER.
GEORGE C. STRONG,
Assistant Adjutant-general, Chief of Staff.

Its effect was to at once arrest all repetitions of similar insults, and order was restored in all sections of the city after the Mayor was arrested and Soulé sent as a prisoner to Fort Warren, for too strongly opposing the measures of General Butler.

General George F. Shepley was appointed Military Governor of New Orleans, upon the consequent suppression of the city government, and at once organized an efficient police force, which secured good order throughout. William B. Mumford, who had taken down the flag from the Mint, and boldly led most of the disturbances, was arrested, tried, and executed as a traitor on the 7th of July. Several soldiers, who had been paroled at Fort Jackson, and had organized themselves as the "Monroe Guard," in order to break through the Federal lines and rejoin the Confederates, were ordered to be shot, but were finally reprieved and sent to Ship Island. Others who had entered houses and carried off property, under color of authority, were hung five days after committing the crime, whilst a number of men and women, guilty of various offenses, were sent to Ship Island, and otherwise punished, apart from the above. General Shepley's administration encountered but few disturbing elements.

On the 25th of July, General Butler issued a proclamation to the effect that all property belonging to prominent Confederate officials, military and civil, would be immediately confiscated, and that such as belonged to other Confederate sympathizers would be liable to confiscation unless they returned to their allegiance by the 22d of the following September.

PANORAMIC VIEW OF THE UNITED STATES FLEET PASSING THE FORTS ON THE MISSISSIPPI, ON ITS WAY TO NEW ORLEANS, APRIL 18TH, 1862.

SKETCHED BY WM. WAUD FROM THE FORETOP OF THE UNITED STATES WAR STEAMER "MISSISSIPPI."

FIRE-RAFT SENT DOWN THE STREAM FROM FORT JACKSON TO DESTROY THE APPROACHING FEDERAL FLEET—THE BOATS OF THE SQUADRON, WITH HELP OF THE FERRYBOAT "WESTFIELD," TOW IT OUT OF ITS COURSE.

On the 27th of October, General Butler occupied the Lafourche District, after an engagement at Labadieville, brilliantly fought by the troops under General Godfrey Weitzel, and remained in charge of the department until relieved, on the 14th of December, 1862, by General Nathaniel P. Banks, General Butler being ordered to New York.

DAVID GLASGOW FARRAGUT.

Born at Campbell's Station, East Tennessee, July 5th, 1801; entered the United States Navy as midshipman, December 10th, 1810, when only nine years of age; first served under Captain David Porter, who had procured his appointment, and was then in command of the frigate *Essex* (32), and accompanied him in the expedition around Cape Horn in 1818. The two following years he passed in several cruises, obtaining the rank of lieutenant, January 1st, 1821. In 1823 he took part in Porter's expedition against the West India pirates, wherein the latter were utterly defeated, after an engagement of fully twelve hours' duration. He spent some time at Tunis, where Mr. Charles Folsom, the United States Consul, ably seconded the young lieutenant's great aptitude and thirst for the study of languages, and of all pertaining to his profession. In 1851 he was second in command to Commodore Skinner, as assistant inspector of ordnance, and when a new navy-yard was built on Mare's Island, near San Francisco, he was placed in charge of it, though at the time standing nineteenth on the list. In 1858 he was given command of the sloop-of-war *Brooklyn*, belonging to the Home Squadron, under Flag-officer McCluney, and remained in that position until the breaking out of the Civil War. He had by that time attained the grade of captain, and was a resident of Norfolk, Va., where he was offered many inducements to join the Confederate Navy. These he refused, however, and taking his family from Norfolk to Hastings-on-Hudson, he sought active duty of the Federal Government.

When the attack on New Orleans was decided upon, Farragut was given the command of the operating fleet, which embraced part of Flag-officer McKean's Western Gulf Squadron, and all of Commander David D. Porter's mortar-boats. On the 20th of April, 1862, after holding a council of captains on board of his flagship, the *Hartford*, preparations were made for the advance, which took place early on the morning of the 24th, in three divisions, led respectively by Farragut in the *Hartford*, by Captain Bell in the *Sciota*, and by Captain Bailey on board the gunboat *Cayuga*. Farragut was posted in the fore-rigging of his vessel, with nightglass in hand, directing the movements of the fleet throughout its perilous advance, and on the same evening had thirteen vessels in safety above the forts close by the Quarantine grounds. The next afternoon he had anchored his vessels off the City of New Orleans, over which he exercised his protection until the city was placed in charge of General Butler. For his services in the capture of New Orleans he received the thanks of Congress, and was made a rear-admiral.

In 1862, Farragut ran the Vicksburg batteries, and early the following year opened communication with Flag-officer Porter on the Upper Mississippi by passing the forts of Port Hudson, afterward joining in the active operations which were directed against the latter, until its fall, on the 9th of July, 1863. After enjoying a short rest, he took part in the important reconnoissances of Fort Gaines and Fort Morgan, and in August, 1864, secured the victory of Mobile Bay. In this battle, his flagship was again the *Hartford*, and from her maintop, where he had caused himself to be lashed in such manner as not to be dislodged by the shock of battle, he again directed the successful movements of the fleet throughout the perilous passage of the forts, and the engagement with the gunboats that ensued. In December, 1864, he was made a vice-admiral, and two years later the grade of admiral was created especially for him. His very arduous duties had, however, so undermined his constitution, that he was not destined long to enjoy the honor thus conferred upon him by a universally grateful people. He was taken seriously ill, early in the Summer of 1870, at Portsmouth, N. H., and there died on the 14th of August of that year.

THEODORUS BAILEY.

Born at Plattsburg, N. Y., April 12th, 1805, and entered the navy as a midshipman, January 1st, 1818, rising to the ranks of lieutenant in 1827, commander in 1849, and captain in 1855. Entered the Mexican War, and did good service on the western coast of Mexico. At the outbreak of the Civil War he was in command of the frigate *Colorado*, attached to the Western Gulf Blockading Squadron, and led the column of the right division of Farragut's fleet in the passage of Forts Jackson and St. Philip. This division consisted of the *Cayuga* (flagship), *Pensacola*, *Mississippi*, *Varuna*, *Oneida*, *Kineo*, *Katahdin*, *Wissahickon*, *J. P. Jackson* and *Portsmouth*. It was the first to pass the forts, the *Cayuga* being far in the lead, and bearing the brunt of the attack from Mitchell's Confederate fleet. Captain Bailey displayed so much gallantry and ability in this engagement that he succeeded in warding off the repeated attempts of the rams to disable his vessels, and only retired, in accordance with Farragut's instructions, after he had compelled the surrender of three and disabled several of the Confederate gunboats. Although the *Cayuga* was struck forty-two times and otherwise suffered injury, Captain Bailey followed on his course up the Mississippi River, shortly after reaching the Quarantine grounds, where he silenced a Confederate battery on the west bank, and received the surrender of its officers and men. When Farragut advanced upon New Orleans, April 25th, 1862, Captain Bailey's *Cayuga* was again in the lead, and bravely withstood the combined fire of the Chalmette batteries, located on both sides of the river, until the fleet came up and aided in silencing them. He was afterward appointed a commodore, and was made the bearer of important dispatches and of many trophies which he carried to Washington. Here he was the recipient of a great deal of attention, and on Friday, the 14th of May, 1864, was given a reception by the Chamber of Commerce of New York City. From the latter year until 1865 he remained in command of the Eastern Gulf Blockading Squadron, and was promoted for his efficient services to the rank of rear-admiral in 1866.

GEORGE F. SHEPLEY.

Born at Saco, Me., January 1st, 1819; graduated at Dartmouth College in 1837, and at the Dane Law School, Cambridge, two years later; was admitted to the Bar of the Bangor Supreme Judicial Court in 1840; removed to Portland in 1844; and was made United States Attorney for the Maine District in 1848. He was reappointed to the same

GEORGE F. SHEPLEY.

position in the years 1853 and 1857, and until the breaking out of the Civil War gave his entire attention to the practice of his profession. In September, 1861, he tendered his services to the Federal Government, was commissioned colonel of the Twelfth Maine Volunteer Regiment, and subsequently formed part of Butler's land force operating against New Orleans. President Lincoln commissioned him a brigadier-general of Volunteers and made him Military Governor of Louisiana on the 3d of June, 1862. While acting as such he carried out many important reforms, especially in sanitary affairs of New Orleans, which secured for that city a greater degree of healthfulness, and it soon regained much of its former commercial influence. In 1864 he was placed at the head of the Military District of Virginia and North Carolina; then served with the Army of the James, entering Richmond with the Twenty-fifth Army Corps on the 3d of April, 1865. He was afterward appointed Military Governor, which position he retained until the close of the war, when he resumed the practice of law, at the same time publishing several law treatises and reports. Although he was once offered and declined the appointment of Judge of the Supreme Court of Maine, he accepted in the year 1869 that of United States Circuit Judge for the First Judicial Circuit.

MANSFIELD LOVELL.

Born in Washington, D. C., October 20th, 1822; entered the United States Military Academy at West Point in 1838, and graduated with great distinction four years later, when he was assigned to the Fourth Regiment of Regular Artillery with the rank of second lieutenant. He served as such with General Zachary Taylor's army of observation at Corpus Christi, Tex., in 1845, and also in Mexico the year following. He was wounded at the battle of Monterey, and on the 6th of October, 1846, was made adjutant-general of Brevet Major-general Quitman's division, which he accompanied to Vera Cruz. He remained with it until the capture of the City of Mexico, where he was severely wounded while leading the storming party that carried the Belen Gate. For his gallantry on the latter occasion, as well as at the battle of Chapultepec, he was made a brevet captain, September 14th, 1847, and soon after assigned to the command of a battery of light artillery.

At the termination of the Mexican War his regiment went into garrison at Fort Pickens, where he remained until 1849 when he went to Baton Rouge, La., on recruiting service. He then did garrison duty at Jefferson Barracks, Missouri, and in 1850 went on frontier duty on the Western prairies of Kansas, where he assisted in establishing Fort Atkinson, Kansas. Garrison duty at Fort Leavenworth, Kansas, Fort Hamilton, New York, and commanding the recruiting depot at Fort Columbus, New York, occupied the next four years of his life, and on December 18th, 1854, he resigned from the army, and went into the commission business in New York City, in partnership with Mr. Herman Livingston. He was Superintendent of Street Improvements from April 20th to November 12th, 1858, and Deputy Street Commissioner from the latter date to September 19th, 1861, acting also at times as the Commissioner of Public Works. From 1859 to 1861 he commanded the City Guard, now the Old Guard, of New York City. Upon the breaking out of the Civil War, he gave up his position, and went South, where he received the appointment of major-general in the Confederate Army. In October, 1861, he was placed at the head of the Department of the South, and had command of the troops at New Orleans when that city was captured by Farragut's fleet in April, 1862. He afterward fought successfully at the battle of Corinth, and became aid to General Joseph E. Johnston. So much fault had been found for his apparent neglect of duty at New Orleans, that he sought a court of inquiry; but the latter was not convened until April, 1863.

The record of the proceedings was transmitted to the Confederate War Department on the 13th of July, but was not acted upon until the following November. The opinion of the court was a vindication of the commander of New Orleans. General Lovell, however, was not restored to his command, and the effect of this course of action, he complained, was to impair his reputation. He made an appeal, which was not noticed by the Confederate administration. After the war, General Lovell, with his family, resided for some years in Savannah, Ga.; then returned to the City of New York, where he took up his residence and practiced his profession as a civil engineer, and where he died on Sunday, the 1st of June, 1884.

PREPARATIONS FOR THE DEFENSE OF NEW ORLEANS.

Commodore D. D. Porter, writing from Ship Island, May 6th, 1862, describes the Confederate rams, floating batteries and forts defending New Orleans:

Four rams and floating batteries, such as the world never before saw, have been destroyed in the late attack. The *Louisiana*, an invincible steam-battery, which was set on fire and sent down on our vessels while the flag of truce was flying and I was drawing up the articles of capitulation, and which exploded within 300 yards of us and sunk in one minute, was 4,000 tons, 270 feet long, and had 16 heavy rifled guns, all made in the South. She intended to take position that night, when she would have driven off all our fleet—for, as a proof of her invulnerability, one of our heaviest ships laid within ten feet of her and delivered her whole broadside, making no more impression on her than if she was firing peas. The *Louisiana's* shot, on the contrary, went through and through the above-mentioned sloop-of-war as if she was glass. By her sinking, this splendid battery of rifled guns was lost to us. The fragments caused by the explosion fairly covered Fort St. Philip, and killed a man of theirs in the fort.

The iron ram *Manassas* hit three vessels before her commander ran her ashore and abandoned her. She has been a troublesome customer all through.

In New Orleans our naval officers found the most splendid specimen of a floating battery the world has ever seen (a sea-going affair), and had she been finished and succeeded in getting to sea, the whole American Navy would have been destroyed. She was 6,000 tons, 270 feet long, 60 feet beam, had four engines, three propellers, four inches (and in some places nine) of iron, and would steam eleven knots an hour. She cost $2,000,000.

The best one I saw floating by me was a dry-dock turned into a floating battery, mounting 16 guns, and the entire engine which was to propel it hermetically sealed by a thick iron turret, against shot. She was sunk, but is now aground on the bar, and can be easily raised.

Besides these monsters, the naval part of the enemy's defenses of the forts consisted of six or seven ironclad gunboats almost impervious to shot, and certainly so against vessels coming bow on. We had nothing there, on our side, but twenty frail mortar-boats, five sloops-of-war, nine or ten poor gunboats (in all, a little over 140 guns), to contend against two of the most impregnable forts in this or any other country, mounting 127 guns (many of them rifled), three iron-plated batteries mounting thirty-one guns, six or seven iron-plated gunboats, and nine or ten things got up for the occasion, soon destroyed, and their power never to be known.

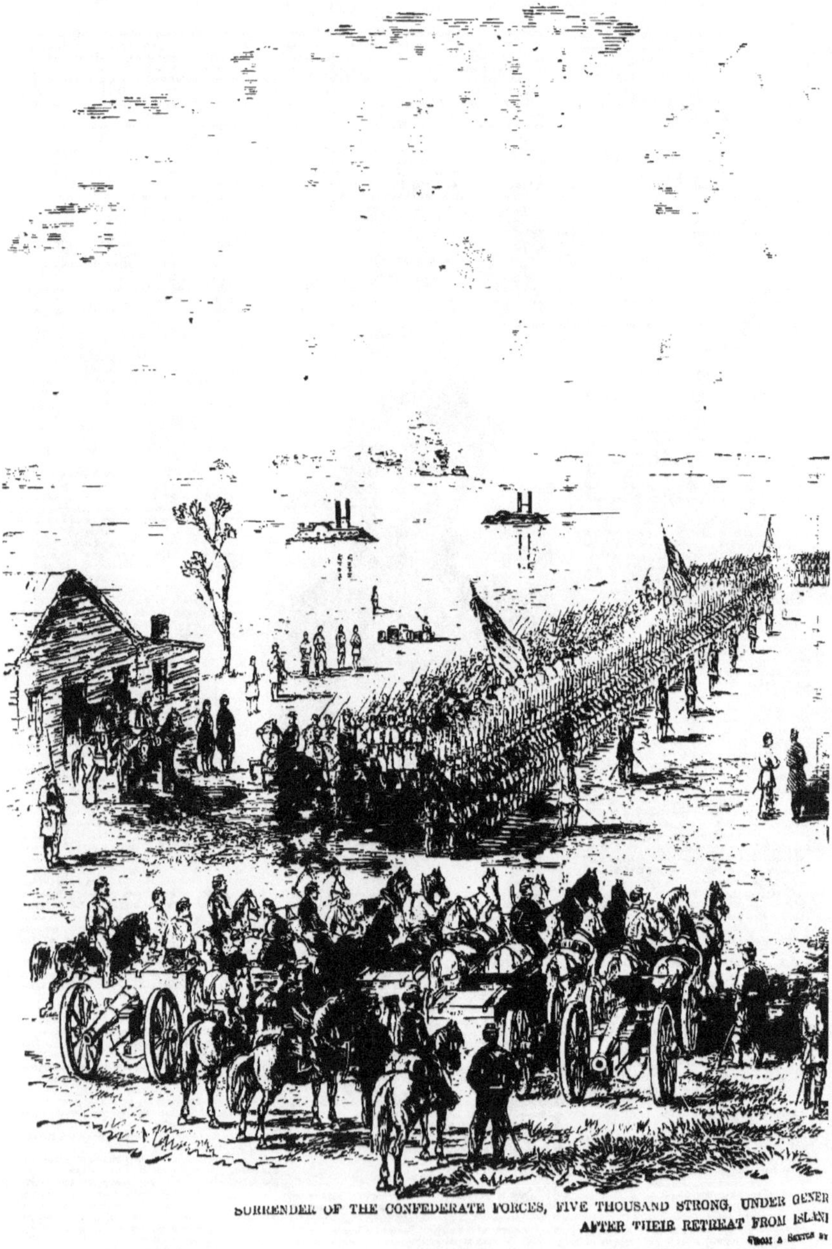

SURRENDER OF THE CONFEDERATE FORCES, FIVE THOUSAND STRONG, UNDER GENER

AFTER THEIR RETREAT FROM ISLAN

FROM A SKETCH BY

SURRENDER OF THE CONFEDERATE FORCES, FIVE THOUSAND STRONG, UNDER GEN[illegible] McCALL AND GANTT, TO GENERAL PAINE, AT TIPTONVILLE, TENN., APRIL [illegible] 1862
AFTER THEIR RETREAT FROM ISLAND NO. 10, AS DESCRIBED ON PAGE [illegible]

[illegible]

MANASSAS JUNCTION AFTER ITS EVACUATION BY THE CONFEDERATE ARMY—ABANDONED FORTIFICATIONS, CAMPS, WAGONS AND BURNED RAILROAD DEPOTS.

From a Sketch by Edwin Forbes.

CAPTURE OF YORKTOWN—BATTLE OF WILLIAMSBURG.

It having been found impracticable to carry out the combined operations of the Federal land and naval forces as President Lincoln had ordered them to take place on the 22d of February, 1862, the Army of the Potomac did not undertake any movement of importance until it learned that General Joseph E. Johnston's army had abandoned Centreville and Manassas, and was falling back upon Richmond.

General McClellan then issued orders for the immediate advance of his army toward the abandoned posts, and on the 10th of March, 1862, Centreville was occupied by Colonel Averill's cavalry. The Confederate troops had retired slowly, and were not very far distant when the Federals had completed their movement but, mainly in consequence of bad weather and roads and the shortness of supplies, no pursuit of any moment was instituted against the Confederates when they encamped either behind the Rappahannock or the Rapidan.

On the 11th of March, 1862, the President issued an order relieving McClellan of part of the responsibility heretofore devolving upon him. The order stated that "General McClellan having personally taken the field at the head of the Army of the Potomac, until otherwise ordered, he is relieved from the command of the other Military Departments, he retaining the command of the Department of the Potomac."

General Halleck was given the command of the new Department of the Mississippi, embracing all the region west of Knoxville, while the Mountain Department, including the region between the Departments of the Potomac and of the Mississippi, was created for General Fremont. All commanders of departments were henceforth to report directly to the Secretary of War.

At a council of war held on the 13th of March, at Fairfax Court House, it was decided to land at Fortress Monroe such of the forces as were not needed for holding Manassas Junction and protecting Washington, the safety of the national capital being insured by the 35,000 men left in the Shenandoah Valley. Fortress Monroe was to be the first base of operations against Richmond, upon which the advance would have to be made by way of Yorktown and of West Point, the latter place furnishing a base of operations later on.

GENERAL McCLELLAN'S HEADQUARTERS AT BIG BETHEL, VA.
From a Sketch by E. S. Hall.

On the 23d of March, the advance, which consisted of Heintzelman's corps, landed at and encamped close by Fortress Monroe, and when McClellan himself reached the latter place on the 2d of April, he found 58,000 men, and much of his artillery, already there. The following day he moved his whole army toward Yorktown, in order to prevent, if possible, Johnston's reinforcement of Magruder, expecting to receive in time the co-operation of the naval force in Hampton Roads, whom he thought would reduce the Confederate batteries both on the James and York Rivers.

The advance was made in two columns, led by General Samuel P. Heintzelman, who had with him the divisions of Generals Charles S. Hamilton and Fitz John Porter, and by General Erasmus D. Keyes, whose force comprised the divisions of General Darius N. Couch and William F. Smith. General Heintzelman's force, accompanied by General McClellan, reached Big Bethel the following day, whilst the left wing under Keyes at the same time occupied Warwick Court House. Thence the two columns proceeded slowly until the 5th of April, when they halted in front of General John B. Magruder's fortified lines, near Yorktown.

April, 1862.

Magruder had first intended making a stand close by Big Bethel, both at Ship Island and in front of Howard's and Young's Mills, but when he learned of the strong force which McClellan was gathering at Fortress Monroe, he changed his base, and established his line from Yorktown to Wynne's Mill on the Warwick River, which McClellan had now reached.

Magruder's force at Yorktown was then reported to be fully 20,000 men. To these were added, toward the middle of April, two divisions of the Army of Northern Virginia, increasing the Confederate force to about 50,000 men.

In the meantime, General Blenker's division of 10,000 men had been sent to reinforce Fremont, and McDowell's entire corps was temporarily detached, by General Wadsworth's suggestion, in order to strengthen the defense of Washington.

From the 5th of April to the 3d of May reinforcements were continually reaching McClellan's army, which, under the direction of General Fitz John Porter, was engaged in throwing up entrenchments, and otherwise preparing for a siege. In response to McClellan's urgent solicitations, General Franklin's division of nearly 12,000 men had been detached from McDowell's corps, and sent in transports on the Posquotin River.

During this period there was frequent skirmishing attending necessary reconnoissances at different points around Yorktown, but none of these developed into anything of moment, except on the 16th of April, when General Smith's division, on the extreme right, attacked the Confederates at what was called Dam No. 1, on the Warwick River.

April, 1862.

McClellan had ordered Smith to make a reconnoissance in force at Wynne's Mill, and if pressed, to open an attack. The Federal vanguard, composed of Vermont troops, waded across the stream, under cover of Ayres's battery, which silenced some of the Confederate guns, and succeeded in driving back two regiments of Georgia and North Carolina troops; but these being strongly reinforced, rallied, and, notably with the aid of General Howell Cobb, drove the Vermonters again to the opposite bank of

THE FEDERAL SOLDIERS REPAIRING THE RAILROAD BRIDGE OVER GOOSE CREEK, DESTROYED BY THE CONFEDERATES IN THEIR RETREAT.
From a Sketch by Edwin Forbes.

THE FEDERAL ARMY, UNDER GENERAL McCLELLAN, BETWEEN BIG BETHEL AND YORKTOWN, APRIL 6TH, 1862

ADVANCE OF THE FEDERAL ARMY ON THE ROAD TO YORKTOWN — HOWARD'S BRIDGE, NEAR BIG BETHEL.

FROM A SKETCH BY E. S. HALL.

the river, with a heavy loss. A second like attempt was made by the Sixth Vermont Regiment, but to no better purpose, and the Federals retired to their works after experiencing a total loss of 35 killed and 120 wounded, nearly one-half of which fell upon four companies of the Third Vermont Regiment.

By the 3d of May McClellan had completed and armed all his works, and had an effective force of 112,000 men, with which he contemplated moving ahead three days later. His works consisted of fifteen different batteries, mounting one hundred and eleven guns and mortars. While constructing them, he had but once departed from his original resolution not to open upon the Confederates until all were finished. That was when he had fired upon vessels discharging at the Yorktown wharf, and had driven them across to Gloucester Point, with both shot and shell from his 100 and 200 pounders.

Late in the afternoon of the 3d, the Confederates began shelling Heintzelman's camp, and kept up firing at intervals until after midnight. At daylight a great conflagration was visible in Yorktown, and the report having been made that the latter place was being evacuated, Heintzelman ascended in his balloon, and found that many of the Confederate guns had in reality been abandoned. The Confederates had, in fact, evacuated Yorktown and Gloucester, and fallen back about twelve miles to Williamsburg, in accordance with the decision arrived at in the council held at the Nelson House, in Yorktown, on the 30th of April.

The Federals entered Yorktown on the 4th of May, and took possession of it, as well as of the fifty-three guns remaining there uninjured, and at once organized a vigorous pursuit, which was directed by General Edwin V. Sumner.

General George Stoneman pushed ahead, in a heavy rainstorm, with cavalry and horse artillery, and was followed by the divisions of Generals Couch, Smith and Silas Casey, which took the Wynne's Mill Road, and by the divisions of Generals Joseph Hooker and Phil Kearney, which entered the Yorktown Road. The divisions of Generals Fitz John Porter, Israel B. Richardson, and John Sedgwick, remained in the immediate vicinity of Yorktown, where McClellan was to complete arrangements for operations along the York River.

Stoneman soon came upon the line of strong earthworks which the Confederates had constructed a few months before about two miles from Williamsburg, and where they had just left a strong rear guard to protect their retreat across the Chickahominy River. There he stopped to await the arrival of the infantry, as he could not well attack the works without it. At five o'clock Smith's division, accompanied by General Sumner, had joined Stoneman's, and at about midnight Hooker had brought his division on Smith's left.

The troops rested as best they could in the midst of the continuous rainstorm, and before daylight on the 5th, Hooker, who was eager for an engagement, pressed forward, and at half-past seven was ready for the attack. The First Massachusetts and the Second New Hampshire Regiments advanced

CAMP OF THE NINTH MASSACHUSETTS, IN THE WOODS ONE MILE FROM THE CONFEDERATE FORTIFICATIONS, YORKTOWN, APRIL 10TH, 1862.

FROM A SKETCH BY E. S. HALL.

ARRIVAL OF McCLELLAN TO TAKE PERSONAL COMMAND OF THE ARMY OF THE POTOMAC IN ITS ADVANCE ON YORKTOWN, VA. APRIL 5TH, 1862.—ENTHUSIASM OF THE TROOPS.

MARTIN'S MASSACHUSETTS BATTERY C OPENING FIRE ON THE CONFEDERATE FORTIFICATIONS NEAR YORKTOWN.

From a Sketch by E. S. Hall.

respectively on the left and right of the principal work called Fort Magruder, with orders to pick off Confederate artillerists and sharpshooters. They were followed by Weber's battery, as well as by part of Bramhall's and Osborn's batteries, which opened upon the fort, and by the Eleventh Massachusetts and Twenty-sixth Pennsylvania Regiments, which formed on the right of the Second New Hampshire. Fort Magruder was soon silenced, and the Confederate rear guard dispersed.

The Federals moved on, and soon came upon quite a large force of Confederates. These afterward proved to belong to Longstreet's corps, which Johnston had sent back from Williamsburg to support the rear guard. The Sixth, Seventh and Eighth New Jersey Regiments were the first engaged, and bravely maintained their ground in force of superior numbers until General Grover brought up the Seventieth and Seventy-second New York and the First Massachusetts to their assistance.

At about noon, Hooker sent for reinforcements, as the Confederates were receiving aid from fresh troops and his losses were already great. With the exception of General J. J. Peck's Brigade, which repelled the Confederate attacks on Hooker's right, no reinforcements came, however, and Hooker's division had to fight unaided until near five o'clock, when Kearney's division came up, and two more of Couch's brigades arrived on Hooker's right.

Sumner could not respond to Hooker's repeated calls for help, as he had sent General Winfield Scott Hancock to the extreme right, toward Queen's Creek, to check the Confederate advance, and take the remaining earthworks in that direction; nor could the other distant troops be moved more rapidly, owing to the extremely bad condition of the roads, which had become almost impassable between Yorktown and Williamsburg. Thus was Hooker forcibly left so long to battle alone against the combined forces of Generals Longstreet, Pryor, Pickett and Wilcox, which depleted his ranks to the frightful extent of 1,700 men, and caused the loss of five of Weber's guns.

General Kearney first sent two companies of Poe's Second Michigan, and afterward the Fifth New Jersey Regiment, for the protection of the batteries, with which Major Wainwright now renewed the fire more vigorously than ever. He also deployed Birney's and Berry's brigades respectively to the right and left of the Williamsburg Road, and sent successively Colonel Ward's Thirty-eighth New York and Colonel Riley's Fortieth New York Regiments to take the rifle-pits in the centre. These were carried by nightfall, under the direction of Captain Mindil, after an unusually severe loss, the Thirty-eighth New York alone losing one-half of its officers.

General Hancock had in the meantime taken possession of one of two unoccupied earthworks which stood upon a high bank, commanding Cub Dam Creek. From these he had opened upon two other redoubts intervening between Fort Magruder and compelled their evacuation. Seeing this and appreciating the danger now threatening the extreme Confederate left, Johnston dispatched the

SUCCESSFUL CHARGE OF COMPANY H, FIRST MASSACHUSETTS REGIMENT, ON A CONFEDERATE REDAN BEFORE YORKTOWN.

GA'LANT ATTACK OF 100 PENNSYLVANIA BUCKTAILS, LED BY COLONEL KANE, UPON A D

FROM A I

GALLANT ATTACK OF 100 PENNSYLVANIA BUCKTAILS, LED BY COLONEL KANE, UPON A DETACHMENT OF "STONEWALL" JACKSON'S ARMY, NEAR HARRISONBURG, VA., FRIDAY, JUNE 6th, 1862

BATTLE OF WILLIAMSBURG, VA., FOUGHT MAY 7TH, 1862, TO COVER THE RETREAT OF GENERAL JOHNSTON'S ARMY.—THE SIXTEENTH, THIRTY-FIRST, AND THIRTY-SECOND NEW YORK AND THE NINETY-FIFTH AND NINETY-SIXTH PENNSYLVANIA REGIMENTS ENGAGED ON THE FEDERAL SIDE.

FROM A SKETCH BY A SOLDIER ON THE FIELD.

Twenty-fourth Virginia and Colonel McRae's Fifth North Carolina Regiments, under General Jubal Early, to dislodge the Federals.

Hancock had anticipated an attack upon the important positions thus secured, and had called repeatedly for reinforcements; but in lieu of receiving any, he had been ordered to fall back to his original line, and this his comparatively small force did reluctantly. He retired slowly, disputing all the way, until he could form a line of battle close by the Dam, where he awaited the Confederate advance, now led by Colonel McRae, who had taken Early's place, as the latter was wounded; and when the enemy reached him, he ordered a bayonet-charge along the entire line, which was at once vigorously executed. The Confederates stood their ground bravely, doubtless in the expectation of reinforcements, which did not reach them, but had finally to yield the ground and retire toward Williamsburg, which they did as darkness came upon the contending forces.

The gallantry of the two Confederate regiments which thus engaged the Federal right wing was such as to afterward call forth the following remark from General Hancock: "The Fifth North Carolina and Twenty-fourth Virginia deserve to have the word 'Immortal' inscribed on their banners."

Hancock's sudden charge decided the battle, for it left the real key of the position in Federal hands. With the reinforcements which McClellan had caused to be sent him immediately upon reaching the scene late in the afternoon, Hancock took possession of all the ground he had previously occupied, and night closed upon what proved to be a dearly bought victory for the Federals. They had, in fact, gained it after sustaining a loss of 2,228 in killed and wounded, the Confederate loss being only about half that number.

Early on the 6th of May, Williamsburg was occupied by the Federals, while Johnston's army was again beyond the Chickahominy. The Federals rested until the main body had come up, and on the 8th, Stoneman was sent with Smith's division to open the road to Franklin. On the 16th the advance reached White House, and four days later McClellan established his headquarters at Cold Harbor, about nine miles from Richmond. Troops were already stationed at Bottom's Bridge, and on the 20th a strong force occupied the heights on the Richmond side of the Chickahominy River.

On the 5th of May, McClellan had ordered Franklin's division to leave its prolonged station in the Poquosin River, and proceed to West Point with the divisions of Generals Richardson, Sedgwick and Porter. Franklin reached the head of the York River the same evening, and early the following day Newton's troops landed on the right bank of the Pamunkey River, where the remainder of General Franklin's division soon joined them.

Late in the evening of the 7th, an unsuccessful attempt was made to drive off the Federals by the Confederates belonging to the rear guard of Johnston's retreating forces. The latter were met by the Sixteenth, Thirty-first and Thirty-second New York, and the Ninety-fifth and Ninety-sixth Pennsylvania Regiments, who kept up for nearly four hours a sharp musketry fire through the woods, until they received the cannon landed by the gunboats. With the aid of the batteries thus landed the Federals soon drove away the Confederates, who continued on their retreat. The Federal losses in this encounter were 49 killed and 151 wounded and missing.

The other divisions were duly landed from the transports, and the Federals thereafter held the position as an additional base of supplies for the Army of the Potomac.

EDWIN VOSE SUMNER

EDWIN VOSE SUMNER.

Born at Boston, Mass., January, 1796, and after completing his studies, entered the army, becoming second lieutenant of infantry, March 3d, 1819, and first lieutenant in July, 1823. He was made assistant commissary of subsistence in June, 1827, captain of dragoons in March, 1833, and major in 1846. During the Mexican War, he greatly distinguished himself, and displayed such marked gallantry, notably while leading the charge at Cerro Gordo, where he received severe wounds, that he was soon after brevetted a lieutenant colonel. This was followed by a brevet colonelcy, for having held the Mexicans in check while he commanded the cavalry at El Molino del Rey. From 1851 to 1853 he was Governor of New Mexico, and in 1857 undertook a successful expedition against the Cheyenne Indians. Upon the breaking out of the Civil War, he was appointed a brigadier-general in place of General David E. Twiggs, and succeeded Albert Sidney Johnston in command of the Department of the Pacific. He commanded the First Corps of McClellan's army throughout the Virginia Peninsular Campaign, in April-May, 1862, where he was twice wounded, and in July of the same year was commissioned a major-general of Volunteers, and placed at the head of the Second Corps. He afterward took part at the battle of Fredericksburg, in December, 1862, and was relieved from service the following month at his own request. In March, 1863, he was placed at the head of the Department of the Missouri, but on the way to his post he was taken ill, and died at Syracuse, N.Y., March 21st, 1863.

JOHN JAMES PECK.

Born at Manlius, N. Y., January 4th, 1821; entered the United States Military Academy at West Point in 1839, was commissioned a brevet-second lieutenant of Artillery in July, 1843; served in the Mexican War, and especially distinguished himself at the battles of Palo Alto, Resaca de la Palma, Contreras, Churubusco, and El Molino del Rey, receiving in return the grades of first lieutenant, of brevet-captain, and of brevet-major. He resigned his army commission on the 31st of March, 1853, to take the position of cashier in a bank of Syracuse, N. Y.; but at the breaking out of the Civil War he tendered his services to the Government, and re-entered the army at the head of a regiment of volunteers. On the 9th of August, 1861, he was made a brigadier-general, and at the time of the Virginia Peninsular Campaign, in April–May, 1862, was given the command of a brigade in the Fourth Corps under General Darius N. Couch. He was appointed a major general in July, 1862, and afterward commanded at Suffolk, Va., where Longstreet conducted a siege against him; also in North Carolina, and on the borders of Canada.

JOHN JAMES PECK

THE OCCUPATION OF NORFOLK.

When President Lincoln and Secretaries Chase and Stanton visited Fortress Monroe after the surrender of Yorktown, General Wool repeated his request to be allowed to break up the Confederate blockade of the James River. He was given the desired leave more readily when it was learned that the Confederate General Benjamin Huger was preparing to leave Norfolk.

May, 1862.

On the 8th of May, arrangements were made for a joint land and naval expedition. Commodore Goldsborough transferred to Captain James L. Lardner the command of a squadron composed of the *Monitor*, *Naugatuck*, *Susquehanna*, *Seminole*, *San Jacinto*, *Stevens* and *Dakota*, and General Wool embarked upon transports a land force consisting of the First Delaware, the Tenth, Twentieth and Ninety-ninth New York, and the Fifty-eighth Pennsylvania Regiments, as well as some mounted riflemen, and two batteries of artillery.

The Sewall's Point and Craney Island batteries were at once engaged by the squadron, the *Monitor* and the *Stevens* being stationed in the immediate front. The Confederates did not respond for some time, and when they finally returned fire, showed that but seventeen guns remained in the main battery at Sewall's Point. At half-past two o'clock the Confederate ram *Merrimack* (*Virginia*) came out from Norfolk, apparently to engage the squadron; but when the *Monitor* advanced toward her, she steamed back, and kept out of reach.

The shelling of the batteries continued during the afternoon, and caused the complete destruction of the Confederate barracks, and of many of the earthworks. Shortly after five o'clock the squadron was ordered back, and the troops were disembarked. A reconnoissance was made the following day by General Wool, in company with Secretary Chase and some leading topographical engineers, when it was decided to land about 5,000 men at

VIEW OF FREDERICKSBURG, VA., FROM THE NORTH BANK OF THE RAPPAHANNOCK RIVER, AFTER ITS EVACUATION BY THE CONFEDERATE TROOPS
FROM A SKETCH BY EDWIN FORBES

GENERAL KEYES'S DIVISION CROSSING THE CHICKAHOMINY RIVER, MAY 23d, 1862, OVER BOTTOM BRIDGE, BUILT BY THE ENGINEERS OF THE FEDERAL ARMY
FROM A SKETCH BY [illegible] S. HALL

Ocean View, on Willoughby's Beach. That same afternoon the troops were re-embarked, the batteries once more engaged, in order to direct attention from the real object of the movement, and early on the morning of the 10th the Federals landed at Ocean View without opposition.

Generals Wool, Viele and Mansfield then took command. A force was immediately sent to take possession of and guard the bridge over Tanner's Creek, in the rear of the Sewall's Point battery; but they found it already on fire, and were attacked with artillery from the opposite bank.

The Confederates had disappeared, however, by the time the Federal guns had been hurried forward, and no opposition was met with when the troops afterward resumed their march.

During the afternoon, the Federals came upon an abandoned camp of the Confederates, which still held twenty-nine guns, and by five o'clock General Wool and his troops were in the immediate vicinity of Norfolk. They were preparing for a vigorous attack of the place, when they were approached by Mayor Lamb of Norfolk and a deputation of its citizens, bearing a flag of truce and an offer to surrender the city. The latter was turned over to General Wool, who at once appointed General Viele its military governor.

General Huger had been ordered not to make any resistance to armed Federal occupation, and he had, therefore, left the city in charge of its Mayor, and retreated to Richmond upon hearing that the Federal forces had occupied Ocean View.

Early on the morning of the 11th, a large fire was seen, and a heavy explosion heard in the direction of the city. It proved afterward to be the burning of the Navy Yard with all its contents, and the blowing up of the *Merrimack* under the direction of Commodore Tatnall.

Norfolk and Portsmouth were taken possession of, and the batteries at Sewall's Point and Craney Island blown up, by Commodore Goldsborough, while the commanding general and Secretary Chase returned to Fortress Monroe. There General Wool soon received, for himself and the soldiers under his command, the thanks of the President.

May, 1862.

OPERATIONS IN THE SHENANDOAH VALLEY.

General James Shields, who had succeeded General F. W. Lander, upon the death of the latter, had followed the Confederates under General Jackson as far as Mount Jackson, but finding them in greater force than he expected, he had fallen back to a point about two and a half miles south of Winchester, closely pursued by Turner Ashby's cavalry. Shields was in hopes that Jackson would attack him, and thus delay the possible junction with Johnston before Richmond.

On the 22d of March, Ashby's cavalry made a dash into Winchester, and drove in the Federal pickets; but after a short though lively skirmish the Confederates were driven back.

March, 1862.

While directing the Federals, General Shields had his arm shattered, and he was also wounded in the side by the fragments of a shell; but, notwithstanding his injuries, he made preparations to meet the renewed encounter, which he thought would be likely to take place the following day.

BLOWING UP OF THE CONFEDERATE FORTS ON CRANEY ISLAND BY COMMODORE GOLDSBOROUGH.
From a Sketch by a Naval Officer.

He sent the same night to Kernstown, about half a mile distant, the brigade commanded by Colonel Kimball of the Fourteenth Indiana Regiment, which was well supported by Daum's battery, and had Colonel Sullivan's brigade as a reserve. A reconnoissance made the next morning showed only Ashby's cavalry in the immediate front, although the Confederates were at that time strongly posted and ready for battle in the woods, half a mile south of Kernstown. Not anticipating an engagement, General Banks went to Washington, in response to a summons he had previously received.

At about twelve o'clock Jackson opened upon Kimball's force with artillery. The fire was immediately returned by Daum's battery, while the reserve was ordered up, and the engagement soon became general. Jackson once made the attempt to turn Kimball's left, but the Confederates were repulsed by the combined efforts of Colonel Carroll's Eighth Ohio Regiment, several companies of the Sixty-seventh Ohio Regiment, and Jenks's battery, which were judiciously thrown forward on both sides of the Valley Turnpike.

Jackson's attempt on the Federal left having proved unsuccessful, he centred his attention upon its right flank, toward which additional batteries were directed, while at the same time a renewed attack was made on the left. The movement was so well directed and so admirably executed, that Daum's artillery gave way, and the rapid Confederate advance at one moment bid fair to endanger the Federal forces.

General Shields, then in bed, was, however, apprised in time of the progress of the battle. He issued an order for Colonel E. B. Tyler's brigade to immediately proceed, and by throwing all of its force upon the Confederate batteries, to endeavor to capture them, and then make an effort to turn Jackson's left.

At three o'clock the First Virginia, Seventh Indiana, Seventh and Twenty-ninth Ohio and One Hundred and Tenth Pennsylvania Regiments commenced the charge, and, after a desperate and prolonged resistance, captured the guns. Then followed an attack upon the Confederates, in which Tyler's brigade was signally aided by the Thirteenth and Fourteenth Indiana, Eighty-fourth Pennsylvania, and Fifth and Sixty-second Regiments, as well as by detachments from the Eighth and Sixty-seventh Ohio Regiments. The Confederates made a bold stand, but they were at last forced back through the woods, and compelled to leave behind their dead and wounded.

Their loss was 60 killed and 343 wounded, whilst that of the Federals was 441 wounded and 103 killed, the latter including Colonel Murray of the Eighty-fourth Pennsylvania. The Federals captured in all about 300 prisoners, besides two pieces of artillery, several caissons and a quantity of small arms. This engagement should properly be called the battle of Kernstown, although it is termed by many the battle of Winchester.

General Banks had been apprised of the progress of the battle by telegraph, and returned the next morning to Winchester, where he took command in person, and a pursuit was made to Woodstock, a distance of about thirty miles, without, however, bringing about any engagement.

Stonewall Jackson's army fell back to Harrisonburg, where it remained until the 19th of April, when it crossed the south fork of the Shenandoah River. There it received, at the end of the month, General Richard S. Ewell's division, and two of General Edward S. Johnson's brigades. General Banks had followed Jackson, and taken position at Harrisonburg; but as soon as General Shields's division was taken from him and given to McDowell, he was ordered to fall

April, 1862.

OLD FORT NORFOLK, BUILT BY THE UNITED STATES GOVERNMENT, ALTERED AND STRENGTHENED BY THE CONFEDERATES.

NAVAL HOSPITAL AND BATTERY AT PORTSMOUTH, VA.

BURNING OF THE NORFOLK NAVY YARD BY THE CONFEDERATES.—UNSUCCESSFUL ATTEMPT TO DESTROY THE DRY-DOCK.

REMOVING SUNKEN SCHOONERS WHICH BLOCKADED THE ENTRANCE TO THE HARBOR

back to Strasburg. A few days later McDowell was ordered to join McClellan before Richmond, by way of the Richmond and Fredericksburg Railroad, and yet hold himself always in such a position as to cover Washington and against a sudden dash of any large body of the Confederate forces. General James Wadsworth was appointed Military Governor of the District of Columbia, and placed at the head of the troops assigned to the defense of the capital.

Jackson had been ordered to watch Banks closely, and to hold him while General Lee would endeavor to cut off the Federal communication between Winchester and Alexandria. As soon, however, as he learned that part of Fremont's forces, under General Milroy, were approaching from Romney, he left Ewell to hold Banks, and moved rapidly toward Staunton, whence he sent E. S. Johnson, with five brigades, to attack Milroy. The latter, finding his forces greatly outnumbered, retired to a place in the Bull Pasture Mountains called McDowell, where he was joined by one of Schenck's brigades at about the time Jackson had concluded to go to Johnson's assistance.

On the 8th of May Jackson appeared with a large force on a ridge overlooking the Federal encampment, and Milroy sent the Third Virginia and the Twenty-fifth, Thirty-second, Seventy-fifth and Eighty-second Ohio, with a 6-pounder of the Twelfth Ohio Battery, in charge of Lieutenant Bowen, to dislodge him. The engagement that followed, and which is called the battle of McDowell, or the battle of Bull Pasture, was fought with great gallantry on both sides. It lasted fully five hours, and did not actually terminate until darkness had set in. The losses were reported at 256 in killed and wounded on the Federal side, the Confederates having lost a still greater number, including General Edward S. Johnson, who was counted among the wounded.

Milroy's position proving untenable, it was decided to abandon it, and during the following night the Federals retired to Franklin. Jackson pursued them to the latter place, but when he learned that Banks was preparing to fall back from Harrisonburg, he returned to McDowell, and crossed the mountains after him. By the time Jackson was ready to leave Lebanon Sulphur Springs, however, Banks was well on his way toward Strasburg. Jackson pushed on to New Market, where he joined Ewell, who had already started in pursuit, and the united forces proceeded thence at once into the Luray Valley, in order to try and cut off, at Front Royal, Banks's possible retreat in that direction. The Confederate forces which were thus consolidated represented about 20,000 men, and embraced Ewell's brigades, led by Generals Elzey, Taylor and Trimble, as well as General E. S. Johnson's; the brigades of Generals Campbell, Folkeston and Winder, and Ashby's cavalry; Colonel Flournoy's Second and Sixth Virginia cavalry, supported by the Brockenborough and First Maryland Batteries.

This advance was so well managed, that the Confederates fell upon Colonel Kenly's small garrison of about 1,400 men stationed at Front Royal, almost before Banks had any intimations of their approach. At about noon of the 23d, Ashby's cavalry attacked Kenly's little force, consisting altogether, at Front Royal proper and on the Road, of companies taken from the Fifth New York, Second Massachusetts, Third Wisconsin, and the Twenty-seventh Indiana and Pennsylvania Regiments, as well as part of Captain Mapes's Pioneers, supported by a section of Knapp's battery. Although the Federals made a very brave resistance, they were before long driven across the river. Kenly tried to burn the bridge, but the flames were soon extinguished by the Confederates, who pursued relentlessly until they had severely wounded Kenly and captured him, as well as about 700 of his men, his guns, and all of his supply-train.

May, 23d.

JAMES SHIELDS.

The news of Kenly's defeat reached Banks at Strasburg, and to avoid the possibility of capture after Jackson would cut off his supplies and reinforcements by taking possession of Winchester, Banks decided to avail of his only means of escape down the Valley. It was likely to prove an even race, for Winchester, the objective point and the real key to the Valley, was about equidistant from Front Royal and from Strasburg.

Banks set out from the latter place on the morning of the 24th, with his train in the immediate front, protected by detachments of infantry and cavalry under Colonel Dudley Donnelly, whilst General John P. Hatch commanded the rear guard, and to Colonel George H. Gordon was given the centre. The rear had proceeded but a short distance beyond Cedar Creek, when reports reached them that the train had been attacked at Middletown. This was soon followed by the train itself, which had been ordered to the rear. The troops were then moved rapidly to the front, where a small Confederate force was encountered and beaten back to the Front Royal Road by Cochran's battery, the Twenty-eighth New York, and the Forty-sixth Pennsylvania Regiments, under Lieutenant-colonels Brown and Knipe.

A reconnoissance made by Broadhead's cavalry showed the road clear to Winchester; but before Banks's main body had gone much beyond Middletown, it was reported that a large portion of Jackson's forces had already reached Winchester. Banks hurried on, and just as he had reached Newtown, was attacked by the advance guard of the Confederates; but the latter were compelled to retire after a spirited engagement, in which the Second Massachusetts, Twenty-seventh Indiana, and Twenty-eighth New York, took a leading part.

By midnight Banks was in Winchester, where he soon posted his infantry and artillery, and prepared actively to meet the Confederate attack, which he justly thought must needs soon follow.

Before daybreak of the 25th, Jackson moved simultaneously against the Federal left, commanded by Colonel Donnelly, and against the right wing, which had been placed in charge of Colonel Gordon and was well posted upon a ridge toward the southern position of the city.

May, 1862.

The Federals repulsed the Confederates, who suffered a heavy loss on the left; but they were not so successful on the right. An attempt to turn the Federal flank from the Perryville Road, and a well-directed movement against the centre, where General Hatch had the cavalry, compelled the Federals to yield in turn. Reinforcements had been continually reaching Jackson, and after a desperate engagement of nearly five hours' duration, the Federals had fully given way along the entire line.

Banks first sent his trains toward the Potomac, and retreated through the City of Winchester under a heavy fire, and with the Second Massachusetts and the Third Wisconsin Regiments acting as a rear guard. When the army had got beyond the city, Banks ordered it to be divided into three parallel columns, each of which was given as powerful a rear guard as could be spared; and after an almost continuous skirmishing with the pursuing Confederates, Banks's army reached Martinsburg, a distance of about twenty-three miles, the same afternoon.

The Federals rested at Martinsburg two and a half hours, and then marched on toward Williamsport, twelve miles farther, reaching the Potomac, opposite the city, at six o'clock in the evening. They had thus covered fifty-three miles in forty-eight hours.

PURSUIT OF GENERAL BANKS'S TROOPS THROUGH THE CITY OF WINCHESTER, VA.

The cavalry waded across the river, but the infantry and artillery could not be successfully moved across until the laying of a ponton-train, which had fortunately been brought along from Strasburg.

By noon of the 26th, all of Banks's army was safely landed on the Maryland side in time to avoid a renewed conflict with the Confederates, who, after pursuing the Federals as far as Martinsburg, had just reached the opposite banks of the river.

HARRY B. HIDDEN.

RECONNOISSANCE OF THE CONFEDERATE POSITION AT STR

FROM A S

BATTLE OF WINCHESTER, VA., MARCH 23D, 1862—DECISIVE BAYO

FROM A SKET

[illegible]

RECONNOISSANCE OF THE CONFEDERATE POSITION [illegible] AND ITS OCCUPATION BY GENERAL [illegible]

[illegible]

BATTLE OF WINCHESTER, VA., MARCH [illegible] —DECISIVE [illegible] OF THE FEDERAL [illegible] LED BY GENERAL E. B. TYLER

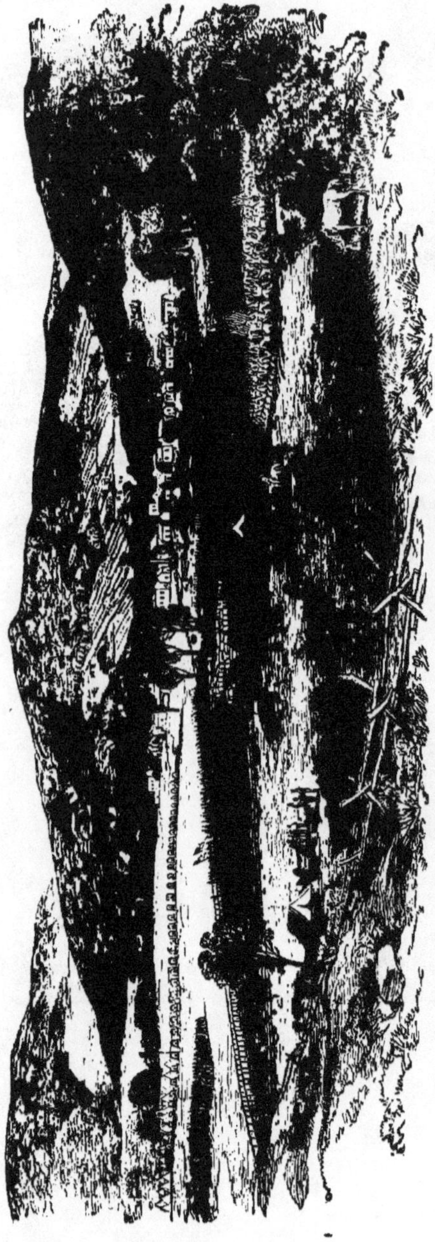

FRONT ROYAL, MANASSAS GAP RAILROAD—BLUE RIDGE MOUNTAINS IN THE DISTANCE—THE FEDERAL ARMY ENTERING THE TOWN.

From a Sketch by Edwin Forbes.

GENERAL FREMONT'S DIVISION CROSSING THE PONTON BRIDGE OVER THE SHENANDOAH RIVER, IN PURSUIT OF "STONEWALL" JACKSON.

From a Sketch by Edwin Forbes.

The loss of the Federals was about 900 men. All the Federal guns, and all but fifty-five of nearly five hundred wagons were saved.

Jackson's advance had caused almost a panic in Washington, and under the belief that the capital was soon to be attacked, orders had been issued to the Governors of the different States to hurry forward all the volunteers and militia they could spare, while the transportation lines were directed to hold themselves in readiness to convey infantry, artillery and cavalry, as well as ammunition and all kinds of army supplies, to the exclusion, if need be, of all other business.

The President countermanded the orders previously given McDowell to move with Shields's division upon Richmond, and ordered him to immediately put 20,000 men into the Shenandoah Valley. This was for the purpose of relieving Banks, and in order that he might there co-operate with the latter, as well as with Fremont, who had been ordered to move in the rear of Jackson's army, by way of Franklin and Harrisonburg.

Perceiving the danger to which he was exposed, Jackson caused Ewell, on the 29th, to make a feigned attack upon Harper's Ferry, then held by General Rufus Saxton, in order to mask his intended retreat, and the following day his entire army was on its march from Winchester to Strasburg, reaching the latter place on the 1st of June, and at once proceeding thence in the direction of Harrisonburg. Jackson destroyed not only all the bridges as he advanced, but he sent, besides, cavalry in different directions to destroy such as were likely to be used by McDowell's army.

June, 1862.

Fremont crossed the mountains with as little delay as was practicable, and, through heavy roads, reached Strasburg just after Jackson had passed through it. There he was joined the following morning by General George D. Bayard, who brought with him the vanguard of Shields's cavalry, and, without waiting either for reinforcements or to afford the fatigued troops their much needed rest, they immediately started in pursuit of Jackson. They shortly after overtook his rear, with which they had a slight skirmish, and followed close upon the retreating force until their advance was checked, on the 3d, by the burning of the

THOROUGHFARE GAP, A PASS IN THE MOUNTAINS ON THE MANASSAS GAP RAILROAD, NEAR STRASBURG, VA.

From a Sketch by Edwin Forbes.

-ENERAL BANKS'S DIVISION RECROSSING THE POTOMAC FROM WILLIAMSPORT, MD., TO ATTACK "STONEWALL" JACKSON.—BAND OF THE FORTY-SIXTH PENNSYLVANIA PLAYING NATIONAL AIRS ON THE VIRGINIA SHORE.

GENERAL FREMONT'S HEADQUARTERS AT MOUNT JACKSON, VA.

Mount Jackson bridge.

Drenching rains had for several days swollen the streams to such an extent that they could not well be forded, and no further progress was feasible until the bridge was replaced. It took a whole day to rebuild it, and by the time the Federals could proceed, Jackson was well on his way to Harrisonburg, which he reached on the 5th. Leaving at the latter place a rear-guard composed of infantry and of the Second and Sixth Virginia Cavalry, he moved toward Port Republic, on the

MARCH OF FREMONT'S ARMY THROUGH THE WOODS, IN PURSUIT OF THE CONFEDERATES.
From a Sketch by Edwin Forbes

north fork of the Shenandoah.

In the meantime, Fremont was making another forced march, and Shields was also moving rapidly in an almost parallel line on the east side of the river.

On the 6th, a reconnoitring party of the First New Jersey Cavalry, led by Colonel Percy Wyndham, engaged Jackson's rear-guard, close by Harrisonburg. Colonel Wyndham was adroitly led into the woods by the apparently retreating Confederates, and soon found he had fallen into an ambuscade. His little

COLONEL PILSON'S BATTERY SHELLING THE REAR-GUARD OF THE CONFEDERATE ARMY AT THE CROSSING OF THE SHENANDOAH RIVER, JUNE 3D, 1862.
From a sketch by Edwin Forbes.

THE BATTLE OF CROSS KEYS, SHENANDOAH VALLEY, SUNDAY, JUNE 8TH, 1862—OPENING OF THE FIGHT.

FROM A SKETCH BY EDWIN FORBES.

The Union Troops, under General Fremont, Advancing to Attack the Confederate Army, Commanded by General Jackson, Posted in the Wood, with its Front Extending for Two Miles. General R. H. Milroy Leading the Centre, General Robert C. Schenck the Right and Generals Louis Blenker and Julius H. Stahl the Left, Wing of the Advancing Army, Consisting of the Eighth New York Volunteers (First German Rifles), Colonel Wutschell; Twenty-ninth New York Volunteers (German), Colonel Soest; Forty-first New York Volunteers (De Kalb), Colonel Gilsa; Forty-fifth New York Volunteers (Fifth German Rifles), Colonel Von Amsberg; Twenty-fifth Ohio Volunteers, Colonel Jones; Eighty-second Ohio Volunteers, Colonel Cantwell; Eighth Virginia, Sixtieth Ohio, and Thirty-ninth New York Volunteers under Colonels Cluseret and D'Utassy.

band fought desperately to get out, but to no purpose, and he was finally made a prisoner, with over sixty of his men. As the latter were being driven ahead, they were met by General Bayard and Colonel Gustave Paul Cluseret, who had followed close upon Wyndham with cavalry and infantry.

The Confederates were fiercely engaged; and, although reinforced by General Stewart's brigade, were, after a sharp fight of several hours, compelled to fall back into a neighboring pine forest, with the loss of a portion of their camp equipage.

Toward evening, General Bayard ordered Colonel Kane, of the Pennsylvania Bucktail Rifles, numbering about 125 men, to explore the forest, and, if possible, dislodge the enemy. They entered a dense pine thicket on the left, but had not proceeded far when they found themselves almost completely surrounded by Confederates, which afterward proved to be detachments from four regiments of cavalry, with a strong support of artillery. The Bucktails flinched only temporarily in face of the almost overwhelming force suddenly opposed to them. Fire was opened upon the Confederates, who promptly returned it, wounding Colonel Kane, and rapidly thinning out the group of Federals opposing them. Such as remained of the Bucktails succeeded, however, in fighting their way out in the darkness, after a loss of 6 killed and 40 wounded and missing, the latter including Colonel Kane, who had been made a prisoner. General Ashby lost his life in this engagement, while gallantly directing the movements of his fine body of cavalry.

Before Jackson's forces could cross the north fork of the Shenandoah, Fremont was close upon them again, and on Sunday, the 7th of June, he attacked the brigades under Generals Stewart, Elzey and Trimble, which formed the rear of Jackson's army, and which were admirably posted upon a ridge commanding the road close by the Cross-Keys Church.

June, 1862.

These were opposed by the Federals under Generals Stahl, Schenck and Milroy, who moved steadily up the slope, under a heavy fire of shot and shell, and gradually pressed back the Confederates until late in the afternoon, when, in view of their heavy loss of nearly 700 in killed and wounded, the Federals were ordered to retire to their original position.

Jackson had, in the meantime, occupied Port Republic, just as Shields's advance guard, led by General Carroll, reached its outskirts. There had been some skirmishing between the two forces, but nothing of moment occurred until the morning of the 9th, when Ewell, having been ordered to Jackson's assistance, attacked the Federal right, then commanded by General E. B. Tyler. The onslaught was borne bravely by the little Federal force of only 3,000 men opposed to more than twice that number, and the Confederates were finally driven into the woods.

Reinforcements were sent to the Confederates, who then made a combined front and flank movement, and with well-served artillery depleted the Federal ranks to such an extent that Tyler was obliged to retreat, with the loss of all but one of his guns, which were abandoned in consequence of the horses being killed.

General Carroll's cavalry protected

ARMY OF GENERAL FREMONT ON ITS MARCH UP THE SHENANDOAH VALLEY — WOUNDED AND RAGGED SOLDIERS.

From a Sketch by Edwin Forbes.

BATTLE ON THE ROAD FROM HARRISONBURG TO PORT REPUBLIC BETWEEN THE FORCES OF GENE

FROM A

BATTLE OF CROSS KEYS, SUNDAY, JUNE 8TH, 1862.—CE

FROM A S

BATTLE ON THE ROAD [illegible] TO PORT REPUBLIC, BETWEEN THE FORCES OF GENERAL [illegible] AND THE CONFEDERATES UNDER GENERALS JACKSON AND EWELL, MAY [illegible] TO JUNE [illegible]

[illegible]

BATTLE OF CROSS KEYS, SUNDAY, JUNE [illegible] FRONT OF THE FEDERAL ARMY IN THE ENGAGEMENT.

[illegible]

WHITE HOUSE LANDING, PAMUNKEY RIVER, VA.—GRAND DEPOT OF THE FEDERAL COMMISSARIAT AND ORDNANCE DEPARTMENTS BEFORE RICHMOND.

FROM A SKETCH BY E. S. HALL.

the retreat during the pursuit which was afterward instituted against it for a distance of nearly five miles. As soon as Tyler had crossed the river the bridge was set afire, and shortly after Fremont's force came upon the scene, whither it had been drawn by the sound of battle.

The Federals lost at the battle of Port Republic 322 in killed, wounded and missing. Their army reached Harrisonburg on the evening of the 9th, Fremont thence going to Mount Harrison and Shields to New Market.

Jackson encamped at Weyer's Cave, where he remained until the 17th, when he was called to assist Lee in the defense of Richmond, whilst a week later the forces under Banks, Fremont and McDowell were consolidated into a body designated the Army of Virginia, and given in command of General John Pope.

JAMES SHIELDS.

Born at Altmore, near Dungannon, in the County of Tyrone, Ireland, December 12th, 1810, and emigrated to the United States about 1826; studied law, and was admitted to practice at Kaskaskia, Ill., at the early age of twenty-two. He afterward gave his attention to politics, and was elected to the State Legislature in 1836, and made State Auditor three years later. In 1843 he became Judge of the Supreme Court, and in 1845 was appointed Commissioner of the United States Land Office. He served in the Mexican War, and was severely wounded both at the battles of Cerro Gordo and Chapultepec, in which he so gallantly conducted himself, that he was given the commissions of brigadier-general and of brevet major-general. He served under General Taylor on the Rio Grande, and under General Wool at Chihuahua. He afterward resigned from the army, and was appointed, by the President, Governor of Oregon Territory in 1848, and settled in California after serving as United States Senator from Illinois, 1849-55, and from Minnesota 1858-60. He again tendered his services upon the breaking out of the Civil War, was made a brigadier-general of volunteers on August 19th, 1861, took a leading part in the battles of Winchester and of Port Republic and resigned from the service in 1863. He then settled in Wisconsin, but soon removed to Carrollton, Mo., where he practiced law and served as a railroad commissioner. In 1874 he was elected to the Missouri Legislature which elected him in 1879 to serve out the unexpired time of the deceased U. S. Senator Bogy. He died at Ottumwa, Iowa, June 1st, 1879.

HARRY B. HIDDEN.

Born in New York City in 1839. He had just returned from a trip to Europe and entered business, when the war broke out, and he volunteered his services, becoming a lieutenant in the First New York (Lincoln) Cavalry, commanded by Colonel Andrew T. McReynolds. On Saturday, the 8th of March, 1862, Companies A and H of the Lincoln Cavalry had been ordered to proceed to Burk's Station, and

JOHN R. KENLY.

guard a portion of the railroad and a bridge then being repaired. They were stationed there at the time General Kearney and his brigade advanced, the following morning. As several Confederate scouts had been seen in the neighborhood, Kearney ordered Lieutenant Hidden to proceed with a detachment of fourteen men of the Lincoln Cavalry to a certain point of the road through which he intended advancing, and to feel and report the enemy's position. They soon came upon one of the Confederate supports, consisting of about 150 infantry, who formed quickly, and commenced firing into them. The temptation for a charge on the part of the cavalry now became irresistible. Quickly Lieutenant Hidden told off his men, and placing himself at their head dashed upon the Confederates at full speed, cheering and shouting to the men to be advanced. Many of the Confederates fled but others fought desperately, and Lieutenant Hidden was one of the first to fall from his horse, having received a ball in the left shoulder, which passed through his neck, killing him instantly.

The command then devolved upon Corporal Eugene Lewis, who continued the fight, both on horseback and afoot, until the enemy had been dispersed, when the detachment returned with eleven prisoners. General Kearney, who had witnessed the charge from an eminence, warmly complimented Lewis and his men, and took down their names for public commendation. Lieutenant Hidden's remains were taken to New York City, and buried from the Fourteenth Street Presbyterian Church, escorted by several companies of the New York Twenty-second Regiment and one company of the New York Seventy-first Regiment, with a troop of horse as a guard of honor, and Captain Adams, Lieutenant Leavitt and a few of the Lincoln Cavalry as mourners.

JOHN R. KENLY.

Born at Baltimore, Md., 1820; after completing his education he devoted his time to the study of law, and achieved great prominence at the Baltimore Bar. He served throughout the Mexican War as major of a Maryland regiment, and distinguished himself in several of the most prominent engagements of that eventful campaign. At its termination he resumed the practice of law in his native State, until the breaking out of the Civil War led him once more to tender his services to the United States Government. He entered the army, receiving the commission of colonel of the First Regiment of Maryland Volunteer Infantry, and gave so much attention to the organization of his command, that it soon obtained a name for proficiency second to none other in the department. He was appointed by General Banks provost-marshal of the City of Baltimore, June 27th, 1861, in place of Colonel George P. Kane, who was confined in Fort McHenry on a charge of treason.

August 22d, 1862, Colonel Kenly was appointed brigadier-general, by President Lincoln, for gallant conduct at the battle of Front Royal, and also appointed major-general of volunteers, March 13th, 1865, for gallant and meritorious services during the war. After the war he resumed the practice of his profession in his native city, where he is now (1884) residing.

BATTLE OF JAMES ISLAND, S. C.

THE Federal army stationed at Port Royal, S. C., being unoccupied by any demonstration of the Confederate troops, General H. W. Benham, in command of the Federal land forces, determined, early in June, 1862, to dash across James Island, and there surprise Colonel J. G. Lamar, who commanded about 8,000 Confederate soldiers stationed at Fort Johnson so as to check any Federal advances on the City of Charleston. General Hunter,

COMMISSARY DEPARTMENT, WITH THREE DAYS' RATIONS AND KITCHEN, ON THE MARCH.

FROM A SKETCH BY EDWIN FORBES.

REPULSE OF THE CONFEDERATE TROOPS ON JAMES ISLAND, S. C., IN T

FROM A SK

in command of the Department of the South, was consulted, and fully agreed to the plan. The troops were transported from Port Royal, up the Stono River, under protection of the Federal gunboats, and were formed in two camps, on the shores of James Island, about two miles apart, and respectively commanded by Generals Stevens and Wright. The Confederate force under Colonel Lamar held possession of a powerful earthwork about two miles from the Federal camps. The first collision took place June 4th, when the Federals were surprised and twenty men captured. Later on the same day, the Federal troops captured a battery of four guns, drivi the Confederates from their position.

On the 10th, a reconnoissance in force was mad the Federals, in order to advance their picket lines a capture an earthwork at Secessionville, which was prov troublesome, as shells were easily thrown into their ca

BATTLE OF SECESSIONVILLE, JAMES ISLAND, S. C.—BAYONET-CHARGE OF THE FEDERAL

REPULSE OF THE CONFEDERATE TROOPS ON JAMES ISLAND, S. C., IN THEIR [illegible] TO CAPTURE THE PICKETS OF GENERAL WRIGHT'S DIVISION

[illegible]

BATTLE OF [illegible]VILLE, JAMES ISLAND, S. C.—BAYONET-CHARGE OF THE FEDERAL [illegible] UNDER GENERAL STEVENS UPON THE CONFEDERATE BATTERIES, JUNE [illegible]

DRESS PARADE AND REVIEW OF THE FIRST REGIMENT, SOUTH CAROLINA (COLORED) VOLUNTEERS AT HILTON HEAD, S. C., UNDER COLONEL FESSENDEN, U. S. A., JUNE 25TH, 1862.

FROM A SKETCH BY W. T. CRANE.

16th ordered General Stevens, with about 4,000 men, to make the attack before daybreak, while General Wright and Colonel Williams, with 3,000 men, were to come up to the left, to protect and support.

By some misunderstanding the movement was delayed, and the troops made a rush upon the fort in broad daylight, and were met by grape and canister, which scattered the assaulting party and drove off all the regiments except the Eighth Michigan and Seventy-ninth New York, who succeeded in reaching the front, and, mounting the parapet, drove the gunners from their guns at the point of the bayonet. Here Lieutenant-colonel Morrison, of the (Highlanders), particularly distinguished himself by leading his men inside the fort; but, failing of support, was obliged to fall back. An officer of his regiment, speaking of his prowess on this occasion, says, "It carried me back to the days of Agincourt."

HEROIC CONDUCT OF LIEUTENANT-COLONEL MORRISON, SEVENTY-NINTH NEW YORK, (HIGHLANDERS), ON THE PARAPET OF THE TOWER BATTERY, JAMES ISLAND.

FROM A SKETCH BY AN OFFICER

Meanwhile Colonel Williams, who had been ordered to reinforce General Stevens, lost his way in the woods, and his men were exposed to a severe cross-fire, in which they lost severely. The Third New Hampshire and Third Rhode Island Regiments drove the Confederates at the point of the bayonet, and thus saved the entire force from capture. The guns of the Tower fort were silenced by these bold assaults, and a prompt reinforcement of a few hundred men would have captured the earthworks.

Before the assaulting party could reorganize, the earthworks were reinforced by two regiments of infantry from Fort Jackson. That fort also began shelling the besiegers, who could not be aided by the gunboats, owing to their too great distance from the field; and the Federals had finally to retire, after having sustained a loss of over 700 killed and wounded, as against but one-third that number lost on the side of the Confederates. It was wisely concluded to withdraw, as it was afterward shown it would have required a much larger force to successfully overcome the large and well armed garrison then at the fort, protected as it was by heavy abatis behind a ditch filled with seven feet of water, and a parapet fully seven feet in height. For a time all further attempts to move upon Charleston were abandoned.

H. W. BENHAM.

Born in Connecticut; entered the United States Military Academy at West Point, July 1st, 1833, and graduated, first in his class, exactly four years later. Entered the army as brevet second lieutenant in the Corps of Engineers, and was promoted to be a first lieutenant on the 7th of July, 1838. From 1839 to 1844, he served as superintending engineer of the repairs of Fort Marion and of the sea-wall at St. Augustine, Fla. In 1844 and 1845 he was engaged on the repairs of the defences of Annapolis Harbor, and in 1845 returned to the work on the sea-wall at St. Augustine, where he remained till 1846. During a part of 1845, however, he was engaged on repairs at Fort Mifflin, Pa., and at Fort McHenry, Md., and during parts of 1846 and 1847 he worked on the repairs of Forts Madison and Washington, Md. In 1847 and and 1848 he fought in the war with Mexico. He was engaged in the battle of Buena Vista, February 22d and 23d, 1846, and on February 23d was brevetted captain for gallant and meritorious services in that battle. In 1848 and 1849 he was engaged as assistant engineer in the repairs of the defences of the harbor of New York, and on May 24th, 1848, was promoted to the rank of captain in the Engineer Corps.

From 1849 to 1852 he acted as superintending engineer of the construction of the sea-wall for the protection of Great Brewster Island, Boston Harbor. In 1852 he superintended the building of the Buffalo Lighthouse, and in part of the same year and part of 1853, superintended the construction of the Navy Yard of Washington.

HENRY W. BENHAM.

In 1853 Captain Benham was assistant in charge of the United States Coast Survey Office at Washington and was in Europe on duty connected therewith from March 20th to November 1st. He was promoted to the rank of major in the Ninth Infantry, March 3d, 1855, but declined. In 1856 and 1857 he was superintending engineer of the building of Forts Winthrop and Independence, Boston Harbor. In 1856 he superintended the survey of the site for a fort at Clark's Point, New Bedford, and the repairs of Fort Adams, Newport, R. I., in 1857 and 1858. He had charge of the building of the fort at Sandy Hook, N. J., from 1858 to 1861, and of the Potomac Aqueduct in 1860. He was a member of the special board of engineers for modifying the Sandy Hook fort in 1860, and was engineer of the Quarantine Commissioners of this port in 1859 and 1860.

He served throughout the Civil War, and as a member of the staff of Brigadier general T. A. Morris, was present at Laurel Hill, July 6th to 11th, 1861. He was brevetted colonel for gallant conduct at the battle of Carrick's Ford, Va., July 13th, 1861, and was in command of the engaged troops on that day. On August 6th, 1861, he became a major in the Corps of Engineers, and on August 13th was made a brigadier-general in the Volunteers. He commanded his brigade at New Creek, August 10th, 1861, and was engaged in the action at Carnifex Ferry, September 10th, and the pursuit of the Confederate forces from Cotton Hill in Raleigh County, Va., November 12th to 16th.

In 1862, he was successively engaged as superintending engineer of the fortifications in Boston Harbor, and as commander of the Northern District of the Department of the South, being present at Tybee Island, Ga., during the bombardment and capture of Fort Pulaski, and at the attack on Secessionville, James Island, S. C. He was severely censured for the result of the last-named attack, and was even for a time deprived of his commission as a general. A subsequent investigation, however, exonerated him from all blame, and he was restored to his rank and position as a general of Volunteers. He was then placed in command of the Engineer Brigade of the Army of the Potomac, that command becoming vacant by the death of Brigadier-general Woodbury. On the 3d of March, 1866, on the consolidation of the Engineers

THE THIRD RHODE ISLAND VOLUNTEERS, COLONEL WILLIAMS, DRIVING, BY A BAYONET-CHARGE, THE CONFEDERATE SHARPSHOOTERS FROM THE WOODS ON JAMES ISLAND, JUNE 16TH 1862

FROM A SKETCH BY AN OFFICER

BATTLE OF CHARLES CITY ROAD, MONDAY, JUNE 30TH, 1862
FROM A SKETCH BY WM. WAUD.

Corps of the Regular Army of the United States, Major Benham was promoted to the rank of lieutenant-colonel of Engineers, which position he subsequently held in the Regular Army.

From April 29th to May 5th, 1863, he was engaged in superintending the throwing of ponton-bridges across the Rappahannock for the passage and retreat of the army at Chancellorsville. During this time he was made lieutenant-colonel of the Corps of Engineers. He was engaged in building pontons at Franklin's Crossing in the face of the enemy, June 5th, 1863; on the Potomac, at Edwards's Ferry, June 21st; was in command of the ponton depot at Washington from July, 1863, to May, 1864; and was in command of the Engineer Brigade from June, 1864, to June 15th, 1865, being engaged in superintending the laying of a ponton-bridge 2,200 feet long across the James River at Fort Powhatan, June 15th, 1864. He constructed and commanded the defenses at City Point, Va., in October, 1864, and on March 13th, 1865, was breveted brigadier-general for gallant services in the campaign terminating with the surrender of Lee. On the same date he was promoted to the rank of major-general of the United States Army. He was mustered out of the Volunteer service on January 15th, 1866.

On March 7th, 1867, he was made a colonel in the Corps of Engineers, and was engaged on works at Plymouth, Salem, Marblehead, Gloucester, and Boston. From October 25th, 1869, till July 30th, 1877, he was engaged on works on Long Island Head. Subsequent to 1877, he was for several years in charge of some of the defenses of New York Harbor. In October, 1877, he became a member of the board for the examination of Engineers for promotion. He retired from active service in 1882, and died in New York City on the 1st of June, 1884. General Benham was the inventor of a method of laying ponton-bridges by simultaneous bays, and of a picket-shovel for infantry on hostile marches.

THE FIRST BATTLES BEFORE RICHMOND.

While the opposing armies stood confronting one another along the Chickahominy River, there occurred a number of skirmishes, but none that proved of moment except when reconnoissances were ordered on the 23d and 24th of May, 1862.

On the first date, McClellan ordered the troops to proceed about three miles up the stream to ascertain whether the right wing could cross in safety. As the Sixth Pennsylvania Regiment, which was in the advance, came near Ellison's Mill, they saw the new bridge, which had just been constructed, and which some Confederate pickets attempted to burn on their approach. This was prevented, however, by a bold dash made by the Pennsylvanians, who took possession of the bridge, and crossed it with Wheeler's, Tidball's and Robinson's batteries.

The Federals pushed their reconnoissance up a hill on the other side, without meeting any opposition, until they reached its summit, when they were fired upon with artillery by Confederates hidden in the wood. The Federal batteries responded promptly, and an exchange of artillery fire continued for some time without apparent advantage on either side, until the Confederates made an attempt to outflank the Federals. In this they were defeated, however, and the Federals encamped on the field for the night.

The Confederates renewed the attempt on the following morning, when they opened upon the Federals from a four-gun battery. Davidson's brigade of Franklin's corps, supported by Wheeler's guns, went forward, and opened upon their assailants, whose line was soon broken, especially when a bayonet-charge was ordered. The Confederates abandoned their ground, and were pursued a short distance, when the Federals were ordered to fall back to their former position.

May, 1862.

On the same day, (24th), a reconnoissance affecting the left wing of the army was made in the direction of the Seven Pines. General Henry M. Nagler was placed in command of the troops selected for the purpose, and soon came upon a body of Confederate infantry and cavalry, supported by two batteries of eight guns, which opened fire on the advance. The engagement that followed was a lively one, and gave the Eighth Pennsylvania Cavalry an opportunity to engage the Confederate horse, which they succeeded in routing completely. The infantry, likewise, did some active work, but the largest share fell to the artillery, which was made to occupy many different positions during the two hours' fight that followed, and which finally secured a Federal victory.

The Confederates were compelled to retire far into a dense forest, where they remained concealed for a while, and thence retreated toward Richmond. They were pursued unavailingly several miles in the direction of the railroad, where it was learned that

REBUILDING THE RAILROAD BRIDGE ACROSS THE RAPPAHANNOCK TO FREDERICKSBURG, VA., BURNED BY THE CONFEDERATES IN THEIR RETREAT.

From a Sketch by Edwin Forbes.

RECEPTION OF THE WOUNDED SOLDIERS OF THE FEDERAL ARMY AT FORTRESS MONROE VA. CARS CARRYING THEM TO THE HOSPITAL. SURGEONS DRESSING THE WOUNDS

From a Sketch by J. H. Schell.

a large Confederate force was stationed, after which the Federals returned to their camp.

Early on the morning of the 27th, the Fifth Corps, under Fitz John Porter, was ordered to Hanover Court House, with the view of clearing the country in that direction of Confederate troops, thus to aid the rapid advance of McDowell, with 40,000 troops, then at Fredericksburg, and ordered to join General McClellan and to form on his right.

On Porter was also enjoined the duty of destroying the railroad bridges across the Pamunkey and other streams — occasionally attempted by cavalry under General Stoneman—for the purpose of preventing a rapid reinforcement of Richmond by Jackson, then in Northern Virginia.

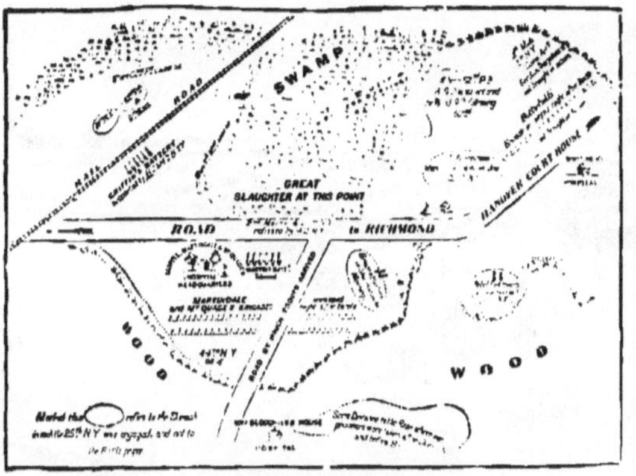

PLAN OF THE BATTLE OF HANOVER COURT HOUSE, VA., MAY 27TH, 1862.

The sudden and rapid advance of Jackson upon Banks in the Valley of Virginia, admirably planned for the purpose of alarming the Administration for the safety of Washington, caused the countermanding of the order to McDowell, the sending him on a futile pursuit of Jackson, and the destruction of McClellan's plans, based on the hope of this reinforcement, deemed by him so essential to maintain his then position along the Chickahominy, and for a successful attack on Richmond.

The recall of McDowell (whose pickets and Porter's connected) was made during Porter's expedition, and Porter was ordered to destroy, as far as practicable, all bridges over the streams along the wagon and rail roads between Richmond and Fredericksburg. This was largely accomplished.

General William H. Emory was in the advance, with two regiments of regular cavalry and Benson's horse battery, and these were closely followed by the brigades of Generals Daniel Butterfield, John H. Martindale, and Colonel McQuade, who had with them Berdan's Sharpshooters and Captain Griffin's three batteries.

They proceeded through a heavy rain-storm, along the New Bridge Road, and over the Hanover Turnpike, and encountered the Confederate pickets at McKinsey's Cross Roads, six miles from Hanover Court House. The pickets fell back, and at noon Emory was brought to a halt within two miles of the last-named place by a line of Confederates drawn up across the road.

Active skirmishing, in which Berdan's Sharpshooters took a leading part, began, and was continued until General Butterfield could bring up his Twelfth and Seventeenth New York, Sixteenth Michigan, and Eighty-third Pennsylvania Regiments. Then a charge was ordered, and the Confederates were driven back, after a contest of over an hour's duration, during the pursuit following which the Seventeenth New York captured one of the Confederate guns. General Martindale had come up in the meantime, and pushed on to Peake's Station, a point on the Virginia Central Railway, then held by a Confederate force, which he had soon driven toward Ashland.

Upon turning in the direction of the Court House, Martindale was attacked by fresh troops. These fell upon him in such great numbers that his centre was finally broken, and his flanks were being

GALLANT CHARGE OF THE SIXTH UNITED STATES REGULAR CAVALRY UPON THE CONFEDERATE CAVALRY UNDER GENERAL J. E. B. STUART MAY 9TH, 1862.

From a Sketch by E. [illegible] Bell.

BATTLE OF WHITE OAK SWAMP, MONDAY, JUNE 30TH, 1862—AYERS'S, MOT

FROM A SKETCH

BATTLE OF WHITE OAK SWAMP, MONDAY, JUNE 30th, 1862—AYRES'S, MOTT'S AND RANDALL'S BATTERIES CHECKING THE PURSUIT OF THE CONFEDERATES

[illegible]

RECRUITING IN PHILADELPHIA FOR THE FAMOUS BUCKTAIL REGIMENT.

THIRTEEN-INCH SHELL MORTAR AS USED BY THE UNITED STATES GOVERNMENT.—WEIGHT OF MORTAR, SEVENTEEN THOUSAND POUNDS.

UNITED STATES MAIL BOAT, PROTECTED BY A GUNBOAT, PASSING THE CONFEDERATE BATTERY OFF FORT POWHATAN, JAMES RIVER ON ITS WAY TO FORTRESS MONROE.

From a Sketch by J. H. Schell.

seriously threatened by Confederates issuing from both sides of the woods, just as Porter sent Captain Griffin's battery and the Thirteenth and Fourteenth New York Regiments to his assistance. Martindale had maintained his ground against superior numbers for nearly an hour. At the same time, General Butterfield was sent with his Sixteenth Michigan and Eighty-third Pennsylvania Regiments to the support of the Ninth Massachusetts and the Sixty-second Pennsylvania Regiments on the Confederate left. A general engagement followed, and continued until evening, when the Confederates under General Lawrence O'B. Branch took to the woods, and left their camp in possession of the Federals, who captured, besides many small arms, one 12-pound howitzer, two railway trains, and 730 prisoners. The Federals had during the day lost in all 53 killed and 326 wounded and missing.

On the 28th and 29th of May, Federal reconnoissances were continued in all directions. Captain William P. Chambliss, at the head of a detachment of cavalry, drove the Confederates from Ashland, and destroyed a railway bridge, as well as the telegraph and road in the vicinity, while Major Williams tore up the Richmond and Fredericksburg Railroad, and destroyed the railway bridge crossing the South Anna. On the 30th, the Confederates advanced a strong reconnoitring party to ascertain the position of the Federals, especially in the direction of General Casey's encampment, but did not bring about any engagement.

General Casey's division was at that time stationed in the advance on both sides of the Williamsburg Road, and just beyond the Seven Pines, at a point about six miles from Richmond. Its right consisted of Naglee's brigade, with the Eleventh Maine, Lieutenant-colonel Plaisted, and the Fifty-second and One Hundred and Fourth Pennsylvania, as well as the Fifty-sixth and One Hundredth New York Regiments, under Colonels T. C. Dodge, W. W. H. Davis, C. H. Van Wyck, and J. M. Brown. The left was held by General J. B. Palmer, with the Fifty-fifth, Eighty-first, Ninety-second and Ninety-eighth New York Regiments, under Colonel T. S. Belknap, and Lieutenant-colonels De Forest, Anderson and Durkee. General Henry W. Wessels's brigade held the centre.

THE FIRST NEW JERSEY BRIGADE, GENERAL TAYLOR, DETACHING ITSELF FROM GENERAL SLOCUM'S DIVISION, AND RUSHING TO THE SUPPORT OF KEARNEY, WHO HAD BEEN DRIVEN BACK AT CHARLES CITY ROAD, JUNE 30TH, 1862

From a Sketch by W. Waud.

BATTLE OF MALVERN HILL, NEAR TURKEY BEND, JAMES RIVER, VA., FOUGHT

BATTLE OF MALVERN HILL, NEAR TURKEY BEND, JAMES RIVER, VA. TUESDAY, JULY 1st, 1862—FINAL REPULSE OF THE CONFEDERATES 7 O'CLOCK P.M.

GREAT NATIONAL BAKERY FOR THE FEDERAL ARMY, IN THE BASEMENT OF THE CAPITOL, WASHINGTON, D.C.

FORT BUILT TO PROTECT THE OFFICERS' QUARTERS OF THE FIRST MINNESOTA REGIMENT, COLONEL SULLY, NEAR FAIR OAKS.

FROM A SKETCH BY AN OFFICER OF THE REGIMENT.

and guarded the turnpike with the Ninety-sixth New York and the Eighty-fifth, the One Hundred and First and the One Hundred and Third Pennsylvania Regiments, led by Colonels J. Fairman, T. B. H Howell, S. H. Wilson, and M. H. Lehman. Palmer's brigade was just in advance of General Couch's division, belonging also to Keyes's corps, which latter stood at the Seven Pines, with its extreme right at Fair Oaks Station, and Heintzelmann's corps was likewise stationed on the left, covering the approaches to the White Oak Swamp.

Johnston decided to heavily attack Keyes's corps in its advanced position before reinforcements could reach it, and for that purpose he sent out, on Saturday, the 31st of May, the entire divisions of Generals James Longstreet, Benjamin Huger, D. H. Hill, and G. W. Smith. They were to move at daybreak, but an unusually heavy rainstorm having set in during the night, Longstreet was not in position until about eight o'clock. He was not, however, willing to endanger the possible success of a combined attack before Huger could join him, and for that reason he moved down the Williamsburg Road, only at a little after twelve o'clock in the afternoon, with Hill's division in the advance.

General Keyes had ordered his troops under arms at eleven o'clock, having become satisfied that an attack was contemplated, as one of Johnston's aids had been captured near the Federal lines, and the cars were heard running in and out of Richmond during almost all of the previous night.

As soon as the Confederates were seen advancing along the Williamsburg Road, Casey ordered forward the One Hundred and Third Pennsylvania Regiment to support the pickets, and called for reinforcements. He then posted Spratt's and Regan's batteries on the right, with the Eleventh Maine, the Ninety-second and One Hundredth New York, and the One Hundredth and Fourth Pennsylvania Regiments, who met the Confederates when the latter had succeeded in forcing back the pickets and the Pennsylvania force sent to their assistance.

At three o'clock the engagement became general. A furious onslaught was being made by General Hill's forces upon the Federal batteries, which were well in the front, and at one time the guns were in serious danger. Naglee's men made a bayonet-charge to relieve the pressure, and drove back the Confederates to the woods; but he was met there by such a furious fire upon his flank, that he had to retire to Fair Oaks Farm with the loss of one of his guns. He was followed here by a force fully three times greater than his own, but he nevertheless maintained his ground until almost completely surrounded by the fresh Confederate troops, which were continually arriving, when he was ordered to retire in front of Couch's division.

The reinforcements which the Federals had asked from Heintzelmann, early in the action, not having by this time come up, Keyes ordered forward to Casey's assistance the Seventh Massachusetts, the Fifty-fifth and Sixty-second New York, and the Twenty-third, Sixty-first, and Ninety-third Pennsylvania Regiments. All of these were, however, forced back, by the superior numbers against them, to the position occupied at Fair Oaks Station by General John Cochrane's First United States Chasseurs and the Thirty-first Pennsylvania Regiment. Here the earthworks, which had been constructed by the Federals, afforded relief to the latter, and from them they were for a while enabled to hold the Confederates at bay.

The Confederate batteries were, however, so well served and so strongly supported, that the struggle proved useless, and the Federals had once more to

DESPERATE SKIRMISH NEAR TUNSALL'S STATION, VA., BETWEEN [illegible] FIFTH UNITED STATES CAVALRY AND STUART'S CONFEDERATE CAVALRY, JUNE 13TH, 186[illegible]

FROM A SKETCH BY WM. WAUD.

HARRISON'S LANDING, JAMES RIVER, VA., THE NEW COMMISSARIAT DEPOT AND BASE OF

BURNING OF THE WHITE HOUSE, VA.—FEDERAL TROOPS, COMMANDED BY McCLELLAN, ABANDONING

FROM A

[illegible] LANDING, JAMES RIVER, VA., THE NEW COMMISSARIAT DEPOT AND BASE OF [illegible] McCLELLAN, OCCUPIED BY THE FEDERAL ARMY, TUESDAY, JULY [illegible], 1862.

[illegible] OF THE WHITE HOUSE, VA.—FEDERAL TROOPS, COMMANDED BY McCLELLAN, ABANDONING THE [illegible] ON THE PAMUNKEY RIVER. DEPARTURE OF THE FEDERAL FLOTILLA FOR THE JAMES RIVER.

[illegible]

HEADQUARTERS OF GENERAL BUTTERFIELD, NEAR HARRISON'S LANDING, JAMES RIVER, VA.

FEDERAL PICKET-BOAT, NEAR FERNANDINA, FLA., ATTACKED BY CONFEDERATE SHARPSHOOTERS STATIONED IN THE TREES ON THE BANKS

FEDERAL TROOPS MARCHING THROUGH THE STREETS OF FERNANDINA, FLA.

CALIFORNIA JOE, THE CELEBRATED SHARPSHOOTER OF BERDAN'S REGIMENT.

FROM A SKETCH BY J. H. SCHELL.

abandon their position and retreat toward the Chickahominy River.

Another line was hurriedly formed by General Couch, and by the time General Kearney had come up, leading Berry's and Jameson's brigades, Longstreet's force had reached the front, and was pressing its way against the Federal left and centre, where the fight was renewed and continued for over an hour. Longstreet's division was closely followed by that of General G. W. Smith, which fell upon the Federals at Fair Oaks Station, where a fierce conflict raged until five o'clock. Then Kearney was forced back toward the White Oak Swamp, and the Confederates established themselves between Couch and Heintzelman, threatening to engulf the entire Federal advance.

Just then, however, General Sumner, who had meanwhile completed two bridges across the heavily swollen river, and hurried forward at the sound of battle, appeared with Sedgwick's troops in the advance. Assuming the command, he formed a line along the edge of a wood near Fair Oaks Station, and awaiting the Confederates, he hurled upon them the concentrated fire of all his guns, following it with an advance along the whole line. He soon recovered almost all the ground Couch had lost, and was still forging ahead, when a large Confederate force appeared at the front, and began a fierce attack with the view of capturing the batteries Sumner had posted there.

The Federal line wavered, but for a few moments only. Sumner quickly brought up the Seventh Michigan, the Fifteenth and Twentieth Massachusetts, and the Thirty-Fourth and Eighty-second New York Regiments, and ordered a bayonet charge, which was so admirably executed, that the Confederates were broken up and forced back into the woods. At eight o'clock all firing ceased.

Richardson's brigade came up in the evening, part of it only having been able to cross the Chickahominy by the lower bridge. It had availed of the upper one, which Sedgwick had already used, and had lost no time in reaching the battle ground, too late, however, to be of any good. It was then posted on Sedgwick's left.

Previous to the final repulse of the Confederates, their commander, General Joseph E. Johnston, had been so severely wounded by the fragments of a shell, that he had to be taken from the field, and the command of the left was for the nonce taken by General G. W. Smith.

On Sunday, the 1st of June, the conflict was renewed at seven o'clock by the Confederates, who fell upon Richardson's division, occupying the centre. The latter was assailed successively at different points; but Heintzelman, who had been given chief command, had so well disposed the artillery, that the Confederates were everywhere repulsed.

JUNE, 1862.

The extreme advance line was given the brigade of General William H. French, who had also with him one of General O. O. Howard's regiments, the remainder of Howard's brigade forming a second line, and General Thomas F. Meagher's brigade completing a third. The Confederates, under Generals George E. Pickett and Roger A. Pryor, with some of Huger's troops, fell upon French's brigade, and were met by a brisk fire, especially from Captain Hazard's 10-pounders; but this did not deter them, and they were moving forward, when Howard went to French's assistance, in which he was afterward aided by Meagher and a part of Hooker's force.

The Confederates, who had been reinforced by Mahone's troops, fought desperately, and subjected the Federals to a very severe fire, in which General Howard lost two horses, and was seriously wounded in the arm.

Part of the Excelsior Brigade, under General Daniel E. Sickles, was sent to Richardson's assistance, and with this reinforcement on the right, the Federals assumed the offensive, and soon compelled the Confederates to fall back. At about the same time Hooker came up from the left, and moved rapidly upon the Confederate rear, following up the advance with a bayonet-charge along the whole line, which ended the battle, as the Confederates were immediately after in retreat toward Richmond. They had failed in their attempt, and, besides temporarily losing the valuable services of their ablest general, had lost altogether 4,233 men, as against 5,739 lost on the side of the Federals.

The Confederate wounded included Generals G. W. Smith and Pettigrew, those on the Federal side being Generals Naglee, Howard, Devens and Wessels.

Heintzelman had given orders to pursue the retreating Confederates; but Kearney had dissuaded him from carrying out his plans, in the anticipation that McClellan would soon order a general advance. Hooker had afterward pushed a reconnoissance up to within four miles of Richmond, but without achieving any important results, the muddy condition of the country not permitting artillery to follow.

Nor did anything of moment occur in the immediate vicinity until the 13th of June, when, with detachments of the First, Fourth and Ninth Virginia Cavalry, the squadron of the Jeff. Davis Legion, and four pieces of horse artillery, the Confederate General James E. B. Stuart commenced a raid which covered most of the territory around the Army of the Potomac.

During the progress of this daring expedition, Stuart encountered and successfully engaged two squadrons of the Fifth United States Cavalry at Hanover Old Church; burned fourteen wagons and two schooners, loaded with forage, at Garlick's Landing, on the Pamunkey River; and captured 165 prisoners, as well as 260 horses and mules, which he brought into Richmond. All this was effected with the loss of only one man on the Confederate side.

EXPLOSION OF A CONFEDERATE MAGAZINE NEAR FREDERICKSBURG, VA., CAUSED BY A TORPEDO.

MAY 25TH, 1862.

VALLEY OF THE CHICKAHOMINY, LOOKING SOUTHEAST FROM MECI

COMMISSARIAT DEPOT OF THE UNITED STATES A[illegible]Y OF THE RAPPAHANNOCK, AT MANASSAS, VA.

[illegible]

PRESIDENT LINCOLN, WITH GENERAL McCLELLAN, REVIEWING THE TROOPS AT HARRISON'S LANDING, JULY 8th, 1862.

SOLDIERS IN CAMP VISITING THE SUTLER'S STORE.

On the 25th of June, "Stonewall" Jackson brought from the Shenandoah Valley into Ashland his army of about 35,000 men; and on the same day McClellan ordered General Heintzelman's corps to proceed, with part of Keyes's and Sumner's troops, on a reconnoissance along the Williamsburg Road. They encountered the enemy at Oak Grove, or King's Schoolhouse; and after a desultory fight, in which there were many casualties on both sides, but mainly in Hooker's and Kearney's ranks, they returned to their former position.

The approach of Jackson, and an intended attack by General Lee upon Porter's troops north of the Chickahominy, were known to Porter who made, as early as the 24th, the necessary preparations to receive him warmly by placing, intrenched and concealed on the high ground just east of Beaver Dam Creek, Reynolds's and Seymour's brigades of McCall's Pennsylvania Reserves, of the Fifth Corps, with ample artillery, under the immediate command of General Reynolds, and withdrew from Mechanicsville all but a few pickets and supports, who were to give warning of Lee's approach, and to retire at once behind Reynolds at Beaver Dam. He next arranged with Generals McCall and Morell to promptly move their divisions to specified positions to the right and rear of Reynolds on the first sound of battle.

On Thursday, the 26th, the Confederates began an advance against the Federal lines. The attack, which was to have taken place early in the morning, did not occur until three o'clock, when General Ambrose P. Hill crossed the Chickahominy, at Meadow Bridge, just above Mechanicsville. Meeting but little opposition from the few forces retiring from Mechanicsville, Hill pushed on to Beaver Dam Creek, even to descending into the valley with large forces, unsuspicious that some 5,000 men and batteries were on the heights overlooking the creek, anxiously waiting his coming within easy range of musketry to give him a warm welcome. Suddenly, when much exposed to the Federal fire, infantry and artillery opened upon his closed and unprepared ranks, mowing the troops down by hundreds. The Confederates, however, pushed on to the creek, over which very few effected a crossing, and from which those who were able quickly retired in confusion.

June, 1862.

The Confederates then directed their attention to the right and left of the line, but they were met by as warm a reception by Griffin's brigade of Morell's division, posted on the right, and some of McCall's, on the left. They were badly repulsed, and at nine o'clock in the evening what has been called the battle of Mechanicsville, or Beaver Dam, came to an end. The Confederates' loss in killed and wounded, was near 4,000; that of the Federals 52. General Fitz John Porter, who was in chief command of the Federals, was present during the entire engagement, giving his attention to all parts of the field, while McCall and Morell specially managed their respective divisions.

After the battle, McClellan learned that Jackson had passed Beaver Dam Creek, and saw that Lee, who was in chief command, and directing the operations of the Confederates since June 3d, intended to cut off the Federals from their base at the White House. He concluded best to be prepared to retreat with his supplies toward the James River, depending on that day's events.

Colonel Rufus Ingalls, the assistant quartermaster-general, was ordered to move the stores and ammunition to Savage's Station, where he also sent all the wounded, and, by daylight of the 27th, the troops and nearly all of the heavy guns and wagons, had crossed the New Bridge, and were just east of Gaines's Mills, between New Cold Arbor (or Cold Harbor) and the Chickahominy River. There the Fifth Corps awaited attack.

DANIEL E. SICKELS.

The Federals were drawn up in a semicircular line, covering the approach to the bridges by which the troops were to cross the Chickahominy. The extreme left was occupied by Morell's division, which stood in advance of McCall's troops, while on the right, along a deep ravine, stood Sykes's division of Regulars and Duryee's Zouaves. Robertson's battery was stationed on Morell's left, Griffin's battery on his right, and Tidball's battery, not far from Seymour's brigade, in the rear.

The detachments of the First and Fifth Regular and of the Sixth Pennsylvania Cavalry, under General Philip St George Cooke, were stationed on the low lands of the valley of the Chickahominy, a little ahead of Alexander's Bridge.

GEORGE STONEMAN.

At about two o'clock in the afternoon, the Confederate advance, under Ambrose P. Hill, opened upon Sykes's division with heavy artillery, but in a little over an hour the guns had to be withdrawn, so sharply did the Regular troops respond. As Jackson had not arrived, Longstreet was ordered up to Hill's support, and made a feint upon the Federal left; but this availed of nothing, and he soon found that the heights must be carried by assault. As he had about completed preparations for the intended attack, Jackson reached the scene, and his right division, commanded by General William H. C. Whiting, was placed upon Longstreet's left, while D. H. Hill's division occupied the extreme Confederate left.

The line then moved ahead, D. H. Hill's troops forcing their way with heavy loss through the swamp, and driving back the Federals to the woods. This done, Ewell's division advanced upon Jackson's right, and the remaining brigades of Jackson's corps joined the forces under A. P. Hill.

In front of a seething infantry fire from the heights, and a still more formidable one from cannon on either side, the Confederates made their way successfully up the heights, where a terrible hand-to-hand encounter took place.

Porter called for reinforcements, but these did not reach him until after he had stood the ground for a long time, and at great sacrifice of life, against superior numbers. When Slocum's division did reach him, it had to be so divided along the line as to add but little comparative strength at any given point in face of the heavy forces thrown on all sides against the Federals.

More reinforcements were urgently called for, but by the time that two of Richardson's brigades, Meagher's and French's, had reached the river, the entire Confederate force, with the exception of Kemper's small reserve brigade, had just been brought into action. The Federal left was attacked by Longstreet's and Whiting's divisions, which Butterfield's men of Morell's division met bravely for a while, but in front of which they could make no successful stand. They were finally driven back so fiercely as to compel the abandonment of several of their guns. A part of the right and centre of the division also gave way at the same time, and retreated toward Alexander's Bridge. There, Richardson's two brigades had just crossed, and served, with Sykes's division, to check the Confederate pursuit by rapidly marching through the lines and making a bold stand while the Federals were being re-formed. The remaining batteries were soon again directed upon the pursuers, and by nightfall the Confederates had retired, and firing ceased.

This day's engagement is variously called the battle of Gaines's Mills, of Gaines's Farm, of the Chickahominy, and of New Cool Arbor (or Cold Harbor).

The Federals lost in all about 6,000 in killed and wounded, besides nearly 2,000 prisoners, including General Reynolds, while the Confederate loss was placed at 9,000 in killed and wounded.

During the ensuing night the Federals crossed the Chickahominy, destroying all the bridges after them, McClellan's headquarters being removed to the vicinity of Savage's Station. On Saturday, the 28th, Ewell's division and the Ninth Confederate Cavalry crossed the river, and opened their artillery upon Smith's division of Franklin's corps, compelling the latter to retire from Golding's Farm, situated close by Woodbury's Bridge.

At three o'clock Sunday morning, McClellan left Savage's Station, after ordering the abandonment of all the Federal works and a retreat toward his

BATTLE OF GAINES'S MILLS, FOUR O'C

FROM

BATTLE OF WILLIS CHURCH, 10 O'CLOCK A.M., MONDAY, JUNE 30TH, 1862.—GENERALS HANCOCK. F

FROM A SKETCH BY A

BATTLE OF GAINES MILLS, [illegible] AFTERNOON, FRIDAY, JUNE [illegible]

BATTLE OF [illegible] CHURCH, [illegible] SUNDAY, JUNE [illegible] GENERALS HANCOCK, [illegible], SUMNER AND [illegible] GENERALS JACKSON, LONGSTREET AND A. P. HILL

NEGRO DRIVERS OF THE BAGGAGE-TRAIN ATTACHED TO GENERAL PLEASANTON'S CAVALRY BRIGADE WATERING THEIR MULES IN THE RAPPAHANNOCK RIVER.

new base along the James River. General Smith's division first got under way, and was closely followed by the forces of Heintzelman, Keyes, Franklin, and Porter, the divisions of Hooker and Kearney bringing up the rear.

As soon as it was ascertained that the Federals were in actual retreat toward the James, General Longstreet and A. P. Hill were ordered to cross the Chickahominy at the New Bridge, which Magruder had rebuilt, and to push along the Darbytown and Long Bridge Roads, while Jackson would cross the Grapevine Bridge, and move along the south side of the Chickahominy to attack the Federal rear. Magruder and Huger were to move respectively by the Charles City and by the Williamsburg Roads, which would allow of an attack on the flank, as well as upon the rear, of the retreating army.

Although McClellan's forces had much the start of the Confederates, Magruder reached the vicinity of Savage's Station at about nine o'clock, and at once engaged the right of Sedgwick's division, which Sumner, then in chief command at that point, had ordered deployed across the railway. From the line of battle which Sumner had thus drawn up, Magruder believed the Federals to be advancing, and he therefore halted, after the engagement had proceeded but a short while, and sent for reinforcements.

By the time two brigades of Huger's division had reached him, Magruder learned that the opposing force was only covering the retreat of the main body. He therefore made preparations for an attack with but one of his divisions and two regiments belonging to another, and at about four o'clock in the afternoon once more engaged Sumner's corps, part of which had, by the misinterpretation of an order, become separated from the main body.

The attack, though a fierce one, was gallantly met, especially by General Burns's brigade and those of Generals Hancock and Brooke. The Confederates had approached through a dense wood, and had planted their cannon in positions from which they did good execution, although the fire from Pettit's, Bramhall's and Osborn's batteries appeared equally well served; but the grape and canister which Captain Pettit was directing on the right, and the repeated charges made by the Irish brigade, were such as to render futile the flanking efforts of the Confederates. They gradually retired, after suffering a total loss of about 400, which proved to be but half that sustained by the Federals.

Not long after the termination of the battle of Savage's Station, the Federals continued on their retreat, and by eight o'clock on the morning of the 30th they had crossed White Oak Swamp and Creek, after destroying the bridge over the latter and warding off the repeated attacks to which they were subjected throughout the night.

JUNE, 1862.

Jackson, who had, on the previous day, been delayed by the necessary rebuilding of the Grapevine Bridge, reached Savage's Station early on the 30th, and there found a large amount of property which the Federals had had no time to destroy, as well as fully 2,500 Federal sick and wounded, which they had likewise been unable to remove.

Jackson had orders to pursue the Federals, which he did, in company with the forces of Longstreet and A. P. Hill, following directly in their track, while a second column, under Generals Magruder and Huger, proceeded to the right, along the Charles City Road, for the purpose of falling upon the flank of the retreating army.

WILLIAM B. FRANKLIN.

After crossing White Oak Creek, the Federals had quickly formed a new line of battle, at Willis Church, General Hancock's forces being on the extreme right, while Porter's occupied the left, and Heintzelman's and Sumner's the intervening space. Jackson's advance was checked by the destruction of the bridge, and when he reached the creek, at about noon, he found the approaches well defended by artillery, under the supervision of Captain Romeyn B. Ayres.

Jackson opened upon Hancock's troops, and made repeated efforts to rebuild the bridge under cover of his heavy artillery; but he was every time repulsed. At length he made a bold effort to cross the stream, but in this he failed likewise, for the brisk fire directed upon him, notably by Smith's infantry and the Federal batteries, almost totally prevented the crossing, as well as any permanent landing on the opposite side.

DARIUS N. COUCH.

While this was going on, Longstreet and A. P. Hill had come upon a Federal force posted some two miles away at a place variously called Frazier's, Glendale's or Nelson's Farm. Here stood Sumner and Hooker on the extreme right, McCall somewhat in advance toward the centre, and Kearney on the extreme left. When Longstreet (who was accompanied by President Davis and General Lee) found this force arrayed against him, he waited for reinforcements to come up, and it was close upon four o'clock when he commenced the attack.

McCall's left was first assailed by Kemper's brigade, which was met by the Pennsylvania Reserves under Colonel S. G. Simmons, who, after a bitter conflict, drove the Confederates into the woods, with a loss of some 250 killed and wounded, and about 200 prisoners. Fresh troops then enabled the Confederates to drive back the Federals, who in turn lost heavily, and could not effect a stand until met by Hooker's division.

Longstreet and Hill now pressed on, and the conflict became a severe one along the entire front. One point, then another, was vainly tried in the determined effort to break the Federal line. At length Wilcox's Alabama brigade rushed across an open field upon McCall's left, directly against Randall's battery, which centred upon the Confederates a most galling fire. Nothing daunted, they moved on, and, finally engaging in a desperate hand-to-hand fight, first captured Cooper's battery and afterward Randall's battery, which had been doing such terrible execution.

A charge was then ordered for the recapture of the guns. The Irish brigade moved forward, but made little progress until the forces under Heintzelman, Meade and McCall, followed later on by those of Hooker and Kearney, had been brought up for a final onslaught.

The Confederates bravely met the severe attacks that followed. A still more severe hand-to-hand struggle took place for the possession of the lost batteries, which were finally recaptured, but not without severe losses on both sides. By dark, the Confederates had retired into the woods, and the Federals remained on that portion of the field which they had lost earlier in the action.

In this engagement, which, in addition to the names already given, is often termed the battle of New Market Cross Roads, of Charles City Cross Roads, or of White Oak Swamp, the Federal loss was about 1,800 killed and wounded, whilst that of the Confederates was somewhat over 2,000. Colonel Simmons and General Meade were both severely wounded, while General G. A. McCall was made a prisoner, and retained as such until exchanged the following August.

During the ensuing night, the Federals moved on to Malvern Hill, where they formed in battle order upon the crest of an elevated plateau, admirably located to resist the attack which could not but follow on the part of the Confederates. Sykes's and Morell's troops occupied the extreme left: next came Couch's division, then the forces of Kearney, Hooker, Sedgwick, Richardson, Smith, Slocum and Casey, in the order named. The whole formed almost a semicircle, and both flanks, resting upon the James River, were protected by the gunboats. There were eight siege

BATTLE OF SAVAGE'S STATION.—GENERAL SMITH'S DIVISION, OF FRANKLIN'S C

FROM A S

BATTLE OF SLAUGHTER'S MOUNTAIN, SATURDAY, AUGUST 9TH, 1862.—FEDERAL ARMY

FROM A SKET

BATTLE OF SAVAGE'S STATION—GENERAL SMITH'S DIVISION, OF FRANKLIN'S CORPS, [illegible] ATTACKING THE CONFEDERATE FORCES UNDER EWELL [illegible]

[illegible]

BATTLE OF SLAUGHTER'S MOUNTAIN, SATURDAY, AUGUST 9TH, 1862—FEDERAL ARMY COMMANDED BY GENERAL BANKS, CONFEDERATES UNDER JACKSON, EWELL AND WINDER.

[illegible]

GORDON'S AND CRAWFORD'S BRIGADES DRIVING THE CONFEDERATE FORCES FROM THE WOODS, AT THE BATTLE OF CEDAR MOUNTAIN. AUGUST 9TH, 1862.

From a Sketch by Edwin Forbes.

guns in position upon the plateau, and the rest of the artillery was so posted along the hill that a concentrated fire of some sixty cannon could be directed either in the immediate front or upon the left.

At nine o'clock on the morning of July 1st the Confederates had formed a line of battle in Couch's immediate front. The divisions of Magruder and Huger occupied the extreme right, while those of Jackson, D. H. Hill, and Whiting, as well as part of Ewell's, extended toward the right. The remainder of Ewell's division, and the divisions of Longstreet and A. P. Hill, were held in reserve.

July, 1862.

After some desultory firing, Lee concluded that the Federal position could be carried only by assault. He therefore ordered a simultaneous attack to take place along the whole line as soon as the concentrated fire from his artillery had succeeded in silencing most, if not all, of the Federal batteries. When this was done, part of Huger's division was to advance with a shout, which was to be the signal for a general movement "to drive the invaders into the James."

The artillery was in position, and began its fire at about three o'clock, and at a little after six the divisions of Couch and Porter were assailed by D. H. Hill's forces, who had misinterpreted a loud shout for the intended signal. The Federals were bitterly assailed, and the Confederates held their ground well, but not having any support, they were soon driven back in confusion near the woods. Thence, brigade after brigade was made to charge upon the Federal batteries, Magruder and Huger advancing boldly upon the Federal left, while Barksdale, Anderson, Mahone and Wright were making a simultaneous attack toward its right and centre.

The dash displayed by the assailants was heroic, but it availed little in face of the artillery and infantry fire, that was studiously reserved until the Confederates were within a short distance of the crest, and then poured destructively into them. A bayonet-charge would then generally follow, and the Confederates would fall back to renew the attack elsewhere and with fresh troops, until finally all were repulsed.

After a short interval the Confederates re-formed their line in the neighboring forest, and renewed the assault more fiercely than ever. They advanced boldly, and, apparently undismayed by the scathing fire, both of artillery and infantry, to which they were exposed, charged with increased vigor, and in successive lines, upon the main Federal batteries. But, despite their determined energy, they were checked and repulsed with terrible slaughter, and promptly pursued by the brigades of Meagher

RUFUS KING.

and Sickles, which had opportunely arrived from Sumner and Heintzelman on Porter's call for help, and were at once led by him into action.

The gunboats had, besides, in the meantime, opened fire from the James River, and were sending into the woods from their heavy guns most destructive volleys of shot and shell, which soon told so heavily upon the Confederates that they had to take shelter some distance beyond.

At a little after nine o'clock all firing ceased, and with it ended the series of Six (though improperly called Seven) Days' Battles which closed the Peninsula campaign in Virginia. In these various engagements, the official reports show the losses in killed, wounded and missing on both sides to have been as follows:

Federals—Porter, 4,278; McCall, 3,024 (McCall was part of Porter's Fifth Corps); Franklin, 2,737; Sumner, 2,111; Heintzelman, 2,073; Keyes, 777; cavalry, etc., 249—Total, 15,249.

Confederates—Magruder and Huger, 4,585; Longstreet, 4,429; A. P. Hill, 3,970; D. H. Hill, 3,954; Jackson, 2,282; Cavalry, etc., 150—Total, 19,370.

Immediately after the battle of Malvern Hill, McClellan issued orders to fall back upon Harrison's Landing, a few miles below, on the James River, where all that remained of the Army of the Potomac was encamped on the evening of July 3d.

On the following day General McClellan issued an address to the soldiers, in which he recounted their exploits of the preceding week.*

The Confederate army remained in the neighborhood of Malvern Hill, and instituted a series of cavalry pursuits against the retreating Federals, until the fire from the gunboats rendered further effective operations impracticable. Lee then ordered his troops withdrawn, and the Army of Northern Virginia reached the defenses of Richmond on the 8th of July.

GEORGE STONEMAN.

BORN at Busti, N. Y., August 8th, 1822; entered the United States Military Academy at West Point in 1842, and upon graduating therefrom, entered the First Dragoons, with which regiment he was stationed at Fort Leavenworth, and went to New Mexico. From 1847 to 1855 he remained on the Pacific Coast, being promoted in the last named year to a captaincy in the Second Regular Cavalry. He was then sent to Texas, and at the time of the commencement of the Civil War troubles, had charge of Fort Brown, which he refused to surrender to General Twiggs, and subsequently evacuated only when an opportunity offered to take his command to New York. In May, 1861, he was promoted major of the First Cavalry, and served on the staff of General

---

* HEADQUARTERS OF THE ARMY OF THE POTOMAC,
Camp near Harrison's Landing, July 4th.

SOLDIERS OF THE ARMY OF THE POTOMAC: Your achievements of the last ten days have illustrated the valor and endurance of the American soldier. Attacked by superior forces, and without hope of reinforcement, you have succeeded in changing your base of operations by a flank movement, always regarded as the most hazardous of military expedients. You have saved your material, all your train and all your guns, except a few lost in battle, taking in return guns and colors from the enemy. Upon your march you have been assailed day after day with desperate fury by men of the same race and nation, skillfully massed and led. Under every disadvantage of numbers, and necessarily of position also, you have in every conflict beaten back your foes with enormous slaughter. Your conduct ranks you among the celebrated armies of history. No one will now question that each of you may always with pride say, "I belong to the Army of the Potomac." You have reached a new base complete in organization and unimpaired in spirit. The enemy may at any time attack you. We are prepared to meet them. I have personally established your lines. Let them come, and we will convert their repulse into a final defeat. Your Government is strengthening you with the resources of a great people. On this our nation's birthday we declare to our foes, who are rebels against the best interests of mankind, that this army shall enter the capital of the so-called Confederacy; that our national Constitution shall prevail; and that the Union, which can alone insure internal peace and external security to each State, "must and shall be preserved," cost what it may in time, treasure and blood.

GEORGE B. McCLELLAN.

CAPTAIN KNAPP'S BATTERY ENGAGING THE CONFEDERATES AT THE BATTLE OF CEDAR MOUNTAIN, AUGUST 9TH, 1862.

CONFEDERATE CAVALRY RETURNING FROM A SUCCESSFUL RAID IN PURSUIT OF FRESH HORSES AND PROVISIONS.

1. Battle of June 26th—Mechanicsville, or Beaver Dam. 2. Battle of the 27th—Gaines's Mills, or New Cold Arbor (Cold Harbor). 3. Retreat of the Federal Army, through Fair Oaks, toward Savage's Station. 4. Battle of the 29th—Savage's Station. 5. Battle of the 30th—White Oak Swamp. 6. Battle of July 1st—Malvern Hill. 7. Extreme Left Flank of the Army after the Battles.
N. B.—The Federal Gunboats were Stationed between Curtis's Neck and Turkey Bend.

MAP OF THE STRATEGICAL MOVEMENTS OF GENERAL McCLELLAN'S ARMY BEFORE RICHMOND, SHOWING THE PLACES WHERE THE SIX BATTLES WERE FOUGHT, FROM THE 26TH OF JUNE TO THE 1ST OF JULY, 1862.

COMPANY A OF THE FIRST SOUTH CAROLINA FEDERAL VOLUNTEERS (COLORED), TAKING THE OATH OF ALLEGIANCE BEFORE GENERAL SAXTON AT BEAUFORT, S. C.

McClellan until the following August, when he was made a brigadier-general, and placed at the head of the Cavalry of the Army of the Potomac, which he organized, and with which he distinguished himself during the Virginia Peninsula campaign.

After the battle of Chantilly, he took the place of much-lamented General Kearney at the head of the First Division of the Third Corps, commanding the corps itself in the fall of November, 1862, when he was made a major-general of Volunteers. He took a leading part at the battle of Fredericksburg, organized and commanded the notable cavalry raid of April-May, 1863; was made chief of the Cavalry Bureau in July, 1863; placed in command of the Twenty-third Corps, January, 1864, and of the Department of the Ohio Cavalry Corps in April, 1864; participated in the Atlanta campaign in May-July, 1864, and conducted a raid against Macon and Andersonville for the liberation of Federal prisoners, but was himself made a prisoner, and held till the latter part of October, 1864. In the following month he was made temporary commander of the Department of the Ohio. He afterward led several brilliant raids, and was placed in command of different departments, until mustered out of service at the end of July, 1866. He was retired from active service early in August, 1871, after having received the commission of colonel of the Twenty-first Regular Infantry, and the brevets of brigadier-general and of major-general for gallant conduct.

DANIEL E. SICKLES.

Born in New York City on the 20th of October, 1822; entered the University of New York, and, upon leaving it, studied law, and was admitted to the Bar in 1843. Four years later he was elected to the New York State Legislature, and in 1853 was made Corporation Attorney of his native city. From the latter part of 1853 until the year 1855, he acted as Secretary of Legation to James Buchanan, when Minister to England, becoming a State Senator upon his return to New York. This was followed in 1858 by his election to a seat in the United States House of Representatives, which latter he was called upon to occupy from 1859 to 1862.

At the breaking out of the Civil War, he raised what was called the Excelsior Brigade, and was soon appointed colonel of the Seventieth New York. This was soon followed by promotions to a brigadier-generalship in September, 1861, and to a major-generalship in November, 1862. He served throughout the Peninsula Campaign, and in April, 1863, was given command of the Third Corps, greatly distinguishing himself notably at the battle of Chancellorsville, and in the second day's fight at Gettysburg, where he lost a leg while gallantly leading his men. Between 1866 and 1867 he commanded the military district comprising North and South Carolina, having in the meantime been appointed colonel of the Forty-second Regiment of Regular Infantry, and received the brevets of brigadier-general and of major-general in the United States Army for gallantry. He retired in 1869 from active service with the rank of major-general, and in the same year was appointed United States Minister to the Court of Spain, which position he resigned five years later.

AMBROSE P. HILL.

DARIUS NASH COUCH.

Born in Putnam County, N. Y., July 23d, 1822; entered the United States Military Academy at West Point, from which he graduated in 1846; served through the Mexican War, and was commissioned a brevet first lieutenant for distinguished services at the battle of Buena Vista; took part in the Florida War, and was on frontier duty from 1848 to 1855, when he resigned from the army to follow mercantile pursuits. He tendered his services to the United States Government at the time of the breaking out of the Civil War; was made colonel of the Seventh Massachusetts Volunteers, and served in the defenses of Washington, as well as throughout the Peninsula, Maryland and Rappahannock campaigns. He was made a major-general of Volunteers on the 4th of July, 1862. From 1863 to 1864 he was in command of the Department of the Susquehanna, and afterward figured in a great many engagements both in Tennessee and in North Carolina. He resigned from the service on the 26th of May, 1865, soon after accepting the nomination of the Democracy for Governor of Massachusetts. He was not, however, elected to the latter post, but became Collector of the Port of Boston, 1866-7, and has, since the latter year, been president of the Virginia Mining and Manufacturing Company.

WILLIAM BUEL FRANKLIN.

Born at York, Pa., February 27th, 1823; entered the United States Military Academy at West Point in June, 1839, whence he graduated four years later. He was assigned to the Corps of Topographical Engineers, and took part in the Mexican War on the staffs of Generals Wool and Taylor, being brevetted first lieutenant for gallantry at the battle of Buena Vista. He served as acting assistant professor of natural and experimental philosophy at the West Point Military Academy from 1848 to 1852; became professor of engineering and of natural and experimental philosophy at the New York Free Academy, and was assigned to lighthouse duty as inspector and engineer from 1853 to 1857, becoming engineer-secretary of the Lighthouse Board from 1857 to 1859. He was the engineer in charge of the Capitol at Washington from November, 1859, to March, 1861, and from the latter date until the month of May following remained in charge of the Bureau of Construction and Repairs.

On the 14th of May, 1861, he was made colonel of the Twelfth United States Infantry, and, three days later, promoted to be a brigadier-general of Volunteers. In July, 1861, he commanded a brigade at the battle of Bull Run, and afterward had charge of a division until March, 1862, when he was assigned to the corps of General McDowell. He took part in the Peninsula Campaign, and organized and commanded the Sixth Corps, which served notably in the engagements at West Point, Golding's Farm, and White Oak Swamp. He was appointed a major-general, July 4th, 1862, and figured more particularly in the battles of South Mountain and Antietam, fought during the subsequent month of September.

In November, 1862, he was assigned to the command of the Left Grand Division of the Army of the Potomac, commanded the left wing at the battle of Fredericksburg, was relieved from duty in the Army of the Potomac January 25th, 1863, assigned to the Department of the Gulf in July, 1863, then successively placed in command of the expedition against the Sabine Pass, in September, 1863, of the troops occupying Northern Louisiana from 1863 to 1864, of the Nineteenth Corps, and of troops of the Department of the Gulf, forming the Red River expedition, in March and April, 1864. He took part in the battles of Sabine Cross Roads and Pleasant Hill, where he was wounded, and conducted the retreat to Alexandria; was absent on sick leave from June to November, 1864, being then

PHILIP KEARNEY.

made President of a Board for Retiring Disabled Officers, which position he retained until November, 1865, when he gave up his commission in the Volunteer service, resigning from the army in the month of March following. He has since been vice-president and general agent of Colt's Fire-arms Manufacturing Company at Hartford, president of the Commission for laying out Long Island City, N. Y., and president and consulting engineer of the Board of Commissioners for building the new State House at the last named locality.

RUFUS KING.

Born in New York City, January 26th, 1814; was the son of Charles King, of Columbia College, New York City, and grandson of Rufus King, the American statesman. Graduated at the United States Military Academy at West Point in 1833, and was appointed lieutenant of Engineers. He resigned from the army September 30th, 1836, became assistant-engineer on the Erie Railway, and from 1839 to 1843 was the Adjutant-general of the State of New York. During part of this time and until the year 1839 he was connected editorially with the Albany *Evening Journal*, which he left to become editor of the Albany *Advertiser*, in which capacity he served six years when he removed to Wisconsin to take charge of the publication of the Milwaukee *Sentinel*, which he conducted until 1861. He was then appointed Minister to Rome. He returned to take part in the Civil War, and commanded a division at Yorktown, Manassas, Fredericksburg, Groveton and Fairfax. He served until the latter part of the year 1863, when he resigned his commission, and was reappointed Minister to Rome. He was recalled July 1st, 1867, and died in New York City, October 13th, 1876.

PHILIP KEARNEY.

Born in New York City, June 2d, 1815; graduated at Columbia College, and studied law, but in 1837 accepted a lieutenancy in the First Dragoons, of which his uncle, General Stephen Watts Kearney, was the colonel. He was afterward sent to Europe by the United States Government, with orders to look into and report upon the French cavalry service; entered the Saumur Military School, and enlisted as a volunteer in the Chasseurs d'Afrique, doing service in Algeria, where he won the cross of the Legion of Honor. He returned to the United States in 1840, and shortly after became attached to the staff of General W. Scott, under whom he served during the Mexican War. He was made captain of dragoons in 1846, and brevetted major for gallantry displayed at the battles of Contreras and Churubusco. He also took a distinguished part in the final assault on the City of Mexico, losing an arm while in the act of directing his troops near the San Antonio Gate. He afterward did service in California, and led an expedition against the Indians on the Columbia River. In 1851 he resigned from the army and went to Europe, where he continued his military studies. He once more entered the French army on the breaking out of the Italian War in 1859, and as a volunteer aid to General Maurier took part in the battles of Magenta and Solferino. Upon the breaking out of the Civil War he returned to the United States and tendered his services to the Government, soon receiving the commission of brigadier-general of Volunteers. During the Peninsula campaign, he

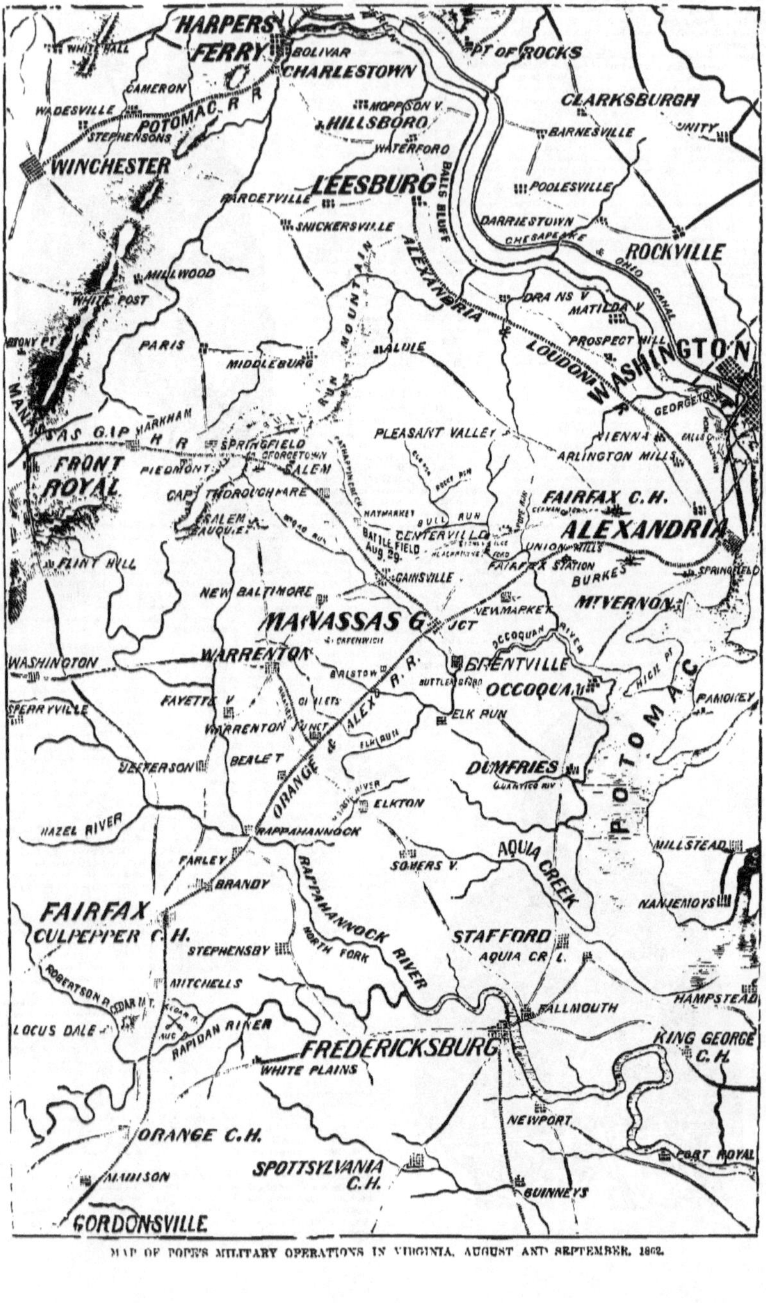

MAP OF POPE'S MILITARY OPERATIONS IN VIRGINIA, AUGUST AND SEPTEMBER, 1862.

commanded the Third (afterward First) Division, Third Corps, of the Army of the Potomac, and greatly distinguished himself, especially at Yorktown, Williamsburg, Fair Oaks, White Oak Swamp, Glendale, and Malvern Hill, being in return promoted to a major-generalship. He likewise took a leading part in the second battle of Bull Run, as well as at Chantilly, and was killed at the last named place on the 1st of September, 1862, while reconnoitring in advance of his troops, and in the act of wheeling his horse around to cheer on his men. He was buried with military honors at Trinity Churchyard, New York City, and his fellow-townsmen afterward erected a monument to his memory in the public square of Newark, N. J.

AMBROSE POWELL HILL.

Born in Culpepper County, Va., in 1825; graduated at the Military Academy at West Point, July 1st, 1847, and entered the army as brevet second lieutenant of artillery. He took part in several of the remaining engagements of the Mexican War, after which he did some frontier duty, and served in the war against the Seminole Indians, having in the meantime been commissioned a second and first lieutenant. From 1855 to 1860 he did duty at the Coast Survey Office in Washington, and was on leave of absence from October of the last named year until March, 1861, when he resigned his commission in the army. Upon the secession of his native State, he accepted the commission of colonel of the Thirteenth Virginia Volunteers, and was stationed at Harper's Ferry until ordered to join the Confederate army at Bull Run. Here he greatly distinguished himself, and was, in consequence, made a brigadier-general, serving as such at the subsequent battle of Williamsburg. He was afterward promoted to be a major-general, and given a division, which he admirably managed during the operations that took place on the Virginia Peninsula, as well during Pope's campaign, ending at Chantilly. He received the surrender of Harper's Ferry, and figured prominently at the battles of Antietam, Fredericksburg, and Chancellorsville, taking the command of Jackson's corps upon the latter's death, and being soon after made lieutenant-general. He displayed great ability throughout the remainder of the civil conflict, notably at Petersburg, where he met his death by a rifle-shot, while engaged in reconnoitring, on the 2d of April, 1865.

WILLIS ARNOLD GORMAN

Born at Flemingsburg, Ky., January 12th, 1816; studied law in Bloomington, Ind., member of the State Legislature for several years; major in General J. H. Lane's regiment of Indiana Volunteers in the Mexican War. At Buena Vista he commanded a rifle battalion, and was severely wounded. He was afterward made colonel of the Fourth Indiana Volunteers, and particularly distinguished himself at the battle of Huamantla. Appointed Military and Civil Governor of Puebla in 1848. Elected to the United States House of Representatives, 1849-53. Entered the Civil War as colonel of the First Minnesota Volunteers. For service at Bull Run he was appointed brigadier-general of Volunteers in September, 1861. Distinguished himself throughout the Peninsula campaign. Mustered out of service in 1864. Resumed practice of law at St. Paul, Minn., where he was elected City Attorney in 1869, and served until his death, May 20th, 1876.

MICHAEL CORCORAN.

Born at Carrowkeel, County Sligo, Ireland, September 21st, 1827; after receiving a thorough English education, he entered the Irish Constabulary Establishment, where he remained three years, being afterward stationed at Creeslough, County Donegal. He resigned in 1849, and emigrated to the United States, settling in New York City. His military career began with his enlistment as private in Company I, Sixty-ninth Regiment of N.Y.S.M., then commanded by Captain John Judge. The regiment greatly distinguished itself in extending and maintaining protection to the Government buildings during the Quarantine troubles in New York Harbor. Corcoran advanced rapidly in rank until, on the 25th of August, 1859, he was made colonel of the regiment. As such he entered the Civil War, and with his regiment took a leading part in the first battle of Bull Run, where he was taken prisoner while gallantly directing the movements of his troops. He was kept in confinement at Richmond, Va., and at Charleston, S.C., nearly a year, when he was exchanged. Upon his way home he was the object of many attentions at Washington, Baltimore and Philadelphia. He left Philadelphia on the morning of the 22d of August, 1862, in company of a delegation from the Common Council of New York City, and, upon his arrival at the Battery, was welcomed by Mayor Opdyke and a large procession of military and firemen, by whom he was escorted to the St. Nicholas Hotel. At the close of the day's festivities he made a speech, in which he declared his intention to raise a brigade, and once more take the field for the Union. He soon after organized and led to the field the Corcoran Legion, and was made a brigadier-general of Volunteers, to date from the day of his capture, July 21st, 1861. He was thrown from his horse, while riding with his staff, near Sawyer's Station, Va., on the 23d of December, 1863, and so fatally injured that he never recovered consciousness, and died the same day.

CAPTURE OF FORT PILLOW AND OF MEMPHIS.

Within a week after the capture of Island No. 10 Commodore Foote had completed preparations for a further advance along the Mississippi, having the City of Memphis for its objective. Above the latter place were two forts (Fort Pillow and Randolph), the more important of which, Fort Pillow, must needs first be reduced before progress could be made.

On the 14th of April, 1862, Foote had his mortars in position at Craighead Point, less than a mile from Fort Pillow. He soon commenced upon the latter a bombardment which was continued almost without intermission, in hope that an early fall in the much-swollen river would soon admit of the co-operation of Pope's land force, then stationed on the Arkansas shore. Pope's troops, with the exception of two regiments, under Colonel Fitch, were, however, withdrawn to Pittsburg Landing, and Foote was left to work alone. The bombardment soon compelled the retirement below Fort Pillow of a flotilla of eight gunboats and four steam-rams, with which Hollins had threatened the Federal advance, and it was not until the 10th of May that they were again brought forward for an aggressive movement.

WILLIS ARNOLD GORMAN.

At that time, the command of the Federal operations had just devolved upon Captain Charles Davis, as Foote had been compelled, by the aggravation of the wound he had received at Fort Donelson, to abandon all further active duty.

May, 1862.

At a little after five o'clock on the morning of the 10th, the largest of Hollins's vessels—the ram *McRea*—swept around Craighead Point, and attacked Acting-master Gregory's mortar-boat, with which it had a fierce encounter. Seeing this, the two Federal gunboats, *Mound City* and *Cincinnati*, hurried forward and engaged the ram, which soon turned upon the last-named, and, in face of terrible broadsides, repeatedly struck the gunboat with her sharp iron prow, inflicting ugly wounds in her side. Before the *Mound City* could effectively engage the *McRea*, another Confederate ram, the *Van Dorn*, had succeeded in severely striking the stem of the *Cincinnati*, and had been joined by a third ram, the *Sumter*, with which she assailed the *Mound City*, just after the latter had silenced the *McRae's* heavy bow-gun. Broadside after broadside was hurled against the three rams, until the *Sumter* struck the *Mound City* with such force as to cause a formidable breach in the bow.

The latter would soon have been totally disabled but for the Federal gunboat *Benton* coming up and engaging the rams with her 50-pound Parrott guns. With these she raked the rams in turn fore and aft, and in a short time had caused the retirement of the *Van Dorn* and *Sumter*, as well as the hauling down of the flag from the *McRae*. A shell had exploded the latter's boiler, killing and scalding many on board, before she floated in a thoroughly disabled condition down the stream. The pilot of the *McRae*, and Captain Stembel, of the *Cincinnati*, were both very severely wounded.

June, 1862.

The Federal and Confederate vessels remained in close proximity to one another, and without bringing about any serious engagement, until the 6th of the following month. Captain Davis had learned on the 4th that Memphis, and the forts defending its approach, had just been evacuated as a natural sequence to the abandonment of Corinth. He had immediately occupied Fort Pillow and Fort Randolph, forcing the Confederate flotilla to fall back along the Arkansas shore in front of the City of Memphis, and had then stationed himself within a mile and a half of the latter city.

Early on the 6th, Captain Davis, whose fleet had been strengthened by several stern-wheel rams, built by and under the command of Colonel Charles Ellett, Jr., moved toward the Confederate vessels. The *Cairo* took the lead, and was first fired upon only by the Confederate gunboat *Little Rebel*; but during the one-and-a-half hours' engagement that followed, the entire fleet on both sides took an active part. The Federals had four rams, the *Monarch*, *Lancaster*, *Switzerland* and *Queen of the West*, besides five gunboats, the *Benton* (flag-ship), *Cairo*, *St. Louis*, *Carondelet* and the *Louisville*, to which were opposed the Confederate rams *Van Dorn* and *Sumter*, and the gunboats *General Bragg*, *General Lovell*, *Jeff. Thompson*, *Beauregard*, *General Price*, and the *Little Rebel*.

The result was most disastrous to the Confederates. The *General Lovell* and *Beauregard* were sunk; the *General Price* and *Little Rebel* were run ashore and abandoned; the *Jeff. Thompson* was burned, and the *Sumter* and *General Bragg* were captured, the *Van Dorn* alone escaping down the river.

Immediately after the engagement was over, the Federal fleet anchored off Memphis, which city was promptly occupied by two regiments under Colonel Fitch, who was appointed its provost-marshal.

MORGAN'S OPERATIONS IN KENTUCKY AND TENNESSEE.

The Confederate cavalry leader, John H. Morgan, under the stimulus given by reason of the successful repulse of the Army of the Potomac before Richmond, planned a raid, from his mountain camp in Tennessee, through Kentucky, with the hope of possibly crossing the Ohio River and striking a blow in the comparatively unprotected territory of Ohio and Indiana.

July, 1862.

The daring leader issued a ringing proclamation announcing the defeats met by the Federal troops, the advance northward of the army of Lee, and calling on all "to rally to their country's call, and drive from their midst the monster of oppression."

Morgan and his band captured Paris and Cynthiana, levying heavy contributions on the inhabitants, which exploits aroused the citizens of Covington, who met and at once determined to drive the raiding party back into Tennessee. Men

FEDERAL ARMY BEFORE RICHMOND RECONNOITERING IN FORCE TO PREVENT THE
GENERAL HOOKER ENGAGE THE CONF
FROM A SKETCH O

[illegible] TO PREVENT THE [illegible] OF REINFORCEMENTS TO [illegible] AGAINST POPE ON THE RAPPAHANNOCK.
GENERAL HOOKER ENGAGE THE CONFEDERATES AT MALVERN HILL, AUGUST [illegible]
[illegible]

THE FIGHT AT LICKING BRIDGE, CYNTHIANA, KY., BETWEEN THE FEDERAL TROOPS AND THE CONFEDERATE RAIDERS UNDER MORGAN.

From a Sketch by H. Lovie.

of all ages seized their muskets, and announced themselves as ready for battle. The only effect of this raid was to show the Confederate Government that the people of Kentucky were determined to unite their fortunes with the Federal States; and from this time forward the Northern army received large accessions of volunteers from the young men of Kentucky, anxious to meet and punish the Confederate raiders. On the 20th of July General Smith arrived at Somerset in pursuit of Morgan, and found that he had made good his escape through the Cumberland Gap, into Tennessee.

MORGAN'S RAIDERS BIVOUACKING IN COURT SQUARE, PARIS, KY., AFTER LEVYING CONTRIBUTIONS ON THE INHABITANTS

From a Sketch by H. Lovie.

NAVAL COMBAT ON THE YAZOO RIVER.

SECOND only to the memorable combat between the *Merrimack* and the *Monitor* in Hampton Roads was the duel between the United States gunboat *Carondelet* and the Confederate ram *Arkansas*, fought July 15th, 1862, at the confluence of the Yazoo and Mississippi Rivers.

The Federal gunboat *Carondelet*, accompanied by the *Tyler*, had been sent by Commodore Farragut to survey the Yazoo River, and ascertain the exact position and condition of the Confederate iron-plated ram *Arkansas*, which reports had represented as a monster of tremendous power. The two gunboats anchored for the night of the 14th at the mouth of the Yazoo, fifteen miles above Vicksburg, and, on the morning of the 15th, steamed up that river, the *Tyler* considerably in the advance. Presently, at a bend, the *Tyler* suddenly came upon the *Arkansas*, steaming down and toward her. The first salute was a Rodman round shot, which howled over the deck of the *Tyler*, followed by another and another. The *Tyler* returning, gave the monster a broadside, but found the shot to glance off her armored decks, doing no harm. Meanwhile, the heavy shot from the *Arkansas* had pierced the armored sides of the *Tyler*, and Captain Gwin soon turned her bow down-stream, closely pursued by the *Arkansas*, which showed great speed. The shot from the *Arkansas* had nearly disabled the *Tyler*, and already killed or wounded 25 of her crew. Her gallant captain, putting on all speed, replied as best he could with the stern gun. Captain Walke of the *Carondelet* now ordered the *Tyler* to proceed down the river and warn the fleet of the danger, while he engaged the *Arkansas*. The bow guns of the *Carondelet*, admirably worked, struck her opponent with rapidity and precision, but the enormous strength of the iron-plating prevented any perceptible effect. In return, the shot from the rifled and smooth-bore guns of the *Arkansas* pierced through and through the *Carondelet*, and soon determined Captain Walke to board the enemy. This they did, only to find no enemy to oppose them; in fact, the crew safely locked themselves inside their iron-proof shell, and from loopholes in her deck poured hot water, steam, and shot from guns and pistols, which was in turn replied to by the same weapons from the *Carondelet*. While this strange warfare was going on, the grapples lost their hold by the vessels running aground, and the boats soon drifted apart, ending the conflict, the *Arkansas* allowing herself to drift down the river, while the *Carondelet* remained aground. Meanwhile, the *Tyler* had alarmed the fleet, and they made hasty preparations to receive the powerful visitor. As the *Arkansas* approached, he first encountered *Gunboat No. 6*, of Farragut's fleet, which sent a ball from a heavy Dahlgren gun through her sides, and received a terrible broadside in return. The *Arkansas* held her way and passed the *Louisville*, which gave her full benefit of broadside and bow guns. Having now gained a position from which every shot told on the fleet, she used all her guns on transports and gunboats indiscriminately, and received in return but slight injury, owing to her rapid movements and impregnable armor. She passed the *Hartford*, *Iroquois* and *Richmond*, pursued by the *Benton*, *Louisville* and *Cincinnati*. The *Essex* managed to send two 100-pound steel shot fairly through her sides; one, below the water-line, caused her to leak. The *Richmond* also sent a 100-pound Parrott shot completely through her. The ram *Lancaster No. 3*

MICHAEL CORCORAN.

EXCITEMENT AT COVINGTON, KY., ON HEARING OF THE CAPTURE OF CYNTHIANA BY THE CONFEDERATE RAIDER MORGAN.
GATHERING OF ARMED CITIZENS.
FROM A SKETCH BY H. LOVIE.

RECEPTION OF GENERAL MICHAEL CORCORAN, BY THE MAYOR AND CITIZENS OF NEW YORK CITY,

DESPERATE NAVAL COMBAT BETWEEN THE CONFEDERATE IRONCLAD RAM "ARKANSAS"

RECEPTION OF GENERAL MICHAEL CORCORAN, BY THE MAYOR AND CITIZENS OF NEW YORK CITY, AUGU[illegible] ON HIS RELEASE FROM THE CONFEDERATE PRISON, IN WHICH HE HAD BEEN CONFINED ONE YEAR

DESPERATE NAVAL COMBAT BETWEEN THE CONFEDERATE IRONCLAD RAM "ARKANSAS" AND THE [illegible] GUNBOAT "CARONDELET," AT THE MOUTH OF THE YAZOO RIVER, TUESDAY, JULY 15th, [illegible]

From a Sketch by an Officer

CONFEDERATE BATTERIES SHELLING THE FEDERAL POSITION ON THE NIGHT OF THE BATTLE OF CEDAR MOUNTAIN, AUGUST 9TH, 1862
WOUNDED MEN LYING ON THE GROUND. M'DOWELL'S CORPS MARCHING ON THE FIELD.

From a Sketch by Edwin Forbes.

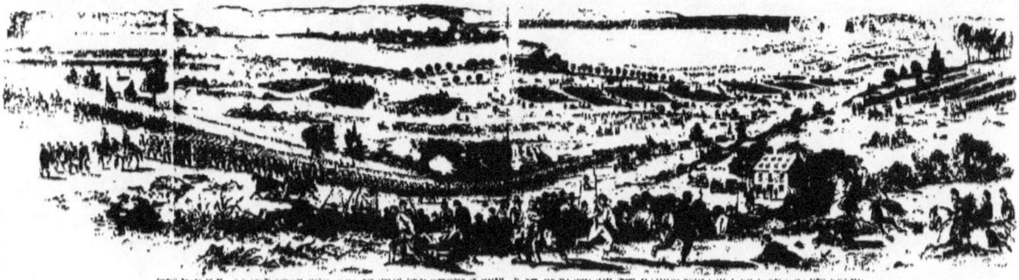

started to run down the intruder, but received a shot which severed her steam-pipe and stopped her progress.

Notwithstanding the large fleet opposed to her, the *Arkansas* passed them all, and gained the protection of the Confederate batteries below. The *Arkansas* was commanded by Captain J. N. Brown, an old steamboat-man and a liberal contributor to the Confederate cause.

POPE'S CAMPAIGN IN VIRGINIA.

The military authorities in Washington, toward the middle of July, 1862, became apprehensive that the Confederates were preparing for an attack upon the capital, and General Halleck immediately made arrangements to offset any demonstration that might be attempted in that quarter. General Pope, who had, on the 26th of June, been placed at the head of the Army of Virginia, was ordered to summon to him General Cox's force, then in Western Virginia, and to cross the Rappahannock in order to threaten the Confederate lines of communication by way of Gordonsville, which latter place was the real key to the southern entrances of the Shenandoah Valley. He issued an address to his army which promised a new system of operations.* McClellan was at the same time seeking to prevent the Confederate army from precipitating their whole force upon Pope, by a succession of reconnoissances in force, which for a time kept Lee's army anxiously on the defensive, and awaiting the next move. The most notable of these reconnoissances took place at daylight of Tuesday, the 5th of August, when a force of cavalry and artillery, commanded by General Hooker, advanced as far as Malvern Hill, and there engaged a Confederate post close by the James River. The latter was in command of Major Pickett, and was defended by the Fauquier Virginia Battery, in charge of Captain Stribling, supported by two regiments of cavalry and the Eighth and Seventeenth Georgia Regiments of Infantry.

The Eighth Illinois Regiment charged upon the battery under cover of Captain Benson's guns, and was promptly followed by the First Brigade of Hooker's division, under General Grover. These made such rapid headway, notwithstanding the excellent range the Confederates had obtained of the Federal position, that by the time the other brigades came up it was found that the post was abandoned. A pursuit was ordered and was continued until dark, when the Federals were recalled, and bivouacked for the night on the field of battle. They had lost 17 in killed and wounded, and had taken nearly 100 prisoners. Hooker's force remained on the field till the following Friday, when they retired to their former position.

McClellan's plans were suddenly broken up by an order from Washington, which directed him to withdraw from the Peninsula, and to transfer his army to Aquia Creek, where Burnside's forces had, some time before, stopping *en route* at Newport News, been ordered to proceed from North Carolina. In the execution of this order, McClellan displayed much of that engineering skill for which he had already become noted. With the aid of an excellent officer and engineer, Colonel McLeod Murphy, and under cover of Commodore Wilkes's gunboat flotilla, he soon built an admirable pontoon-bridge extending across the Chickahominy River—nearly a mile from its confluence with the James—which enabled him to transport his entire force of infantry, cavalry and artillery, on the 15th, 16th, 17th and 18th of August. This was effected without the loss of a single man, or of anything excepting twenty pontons, which were destroyed after the army had passed.

August, 1862. On the 7th of August, Pope concentrated his infantry between Sperryville and Culpepper Court House, and sent the cavalry in the direction of Gordonsville. He lost no time completing reconnoissances in all directions, one of the reconnoitring parties under General Samuel W. Crawford being successful in driving away a Confederate force stationed at Orange Court House, which place the Federals immediately occupied.

Seeing this, Jackson and Ewell crossed the Rappidan, near Burnett's Ford, on the following day, and, in turn, forced back the Federal cavalry that had been stationed there. Crawford was at once sent forward, and on the morning of the 9th Banks followed with his entire corps to aid Crawford, who, by that time, had his force well deployed near Cedar or Slaughter's Mountain.

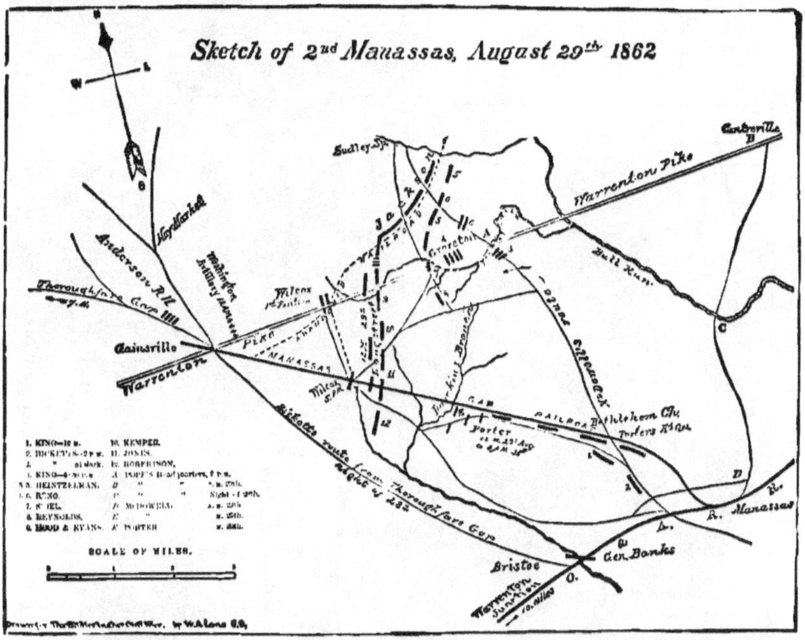

SHOWING THE POSITION OF THE TROOPS, PREPARATORY TO THE SECOND BATTLE OF BULL RUN, AUGUST 29TH, 1862.

* WASHINGTON, July 14, 1862.

TO THE OFFICERS AND SOLDIERS OF THE ARMY OF VIRGINIA: By special assignment of the President of the United States, I have assumed command of this army.

I have spent two weeks in learning your whereabouts, your condition, and your wants; in preparing you for active operations, and in placing you in positions from which you can act promptly, and to the purpose.

I have come to you from the West, where we have always seen the backs of our enemies—from an army whose business it has been to seek the adversary, and to beat him when found—whose policy has been attack, and not defense.

In but one instance has the enemy been able to place our Western armies in a defensive attitude.

I presume that I have been called here to pursue the same system, and to lead you against the enemy.

It is my purpose to do so, and that speedily.

I am sure you long for the opportunity to win the distinction you are capable of achieving. That opportunity I shall endeavor to give you.

Meanwhile, I desire you to dismiss from your minds certain phrases which I am sorry to find much in vogue amongst you.

I hear constantly of taking strong positions and holding them—of lines of retreat and of bases of supplies. Let us discard such ideas.

The strongest position a soldier should desire to occupy is one from which he can most easily advance against the enemy.

Let us study the probable lines of retreat of our opponents, and leave our own to take care of themselves.

Let us look before, and not behind.

Success and glory are in the advance.

Disaster and shame lurk in the rear.

Let us act on this understanding, and it is safe to predict that your banners shall be inscribed with many a glorious deed, and that your names will be dear to your countrymen forever.

JOHN POPE,
Major-General Commanding.

FEDERAL BAGGAGE-TRAIN OF POPE'S ARMY MAKING THEIR WAY TOWARD MANASSAS JUNCTION.

From a Sketch by Edwin Forbes

That same afternoon, Jackson came upon the Federal advance, and decided to engage it before reinforcements should come up. General Ewell was ordered forward, and with two of his brigades advanced to the west of the mountain, while Early took the remaining brigade along the Culpeper Road, and with part of Jackson's division formed in line of battle upon a ridge to the right, directly facing the Federal position. General Charles S. Winder, with "Jackson's Own," afterward marched upon the left of the road, his own brigade being then held in by Colonel Roland, while Campbell's and Taliaferro's brigades remained to support the artillery.

At about four o'clock, one of Early's small batteries opened upon Gordon's and Crawford's position, and in a short time nearly all the artillery on both sides became engaged. Under cover of its fire, Winder's force was thrown forward in the direction of the woods, and was followed by Thomas's brigade of A. P. Hill's division, which came upon the scene at about five o'clock, when the conflict was at its height.

Banks was at a disadvantage, for he had not only superior numbers to contend against, but the Confederates were stationed upon an elevation from which their batteries proved very effective. He therefore concluded to assail the latter, and ordered a charge to be at once made upon them.

The Federal advance met with a perfect storm of shot and shell, but, nevertheless, moved ahead across the open fields, and scarcely faltered until the base of the mountain was reached. There a large force of fresh Confederate troops suddenly emerged from the woods, and fell so heavily upon part of his force as to compel it to fall back.

The remainder, however, pushed ahead, and made such an onset that the extreme of the Confederate line was turned and broken up in confusion; but this was only momentary, for Jackson himself had rapidly come forward, reformed the lines, and brought the fresh troops of Archer's and of Pender's brigades into action.

The Federal progress was thus rapidly checked, and the Confederates, with Hill's division in the lead, soon pressed forward with so much vigor as to compel the prompt retreat of the Federals along the entire front. The latter were pursued relentlessly until they reached the line which Pope had already formed with Ricketts's division of McDowell's corps. The artillery here directed its fire so actively upon the pursuers, that they were compelled to desist from any further aggression. This story of the battle is vividly described by Edwin Forbes, the artist, who was on the field, and furnishes the sketches as given herewith. He says: "The scene at night was very striking. It was past ten o'clock. There was a bright moonlight and a clear blue sky. We were on rising ground while the enemy's batteries were shelling us from the woods, our batteries replying, and one by one driving them further back. The hospital was near our position, and wounded men were lying on the ground, waiting their turn to receive surgical attention. Near them were groups of stragglers, and ulances, ammunition-wagons, etc. I have taken my sketch just as McDowell's corps was marching on the field."

General Sigel had marched his corps all the night preceding the battle, but by reason of the misinterpretation of orders as to which route he was expected to take, did not come upon the scene until nightfall.

In this day's engagement, which is called the battle of Cedar Run, or Cedar Mountain, the Confederates lost nearly 1,300 men, and the Federals about 1,800 in killed, wounded and missing. The most serious loss experienced by the Confederates was that of General Winder, who died in a few hours from wounds received while directing the artillery fire at the commencement of the action. On the Federal side, Generals Christopher C. Augur and John W. Geary were wounded, and General Henry Prince made a prisoner, the latter being held as such until the following December.

During the two subsequent days, nothing of importance occurred on either side; but on the evening of the 11th, heavy reinforcements having reached Pope's army, Jackson withdrew from the field across the Rapidan, being made aware that other troops were rapidly coming forward to strengthen the Federal forces.

Reinforcements were, in fact, likewise hurried forward on the side of the Confederates, whose intention it was to strike Pope's army before it could possibly be strengthened, especially by additions from McClellan's forces, which had already reached Aquia Creek. By the 25th of the same month, Lee had matured his plans for the proposed movement.

It was originally intended that Longstreet and Jackson should advance together, but when it was

J. B. RICKETTS.

found that the river had become so much swollen by incessant rains as to render impossible any advantageous crossing, Jackson was ordered to move around the Bull Run range, and to attempt a flank movement by way of Thoroughfare Gap.

Pope had meanwhile been strengthened to such an extent, that when he fell back behind the Rappahannock, there was a Federal force of 45,000 men posted between the Station and Warrenton Springs. He had been ordered to keep up his communication with Fredericksburg, and he was in a position to check any advance upon the capital, and to protect the line by which reinforcements could reach him from Aquia Creek; but the *détour* of Jackson made it imperative on Pope to extend his lines. He called for more troops; but up to the

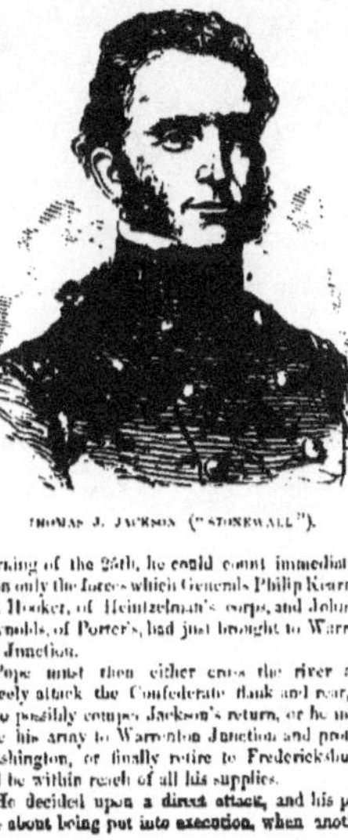

THOMAS J. JACKSON ("STONEWALL").

morning of the 25th, he could count immediately upon only the forces which Generals Philip Kearney and Hooker, of Heintzelman's corps, and John F. Reynolds, of Porter's, had just brought to Warrenton Junction.

Pope must then either cross the river and fiercely attack the Confederate flank and rear, so as to possibly compel Jackson's return, or he must take his army to Warrenton Junction and protect Washington, or finally retire to Fredericksburg, and be within reach of all his supplies.

He decided upon a direct attack, and his plan was about being put into execution, when another heavy rainstorm set in, and so destroyed all means of crossing, that the movement had to be given up. He then determined, Jackson being in his rear, to abandon the river line, and to move upon Manassas Junction.

Longstreet had, in the meantime, been slowly moving his forces away from the Rappahannock so as to unite them with Jackson's corps, which, as it afterward turned out, had passed Thoroughfare Gap, and reached Bristoe Station by the evening of the 26th. Jackson had thus made a forced march of nearly fifty miles in thirty-six hours, and had now at his mercy all of Pope's most important supplies and munitions of war, which were at Manassas Junction, and which Stuart, with a strong force of cavalry and some infantry under Colonel Trimble took possession of, or destroyed, the same evening.

While Pope was advancing with Hooker's division toward Manassas Junction, the forces under McDowell, Sigel and Reynolds were ordered to intercept, if possible, Longstreet's approach by way of Gainesville, which latter commanded the road leading through Thoroughfare Gap. Reno and Kearney were to move toward Greenwich so as to support McDowell if necessary, and Fitz John Porter had orders to remain at Warrenton Junction, and not to move thence to Gainesville until Banks could come up and take his place in holding the Junction.

When Jackson left for Manassas, early on the 27th, Ewell remained at Bristoe Station. There Hooker's force, which was in the advance, encountered Ewell in the afternoon, and after a short engagement, compelled him to fall back upon Manassas, without, however, being able to pursue him in consequence of the destruction of both the railway track and bridge, as well as of the shortage of ammunition.

August, 1862.

As soon as Pope's forces were well in hand, he decided to make the attempt of capturing Jackson's army, and issued the following orders for execution early on the morning of the 28th:

HEADQUARTERS ARMY OF VIRGINIA,
August 27th, 1862—6:30 P.M., Bristoe Station.

GENERAL: The major-general commanding directs that you start at one o'clock to-night, and come forward with your whole corps, or such part of it as is with you, so as to be here by daylight to-morrow morning. Hooker has had a very severe action with the enemy, with a loss of about 300 killed and wounded. The enemy has been driven back, but is retiring along the railroad. We must drive him from Manassas, and clear the country between that place and Gainesville, where McDowell is. If Morell has not joined, you send word to him to push forward immediately; also send word to Banks to hurry forward with all speed to take your place at Warrenton Junction. It is necessary, on all accounts, that you should be here by daylight. I send an officer with this dispatch, who will conduct you to this place. Be sure to send word to Banks who is on the road from Fayetteville, probably in the direction of Bealeton. Say to Banks, also, that he had best run back the railroad trains to this side of Cedar Run. If he is not with you, write him to that effect.

By command of Major-general Pope,
GEORGE D. RUGGLES
Colonel and Chief of Staff

MAJOR-GENERAL F. J. PORTER, *Warrenton Junction*.

P.S.—If Banks is not at Warrenton Junction, leave a regiment of infantry and two pieces of artillery as a guard till he comes up, with instructions to follow you immediately. If Banks is not at the Junction, instruct Colonel Clary to run the trains back to this side of Cedar Run, and post a regiment and section of artillery with it.

By command of Major-general Pope,
GEORGE D. RUGGLES,
Colonel and Chief of Staff

HEADQUARTERS ARMY OF VIRGINIA,
Bristoe Station, August 27th, 1862—9 o'clock P.M.

MAJOR-GENERAL MCDOWELL: At daylight to-morrow morning march rapidly on Manassas Junction with your whole force, resting your right on the Manassas Gap Railroad, throwing your left well to the east. Jackson, Ewell and A. P. Hill are between Gainesville and Manassas Junction. We had a severe fight with them to-day, driving them back several miles along the railroad. If you will march promptly and rapidly at the earliest dawn of day upon Manassas Junction, we shall bag the whole crowd. I have directed Reno to march from Gainesville at the same hour upon Manassas Junction, and Kearney, who is in his rear, to march on Bristoe at daybreak. Be expeditious, and the day is our own.

JOHN POPE,
Major-general Commanding.

HEADQUARTERS, BRISTOE,
August 27th, 1862—9 o'clock, P.M.

MAJOR-GENERAL KEARNEY: At the very earliest blush of dawn push forward with your command with all speed to this place. You cannot be more than three or four miles distant. Jackson, A. P. Hill, and Ewell are in front of us. Hooker has had a severe fight with them to-day. McDowell marches upon Manassas Junction from Gainesville to-morrow at daybreak; Reno upon the same place at the same hour. I want you here at day-dawn, if possible, and we shall bag the whole crowd. Be prompt and expeditious, and never mind wagon trains or roads till this affair is over. Lieutenant Brooks will deliver you this communication. He has one for General Reno and one for General McDowell. Please have these dispatches sent forward instantly by a trusty staff officer, who will be sure to deliver them without fail, and make him bring back a receipt to you before daylight. Lieutenant Brooks will remain with you and bring you to this camp. Use the cavalry I send you to escort your staff officer to McDowell and Reno. JOHN POPE,

Major-general Commanding.

BRISTOE STATION, August 27th, 1862—9 P.M.

TO MAJOR-GENERAL RENO: March at earliest dawn of day, with your whole command, on Manassas Junction. Jackson, Ewell and A. P. Hill are between Gainesville and that place, and if you are prompt and expeditious we shall bag the whole crowd. McDowell advances upon Manassas Junction from Gainesville at the same hour; Kearney on Bristoe. As you value success, be off at the earliest blush of day. Acknowledge the receipt of this, and do not stop to look for roads; and, if necessary, leave guards with your trains. Push across the country whatever artillery can be hauled. I rely on your speed. JOHN POPE,

Major-general Commanding.

WOMEN OF MARYLAND ENTERTAINING THE FEDERAL RECRUITS WHILE EN ROUTE THROUGH BALTIMORE, MD.

The forces of McDowell—including his own, Sigel's and Reynolds's—and Reno were thus to move respectively from Gainesville and from Greenwich to Manassas Junction, while Kearney and Porter were to join Hooker at Bristoe Station, in order to aid in driving Jackson from Manassas.

Jackson had, however, realized in time the dangers by which he was being surrounded, and he had, without unnecessary delay, availed of the only alternative left him. This was to endeavor to effect a junction with Longstreet. He could not do it openly, and therefore resorted to a ruse, in order to deceive the Federals as to his real purpose.

"Jackson's Own" division, which, since Winder's death at Cedar Run, had been placed in charge of General August Taliaferro, was ordered at three o'clock on the morning of the 28th to move directly north, while Ewell and Hill would go to the northeast, as if advancing upon Washington. This they did, and, when at Centreville, a sharp turn to the west brought the different divisions of Jackson's corps once more together later in the day.

Pope's orders could not be literally carried out. Porter had a distance of ten miles to go, along a heavily wooded road, intersected by a great number of streams and marshy lands, and in many places encumbered by some of the two or three thousand wagons belonging to Pope's army. He, nevertheless, so ably directed his already much fatigued force during the extremely dark and occasionally rainy night which followed the reception of Pope's order, that the distance was successfully covered in seven hours; and at eight o'clock on the morning of the 28th he reached Bristoe Station almost simultaneously with the force led by General Kearney.

After holding an interview with Porter, General Pope started for Manassas with Hooker's force, leaving instruction for the divisions of Reno and Kearney to follow promptly. They reached Manassas at about noon, in time for Kearney to engage for a while the rear guard left by Jackson before it fled in the direction of Sudley Springs Road.

Believing that the main portion of Jackson's army had gone to Centreville, Pope began a pursuit in that direction, and ordered McDowell to advance upon Centreville, and Porter to remain at Bristoe till sent for.

Upon receiving Pope's order, McDowell had, on his own responsibility, detailed Ricketts to observe Thoroughfare Gap, and had proceeded with the rest of his force along the main road. His route toward Centreville led him close by Jackson's right, and toward sunset King's division accidentally stumbled upon the Confederates close by Groveton.

Then followed an engagement of nearly four hours' duration, in which the Federal brigades of John Gibbon and part of Abner Doubleday alone took part. The artillery was brought into play so effectively as to cause severe losses on both sides, and fire did not cease until about nine o'clock in the evening, when the Federals fell back some distance for the night. In this engagement General Taliaferro was severely wounded, and General Ewell lost a leg.

Pope's advance reached Centreville in the afternoon, and, believing that McDowell's corps must have intercepted Jackson's retreat, ordered a general movement for the morning of the 29th. King's division and McDowell were to maintain their position on the Warrenton Pike, at all cost; Kearney was to push ahead from Centreville along the Warrenton Turnpike, in order to engage Jackson's front; and Porter was to advance toward Centreville, in the vicinity of which Pope expected a battle.

Jackson, in the meantime, took position between Sudley Springs and Groveton, there to await Longstreet's arrival. He was well posted under shelter of thick woods, with "Jackson's Own," now in charge of General Starke, on the right, supported by the main portion of his artillery, while General A. P. Hill was on the left, and General Alexander R. Lawton, with Ewell's late division, occupied the centre.

Longstreet, however, passed through the Gap much earlier than Pope had contemplated, and after forcing back Ricketts, first to Gainesville and then toward Bristoe Station, took up his position on Jackson's extreme right. King felt compelled during the night to abandon the Warrenton Turnpike, and he retreated toward Bristoe Station, thus facilitating a junction of Longstreet with Jackson.

As soon as Pope learned of King's retreat, he issued another order for Sigel and Reynolds to march upon Groveton and attack Jackson at daylight, while Heintzelman, Reno, Hooker and Kearney would advance from Centreville toward Gainesville. Porter was directed to march upon Gainesville, taking with him King's division in accordance with the following order:

HEADQUARTERS ARMY OF VIRGINIA,
Centreville, August 29th, 1862.

TO MAJOR-GENERAL FITZ JOHN PORTER: Push forward with your corps and King's division, which you will take with you, upon Gainesville. I am following the enemy down the Warrenton Turnpike. Be expeditious, or we will lose much. JOHN POPE,

Major-general Commanding.

When Porter received the last named order he was two and a half miles beyond Manassas, *en route* for Centreville. He immediately retraced his steps, and at about half-past nine o'clock in the morning was again at Manassas. There he was joined by McDowell, and from him learned all concerning the previous night's engagement, and of the proximity of Longstreet's army. Both commanders felt aggrieved, among other things, at the conflicting orders received. McDowell decided to hunt up Ricketts, and join his other forces near Groveton. Porter, meanwhile, advanced his troops, now joined by King's division, in accordance with the orders then in force.

To satisfy McDowell and Porter, each of whom had, unbeknown to the other, asked for specific instructions, the following joint order was issued at 10.30 P.M.:

HEADQUARTERS ARMY OF VIRGINIA,
Centreville, August 29th, 1862.

GENERALS MCDOWELL AND PORTER: You will please move forward with your joint commands toward Gainesville. I sent General Porter written orders to that effect an hour and a half ago. Heintzelman, Sigel and Reno are moving on the Warrenton Turnpike, and must now be not far from Gainesville. I desire that as soon as communication is established between this force and your own the whole command shall halt. It may be necessary to fall back behind Bull Run at Centreville to-night. I presume it will be so on account of our supplies. I have sent no orders of any description to Ricketts, and none to interfere in any way with the movements of McDowell's troops, except what I sent by aide-de-camp last night, which were to hold his position on the Warrenton Pike until the troops from here should fall on the enemy's flank and rear. I do not even know Ricketts's position, as I have not been able to find out where General McDowell was until a late hour this morning. General McDowell will take immediate steps to communicate with General Ricketts, and instruct him to join the other divisions of his corps as soon as practicable. If any considerable advantages are to be gained by departing from this order it will not be strictly carried out. One thing must be held in view: That the troops must occupy a position from which they can reach Bull run to-night or by morning. The indications are that the whole force of the enemy is moving in this direction at a pace that will bring them here by to-morrow night or the next day. My own headquarters will, for the present, be with Heintzelman's corps or at this place.

JOHN POPE,
Major-General Commanding.

This found them a little east of Dawkins Branch. Previous to its reception, however, Porter's skirmishers had exchanged fire with what proved to be Longstreet's men, several of whom had been captured, and informed Porter of Longstreet's arrival.

In the meantime, Sigel had opened upon Jackson's right, as directed, and from a little after six o'clock until half-past ten o'clock much of the infantry and artillery on both sides had at intervals been brought into action. The Federal attacks were so well executed by the divisions of Generals Schurz, Milroy and Schenck, that Jackson had to fall back as far as the abandoned railroad, where the Confederates made a most determined stand. The Federals charged repeatedly upon a steep embankment that here shielded the Confederates, but had to retire before the artillery fire which was there concentrated upon them. Nor did the Federals yield the ground until it became evident that, with the arrival of new troops and batteries, which proved afterward to be Longstreet's, the offensive was about to be taken by Jackson.

The Federals retreated a short distance, and a little after noon were joined by Pope, who placed his newly arrived troops in position. Kearney was given Sigel's right, Reynolds's held the extreme left, and Reno was divided, part being on Reynolds's right, and part placed in support of the centre, between Sigel and Heintzelman, the latter being on the extreme right.

By this time Longstreet had established himself immediately on Jackson's right, extending his line across the Warrenton Turnpike southward to and beyond the Manassas Gap Railroad. General Stuart's cavalry protected the extreme right flank—with General Robertson's brigade in advance—while Longstreet's infantry, with artillery, connected with Jackson in the following order: The divisions of General D. R. Jones, J. L. Kemper, and J. B. Hood, with the Washington Artillery on Hood's left and Wilcox's three brigades supporting.

There was active skirmishing at different points along Pope's line, soon after the arrival of his troops on the ground, and until about four o'clock, when Heintzelman, the divisions of Hooker, Kearney and Reno, were ordered to attack Jackson's left and centre, Pope still apparently ignoring Longstreet's arrival, and believing that McDowell and Porter could be able to turn Jackson's right.

Grover's brigade of Hooker's division advanced boldly in face of a very destructive artillery and infantry fire, and at the point of the bayonet overcame the force holding the abandoned railroad embankment. They soon penetrated a space of about one hundred and fifty yards in width between the brigades of Generals Bryan M. Thomas and Maxey Gregg, for a while completely isolating the latter from the main body. But the Forty-ninth Georgia and the Fourteenth South Carolina Regiment, held in reserve, being quickly brought up, and supported first by Colonel Forno, who then led Hayes's Louisiana brigade, and afterward by the Eighth Louisiana Regiment and Early's brigade, the Federals had to fall back to their first position, after a bitter and prolonged hand-to-hand fight, in which the loses were very severe on both sides.

General Kearney, later, attacked A. P. Hill's division toward its right, and succeeded in doubling its flank upon the centre, but for a short time only, as heavy reserves impeded the further progress of the small Federal force, which had to fall back. There was no combined attacks, the attacks all day being with small bodies, and disconnected with considerable intervals; a series of "spurts," as Heintzelman termed them.

While all this was going on, Porter had conferred with his ranking officer, McDowell, with whom he had ridden over to the right, in order to see if they could establish the communication directed by the joint order. The execution of the latter was found impracticable, and after duly weighing all the suggestions made relative to a possible advance upon Longstreet, McDowell concluded that Porter had better suspend his preparations for attack, and place his troops back into the woods, where they would be concealed, and ready for any emergency of attack or defense, while he would go back and take with him King's division of 8,000 men, which had before been given to Porter, and also Ricketts's division, which would immediately follow King along the road running from Bethlehem Church to Sudley Springs.

McDowell thus left Porter shortly after twelve o'clock, and about half-past five King's division, led by General John P. Hatch, of McDowell's corps, reached Groveton, and at once took place between the positions then held by Sigel.

Hatch, with three brigades of King's division, was ordered to attack by McDowell, who declared, by Pope's direction, the enemy in full retreat. Hatch advanced rapidly a little west of Groveton, when he suddenly encountered Longstreet's troops, in overpowering numbers, advancing to attack.

A fierce encounter took place, lasting till darkness brought it to an end, and resulting in the loss of the field by Hatch, and many killed, wounded, and prisoners.

Porter had frequent skirmishes during the afternoon with the forces of Longstreet in front of him, and at one time believing Sigel was retiring, prepared to go to his assistance. He soon was convinced of his erroneous impressions, and held to his ground, anxiously expecting to hear of McDowell, according to agreement, having taken his position between him and the troops at Groveton. To have gone to Sigel would have been dangerous, if not disastrous. A flank march across the hilly and wooded country was impracticable, especially for artillery, as there was no road and no open space except along the front of Longstreet's lines. Porter could not retire to the Sudley Springs Road, as by doing so his flank and rear would become exposed, and Longstreet's army be free to advance upon Pope. As it afterward proved, he did best by merely keeping his ground, and holding Longstreet in his front, in accord to agreement with McDowell.

Porter, in order to hold Longstreet before him, issued orders about four o'clock for Morell to advance, but upon receiving remonstrances on all sides from his officers, and being shown conclusively the uselessness of the movement, he wisely recalled the orders. The movement of Morell's troops, in consequence of these orders, had the effect of causing Wilcox's division of Longstreet's corps to be taken from in front of Pope and sent over to resist Porter, thus having a better effect than by going to Pope's aid.

Toward sunset the following was received:

HEADQUARTERS IN THE FIELD,
August 29th, 1862—4.30 p. m.

MAJOR-GENERAL PORTER: Your line of march brings you in on the enemy's right flank. I desire you to push forward into action at once on the enemy's flank, and, if possible, on

INFANTRY CHARGE BY THE FEDERALS, AND ROUT OF THE CONFEDERATES, AT BLUE RIDGE PASS, MD., SUNDAY, SEPTEMBER 14TH, 1862.

CENTRE AND RIGHT WING OF McCLELLAN'S ARMY, COMMANDED BY GENERALS HOOKER, SUMNER A
AT THE BATTLE OF ANTIETAM, OR SHA

From a Sketc

BURNSIDE'S DIVISION (LEFT WING).—HAWKINS'S ZOUAVES, COLONEL KIMBALL, CHARGING ON TH

CENTRE AND RIGHT WING OF McCLELLAN'S ARMY, COMMANDED BY GENERALS HOOKER, SUMNER AND [illegible], ENGAGING THE CONFEDERATE FORCES COMMANDED BY LEE, JACKSON AND LONGSTREET, AT THE BATTLE OF ANTIETAM, OR SHARPSBURG, WEDNESDAY, SEPTEMBER 17th, 1862

From a sketch [illegible]

BURNSIDE'S DIVISION (LEFT WING)—HAWKINS'S ZOUAVES, COLONEL KIMBALL, CHARGING ON THE CONFEDERATE BATTERY ON THE HILL, SEPTEMBER 17th, 1862. ROUT OF THE CONFEDERATES

From a sketch [illegible]

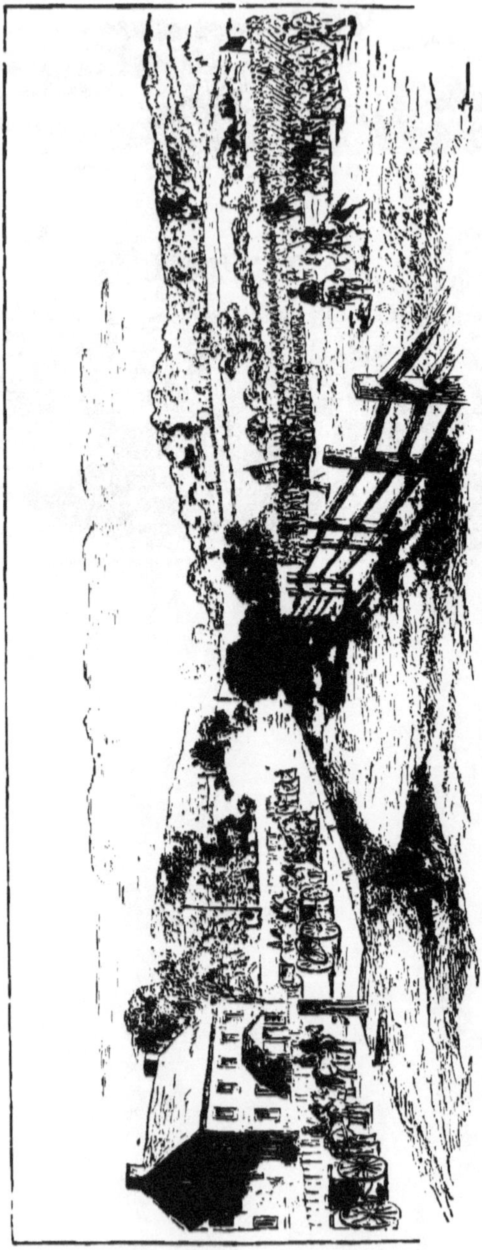

BATTLE OF BLUE RIDGE PASS, MD., SUNDAY, SEPTEMBER 14TH, 1862.—THE CONFEDERATES DRIVEN FROM THE PASS.—VIEW FROM THE NATIONAL ROAD.

FROM A SKETCH BY F. H. SCHELL.

his rear, keeping your right in communication with General Reynolds. The enemy is massed in the woods in front of us, but can be shelled out as soon as you engage their flank. Keep heavy reserves, and use your batteries, keeping well closed to your right all the time. In case you are obliged to fall back, do so to your right and rear, so as to keep you in close communication with the right wing.

JOHN POPE,
Major-general Commanding.

When Pope issued it, he was evidently still ignorant of even the close proximity, much less the actual presence, of Longstreet's corps. The carrying out of the order, as Pope intended it, was of course impossible. Porter's line of march would bring him in Longstreet's front, not on Jackson's right flank, nor could he connect with Reynolds, who was on the other side of the hills, nearly two miles away. But the order was received near dark, too late to execute. Though Porter made preparations to attack, darkness put an end to them.

At half-past eight o'clock Pope sent Porter another order, requiring him to march his command to the field of battle, so as to reach the latter at latest after daybreak the following morning. In accordance therewith, Porter joined Pope early on the 30th with 7,000 of his men, the brigades of Generals Piatt and Griffin having by a misinterpretation of orders marched toward Centreville.

AUGUST, 1862.

Thus, soon after daybreak of the 30th, Pope had concentrated at Groveton all of his army, with the exception of Porter's two brigades alluded to, and of Banks's corps, then in charge of the railroad and wagon-trains at Bristoe Station.

During the night General Lee had made preparations for attacking Pope. He had drawn in Jackson's left from the ground upon which it lay exposed the day previous, and, by the morning of the 30th, Jackson's entire line was much contracted from what it was the previous day, while a small part on the left was at right angles with Longstreet's left, which latter was hidden from view by the intervening woods and hills. Behind a high knoll of land, which commanded nearly all of Lee's front, he had posted forty-eight heavy guns in such manner that he could sweep the ground to the right and left.

Pope thought the Confederate army was retreating along the Warrenton Turnpike, and was confirmed in this belief by the report of a paroled prisoner who had first entered Porter's lines, where his representations had, however, found discredit on all sides. He, therefore, ordered McDowell to pursue the Confederates on their right along the turnpike, which he did, with Porter's corps in the advance, closely followed by King and Reynolds in the centre, while Ricketts, followed by Heintzelman, was to take the Haymarket Road, thereby to turn the enemy's left. Reynolds at first stood on Porter's left, but, in pursuance of Pope's order, moved to Porter's rear—thus leaving the left unguarded against Longstreet.

As the Federals under Porter advanced upon Jackson, the Confederates under Longstreet, massed at the edge of the woods near Groveton, suddenly opened a terrific and destructive fire of shot and shell, enfilading Porter's ranks. At the same time, Longstreet swung his right around, in order to outflank the Federal left, now unprotected by the withdrawal of Reynolds. As soon as discovered, Schenck and Milroy, of Sigel's corps, were sent to Bald Hill to meet this attack, and Reynolds was immediately recalled to their assistance, going in on their left, where Tower, of Ricketts's division, and Sykes, of Porter's corps, subsequently joined them.

Warren had seen the error of removing Reynolds from the left, and had promptly replaced the latter by his own brigade, which, however, was almost destroyed by the advancing enemy under Hood. But his prompt action had held the enemy long enough for Schenck and Milroy to form on his left on Bald Hill.

In the meantime Porter, with his own corps and the division of King, under Hatch, vigorously attacked Jackson, covered by the embankment of the railroad cut. In successive lines, thrice did his troops advance and vigorously attack, and thrice, after damaging inroads upon Jackson, were his lines repulsed, with great slaughter, by the enemy's direct infantry and flanking artillery fires. Forced to desist in his attacks, Porter fell back to hold a defensive position till dark, with part of his troops against Jackson, while another portion under Sykes was sent to the Henry House Hill in support of the left wing.

Longstreet, on the south of the Warrenton Pike, attacking direct with Hood and Evans, and swinging around Kemper's and Jones's divisions (the withdrawal by Pope of Porter's troops from Dawkins Branch having left them free) to the attack of the Federals on Bald Hill and south of Henry Hill, gradually forced the latter back until dark, when the battle ceased much to the relief of both wearied and decimated armies.

The night of the 30th was dark, but Pope successfully effected his retreat across Bull Run to Centreville, where he reformed his troops, to meet any advance of Lee's army.

The corps of Generals Franklin and Sumner joined Pope's army at Centreville in time to have checked the flanking movement which Jackson had intended early on Monday, the 31st. For that purpose Jackson took his own and Ewell's division across Sudley Ford and on the Little River Turnpike, but a furious storm delayed all further advance, and the contemplated attack was forcibly abandoned.

A perfect tempest of unusually cold rain raged during the whole night, and continued throughout all of the 1st, but, notwithstanding this, Lee's heavy columns followed the course taken by Jackson and Ewell along the Little River Turnpike, and in the afternoon of the last-named day it became evident to the Federals that an attempt would soon be made to turn Pope's right, then near Germantown, thus opening the road to Washington.

SEPTEMBER, 1862.

To prevent this, Pope ordered Hooker to push ahead toward Germantown, which he did, taking position across the turnpike. At Hooker's left, and along the Centreville Road, stood McDowell, Franklin, Heintzelman, Porter, and Sumner, in the order named, while Reno, closely supported by Kearney, occupied the Ox Hill Heights, near Chantilly. Banks, who had brought the wagon-train from Bristoe Station, was ordered to move along the old Braddock Road toward Alexandria.

At about five o'clock "Stonewall" Jackson appeared in Reno's front, and, with Ewell's division, under Lawton, in the centre, and Hill on the extreme right, fiercely engaged the Federal advance. The contest was telling severely upon Reno, when General Isaac I. Stevens, commanding the Second Division, ordered a charge, which he led in person, but this proved unavailing against the serried Confederate ranks. Stevens was shot dead, and for a moment Reno's whole forces seemed about to fall back in disorder, but Kearney advanced to Reno's aid with Birney's brigade in the front, closely followed by McDowell's and Hooker's forces.

Just then a furious thunderstorm burst over the field, almost precluding the use of ammunition, and, nothing daunted, Kearney moved his batteries ahead, and, planting one himself, personally directed their fire upon the Confederates. Then, perceiving a gap left by Stevens's retiring division, he pushed forward to reconnoitre the ground, but was shot dead while he was unwittingly in the Confederate lines.

The command of Kearney's division now devolved upon General David B. Birney, who at once ordered a bayonet-charge, which was brilliantly executed by Colonel Tom Egan with the First, Thirty-eighth and Fortieth New York Volunteer Regiments. The Confederates were driven back, and darkness put an end to the conflict, which has been variously designated as the battle of Chantilly, of Germantown, and of Ox Hill.

Pope found himself in no condition to continue his campaign, and retired within the fortifications of Washington. The casualties of his forces, from August 16th to September 2d, were, exclusive of Porter's corps, in killed, wounded and missing, 10,509. Porter, who joined his corps to Pope's army at Warrenton Junction on the 27th of August, lost 2 151 on the 29th and 30th.

LETTER FROM EDWIN FORBES,

FROM THE BATTLEFIELD OF THE SECOND BATTLE OF BULL RUN, AUGUST 30TH, 1862.

(OUR SPECIAL ARTIST.)

FIELD OF BATTLE, Monday, September 1st, 1862.

MR. FRANK LESLIE: DEAR SIR—I send with this letter my sketches of the hard-fought battles on the old field of Bull Run. I arrived on the ground just before the beginning of the fight. The scene looking from the crest of the hill on our left was very impressive. On the plain below lay large bodies of infantry; some in line of battle, and others en masse. It reminded the spectator more of a grand review than of the beginning of an affair in which thousands would probably lay down their lives.

Our men were weary, tired and worn out by the long marches and excitement of the past ten days, and required a stimulant until they got into the thickest of the fight; a hearty cheer and yell would be worth a thousand men at such a time, yet nobody seemed to feel the greatness of the occasion.

The fight was opened by our batteries in front of the hill and woods on the centre and left. It was immediately replied to by the enemy's batteries in the orchard and along the crest of the hill about a quarter of a mile distant. After the artillery fighting had lasted some time, our infantry

FITZ JOHN PORTER.

attacked the enemy's left flank. The fighting here was very severe; huge columns of yellow smoke rolled up from the roads; the faint rattle and roll of distant musketry came across the open fields, interrupted occasionally by the boom of a heavy gun. Meanwhile, the enemy were making a very serious attempt to turn our left. Part of McDowell's corps was sent to drive them back. They moved in solid column across the field from the right, while the enemy, in overwhelming force, was pushing our small number back.

The fighting was terribly fierce at this point, the enemy throwing all their force on this flank. Our men retired across the field in the foreground and into the woods. On the right the enemy was driven from his position.

I have been at four battles where Jackson commanded the enemy's forces, and could not help remarking the similarity of the ground chosen by him in his several actions. His position is such that he invariably has a dense wood on one of our flanks and open ground on the other, and by moving his whole force under cover of the wood, outflanks us.

I was in the hottest of the fire for quite a while. When I attempted to get away I found myself cornered. I started with a party of skirmishers through a dense wood, leading my horse, and after passing under a severe fire of shell, I got a safe position. Yours, EDWIN FORBES.

FITZ JOHN PORTER.

BORN at Portsmouth, N. H., August 30th, 1822; was admitted to the United States Military Academy at West Point, July, 1841, from which he graduated on the 11th of July, 1845, and entered the army as brevet second lieutenant of artillery. He served throughout the Mexican War, and was wounded at the assault on the City of Mexico, September 13th, 1847. For his gallantry at Chapultepec and Molino del Rey, he was given the brevets of captain and major. From 1849 to 1855, he was stationed at West Point as instructor of artillery and cavalry, and was for a year the adjutant of the post. From West Point he was transferred to the adjutant-general's department, and during the years 1857-60, was adjutant-general of the Utah expedition.

Upon the breaking out of the Civil War, he was appointed colonel of the Fifteenth United States Infantry, and soon promoted to be a brigadier-general of Volunteers, serving as chief of staff with Generals Patterson and Banks until sent, in August, 1861, to command a division in the Army of the Potomac. He directed successfully the siege of Yorktown, and upon the Federal occupation of the latter place, was given the command of the Fifth Corps, which comprised the divisions of Morell and Sykes, to which was added Hunt's Reserve Artillery and McCall's division of Pennsylvania Reserves, and formed the right wing of McClellan's army. This corps took a leading part notably in the battles of New Bridge, Hanover Court House, Mechanicsville, Gaines's Mills and Malvern Hill, suffering great losses during the last named engagement. It also distinguished itself at the second battle of Bull Run, fought August 30th, 1862, as well as at the battle of Antietam, September 16th and 17th, and of Shepherdstown on September 18th and 19th of the same year. In the following November, General Porter was arraigned before a court-martial upon the charge of disobedience of orders at the second battle of Bull Run, and he was cashiered, January 21st, 1863.

Since that date he has been engaged in civil life—at times in Colorado in charge of mines belonging to New York associations, and also in business in New York City. He was likewise employed by the State of New Jersey, and, as superintendent, built the Asylum for the Insane at Morristown, one of the finest buildings of the kind in the world, requiring the careful expenditure of over $2,000,000.

In 1875 he was appointed Commissioner of Public Works of the City of New York, and subsequently was assistant-receiver of the New Jersey Central Railroad. At the time of writing (July, 1884), General Porter has, after a thorough revision of all the facts in the case, and an ample discussion of the same by both political parties in the two Houses of Congress, been completely exonerated from the charges made before the court-martial, by the passage of a Bill restoring him to the rank of colonel in the Regular Army. But the President has declined to give that Bill his approval, assigning as a reason that it trespassed upon the powers and privileges of his position granted by the Constitution. The Bill was passed by the House of Representatives over the President's veto, but failed so to pass the Senate, just before the adjournment of that body. General Porter resides at Morristown, N. J.

GEORGE W. PRATT.

BORN at Prattsville, Greene County, N. Y., April 18th, 1830; commenced his studies in his native State and completed them abroad. After an extended tour of Europe he returned home in 1850, was made a captain, and afterward succeeded his father, Zadock Pratt, in the colonelcy of the Twentieth New York Militia Regiment. He also was cashier of his father's bank at Prattsville; represented his district in the State Senate, 1858-9; on the breaking out of the Civil War, he equipped his Militia Regiment, which left Kingston, N. Y., for the capital, on the 28th of April, 1861, and completed the three months' service for which it had enlisted. The regiment, on its return, re-enlisted under the name of the Ulster County Guard, or Twentieth Regiment, New York Volunteers, and under Colonel Pratt took the field for three years, and on the 7th of November, 1861, joined General Wadsworth's brigade across the Potomac, remaining in camp at Upton's Hill, Va., up to the end of the year. With it Colonel Pratt afterward participated in engagements at Falls Church, Rappahannock Station, and White Sulphur Springs, Va., distinguishing himself more particularly at the second battle of Bull Run, where, on the 30th of August, 1862, he received the wound which compelled his immediate retirement from the field, and from which he died at Albany, on the 11th of the subsequent month.

ISAAC INGALLS STEVENS.

BORN at Andover, Mass., March 25th, 1818; entered the United States Military Academy at West Point, whence he graduated, July 1st, 1839, at the head of his class; served in the Mexican War, and was breveted captain for gallant and meritorious service at Contreras, Churubusco, and Chapultepec, as well as breveted major for bravery displayed at the storming of the San Cosme Gate. From 1849 until his resignation from the army in March, 1853, he was principal assistant in charge of the office of the United States Coast Survey at Washington. He afterward conducted the pioneer survey of the route for the Northern Pacific Railway, was appointed by President Pierce Governor of Washington Territory, and represented the latter in Congress from 1857 to 1861. When the Civil War broke out he was on the Pacific Coast, and lost no time in reaching Washington, where he tendered his services to the Government. He was made colonel of the Seventy-ninth New York Regiment of Highlanders upon the death of its commander, James Cameron, and on the 28th of September, 1861, was promoted to be a brigadier-general of Volunteers. He accompanied General T. W. Sherman to South Carolina, and participated in the engagements around Port

GENERAL McCLELLAN AND HIS ARMY PASSING THROUGH FREDERICK CITY, MD., IN PURSUIT OF THE CONFEDERATES, SEPTEMBER 12TH, 1862.

FROM A SKETCH BY EDWIN FORBES.

Royal. Upon returning from North Carolina with General Reno to the Army of Virginia, he was made a major-general, July 4th, 1862. He greatly distinguished himself with the Ninth Corps at the second battle of Bull Run and at Chantilly, and at the last named engagement was shot through the head and instantly killed, while gallantly leading a charge, on the 1st of September, 1862.

CAPTURE OF HARPER'S FERRY,

AND

BATTLES AT SOUTH MOUNTAIN, ANTIETAM CREEK AND SHARPSBURG.

AFTER the battle of Chantilly, Pope renewed the request he had previously made to be relieved of command and allowed to return West. His request was more favorably received, and on the 2d of September, President Lincoln and General Halleck called upon McClellan and placed in his hands the "command of the fortifications of Washington, and of all the troops for the defense of the capital."

SEPTEMBER, 1862.

The Federal army, which had fallen back from Chantilly to the fortifications around Washington and Alexandria, was at once reorganized. Burnside, Porter, Franklin and Sumner retained the command of their respective corps, but McDowell's army was placed in charge of General Hooker, and to General Mansfield was given the command of the corps heretofore led by General Banks, who now had charge of the fortifications around the capital.

The day following the battle of Chantilly, General Lee was joined by General D. H. Hill with his five brigades, thus increasing the Confederate army to about 70,000 men. With these he determined upon the immediate invasion of Maryland. The Potomac was crossed about midway between Harper's Ferry and Washington, not far from Ball's Bluff, and on the 7th of September, Lee's army encamped at Frederick City, the passage of the river having been accompanied by a general uncovering of heads under the strains of "My Maryland," which issued from all the bands, and the words of which were likewise simultaneously taken up in every direction.

Lee had supposed that his advance would lead to the Federal evacuation of Harper's Ferry and of Martinsburg. This not occurring, he determined upon the attempt to capture both places, and for that purpose he divided his army, sending Jackson's corps and half of Longstreet's to Martinsburg to take the latter place, and then move down to Harper's Ferry. Lee retained with him the remainder of Longstreet's corps, D. H. Hill's division, and nearly all of the cavalry. General Lafayette McLaws was ordered to seize Maryland Heights, on the north side of the Potomac, opposite Harper's Ferry, with his own and R. H. Anderson's force, while General W. S. Walker would capture London Heights, situated at a point on the southeastern side of the Shenandoah River, where it unites with the Potomac.

BURNSIDE'S DIVISION CARRYING THE BRIDGE OVER ANTIETAM CREEK, AND STORMING THE CONFEDERATE POSITION, SEPTEMBER 17TH, 1862.

FROM A SKETCH BY EDWIN FORBES.

McLaws engaged Maryland Heights on the 13th, and occupied the place, after a spirited though brief contest, the Federals under Colonel Ford falling back across the Potomac to Harper's Ferry. London Heights was taken possession of on the same day without opposition. In the meantime, Jackson had pushed on rapidly, reaching Williamsport on the 11th, and entered Martinsburg on the 12th, while Lee's force had crossed to the west of South Mountain, Longstreet going to Hagerstown and D. H. Hill to Boonsboro', where the army headquarters would be established after the intended reduction of Harper's Ferry. The cavalry under General Stuart remained northeast of South Mountain to retard the Federal advance, and the force at Boonsboro' would prevent any possible Federal escape through Pleasant Valley.

General McClellan took the field on the 7th, having previously brought his army north of Washington into Maryland, and advanced toward Frederick City in five parallel lines, covering both Washington and Baltimore. The right wing was commanded by General Burnside, who had Hooker's (McDowell's First) corps, besides his own Ninth Corps, under Reno; General Sumner held the centre with his own Second Corps and Banks's Twelfth Corps, under Mansfield; and General Franklin had the Sixth Corps and Couch's division on the extreme left. Porter's corps, except Sykes remained in Washington until the 12th, and reached the army on the 14th, near Turner's Gap.

The Federal advance entered Frederick City on the 13th, after a brisk skirmish with the Confederate rear guard, and there found a copy of Lee's order of the 9th directing the movements of the Confederate army from Frederick. This order, which had been accidentally left behind, revealed to McClellan the actual disposition of Lee's forces, which did not have in view any immediate attack upon either Baltimore or the capital, so long as McClellan's army remained between the two cities.

SEPTEMBER, 1862.

McClellan immediately ordered an advance toward South Mountain, Burnside, followed by Sumner, going in the direction of Boonsboro' through Turner's Gap, and Franklin proceeding through Crampton Gap, which lies directly in front of Burkittsville, and opens into Pleasant Valley.

General Pleasanton, who commanded the Federal cavalry, was close to Turner's Gap on the afternoon of the 13th, but the heads of the Federal infantry columns did not reach the passes until the morning of the following day. Reconnoissances having been made by Pleasanton's cavalry, and by the First and Second Brigades of Cox's division, commanded respectively by Colonels E. P. Scammon and George

OPENING OF THE BATTLE OF ANTIETAM.—HOOKER'S DIVISION FORDING THE CREEK TO ATTACK THE CONFEDERATES.

From a Sketch by F. H. Schell.

THE FEDERAL ARTILLERY TAKING POSITION AT THE BATTLE OF SOUTH MOUNTAIN.

From a Sketch by F. H. Schell.

Crook, Reno ordered an assault in the Confederate position south of Turner's Gap.

Under cover of McMullin's and Simmons's batteries the Federals led by Rodman, Wilcox, Sturgis, and Cox, with the latter in the immediate advance, rapidly marched up the sides of the mountain. Cox soon encountered General Garland's brigade of Hill's division, with which he had a fierce engagement, resulting in the death of the Confederate commander, and the consequent falling back of the brigade. Longstreet hurried from Hagerstown at Hill's request, and by the time Rodman, Sturgis and Wilcox reached the scene the Confederate force in command of the Gap, and of both crests, had been swollen to nearly 30,000 men.

At about two o'clock Hooker's corps arrived, and moved toward the Confederate left along the old Hagerstown Road, closely followed by Meade from the Kittocton Creek. Ricketts was shortly after ordered to move in the same direction along the turnpike simultaneously with Cox's advance by Reno's division on the extreme Federal left, and by King's division, commanded by General John P. Hatch, in the centre.

The Federal movement was admirably executed, in face of a well-directed fire from the Confederates, who had the advantage of position, and could contest almost every inch of the steep, wooded and rocky approach. By four o'clock the engagement became general, and the entire ground was vigorously contested until the crest was reached, and darkness put an end to the fight.

In the last named engagement, the total loss on both sides in killed, wounded and missing, was nearly 3,000. General Jesse L. Reno was killed while at the head of his command, and was replaced by General Cox, General Hatch and Colonel W. P. Wainwright being severely wounded.

Franklin had been successful in his attempt to force the passage of Crampton's Gap, where McLaws stood with three brigades, under Howell Cobb. He had advanced boldly against the Confederate front with the division of General Henry W. Slocum, while General William F. Smith's division charged up the mountain on the left, and he had gained the crest after sustaining a loss of 533 in killed and wounded. He captured, however, 400 prisoners and several hundred stand of arms from the Confederates, who were compelled to flee down the western side of the mountain after experiencing a loss of nearly 600 men.

Both these engagements, fought on the 14th of September, constitute what has been called the battle of South Mountain.

Early on the same day, the Confederates had almost completely invested Harper's Ferry, then in charge of Colonel G. H. Miles, who had a total force of nearly 12,000 men, including the troops which General Julius White brought with him there after abandoning Martinsburg. Miles still held batteries on Bolivar Heights in the rear; but the Confederates commanded both the Maryland and Loudon Heights across the Potomac and Shenandoah Rivers, and from these an artillery fire was opened in the afternoon.

Instead of holding out to the last extremity, and endeavoring to reoccupy Maryland Heights, as McClellan had directed, Miles sent away his cavalry in the evening, and made no effort to regain the Heights, which Colonel T. H. Ford, after repelling a heavy Confederate attack, had been compelled to abandon during the night of the 13th.

At dawn on the 15th the investment was complete, for Jackson had brought up his force in the rear of Harper's Ferry, and opened upon the Bolivar Heights batteries simultaneously with the firing from Loudon and Maryland Heights.

The position was, of course, untenable, and a white flag was soon displayed by

JOSEPH HOOKER

Colonel Miles, who, however, was mortally wounded before it could be distinguished. The surrender devolved upon General White, who had waived command in Miles's favor, and to the Confederates Harper's Ferry was transferred, with 11,583 prisoners, 13,000 stand of arms, 200 wagons, 73 cannon, some ammunition, and a large quantity of stores and camp equipage.

Miles died shortly after the surrender, with a strong suspicion of disloyalty unjustly attaching to him, and Ford was dismissed on the ground of such "lack of military capacity as to disqualify him from a command in the service."

When Lee saw the danger threatening his army from Turner's and Crampton's Gap, he determined to fall back to Sharpsburg. The forces under Longstreet and D. H. Hill reached the latter place

JOSEPH K. F. MANSFIELD.

early on the 15th, and those under Jackson and Walker on the 16th; but McLaws could not cross over to Harper's Ferry until the morning of the last named date, and reached Sharpsburg, by way of Shepherdstown, only on the 17th, after the battle of Antietam had commenced.

Lee posted his troops along the range of heights and in the woods between the Antietam Creek and the town of Sharpsburg, Longstreet being placed on the right of the Boonsboro' Road, and D. H. Hill on the left, while Jackson, protected by Stuart's cavalry, stood to the left of the road leading to Hagerstown, and Walker occupied Longstreet's right, near Shaveley' Farm.

As soon as McClellan learned of Lee's retreat he ordered a pursuit, which brought about, on the 15th, quite a lively cavalry skirmish at Boonsboro', and a still more important infantry and artillery engagement on the Keedysville and Sharpsburg Road.

On the afternoon of the 16th Hooker was ordered to cross the Antietam Creek, with Ricketts, Meade, and Doubleday (the latter in charge of Hatch's division), and to attack the Confederate left.

Hooker crossed by the upper one of the four stone bridges spanning the creek below Pry's Mill, near Keedysville, and moving to the west and south, occupied, after some skirmishing with Hood's force, the woods east of the road to Hagerstown. Here he remained during the night, and was joined by General Mansfield's Twelfth Corps, which bivouacked about a mile in the rear.

During the night, Hood's troops were relieved by two brigades of Ewell's, led by General Alexander R. Lawton, who had on his left "Jackson's Own," under General J. K. Jones, supported by the remainder of Ewell's division.

SEPTEMBER, 1862.

At dawn of the 17th, Hooker's artillery opened a vigorous fire against the Confederate left under Jackson, following it with an attack by Meade's Pennsylvania Reserves, occupying his centre. Doubleday stood on Meade's right and Ricketts on his left. After a severe contest, marked by a most stubborn resistance on the part of the Confederates, they were driven with heavy losses beyond the line of woods across the Hagerstown Road, where stood Jackson's reserves. Hooker further advanced Meade's force in order to seize the road and occupy the woods; but as it approached, Jackson's reserves, and the force just sent him by Hood, fell heavily upon it, and fought it with such tenacity, that Meade had to summon immediate aid.

Doubleday and Ricketts came at once to his support, and for a while the opposing forces fought with a determination and obstinacy rarely witnessed. The struggle did not cease, in fact, until the ranks on both sides had been fearfully decimated by the heavy and very effective artillery brought on the field. Hooker's corps, and his opponents, "Jackson's Own," and the brigades of Hays, Lawton, and Trimble, were completely shattered. General Hartsuff, of Doubleday's force, was badly wounded, General Starke, commanding the Stonewall division, and Colonel Douglas, commanding one of Lawton's brigades, were killed, and General Lawton in charge of the division, and Colonel Walker, commanding a brigade, were severely hurt.

A temporary lull occurred, during which Mansfield's corps was brought up and formed, at about half-past seven o'clock, with Williams's division on the right and Greene's on the left. While deploying, however, General Mansfield was mortally wounded, and his place was taken by General Crawford. The latter lost no time in advancing toward the woods, leaving Greene's division to take position close by the Dunker church and soon encountered D. H. Hill's division, which had replaced the exhausted Confederate troops. Guns were soon again placed in position on both

CONFEDERATE BATTERY AT HARPER'S FERRY, VA, ERECTED ON THE HEIGHTS

CONFEDERATE BATTERY AT HARPER'S FERRY, VA., ERECTED ON THE HEIGHTS OVERLOOKING THE TOWN, AND COMMANDING THE RAILROAD BRIDGE AND CANAL

WOMEN AND CHILDREN OF SHARPSBURG, MD., TAKING REFUGE IN THE CELLAR OF THE KRETZER MANSION, DURING THE BATTLE. BURSTING OF A SHELL IN THE WINDOW OF THE CELLAR.—From a Sketch by F. H. Schell.

sides, and the attack was renewed more fiercely than ever.

One of the Confederate batteries was silenced on their extreme right by Doubleday's guns, which latter had been doing such terrible execution, that an unsuccessful attempt was made to capture them by the Fourth Alabama and the First Texas Regiments. Both sides fought with desperation, alternately advancing and retreating, as reinforcements came upon the field, until about nine o'clock, when, under a more determined onslaught than any of the preceding ones, the Federal line began to waver.

Just then Sumner opportunely arrived, and took the place of General Hooker, who had just been so severely wounded in the foot as to have to be carried from the field. Sedgwick was sent with the First Division to aid Crawford, while Richardson and French advanced further to the left, toward the Dunker church. The woods were taken possession of west of the church, and Hood's troops were being rapidly driven back, when fresh troops under McLaws and Walker came upon the scene.

Sedgwick's impetuosity had carried him so far forward, that a huge gap separated him from all support on the left, where stood French's division, and toward this gap the Confederates advanced boldly. They penetrated it, compelling the Federals to fall back to the first line of woods, and were making their way toward an unprotected Federal battery, which, for want of infantry support, would doubtless have been easily captured, when Franklin reached the ground with Slocum's and Smith's divisions, and promptly covered the exposed point.

Slocum was placed to the left of General O. O. Howard, who had just taken Sedgwick's division, as the latter was twice wounded, and had to be carried from the field; and Smith was ordered to retake the ground near the Dunker church, which he did, after making several charges, in which Colonel Irwin's First Brigade, and notably the Seventh Maine Regiment, greatly distinguished themselves. French and Richardson were ordered at the same time to make a diversion in favor of the right, which was also rapidly carried out. Three of General Hill's brigades were driven back in disorder to a sunken road, and thence upon the Hagerstown Road, leaving the Federals once more in possession of the much-contested ground.

Pleasanton's cavalry and horse artillery were brought on Richardson's left in front of the second bridge, and did excellent service in repelling the many assaults made upon the Federal centre during the afternoon. With the reinforcements that General R. H. Anderson brought General Hill, an effort was made to seize a ridge on the Federal left, which was successfully opposed by Colonel Cross with his well-known Fifth New Hampshire Regiment and the Eighty-first Pennsylvania, while another and more important attempt was being made to flank the Federal right. The latter was frustrated by Kimball's brigade, and the Sixty-first and Sixty-fourth New York Regiments, with which Colonel Francis C. Barlow made a most determined attack.

The Federal lines were finally advanced close on to Dr. Piper's house, where another stand was made by the Confederates. A fierce artillery duel here took place, and while directing the fire of one of the batteries, General Richardson was so very severely wounded, that he had to resign his command to General W. S. Hancock. At about the same time, Colonel Burke had to take the place of General Meagher, who was likewise taken away seriously wounded. The fight continued fiercely until toward nightfall, when a charge was ordered by General Hancock, and Dr. Piper's house was abandoned to the Federals.

RAPHAEL SEMMES.

ISAAC PEACE RODMAN.

While the Federal right and centre had been thus engaged, the left was not altogether idle. Burnside had been ordered at eight o'clock to carry the lower stone bridge, take possession of the Sharpsburg Heights, and then advance along their crest upon the town. He made several attempts, but failed in presence of the raking fire which Confederate infantry and sharpshooters directed upon him.

Failing to hear of any progress, McClellan twice sent to him; but this not producing any result, he commanded Burnside to carry the bridge at the point of the bayonet. This was finally done at one o'clock in the afternoon, when the Fifty-first New York and the Fifty-first Pennsylvania drove the Confederates from the bridge to the heights. The divisions of Sturgis, Wilcox, Rodman, and Cox crossed the bridge, with their accompanying batteries, and, after a most spirited attack, the Confederates were driven back toward Sharpsburg, leaving Burnside's force in possession of the crest.

Had this been done a few hours earlier, as McClellan had ordered it, Lee's line would have been fatally pierced at Sharpsburg. As it was, the delay enabled A. P. Hill's division to reach the ground. Though fatigued after its hurried march from Harper's Ferry, it immediately directed such a heavy fire, mainly upon Burnside's left flank, that the Federals were compelled, not long after, to fall back to the protection of the bluffs, near the bridge they had crossed. In one of the charges that followed Hill's arrival, General Rodman was mortally wounded, and General L. O'B. Branch was killed.

The Federal reserve infantry, and the artillery under Sturgis, aided materially in checking the Confederate advance, and Hill made no attempt to retake the bridge. Night closed upon another sanguinary chapter of the war—a loss of over 12,000 men being credited to each side during the brief time that the battle of Antietam lasted.

On the morning of the 18th neither side appeared ready for the offensive. McClellan's army was reinforced during the day by about 18,000 men under Couch and Humphreys, and General Lee was also strengthened by the last division from Harper's Ferry.

SEPTEMBER, 1862.

McClellan delayed resuming the attack on the 18th. He knew that Lee was being largely reinforced, and to take the aggressive he needed reinforcements, which, though promised and expected on the 17th, had been held back at Frederick by directions from Washington, in order to guard against the enemy getting in rear of the army.

Porter, on the 17th, in the centre of the line, covered the supply-trains, protected Burnside's right flank, and assisted him as he advanced; supplied Pleasanton with infantry and artillery, and sent two of Morell's brigades to Sumner. Humphreys's arrival on the 18th enabled him to replace Burnside's wearied troops, which were withdrawn east of the Antietam.

At dawn on the 19th, it was discovered that the enemy had abandoned his position, and withdrawn across the Potomac. Pursuit was, as soon as possible, organized by Porter, which resulted in the capture of many prisoners, near the Shepherdstown Ford, where, on the south bank, the enemy had made a stand, with artillery and considerable infantry.

Griffin's and Barnes's brigades were ordered to take the eight batteries which Lee had left for the defense of the river approaches, and after a spirited and rather prolonged engagement, in which the Federals lost 220 killed and wounded, four of the guns were captured. Two of these had been lost by Griffin at first Bull Run battle, in 1861.

The next day Porter undertook a reconnoissance in force—the advance of which, being attacked by A. P. Hill before the main body could cross the river, was withdrawn to the north bank.

Lee's army marched to the Opequan River, near Martinsburg, where it remained a few days, and thence moved up the Shenandoah Valley to the vicinity of Bunker Hill and Winchester.

McClellan sent General Williams to retake Maryland Heights, which he did on the 20th, and two days later General Sumner occupied Harper's Ferry, which was soon placed in communication by ponton-bridges with the Shenandoah and Potomac shores. The Federal army lay in the vicinity of Sharpsburg until the 26th of October, when it began crossing the Potomac, and, a week later, was safely on Virginia soil, McClellan's headquarters being, on the 6th of November, established at Rectortown near Front Royal.

CONFEDERATE CAVALRY DRIVING STRAGGLERS AND SKULKERS BACK TO THEIR DUTY AT THE BATTLE OF ANTIETAM, MD

From a sketch by F. H. Schell.

KILLING'S CAVE, ON THE BANKS OF THE POTOMAC, NEAR SHARPSBURG, MD., USED AS A PLACE OF SAFETY DURING THE BATTLE OF ANTIETAM

From a sketch by F. H. Schell.

THOMAS JONATHAN JACKSON,

Popularly Known as "Stonewall" Jackson.

Born in Clarksburg, Harrison County, W. Va., January 21st, 1824; at the age of three years was left an orphan, and likewise penniless, but was taken charge of by one of his relatives until his fourth year, when he was turned over to an uncle, Cummings E. Jackson, with whom he remained until he was sixteen. He had, in the meantime, attended an old-field school, but had mainly given attention to the care of his uncle's farm. Upon leaving the latter he was elected county constable, and remained such for two years, when he was induced to apply for and did obtain, on the 1st of July, 1842, a cadetship in the United States Military Academy at West Point. He was a classmate of McClellan, Reno, Stoneman, Couch, Foster, Gibbons, Hill, Maury, and others, who subsequently became generals, and, after four years' study, graduated seventeenth in a class of seventy.

On the 1st of July, 1846, he was appointed a second lieutenant of artillery, and at once entered the Mexican War, where he distinguished himself greatly. He took a conspicuous part at the reduction of Vera Cruz, and in the battles of Contreras, Churubusco, Molino del Rey, Chapultepec and Mexico, being twice commended in General Scott's reports, and receiving the commissions of first lieutenant and of brevet-major for skill and gallantry. Upon the termination of the Mexican War he was ordered to duty in Florida, but, after remaining there three years, his health became so impaired, that he was compelled to resign from the service.

On the 1st of September, 1851, he became professor of natural philosophy and instructor of artillery in the Virginia Military Institute at Lexington, and remained there until April, 1861, when he tendered his services to his native State. He was soon placed in charge of the Confederate Volunteers assembled at Harper's Ferry, and was made a brigadier-general, after being given by General Joseph E. Johnston the command of a brigade of four infantry regiments. When McDowell advanced upon Manassas, in July, 1861, Jackson's force, which had meanwhile taken a distinguished share in the engagement at Falling Waters, was detached from the "Valley of Virginia," and sent to Beauregard's assistance.

Jackson's conduct throughout the first battle of Bull Run was such as to merit the highest encomiums on all sides, and to him is attributed the success gained by the Confederates at this, the first important engagement of the Civil War. At a period of the battle when the Federal troops were fiercely beating back the Confederate lines, Jackson's brigade stood its ground manfully, and was pointed at with admiration by General Bee, who exclaimed to his men: "Look! There is Jackson, standing like a stone wall. Let us determine to die here, and we will conquer!" The words electrified the men, who, upon being rallied beside Jackson's line, advanced with it doggedly, and repulsed the Federal advance. The name of "Stonewall" was always afterward used to denote him, and was likewise given to his brigade. His gallantry on that occasion won for him the grade of major-general. He was afterward placed in command of the Confederate forces in the lower Shenandoah Valley, and took part in the battles of Kernstown, McDowell, Winchester, Cross Keys, Port Republic, New Cold Arbor (Cold Harbor), and Cedar Run.

Advancing with Lee into Maryland, his troops led the van to Frederick City, and shortly afterward the capitulation of Harper's Ferry with 11,000 men, a large quantity of small arms, and a number of pieces of artillery, wagons, etc.

Jackson afterward took a leading part in the battles of Antietam, Fredericksburg and Chancellorsville, meeting his death at the last-named engagement. Late on the 2d of May, 1863, he surprised General Hooker's forces, and pursued them until nightfall, evidently only to completely rout the Federals, with heavy loss. Late the same evening, Jackson, with his staff, rode a little ahead of his lines to reconnoitre with the intention of continuing the pursuit early the following day. He was so engrossed with the object in view, that he proceeded much further than he had intended in advance of his troops. Being warned of the danger he was in, he hesitated to return, but had not gone far when a heavy volley was fired at him by his own infantry. The party scattered, and Jackson turned rapidly into the forest. There he was fired upon by more of his infantry in the attitude of kneeling to repel cavalry, and received the three wounds which caused his death. One ball had entered his left arm, just below the shoulder-joint, severing the main artery; another had entered the wrist; and a third passed through the palm of his right hand. While in this helpless condition his horse ran away, but he managed to keep the bridle with his bleeding right hand till the horse was stopped, and he was taken down in an almost fainting condition. He was laid under a tree near the road until an ambulance-litter could be brought forward, and, amid a terrific fire of shot and shell which the Federals had just opened in that direction, it made its way to an ambulance-wagon.

The fact of his being wounded was studiously kept from his troops, lest they become discouraged in consequence, but he was recognized by one of his division generals, General W. D. Pender, who approached, and said, "Ah, general, I am sorry to see you have been wounded. The lines here are so much broken by the enemy's fire, that I fear we will have to fall back." Raising his drooping head, Jackson exclaimed, "You must hold your ground, General Pender! You must hold your ground, sir!" It was his last order on the field. The next day his arm was amputated by Dr. Hunter McGuire, an eminent Richmond physician; but, pneumonia setting in, he rapidly declined, and died on the following Sunday, May 10th, 1863. His last words: "Let us cross over the river and rest under the shade of the trees," were whispered to his wife, whom he had sent for, and by whom he was tenderly nursed after the performing of the operation.

His body was taken to Richmond, where it lay in state at the Capitol, the entire city going into mourning; thence it was carried to Lexington, where it was received by the superintendent, professors and cadets of the institute and the citizens. The body lay in state in the old lecture-room of the deceased until it was borne under a large escort of infantry, cavalry and artillery to its last resting-place "in Lexington, in the Valley of Virginia," where Jackson had expressed a wish to be buried, and where a simple monument marks what is known as "Jackson's grave." A bronze statue of heroic size has been erected to Jackson's memory on the Capitol Square at Richmond, and at the time of writing (1884) a still more elaborate monument is in contemplation to properly honor the last resting-place of one who may well be regarded the most popular chieftain the Southern Confederacy had, and who doubtless was the ablest strategist produced on either side during the entire Civil War.

CAPTAIN SEMMES, OF THE PRIVATEER "290," OR "ALABAMA," DECOYING SHIPS TOWARD HIM BY BURNING A PRIZE VESSEL.

JOSEPH K. F. MANSFIELD.

Born at New Haven, Conn., December 22d, 1803; entered the Military Academy at West Point, and, upon graduating therefrom, was appointed a second lieutenant of Engineers in 1822; engaged in engineering upon the Atlantic and Pacific Coasts until the breaking out of the Mexican War, having meanwhile gained a captaincy in 1838; served in Mexico as chief engineer of General Taylor's army, and gained the brevets of major, lieutenant-colonel and colonel for gallantry in the defense of Fort Brown, and at the battles of Monterey and at Buena Vista, where he was severely wounded.

During the five years following the close of the Mexican War he was a member of the Board of Engineers for Fortifications on the Atlantic and Pacific Coasts, and from 1853 until 1861 was inspector-general of the Army, with the rank of colonel. In April, 1861, he was placed in command of the Department of Washington, and lost no time in fortifying the capital, receiving the appointment of brigadier-general of Volunteers the following month. In October, 1861, he was transferred to Camp Hamilton, Va., and one month later was ordered to take command at Newport News, participating in the capture of Norfolk, May 10th, 1862. He was in command of Suffolk from June to September, 1862, being promoted to be a major-general of Volunteers in July, 1862, and afterward commanded a corps of the Army of the Potomac, at the head of which he received, at the battle of Antietam, the wounds from which he died, on the 18th of September, 1862.

ISAAC PEACE RODMAN.

Born at South Kingston, R. I., August 29th, 1822; died near Hagerstown, Md., September 30th, 1862. At the breaking out of the Civil War, he took the field as a captain in the Second Rhode Island Regiment. Was at the first battle of Bull Run, participated in the capture of Roanoke Island, and of New Berne, N. C., receiving the commission of brigadier-general for gallantry at the latter place, where he took possession of the Confederate works at the point of the bayonet. He commanded General Parke's division, and greatly distinguished himself at the battles of South Mountain and Antietam, being mortally wounded while fighting for the possession of the stone bridge.

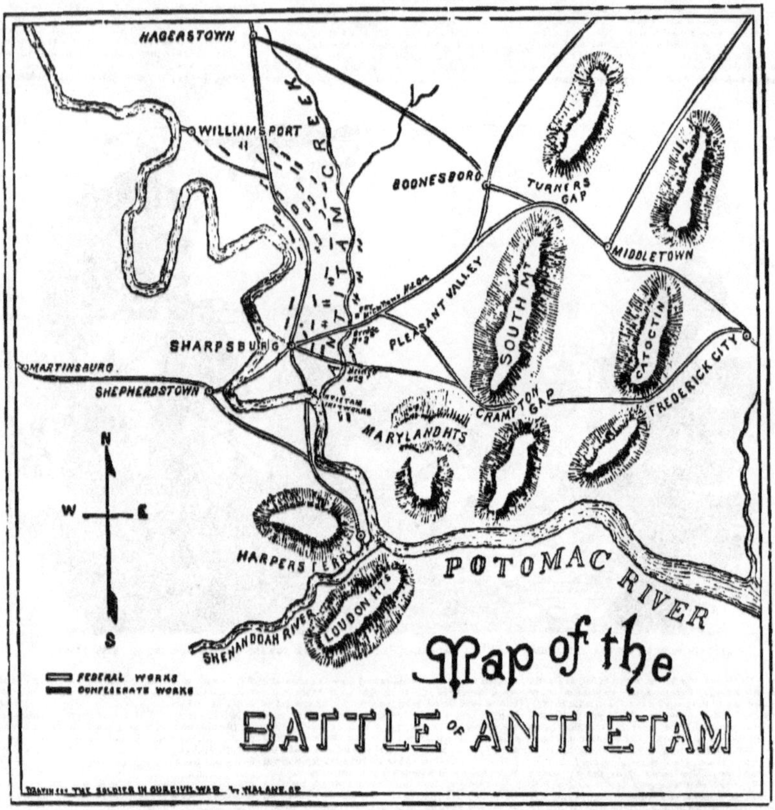

Map of the BATTLE OF ANTIETAM

DRAWN FOR THE SOLDIER IN OUR CIVIL WAR

BATTLE OF MUMFORDSVILLE, KY.

As soon as Buell learned that Bragg intended moving upon Louisville he posted troops and erected defenses at all assailable points along the Louisville and Nashville Railway, and made preparations to head off Bragg, also, in his evident ultimate advance upon Nashville.

One of the threatened points was Mumfordsville, situated on the Green River. It was held by Colonel T. J. Wilder, who had erected there several strong earthworks on both sides of the railway, and who had with him a small force of recruits from the Seventeenth, Sixty-seventh and Eighty-ninth Indiana Regiments, as well as several batteries, and a company each from the Louisville Provost Guard and the Eighteenth Regular Cavalry.

General J. K. Duncan, who commanded two of General Buckner's brigades, belonging to Bragg's advance, which was led by General J. R. Chalmers, appeared before Mumfordsville on the evening of Saturday, the 13th of September, and at once demanded its unconditional surrender. This was refused by Colonel Wilder, and on the following morning Duncan opened upon the Federals; but these being reinforced by Colonel C. L. Dunham with about four hundred men belonging to the Fiftieth Indiana, the Confederates were driven back with considerable loss, after an engagement of several hours' duration.

Duncan withdrew his force and posted it on each side of the Louisville and Nashville Railway, where it remained, facing the earthworks, until the arrival of General Polk's contingent of Bragg's army, on the 16th. The Confederate force surrounding Mumfordsville was thus increased to about 25,000 men.

The Federals had meanwhile been strengthened by the Sixtieth and Eighty-fourth Indiana Regiments, which made their total force about 4,000 men. Notwithstanding the great disparity in numbers, the Federals made a vigorous resistance when they were attacked by the Confederates, and throughout most of the 16th directed such an effective fire from behind their earthworks as to cause serious losses to their opponents. By evening the Confederates had in position 45 cannon ready to open upon Mumfordsville, and made a renewed demand for the surrender of the place.

Wilder had asked for aid from General Buell, then at Bowling Green, but this not coming, and there being no likelihood of its soon reaching him from that or any other quarter, he called a council of officers, by whom it was decided to surrender, as further resistance would be useless. In accordance therewith, the Federal commander capitulated early on the 17th, when his force marched out of the place with all the honors of war.

JOSEPH HOOKER.

Born at Hadley, Mass., November 13th, 1814; entered the United States Military Academy at West Point in 1833, and upon graduating therefrom, in February, 1838, was appointed a second lieutenant of Artillery, July 1st, 1837 served in the Florida War against the Seminole Indians, and did garrison and frontier duty until the breaking out of the war with Mexico, taking part in the latter on the staffs of Generals Butler, Hamer and Smith. In 1847 he was appointed assistant adjutant general, serving as such in Pillow's division, and received the brevets of captain, major and lieutenant-colonel for gallantry at Monterey, at the National Bridge and at Chapultepec. In 1853 he resigned from the army and engaged in commercial and agricultural pursuits in California, and was also superintendent of Military Roads in Oregon until 1861, when he tendered his services to the United States Government. On the 17th of May, 1861, he was made a brigadier-general of Volunteers, serving in the defenses of Washington and on the lower Potomac until March, 1862, when he was placed at the head of the Third Corps of the Army of the Potomac. He took part in the Virginia Peninsula Campaign—in the engagements before Yorktown, as well as in the battles of Williamsburg, Fair Oaks, Frazier's Farm and Malvern Hill. Was made a major-general, to date from the battle of Williamsburg, and figured conspicuously in the battles of the second Bull Run, Chantilly, South Mountain and Antietam, being so severely wounded at the last-named battle, that he had to abandon

A B DAVIES

T J Jackson

all active service until the following November. He had meanwhile been relieved of command [illegible] Harper's Ferry [illegible] in the following month [illegible] of the Army of the Potomac, and fought the battle of

Artillery, [illegible] served in Mexico [illegible] Cerro Gordo, and the City of Mexico, [illegible] received the brevets of

[illegible] Alabama, that she had to be sold early in 1862, [illegible] with one hundred and sixty- [illegible] property valued at \$6,000,000 [illegible] generally fly the Red Cross of St. George upon nearing a vessel, and, when the latter was

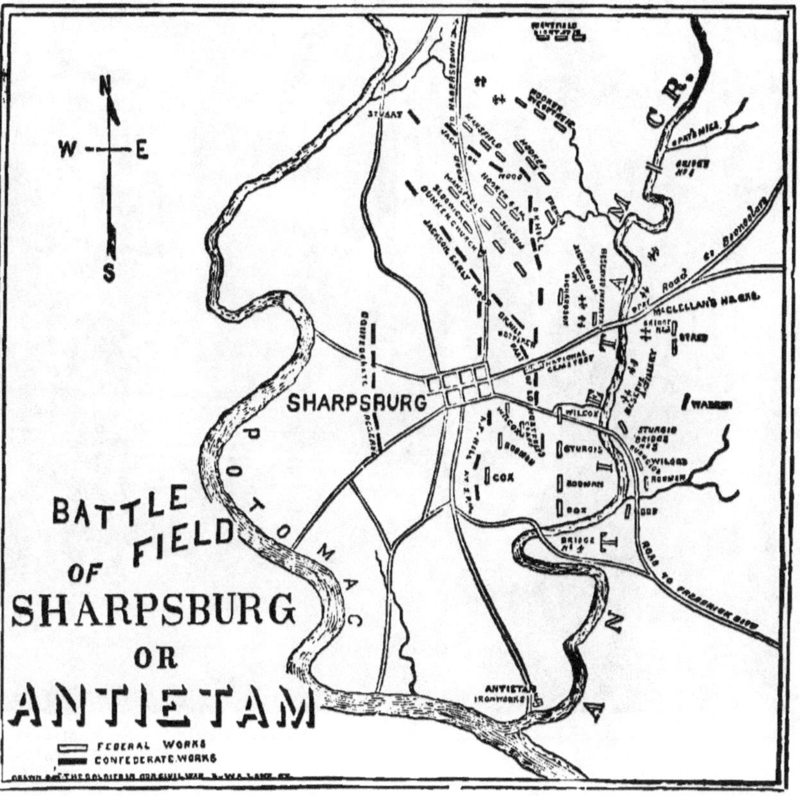

Chancellorsville, May 2d, 1863. He pursued Lee toward Pennsylvania, and at Frederick City, June 28th, 1863, asked to be relieved, and Meade was placed in command. He [illegible] Twentieth Army Corps, participating in the battles of Lookout Mountain, Missionary Ridge, and Chattanooga [illegible] November, 1863 [illegible] In the movement of Georgia by General Sherman's army, Hooker led his corps in almost constant fighting up to the time of the capture of Atlanta, and was then relieved at his own request. He subsequently commanded the departments of the North, of the [illegible] was brevetted major-general in the Regular Army for his gallantry at Chattanooga, and in October, 1868, was retired upon the full rank of major-general. Died October 31st, 1879.

JAMES B. RICKETTS

Born in New York City, 1816; graduated at the United States Military Academy at West Point, and entered the

lieutenant-colonel, colonel, brigadier-general and major-general for gallantry [illegible] retired [illegible] full rank of major-general in the Regular Army.

RAPHAEL SEMMES

Born in Charles County, Md., September 27th, 1809; [illegible] Navy in 1826 [illegible] Worth in the Valley of Mexico, in 1847; [illegible] The Sumter [illegible] blockade at the mouth of the Mississippi, June 30th, 1861, and destroyed much Federal property before she was forced into Gibraltar, and there so closely watched by the United States

brought under his guns, would run up the Confederate flag [illegible] The majority of the prizes were [illegible] in many instances [illegible] 1851 published two works on the Mexican War. He [illegible] of the *Alabama* and *Sumter*, and [illegible] in 1864 [illegible] 1869 [illegible] 1877.

HOLD OF THE CONFEDERATE PRIVATEER "ALABAMA," CAPTAIN SEMMES, IN WHICH WERE CONFIN
LETTING DOWN WATER T

From a Sketch

[illegible] OF THE CONFEDERATE [illegible] ALABAMA [illegible] IN WHICH WERE CONFINED THE OFFICERS AND CREWS OF THE WHALERS AND MERCHANTMEN CAPTURED BY THAT VESSEL
LETTING DOWN WATER TO THE PRISONERS IN IRONS

VOLUNTEERS FOR THE FEDERAL ARMY CROSSING FROM CINCINNATI, O., TO COVINGTON, KY., ON A BRIDGE OF COAL-BOATS, HASTILY CONSTRUCTED THAT THEY MIGHT DEFEND KENTUCKY FROM THE INVASION OF GENERAL KIRBY SMITH.

From a Sketch by H. Lovie.

THE SONS OF VETERANS OF THE UNITED STATES OF AMERICA.

The material for the following outline of the origin, organization, purposes, progress and aims of the National Association, now so widely spread and so well known under the above-named simple and highly appropriate official title, has been furnished by Comrade A. P. Davis, the originator of the Order, with the assistance of Brother Frank P. Merrill, the Commander-in-chief of the Organization, and is approved by the officers of the National Association.

The term "veteran" would indicate one who was experienced in any art or calling, but more particularly that of war. Therefore, before our late civil struggle of 1861-5 had closed, we had what was termed veteran soldiers and veteran regiments. When the end had come, and the Union no longer required the services of her well-trained and faithful volunteer hosts, those who had passed through the ordeal and were still alive returned to their several homes and vocations as "citizens," with the feeling that each and all had done something to save and perpetuate a great and good nation; and so it came that in due time, and as it were by common consent, the mantle and title of "veteran" slowly and surely fell upon all who had drawn a sword or shouldered a musket for our national existence.

The "Military Order of the Loyal Legion," the "Grand Army of the Republic," and all of the various army societies which grew out of the late war, had their conception in that feeling of fraternity which ever takes root and springs up among large bodies of men who are, from circumstances, one in vocation, especially if the same be hazardous in its nature.

In the foundation and organization of the Loyal Legion, it was deemed best to look to the future as well as the present, and therefore a perpetual feature was engrafted into its organic laws, making proper provision for the transmission of membership from father to son, the rules governing the line of succession being in substance the same or akin to those of the "Society of the Cincinnati," formed at the close of the war for our national independence, with General Washington as its first Commander-in-chief.

In the foundation and organization of the Grand Army of the Republic, no provisions were made looking to a continuation of the Association beyond the termination of the lease of life held by its several members. As it is not at this late day at all probable that any change in the foregoing direction will be deemed expedient, the results will be that, through the wearing effects of time, the membership of the Association will weaken and pass away, and that, when the eyes of the last Comrade are closed in the long sleep of death, the Grand Army of the Republic, with all of its glorious recollections and associations, will have passed away for ever. And still, and though gone never to return, the day is far distant when its influence for the common good will not be felt and appreciated by future generations. The feeling that an omission had been made, and that a deficiency existed in the make-up of the Grand Army of the Republic as regarding the future, has for years existed in the minds of many of its more earnest and faithful workers, and during this time, from various legitimate causes and reasons, no happy or satisfactory solution of the question could be reached.

The idea of a permanent and perpetual organization, composed solely of the sons of deceased or honorably discharged soldiers, sailors, and marines, who served in the Union Army or Navy during our late Civil War, and descending in due time to their eldest male lineal descendants, had its origin in the mind of Comrade A. P. Davis, a member of the Grand Army of the Republic residing in the City of Pittsburg, Pa., and through his agency and exertions the movement was developed and brought to an assured success. After agitating the subject for a number of years, in one form or another, Comrade Davis became fully convinced that the only right and practical course to take was for the sons of veterans to start and organize as a wholly separate and distinct Order, and then by their merits win their way to popular favor. To this end, during the month of November, 1881, Davis Camp No. 1 of the Sons of Veterans of Pennsylvania* was organized in the City of Pittsburg, and from this humble commencement the Organization started out on its national mission of "*Friendship, Charity and Loyalty.*"

The original elected officers of Camp No. 1 were H. T. Rowley, captain; John H. Seiferth, first lieutenant; and Walter E. Morris, second lieutenant. Shortly after other Camps were organized in the vicinity of Pittsburg, and during the succeeding month of December a charter was obtained from the Commonwealth of Pennsylvania, which was not only good for and covered the whole State, but under United States statute law was valid in any State of the Union.

COAT-OF-ARMS OF THE SONS OF VETERANS.

During the early part of the year 1882, sufficient progress had been made in Pittsburg and vicinity to form a Division Organization, with H. T. Rowley, the senior officer of the Order, as its Commander; Henry W. Orth, Commander of Lieutenant James M. Lysle Camp No. 2, located in Allegheny City, as the second in command; and John A. Woods, Commander of Garfield Camp No. 3, located in McKeesport, Allegheny County, as the third in command.

While the foregoing progress was being made in and about the city of its birth, arrangements were being made by Comrade Davis, and the Order was being spread both East and West. It soon made its way into the adjoining States, and in due time permanent establishments were secured in the same, and they were duly organized as separate Divisions of the Order. These labors were continued for some months, and during the period Comrade Davis discovered that, owing to the magnitude of the work, and through long-standing disabilities, he was incapacitated for vigorously carrying on the same without more substantial support, coupled with experience; and to secure the desired aid, he divided the country into five Grand Divisions, and solicited the co-operation and assistance of prominent members of the Grand Army of the Republic.

FRANK P. MERRILL.

* So named "in honor of the memory of Captain Isaac Davis, who fell at Concord Bridge, in the Revolutionary War; Captain Jacob Davis, who served during the war of 1812; and as a compliment to Major A. P. Davis of this city."

The results were all that could be desired. Comrade Paul Vandervoort, Commander-in-chief of the Grand Army of the Republic, developed a kindly interest, and gave the movement encouragement.

Comrade William E. W. Ross, of Baltimore, Md., the Senior Vice Commander-in-chief, was induced to take charge of and, as their Commander, organize the Second and Fifth Grand Divisions; and Comrade Isaac S. Bangs, of Waterville, Me., Junior Vice Commander-in-chief, consented to perform a like service in the First Grand Division. Comrade William J. Maskell, of Chicago, Ill., prominently known throughout the Northwest as an active and earnest worker in the ranks of the Grand Army of the Republic, offered to assume command, and organize the Third Grand Division.

The Fourth Grand Division was placed in the charge of Comrade A. V. Bohn, of Leadville, Col., equally well known in Grand Army of the Republic circles in his State and section of the country.

Comrades Ross and Bangs were particularly fortunate in their exertions to establish the Order in their respective localities; and the time and means which all of these gentlemen so freely gave, and the success and substantial results they secured, entitle them to the lasting respect and gratitude of each and every Son of a Veteran.

In the meantime, and prior to the consummation of the foregoing, it was decided that the Order was far enough advanced to have a nominal head and to organize on a national basis. To this end, in July, 1882, H. T. Rowley, as the Senior Camp and Division Commander, was duly declared Provisional Commander-in-chief, and the first regular national meeting was called the same day, to be held in the City of Pittsburg, Pa., on the 18th day of the succeeding October.

At this meeting, at which thirteen States were duly represented, a permanent national organization was effected. The various organic laws, ritual, insignia, etc., of the Order, as prepared by Comrade Davis, were unanimously approved and adopted, and the following executive officers elected in due form:

Commander-in-chief, H. T. Rowley, Pittsburg, Pa.
Lieutenant Commander-in-chief, Charles M. Durfee, Decatur, Ill.
Vice Lieutenant-Commander-in-chief, Wheeler D. Wilcox, Columbus, O.

The meeting having adjourned, the work of organization and extension under the guidance of the Grand Army of the Republic Comrades named, assisted by many others equally earnest and energetic, was vigorously pushed forward. During the balance of the year 1882, and for the next six months of 1883, rapid progress was made in all directions, and the Order gained a substantial foothold in many new localities.

On the 25th day of July, 1883, the National Encampment of the Grand Army of the Republic met in the City of Denver, Col. At this meeting Comrade Vandervoort, Commander-in-chief, officially brought the question of the sons of veterans before the Encampment, and, as a result, the Order was, under its legitimate and legal title of the "Sons of Veterans of the United States of America," and, without a single dissenting voice, unanimously recognized as one "*entitled to the confidence and support of all Comrades of the Grand Army of the Republic.*"

On the 6th day of the succeeding August, the second annual meeting of the national body of the Sons of Veterans was held in the City of Columbus, Ohio. At this meeting, twenty-one different State or Division organizations were duly represented, *viz.:* Maine, New Hampshire, Vermont, Massachusetts, New York, New Jersey, Delaware, Eastern Pennsylvania, Western Pennsylvania, Ohio, Maryland, Illinois, Indiana, Michigan, Wisconsin, Minnesota, Iowa, Missouri, Kansas, Nebraska and Colorado.

The proceedings of the meeting were marked by unusual harmony and concert of action on the part of all present.

For various reasons, the delegates present did not deem it wise or expedient at that time to consider or entertain any measures looking to a revision or change in any portion of the organic laws or ritual of the Order, and, in consequence of this feeling the time of the meeting was in substance devoted to the winding up of the affairs of the retiring administration, necessary legislation for the support

BATTLE OF MUMFORDSVILLE, KY., SUNDAY, SEPTEMBER 14th, 1862. THE CONFEDERATES CHARGING THROUGH THE ABATIS IN FRONT OF THE FORTIFICATIONS NEAR GREEN RIVER.

From a Sketch by H. Lovie.

of the Order for the coming official year, and the election of new officers.

The following is a full list of the same:

Commander-in-chief, Frank P. Merrill, Auburn, Me.
Lieutenant-commander-in-chief, Augustus Saltzman, St. Joseph, Mo.
Vice Lieutenant-commander-in-chief, Charles C. Morton Philadelphia, Pa.
Chief-of-staff, Horace L. Wright, Auburn, Me.

COUNCIL-IN-CHIEF.

Edward J. Thornton, Philadelphia, Pa.
Herbert A. Gross, Auburn, Me.
Frank H. Challis, Manchester, N. H.
Joseph B. McCabe, East Boston, Mass.
John A. Wood, McKeesport, Pa.
Edgar R. Vincent, Columbus, O.
George M. Allen, Terre Haute, Ind.
J. A. Wiedmuller, St. Louis, Mo.
C. F. Rick, Danville, Ill.
F. E. Brown, Denver, Col.
Fred. H. Storah, Auburn, Me.
Will Valentine, Bennington, Vt.
S. Ellis Ripley, Livermore Falls, Me.
A. S. Libby, Portland, Me.
H. F. Baker, Trenton, N. J.

After the installation of the above-named officers, the Commander-in-chief announced the names of the following Brothers as members of his official staff.

Adjutant-general, Fred. L. Edgecomb, Auburn, Me.
Quartermaster-general, John C. Blake, Auburn, Me.
Judge Advocate-general, Edmond M. Amies, Altoona, Pa.
Inspector-general, E. H. Oilkey, Columbus, O.
Chief Mustering Officer, John J. Miller, Trenton, N. J.
Chaplain-in-chief, W. R. Byers, Columbus, O.
Surgeon-general, Edwin R. Bennett, Chicago, Ill.
Chief Ordnance Officer, Harvey M. Burrell, Leadville, Col.

The business of the meeting being completed, it adjourned on the evening of August 7th, to meet on the call of the Commander-in-chief in the City of Philadelphia, Pa., during the month of August, 1884.

In the foregoing, we have in brief outlined the origin of the Order—its history and progress during the first two years of its existence. From an humble start of a single Camp of less than a dozen members, we have seen it grow and spread out to Division or State organizations, and then to Grand Division and National proportions. Its progress has in all directions been steady and sure, and in all cases its extension and growth has been marked by those features which indicate permanency and lasting success.

In the short space of time named, a firm establishment has been secured in twenty-five (25) States and Territories of the Union, having an active and growing membership of over seventeen thousand; and, in short, the Order has been so kindly received, and is now so well seated and firmly welded to the interests of the old soldier element, that it cannot, under its carefully arranged, full, and complete system, possibly weaken or hesitate in its onward march.

The Grand Army of the Republic was conceived amid the storms and clouds, the trials and dangers, of four long and weary years of civil strife. Born at the close of the contest, it is now in the full noontide hour of its power and glory.

As time has passed on, and from year to year its members, from North to South and from ocean to ocean, have, on the 30th day of May, gathered together and wended their way to the several places where their dead comrades are laid at rest, and have bedecked their graves with the brightest and sweetest flowers of Spring, the question has often been asked, Who will observe these beautiful ceremonies when we have passed beyond? Again, many a thinking Comrade has studied long and deeply as to how his children and descendants could be best and permanently made to fully understand and properly sustain the principles he fought for, and sacrificed so much to maintain. The desire to instruct those who are to follow him, and the people as a whole, so that, as citizens, they may act considerately and well, and at all times consult the common welfare and good, has been strong in his heart, and many an earnest prayer has gone forth, asking for some conclusion that would meet the present requirements and provide for the future.

In the advent of the Sons of Veterans of the United States of America, it is believed that the hope and wish of so many Comrades of the Grand Army of the Republic has been amply answered.

Having proceeded thus far, we will, by request, now present a few of the more important and peculiar features of the Organization, as the same appear in its organic laws and other written work, commencing with the articles on title, principles and objects:

Title.

This Association shall be known as the *Sons of Veterans of the United States of America.*

Principles.

SECTION 1. A firm belief and trust in Almighty God, and a realization that under His beneficent guidance the free institutions of our land—consecrated by the services and blood of our Fathers—have been preserved, and the integrity and life of the nation maintained.

SECTION 2. True allegiance to the Government of the United States of America, based upon a respect for and devotion and fidelity to its Constitution and Laws, manifested by the discountenancing of anything that may tend to weaken Loyalty, incite to Insurrection, Treason or Rebellion, or in any manner impair the efficiency and permanency of our National Union.

Objects.

SECTION 1. To keep green the memories of our Fathers, and their sacrifices for the maintenance of the Union.

SECTION 2. To aid the members of the Grand Army of the Republic in the caring for their helpless and disabled Veterans; to extend aid and protection to their widows and orphans; to perpetuate the memory and history of their heroic dead, and the proper observance of Memorial Day.

SECTION 3. To aid and assist worthy and needy members of our Order.

SECTION 4. To inculcate patriotism and love of country, not only among our membership, but among all the people of our land, and to spread and sustain the doctrine of equal rights, universal liberty, and justice to all.

Membership.

FIRST CLASS.—The sons, not less than eighteen years of age, of deceased or honorably discharged soldiers, sailors, or marines, who served in the Union Army or Navy during the Civil War of 1861–5, shall be eligible to membership in the First Class; also, upon attaining the prescribed age, the eldest lineal male descendants of deceased members of the First Class, and if there are no descendants, male or female, then the male heirs of such deceased members in the collateral branches of their families in the order of genealogical succession according to the rules of descent.

SECOND CLASS.—The eldest sons of living members of the First Class, not less than eighteen years of age, shall be eligible to membership in the Second Class, and upon the death of a member of the First Class, through whom eligibility is derived, a member of the Second Class shall become a member of the First Class.

THIRD CLASS.—The eldest sons of living members of the Second Class, not less than eighteen years of age, shall be eligible to membership in the Third Class, and upon the death or advancement to the First Class, of a member of the Second Class, through whom eligibility is derived, a member of the Third Class shall become a member of the Second Class.

Organization.

The several Constituted Bodies of the Association shall be as follows:

First—Of subordinate organizations, known as Camps; each Camp to have an appropriate name and number, providing, however, that no two Camps in the same Division shall be allowed to use the same name and number.

Second—Of State organizations known as Divisions; providing, however, that the State of Pennsylvania shall be divided into Eastern and Western Divisions, in accordance with an agreement concluded between representatives of each Division; and that all that portion of the State east of the eastern boundaries of the counties of Potter, Clinton, Centre Huntingdon, and Fulton, shall comprise the Eastern Division; and all that part of the State west of the western boundaries of Tioga, Lycoming, Union, Mifflin, Juniata, and Franklin, shall comprise the Western Division; and that the established boundary-lines shall not hereafter be altered or changed except at the request of the two Divisions, made in due form to the Commandery-in-chief.

Third—Of five Grand Divisions as the same are hereinafter defined and bounded.

Fourth—Of the Commandery-in-chief.

GRAND DIVISIONS—CONSTRUCTION.—The different Grand Divisions shall be made up and continued as follows: The first will be composed of Maine, New Hampshire, Vermont Massachusetts, Rhode Island and Connecticut. The second, of New York, New Jersey, Delaware, Pennsylvania, Ohio West Virginia, Maryland District of Columbia, and Virginia The third, of Illinois, Indiana, Michigan, Wisconsin, Minnesota, Iowa, Kentucky, Missouri, Kansas, Nebraska and Dakota. The fourth, of California, Oregon, Washington, Montana, Wyoming, Nevada, Utah, Idaho, Colorado, Arizona and New Mexico. The fifth, of North Carolina, South Carolina, Tennessee, Georgia, Florida, Alabama, Mississippi Louisiana, Arkansas, Indian Territory and Texas.

COMMANDERY-IN-CHIEF—POWERS AND AUTHORITY.—The Commandery-in-chief shall be the supreme source of power for the Sons of Veterans, and under its complete and continued authority shall make all needful rules and regulations to insure a uniform system in all things, and the permanency and continued success of the Order throughout the whole country. To this end, no form of government, either general or local, shall be considered as legally established until the same has been submitted to and duly approved by the Commandery, at a stated yearly meeting of the same. The Commandery shall, through its proper officers, from time to time publish all necessary orders, and give all detailed instructions necessary to maintain uniformity, and for the information and guidance of all concerned, and shall make it its especial duty to see that in all the different branches of the Order the same are faithfully and fully complied with.

Religion and Politics.

The Order being strictly non-sectarian and non-political, the introduction or discussion of sectarian or political topics is strictly prohibited, under penalty of a fine, suspension, or expulsion from the Order.

It shall be the special duty of the Commandery-in-chief to see that the Order fully maintains for all coming time, and in all respects, its claims of being a strictly non-sectarian and non-political association.

Applications for Office.

No officer or past officer of the Order shall, under any circumstances, affix his official signature to any recommendation or application for a political position or of a political character.

Relief Funds.

A Relief Fund for the assistance of needy soldiers, sailors and marines, and the widows and orphans of deceased soldiers, sailors and marines, shall be established by each Camp, and any donations to this fund shall be held sacred for such purposes.

Coat-of-arms.

The following instructions for painting the coat-of-arms of the Order shall be strictly adhered to:

Shield—The field is white; two sabres crossed, points up, in proper colors, enclosed by a wreath of laurels, green; on a chief azure (heraldic blue cobalt); the rising sun, gold; in the disk the monogram S. V. in vermilion; on the white field, arrange thirteen stars of five points, as in the cut, in vermilion.

Supporters—On the right, a soldier in fatigue uniform (without arms) of 1861–5, viz.: dark-blue blouse, light-blue pants, Zouave cap, cross and waist belts of brown leather. On the buckle the letters U. S. On the left a sailor—navy-blue shirt and pants, black silk necktie and regulation-cap.

Crest—An eagle (American) on rocks in proper colors.

The scroll containing the mottoes are white, shaded at the ends with crimson lake; letters black; the ornaments bordering the shield, and under the same, of gold; the flags, naval and military, with cannon and muskets, all in their proper places and colors.

Seals.

The seals of the Commandery-in-chief, the several Grand Divisions and Divisions, of the Order, shall consist of the full coat-of-arms of the Order, surrounded, for the Commandery with the words: Commandery-in-chief Sons of Veterans United States of America; for the Grand Divisions, with the words: ——— Grand Division Sons of Veterans, United States of America; and for the several Divisions of the Order with the words: ——— Division Sons of Veterans, United States of America.

The Camp seals shall consist of the crest of the coat-of-arms, surrounded by thirteen stars, and under the roll shall appear, in Roman numerals, the year of the organization of the Order (to wit, 1881). The whole shall be surrounded with the words: Camp No. ——— Sons of Veterans—and the location, town, or city and State, shall be added to the same.

BATTLE AT DAM NO. 4, POTOMAC RIVER, BETWEEN GENERAL BUTTERFIELD'S BRIGADE AND GENERAL LEE'S ADVANCE ARMY.

FROM A SKETCH BY J. H. SCHELL.

OFFICIAL MOTTO, ETC. - The Latin motto, "*Gratia Dei Servatus,*" which appears on the Coat-of-arms of the Order, its Bronze Medal, etc., reads, when translated into English, "*Preserved by the special favor of God.*"

The sentiment is so entirely appropriate, and it meets the requirements of the case so fully, that it was most cordially received from the start.

On the bar of the Medal or Badge of general membership in the Order, and above the eagle on the crest of the Coat-of-arms, appears in a scroll the Latin phrase, "*Filii Veteranorum,*" which is also expressed under the term, "*Son of a Veteran.*"

The Badge is constructed of fine bronze metal, and is pendent from the bronze bar by a tri-colored ribbon of red, white and blue.

The coat-of-arms, including mottoes, and all of the foregoing, as well as the iron cross,* buttonhole-decoration, and other decorative honors, and various ribbons of the Order, are all from suggestions and designs prepared by Comrade Davis, and the same were, after elaboration by Messrs. Bailey, Banks and Biddle, of Philadelphia, Pa., in due form legally adopted. They are all neat, compact in proportions and outline, and, in general appearance, are specially attractive and suitable to the wants of the Order.

CAMP CEREMONIES. -The camp ceremonies are all simple and beautiful in form, as well as highly impressive and appropriate in their nature.

BADGE OF THE ORDER.

The hour of meeting having arrived, the commanding officer assumes his seat, the Camp bugler sounds the usual call, the drummer beats an appropriate air, and the officers and members take their respective stations. The commanding officer then satisfies himself that all present are entitled to remain. This being accomplished, the established opening prayer is rendered by the Chaplain, and the following hymn is sung:

God bless our native land!
Firm may she ever stand,
Through storm and night.
When the wild tempests rave,
Ruler of wind and wave,
Do thou our country save
By thy great might!

DRUMS.—The drums then softly roll, and the commanding officer in due form declares the Camp open for the transaction of such business as may legally and properly come before it.

The regular order of business is then proceeded with. This having been gone through with, and the commanding officer having previously ascertained that no Brother has anything more to offer for the good of the Order, states that, "there being no further business to come before the Camp, we will proceed to close." The Chaplain then asks the blessings of God on the deliberations of the evening, the Doxology is sung, and the drums softly roll. The Commanding Officer then closes the Camp in due form, and the officers and members

THE GOLD STAR.

retire to their respective homes. The muster of recruits, the installation of officers, and other Camp ceremonies, are each and all marked by original and highly interesting features.

The reader will now have, in a general way, a very clear view of the Order as it now exists. From all of the foregoing it must not be gathered that the course of the organization has been wholly one that has not been beset by obstacles, for such has not been the case. As the Order spread out from its central point, it soon developed and met with opposing elements and influences, who were both anxious and determined that their peculiar views and wishes should prevail. Fortunately, by prudent and judicious treatment and management, these and many other minor obstacles and difficulties have been most happily overcome, and harmony and unity of action to all practical intents is now substantially secured.

It has been suggested that we outline and picture the future of the Order. In approaching this subject, we do so with some hesitation. In all events of more than ordinary importance, and especially in those of the character in hand, it is difficult to look far ahead, and to define what time will bring forth. Various hopes have been indulged in, and various opinions have been expressed.

From one standard authority we quote as follows:

"Major A. P. Davis has builded wiser than he knew. The Sons of Veterans is destined to become the great military organization of this country, while at the same time its devotees, the American youth, will be permeated with that love of our country, that glory in its supremacy, that thrilling of the senses when its National hymns are sung, that none others not thus reared can know or feel. Through this organization the declining days of the Union veteran will be made pleasant, his record of service to his country preserved, his memory honored, patriotism protected, while, if the dire necessity of the Nation should demand, the Sons of Veterans, uniformed, drilled, and equipped, would come at once to her defense with the glory of their fathers surrounding them, each heart pulsating in unison with the rising and falling of the Nation's emblem, and who would be powerful to prevail against such a host."

THE IRON CROSS.

it may be that such will be the case, and that the Sons of Veterans will become the great military organization of the country. It may be that the dire necessity may arise in which they would feel obliged as an organization, and not as individuals, to resort to arms; and still such a conclusion was never reached in the minds of those who are entitled to so much respect and credit for their exertions to establish the Order on a firm, durable basis.

Not as a military organization, but as the great civil *military* society of the country, it is to be hoped, and it is believed, that the Sons of Veterans will long exist, possibly while the life of the nation lasts.

As such, and as a peaceful, unarmed association, they can work no harm, and can accomplish much for the common good.

It is not impossible that, in the dim future, and as the wheel of time turns around, there will, in one section of the country or another, be found those who, to suit the wishes of a faction or locality, or to advance their own personal ends, will attempt to ignore the legal authorities under which we live, and destroy our national compact.

In the event that such an unfortunate conclusion should be reached, may we not hope and believe that the Sons of Veterans will, as a great non-political and non-sectarian moral power and force, leavening and quickening the whole, rise up in

THE GOLD CROSS.

their union and strength, and proclaiming a halt, say: "*Stop! No, you may do as you will. You may legislate as you can, but if you do aught toward blotting out from among the nations of the earth the Union our fathers risked life and limb to save, we will rally to its support, and save it from the Vandal hands of all who are raised against it and seek its destruction.*"

Whatever may come in the future, the present is all bright and clear, and we are a happy, united people.

With their principles and objects constantly before them, the Sons of Veterans, with gathering numbers, will move forward and onward, performing with prudence and consideration the obligations which devolve upon them, and fulfilling the mission which the Ruler of all things has in His forethought and wisdom marked out for them.

NOTE.—The foregoing article traces the history of the Sons of Veterans from their birth up to about January 1st, 1884. Since then steady and, especially of late, rapid progress has been made, and at the present date (July 1st, 1881,) the Order has a membership in good standing of over 21,000. The First Grand Division was permanently organized by Comrade Baugs, of Maine, December 27th, 1883, at Manchester, N. H., and Frank H. Challis, of that city, was duly elected Commander. Comrade Ross, of Maryland, will permanently organize the Second Grand Division at Philadelphia, Pa., August 26th, and at that date he will retire as Provisional Commander. The Third Grand Division will be permanently organized by Commander Markell of Chicago, Ill., July 8th, and a Son of a Veteran will then be elected to assume command. It is proposed to establish permanent organizations in the near future in the Fourth and Fifth Grand Divisions, and action looking in this direction will be taken at the next meeting of the Commandery-in-chief, which is to be held in Philadelphia, Pa., August 27th. The Order is now, to all practical intents and purposes, in the hands of the young men who make up its membership, and at no period in its existence have the prospects been more bright and flattering.

* The Iron Cross is the highest decorative honor known to the Order, and the only persons entitled to wear it are the Past Commanders of its several branches, who have, by faithful service, as is duly defined, entitled themselves to the distinction. Each branch is designated by its peculiar ribbon attached to the Decoration. The Gold Cross and Gold Star are more intended as presentation decorations to be bestowed upon certain officers who may, "*by special adherence and devotion to the principles and objects of the Order, the exercise of particular discretion and vigilance in the discharge of their duties, coupled with long and faithful service in the Order, merit some special reward.*" The whole matter of awarding any and all of the decorative honors is placed under a carefully arranged system in the hands of the proper legislative bodies of the Order, who pass upon and decide each individual case as it is duly presented to them.

DELAWARE INDIANS ACTING AS SCOUTS FOR THE FEDERAL ARMY IN THE WEST.

FROM A SKETCH BY H. LOVIE

INDEX

TO

ILLUSTRATIONS.

VOL. I.

Donelson, Fort, Charge of the Second Iowa Regiment........ 238-239
Donelson, Fort, Gallant charge of the 17th, 46th, and 49th Illinois Volunteers.......................... 234-235
Douglas Camp, Chicago, Ills.......... 283
Dranesville, Va., Battle of 198
Dupont, Samuel Francis, Portrait...... 177
Duryea's Zouaves carrying the body of Lieutenant Greble from the field at Big Bethel........... 94

E.

Edwards Ferry, Engagement at, and Retreat of Federal Troops 150-151
Effect of Shells on Fleeing Confederates.....'''' 181
Election of Lincoln and Hamlin, Reception at Charleston, S. C. of the News. 13
Ellis, E. F. W., Portrait.............. 270
Elk Ridge, Battery on 71
Eleventh Indiana Zouaves Crossing the Potomac at "Romney," 86-87; The Day After "Romney"............... 89
Ellsworth's Chicago Zouave Cadets, Group of.... 73
Ellsworth's Zouaves, Departure of, from New York. 74-75
Ellsworth's Zouaves at Washington, D. C. 74-76
Ellsworth's (Fire) Zouaves Fighting their Old New York Enemy in their usual way........ 76
Ellsworth's Zouaves at Alexandria, Va., 103
Ellsworth Ephraim Elmore, Portrait.. 76
Death of... 77
Encampment of Ellsworth's Zouaves at Washington, D. C. 74-75
Encampment of Federal Troops at Annapolis, Md. 133
Engagement at Romney, Virginia, the Eleventh Indiana Zouaves Crossing the Potomac.....................86-87
Engagement at Sællington, Va......... 94
Ericsson, John, Portrait............... 245
Excitement at Covington, Ky., Gathering of armed citizens................. 373
Explosion of a Confederate Magazine near Fredericksburg............... 353

F.

Fairfax Court House, Va., United States Cavalry Scouting................... 140
Fanny, U. S. Propeller, Capture of.... 120
Farragut, David G., Portrait........... 301
Fascines and Gabions, Making of....... 218
Federal Hill, Baltimore............... 73
Federal foraging parties, near Annandale Chapel, Va... 130
Federal Troops foraging in Missouri... 163
Federal Troops rebuilding Bridge over Bacon's Creek, Ky................. 217
Federal Troops landing in Kentucky... 164
Federal Squadron passing Forts Jackson and St. Philip........ 302
Federal Picket Boat attacked by Confederate sharpshooters near Fernandina, Fla.... 352
Federal Troops marching through Fernandina, Fla.................. 353
Field-øven of the Nineteenth N. Y. Volunteers.......................... 191
First Massachusetts Regiment, Charge of, at Yorktown 313
Fire Raft, sent from Fort Jackson...... 304
First Regiment Ohio Volunteers fired into by a Masked Battery near Vienna, Va.............................. 90
First Michigan Regiment, at Alexandria, Va............................... 103
First Iowa Regiment, Charge of, at battle of Wilson's Creek 112
First New Jersey Brigade, going to support of General Kearny. 346
First Regiment South Carolina (Colored) Volunteers, Dress Parade at Hilton Head, S. C........................... 336
First South Carolina Federal Volunteers, (Colored) at Hilton Head, 336; Taking the Oath of Allegiance............ 368
Flag of the Confederacy ....'' 10
Flag of Fort Sumter.................. 39
Flag the Palmetto................... 16
Floating Battery, Scene on, During Bombardment of Fort Sumter 38
Foot, A. H. Portrait.................. 225
Fort Beauregard, Interior View of..... 180
Forts Clark and Hatteras, General View of, 118, 121; Bombardment of,....122-123
Forts at Craney Island, Blown Up by Commodore Goldsborough 310
Fort Donelson, Charge of the 8th Missouri and the 11th Indiana Regiments, 236; Confederate Prisoners Captured at, 237; Charge of the 2d Iowa Regiment, 238-239; Gallant Charge of the 17th, 48th, and 49th Illinois Regiments............................254-255
Fort Henry, Plan of, 227; Bursting of 42-pound Gun....... 230-231
Fort Huger, Bringing in Confederate Prisoners.........................210-211
Forts Jackson and St Philip, Passage of Second Division, 303; First Day's Bombardment, 294; Sketch of Naval Engagement, 296; Discharge of Grape upon the *Iroquois*, 300; Disguise of Federal Vessels, 302; Sending of Fire-raft from............................ 304
Fort Lafayette, New York Harbor..... 173
Fort Macon, Firing Guns, Mortar Practice, 10-inch Mortar Battery, 260; Fighting the Mortar; Surrender of the Fort 261
Fort Moultrie, Exterior View of, 17; Spiking the Guns, 23; Evacuation of, 26-27; Review of South Carolina Volunteers in, 30-31; Interior View of.. 37
Fort Norfolk (old)................... 310
Forts on the Mississippi Being Passed by the U. S. Fleet........ 303
Fort Pickens, Santa Rosa Island, 45; Relief of by U. S. Fleet.......... 46-47
Fort Powhatan, U. S. Mail Boat Passing Confederate Battery at.......... 345
Fort Pulaski 281, 284, 288, 290-291
Fort Runyon, Searching Wagons at Gate of............................... 127
Fort Sumter, Raising the Flag by Major Anderson, 21; Bombardment of, 34-35; Flag of, 39; View of Interior after the Bombardment, 42; Demonstrations at Charleston during the Bombardment of......................... 43
Fort Walker, Landing of U. S. Troops at...........160, 174-175, 176, 178, 179
Forging Work, for the gun-carriages at the Watervliet Arsenal, Troy, N. Y... 83
Forsyth, John, Portrait 13
Fortress Monroe, Drumming out thieves from, 127; Reception of wounded soldiers.................................. 340
Franklin, William B., Portrait.......... 361
Frederick City, McClellan and his army passing through in pursuit of the Confederates 390
Fremont's Bodyguard, Charge of, at Springfield, Mo., 156; Dragoons's Kitchen.............................. 161
Fremont, John Charles, Portrait 157
Fremont, General, March from Tipton to Warsaw, 163; Headquarters at Mount Jackson, Virginia.... 327
Fremont's Hussars fording the Osage River........... 162
Fremont's Division crossing the Shenandoah, in pursuit of "Stonewall" Jackson.................................. 325
Fremont's Army marching through the woods in pursuit of the Confederates, 327; on its march up the Shenandoah Valley......................... 329
Front Royal, Federal Army entering the town 324
Funeral Cortège, at Boston, Mass...... 78

G.

Gaines Mills, Battle of............ 358-359
Galveston, Texas, Shelling of Batteries at 137
Garfield, James A., Portrait............ 217
General McGowen addressing South Carolina Volunteers in front of the Charleston Hotel 20
General Rosecrans and Staff........... 134
General Banks in Western Maryland, Incident in the march of............... 199
General View of Forts Hatteras and Clark. 118; 121
Georgetown, D. C., General Hospital at, 109
Girardeau Cape, occupied by Federal Troops.................................. 164
Goldsborough, Louis M., Portrait, 201; Blowing up Forts at Craney Island... 310
Gorman, Willis Arnold, Portrait 340
Gosport Navy Yard, Norfolk, Va., Burning of..............................62-63
Goose Creek, Bridge over, destroyed by Confederates 360
Governor, U.S. Steamer, Marines rescued by the U. S Frigate *Sabine* 120
Governor Moore, Confederate Gunboat, engaging U. S. Gunboat *Varuna*.... 297
Gradine, A., Portrait................... 244
Grafton, Va., View of McClellan's Headquarters.................................. 66-67
Grant, General, Bodyguard passing over Mayfield Bridge..................... 228
Grand Review of General Thomas' Brigade in Maryland.................. 193
Graves of Federal forces killed at Port Royal......... 179
Greble, Lieutenant John T., Carried from the Field of Big Bethel........ 91
Group of Colored Men who Captured the Confederate Steamer *Planter*.... 244
Group of Ellsworth's Chicago Zouave Cadets............ 73
Guardhouse at Langley, Va........... 201
Gunpowder Bridge, burning of 69
Guns and Ammunition Shipped from Watervliet Arsenal................ 61

H.

Hall, Lieutenant, with Flag of Truce to Governor Pickens..................... 34
Hall, Nosman J., Portrait. 21
Halleck, Henry Wager, Portrait...... 212
Hampton Roads, Naval Battle at....246-247
Hampton, Va., Evacuation of.......... 117
Hanover Court House, Plan of the Battle..... 341
Harper's Ferry, Burning of Arsenal at, 61; Confederate Battery at 394-395
Harrisonburg to Port Republic, Battle on the Road from.... 330-331
Harrison's Landing, James River, Va., 350-351; Headquarters of General Butterfield, 353; Lincoln and McClellan at.................................. 350
Hardee, William J., Portrait.......... 265
Harper's Ferry, Confederate Battery at.................................394-395
Harvey Birch, Burning of by the Privateer *Nashville* in the British Channel, 200
Hatteras, U. S. Fleet Off the Cape in a Storm 204
Hatteras Island, and Chicamacomico, N.C. 121
Hatteras and Clark, Forts, View of, 118, 121; Bombardment of, 122-123; Camp of the 20th Indiana Regiment, 124
Hawkins' N. Y. Zouaves, Recruiting for the............ 65
Hawkins, Rush C., Portrait.... 221
Hayne, Isaac W., Portrait............. 25
Huyne, Paul H., Portrait............... 43
Hay and Straw Department, Washington, D. C.......................158-159
Headquarters of General Butterfield, Harrison's Landing, James River.... ... 353
Henry, Fort, Plan of, and its Approaches, 227; Bursting of a 42-pound Gun. 230-231
Herron, F. J., Portrait................ 253
Hidden, Harry B., Portrait.. 323
Hill, Ambrose P., Portrait............ 307
Hilton Head, Map of, 191; Morning Detail, 4th New Hampshire Volunteers going to work, 190; Government works at, 186-187; 218-219; View of Fortifications; 290-291; Dress Parade of 1st South Carolina Colored Regiment.................................. 336
Hooker, Joseph, Portrait............... 393
Horses swung overboard for Santa Rosa Island.............................. 48
Horse Depot, near Washington.... 158-159
Huger, Fort, Bringing in Confederate prisoners 210-211
Hunter, David, Portrait................ 249
Hyattstown, Md., Bivouac of the officers of the 12th Massachusetts Regiment.. 193

I.

Incident of General Banks' March in Maryland 199
Indians, Delaware, Acting as Scouts for the Federal Army in the West....... 410
Indignities shown a Massachusetts Editor. 148
Indiana Volunteers, The Burial of 101
Iroquois, U. S. S., Bursting of a Shell on, 300
Island No. 10, Night Expedition to, 240; U. S. Transport, *W. B. Terry*, Pushing Her Way Through the Swamps, 202; Night Bombardment of, 250; Night Attack on March 18th, 1862, 256-250; Bombardment of, 258-259, Surrender of Confederate Forces at Tiptonville.......................306-307

J.

Jackson, Thomas J. "Stonewall," Commencement of Great Flank Movement, 378-379; Portrait of 383
Jackson and St. Philip, Forts, 292, 294, 295, 300, 302, 304
James Island, S. C., Repulse of the Confederate troops, 334-335; Charge of the 3d Rhode Island Regiment at..... 307
Jamestown, *Merrimack*, and *Yorktown*, Confederate vessels, engaging the *Monitor* and Federal Frigates... 246-247
Jeffers, William N., Portrait....... ... 249
Johnson, The Deserter............ 194-195

K.

Kearny, Philip, Portrait............... 367
Keely, John H., Portrait.............. 393
Keyes, General, Division crossing the Chickahominy River................ 318
Kimball, E. A., Portrait.............. 307
King, Rufus, Portrait................. 365

L.

Lafayette, Fort, New York Harbor..... 173
Landing of Troops at the Naval Academy, Annapolis, Md.................. 68
Landing of United States Troops at Fort Walker 169
Landing Federal Troops in Kentucky.. 161
Lane, James H., Portrait.............. 129
Lofferts, Marshall, Portrait........... 57
Lexington, Mo., Siege of........... 180-181
Licking Bridge, Cynthiana, Ky., Fight at................................. 372
Lighthouse at the entrance to Charleston Harbor, S. C........... 25
Lighter with Supplies for shipment by steamers 85
Lillie, Camp.............. 157
Lincoln, Abraham .... Frontispiece.
Lincoln, Abraham, Members of his first Cabinet....... 14-15
Lincoln and Cabinet reviewing Cavalry, 146-147
Lincoln, President, with General McClellan, at Harrison's Landing.......... 350
Louisiana, U. S. Steamer, Scene on.... 184
Lyon, General Nathaniel, death of, 116; Portrait of 117

M.

Macon, Fort, Firing on, 260; Shelling of, 261; Surrender of, and lowering the Confederate Flag. 261
Machine Designed to Destroy the United States Flotilla in the Potomac....... 111
Malvern Hill, Battle of, 346-347; General Hooker Engages the Confederates....... 370-371
Manassas Junction, after its Evacuation by the Confederate Army............. 308
Mansfield, J. K. F., Portrait.......... 390
Map of the Battle of Antietam, or Sharpsburg 400
Map of the Battle of Balls Bluff....... 149
Map of the Battle of Belmont, Mo...., 171
Map of the Battle of Big Bethel....... 91
Map of the Battle of Bull Run, 1st... .. 109
Map of the Battle of Bull Run, 2d..... 381
Map of the Battle of Hanover Court House, Va.......................... 341
Map of the Battle of Peach Orchard, Pittsburg Landing............ 271
Map of the Battle of Pea Ridge....... 251
Map of the Battle of Philippi......... 85
Map of the Battle of Pittsburg Landing................. 265
Map of the Battle of Sharpsburg, or Antietam........ 400
Map of the Battle of Shiloh.......... 265
Map of the Battlefield of Antietam, or Sharpsburg...................... 401
Map of Charleston Bar................ 291
Map of Charleston Harbor............. 50
Map of Forts Hatteras and Clark...... 121
Map of Fort Henry and its approaches. 227
Map of Fort Pulaski.................. 281
Map of Fort Walker 178
Map of Hatteras Island............... 121
Map of Hilton Head 191
Map of Pamlico Sound, N. C........... 121
Map of Pea Ridge and vicinity........ 251
Map of Pensacola Bay, Florida........ 45
Map of Pope's Military Operations in Virginia.... 308
Map of Port Royal Harbor 177
Map of Richmond and vicinity........ 368
Map of Roanoke Island, N. C.......... 205
Map of Sharpsburg, or Antietam, Plan of Battle.......................... 401
Map of the Southern Coast of the United States........ 214
Marshall House, Alexandria, Va...... 77
Martin's Massachusetts Battery opening fire upon Yorktown................. 313
Mason, James Murray, Portrait... ... 153
Members of Lincoln's First Cabinet....14-15
Merrill, Frank P., Commander-in-Chief Sons of Veterans. 408
Meseeck's Point, Discovery of Confederate Battery at.................. . 127

Merrimack, Engagement with the *Monitor*, the *Cumberland*, and the *Congress*, 246-247; Destruction of...... 248
McCulloch, Ben., Portrait.......... 113
McClernand's Headquarters at Shiloh captured by the Confederates.... ..270
McClellan, George B., Headquarters at Grafton, 80-87; Portrait, 95; Witnessing Trial of Skill by Berdan's Sharpshooters, 138-139; Present at Experimental Practice of Building Ponton Bridges, 166-167; Arrival at Yorktown, 312; Passing Through Frederick City.......................... 390
McDowell, Irvin, Portrait.............. 105
McGowan, General, Addressing the Thirty-fifth Abbeville (S. C.) Volunteers at Charleston.................. 29
McKinstry, Justus, Portrait........... 163
Military Execution................ 104-105
Millersville Bridge, Troops repairing the 71
Mill Spring, Battle of............ 222-223
Minnesota, U S. Steamer, rescued by the *Monitor* 246-247
Mississippi, Forts being passed by the U. S. Fleet.... 309
Mitchell, Ormsby M., Portrait.. 211
Monitor, engaging the *Merrimack*. 246-247
Monitor, loss of the.. 248
Monument Square, Baltimore, Md...... 124
Morgan's Raiders, in Paris, Kentucky.. 372
Mortar Batteries, Construction of, at St. Louis, Mo........ 216
Mortar Practice, Putting in a shell..... 200
Mortar Battery, the 10-inch at Fort Macon.. 200
Morrison, William, Portrait........... 244
Morrison, Lieutenant-Colonel, 79th N.Y. Highlanders, his heroic conduct at James Island 337
Moultrie, Fort, Exterior view of, 17, Spiking the Guns, 23; Evacuation of, 26-27; Review of South Carolina Volunteers in, 30-31; Interior view of. . 37
Movement of Troops and Munitions of War 63
Mumfordsville, Ky., Battle of, Confederate Charge, September 14th, 1862 ... 406

N.

Nashville, Confederate Privateer, burning the *Harvey Birch* in the British Channel 315
Naval Academy, Annapolis, Md., Landing of troops at........ 68
Naval Battle, Plan of, at Port Royal Harbor. 177
Naval Battle, at Hampton Roads, Va., 246-247
Naval Brigade, at Alexandria, Va...... 200
Naval Battle on the Yazoo River ...374-375
Naval Battery at New Berne, N. C..... 200
Naval Practice Battery at Washington, D. C............................... 142
Naval Recruiting Office in New York... 65
Negley's Pennsylvania Brigade passing down the Ohio River 212
Negley, James S, Portrait............. 213
Negro Drivers of the Baggage Train Watering their Mules in the Rappahannock River...................... 300
New Berne, N. C., View of, 208; Naval Battery at, 209; From the Interior of Fort Thompson...... 218-219
New Orleans and Algiers, Burning of Confederate Gunboats, Rams and Vessels... 293
New Orleans, Landing of Captain Bailey and Lieutenant Perkins, with a Flag of Truce.......................... 296
New Orleans, Panoramic View of, 298-299; View of Fleet Passing the City, 303; *Westfield* Protecting Fleet from the Fire-raft........ 301
New York Rifles, Firing upon Captain Crosto's Company of the same regiment 139
Niagara, U. S. Steamer, Explosion of a Shell in the Cutter of 126
Norfolk Navy Yard, Burning of, by Confederates 320
Norfolk, Va., Removing Sunken Vessels in the Harbor 320
North Battery, on the Potomac River... 199
Ninth Massachusetts Regiment, Camp at Yorktown....... 311
New Hampshire, Fourth Volunteers going to work on the Fortifications at Hilton Head........ 190

O.

Oak Hill, Springfield, Mo., Battle of, 114-115
Officers' Quarters, 1st Minnesota Regiment, Colonel Sully 349
Ohio and Mississippi Railroad, Accident on 170
Old State House at Columbia.......... 25
Old Fort Norfolk................ 319
Ordnance Bureau at Charleston, S. C.. 33
Osage River, Forded by Fremont's Hussars 162

P.

Paducah, Occupation by Gen'l Grant, 169; Earthworks Erected to Defend .. 169-171
Palmetto Flag, The.................. 16
Pamlico Sound, N. C., Map of, 121, Transfer of Prisoners in............ 261
Peabody, Everett, Portrait........... 269
Peach Orchard, (Shiloh), Plan of the Defense at the...... 271
Pea Ridge, Battle of, 186-187; Map of the country around.. 251
Pea Ridge, General Asboth and Staff.. 253
Peck, John James, Portrait.. 317
Pennsylvania Volunteers, Return to Baltimore Harbor.......... 81
Pennsylvania "Bucktails," Gallant Attack of, Upon a Detachment of "Stonewall" Jackson's Army, 314-315; Recruiting in Philadelphia........... 344
Perkins, Lieutenant, Landing at New Orleans with Flag of Truce...... 59
Pensacola Bay, Fla., U. S. Navy Yard Map of 42
Philadelphia, Arrival and Departure of Troops 26
Philippi, Va., Fight at, 64; Plan of the Fight.... 65
Pickens, Fort, Santa Rosa Island, 46; Relief of, by U. S Fleet.......... 46-47
Pierce, Frank, of the Eighth Massachusetts, diving for a missing rail....... 71
Pierpont, Francis H., Portrait......... 185
Pilson's Battery shelling Confederates on the Shenandoah River............ 327
Pinckney (Castle,) Charleston Harbor, S. C..... 46-47
Pittsburg Landing, Battle of, 234, 261, 266-267, 269; Incident of, 269; Capture of McClernand's Headquarters by the Confederates, 270; The 44th Indiana Regiment, 271; Defense at the Peach Orchard, 271; Recapture of Artillery, 272; Soldiers burning dead horses, 273; Final stand of General Grant's Army, 274-275; Where the Battle commenced, 280; Map of, 265. 265
Plan of the Fight at Philippi, June 3d, 1861........ 65
Plan of the Battle of Ball's Bluff. 149
Plan of Fort Henry and its Approaches, 227
Plan of Fort Walker. 170
Planter, Steamer, Portraits of Four of the Nine Colored Men who Captured her..... 244
Ponton Bridges, Experimental Practice in Building, at Camp Alexander, near Washington, D. C... 166-167
Pope's, General, Military Operations in Virginia 368
Pope, John, Portrait................ 237
Porter, Fitz John, Portrait of...... ... 380
Portraits.
Allen, J. H., Portrait 207
Anderson, Robert, Portrait, 40; Biography, ... 40
Bailey, Theodorus, Portrait, 301; Biography 305
Baker, Edward Dickinson, Portrait, 149; Biography.... 152
Bates, Edward, Portrait 14-15
Beauregard, P. G. T., Portrait, 41; Biography...................... 41
Benham, Henry W, Portrait, 337; Biography.... 337
Blair, Montgomery, Portrait 14-15
Blenker, Louis, Portrait, 235; Biography.................. 235
Bragg, Braxton, Portrait, 137; Biography...... 137
Brittan, S. P., Jr., Portrait 225
Buckner, Simon Bolivar, Portrait, 237; Biography 235
Buell, Don Carlos, Portrait, 241; Biography 245
Burnside, Ambrose E., Portrait, 207, Biography. .... Vol. II.
Butler, Benjamin F, Portrait, 73; Biography 73
"California Joe," Portrait........... 353
Cameron, James, Portrait, 108; Biography............. 109
Cameron, Simon, Portrait..........14-15
Chase, Salmon P., Portrait.........14-15
Corcoran, Michael, Portrait, 373; Biography 369
Couch, Darius N., Portrait, 381; Biography.......................... .. 367
Crawford, Martin J., Portrait........ 18
Davis, A. P., Portrait... 407
Davis, Charles Henry, Portrait, 290; Biography. 290
Davis, Jefferson, Portrait, 19; Biography 19
Dix, John Adams, Portrait, 23; Biography............ 23
Dupont, Samuel Francis, Portrait, 177; Biography....... 177
Ellis, E. F. W., Portrait......... ... 279
Ellsworth, Ephraim, Elmore, Portrait, 76; Biography...... 76
Ericsson, John, Portrait, 245; Biography....... 249
Farragut, David Glasgow, Portrait, 301; Biography... 305
Foote, Andrew H., Portrait, 225; Biography........................ 225
Forsyth, John, Portrait... 19
Franklin, William B., Portrait, 361; Biography.... 367
Fremont, John Charles, Portrait, 157; Biography 163
Garfield, James A., Portrait, 217; Biography 217
Goldsborough, Louis M., Portrait, 201; Biography......... .... Vol II.
Gorman, Willis Arnold, Portrait, 390; Biography 369
Gradine, A., Portrait................ 241
Hall, Norman J., Portrait........... 24
Halleck, Henry Wager, Portrait, 243; Biography 213
Hardee, William J., Portrait, 285; Biography 279
Hawkins, Rush C., Portrait........... 121
Haynes, Paul H., Portrait............ 43
Haynes, Isaac W., Portrait........... 25
Heintzelman, J., Portrait 251
Hildreth, Harry B, Portrait, 312; Biography 331
Hill, Ambrose P., Portrait, 367; Biography... 369
Hooker, Joseph, Portrait, 308; Biography.......................... 400
Hunter, David, Portrait, 289; Biography..................... 280
Jackson, Thomas J. "Stonewall," Portrait, 383; Biography.......... 380
Jeffers, William N., Portrait........ 240
Johnston, Albert Sidney, Portrait....; Biography.... 260
Kearny, Philip, Portrait, 307; Biography.......................... 307
Keely, John R., Portrait, 333; Biography............ 333
Kimball, E. A, Portrait... 207
King, Rufus, Portrait, 365; Biography 367
Lander, Frederic West, Portrait.... Biography......................... 264
Lane, James H., Portrait, 120; Biography.......................... 133
Lefferts, Marshall, Portrait, 57; Biography......................... 67
Lincoln, Abraham, Portrait.. Frontispiece.
Lovell, Mansfield, Portrait ...; Biography............................ 365
Lyon, Nathaniel, Portrait, 117. Biography.......................... 117
Mansfield, Joseph K. F., Portrait, 393; Biography........ 399
Mason, James Murray. Portrait, 155; Biography.... 155
McClellan, George B., Portrait, 95; Biography.... ... .Vol. II.
McCulloch, Ben., Portrait, 113; Biography...... 116
McDowell, Irvin, Portrait, 105; Biography... ....Vol. II
McKinstry, Justus, Portrait, 163; Biography........ 163
Morrill, Frank P., Portrait...... 405
Mitchell, Ormsby M., Portrait, 241; Biography 235
Morrison, William, Portrait 244
Negley, James S., Portrait, 213; Biography.......... 213
Peabody, Everett, Portrait.... 269
Peck, John James, Portrait, 317; Biography... 317
Pierpont, Francis H., Portrait.... . 135
Pope, John, Portrait, 257; Biography 257
Porter, Fitz John, Portrait, 380, Biography.... 380
Pratt, George W., Portrait, 370; Biography...................... 380
Price, Sterling, Portrait, 113; Biography........................... 116
Ricketts, J. D., Portrait, 382; Biography... 401
Roman, A. B., Portrait 18
Rodman, Isaac Peace, Portrait, 397; Biography......................... 399
Rousseau, Lovell H., Portrait, 269; Biography 271
Ruffin, Edmund, Portrait.......... 37
Semmes, Raphael, Portrait, 397; Biography. 401
Seward, William H., Portrait......14-15
Shepley, George F., Portrait, 305; Biography 305
Shields, James, Portrait, 331; Biography. 333
Sickles, Daniel E., Portrait, 357; Biography.... 357
Sigel, Franz, Portrait, 251; Biography........ 252
Slemmer, Adam J., Portrait, 40; Biography.... 40
Slidell, John, Portrait, 153; Biography. 155
Smalls, John, Portrait.............. 244
Smalls, Robert, Portrait.... 244
Smith, Caleb B., Portrait 14-15
Sprague, William, Portrait, 67; Biography............................ 67
Stevens, Isaac Ingalls, Portrait, 378; Biography 380
Stoneman, George, Portrait, 357; Biography.... 363
Stringham, Silas H., Portrait, 119; Biography............... 129
Sumner, Edwin Vose, Portrait, 317; Biography 317
Tyler, E. B., Portrait............ .. 323
Wallace, Lewis, Portrait, 263; Biography 270
Welles, Gideon, Portrait... 14-15
White, Frank J., Portrait 161
Wilkes, Charles, Portrait, 155; Biography.......................... 155
Worden, John Lorimer, Portrait, 249, Biography........ 249
Zollicoffer, Felix, Portrait, 231; Biography....... 235
Port Republic, Battle of......... ..330-331
Port Royal, S. C., Plan of Naval Battle, 177; Graves of Federals killed at.... 180
Portsmouth, Va. Naval Hospital and Battery at 320
Potomac River, Attack upon the Confederate Batteries.................. 83
Potomac, Banks Crossing from Williamsport, Md., to attack "Stonewall" Jackson....... 320
Pratt, George W., Portrait........ 379
Prentiss', General B. M., Division gathering "Secesh" Oats 166
Price, Sterling, Portrait... 118
Provost Marshall Examining Passes at Washington........ 110
Pulaski, Map of, 281; Outside View of, 284; During the Bombardment, 288; Mortar Battery "Stanton" throwing a 13-inch Shell 290-291

Q.

Quaker City, U. S. Steamer, in Lynn Haven Bay, Va...................... 111
Quantico Creek, Burning of a Confederate Schooner....................... 283

R.

Railroad Battery.... 76
Rappahannock River, Rebuilding the Bridge over 380
Recruiting in Philadelphia for the famous Bucktail Regiment........... 344
Reception at Charleston, S. C., of the news of the election of Lincoln and Hamlin 17
Recruiting for the Hawkins' New York Zouaves 62
Refugees from Southern Missouri....... 256
Relief of Fort Pickens, Santa Rosa Island 46-47
Released Prisoners, Transfer of, in Pamlico Sound, S C.. 261
Rescue of Marines from the Steamship *Governor*, by U. S. Frigate *Sabine*.. 124
Review of Cavalry, by President Lincoln and Members of his Cabinet..... 146-147
Review of the Clinch Rifles, at Augusta, Ga.,............. 33
Review of Confederate Troops en route to Virginia, at Savannah, Ga....... 185
Review of South Carolina Volunteer Troops in Fort Moultrie......... ... 30-31
Rhode Island Regiments embarking at Providence for New York and Washington........... 68
Richmond, Va, Salute of one hundred guns 109
Rich Mountain, General Rosecrans advancing, 97; Battle of....... 98-99, 100
Ricketts J. D., Portrait of........... 382

INDEX

TO

HISTORICAL MATTER.

A.

Adams, Captain, *U. S. S Sabine.* 105
Adams, J. H., Commissioner from South Carolina to Washington.......... 21
Adelaide, U. S. Str., Commander Stellwagen........ 110
Alabama (No. 290), Confederate Privateer, Captain Semmes 399; 401
Alabama, Date of Secession...... ... 18
Alden, Captain of the *U. S. S Richmond*. 203
Allen, Colonel J. W., *9th New Jersey Volunteers* 201
Allen, Commodore 61
Allen, Major John H., *4th Rhode Island Volunteers*....... 135
Allston, Abram 244
Ammen, Daniel, Commander of the *U. S. S Seneca* 177
Anderson, B. H 391; 397
Anderson, Major Robert, Evacuation of Fort Moultrie, 18; 19, 20; private letter from, 19, raising the Flag on Fort Sumter, 20; writes to Governor Pickens, 22; sketch of........ 40
Anderson, Mrs Robert, search for Peter Hart; at Fort Sumter.............. 23
Anderson, General, *Confederate*.85; 135; 305
Anderson, Lieutenant-Colonel Frank.205. 351
Andrews, Major W S G 110, 121; 173
Annapolis and Baltimore occupied by General Butler 69
Antietam Creek, Battle of 391-397
Aquia Creek, Attack on by the Confederates.... 85
Arkansas, Confederate ram, Fight with U. S. Gunboats *Carondelet* and *Tyler*. 373.................................. 381
Arkansas, Date of Secession............ 19
Arkansas Regiment, Thirteenth........ 17a
Arnold, Major.... 133
Armstrong, Commodore............... 48
Arsenal at Augusta, Ga., Seizure of.... 33
Arsenal at Little Rock seized.......... 16
Artillery, U. S. Regular: First, 49, Second.............................. 49
Asboth, General Alexander S 161; 251
Asboth, Colonel A, ... 249
Ashby, General Turner................. 329
Army Office in New York City......... 141
Augusta, Ga., Seizure of Arsenal at 33
Augusta, U. S. Str.. ....177; 244
Augur, General Christopher C..... .. 383
Avery's History of Georgia... 88
Ayres, Captain Romeyn B.......... ... 361

B.

Battle of Antietam Creek (Sharpsburg). 391-397
" Ball's Bluff 148
" Bealington 95
" Beaver Dam.................. 357
" Belmont, Mo.................. 171
" Big Bethel 89
" Bull Run (The First)....103; 141
" Bull Run (The Second)..381; 383, 384, 385, 386........... 387
" Bull Pasture (McDowell).... 321
" Carnifex Ferry............... 135
" Carrick's Ford, Va.......... 95
" Cedar Mountain.............. 381
" Chantilly..................... 389
" Charles City Cross Roads..... 361
" Chickahominy River..... .. 357
" Cross Keys..................... 329
" Cross Roads................... 361
" Donelson, Fort................ 237
Battle of Dranesville.................. 197
" Gaines Mills................ 357
" Germantown.................. 389
" Groveton, 381; 383; 384; 385; 386..................... 387
" Hampton Roads (Naval Battle). 215
" Hanover Court House.... .. 341
" James Island, S C............ 333
" Kernstown................... 319
" Leesburg..................... 148
" Lexington 129
" Logan's Cross Roads (Mill Springs) 221
" Malvern Hill.... 363
" Manassas, 103, 141; 381; 383; 384; 385; 386.... 387
" Mechanicsville.... 357
" Mill Springs (Logan's Cross Roads) 221
" Munfordsville................ 409
" McDowell (or Bull Pasture).. 321
" New Berne, N. C..... 268
" New Cold Arbor (Cold Harbor). 357
" New Market Cross Roads.... 361
" Oak Hill (Wilson's Creek).. 113
" Ox Hill 389
" Pea Ridge.................... 249
" Philippi 84
" Pittsburg Landing (Shiloh).. 263
" Port Republic 329; 333
" Port Royal................ 177
" Prestonburg 237
" Rich Mountain.............. 95
" Roanoke Island.............. 199
" Romney 85
" Savage's Station........357; 361
" Secessionville............... 333
" Second Bull Run, 381; 383; 384, 385; 386..... 387
" Sharpsburg (Antietam)...391; 397
" Shiloh (Pittsburg Landing)... 263
" Slaughter's Mountain 381
" South Mountain 391; 397
" White Oak Swamp 361
" Wilson's Creek (Oak Hill).... 113
" Williamsburg......... 309
" Willis Church.....359; 360; 361
" Winchester 310; 323; 323
Battles fought before Richmond.... ... 339
" along the Chickahominy River.......... .354; 355
Badges and Crosses of S. O. V. 409
Bailey, Captain Theodorus, of the *U. S. S. Colorado*........ ....135; 285; 301; 305
Baker, General Edward Dickinson, 148; sketch of his life... 153
Baker, Senator E. D from Oregon, Speech at New York.... 53
Baker, Captain, of the *U. S. S. Pioneer*. 201
Baldwin, Colonel, of the *57th Illinois Regiment*.......................... 241
Baldwin, Colonel S. D.......... 263
Baltimore and Annapolis occupied by General Butler......... 69
Balmstead, Lieutenant-Colonel, *11th Maine Volunteers* 345
Ball's Bluff, Battle of............. ... 148
Bancroft, George, Secretary of the Navy. 68
Bankhead, Commander J. P., *U. S. S. Pembina* 177; 249
Banks, General Nathaniel P., 148; 191; 305; 319, 321; 333.......... . 391
Bates, Edward, Attorney-General...... 19
Barksdale, Colonel... ....149; 365
Barnwell, R. W., Commissioner from South Carolina to Washington....... 21
Barlow, Colonel Francis C.... 397
Baltimore *Sun*, Account of the Riot.... 60
Barrancas, Fort, 10; 45; 48, 49........ 211
Barron, Samuel..... ....121; 137
Bartow, Fort....... 205
Bayard, General George D., 58; 109; 325....................... 329
Bealington, Carrick's Ford, and Rich Mountain, Battles of 95
Beaufort, N. C., Occupation of. 209
Beaufort, S. C., Capture of 177
Beauregard, General P. G. T., 37; 41; 257; 271............................ 273
Beauregard, Confederate Ram........ 309
Beauregard, Fort.................... 177
Beaver Dam, Battle of................ 357
Bebee, Lieutenant..... 201
Beird, Captain....... 149
Belmont, Mo., Battle of, ... 171
Belknap, Colonel T. S................. 315
Belzhoover's Battery................. 171
Bell, Captain Henry W............... 205
Bell, Major Joseph W................ 303
Benham, General Henry W., U. S. Engineers 109; 135; 289; 336; 347
Bendix, Colonel John E, "Steuben" Volunteers 82
Benjamin, Judah P., Attorney-General Confederate States..... 10
Benton, U. S. Gunboat,...... 373
Berrett, James W., At Fort Lafayette,. 173
Berge, Colonel, *66th Illinois Sharpshooters*..... 237
Berryman, Captain, of the *U. S. S. Wyandot*...... 48
Bienville, U. S. Str. 177
Big Bethel, Battle of..... 89
Big Tybee Island, Capture of.......... 177
Bissell, Colonel J. W............ ... 257
Blake, Captain, of the *U. S. S Maryland*. 69
Blair, Frank P., of Missouri.......... 79
Blair, Montgomery, Postmaster-General. 18
Blanchard, Fort 205
Blenker, Colonel Louis, 103; sketch of.. 235
Boggs, Captain, of the *Varuna*.263; 297; 301
Bonds, Coupon U. S... 143
Bonds, U. S. Government............. 143
Bonham, General M. L. 105
Bowling Green, Reoccupation of....... 243
Bragg, General Braxton......137; 273; 279
Bramhall, Lieutenant.............. . 149
Branch, General Lawrence O'B.208; 345; 397
Breckenridge, General J. C 305; 259
Brushwood, Captain John G., of the *U. S. Revenue Cutter McClelland*....... 22
Britten, Lieutenant S. B, Jr........... 327
Brown, Joseph E., Governor of Georgia. 33
Brown, Major, 6th Mass. Regt..... .60, 61
Browne, William M., Assistant Secretary of State, Confederate States......... 19
Brown, Colonel J. M.. 346
Brown & Derby, Publishers 21
Brownell, Private Francis E........... 56
Brooks, General Wm. T. H........... 391
Brooklyn, U. S. Str., 45; Captain Walker, 135 · Captain Craven....... 203
Brown, Colonel Harvey............49; 135
Brown, Captain J N., Commander of the Confederate Ram *Arkansas* 381
Buchanan, Captain, of the *Merrimack*. 246
Buchanan, Franklin... 68
Buchanan, James, President, 10; interview with the South Carolina Commissioners... ....19; 21; 45
Buckner, General Simon Bolivar, Sketch of,...........................235; 243
Buell, General Don Carlos, 10; 237; 243; 273 400
Budd, Captain F. A., of the *U. S. S. Penguin*............ 177
Buford, Colonel N. B., *27th Illinois Regiment*............................ 171
Bunting's R. I. Battery...........148, 149
Burns, General W. W... 391
Bull Run (First Battle of).........103; 141
Bull Run (Second Battle of)..381 · 384, 384; 385; 386. 387
Bull Pasture, Battle of 321
Burnside, General Ambrose E., 67; 199; 208, 261 391
Burt, Colonel E R..................... 149
Butterfield, General Daniel, Colonel of the 12th N. Y S. M.... ...67; 341; 345
Butler, Major, *11th Louisiana Regiment*, Death of... 171
Butler, Pierce, at Fort Lafayette....... 173
Butler, General Benjamin F..57; 69; 73; 121; 113; 209; 301, 302, 303; 305

C.

Cadwallader, General George......... 73
Cahill, Colonel, *9th Connecticut Volunteers*............ 293
Cairo, *U. S. S*.... 309
Calhoun, Lieutenant,. 201
Caldwell, Lieutenant, *U. S. S. Itasca* . 298
Cameron, Simon, Secretary of War.... 18
Carpenter, Frank B., "Six Months in the White House." Portrait of Lincoln (frontispiece)... 16
Cameron, Colonel James.........104; 105
Campbell, General.... 383
Carnifex Ferry, Battle of............. 135
Carrick's Ford, Battle of............. 95
Carr, General Joseph B 88; 91; 231
Carr, Colonel Eugene A............... 249
Carr, Commander, of the U. S.S. *Quaker City*................ 110
Carondelet, U. S. S., 250; Fight with Confederate Ram *Arkansas*.....379, 381
Carroll, Colonel, *8th Ohio Volunteers* .. 319
Carroll, General.................... 320
Catlin Lieutenant J. H......... 171
Castro, General (Mexican) 163
Casey, General Silas.........311; 345; 361
Cass, General, Speech of.... 55
Cass, Commander..................... 161
Castle Pinckney.....................19; 21
Caswell, Fort, at Macon, S. C...... ... 16
Cayuga, U. S. Str..................... 293
Cedar Mountain, Battle of............ 381
Cease, Ullery, at Fort Lafayette, ... 173
Chase, Salmon P., Secretary of the Treasury, 18; resigns............. .. 22; 141
Chase, Colonel William H............ 48
Chatfield, Colonel, *3d Connecticut Volunteers*..........................104; 285
Chatfield, Colonel James L., *6th Connecticut Volunteers*.............. 177
Chantilly, Battle of.................. 389
Chambliss, Captain William P........ 345
Chasseur, U. S. Str., Captain West .. 201
Chalmers, General J. B 400
Charles City Cross Roads, Battle of.... 361
Charleston Harbor, Forts and defences of, 36; Daring exploit of colored men. 214
Charleston, S. C., Rejoicings in........ 43
Chickahominy River, Battles along the, 354............................. 355
Chickahominy River, Battle of the.... 357
Chesnut, James, Letter to Major Anderson........................... 37
Chew, R. A., State Department.... .. 37
Cheatham, Major R. B............... 148
Cheatham, General B. F.....171; 209 271

D.

E.

F.

G.

T.

U.

V.

W.

Y.

Z

CHRONOLOGICAL

LIST OF EVENTS

(1860-1863)

AND

MISCELLANEOUS STATISTICS.

COMPILED AND ARRANGED

BY

T. CAMPBELL-COPELAND,

Editor of "Modern Military Maxims," etc., etc.

FROM "OFFICIAL RECORDS OF THE FEDERAL AND CONFEDERATE ARMIES;" THE "REBELLION RECORD;" "PHISTERER'S STATISTICAL RECORD;" "HAMERSLEY'S ARMY REGISTER;" THE "OFFICIAL ARMY REGISTER;" STATISTICAL VOLUMES AND PAMPHLETS OF THE DEPARTMENT OF THE INTERIOR; "THE ANNUAL CYCLOPÆDIA;" "TWENTY YEARS OF CONGRESS;" AND SUCH OTHER THOROUGHLY RELIABLE BOOKS AND DOCUMENTS AS HAVE BEEN MADE AVAILABLE.

CHRONOLOGICAL LIST OF EVENTS (1860-1865).

DATE.	EVENT	LOCATION.	DURATION.	FORCE. F.	FORCE. C.	COMPOSITION OF FORCE.	COMMANDERS.	KILLED. F.	KILLED. C.	WOUNDED. F.	WOUNDED. C.	PRISONERS TAKEN AS F.	PRISONERS TAKEN AS C.	MISSING. F.	MISSING. C.	[illegible]	[illegible]	ADVANTAGE.
1860																		
Nov. 6	President Lincoln elected.																	
Nov. 7	Palmetto Flag raised at Charleston, South Carolina.																	
	Indignation meetings held in Southern cities.																	
	Major Fitz-John Porter, A. A. G., inspected Forts and Garrisons in Charleston Harbor.																	
	Major Robert Anderson assigned to command of defences in Charleston Harbor.																	
	Captain T. Seymour arrested by Charleston City Authorities for attempting to transfer supplies from Charleston Arsenal to Fort Moultrie.																	
Nov. 13	State of South Carolina resolved to raise 10,000 Volunteers.																	
Nov. 18	Legislature of Georgia voted $1,000,000 to arm the State.																	
Nov. 26	Legislature of Mississippi specially convened.																	
Dec. 1	Legislature of Florida specially convened.																	
Dec. 10	Legislature of Louisiana specially convened.																	
Dec. 20	South Carolina seceded.																	
Dec. 23	Louisiana seceded.																	
Dec. 26	Fort Moultrie, S. C., evacuated by Major Anderson.																	
Dec. 27	Fort Pinckney, S. C., seized by Confederates.																	
	Flag raised on Fort Sumter by Major Anderson.	CHARLESTON HARBOR, S. C.																
	Cutter *William Aiken* surrendered to Confederates by Capt. Coste.																	
Dec. 29	Palmetto Flag raised at Charleston.																	
Dec. 30	Arsenal at Charleston seized by Confederates.																	
1861																		
Jan. 2	Fort Johnston, S. C., seized by Confederates.																	
Jan. 3	Fort Pulaski, Ga., seized by Confederates.																	
	Enrollment of Volunteers commenced at New York City.																	
Jan. 4	Arsenal at Mount Vernon seized by Confederates.																	
	U. S. Revenue Cutter *Dolphin*, seized at Savannah, Ga., and released.																	
Jan. 5	First expedition for the relief of Fort Sumter sails from New York Harbor.	NEW YORK HARBOR, N. Y.		230		Federal Steamer *Star of the West*, with Artillery and Marines												
	Forts Morgan and Gaines, Ala., seized by State Troops.																	
Jan. 6	U. S. Arsenal at Apalachicola, Fla., seized by State Troops.																	
Jan. 7	Fort Marion, Fla., seized by Confederates.																	
	Legislature of Virginia specially convened.																	
	Senators Toombs and Wigfall arrested for treason.																	
	Fort Johnston, N. C., seized by citizens of Smithville.																	
Jan. 9	Mississippi seceded.																	
	Star of the West fired at in Charleston Harbor.																	
Jan. 10	Fort Caswell, N. C., seized by citizens of Smithville and Wilmington.																	
	Fort Livingston, La., seized by Confederates.																	
	U. S. Arsenal and Barracks at Baton Rouge, La., seized by Confederates.																	
	Alabama and Florida seceded.																	
Jan. 11	U. S. Marine Hospital, New Orleans, seized by Confederates.	NEW ORLEANS, LA.				Party of Louisiana Militia. (Confederate.)												
	Forts Jackson and St. Philip, La., seized by Confederates.																	
	Formal demand made for surrender of Fort Sumter, and refused by Major Anderson.																	
Jan. 12	Surrender of Fort Pickens, Fla., demanded.																	
	Fort Barrancas, Fla., seized by Confederates.																	
	Fort McRee, Fla., seized by Confederates.																	
	Navy Yard, Pensacola, Fla., seized by Confederates.																	
Jan. 14	Fort Taylor, Key West, Fla., garrisoned by U. S. Troops.																	
	Fort Pike, La., seized by Confederates.																	
Jan. 15	U. S. Schooner *Dana* seized by Florida State authorities.																	
	Second demand for surrender of Fort Pickens, Fla.																	
Jan. 18	Fort Jefferson, Tortugas, garrisoned by U. S. Troops.																	
	Third demand for surrender of Fort Pickens.																	
Jan. 19	Georgia seceded.																	
Jan. 20	Fort on Ship Island, Miss., seized by Confederates.																	
Jan. 24	Re-enforcements for Fort Pickens, Fla., sail from Fort Monroe, Va.																	
	Arsenal at Augusta, Ga., seized by Confederates.	AUGUSTA, GA.				Local Militia. (Confederate.)	*By order of* The Governor of Georgia.											
	Catawba Indians, S. C., enter Confederate State Service.																	
Jan. 26	Oglethorpe Barracks, Savannah, Ga., and Fort Jackson, seized by State Troops.																	
	Louisiana seceded.																	
Jan. 28	Fort Macomb, La., seized by Confederates.																	
	U. S. property in the hands of Army Officers seized at New Orleans.																	
Jan. 29	U. S. Cutter *Robert McClelland* surrendered at New Orleans to State Authorities.																	
Jan. 31	Mint at New Orleans, La., seized by Confederates.																	
	Attorney General of S. C. offers to purchase Fort Sumter.																	
Feb. 1	Texas seceded.																	
Feb. 2	U. S. Cutter *Lewis Cass* surrendered at Mobile to State of *Louisiana*.																	
Feb. 6	U. S. Steamer *Brooklyn* arrives off Pensacola, Fla., with re-enforcements for Fort Pickens.																	
Feb. 7	The Choctaw Nation declares its adherence to the Southern States.																	
Feb. 8	Five vessels from New York seized at Savannah—released again on 10th February.																	

CHRONOLOGICAL LIST OF EVENTS (1860-1865).—Continued.

DATE.	EVENT.	LOCATION.	DURATION.	FORCE. F.	FORCE. C.	COMPOSITION OF FORCE.	COMMANDERS.	KILLED. F.	KILLED. C.	WOUNDED. F.	WOUNDED. C.	PRISONERS TAKEN BY F.	PRISONERS TAKEN BY C.	MISSING. F.	MISSING. C.	[illegible]	[illegible]	ADVANTAGE.
1861																		
Feb. 8	U. S. Arsenal at Little Rock, Ark., seized by Confederates.																	
Feb. 12	U. S. Ordnance Stores seized at Napoleon, Ark.																	
Feb. 16	U. S. Arsenal and Barracks at San Antonio, Texas, seized by Confederates.																	
Feb. 18	Jefferson Davis inaugurated as "President of the Confederate States."																	
	U. S. Military Posts in Department of Texas surrendered by General Twiggs, U. S. A.																	
Feb. 19	Fort Kearney, Kansas, seized by Confederates and retaken by Federal Troops.																	
	General Twiggs superseded by Colonel Waite.																	
	U. S. Paymaster's office at New Orleans seized by Confederates.																	
Feb. 21	Three New York vessels seized at Savannah, Ga.																	
	Camp Cooper, Texas, abandoned.																	
	U. S. property at Brazos Santiago, Texas, seized by Confederates.																	
Feb. 23	President Lincoln entered Washington.																	
Feb. 26	Camp Colorado, Texas, abandoned.																	
Feb. 28	Mint at Dahlonega, Ga., seized by Confederates.																	
Mar. 1	General Twiggs expelled from U. S. Army.																	
	The Government of the Confederate States assumes control of Military affairs at Charleston.																	
Mar. 2	U. S. Cutter *Dodge* seized in Galveston Bay, Texas.	GALVESTON, TEXAS																
Mar. 3	Mint at Charlotte, N. C., seized by Confederates.																	
	Brigadier-General Beauregard, C.S.A., assumes command at Charleston.																	
Mar. 4	Arkansas seceded.																	
	President Lincoln inaugurated.	WASHINGTON, D. C.																
Mar. 5	Fort Brown evacuated.																	
	General Beauregard ordered by Jefferson Davis to command the Confederate Forces at Charleston.																	
Mar. 6	Fort Brown, Texas, surrendered.																	
Mar. 7	Ringgold Barracks, Texas, abandoned.																	
	Camp Verde, Texas, abandoned.																	
Mar. 11	Brigadier-General Bragg, C.S.A., assumes command of Confederate Forces.																	
Mar. 12	Southern Commissioners request interview with Secretary of State, who declines to receive them.																	
	Fort McIntosh, Texas, abandoned.																	
Mar. 15	Camp Wood, Texas, abandoned.																	
Mar. 17	Camp Hudson, Texas, abandoned.																	
Mar. 19	Fort Clark, Texas, abandoned.																	
	Fort Inge, Texas, abandoned.																	
	Fort Lancaster, Texas, abandoned.																	
Mar. 20	Sloop *Isabel* seized at Mobile by Confederates.																	
	Fort Brown, Texas, abandoned.																	
	Fort Duncan, Texas, abandoned.																	
Mar. 21	Seizure of the Sloop *Isabella*.																	
Mar. 22	Colonel W. W. Loring, U.S.A., assumes command of the Department of New Mexico.																	
Mar. 28	Fort Chadbourne, Texas, abandoned.																	
Mar. 29	Fort Mason, Texas, abandoned.																	
Mar. 31	Fort Bliss, Texas, abandoned.																	
Apr. 3	Schooner *Rhoda H. Shannon* fired upon by the Confederate Batteries.																	
Apr. 5	Fort Quitman, Texas, abandoned.																	
Apr. 7	Re-enforcements for Fort Pickens, Fla., sail from New York.																	
Apr. 10	Second expedition for the relief of Fort Sumter sails from New York Harbor.																	
Apr. 11	Evacuation of Fort Sumter demanded by General Beauregard.																	
*12&13	*Bombardment.	FORT SUMTER, S. C.	33 hours.			Battery E, 1st U. S. Artillery.	Major Anderson, F. Gen. Beauregard, C.	1		4								Conf'd
	Re-enforcements from Fort Monroe, and detachment of Marines, landed at Fort Pickens, Fla.																	
Apr. 13	Brevet-Colonel Harvey Brown assumes command of the Department of Florida.																	
	Fort Davis, Texas, abandoned.																	
Apr. 14	Fort Sumter evacuated by Major Anderson.																	
	Arsenal at Charleston seized by Confederates.																	
Apr. 15	Fort Macon, N. C., seized by Confederates.																	
	The Governor of Kentucky, and of North Carolina, refuses to supply *Federal Troops* for service.																	
Apr. 16	Fort Washita, Indian Territory, abandoned.																	
	Fort Caswell, N. C., seized by Confederates.																	
	Fort Johnston, N. C., seized by Confederates.																	
Apr. 17	Virginia seceded.																	
	Steamer *Star of the West* seized by Galveston Volunteers.																	
	Re-enforcements from New York arrive at Fort Pickens, Fla.																	
	The Governor of Missouri refuses to supply quota of Federal Militia.																	
Apr. 18	Major-Gen. Taliaferro assigned to command of Virginia forces at Norfolk, Va.																	
	Arsenal at Harper's Ferry burned by Federal forces.	HARPER'S FERRY, VA.		43		Detachment, Ordnance Men.	Lieut. Jones, F.											

*Owing to the conflicting accounts issued officially and semi-officially respecting the casualties, etc., in several important engagements, the totals given in the list of events will be found to vary occasionally from those given in the text.

CHRONOLOGICAL LIST OF EVENTS (1860-1865).—Continued.

DATE.	EVENT	LOCATION.	DURATION	FORCE. F.	FORCE. C.	COMPOSITION OF FORCE.	COMMANDERS	KILLED. F.	KILLED. C.	WOUNDED. F.	WOUNDED. C.	PRISONERS TAKEN BY F.	PRISONERS TAKEN BY C.	MISSING. F.	MISSING. C.			ADVANTAGE.
1861																		
Apr. 16	Federal Subsistence stores seized at Pine Bluff, Ark.																	
	The Governor of Tennessee refuses to supply Federal troops for service.																	
	Custom House and Post Office at Richmond seized by Confederates																	
	Secession Flag raised and torn down in Baltimore.																	
Apr. 19	Major-General Pattern-n assigned to command over the States of Delaware, Pennsylvania and Maryland, and the District of Columbia.																	
	Street fight	STREETS OF BALTIMORE, MD.		[illegible]		6th Mass. State Militia 26th Penn. Volunteers	Col. Jones, F. Capt. Follansbee, F.	3		9								
	Steamer *St. Nicholas* seized at Washington																	
	Bridges near Baltimore burned by Secessionists.																	
	Southern ports blockaded by order of President Lincoln.																	
Apr. 20	General Butler's command arrives at Annapolis, Md.																	
	Mass meeting of citizens in Union Square, New York.																	
	Gosport Navy Yard, Va., burnt.																	
	U. S. arsenal at Liberty, Mo., seized by Confederates																	
	Steam tug, *Uncle Ben*, seized at Wilmington, N. C., by Secessionists.																	
Apr. 21	Fort Norfolk seized by Secessionists.																	
	U. S. Branch Mint at Charlotte, N. C., seized by State Authorities																	
	Colonel Van Oern, C. S. A., assumes command in Texas.																	
Apr. 22	U. S. arsenal at Fayetteville, N. C., seized by Confederates.																	
	The Governor of Arkansas refuses to supply quota of Federal Militia.																	
Apr. 23	Major-General R. E. Lee, assigned to command of Confederate Military and Naval forces of Virginia.																	
	Federal officers at San Antonio, Texas, seized as prisoners of war.																	
	Company of Eighth U. S. Infantry, (Lee's), captured near San Antonio, Texas.																	
	Fort Smith, Arkansas, seized by Confederates.																	
Apr. 24	The Governor of Virginia, releases all vessels except *Jamestown* and *Yorktown*.																	
Apr. 25	General Harney arrested at Harper's Ferry, by Virginia Authorities.																	
	Stores in Federal Arsenal at St. Louis, seized by Illinois Volunteers.																	
	Steamer *Catawba* seized at New Orleans—afterwards released																	
	Federal troops captured at Saluria, Texas.	SALURIA, TEXAS			800		Maj. Sibley, F. Col. Van Dorn, C.						630					Conf'd.
	Sioux and Chippewa Indians volunteer to serve under the Federals.																	
	Fort Stockton, Texas abandoned.																	
Apr. 26	Bridges over Gunpowder River burnt by Baltimore Secessionists.																	
	Steamer *Hillman* seized at Cairo by Illinois Troops.																	
	Major Gen. J. E. Johnston assigned to command of State Forces in and about Richmond, Va.																	
	Major-Gen. Gwynn assigned to command of State Forces in and about Norfolk, Va.																	
Apr. 27	Harbor Police of New York detain six vessels.																	
	Major-Gen. Patterson assigned to command of the Department of Pennsylvania.																	
	Brig.-Gen. Butler assigned to command of the Department of Annapolis.																	
	Colonel J. K. F. Mansfield U. S. A., assigned to command of the Department of Washington.																	
	Colonel T. J. Jackson assigned to command of State Troops in and about Harper's Ferry, W. Va.																	
Apr. 29	Books and Cash in possession of the Collector, Nashville, Tennessee, seized by order of State Governor.																	
Apr. 30	General Harney released.																	
May 1	Volunteer Forces called out in Virginia.																	
May 3	Confederate Privateer *Savannah* captured by U. S. Brig *Perry*.																	
	The Governor of Virginia issues call for additional forces.																	
May 4	U. S. Ordnance Stores seized at Kansas City, Mo.																	
	Colonel Porterfield assigned to command of State Forces in North-Western Virginia. (W. Va.)																	
May 5	Relay House near Baltimore, seized by General Butler																	
	Forts Arbuckle and Cobb, Indian Territory, abandoned.																	
	Alexandria, Virginia, abandoned by State Troops, (re-occupied).																	
May 6	Tennessee seceded.																	
	Arkansas seceded.																	
May 7	Routes between Philadelphia, Harrisburg and Washington, via Baltimore, re-established.																	
May 8	Privateer captured at mouth of the Chesapeake by steamer *Harriet Lane*.																	
May 9	Capture of Federal Troops at San Lucas Spring, Texas.																	
	Exchange of shots between the Federal Steamer *Yankee* and the batteries at Gloucester Point, Va.																	
May 10	Capture of Camp Jackson by Federal Forces	CAMP JACKSON, MO.		7000		1st, 3rd and 4th Missouri Reserve Corps 3rd Missouri Volunteers	Capt. Lyon, F. Gen. Frost, C.					639						Federal.
	Major-General R. E. Lee assigned to command of the Confederate States Forces serving in Virginia.																	
May 11	Riot in St. Louis, Mo.					4th Missouri U. S. Reserve Corps			7									
	Brig.-Gen. W. S. Harney, U. S. A., resumes command of the Department of the West.																	
May 13	Baltimore, Maryland, occupied by Federal Troops																	
	Major-Gen. Geo. B. McClellan, U. S. A., assumes command of the Department of the Ohio.																	

CHRONOLOGICAL LIST OF EVENTS (1860-1865).—Continued.

DATE	EVENT.	LOCATION.	DURATION.	FORCE. F.	FORCE. C.	COMPOSITION OF FORCE.	COMMANDERS.	KILLED. F.	KILLED. C.	WOUNDED. F.	WOUNDED. C.	PRISONERS TAKEN BY F.	PRISONERS TAKEN BY C.	MISSING. F.	MISSING. C.	[illegible]	[illegible]	ADVANTAGE.
1861																		
May 13	Brig.-Gen. B. McCulloch, C. S. A., assigned to command in the Indian Territory.																	
May 14	Seizure of a train of cars at Harper's Ferry, West Virginia.																	
	Schooner with arms, etc. for Confederates, seized at Baltimore.																	
May 16	Bark *Ocean Eagle* seized by Confederate steamer, near New Orleans.																	
	Expedition from St. Louis to Potosi, Mo.																	
May 18 / May 19	Engagement	SEWALL'S POINT, VA.	1½ hours			U. S. Steamer *Monticello*; Steam-tug *Federal* / (Confederate) City Light Guards; Wood's Rifles; Det. Norfolk Juniors; Det. Light Artillery Blues	Com. Eagle, U. S. N. / Captain Colquitt, C.			2								Conf'd.
May 19	2 Schooners, carrying Confederate Troops, seized by steamer *Freeborn*, near Fort Washington, Potomac.																	
May 20	North Carolina seceded.																	
	Mass Meeting of citizens, Union Square, New York.																	
May 21	Arms seized by Federal Troops near Greenmount Cemetery, Baltimore																(600)	
	Colonel John B. Magruder, C.S.A., assigned to command at Yorktown, Va.																	
	Brigadier-General M. L. Bonham, C.S.A., assigned to command on the "Alexandria Line," Va.																	
	Convention between General Harney and Major-General S. Price, Missouri State Guard.																	
May 22	Fortress at Ship Island, Gulf of Mexico, destroyed by Federal Troops, to prevent occupation.																	
	Steamer *J. C. Swan* seized near St. Louis, by order of General Lyon.																	
	Brigadier-General B. F. Butler, Mass. Militia, assigned to command at Fort Monroe, Va.																	
May 23	Demonstration on Hampton, Va.			800			Colonel Phelps, F.											Federal.
	Brigadier-General Benj. Huger, Virginia Volunteers, assigned to command at Norfolk, Va.																	
May 24	Occupation of Alexandria, Virginia, by Colonel Ellsworth and New York Fire Zouaves							1										Federal
	Advance of Federal Army into Virginia.																	
	Occupation of Arlington Heights, Va.					5th, 7th, 11th, 12th, 25th, 28th, 69th N. Y., 1st Michigan, 1st and 2nd Va. Volunteers, 14th, 16th and 18th Ohio, and 2 Guns	Maj.-Gen. Sandford, F. / Maj.-Gen'l McClellan, F.											
May 26	Advance upon Grafton, W. Va., by Federal Forces																	
May 28	Brigadier-General Irvin McDowell, U.S.A., assumes command of Department of N. E. Virginia.																	
May 29	Occupation of Newport News, Va., by Federal Forces.																	
May 30	Occupation of Grafton, Virginia, by Federal Forces.																	
May 31	Confederate Batteries at Aquia Creek attacked by Captain Ward, U.S.N., with 3 Gunboats		2 hrs. / 5 hrs.			Gunboats *Freeborn*, *Anacostia* and *Pawnee*	Capt. Ward, U.S.N. / Colonel Ruggles, C.											
	Ex-Governor Pratt of Maryland, arrested																	
	Brigadier-General Lyon, U.S.A., supersedes General Harney.																	
June 1	Skirmish	FAIRFAX COURT HOUSE, VA.		50	1000	Company B, 2nd U. S. Cavalry	Lieut. Tompkins, F. / Lieut.-Col. Ewell, C.	1	25	1		5		1				Conf'd.
	Skirmish	WILLIAMSPORT	1 hour.								4							Federal.
	Skirmish	ARLINGTON MILLS			9 Sc'ts	Company Zouaves / Company E Michigan Regiment	Capts. Brown & Hoth, F.	1		1	1							Federal.
June 2	Brigadier-General G. T. Beauregard, C.S.A., supersedes General Bonham in command of the "Alexandria Line," Va.																	
June 3	Action	PHILIPPI, W. VA.			2000	1st W. Va.; 16th Ohio; 7th and 9th Indiana; and 14th Ohio Volunteers; 4 Companys 6th Indiana, Det. Burnett's Ohio Artillery	Cols. Kelley & Dumont, F. / Col. Porterfield, C.	2	16	25		10						Federal.
June 5	Attack on Pig Point Batteries, Va.		20 minutes			U. S. Steamer *Harriet Lane*	Com. Pegram, C.											
June 6	Brigadier-General Henry A. Wise, C.S.A., ordered to command troops in Kanawha Valley, W. Va.																	
	Missouri transferred to the Department of the Ohio																	
June 7	Reconnaissance from Yorktown to Newport News, Va.				22		Capt. Werth, C.											Conf'd.
June 8	Six Bridges burned by Confederates.																	
	Virginia State Troops transferred to the Confederate States.																	
	Brigadier-General R. S. Garnett, C.S.A., assigned to command troops in N. W. Virginia.																	
June 10	Engagement	BIG BETHEL, VA.	2½ hours	3000	1800	1st, 2nd, 3rd, 5th, and 7th N. Y.; 4th Mass Volunteers; and Detachment 2nd U. S. Artillery	Br.-Gen'l Pierce, F. / Col. C. P. Stone, F.	18	8	53	20		8	5				Conf'd.
	Brigadier-General Beauregard in command of all Confederate Forces in Prince William, Fairfax, and Loudoun Counties, Va.																	
June 11	Engagement	ROMNEY, W. VA. (Hanging Rock)			300	11th Indiana Volunteers	Col. Wallace, F.		2	1	1							Federal.
	Major-General Banks supersedes Brevet-Major-General Cadwalader in Department of Annapolis.																	
	Colonel E. R. S. Canby, 10th U. S. Infantry placed in charge of Department of New Mexico.																	
June 13	Expedition from St. Louis up the Missouri River.																	
June 14	Skirmish	SENECA'S MILLS, MD.		200	Cav. 100	District Volunteers	Lieut.-Col. Everett, F. / Capt. Shreves, C.		3		1							Federal
	Jefferson City, Missouri evacuated by Confederates.																	
June 16	Skirmish at Bowman's Place, Cheat River, West Virginia.																	
	Harper's Ferry, West Virginia, evacuated by Confederates.																	
June 17	Action	VIENNA, VA.		271	2600	1st Ohio Volunteers	Brig.-Gen. Schenck, F. / Col. M. Gregg, C.	5	6	6			24					Federal
	Engagement	BOONEVILLE, MO.		2000	4000	2d Missouri (3 Months) Batteries H and L, and 1st Missouri Light Artillery Volunteers	Gen. Lyon, F. / Col. Marmaduke, C.	2	35	9	50	10	20					Federal.

CHRONOLOGICAL LIST OF EVENTS (1860–1865).—Continued.

DATE.	EVENT.	LOCATION.	DURATION.	FORCE. F.	FORCE. C.	COMPOSITION OF FORCE.	COMMANDERS.	KILLED. F.	KILLED. C.	WOUNDED. F.	WOUNDED. C.	PRISONERS TAKEN BY F.	PRISONERS TAKEN BY C.	MISSING. F.	MISSING. C.	[illegible]	[illegible]	ADVANTAGE.
1861																		
June 17	Skirmish	Edward's Ferry, Va.	8 hours.	300		1st Pennsylvania Volunteers.	Capt. Gardner, F.	1	30	3								Federal.
	Attack on Federal Troops whilst carrying Flag of Truce.	Independence, Mo.				Detachment Missouri Volunteers.	Capt. Stanley, F. Capt. Prince, F.		2									Federal.
June 18	Skirmish	Conrad's Ferry, Md.		20	Art'y.			25	4	32	20							
June 19	Engagement	Camp Cole, Mo.		900		Union Home Guards.	Capt. Cook, F.	15	40	26			23					Conf'd.
	Skirmish	New Creek, W. Va.		250	4 Co's	(Organizations not recorded).	Col. Vaughn, C.									2		Conf'd.
	Bridge at New Creek, Cumberland, Md., burnt by Confederates.																	
	Detachment of Federal Regulars from Kansas, capture 35 Confederates at Liberty, Missouri.											35						Federal.
June 20	3rd Virginia Regiment capture 13 Confederates at Clarksburg, Penn.											13						Federal.
June 23	Maj. Gen. McClellan takes command of Federal Forces in Western Va.																	
	Skirmish	Rigoter, W. Va.				(Organizations not recorded.)												
June 24	Crew of steamer *Monticello*, attacked on Rappahannock River by 50 Confederates.							2		6								Federal.
	U. S. Steamer *Quaker City*, engages a number of Confederate Dragoons.							1										
	Skirmish	Jackson, Mo.																
June 25	Descent on Mathias Point, Virginia.																	
June 26	Skirmish Skirmish	Frankfort, W. Va. Patterson Creek, W. Va. (Kelly's I.)		13	75	11th Indiana Volunteers.		1	17									Federal.
June 27	Attack	Mathias Point, Va.				Crews of U. S. Gunboats *Pawnee* and *Freeborn*.	Capt. Ward, U.S.N.	1		4								
June 28	Skirmish	Fall's Church, Va.				New Jersey Zouaves		1	2									
June 29	Steamer *St. Nicholas*, captured on Potomac River, by Confederates.																	
June 30	Skirmish	Shuter's Hill, Va.		3 Pls.	14	14th Pennsylvania Regiment Confederate Scouts		1	2	1	1							Federal.
July 1	Skirmish	Farmington, Mo.		50	250	Home Guards Confederate Mounted Guards	Capt. Cook, F.		4									Conf'd.
	Orders issued for raising U. S. Troops in Kentucky and Tennessee.																	
	Arrest of the Baltimore Police Commissioners.																	
July 2	Engagement	Falling Waters Va. (Haynesville and Martinsburg).	6½ hours.			1st Wisconsin and 11th Pennsylvania Volunteers.	Brig.-Gen. Thomas F. Gen. Jackson, C.	3	31	10	50	10						Federal.
	Operations in the Shenandoah Valley. (July 2–25).																	
July 3	$27,000 taken from Exchange Bank of Weston, Virginia, by State Authorities.																	
	New Mexico included in the Western Department.																	
	Fort McLane, New Mexico, abandoned.																	
	The Western Department organized.																	
July 4	Skirmish	Harper's Ferry, Va.						2		3								Conf'd.
	Skirmish	Farmington, Mo.				(Organizations not recorded.)												
July 5	Engagement	Carthage, Mo. (Dry Fork Creek and Brier Fork)	3½ hours.	1500		3rd and 5th Mo. (3 mos.), and Battery Mo. Art. Vols.	Gens. Sigel & Solomon, F Gens. Rains & Price, C	13		31								Federal.
	Skirmish	Newport News, Va.		25	150	9th N. Y. (one company.)		6	3									Federal.
	Capture of Federal Troops at Neosho, Mo.																	
	Regiment of Confederate Infantry fire into Company of Confederate Cavalry by mistake, at Fairfax Court House, Va.								7									
July 6	Skirmish	Middle Creek Fork, W. Va.		45		3rd Ohio Volunteers (one company).		1		13			7					Conf'd.
	Skirmish	Buckhannon, W. Va.				3rd and 4th Ohio Volunteers.	Brig. Gen. Morris, F. Gen. Wise, C.		23			200						Federal.
	Campaign in West Virginia (July 6–17).																	
July 7	Skirmish	Great Falls, Md.				8th N. Y. Volunteers	Major Gerhardt, F.	2	100									Federal.
July 8	Skirmish	Laurel Hill, W. Va. (Bealington.)			1200	14th Ohio Volunteers 9th Indiana Volunteers	Gen. Morris, F. Gen. Pegram, C.	2	30	6	40							Federal.
	Brigadier-General Sibley, C. S. A., ordered to Texas to expel Federal Forces from New Mexico.																	
July 9	Skirmish	Vienna, Va.		2 Cos			Lieut. Col. Young, F.			4								Federal.
July 10	Skirmish	Monroe Station, Mo.		600	1600	16th Illinois Volunteers; 3rd Iowa Volunteers; Hannibal Home Guards.	Col. Smith, F. Brig.-Gen. Harris, C.		4									Federal.
	Bill passed in Senate authorizing employment of 500,000 Volunteers and an appropriation of $500,000,000.																	
	Fort Breckinridge, New Mexico, abandoned																	
July 11	Battle	Rich Mountain, W. Va.	1½ hours		2500	8th, 10th and 13th Indiana Volunteers 19th Ohio Volunteers.	Gen. Rosecrans, F. Gen. Pegram, C.	20	60	40						1		Federal.
	Engagement	Hannibal, Mo.			1200	Burdall's Cavalry	Col. Smyth, F. Gen. Harris, C.					75				1		Federal.
	Skirmish	Martinsburg, Va.						1										
July 12	Engagement	Barboursville, W. Va. (Red House.)		3 Cos	600	2nd Kentucky Volunteers.	Lieut.-Col. Neff, F.	2	20	6	40							Federal.
	Engagement	Beverly, W. Va.				4th and 9th Ohio Volunteers.	Col. Pegram, C.	13	150	40		600						Federal.
	Skirmish	Newport News, Va.		200		7th N. Y. Infantry	Lieut. Col. Kapff, F.						12					Conf'd.
July 13	Major-General Polk, C.S.A., assumes command of Department No. 2.																	
July 14	Battle	Carrick's Ford, W. Va.				14th Ohio and 9th and 7th Indiana Volunteers.	Gen. Morris, F. Gen. Garnett, C.	2	20	12	10	50						Federal.
	Reconnaissance from Alexandria, Va.																	
July 15	Skirmish	Bunker Hill, Va.			600	General Patterson's Division	Gen. Patterson, F. Col. Stuart, C.		4			5						Federal.
	Skirmish	Mexico, Mo.																
	Military Forces, Stores, &c., of Arkansas transferred to the Confederate States.																	
July 16	Skirmish (15th–17th).	Millsville, Mo. (Wentzville.)		600		8th Missouri Volunteers.			7									Federal.
	The Bull Run or Manassas Campaign, Va. (July 16–22).																	
	Fairfax Court House, Va., occupied by Federal Troops.																	
July 17	Skirmish	Fulton, Mo.			400	3rd Missouri Reserves.												
	Attack on Confederates	Scarytown, W. Va.				2nd Ky., 12th and 21st Ohio Vols., and 1st Ohio Battery			7		28							Conf'd.
July 18	Skirmish	Martinsburg, Mo.	4 hours.	170	300	1st Missouri Reserves (one company). Detachment.	Maj. Van Horn, F. Capt. Duncan, C.	1	14									Federal.

CHRONOLOGICAL LIST OF EVENTS (1860-1865).—Continued.

Date.	Event.	Location.	Duration.	Force F.	Force C.	Composition of Force.	Commanders.	Killed F.	Killed C.	Wounded F.	Wounded C.	Prisoners taken F.	Prisoners taken C.	Missing F.	Missing C.	[illegible]	[illegible]	Advantage.
1861																		
July 18	Engagement	Blackburn's Ford, Va.	3 hours			1st Mass., 2nd and 3rd Mich., 12th N.Y. Volunteers; Det. 2nd U.S. Cavalry and Battery E 3d U.S. Art.	Gen. Tyler, F.	19	15	38	53		26					Conf'd.
	Skirmish and Action (17th–19th)	Harrisonville, Mo. (Parkersville.)	4 hours	170	500	Van Horn's Battalion (Mo.) / Cass County Home Guards.	Major Van Horn, F. / Captain Duncan, C.	1	14									Federal.
July 19	Affair on the Back River Road, Va.																	
	Affair near New Market Bridge, Va.																	
July 20	Brigadier-General Loring, C.S.A., assigned to command of "North-western Army," W. Va.																	
	Expedition from Springfield to Forsyth, Mo.																	
July 21	Battle	Bull Run (First), Va. (Manassas.)	6 hours	35,000	40,[illegible]	Infantry Volunteers or Militia:—2nd Maine, 2nd N.H., 2nd Vt.; 1st 4th and 5th Mass.; 1st and 2nd R.I.; 1st, 2nd and 3rd Conn.; 8th, 11th, 12th, 13th, 16th, 18th, 27th, 29th, 31st, 32nd, 35th, 38th, and 69th N.Y. Volunteers; 2nd, 8th, 14th, 69th, 71st, and 79th N.Y. Militia; 27th Penn. Volunteers; 1st, 2nd and 3rd Mich.; 1st and 2nd Minn.; 1st and 2nd Ohio; Det. of 2nd, 3rd and 8th Regular Infantry, and a Battalion of Marines. Artillery:—Batteries D, E, G, and M, 2nd, E, 3rd Artillery; D, 5th Artillery, and 2nd R.I. Battery. Cavalry:—Det. from 1st and 2nd Dragoons	Gen. McDowell, F. / Gen. Beauregard, C.	481	200	1011	1483		1421	1460	30	20	4000	Conf'd.
	Major-General N. P. Banks, U.S.A., ordered to relieve Major-General Patterson in command of the Department of the Shenandoah.																	
July 22	Skirmish	Etna, Mo.				21st Missouri Volunteers.												
	Skirmish	Forsyth, Mo.	1 hour		150	1st Iowa Volunteers and 2nd Kan. Volunteers; Stanley Dragoons and Totten's Battery	Gen. Sweeney, F.		5	3								Federal.
	Major General G. B. McClellan, U.S.A., ordered to Washington, D. C.																	
	Brigadier-General W. J. Hardee, C.S.A., assumes command in North-western Arkansas.																	
July 23	Major-General J. A. Dix, U.S.A., assumes command of the Department of Maryland.																	
	Brigadier General W. S. Rosecrans, U.S.A., assumes command of the Department of the Ohio, embracing portion of W. Va.																	
	Fort Buchanan, New Mexico, abandoned.																	
July 24	Action	Blue Mills, Mo.				5th Missouri Reserves.												
	300 men under Lieutenant Crosby, U.S.A., burn 9 Confederate Sloops and Schooners, and seize 1 Schooner																	Federal.
	Operations on Back River, Va.																	
	Retreat of General Wise's command up the Kanawha Valley.																	
July 25	Skirmish	Dug Springs, Mo.				(Organizations not Recorded.)												
	General Cox occupied Charleston on the Kanawha.																	
	Major-General Banks, U.S.A., assumes command of the Department of the Shenandoah.																	
	Major-General Dix, U.S.A., assumes command of the Department of Pennsylvania.																	
	Major-General Fremont, U.S.A., assumes command of the Western Department.																	
	Skirmish	Mesilla, New Mexico	1½ hours	380	700	7th U.S. Infantry, Battery and Detachment Rifles	Major Lynde, F.	8	K&W 11	6								Conf'd.
July 26	Skirmish	Lane's Prairie, Mo.		15	65	Missouri Home Guards			4	3								Federal.
	Skirmishes (25th–27th)	Harrisonville, Mo.				Missouri Home Guards and Kansas Cavalry			14									Federal.
	Skirmish	McCulla's Store, Mo.				(Organizations not Recorded.)												
	Fort Fillmore, New Mexico, abandoned.																	
	Brigadier-General Zollicoffer, C.S.A., assigned to command in East Tennessee.																	
July 27	Hampton, Virginia, evacuated by Gen. Butler.																	
	Major-Gen. McClellan assumes command of the Division of the Potomac																	
	Surrender of Federal Forces at St. Augustine Springs, New Mexico			410		7th U.S. Infantry and U.S. Mounted Rifles	Major Lynde, F.											
July 28	New Madrid, Mo., occupied by Confederate Troops.																	
	The Privateer *Gordon*, of Charleston, S.C., captured 2 vessels; The *Mariner* captured 1 vessel; The *York* captured 1 vessel																	Conf'd.
	Attack on Federal Troops	Hickory Hill, Mo.				2 Cos. Col. Mulligan's Regt. 3 Cos. Home Guards.						28						Federal.
July 29	Engagement	Mathias Point, Va.		50		Federal Steamer *Freeborn* and Det. Federal Troops.	Col. Ruggles, C.	1	4									Conf'd.
	Skirmish	Shooter's Hill, Va.				(Organizations not Recorded)		1	2	1	1							
	Brig. Gen. Pope, U.S.A. assumes command in Northern Missouri.																	
	Skirmish	Edward's Ferry, Md.																
July 31	The Army of the State of Tennessee transferred to the Confederacy.																	
Aug. 1	Skirmish	Eureka, Mo.																
	Gen. R. E. Lee, C.S.A., commanding in West Virginia.																	
Aug. 2	Skirmish	Dug Springs, Mo.	3 hours			1st Iowa Vols. and 3rd Mo. Vols. and 5 Batteries, Mo. Light Artillery	Gen. Lyon, F. / Gen. McCulloch, C.	8	40	30	44							Federal.
	Reconnoissance from Ironton to Centreville, Mo.																	
	Fort Stanton, New Mexico, abandoned.																	
Aug. 3	Engagement	Mesilla, New Mexico			700	7th U.S. Infantry and U.S. Mounted Rifles	Capt. Baylor, C.		12	2								Federal.
	Skirmish	McCulla's Store, Mo.				(Organizations not Recorded.)												
Aug. 5	Attack on Federal Camp	Athens, Mo.	1 hour	400	1850	Home Guards and 21st Missouri Volunteers	Col. Moore, F. / Col. Martin Green, C.	13	23	8	44							Federal.
	Skirmish	Point of Rocks, Md.		60	Cav'l	28th N.Y. Volunteers	Lieut.-Col. Brown, F. / Capt. Mead, C.		3		2	7						Federal.
	The *Alvarado* burned off Fernandina by U.S. Steamer *Vincennes*																	

CHRONOLOGICAL LIST OF EVENTS (1860-1865).—Continued.

Date	Event	Location	Duration	Force F.	Force C.	Composition of Force	Commanders	Killed F.	Killed C.	Wounded F.	Wounded C.	Prisoners Taken F.	Prisoners Taken C.	Missing F.	Missing C.	[illegible]	[illegible]	Advantage
1861																		
Aug. 7	Hampton, Virginia, destroyed by Gen. Magruder	Hampton, Va.			500	20th N. Y. Volunteers	Col. Weber, F.		3		6							
	Expedition to Price's Landing, Commerce, Benton and Hamburg, Mo. (7th–10th).																	
Aug. 8	Skirmish	Lovettsville, Va.		100	130	19th N. Y. Volunteers	Capt. Kennedy, F		1		0							Federal.
	Brig.-Gen. U. S. Grant, U. S. A., assumes command of the District of Ironton, Mo.																	
Aug. 10	Battle	Wilson's Creek, Mo. (Springfield and Oak Hill)	8 hours.	5200	22,000	Cavalry 6th and 10th Mo., 2nd Kan. Mounted Vols. and one company U. S. Infantry, 1st Iowa, 1st Kan., 1st, 2nd, 3rd and 5th Mo. detachments, 1st and 2nd Regulars, Mo. Home Guards. Artillery, 1st Mo. Light and Battery F, 2nd U. S.	Brig.-Gen. Lyon, F. / Gen. McCullough, C.	223	421	721	1300	296		291				Conf'd.
	Skirmish	Potosi, Mo.			80	Missouri Home Guards	Capt. White, C.	1	2		3							Federal.
Aug. 11	Affair at Hamburg, Mo.																	
	Brig.-Gen. Floyd, C. S. A., assumes command in the Kanawha Valley, W. Va.																	
Aug. 13	Skirmish	Grafton, W. Va.	1 hour.	50	200	One Company 4th W. Va. Volunteers	Capt. Dayton, F. / Sher. Cochrane, C		21									Federal.
Aug. 14	79th New York Regiment are deprived of their colors for mutiny.																	
	Martial law declared at St. Louis, Mo.																	
	Brig.-Gen. Earl Van Dorn relieved from, and Brig.-Gen. Hébert assigned to command of Confederate Forces in Texas.																	
Aug. 15	Expedition to Saint Genevieve, Mo.																	
	Brig.-Gen. Anderson, U. S. A., placed in command of the Army of the Cumberland (Kentucky and Tennessee).																	
Aug. 16	Expedition to Fredericktown, Mo.																	
	Operations around Kirksville, Mo. (16th–21st).																	
Aug. 17	Skirmish	Brunswick, Mo.				5th Missouri Reserves.												
	Affairs at Hunnewell and Palmyra, Mo.																	
	Brt. Major-Gen. Wool, U. S. A., supersedes Major-Gen. Butler in command of the Department of Virginia.																	
	Departments of N. E. Virginia, Washington and Shenandoah included in Department of the Potomac.																	
Aug. 18	Skirmish	Lady's Fork, Va.						3		2		2						Conf'd.
	Scout to Accotink, Va.																	
	Skirmish	Pohick Church, Va.		Scts.	Cav.	Lincoln Cavalry	Lieut. Gibson, F	1										Federal.
	Skirmish	Sandy Hook, Md.		2Co's	300	2nd Mass. Regiment			2		5							Federal.
Aug. 19	Battle	Charleston, Mo. (Bird's Point)		220	650	22nd Illinois Volunteers	Col. Dougherty, F. / Col. Hunter, C.	1	40	4		17						Federal.
	Skirmish	Klapsford, Mo.				(Organizations not recorded).												
Aug. 20	Skirmish	Laurel Fork Creek, W. Va.				(Organizations not recorded).												
	Skirmish	Hawks' Nest, W. Va.		600		11th Ohio Volunteers	Col. Croghan, C.	3		2				1				Federal.
	Attack on Union Troops while riding in train	Lookout Station, Mo.				(Organizations not reported)		1		6								
	Major-Gen. McClellan, U. S. A., assumes command of the Army of the Potomac.																	
	Skirmish	Fish Lake, Mo.	15 min.	50	50	Centralia Cavalry	Capt. Noleman, F.					35					80	Federal.
	Brig.-Gen. Gatlin, C. S. A., assumes command of the Defences of North Carolina.																	
Aug. 21	Skirmishes (21st–22d)	Jonesboro, Mo.				Missouri Home Guards.												
	Brig.-Gen. Shipley, C. S. A., assigned to command of the Department of South Carolina.																	
	Brig.-Gen. Grayson, C. S. A., assigned to command of the Department of Middle and East Florida.																	
Aug. 22	Capture of Steamers *W. B. Terry* and *Samuel Orr*, at Paducah, Ky.																	
Aug. 23	Engagement of U. S. Steamers *Yankee* and *Release* with batteries at the Mouth of Potomac Creek, Va.		40 min.															
	Skirmish	Fort Craig, New Mexico		9	Cav.	New Mexico Volunteers	Capt. Hubbell, F. / Lt.-Col. Baylor, C.						10					Conf'd.
	Skirmish	Medoc, Mo.				(Organizations not recorded).												
	Skirmish	Springfield, W. Va.				(Organizations not recorded).												
Aug. 24	Department of Pennsylvania included in the Department of the Potomac.																	
Aug. 25	Operations against Indians about Fort Stanton, New Mexico (Aug. 25th–Sept. 8th).																	
	Skirmish with Indians near Fort Bliss, Texas.																	
	Skirmish	Piggot's Mill, W. Va.							1		5							Federal.
	Scout into Virginia from Great Falls, Md.																	
Aug. 26	Battle	Cross Lanes, W. Va. (Summerville)			2400	7th Ohio Volunteers	Col. Tyler, F.	15		40			4	200				Conf'd.
	Skirmish	Blue's House, W. Va.				(Organizations not recorded).												
Aug. 27	Skirmishes (26th–27th)	Wayne Court House, W. Va.				5th West Virginia Volunteers	Capt. Smith, F.											
	Skirmishes (27th–28th)	Ball's Cross Roads, Va.			600	Two Companies, 23rd N. Y. Volunteers	Col. Hoffman, F.	1		1								Conf'd.
	Skirmish	Antietam Iron Works, Md.				(Organizations not recorded).												
Aug. 28	Skirmish (28th–29th)	Hall's Mills, Mo.				(Organizations not recorded)												
	Capture of Confederate Batteries (28th–29th)	Fort Hatteras, N. C.				9th, 20th and 99th N. Y. Volunteers and Naval Forces	Col. Hawkins, F. / Com. Stringham, F.	1	49	2	49	716				81	1000	Federal.
	Operations in Southwestern Missouri. (Aug. 28–Sept. 5th.)																	
	Fort Clark, N. C., evacuated by Confederates.																	
Aug. 29	Skirmish	Lexington, Mo.		430	4300	Missouri Home Guards		1	8	6	52	2						Federal.

CHRONOLOGICAL LIST OF EVENTS (1860-1865).—Continued.

Date.	Event.	Location.	Duration.	Force. F.	Force. C.	Composition of Force.	Commanders.	Killed. F.	Killed. C.	Wounded. F.	Wounded. C.	Prisoners Taken by F.	Prisoners Taken by C.	Missing. F.	Missing. C.	Guns taken.	Stands of Arms taken.	Advantage.
1861 Aug. 29	Skirmish	Moore's Mills, Mo.				(Organizations not recorded).												
Aug. 30	Skirmishes (29th–30th)	Bailey's Corners on Cross Roads, Va.		250	200		Major Champlin, F.; Captain Dillman, F.		4	3								Federal
	"Emancipation Proclamation" issued by Gen. Fremont.																	
	Operations in Northeastern Missouri (Aug. 30th, Sept. 7th).																	
Aug. 31	Skirmish	Munson's Hill, Va.			Pkts	Two Companies, 3rd New Jersey Volunteers		1		2								Conf'd.
Sept. 1	Skirmish	Burlington, W. Va.				(Organizations not recorded.)												
	Skirmish	Blue Creek, W. Va.				(Organizations not recorded.)												
	Skirmish	Bennight's Mills, Mo.	½ hour	85	350	Missouri Home Guards		3		6								Conf'd.
	Skirmish	Boone Court House, W. Va.				1st Kentucky Volunteers			30	6		40						Federal.
	Skirmish	Fort Scott, Kan.																
	Brig.-Gen. U. S. Grant, U. S. A., assumes command in Southeastern Missouri.																	
	Cairo, Illinois, occupied by Union Troops.																	
	Expeditions through Jefferson County, Mo.																	
Sept. 2	Expeditions toward Columbia and Iberia, Mo.																	
	Skirmish	Bever's Mill, Va.			H'me G'ds	13th Massachusetts Volunteers			3		5	20						Federal.
	Skirmish	Dallas, Mo.				11th Missouri Volunteers.												
	Destruction of U. S. Dry-dock at Pensacola, Fla.																	
	Action	Dry Wood Creek, Mo. (Fort Scott)	3 hours	500	600	3rd and 4th Kansas Volunteers; 1 Company, 9th Cavalry; 1st Kansas Battery	Montgomery, F.; General Rains, C.											Conf'd.
	Skirmish	Hawk's Nest, W. Va.				(Organizations not recorded.)												
	Skirmish	Worthington, W. Va.			400	3 Companies Federal Troops	Col. Crossman, F.	2										Conf'd.
	Major-Gen. Polk, C. S. A., placed in command of Arkansas and Missouri Military Forces.																	
Sept. 3	Dry-dock at Pensacola, Fla., burnt.																	
	Destruction of bridge on the Hannibal and St. Joseph Railway	Platte River, Mo.						17										
	Advance of Confederate Forces into Kentucky (3d–12th).																	
	Columbus and Hickman, Ky., occupied by Confederate Forces.																	
	Brig.-Gen. Anderson, C. S. A., ordered to North Carolina.																	
Sept. 4	Action	Shelbina, Mo.	1½ hours	1100	1500	3rd Iowa Volunteers	Col. Williams, F.; Col. Martin Green, C.			1								Conf'd.
	Command of C. S. A., in Texas transferred to Col. McCulloch, 1st Texas Rifles.																	
	Skirmish	Great Falls, Md.				7th and 8th Infantry, Brig.-Gen. McCall's Command	Colonel Harvey, F.	2										Federal.
Sept. 6	Skirmish	Papinsville, Kan.				(Organizations not recorded.)												
Sept. 6	Skirmish	Bowkin's Run, W. Va.				(Organizations not recorded.)												
	Skirmish	Fort Craig, New Mexico				(Organizations not recorded.)												
	Paducah, Ky., occupied by Federal Forces.																	
	Skirmish	Monticello Bridge, Mo.				(Organizations not recorded.)												
	Brig.-Gen. C. F. Smith, U. S. A., assigned to command in Western Kentucky.																	
Sept. 7	Skirmish	Petersburg, W. Va.				Three Companies, 4th Ohio Volunteers.												
	Expedition to Big Springs, Mo.																	
Sept. 8	Operations against Green's Guerrillas in Missouri (8th–9th.)																	
	Reconnoissance from Cairo, Ill. (8th–10th.)																	
Sept. 9	Skirmish	Shepherdstown, W. Va.				(Organizations not recorded.)												
Sept. 10	Battle	Carnifex Ferry, W. Va.	4 hours	4000	2000	9th, 10th, 12th, 13th, 28th and 47th Ohio Volunteers	Gen. Rosecrans, F.; Gen. Floyd, C.	16		80								Federal.
	Attack on Federal Gunboat	Lucas Bend, Mo.			Btt's	Federal Gunboat *Lexington*	Colonel Waagner, F.											
	Brig.-Gen. Thomas, U. S. A., assigned to command at Camp Dick Robinson, Eastern Kentucky.																	
	Reconnoissance toward Norfolk, Mo.																	
	Skirmish	Lewinsville, Va.		100	Cav.	79th New York Infantry	Captain Ireland, F.	1	4		3	1						Federal.
Sept. 11	Skirmishes	Elkwater, W. Va.				3rd Ohio, 15th and 17th Ind. Volunteers		6	20	4	14							Federal.
	Reconnoissance from Chain Bridge, Va.																	
	Engagement	Lewinsville, Va.		1500		19th Ind., 3rd Vt. and 63th N. Y. Vols. and 79th N. Y. Militia	Col. Stevens, F.; Col. Stuart, C.	3	4	9			4					Federal
	Operations in Cheat Mountain, W. Va., including Actions and Skirmishes at Cheat Mountain *Pass*, Cheat Summit, Point Mountain Turnpike, and Elk Water (11th–17th)				9000	1st Brigade, Army of the Ohio	Brig.-Gen. Reynolds, F.; Gen. R. E. Lee, C.	9	100			20	60	2				
Sept. 12	Skirmish	Parkersburg, W. Va.				(Organizations not recorded.)												
	Skirmish	Peytona, W. Va.				(Organizations not recorded.)												
	Skirmish	Black River, Mo.				Three Companies, 1st Indiana Cavalry	Major Gavitt, F.; Ben Talbot, C.		5			4						Federal.
	Siege (12th to 20th)	Lexington, Mo.				8th, 25th and 27th Mo. Vols., 13th and 14th Mo. Home Guards, Berry's and Van Horn's Mo. Cavalry, 1st Cavalry and 23rd Infantry Ill. Vols.	Col. Mulligan, F.; Gen. Rains, C.; Gen. Price, C.	12	25	105	75		3500	1624				Conf'd
	Engagement (12th to 13th)	Cheat Mountain, W. Va.	½ hour	320	3000	13th, 14th, 15th and 17th Ind., 3rd, 6th, 24th and 25th Ohio and 2nd W. Va. Volunteers	Gen. Reynolds, F.; Gen. Anderson, C.	9	80	2	20	20	60					Federal
	Capture of Confederate Camp at Petersburg, Va.																	
	Arrest of members of the Maryland Legislature and other citizens of that State.																	
Sept. 13	Engagement	Booneville, Mo.			1000	Missouri Home Guards	Capt. Eppstein, F.; Col. Brown, C.	1	12	4	30							Federal.
	Skirmish	Ball's Cross Roads, Va.				(Organizations not recorded.)		4										
	Occupation of St. Joseph's, Mo., by Federal Forces.																	
Sept. 14	Skirmish	Old Randolph, Mo.				(Organizations not recorded.)												
	Skirmish	Shepherdstown, W. Va.						4		18								

CHRONOLOGICAL LIST OF EVENTS (1860-1865).—Continued.

DATE	EVENT	LOCATION	DURATION	FORCE F	FORCE C	COMPOSITION OF FORCE	COMMANDERS	KILLED F	KILLED C	WOUNDED F	WOUNDED C	PRISONERS TAKEN BY F	PRISONERS TAKEN BY C	MISSING F	MISSING C	[illegible]	[illegible]	ADVANTAGE
1861																		
Sept. 14	Descent on Pensacola Navy Yard by boats from U. S. Squadron. Steamer *Judah* burnt by Federal Forces.	NEAR PENSACOLA, FLA.				Force from Federal Frigate *Colorado*.	Lieut. Russell, U.S.N.	3		4								Federal.
Sept. 15	Skirmish	PRITCHARD'S MILLS, VA. (Damestown)	3 hours.		600	28th Pennsylvania Volunteers. 13th Massachusetts Volunteers.	Col. Geary, F.	1	k. & w. 19	3	23					2		Federal.
	Gen. A. S. Johnston, C. S. A., supersedes Major-Gen. Polk in command of Department No. 2																	
Sept. 16	Skirmish	SENECA CREEK, MD.		15	3 Cos.	34th N. Y. Regiment.		2										Federal.
	Colors restored to 79th N. Y. Regiment, at Washington.																	
	Action	PRINCETON, W. VA.				(Organizations not recorded.)												
	Skirmish	MAGRUDER'S FERRY, VA.				(Organizations not recorded.)												
	Attack on Lexington	LEXINGTON, MO.			2400		Gen. Price, C.											Federal.
Sept. 17	Action	BLUE MILLS LANDING, MO.	1 hour	500	4000	3rd Iowa Volunteers.	Lieut.-Col. Scott, F.	16	10	80	60							Conf'd. / Federal.
	Skirmish	MORRISTOWN, MO.		600	400	5th, 6th and 9th Kansas Cavalry, 1st Kansas Battery.	Col. Montgomery, F. / Col. Smith, F.	2	7	6								Federal.
	Accident on the Ohio & Mississippi Railroad. 19th Illinois Reg't. Lost 100 men killed and wounded.																	
	Brig.-Gen. Prentiss, U. S. A., assigned to command along and north of the Hannibal and St. Joseph Railroad.																	
Sept. 18	Skirmish	BARBOURSVILLE, (also Red House, W. Va.)		27	300	Kentucky Home Guards.		1	7	1			1					Federal.
	Bowling Green, Ky., occupied by Confederate Troops.																	
	Brig.-Gen. Hébert, C. S. A., assumes command of the Department of Texas.																	
	Brig.-Gen. Buckner, C. S. A., assumes command of the Central Division of Kentucky.																	
	Skirmish	BERLIN, MD.				(Organizations not recorded.)												
Sept. 19	Engagement	BARBOURSVILLE, KY.		300	800		Colonel Battle, C.	12	2		3		2				23	Conf'd.
	Department of the Ohio reorganized.																	
	Department of Western Virginia constituted.																	
Sept. 20	Lexington, Mo., surrendered by Federal Troops. (Engagement)	LEXINGTON, MO.	50 hours.	2640		Irish Brigade, Home Guards, and 8th Missouri Regt.	Col. Mulligan, F. / Gen. Price, C.	42	23	108	75		2400			6	3000	Conf'd.
	Mayfield, Ky., evacuated by Confederate Troops.																	
	Skirmish	SENECA CREEK, MD.				(Organizations not recorded.)												
Sept. 21	Engagement	PAPINSVILLE, MO.				5th, 6th and 9th Kansas Cavalry.	Gen. Lane, F.	17	10			100						Federal.
	Gen. R. E. Lee, C. S. A., in command of forces in the Valley of the Kanawha.																	
	Gen. Johnston, C. S. A., calls upon Tennessee for 30,000 men.																	
	Brig.-Gen. Mitchel, U. S. A., assumes command of the Department of the Ohio																	
	Major-Gen. Polk, C. S. A., assigned to command of Western Division Department No. 2.																	
	Reconnoissance toward Columbus (21st–22d).																	
	Skirmish	MAYFIELD CREEK, KY.		10	100				k. & w. 4									Federal.
Sept. 22	Skirmish	ELLIOTT'S MILLS, MO. (Camp Crittenden)			50	7th Iowa Volunteers												Federal.
	Arkansas and Mississippi called upon for 10,000 men each for service in Department No. 2.																	
	Destruction of Osceola, Mo.																	
Sept. 23	Engagements (23d–25th)	ROMNEY, W. VA. (Hanging Rock)		975	700	Ringgold's Cavalry, 4th and 8th Ohio Volunteers.	Cols. Cantwell and Parke, F.	3	33	10								Federal.
	Affair at Albany, Ky.																	
	Skirmish	CASSVILLE, W. VA.				(Organizations not recorded.)												
Sept. 24	Skirmish	POINT OF ROCKS, MD.			200	(Organizations not recorded.)												
Sept. 25	Major-Gen. G. W. Smith, C. S. A., assigned to command of Second Corps, Army of the Potomac.																	
	Brig.-Gen. Wise, C. S. A., relieved from command in West Virginia.																	
	Reconnoissance to, and Skirmish near Lewinsville, Va.																	
	Engagement	FREESTONE POINT, VA.			Bats.	Federal Gunboats.	Colonel Wigfall.											
	Engagement	CHAPMANSVILLE, W. VA.				1st Ky. Regiment and 34th Ohio Volunteers.	Col. Enyart, F. / Col. Davis, C.	1	60	9	50	47						Federal.
	Smithland, Ky., occupied by Federal Troops.																	
	Skirmish	CAÑADA ALAMOSA, NEW MEXICO			114	New Mexico Mounted Volunteers.	Captain Minks, F.						9					Conf'd.
Sept. 26	Expedition from Cumberland Ford (26th–30th).																	
	Skirmish	LUCAS BEND, KY.		75	40	Captain Stewart's Cavalry.	Captain Stewart, F.		4			6						Federal.
	Skirmish	HUNTER'S FARM, MO.			40	Federal Cavalry.	Captain Stewart, F.		10			4						Federal.
	Destruction of Dock at the Mouth of Muddy River, Ky.	FORT THORN, NEW MEXICO	1½ hours.	101		3d Cavalry.	Captain Morris, F.											Federal.
Sept. 27	Skirmish	SHANGHAI, MO.				(Organizations not known.)												
	Skirmish	NORFOLK, MO.		200	400	22d Illinois Infantry.	Colonel Oglesby, F.											Federal.
Sept. 28	Munson's Hill, Va., evacuated by Confederate Troops.																	
Sept. 29	69th Penn. fire into the 71st Penn. Volunteers through mistake.	MUNSON'S HILL, VA.						9		23								
	Skirmish	BERLIN, MD.				(Organizations not reported.)												
	Skirmish	FALLS CHURCH, VA.						10		20								Federal.
	Engagement	JAMES BAYOU BRIDGE, KY.		100	250				3		1							
	Brig.-Gen. D. H. Hill, C. S. A., ordered to North Carolina.																	
	Affairs at Albany, Ky., and Travisville, Tenn.																	
	Skirmish	HOPKINSVILLE, KY.				Home Guards.			1		1		2					Conf'd.
Sept. 30	Operations against Indians from Fort Robeldo, New Mexico (Sept. 30th–Oct. 7th).																	

CHRONOLOGICAL LIST OF EVENTS (1860-1865).—Continued.

DATE	EVENT	LOCATION	DURATION	FORCE F.	FORCE C.	COMPOSITION OF FORCE	COMMANDERS	KILLED F.	KILLED C.	WOUNDED F.	WOUNDED C.	PRISONERS TAKEN F.	PRISONERS TAKEN C.	MISSING F.	MISSING C.	GUNS	STANDS OF SMALL ARMS	ADVANTAGE
1861 Oct. 1	Department of New England constituted, under command of Major-Gen. Butler, U. S. A.																	
	The *Fanny* captured by Confederate Steamers in Pamlico Sound												31					
	Skirmish	Edsall's Hill, Va		11	80		Surgeon Cox, F.	1		3								
	Confederate Council of War at Centreville, Va																	
Oct. 2	Expedition from Bird's Point / Confederate Camp broken up	Charleston, Mo.										40						Federal.
	Skirmish	Springfield Station, Va.																
Oct. 3	Engagement	Green Brier, W. Va	1 hour	5000	6000	Battery G, 4th U. S. Artillery, Battery A, 1st Mich. Artillery, 24th, 25th and 32nd Ohio, 7th, 9th, 13th, 14th, 15th and 17th Ind. Volunteers	Brig.-Gen. Reynolds, F. / Gen. Lee, C.	6	100	32	75	13						Federal.
	Expedition to, and occupation of Pohick Church, Va., by Federal Forces																	
	Skirmish	Springfield Station, Va.		600	Pkts.	Federal Troops of General Newton's Brigade	Colonel Pratt, F.											Federal.
Oct. 4	Attack on Federal Troops	Alamosa, New Mexico			110	Mink's New Mexico Cavalry and U. S. Regulars	Captain Mink, F. / Captain ——, F.		11		30							Federal
	Skirmish	Edward's Ferry, Md.					Brig.-Gen. Stone, F.											Federal
	Skirmish	Buffalo Hill, Ky.				(Organizations not reported)		20	30									Federal
	Capture reported of 2 Confederate Schooners by Steamer *South Carolina* off S. W. Pass of Mississippi.																	
Oct. 5	Affair at	Chicamicomico, N. C.	4 hours			U. S. Gunboat *Monticello*, 20th Indiana Volunteers	Lieut. Braine, U. S. N.		28									Federal.
	Brig.-Gen. Mansfield, U. S. A., assigned to command at Hatteras Inlet.																	
Oct. 6	Confed. Schooner *Alert* captured by U. S. Steamer *Flag* off Charleston, S. C.																	
Oct. 7	Reconnoissance from Cairo, Ill., to Lucas Bend, Mo.																	
	Major-Gen. Braxton Bragg's command, (C. S. A.) extended over Coast and State of Alabama.																	
Oct. 8	Attack on Confederate Troops	Hillsboro, Ky.	20 minutes	50		Flemingsburg Home Guards	Lieut. Sadler, F. / Capt. Holliday, C.	5	11	2	29	22						Federal.
	Brig.-Gen. Sherman, U. S. A., supersedes Brig.-Gen. Anderson in command of the Department of the Cumberland.																	
Oct. 9	Action	Santa Rosa, Fla.	3 hours	200	1400	6th N. Y. Volunteers, Detachments of Cos. A, 1st, and H 2nd U. S. Artillery and Cos. C and E 3rd U. S. Infantry	Col. Wilson, F. / Brig.-Gen. Anderson	14		29	350	30	24					Federal.
Oct. 10	Attack on Federal Pickets	Paducah, Ky.				Six Pickets of 4th Cavalry Regiment		2					6					Confed.
	Brig.-Gen. Mitchel, U. S. A., ordered to organize an expedition into East Tennessee.																	
Oct. 11	Skirmish	Harper's Ferry, W. Va.				(Organizations not recorded												
	Operations against Indians from Fort Inge, Texas (11th-16th).																	
	Brig.-Gen'l Rosecrans, U.S.A., assumes command of the Department of Western Virginia.																	
Oct. 12	Skirmish	Barren Co., Ky.		40	150		Capt. S. Taylor, F.	5	4									Conf'd.
	Skirmish	Bayle's Cross Roads, La.				79th N. Y. Volunteers												
	Skirmish	Cameron, Mo.		80	230	30th Indiana Volunteers, Maj. James' Cavalry		1	8	4		6						Federal.
	Skirmish	Upton's Hill, Ky.			Cav	Detachment 38th Indiana Regiment	Captain Herring, F.		5		3		22					Federal.
	Skirmishes near Clintonville, and on the Pomme de Terre, Mo.																	
	Operations about Ironton and Fredericktown, Mo.																	
	Skirmish	[illegible] River, Va.		40	300				5		3							Federal.
Oct. 13	Action	Wet Glaze, Mo. (Shanghai, Henrytown, and Monday's Hollow)	3 minutes			10th and 6th Mo. Cavalry and Fremont Battalion Cavalry		1	20			30						Federal.
	Brig.-Gen'l T. Williams, U.S.A., supersedes Brig.-Gen'l Mansfield																	
	Skirmish	Beckwith's Farm, Mo.		20	100	Lieut. Tuff's Detachment Cavalry	Lieut. Tuff, F.	2	abt 12	5				8				Conf'd.
	Skirmish	Cotton Hill, W. Va.																
Oct. 14	Affair at Linn	Linn Creek, Mo.	½ hour		45	6th Mo. Cavalry, 13th Ill. Volunteers	Major Wright, F. / —— Bolarie, C.					37						Federal.
	Skirmish	Underwood's Farm, Mo.		20	100	Captain Holeman's Centralia Cavalry	Lieut. Tufts, F.		abt 6	4								Federal.
	Department of Alabama and West Florida constituted, under command of Maj.-Gen. Bragg, C.S.A.																	
Oct. 15	Engagement	Big River Bridge, Mo.	10 minutes	40	600	38th Illinois Volunteers; 2d and 3d Dragoons (Confed.)	Jeff Thompson, C.	1	20	7	4		33					Conf'd.
	Skirmish	Little River Turnpike, Va.		6	20	1st New Jersey Volunteers	Lieut. Tilden, F.	1	1					2				Federal.
Oct. 16	Skirmish	Bolivar Heights, Va.	6½ hours			Detachments from 28th Penn., 3rd Wis. and 13th Mass. Volunteers	Col. Geary, F. / General Evans, C.	4	150	7		4	3			1		Federal.
	Skirmish	Linn Creek, Mo.		15	45	Fremont Cavalry	Lieut. Kirby, F.		5		1						10	Federal.
	Skirmish	Warsaw, Mo.		40	35	(Organizations not reported)			8			3						
	Recapture of Lexington	Lexington, Mo.		220	Pkts.	Detachments 1st Mo. Cavalry and Irish Dragoons	Major White, F.		60							2	60	Federal.
Oct. 17	Confederates routed	Fredericktown, Mo. (including skirmish at Ironton)				Co. A, 1st Mo. Light Artillery, 11th Mo. and 17th, 20th, 21st, 33rd and 38th Ill., 1st Ind. and 8th Wis. Vols.	Col. Alexander, F.											Federal.
Oct. 18	Skirmish	Warrensburg, Mo.				(Organizations not recorded.)												
	Reconnoissance down the Mississippi River.																	
	Reconnoissance towards Occoquan River, Va.																	
	Skirmish	Rockcastle Hills, Ky.				(Organizations not recorded.)												
	Major-Gen. M. Lovell, C. S. A., supersedes Major-Gen. Twiggs in command of Department No. 1.																	
Oct. 19	Action	Big Hurricane Creek		220	400	18th Missouri Volunteers	Colonel Morgan, F.	2	14	14		9						Federal.
	Operations in the Kanawha and New River region, W. Va.																	
Oct. 20	Skirmish	Butler, Mo.				(Organizations not recorded.)												
	Reconnoissance to Hunter's Mill and Thornton Station, Va.																	
	Engagement	Fredericktown, Mo.	2 hours	2000	8700	Portion of General Grant's Command	Col. Carlin, F. / Col. Thompson, C.	6	abt 200	40		80				4		Federal.
Oct. 21	Operations on the Potomac near Leesburgh, Va.																	
	Skirmish	Leesburgh Roads, Va.	20 minutes	1 Co.	3 Co's	17th Miss. Infantry	Captain Duff, F.			3		8					35	Federal.

CHRONOLOGICAL LIST OF EVENTS (1860-1865).—Continued.

DATE.	EVENT.	LOCATION.	DURATION	FORCE. F.	FORCE. C.	COMPOSITION OF FORCE.	COMMANDERS.	KILLED. F.	KILLED. C.	WOUNDED. F.	WOUNDED. C.	PRISONERS TAKEN BY F.	PRISONERS TAKEN BY C.	MISSING. F.	MISSING. C.	GUNS TAKEN.	[illegible]	ADVANTAGE.
1861																		
Oct. 21	Battle	Ball's Bluff, Va., also Edward's Ferry, Va.	2½ hours	2100	2500	15th and 20th Mass., 40th N. Y. and 71st Penn. Vols. and Battery B, R. I. Artillery	Col. Baker, F.; Gen. Evans, C	223	30	220	204	2	435					Confd.
	Action	Wild Cat, Ky.			7000	33rd Ind., 14th and 17th Ohio Vols., 1st Ky. Cavalry and 1st Ohio Battery	Gen. Schoepf, F.; Gen. Zollicoffer, C	4		21								Federal.
	Skirmish	Young's Mill, Va.		150		3rd Massachusetts Regiment	Capt. Barnes, F.											Federal.
	Expedition sails from Annapolis, Md., for the South Carolina coast under Brig. Gen. Sherman, U. S. A.																	
	Affairs around Budd's Ferry, Md.																	
Oct. 22	Skirmish	Buffalo Mills, Mo.				(Organizations Not Recorded).												
	Brig.-Gen. Trapier, C. S. A., assigned to command of the Department of Middle and East Florida.																	
	Reconnoissance	Goose Creek, Va.		31	Videt	Van Alen Cavalry	Major Mix, F.											Federal.
	Brig.-Gen. B. F. Kelley, U. S. A., assigned to command of the Department of Harper's Ferry and Cumberland.																	
	Department of Northern Virginia constituted under command of Gen. Johnston, C. S. A.																	
	Gen. Beauregard and Major-Generals Holmes and Jackson, C. S. A., assigned to command respectively of Potomac, Aquia and Valley Districts.																	
Oct. 23	Skirmish	Hodgenville, Ky.		50	100	Detachment 6th Indiana Volunteers	Lieut. Grayson, F.		8	8	6							Federal.
	Skirmish	West Liberty, Ky.				2nd Ohio Vols., 1st and Loughlin's Ohio Cavalry and 1st Ohio Artillery	Col. Harris, F.		21	2	30	34						Federal.
	Reconnoissance in the Kanawha Valley, W. Va. (23d-27th).																	
Oct. 24	Skirmish	Green Co., Ky.			100	General Ward's Pickets	Capt. ——, F		2				1					Conf'd.
	Major-Gen. Hunter, U. S. A., ordered to supersede Gen. Fremont.																	
	Attack on Camp Joe Underwood, Ky.																	
Oct. 25	Action (Zagonyi's Charge)	Springfield, Mo.	3 minutes	300	2000	Fremont's Body Guard and White's Prairie Scouts	Major Zagonyi, F.	23	60	17		27	10					Federal.
Oct. 26	Skirmish	Springfield, W. Va.				(Organizations not Recorded.)												
	Skirmish	South Branch Bridge, W. Va.		700	600	2nd Maryland Infantry	Colonel Johns, F.	1		9								Conf'd.
	Action, and capture of	Romney, W. Va. (Mill Creek Mills)	2 hours			4th and 8th Ohio and 7th W. Va. Vols., 2nd Regt. Potomac Home Brigade, Maryland Vols. and Ringgold's Cavalry Battalion	General Kelley, F.	2	20	13	15	300					[illegible]	Federal.
	Expedition to Eddyville, Ky.																	
	Skirmish	Saratoga, Ky.		3 Co's		9th Illinois Volunteers and Federal Gunboat *Conestoga*	Maj. Phillips, F.; Lt.-Cm. Phelps, F		13	2		24						Federal.
	Brig.-Gen. Lawton, C. S. A., assigned to command of the Department of Georgia.																	
Oct. 27	Attack on Confederate Camp	Plattsburg, Mo.		700		(Organizations Not Recorded).			8			13				1		Federal.
	Skirmish	Spring Hill, Mo.				1 Company 7th Missouri Cavalry.												
Oct. 28	Expedition to Fulton, Mo.																	
	Skirmish	Laurel Bridge, Ky.				(Organizations not Recorded.)												
	Skirmish	Budd's Ferry, Md.			Batts	Federal Steamer.												
	General Johnston, C. S. A., assumes command of the Army Corps of Central Kentucky.																	
Oct. 29	Skirmishes	Woodbury, Ky.		250	400	17th Ky. Infantry and 3rd Ky. Cavalry Vols.	Colonel Burbridge, F.		50	1								Federal.
	The Sherman Expedition sails from Hampton Roads, Va.																	
Oct. 31	Skirmish	Morgantown, Ky.			300	Home Guards and 1 Company Kentucky Volunteers	Capt. Porter, F.; Lieut. Rogers, F.											Federal.
	Skirmish	Greenbrier, W. Va.				(Organizations not Recorded.)												
	Skirmishes (1st, 3rd)	Cotton Hill, W. Va.				(Organizations not Recorded.)												
Nov. 1	Confederates routed	Renick, Mo.		400	500	(Organizations not Recorded).	Lieut.-Col. Morse, F.											Federal.
	Expedition from Rolla, Mo., against Freeman's Forces (1st-9th).																	
	Skirmish with Indians on the Peel River, Texas.																	
	Brig.-Gen. H. Marshall, C. S. A., ordered to Eastern Kentucky.																	
	Major-Gen. McClellan supersedes Lieut.-Gen. Winfield Scott in command of the Armies of the United States.																	
Nov. 2	Skirmish	Platte City, Mo.				(Organizations not Recorded).			13			80						Federal.
	Gen. Fremont, U. S. A., relieved by Major-Gen. Hunter.																	
	Operations from Bird's Point, Cape Girardeau, and Ironton, Mo., against Gen. Thompson's Confederate Forces.																	
Nov. 3	Expedition into Lower Maryland (3d-11th).																	
Nov. 4	Expedition in quest of Confederates and capture of	Houston, Mo.				Federal Troops.	Colonel Dodge, F.					82						Federal.
	Operations in the Valley District (Nov. 4, 1861-Feb. 21st, 1862.)																	
Nov. 5	Gen. R. E. Lee, C. S. A., assigned to command of the Department of South Carolina, Georgia and East Florida.																	
	Coast of South Carolina, Georgia and East Florida constituted a Department under command of Gen. R. E. Lee, C. S. A.																	
Nov. 6	Action	Little Santa Fe, Mo.		120	600	4th Missouri Cavalry; 5th Kansas Cavalry	Capt. Shields, F.						120					Conf'd.
Nov. 7	Engagement	Belmont, Mo.	6½ hours	3500	6500	Kowald's Missouri Battery; 22nd, 27th, 30th, 31st Ill. and 7th Iowa Vols., Battery B, 1st Ill. Artillery and 2 Companies 15th Ill. Cavalry and Gunboats *Tyler* and *Lexington*	Brig.-Gen. Grant, F.; Gen. Cheatham, C.; Capts. Walker and Stemble, U. S. N.	80	261	173	427	278	233			19		1 Fed. 2 Con.
	Demonstration from Paducah upon Columbus, Ky.																	
	Naval Engagement	Port Royal, S. C.	4 hours		Batts, etc.	Federal Navy	Com. S. F. Dupont, F.; Com. Tatnall, C	8	100	23	100	2500				42		Federal.
	Forts Beauregard and Walker, Port Royal Bay, South Carolina, captured by U. S. Navy.																	
Nov. 8	Arrest of Commissioners Mason and Slidell by Captain Wilkes.																	
	Gen. R. E. Lee, C. S. A., assumes command of the Department of South Carolina, Georgia and East Florida.																	

CHRONOLOGICAL LIST OF EVENTS (1860-1865).—Continued.

DATE.	EVENT.	LOCATION.	DURATION	FORCE. F.	FORCE. C	COMPOSITION OF FORCE.	COMMANDERS.	KILLED. F.	KILLED. C.	WOUNDED. F.	WOUNDED. C.	PRISONERS TAKEN BY F.	PRISONERS TAKEN BY C.	MISSING. F.	MISSING. C.	Guns taken	Stands of Arms taken	ADVANTAGE.
1861																		
Nov. 8	Capture of the *Royal Yacht* in Bolivar Channel, Texas.																	
	Reconnoissance on Hilton Head Island, S. C.																	
	Revolt of Unionists in East Tennessee (8th–18th).																	
Nov. 9	Skirmish and Engagement (8th–9th)	PIKETON, KY. (Ivy Mountain)	1½ hours			2nd, 21st, 33rd, 59th Ohio and 16th Ky. Vols	Col. J. W. Sill, F. / Col. J. S. Williams, C	4	410	20	15	2000			40			Federal.
	Expedition to Mathias Point, Va.																	
	City of Branford captured by crew of the *Sceneca*.																	
	Department of New Mexico re-established under Colonel Canby, U.S.A.																	
	Department of the Missouri and Department of Kansas constituted.																	
	Department of the Ohio to include Kentucky and Tennessee.																	
Nov. 10	Retreat of Gen. Wise, Confederate	GAULEY'S BRIDGE, W. VA.				11th Ohio Volunteers and 2nd Kentucky Cavalry	Gen. Cox, F. / Col. DeVilliers, F	8		11							1200	
	Skirmish	TAYLOR'S FORD, TENN.	½ hour	300	22	Loyal Citizens	Capt. Miller, C.	9		7								Conf'd.
	Affair at	GUYANDOTTE, W. VA.		160	700	Recruits from 9th W. Va. Volunteers	—— Jenkins, C	7	7	20	15	12	10					Conf'd.
	Expedition from Hilton Head to Braddock's Point, S. C.																	
Nov. 11	Attack on Confederate Camp	LITTLE BLUE, MO.		110	Guer	7th Kansas Cavalry ("Kansas Jayhawkers")	Col. Anthony, F. / Col. Hays, C.	8		8								Federal.
	Major-Gen. Crittenden, C. S. A., assigned to command of the District of Cumberland Gap.																	
	Skirmish	NEW MARKET BRIDGE, VA.				(Organizations not recorded)	Col. Weber, F.		2									Federal.
Nov. 12	Reconnoissance to Pohick Church, Va.																	
	Skirmish	OCCOQUAN CREEK, VA.				Reconnoitering Party from 1st N. Y. Cavalry	Capt. Todd, F.	3		1			6					Conf'd.
Nov. 13	Expedition from Greenville to Doniphan, Mo. (13th–15th).																	
	Scout through Texas and Wright Counties, Mo. (13th–18th).																	
	Skirmish	ROMNEY, VA.				Pickets of General Kelly's Brigade		2				12						Federal.
Nov. 14	Confederates routed	POINT OF ROCKS, VA.		23		—— Pennsylvania Regt.	Col. Geary, F.		3									Federal.
	Affair at the Mouth of Mattawoman Creek, Md.																	
	Skirmish on the road from Fayetteville to Raleigh, W. Va.																	
	Skirmish	McCOY'S MILLS, VA.				7th and 37th Ohio Vols. and Capt. Schneider's Rifle Artillery	Gen. Benham, F. / Col. Creighton, F / Gen. Floyd, C.		15									Federal.
	Expedition through Accomac and Northampton Counties, Va.																	
Nov. 15	Brig.-Gen. Buell, U. S. A., assumes command of the Department of the Ohio.																	
Nov. 16	Capture and Re-capture of Wagons and Cattle	CASS COUNTY, MO.				Federal Troops		1	40	6	17							1 Con. 2 Fed.
	Capture of Union foraging party at Doolan's Farm, Va.																	
	Captain G. N. Ingraham, C. S. N., assigned to duty in Charleston Harbor, S. C.																	
Nov. 17	Confederates routed	CYPRESS BRIDGE, KY				(Organizations Not Recorded)	Col. Alcorn, F. / Col. Hawkins, C.	10		15								Federal.
Nov. 18	Skirmish	PALMYRA, MO.				Detachment 3rd Missouri Cavalry			3		5	10						Federal.
	Skirmish	FALLS CHURCH, VA.				Pickets 14th N. Y. S. Militia				1								1 Con. 2 Fed.
	Affair near Warrensburg, Mo.																	
	Attack on Steamer *Platte Valley* at Price's Landing, Mo.																	
Nov. 19	Operations in the Indian Territory. (Nov. 19, 1861, Jan. 4, 1862).																	
		WIRT COURT HOUSE			Rgs.	Detachment 1st W. Va. Cavalry			1		6							Federal.
	Major-Gen. H. W. Halleck, U. S. A., assumes command of the Department of the Missouri.																	
	Gen. Johnston, C. S. A., calls upon Tennessee for all Militia and Volunteers.																	
Nov. 20	Skirmish	BUTLER, MO.		24			Col. Burchard, F.		5		8							Federal.
	Skirmish	LITTLE SANTA FE, MO.				(Organizations not recorded).												
	Skirmish	BROWNSVILLE, KY.			50	Col. Jackson's Regiment	Brig.-Gen. Hindman, C	7		4	1							Conf'd.
	Major-Gen. Hunter, U. S. A., assumes command of the Department of Kansas.																	
Nov. 21	Destruction of U. S. Stores at Warsaw, Mo.																	
	10,000 Volunteers called out in Mississippi for the defense of Columbus, Ky., etc.																	
	Brig.-Gen. Tilghman, C. S. A., assigned to command of Forts Henry and Donelson, Tenn.																	
Nov. 22	Department of the Indian Territory established under the command of Brig.-Gen. A. Pike, C. S. A.																	
Nov. 23	Bombardment of Confederate lines. (22d–23d)	PENSACOLA, FLA.	27 hours	1300	8000	Batteries A, F, L, 1st U. S. Art., C, H and K, 2nd U. S. Art., Companies C and E, 3rd U. S. Infantry, and Cos. G and I, 6th N. Y. Volunteers, and Federal gunboats *Niagara* and *Richmond*	Col. Harvey Brown, F / Flag Officer McKean, F. / Gen. Bragg, C.	1	7	6	8							Federal.
Nov. 24	Forrest's Expedition to Caseyville, Eddyville, etc., Kentucky, (Nov. 24th, Dec. 5th).																	
	Skirmish	JOHNSTOWN, MO.				Missouri Home Guards.												
	Skirmish / Confederates routed	LANCASTER, MO.	½ hour.	460	420	21st Missouri Volunteers	Col. Moore, F. / Lieut. Col. Blanton, C.	2	13	1								Federal.
	Union Forces occupy Tybee Island, Ga.																	
	Expedition to Dranesville, Va.																	
Nov. 26	Skirmish	DRANESVILLE, VA.		7 Cos	Cav.	1st Pennsylvania Cavalry	Col. Bayard, F. / Capt. Farley, C.		2	2		4						Federal.
	Reconnoissance and Skirmish	HUNTER'S MILLS, VA.		1 Squ		3rd Pennsylvania Cavalry	Capt. Bell, F.		1					20				Conf'd.
	Skirmish	INDEPENDENCE, LITTLE BLUE, MO.		6	66	7th Kansas Cavalry				1				2				Conf'd.
Nov. 27	Skirmish	FAIRFAX COURT HOUSE, VA.		1 Squ		Lincoln Cavalry	Capt. Boyd, F.				1							Conf'd
	The Ship Island Expedition sails from Hampton Roads, Va.																	
Nov. 28	Missouri admitted as a member of the Confederate States of America																	
	Brig.-Gen. Prentiss, U. S. A., assumes command of District of North Missouri.																	
	Reconnoissance of Federal Troops from Springfield, Va.							37th and 61st N. Y. Regiments	Col. Cone, F.											

CHRONOLOGICAL LIST OF EVENTS (1860-1865).—Continued.

Date	Event	Location	Duration	Force F.	Force C.	Composition of Force	Commanders	Killed F	Killed C	Wounded F	Wounded C	Prisoners Taken by F	Prisoners Taken by C	Missing F	Missing C	Guns taken	Stands of Arms taken	Advantage
1861																		
Nov. 29	Engagement	Black Walnut Creek, Mo.		4 Co's		1st Missouri Cavalry	Major Hough, F.		k&w: 17	5		5						Federal.
	Engagement	New Market Bridge, Va.		40	35	Prince Edward Cavalry (Confed.)	Drake DeKay, A.D.C., F.		2		5							Federal.
	Brig.-Gen. Schofield, U. S. A., assumes command of the Missouri Militia.																	
Nov. 30	Skirmish	Grand River, Mo.				(Organizations not recorded.)												
	Skirmish	Little Cacapon River, W. Va.				Confederate "Bushwhackers"	Captain Dyche, F.			3								1 Con. 2 Fed.
Dec. 1	Hostile Demonstration on Fort Holt, Ky.																	
	Operations about Mill Springs and Somerset, Ky. (1st–13th).																	
	Skirmish	Morristown, Tenn.			Pkts.	(Organizations not recorded.)												Federal.
	Skirmishes (1st–2nd)	Camp Goggin, Ky.				(Organizations not recorded.)												
	Skirmish	Shanghai, Mo.				(Organizations not recorded.)												
	Skirmish	Whippoorwill Creek, Ky.				(Organizations not recorded.)												
Dec. 2	Brig.-Gen. Denver, U. S. A., assigned to the command of all the Troops in the State of Kansas.																	
	Skirmish	Anandale, Va.		30	40	3rd New Jersey Volunteers	Col. Taylor, F.	1	7			3						Federal.
Dec. 3	Scout through Saline County, Mo. (3d–12th).																	
	Action	Salem, Mo.			300	Detachment 10th Missouri Cavalry	Major Bowen, F. Col. Freeman, C.	3	10	8	20	10	3					Federal.
	Engagement	Vienna, Va.		1 Squ.	700	Detachment 3rd Pennsylvania Cavalry	Capt. Bell, F.		3	4			0			45		Conf'd.
	Brig.-Gen. Pope, U. S. A., assumes command of all the Forces between the Missouri and Osage Rivers.																	
	Ship Island, Miss., occupied by Federal Forces																	
Dec. 4	Attack of Citizens on Confederate Troops	Dunksburg, Mo.				Citizens	Capt. Wheatley, C.		10		7							Federal.
	Skirmish	Burke's Station, Va.				(Organizations not recorded.)												
	Expedition to and Destruction of Bacon Creek Bridge, Ky.																	
Dec. 5	Expedition through the Current Hills, Mo. (5th–9th).																	
	Major-Gen. Hardee, C. S. A., assumes command of the Central Army of Kentucky.																	
	Scout in vicinity of Russellville, Ky. (5th–8th).																	
Dec. 6	Expedition to Gunnell's Farm near Dranesville, Va.																	
	Expedition to Port Royal Ferry and Beaufort, S. C.																	
Dec. 7	Capture of Confederates	Glasgow, Mo.				Detachment Federal Cavalry	Capt. Merrill, F. Capt. Sweeney, C.					35						Federal.
Dec. 8	Skirmish	Romney, W. Va.				(Organizations not recorded.)												
	Skirmish	Dam No. 5, C. & O. Canal			600	13th Mass. Regiment and an Illinois Regiment	Colonel Leonard, F.											Federal.
	Skirmish	Fishing Creek, Ky.				(Organizations not recorded.)												
Dec. 9	Engagement	Bushy Creek, Ark.		4000	1300	Federal Indians	Opothleyholo, F. Col. Cooper, C.			200								Conf'd.
	Skirmish	Union Hills, Mo.				(Organizations not recorded.)												
Dec. 11	Skirmish	Dam No. 4, Potomac, Va.		Pkts.		12th Indiana Volunteers			7									Conf'd.
	Skirmish	Berthand, Mo.		2 Co's		2nd Illinois Cavalry and Infantry	Lieut.-Col. Rhodes, F. Major Mudd, F.	1				16						Federal.
	Skirmish	Greenbrier Bridge, W. Va.				(Organizations not recorded.)												
Dec. 12	Skirmish	Bagdad, Ky.		8	40	6th Kentucky Volunteers				1								Conf'd.
	Skirmish	Gradyville, Ky.				(Organizations not recorded.)												
	Pascagoula Bay and Mississippi, east of Pascagoula River, included in Department of Alabama and West Florida																	
	Skirmish	Charleston, Mo.				(Organizations not recorded.)												
Dec. 13	Engagement	Buffalo Mountain, W. Va., also Camp Allegheny, W. Va.	7 hours	1750	2000	9th and 13th Ind., 25th and 32nd Ohio and 2nd W. Va. Vols.	Brig.-Gen. Milroy, F. Gen. Johnson, C.	21	20	107	96							Federal.
Dec. 14	Brig.-Gen. Sibley, C. S. A., assumes command of the Forces on the Upper Rio Grande and in New Mexico and Arizona.																	
Dec. 15	Affair in Roane Co., W. Va.																	
	Capture of the Sloop Victory																	
	Operations on the lower Potomac. (15th–17th).																	
	Expedition to Meadow Bluff, W. Va. (15th–21st).																	
Dec. 17	Jackson's Operations against Dam No. 5, Chesapeake and Ohio Canal.																	
	Action	Rowlett's Station, Ky. (Munfordville and Woodsonville)		4 Co's		32nd Indiana Volunteers	Col. Willich, F. Col. Terry, C.	9	33	16	50							Federal.
	Skirmish	Chisholms Island, S. C.				(Organizations not recorded.)												
	Evacuation of Rockville, S. C., by Confederate Forces.																	
Dec. 18	Skirmish	Milford, Mo. (Shawnee Mound and Blackwater)		2200		27th Ohio and 8th, 18th, 22nd and 24th Ind. Vols., 1st Kan. Cavalry and 1st Iowa Cavalry, a detachment U. S. Cav., and 2 Bat. 1st Mo. Light Art.	Gen. Pope, F.	2		8		150					1000	Federal.
	Scout from Rolla towards Houston, Mo.																	
	Reconnoissance to Pohick Church, Va.																	
	Reconnoissance from Somerset to Mill Springs, Ky.																	
Dec. 19	Skirmish	Point of Rocks, Md.	½ hour	6 Co's	200	Pennsylvania Regiment	Col. DeKorponay, F.		14									Federal
	Stone Fleet sunk in Charleston Harbor, S. C.																	
Dec. 20	Engagement	Dranesville, Va.	1 hour			1st, 6th, 9th, 10th and 12th Regt. Penn. Reserve Corps, 1st Penn. Artillery and 1st Penn. Cavalry	Gen. McCall, F. Col. J. H. Forney, C.	7	30	63	10	6	3					Federal.
Dec. 21	Skirmish	Hudson, Mo.		103	400	Detachment 7th Missouri Cavalry	Major McKee, F.		10	5		17						Federal.
	Brig.-Gen. Anderson, C. S. A., assigned to duty in North Carolina																	

CHRONOLOGICAL LIST OF EVENTS (1860-1865).—Continued.

Date.	Event.	Location.	Duration.	Force F.	Force C.	Composition of Force.	Commanders.	Killed F.	Killed C.	Wounded F.	Wounded C.	Prisoners Taken F.	Prisoners Taken C.	Missing F.	Missing C.	Guns Taken.	[illegible]	Advantage.
1861																		
Dec. 22	Skirmish	New Market Bridge, Va.	6 hours	4 Co's		20th New York Volunteers	Col. Max Weber, F.			5								
Dec. 23	Skirmish	Dayton, Mo.				(Organizations not recorded.)												
	Expedition to Lexington, Mo.																	
	Garfield's and Marshall's Operations in Eastern Kentucky (Dec. 23, 1861, Jan. 30, 1862).																	
Dec. 24	Skirmish	Wadesburg, Mo.				Missouri Home Guards.												
	Scout towards Fairfax Court House, Va., (24th, 25th).																	
Dec. 25	Brig.-Gen. Curtis, U. S. A., assigned to command of Southwestern District of Missouri.																	
	Skirmish	Cherry Run, W. Va.				(Organizations not recorded.)												
	Skirmish	Fort Frederick, Md.				(Organizations not recorded.)												
	Skirmish	Grider's Ferry, Ky.				(Organizations not recorded.)												
	Expedition to Danville, Mo.																	
Dec. 26	Skirmish	Camp Boyle, Ky.		Pkts	600	Federal Troops	Major Dudley, F.		6									Federal.
	Martial Law proclaimed in St. Louis, Mo., and in and about all railroads in the State of Missouri.																	
Dec. 27	Skirmish	Hallsville, Mo.		300	1 Co.	6 Troops Federal Cavalry and 5 Companies Sharpshooters	Capt. Howland, F.; Col. Glover, F.; Capt. Johnson, C.		8	2		7						Federal.
Dec. 28	Expedition to Camp Beauregard and Viola, Ky. (28th-31st).																	
	Action	Mount Zion Church, Mo		470	900	Birge's Sharp-shooters and 3rd Missouri Cavalry	Gen. Prentiss, F.; Col. Dorsey, C.	3	150 k&w	11		35				105		Federal.
	Action	Sacramento, Ky.	½ hour	2 Sqds.	700	3rd Kentucky Cavalry	Major Murray, F.; Col. Forrest, C.	1	30 k&w	8								Conf'd.
	Beckley (Raleigh Court House), W. Va., occupied by Union Forces.																	
Dec. 29	Capture of Suttonsville (Braxton Court House), and Skirmishes in Clay, Braxton and Webster Counties, W. Va. (29th-30th).																	
	Descent upon Commerce, Mo., and attack on Steamer *City of Alton*.																	
1862																		
Jan. 1	Engagement	Port Royal, Coosa River, S. C.		3000	8000	3 Gunboats, 3rd Michigan, 47th, 48th and 79th New York and 50th Pennsylvania Volunteers	Flag Off. Du Pont, F.; Com. Rogers, F.; Brig.-Gen. Stevens, F.	2	8	12	24			1				Federal.
	Expedition from Morristown to Dayton and Rose Hill, Mo., Skirmish en route, and Destruction of Dayton. (1st-3d).																	
	Bombardment of Forts McRee and Barrancas, Pensacola Harbor.						Col. H. Brown, F.; Gen. Bragg, C.			2								
Jan. 2	Skirmish	Hunnewell, Mo				4 Companies of 10th Missouri Cavalry.												
	Descent upon, and Skirmish at	Huntersville, W. Va.		738	250	Det. 25th Ohio Volunteers and 2nd W. Va. and 1st Indiana Cavalry	Major Hunter, F.			1	8							Federal.
	Skirmishes. (3d-4th)	Bath, W. Va				28th Illinois Volunteers	Capt. Linton, F.			3			8					Conf'd.
	Reconnoissance from Camp Hamilton to Big Bethel, Va																	
Jan. 4	Skirmishes	Slanes Cross Roads, W. Va.; Great Cacapon Bridge, W. Va.; Sir John's Run, W. Va.; Alpine Depot, W. Va.				39th Illinois Volunteers.	Capt. Hother, F.		6	1								Federal.
	Skirmish	Calhoun, Mo.				(Organizations Not Recorded).												
Jan. 5	Operations in Johnson and La Fayette Counties, Mo.																	
	Bombardment of Hancock, Md. (5th-6th).																	
Jan. 6	Brig.-Gen. S. Hamilton, U. S. A., assumes command of the St. Louis District.																	
Jan. 7	Occupation of Paintsville, Ky., by Federal Forces.					42nd Ohio, 40th Ky., and 300 of 2nd Va. Cavalry	Col. Garfield, F.	2	3	1		15						Federal.
	Skirmish	Blue Gap, near Romney, Va.			2000	4th, 5th, 7th and 8th Ohio and 14th Indiana Vols., and 1st W. Va. Cavalry.	Col. Dunning, F.		15			20				2		Federal.
	Skirmish	Jennie's Creek, Ky		60	200	4 companies of 1st West Virginia Cavalry	Colonel Bolles, F.	2	6	1								Federal.
	Department of North Carolina constituted, to be commanded by Brig.-Gen. Burnside, U. S. A.																	
Jan. 8	Skirmish	Fishing Creek, Ky.				(Organizations not recorded.)												
	Skirmish	Charlestown, Mo.			80	10th Iowa Vols., Detachments, 11th, 20th and 22nd Illinois	Col. Perczel, F.	7		15								Conf'd.
	Skirmish	Dry Forks, Cheat River, W. Va.				1 company West Virginia Cavalry												
	Action	Silver Creek, Mo. (Roan's Tanyard)	40 minutes	450	1000	Detachments 1st and 2nd Mo., and 4th Ohio and 1st Iowa Cavalry	Major Torrence, F.; Major Hubbard, F.; Col. Poindexter, C.	6	40	10	60	28					200	Federal.
Jan. 9	Skirmish	Columbus, Mo.		50	300	1st Kansas Cavalry.	Capt. Merriman, F.; Col. Elliott, C.	6										Conf'd.
	Skirmish	Pohick Run, Va.				(Organizations not recorded.)												
Jan. 10	Engagement	Middle Creek and Prestonburg, Ky.	9 hours	2100	3000	40th and 42nd Ohio, 14th and 22nd Ky. Vols.	Col. J. A. Garfield, F.; ——— Marshall, C.	2	27	25		25						Federal.
	Expedition into Kentucky from Cairo, Ill. (10th-21st)			5000		10th, 18th, 27th, 29th, 30th, 31st and 48th Regts. of Infantry, 2 Batteries Light Artillery, 6 Companies of Cavalry	Brig.-Gen. McClernand, F.											
	The Trans-Mississippi District of Department No. 2 organized under command of Major-Gen. Earl Van Dorn, C. S. A.																	
Jan. 11	The Burnside Expedition sails from Hampton Roads for the Coast of North Carolina																	
	Department of Key West, Fla., constituted under command of Brig.-Gen. Brannan, U. S. A.																	
Jan. 12	Expedition to Logan Court House and the Guyandotte Valley, W. Va. (12th-23d)					27th Ohio Volunteers	Col. Siber, F.	2										
Jan. 13	Expedition arrives at Hatteras Inlet.																	

CHRONOLOGICAL LIST OF EVENTS (1860-1865).—Continued.

Date.	Event.	Location.	Duration.	Force F	Force C	Composition of Force.	Commanders.	Killed F.	Killed C.	Wounded F.	Wounded C.	Prisoners Taken by F.	Prisoners Taken by C.	Missing F.	Missing C.	Guns Taken	[illegible]	Advantage
1862																		
Jan. 13	Brig.-Gen. Burnside, U. S. A., assumes command of the Department of North Carolina.																	
Jan. 14	Gunboat Reconnoissance to Columbus, Ky.																	
Jan. 16	(15th–25th). Reconnoissance from Paducah, Ky., to Fort Henry, Tenn., under Brig.-Gen. C. F. Smith, U. S. A.																	
	(15th–17th). Expeditions to Benton, Mo., Bloomfield and Dallas, Mo.					17th Illinois Volunteers, 7th Illinois Cavalry	Maj. F. M. Smith, F.; Capt. Murdock, F.; Capt. Welker, F.; Maj. Rawalt, F.					57						
Jan. 16	Naval Descent by Federals upon Cedar Keys, Fla.											16						Federal.
Jan. 17	(17th–22d). Gunboat Demonstrations on Fort Henry, Tenn.																	
Jan. 19	Engagement	Mill Spring, Ky. (Logan's Cross Roads).	41 hours.	8000	8000	9th and 14th Ohio, 2nd Minn., 4th and 10th Ky. and 10th Ind., Vols. and 1st Ky. Cavalry. 15th Miss., 17th, 19th, 20th, 25th 28th and 29th Tenn., 16th Alabama (Confederates)	Brig.-Gen. Thomas, F.; Maj.-Gen. Crittenden, C.	39	125	207	309	89				12		Federal.
	Operations in and about Atchison, Kansas. (20th–24th).			1 Co		1st Missouri Cavalry	Capt. Fuller, F.		1			15						Federal.
Jan. 20	Second Stone Fleet sunk at the Entrance to Charleston Harbor, S. C.																	
	Contest over the British Schooner *Anthracite* on the coast of Alabama.					2 Federal Steamers, Capt. Cottrill commanding Confederates	Capt. Cottrill, C.											
Jan. 22	Skirmish	Knob Noster, Mo.				2nd Missouri Cavalry.												
	Expedition to Edisto Island, S. C., (22d, 25th).						Col. Stevens, C.											
	Occupation of Lebanon, Mo.					Wright's Battalion of Missouri Cavalry	Lieut.-Col. Wright, F.											
	Brig.-Gen. Wise, C. S. A., assigned to command at Roanoke Island.																	
Jan. 24	(24th–30th). Expedition to the Little Sandy and Piketon, Ky.																	
Jan. 26	Reconnoissance to Wilmington Narrows, Ga., Naval Engagement (26th, 28th)	Wilmington Narrows, Ga.	1 hour.		5 G'bts	Federal Gunboats *Ottawa*, *Seneca*, *Isaac H. Smith*, *Potomska*, *Ellen* and *Western World*, and Federal Troops	Capt. C. H. Davis, U. S. N.; Brig.-Gen. Wright, F.; Flag Officer Tatnall, C.											Federal.
	General Beauregard, C. S. A., ordered from the Potomac District to Columbus, Ky.																	
Jan. 27	Brig.-Gen. Withers, C. S. A., assigned to command of the Army of Mobile.																	
	Brig.-Gen. Samuel Jones, C. S. A., assigned to command of the Army of Pensacola.																	
Jan. 28	Operations near Greensburg, Ky., and Lebanon (Jan. 28th, Feb 2nd).				Cav.	2 Companies 1st Ohio Cavalry	Lieut.-Col. T. C. A. Smith, F.; Capt. Morgan, C.						3					
Jan. 29	Affair at Occoquan Bridge, Va.					Detachment 37th N. Y. Volunteers and 1st N. J. Cavalry												
	(Jan. 29th, Feb. 3rd). Expedition to Blue Springs, Mo.						Capt. Oliver, F.; —— Quantrill, C.	1		2								
	Major-Gen. Earl Van Dorn, C. S. A., assumes command of the Trans-Mississippi District.																	
Feb. 1	Skirmish	Bowling Green, Ky.				One company, 2nd Indiana Cavalry.												
Feb. 2	Skirmish	Morgan County, Tenn.			Cav.	Detachment 1st Tennessee Cavalry, (Confederate)	Col. Leadbetter, C.	6					1					Conf'd.
Feb. 3	Call for 71,000 men from the State of Missouri for Confederate service.																	
	Reconnoissance to Occoquan Village, Va.			78		3rd Michigan Infantry	Capt. Lowing, F.				4							
Feb. 4	Gunboat Reconnoissance to Fort Henry, Tenn.																	
Feb. 6	Expedition to Florence, Ala. (6th–10th.)					Federal Steamers *Tyler*, *Lexington* and *Conestoga*	Lieut.-Com. Phelps, U. S. N.										200	Federal.
	Capture of Fort Henry, Tenn.		1¼ hours.		6000	Federal Gunboats *Essex*, *Carondelet*, *St. Louis*, *Cincinnati*, *Conestoga*, *Tyler* and *Lexington*	Brig.-Gen. U. S. Grant, F.; Flag Off. Foote, F.; Gen. Tilghman, C.	[illegible] 44				81				17		Federal.
	Reconnoissance of Fed. Troops to Wright River, S.C., under Maj. Beard.																	
Feb. 7	Expedition to Flint Hill and Hunter's Mill, Va.			6 Sqd		Cameron Dragoons	Major Bliss, F.	1	1			4						
Feb. 8	Brig.-Gen. B. R. Johnson, C. S. A., assumes command at Fort Donelson, Tenn.																	
	Skirmish	The Bluestone, W. Va.		450	225	45th Virginia Regiment (Confederates)	Lieut.-Col. Peters, C.											Conf'd.
	Skirmish	Linn Creek, Va.				(Organizations not recorded.)												
	Battle	Roanoke Island, N. C.	14 hours.	1484	2000	Detachment 5th W. Va. Vols., U. S. Gunboats *Southfield*, *Delaware*, *Stars and Stripes*, *Louisiana*, *Hetzel*, *Commodore Perry*, *Underwriter*, *Valley City*, *Commodore Barney*, *Hunchback*, *Ceres*, *Putnam*, *Morse*, *Lockwood*, *J. A. Seymour*, *Granite*, *Brinker*, *Whitehead*, *Shawsheen*, *Picket*, *Pioneer*, *Hussar*, *Vidette*, *Chasseur*, 21st, 23rd, 24th, 25th, 27th Mass., 10th Conn., 9th, 51st and 53rd N. Y., 9th N. J., 51st Penn., and 4th and 5th R. I. Vols.	Brig.-Gen. Burnside, F.; Com. L. M. Goldsborough, F.; Col. Shaw, C.	37	23	214	58	2500		13	62	40		Federal.
	Martial Law declared throughout the State of Kansas.																	
	Affair at Bolivar, Mo.						Lieut. Col. Lewis, F.					2						Federal.
Feb. 9	Brig.-Gen. Pillow, C. S. A., assumes command at Fort Donelson, Tenn.																	
	Skirmish	Marshfield, Mo.				Cavalry Battalion	Lieut.-Col. Wright, F.		2		2	3						Federal.
Feb. 10	Action	Elizabeth City, N. C.				Federal Gunboats *Delaware*, *Underwriter*, *Louisiana*, *Seymour*, *Hetzel*, *Shawsheen*, *Valley City*, *Putnam*, *Commodore Perry*, *Ceres*, *Morse*, *Whitehead*, and *Brinker*	Col. Henningsen, C.											Federal.
	Skirmish	Barnwell Island, S. C.		Pkts.			Capt. Dimock, F.; Lieut. Foot, F.											Federal.
Feb. 11	Occupation of Edisto Island, S. C., by Federal Forces					47th N. Y. Infantry	Col. H. Moore, F.											Federal.

CHRONOLOGICAL LIST OF EVENTS (1860-1865).—Continued.

Date.	Event.	Location.	Duration.	Force F.	Force C.	Composition of Force.	Commanders.	Killed F.	Killed C.	Wounded F.	Wounded C.	Prisoners Taken F.	Prisoners Taken C.	Missing F.	Missing C.	Guns taken.	Stands of Arms taken.	Advantage.
1862																		
Feb. 11	(11th, 18th.) Operations at Aransas Bay, Texas.																	
Feb. 12	(12th-16th.) Siege of Fort Donelson, Tenn., commenced (see 16th).																	
	Skirmish	Springfield, Mo.				Brig.-Gen. Curtis' Command. Regt. of Confederates	Brig.-Gen. Curtis, F.		2									Federal.
Feb. 13	Skirmish	Fort Heiman, Ky.		200		Hill's and Herndon's Battalions (Confederates)	Lieut.-Col. Miller, C.	3	1		2							Federal.
	Brig.-Gen. Floyd, C. S. A., assumes command at Fort Donelson, Tenn.																	
Feb. 14	Skirmish	Bloomery Gap, W. Va.		400	400	67th and Co. A, 39th Virginia Vols. and Federal Cavalry	Brig.-Gen. Lander, F.		11					50				Federal.
	Skirmish	Flat Lick Ford, Ky.				40th Ind. Vols., 6th Ky. Cavalry.												
	Skirmish	Crane Creek, Mo.				Cavalry of Brig.-Gen. Curtis' Command.												
	Attack on Confederate Troops	Mashfield, Mo.				9th Mo. Cavalry and 3rd Ill. Cavalry	Capt. Montgomery, F.		2		3	8						Federal.
	Attack on Confederate Pickets	Cumberland Gap, Tenn.				Company 1st Battalion Kentucky Cavalry	Lieut.-Col. Munday, F.		3		2	9						Federal.
	Brig.-Gen. U. S. Grant, U. S. A., assigned to command of the District of West Tennessee.																	
	Brig.-Gen. Sherman, U. S. A., assigned to command of the District of Cairo.																	
Feb. 15	Brig.-Gen. Schofield, U. S. A., assumes command of the District of St. Louis, Mo.																	
	(14th, 15th.) Evacuation of Bowling Green, Ky., by Confederates and Occupation by Federal Forces					Troops of Brig.-Gen. Buell's Army.												
	Action	Venus Point, Ga.	1 hour			Detachment 3rd R. I. Regt., 4 Confederate Gunboats	Capt. Gould, F.											Federal.
	(16th-22d.) Expedition from Cairo, Ill., to Eastport, Miss.																	
	Skirmish	Flat Creek, Mo.				Federal Troops	Brig.-Gen. Curtis, F.											Federal.
Feb. 16	Action	Pott's Hill, Ark.				Wright's Battalion Miss. Cavalry, 3rd Ill. Cavalry, 1st Mo. Cavalry, Major Bowen's Battery	Lieut.-Col. Wright, F.	1		3								Federal.
	Engagement	Fort Donelson, Tenn.	(Actual) 4 hours	15,000	10,000	17th and 25th Ky., 11th, 25th, 31st and 44th Ind., 2nd, 7th, 12th and 14th Iowa, 1st Neb., 68th and 76th Ohio, 8th and 13th Mo., 8th Wis., 8th, 9th, 11th, 12th, 17th, 18th, 20th, 28th, 29th, 30th, 31st, 41st, 45th, 46th, 48th, 49th, 57th and 58th Ill. Vols., Batteries, B and D 1st, and D and E 2nd Ill. Artillery, 4 companies Ill. Cavalry, Birge's Sharpshooters and 6 Gunboats	Brig.-General U. S. Grant, F. Com. A. H. Foote, F. Brig.-Gen. Buckner, C.	446	k., w. & m. 15,067	1780				150		40		Federal.
Feb. 17	Action	Sugar Creek, Ark.				1st and 6th Missouri and 3rd Illinois Cavalry	Brig.-Gen. Curtis, F.	13		13								Federal.
Feb. 18	Skirmish	Independence, Mo.				2nd Ohio Cavalry.												
	Action	Bentonville, Ark.				Detachments Benton and Fremont Hussars, and Capt. Elberts' Battery	Brig.-Gen. Asboth, F. Col. Rector, C.					27					24	Federal.
	(18th, 19th.) Expedition to Mount Vernon, Mo.			30		3rd Iowa Cavalry	Capt. Mudgett, F.					5						Federal.
	(19th-20th.) Expedition to Winton, N. C.																	
Feb. 19	Skirmish	West Plains, Mo.		203		3rd Iowa Cavalry, 6th Missouri Cavalry	Lieut.-Col. Wood, F.		8		8	80					60	Federal.
	Occupation of Clarksville, Tenn., by Federal Forces under Gen. Grant.																	
	(19th, 20th.) Expedition into Currituck Sound, N. C.					U. S. Gunboat *Delaware*	Brig.-Gen. Burnside, F. Col. Hawkins, F. Com. Rowan, F.											Federal.
	Skirmish	Winton, N. C.			600	9th New York Regt. and Gunboats.												
Feb. 21	Engagement	Valverde, New Mexico (Fort Craig)	11 hours	3810	1300	Detachments of 1st, 2d and 5th New Mexico Vols., 1st N. Mex. Cavalry and 2d Col. Cavalry. Detachments 5th, 7th and 10th U. S. Infantry and Hall's and McRae's Batteries	Col. Canby, F. Gen. Sibley, C.	68	36	160	150			35	1	7		Conf'd.
Feb. 22	Engagement	Aransas Bay, Texas				2 Federal Steam Launches	Capt. Neal, C.											Federal.
	Expedition to Vienna and Flint Hill, Va.					5th Penn. Cavalry, Cameron Dragoons	Col. Max. Friedman, F.					9						
	Skirmish	Independence, Mo.				(Organizations not recorded.)												
	Brig.-Gen. Arnold, U. S. A., supersedes Colonel Harvey Brown in command of the Department of Florida.																	
Feb. 23	Occupation of Fayetteville, Ark., by Federal Forces.																	
	Reconnoissance on Bull River and Schooner Channel, S. C. (23d-26th.)			23		8th Michigan Volunteers	Capt. Ely, F.											
	Evacuation of Nashville, Tenn., by Confederates and Occupation by Federal Forces. (23d-25th.)			10,000												24		
	General A. S. Johnston, C. S. A., assumes command of the Central Army.																	
	Department of the Gulf constituted under command of Major-Gen. B. F. Butler, U. S. A.																	
	Brig.-Gen. Pope, U. S. A., assumes command of the Army of the Mississippi.																	
Feb. 24	Skirmish	Mason's Neck, Va.				37th N. Y. Volunteers.												
	(23d, 24th.) Reconnoissance to Pea Ridge Prairie, Mo., and Skirmish			41		Missouri Mountain Rangers	Capt. Richardson, F.		3		1	8						Federal.
	Skirmish	Mingo Creek, Mo.				(Organizations not recorded.)												
	(Attack on Federal Pickets.) Affair at	Lewis's Chapel, Va.		2500		(Organizations not recorded)	Gen. Richardson, F.											
	Skirmish	New Madrid, Mo.				(Organizations not recorded.)												
Feb. 25	(23d-25th.) Reconnoissance from Greenville, Mo., and Skirmish near St. Francisville			200	200	2 companies 1st Ind. Cavalry, Captain Hawkins' Co. Mo. Vols., Captain Leeper's Co. Mo. State Militia	Major Clendenning, F.	1		2			6					Conf'd.
	Operations in Loudoun Co., Va. (Feb. 25th-May 6th.)					Artillery, 28th Pennsylvania Infantry	Col. J. W. Geary, F.	4		7		15	7					
	Skirmish	Keytesville, Mo.			500	9th Mo. Cavalry. Texas Rangers, (Confederates)	Capt. Montgomery, F. Maj. Ross, C.	2					1					Confd.

CHRONOLOGICAL LIST OF EVENTS (1860-1865).—Continued.

DATE.	EVENT.	LOCATION.	DURATION.	FORCE F.	FORCE C.	COMPOSITION OF FORCE.	COMMANDERS.	KILLED F.	KILLED C.	WOUNDED F.	WOUNDED C.	PRISONERS TAKEN BY F.	PRISONERS TAKEN BY C.	MISSING F.	MISSING C.	GUNS TAKEN.	STANDS OF ARMS TAKEN.	ADVANTAGE.
1862																		
Feb. 25	Major-Gen. E. K. Smith, C. S. A., assigned to command in East Tennessee.																	
Feb. 26	Scout to	Nashville, Tenn.			12		Capt. Morgan, C.											
	Major-Gen. McCown, C. S. A., assumes command at Madrid Bend.																	
Feb. 28	Operations at New Madrid, Mo., and Island No. 10, and Descent upon Union City, Tenn. (28th–April 8th.)																	
	Florida Expedition sails from Warsaw Sound.																	
	Affair at	Osage Springs, Ark.				(Organizations not recorded.)												
	Brig.-Gen. Samuel Jones, C. S. A., supersedes Major-Gen. Bragg in command of the Department of Alabama and West Florida.																	
Mch. 1	Engagement	Pittsburg, Tenn.				Federal Gunboats *Lexington* and *Tyler*, and 32d Ill. Vols.	Brig.-Gen. Cullum, F. / Col. Mouton, C.	2		0				3				Conf'd.
	Engagements	Sikeston, Mo.				7th Cavalry, 10th Infantry Illinois Volunteers.	Col. Morgan, F. / Jeff. Thompson, C.									8		Federal.
Mch. 2	Evacuation of Columbus, Ky., by Confederates and Occupation by Federal Forces. (2d–3d.)																	
	Abandonment of Albuquerque, New Mexico, by the Federal Forces.																	
	Skirmish	New Madrid, Mo.	2½ hours.			5th Iowa, 59th Ind., 39th and 63rd Ohio Infantry and 2nd Mich. and 7th Ill. Cavalry Vols.	Gen. Pope, F.	1		4								Conf'd.
Mch. 3	(3d–7th.) Reconnoissance to Berryville, Ark.			140			Col. Ellis, F.					50					60	Federal.
	Skirmish	Martinsburg, W. Va.				(Organizations not recorded.)												
	(3d–14th.) Siege of New Madrid, Mo.																	
	Capture of Cubero, New Mexico			47	20		Capt. Aragon, F. / Cpt. Thurmond, C.						47				60	Conf'd.
	Amelia Island, Fla., evacuated by the Confederate Forces.						Col. McBlair, C.											
	Gen. R. E. Lee, C. S. A., called to Richmond, Va.																	
Mch. 4	Scout through Laclede, Wright and Douglas Counties, Mo. (4th–11th.)			92		Federal Troops	Capts. Ludlow and Holden, F.	1	13	4	4	31					50	
	Abandonment of Santa Fé, New Mexico, by the Federal Forces.																	
	Major-Gen. Pemberton, C. S. A., assumes command of the department of South Carolina, Georgia and East Florida.																	
	Amelia Island, Fla., occupied by the Federal Forces.						Brig.-Gen. Wright, F.											
Mch. 5	Skirmish	Bunker Hill, Va.				(Organizations Not Recorded).	Brig.-Gen. A. S. Williams, F.											Federal.
	Skirmish	Pohick Church, Va.		50	30	63rd Pennsylvania Volunteers.	Lieut. Col. Morgan, F.	3		1								Conf'd.
	Skirmish	Occoquan, Va.				Reconnoitering Party of 63rd Pennsylvania Volunteers.												
	Gen. Beauregard, C. S. A., assumes command of Confederate Army of the Mississippi.																	
Mch. 6	Skirmish	Bentonville, Ark.				(Organizations not recorded.)												
	Battle. (6th–8th.)	Pea Ridge, Ark.			14,000	The Army of the Southwest	Brig.-Gen. Curtis, F.	203	600 K. & W.	972		200	800	171				Federal.
Mch. 7	Engagement, and Occupation of	Point Pleasant, Mo.				11th Mo., 26th and 47th Ill., 2nd and 3rd Mich. Cav., 1st Mo. Light Artillery, one company Engineers.	Brig.-Gen. Plummer, F.											Federal.
	Skirmish	Fox Creek, Mo.				4th Missouri Cavalry	Capt. Ludlow, F.			5								Federal.
	Skirmish	Bob's Creek, Mo.		120		1st Missouri Cavalry	Capt. Windmueller, F.		12	8								Federal.
	Skirmish	Winchester, Va.				Cole's Cavalry, Mathew's Battery, 46th Penn. and 5th Conn. Infantry	Capt. Cole, F. / Lt.-Col. Ashby, C.	3	6		7							Federal.
	Operations in Saline Co., Mo. (7th–10th.)					Federal Troops.	Col. Kaiser, F.		1			10	11					Conf'd.
	Withdrawal of the Confederate Forces from Evansport, Dumfries, Manassas and Occoquan, Va. (7th–9th.)																	
	Federal advance to Centreville and Manassas, Va.																	
	Advance of the Federal Forces to Centreville and Manassas, Va. (7th–11th.)																	
	Reconnoissance up the Savannah River and to Elba Island. (7th–11th.)			371		3rd N. H. Infantry.	Lieut.-Col. Jackson, F.											
	Attack of Federal Gunboats on Batteries, from Liverpool Point to Boyd's Hole, and at Aquia Creek, Potomac.																	
Mch. 8	Reconnoissance from Ship Island to	Mississippi City, La.				30th Mass. Volunteers.	Col. E. F. Jones, F.											Conf'd.
	Morgan's Operations near Nashville, Tenn.				25	1st Wis. Vols. and 4th Ohio Cavalry			4		2							Federal.
	Operations about Rolla, Mo. (8th–9th.)			15		Detachment Wood's Battalion	Maj. Joslyn, F.											
	Occupation of Leesburg, Va., by the Federal Forces.																	
	Sherman's Division embarks at Paducah, Ky., for the Tennessee River.																	
	Naval Engagement in Hampton Roads, Va., and Destruction of the Federal Frigate *Congress* and Sloop-of-War *Cumberland* by the Confederate iron-clad *Virginia* (formerly the *Merrimac*).					Federal Frigates *Cumberland*, *Congress*, *Minnesota*, *St. Lawrence*, and Gunboats *Oregon* and *Zouave*.	Flag Off. Marston, F. / Flag Off. Buchanan, C.	0		10				7				Conf'd.
	Occupation of Chattanooga, Tenn., by the Confederate Forces.						Brig.-Gen. Floyd, C.											
	Colonel Thomas M. Jones assigned to command at Pensacola.																	
	Expedition towards Purdy, and Operations about Crump's Landing, Tenn. (9th–14th.)																	
Mch. 9	Skirmish	Sangster's Station, Va.				(Organizations not recorded.)												
	Skirmish	Granny White's Pike, Tenn.		160	46	1st Louisiana Cavalry. (Confederates).	Capt. Scott, C.	12	8									Conf'd.
	Skirmish	Big Creek, Mo.				Cavalry	Capt. Wiedmueller, F.		2									Federal.
	Skirmish	Mountain Grove, Mo.		110	40	10th Missouri Cavalry	Capt. J. G. Rich, F.		13		7	20						Federal.
	Major-Gen. E. K. Smith, C. S. A., assumes command in East Tennessee.																	
Mch. 10	Skirmish	La Fayette Co., Mo.		30	25	1st Iowa Cavalry	Lieut. J. D. Jenks, F.	1	9	4	3	1						Federal.
Mch. 11	Skirmish	Paris, Tenn.				Detachment 5th Iowa Cavalry, and 1st Nebraska Cavalry and Bat. K., 1st Missouri Artillery	Capt. Croft, F.	5		5		6						Federal.
	Skirmish	Stephenson's Station, Va.				1 Company 1st New York Cavalry.												
	Winchester, Va., abandoned by the Confederates and occupied by the Federal Forces. (11th–12th.)																	

CHRONOLOGICAL LIST OF EVENTS (1860-1865).—Continued.

DATE	EVENT.	LOCATION.	DURATION	FORCE. F.	FORCE. C.	COMPOSITION OF FORCE.	COMMANDERS.	KILLED. F.	KILLED. C.	WOUNDED. F.	WOUNDED. C.	PRISONERS TAKEN BY. F.	PRISONERS TAKEN BY. C.	MISSING. F.	MISSING. C.	Guns taken	Stands of Arms taken	ADVANTAGE.
1862																		
Mch. 11	Department of Western Virginia merged into the Mountain Department																	
	Major-Gen. McClellan relieved from command of the Armies of the United States—retaining command of the Army of the Potomac.																	
	Departments of Kansas, of the Missouri, and in part of the Ohio merged into the Department of the Mississippi, under Major-Gen. Halleck, U. S. A.																	
Mch. 12	Jacksonville, Fla., occupied by the Federal Forces																	
	Skirmish	Lexington, Mo.				1st Iowa Cavalry.												
	Skirmish	Aubrey, Ark.		30			1st Lieut. Ross, F. —Quantrill, C.	...	9	1								Federal.
	Skirmish	Lebanon, Mo.				(Organizations Not Recorded).												
Mch. 13	Major-Gen. Halleck, U. S. A., assumes command of the Department of the Mississippi.																	
	Army Corps organized in the Army of the Potomac, and Generals McDowell, Sumner, Heintzelman, Keyes and Banks assigned as commanders.																	
	Action	Spring River, Ark.	4 hours.	250	800	3rd Iowa and 6th Missouri Cavalry	Lieut.-Col. Wood, F. Col. Coleman, C.	4	...	11	...	20						Federal
	Destruction of Beach Creek Bridge, Mobile and Ohio Railroad, Tennessee.																	
	Gen. R. E. Lee "charged with the conduct of Military Operations in the Armies of the Confederacy."																	
Mch. 14	Skirmish	Big Creek Gap, Tenn.		3300	...	2nd East Tenn., Co. A, 1st East Tenn., Co. B, 49th Ind., and Detachment 1st Battery Ky. Cavalry	Col. Carter, F. Lt.-Col. White, C.	...	5	1	15	15						Federal.
	Capture of	New Madrid, Mo.		9,000	...	10th and 16th Ill., 27th, 39th, 43rd and 63rd Ohio Vols., 2d Mich. Cav., 1st U. S. Inf., Birdsall's Mo. Engineers	Brig.-Gen. Pope, F.	51	...							33	[illegible]	Federal.
	(14th–17th.) Expedition from Savannah, Tenn., to Yellow Creek, Miss., and occupation of Pittsburg Landing, Tenn.																	
	Skirmish	Jacksborough, Tenn.				2nd Tennessee Volunteers.	Colonel Carter, F.	...	1	...	...	1						Federal.
	Reconnoissance to Cedar Run, Va. (14th–16th)					57th N. Y. Vols. and a Brigade of Cavalry	Bg.-Gen. Stoneman, F.											
	Major-Gen. Pemberton, C. S. A., assigned to command of South Carolina and Georgia Department, and Brig.-Gen. Trapier, C. S. A., assigned to command of Middle and East Florida Department																	
	Brig.-Gen. Rosecrans, U. S. A., assumes command of the Mountain Department																	
	Battle	New Berne, N. C.	4 hours.			51st N. Y., 8th, 10th and 11th Conn., 21st, 23rd, 24th, 25th and 27th Mass., 9th N. J., 51st Penn., 4th and 5th R. I. Vols.	Bg.-Gen. Burnside, F.	90	64	380	101	200	...	1	413	64		Federal.
Mch. 15	The States of South Carolina, Georgia and Florida constituted the Department of the South, to be commanded by Major-Gen. David Hunter, U. S. A.																	
	Morgan's Operations about Gallatin, Tenn. (15th–18th.)																	
	Skirmish	Marshall, Mo.		30	50	Lieut. Turley's Co., Missouri State Militia	Lieut. Turley, F.	...	...	...	2							Federal.
	(March 15th–April 7th.) Siege of Island No. 10																	
	Department of Florida merged into the Department of the South, Major-Gen. Hunter, U. S. A., commanding.																	
	Engagement	Aquia Creek, Va.				U. S. Gunboats Yankee and Anacostia												Conf'd.
Mch. 16	Skirmish	Marshall, Mo.				Booneville Battalion Mo. Cavalry	Capt. Kaiser, F.	...	8	...	...	3						Federal.
	Action	Pound Gap, Ky.	30 minutes	700	600	Detachments 22nd Ky., 40th and 42nd Ohio Vols., 1st Ohio Cavalry	Bg.-Gen. Garfield, F. Maj. Thompson, C.	...	7	...	...							Federal.
	Skirmish	Pittsburgh Landing, Tenn.			Cav.	Cavalry of General Sherman's Division		...	...	4	...							Federal
	Skirmish	Black Jack Forest, Tenn.		86	500	Detachments 4th Ill. Cavalry and 5th Ohio Cavalry.	Lieut.-Col. Heath, F.	...	...	4	...	2						Federal
Mch. 17	Embarkation of the Army of the Potomac for the Peninsula, commenced at Alexandria.																	
	Action	Battery No. 1, New Madrid, Mo. (Willow Point.)	9 hours.	...	Batty	5 Federal Gunboats and 1 Mortar Boats	Brig.-Gen. Trudeau, C.	...	1	...	...							Conf'd.
Mch. 18	Operations in Johnson, St. Clair and Henry Counties, Mo. (18th–30th)						Col. Fitz Henry Warren, F.	...	...	...	...	75						
	Skirmish	Salem, Ark.				Detachments 6th Mo. and 3rd Iowa Cavalry.												
	Engagement	Point Pleasant, Mo.				(Organizations not recorded.)												
Mch. 19	Reconnoissance on May River, S. C. (19th–24th.)																	
	Skirmish	Leesville, Mo.				Detachment 1st Iowa Cavalry	Capt. Ankeny, F.	...	5	4	1	...	...	...	...	...	7	Federal.
	(19th–23d). Operations in	Johnson Co., Mo.		85	4	Missouri State Militia	Lieuts. Christian and Jewell, F.	1	4	1	...	...	...	...	...	...	...	Federal.
	(19th–20th). Expedition to	Carthage, Mo.				5th Kansas Cavalry	Lieut.-Col. Clayton, F.	...	...	3	...	20	1	...	...	...	...	Federal.
	Colonel W. S. Dilworth, Florida, assigned to command of the Department of Florida, vice Trapier ordered to Alabama.																	
	Brig.-Gen. J. R. Anderson supersedes Brig.-Gen. Gatlin in command of the Confederate Department of North Carolina.																	
Mch. 20	(20th–24th.) Operations near Bluffton, S. C., including affairs at Buckingham and Hunting Island.					3rd N. H. Vols. and 3rd R. I. Vols.	Lieut. Col. Jackson, F.											
	(20th–21st.) Expedition to	Washington				24th Mass. Vols., U. S. Gunboats Delaware, Louisiana and Commodore Barney.	Col. Stevenson, F.											
	Major-Gen. B. F. Butler, U. S. A., assumes command of the Department of the Gulf.																	
Mch. 21	Affair at	McKay's Farm, Mo.		40	100	Missouri State Militia	Lieut. McCabe, F.	1	...	1	...	...	...	...	...	...	...	Conf'd.
	Reconnoissance and Skirmish. (21st–23d.)	Cumberland Gap, Tenn.		2300	...	1st East Tenn., 7th Ky., 16th Ohio, 49th Ind., 1st Ky. Cavalry, 9th Ohio Battery	Col. Carter, F.	...	...	...	5	...	...	...	...	...	...	Federal.
	Engagement	Mosquito Inlet, Fla.		...	...	U. S. Gunboats Penguin and Henry Andrew.	Lieut. Budd, U. S. N.	8	...	...	...	...	2	...	...	...	...	Conf'd.
Mch. 22	Skirmish	Post Oak, Mo.		...	...	(Organizations not recorded.)												

CHRONOLOGICAL LIST OF EVENTS (1860-1865).—Continued.

DATE.	EVENT.	LOCATION.	DURATION.	FORCE.		COMPOSITION OF FORCE.	COMMANDERS.	KILLED.		WOUNDED.		PRISONERS TAKEN BY		MISSING.		GUNS TAKEN.	STANDS OF ARMS TAKEN.	ADVANTAGE.
				F.	C.			F.	C.	F.	C.	F.	C.	F.	C.			
1862																		
Mch. 22	Skirmish	LITTLE SANTA FE, MO.		300	20	2nd Kansas	Col. Mitchell, F.	1	7	1	...	6						Federal.
Mch. 23	Battle	WINCHESTER, VA		7500	10,000	1st W. Va., 84th and 110th Penn., 5th, 7th, 6th, 29th, 62nd and 67th Ohio, 7th, 13th and 14th Ind., 39th Ill. Vols., 1st W. Va. and 1st Ohio and Co. E, 1st U. S. Artillery, 1st Mich. and 1st Ohio Cav.	Brig.-Gen. Shields, F. Gen. Ashby, C.	103		440	...	300	...	24	...	2	1000	Federal.
	Affair at	SMYRNA, FLA.					Capt. Bird, C.	7		30			3					Conf'd.
	Expedition to	LITTLE RIVER, MO.		200	40	7th Illinois Cavalry	Maj. Rawalt, F.	2	...	2		4						Federal.
	Skirmish	CARTHAGE, MO.				6th Kansas Cavalry.												
	(23d-April 26th.) Siege of	FORT MACON, N. C.		...	...	12 Regiments and 1 Battery	Brig.-Gen. Parke, F.	1	7	3	18	400		...		54	500	Federal.
Mch. 24	Scout in St. Clair and Henry Counties, Mo.																	
	Skirmish	CAMP JACKSON, TENN		...		(Organizations not recorded.)												
	Major-Gen. T. H. Holmes, C. S. A., supersedes Brig.-Gen. J. R. Anderson																	
Mch. 25	Skirmish	MONAGHAN SPRINGS, MO.		...		(Organizations not recorded.)												
	Expedition in Moniteau Co., Mo., (25th-28th) and Skirmish en route			...	200	Co. A, 6th Mo. Vols., Capt. Adam's Co. 6th Mo. Vols., 2 Cos. Militia and Section Artillery	Lieut.-Col. Blood, F.	...	7	...		2						Federal.
	Reconnoissance from Murfreesborough to Shelbyville, Tullahoma, Manchester and McMinnville, Tenn																	
	Reconnoissance to Agnew's Ferry, Tenn						Col. Kennett, F.											
Mch. 26	Skirmish	APACHE CAÑON, NEW MEXICO.		418	300	1st Colorado Infantry, 3rd Cavalry, 1st Cavalry, Colorado Volunteers	Maj. Chivington, F.	5	32	14	43	71						Federal.
	Action	POST OAK, MO		60	200	Missouri State Militia	Maj. Foster, F. —Maj. Hoss, C.	2	6	7		16						Federal.
	Action	HUMANSVILLE, MO.		...	400	Companies A, B, D and E, 8th Mo. Militia Cavalry	Capts. Stockton, Cosgrove, Garrely and Smith, F.	.	20	13	20	3						Federal.
	Skirmish	GOUGE'S MILL, MO		25	40	8th Missouri	Capt. Ostermayer, F.	..	*									Federal.
Mch. 27	Reconnoissance on Santa Rosa Island, Fla. (27th-31st.)			...	...	Company L, 1st Artillery, Companies D and F, 6th N. Y. Vols.	Capt. Closson, F.											
	Attack on Federal Camp	STRASBURG, VA.		...	...	Portion of Brig.-Gen. Banks's command.	—— Ashby, C.	1	...	1								Federal
	Expedition into Scott and Morgan Counties, Tenn.			...	...	Tennessee Infantry and Cavalry (Confederate)	Col. Vaughn, C.	6	15	...	19	...	7					
Mch. 28	Reconnoissance near the Mouth of St. Augustine Creek, Ga.			...	...		Maj. O. T. Beard, F.											
	Engagement	MIDDLEBURG, VA		...	...	28th Pennsylvania Volunteers.	Col. Geary, F.											Federal.
	Engagement. (26th-28th)	GLORIETA, NEW MEXICO	6 hours	1300	1000	1st and 2nd Colorado Cavalry	Col. Slough, F. L.-Col. Scurry, C.	29	33	42	25	...	18					Federal.
	Skirmish (26th)	WARRENSBURG, MO.		60	Guer	Detachment Col. Phillips' Mo. Regiment	Maj. Foster, F. —— Quantrill, C.	3	9	11	17							Federal.
	The Cumberland Gap Campaign. (March 28th-June 18th.) Brig.-Gen. Morgan, U. S. A., assigned to command of Seventh Division, Army of the Ohio, and ordered to operate against Cumberland Gap																	
Mch. 29	Affair on	EDISTO ISLAND, S. C.		...	650	Enfield Battalion, Conf'd, Holcombe Legion, Conf'd	Col. Stevens, C.	3		...	2	...	18	...			11	Conf'd
	Skirmish on the	BLACKWATER, MO.		...	65	Detachments 1st Iowa Cavalry and 1st Mo. Artillery	Capt. Thompson, F. Col. Parker, C.	1	10	2	5	13						Federal.
	The Confederate Armies of Kentucky and the Mississippi consolidated under the latter designation, General A. S. Johnston commanding, and General Beauregard second in command. Major-Generals Polk, Bragg, Hardee and Crittenden assigned to the First, Second, Third and Reserve Corps respectively.																	
Mch. 30	(30th-31st.) Affairs on	WILMINGTON & WHITEMARCH ISLAND, GA.		50	...	Detachments 46th N. Y. Regt., 13th Georgia Regt., (Confederates)	Col. Rosa, F. Capt. Crawford, C.	1		...	1	...	19	...		1		Conf'd.
	Skirmish	CLINTON, MO.		...	...	Detachment 1st Iowa Cavalry			1	1	7	10						Federal.
	Descent upon	UNION CITY, TENN		...	...	27th Ill. Vols., 15th Wis. Vols., Captain Hotchkiss's Cav., Sparrestrom's Battery, 2nd Illinois Cav.	Col. Buford, F. L.-Col. Hogg, F. Col. Pickett, C.					11						Federal.
Mch. 31	Skirmish	PURDY ROAD, TENN.		25	...	Co. I, 5th Ohio Cavalry	Lieut. Murray, F.						3					Conf'd.
	Major-Gen. Hunter, U. S. A., assumes command of the Department of the South.																	
	(31st-April 2d.) Expedition to	PARIS, TENN.		73			Capt. Haw, F.											
	Skirmish	PINK HILL, MO		65	150	Detachment 1st Missouri Cavalry	Capt. Peabody, F.		6	8								Federal.
	Skirmish	DEEP GULLY, N. C.				(Organizations not recorded.)												
	Brig.-Gen. Mackall, C. S. A., supersedes Major-Gen. McCown in command at Madrid Bend, Mo.																	
	Reconnoissance of Federal Troops, from Newport News to Watts' Creek, Va.																	
Apr. 1	Skirmish on the	LITTLE SNI, MO.		50	...	—— Missouri Cavalry	Capt. Murphy, F.		5	2	6	1						Federal.
	Skirmish	DONIPHAN, MO.			...	Advance Guard	Col. Carlin, F.	1										Federal.
	Expedition from Pittsburg Landing, Tenn., to Eastport, Miss., and Chickasaw, Ala.																	
Apr. 2	Reconnoissance from Cape Girardeau to Jackson, Whitewater and Dallas, Mo. (2d-8th).						Col. Tyler, F.											
	Skirmish	WALKERSVILLE, MO		...	...	(Organizations not recorded).												
	Engagement	PUTNAM'S FERRY, MO			...	15th Ill. Cavalry, 21st and 38th Ill. Vols., 16 Ohio Battery, Colonel Carlin's Brigade.	Col. Carlin, F.	...	1			4						Federal.
	Occupation by Federal Troops of	THOROUGHFARE GAP, VA.			...	28th Pennsylvania Volunteers	Col. Geary, F.	1	...			3						Federal.
	Brig.-Gen. J. W. Denver, U. S. A., assumes command of District of Kansas																	
Apr. 3	Expedition from Ship Island to Biloxi and Pass Christian, Miss. (3d-4th.)																	
	Reconnoissance from Savannah, Tenn., to Eastport, Miss., and Chickasaw, Ala.			...	...	U. S. Gunboat *Tyler*	Col. Webster, F.											
	Affairs at Biloxi and	PASS CHRISTIAN, MISS.		1200	1000	9th Conn., 6th Massachusetts Artillery and Gunboats	Maj.-Gen. Lovell, C.			2								Federal.

CHRONOLOGICAL LIST OF EVENTS (1860-1865).—Continued.

Date.	Event.	Location.	Duration.	Force. F.	Force. C.	Composition of Force.	Commanders.	Killed. F.	Killed. C.	Wounded. F.	Wounded. C.	Prisoners Taken by F.	Prisoners Taken by C.	Missing. F.	Missing. C.	[illegible]	[illegible]	Advantage.
1862																		
Apr. 2	Skirmish	Monterey, Tenn.		400		5th Ohio Cavalry	Col. Taylor, F.; Col. Clanton, C.				1	1						Federal.
Apr. 4	Skirmish	Adamsville, Tenn.				5th Ohio Cavalry, 48th, 70th and 72nd Ohio Volunteers	Lieut. Murray, F.						3					Conf'd
	Skirmishes	Big Bethel, Va.				Advance of the Third Corps Army of the Potomac.												
	Skirmish	Lawrenceburg, Tenn.			76	28th Ohio, 17th Indiana, 3rd Ohio Cavalry	Brig.-Gen. Hascall, F				2							Federal.
	Skirmish	Pittsburg Landing, Tenn.				Guard of 70th Ohio and Co. B, 72nd Ohio Regiment.	Lieut. Herbert, F.; Maj. Crockett, F.			8	2	10	11					2 Fed. 1 Con.
Apr. 5	Occupation of Edisto Island, S. C., by the Federal Forces.					3rd New Hampshire Regiment.	Col. Fellows, F.											
	(5th, 6th.) Affair at	San Luis Pass, Texas.			25	13th Texas Infantry (Confederate).	Maj. Perry, C.					8						Federal.
	Siege of Yorktown (April 5th–May 3d.)					Second, Third and Fourth Corps Army of the Potomac.												
Apr. 6	Battle. (6th, 7th.)	Shiloh, Tenn.	(Actual) 19½ hours		40,335	Army of the Tennessee and Army of the Ohio, Army of the Mississippi. (Confederate).	Maj.-Gen. Grant, F; Maj.-Gen. Buell, F; Gen. Beauregard, C; Gen. A. S. Johnston, C	1754	1723	8408	8012			2885	959			Federal.
	Expedition from Greeneville, Tenn., into	Laurel Valley, N. C.		3 Co's		3rd Tennessee Regiment (Confederate.)	M.-Gen. K. Smith, C; Lieut.-Col. Key, C.	15	2		1							
Apr. 7	Capture of Island No. 10.						Maj.-Gen. Pope, F.									124		Federal.
	Raid on Confederate line of communication between Chattanooga, Tenn. and Marietta, Ga.																	
	Major Gen. Pemberton's command extended over Middle and Eastern Florida.																	
	(7th–8th.) Expedition to	Elizabeth City, N. C.		3 Co's	2 Co's	9th New York Regiment.	Lieut.-Col. Griffin, F.		1		1	78					30	Federal.
	Affair at	St. Andrew's Bay, Fla.				Marianna Dragoons. (Confederate).	Capt. R. S. Smith, C.	5										Federal.
	Skirmish	Newport, N. C.			60	Pickets	Capt. Boothe, C.			1			10					Conf'd.
	Skirmish	Foy's Plantation, N. C.				(Organizations not recorded.)												
Apr. 8	Garrison of Island No. 10 surrendered at Tiptonville, Tenn.																	
	Skirmish	Warrensburg, Mo.				(Organizations not recorded.)												
	Skirmish	Warsaw, Mo.				(Organizations not recorded.)												
	Skirmish	Medicine Creek, Mo.				A Guard (Federal), a party of Guerillas (Confederate)		1		2								Federal.
	Scout through Gadfly, Newtonia, Granby, Neosho, and the Valley of Indian Creek, Mo., and Skirmishes.						Col. Clark Wright, F											
	Martial Law proclaimed in East Tennessee.																	
	Brig.-Gen. Finegan, C. S. A., assigned to command of the Department of Middle and Eastern Florida																	
	Skirmish	Albuquerque, New Mexico		1216		Federal Troops	Col. Canby, F.		1									Federal.
	Reconnoissance from Shiloh Battlefield						Brig.-Gen. Sherman, F											
Apr. 9	Skirmish	Jackson, Mo.		65	56	Detachments Companies A, B and C Missouri Cavalry Militia	Capt. Fleetz, F.; Capt. Jefferies, C.	8	3		3		1	1				Conf'd.
		Owen's River, Cal.				2nd California Cavalry.	Brig.-Gen. Wright, F											
	Evacuation of Jacksonville, Fla., by the Federal Forces.																	
	Scout to Shiloh Camp on Hoyle's Run, near Quincy, Mo., and Skirmishes; scout to Little Niangua, Hickory County, Mo., and scout from Humansville to Montevallo, Vernon County, Mo. (9th–16th.)							4	3	4	1	12						
	Brig.-Gen. Parsons assumes command of Missouri State Guard (Confederate).																	
Apr. 10	Skirmish	Fernandina, Fla.		7	40	Detachments, 9th Maine Regt., 1st Florida Cav., (Conf'd)	Capt. Baker, F.; Capt. Footman, C	1					6					Conf'd.
	Brig.-Gen. Sturgis, U. S. A., assumes command of the District of Kansas.																	
Apr. 11	(10th, 11th.) Bombardment and Capture of	Fort Pulaski, Ga.	30 hours.			46th and 48th N. Y. Vols., 6th and 7th Conn., 8th Maine, 2 companies N. Y. Vol. Engineers, 2 companies 3rd R. I. Artillery and detachment Co. A, Corps of Engineers, 15th U. S. Infantry, Federal Steamer *Wabash*	Maj.-Gen. Hunter, F	1			3	360				47		Federal.
	Occupation of Huntsville, Ala., by the Federal Forces.					3rd Division Army of the Ohio.	Brig.-Gen. Mitchell, F					200						
	Skirmish	Yorktown, Va.			700	12th N. Y., 57th and 63rd Pennsylvania Volunteers.	Col. Campbell, F.											Conf'd.
	Skirmish	Wartrace, Tenn.		600	200	8th Tennessee Cavalry, (Confederates).	Lieut.-Col. Starnes, C		3		6							Federal.
Apr. 12	(12th, 13th.) Expedition to	Bear Creek, Ala.				Detachment 4th Illinois Cavalry, General Fry's Brigade and Gunboats *Tyler* and *Lexington*	Brig.-Gen. Sherman, F											
	Skirmish	Little Blue River, Mo				(Organizations not Recorded)												
	Attack on Federal Pickets	Monterey, Va				75th Ohio Volunteers, 1st W. Va. Cavalry.	Major Webster, F.			3								Federal.
Apr. 13	Expedition from Southern California, through Arizona, to northwestern Texas and New Mexico. (April 13th–Sept. 20th.)																	
	Skirmish	Gillett's Farm, N. C.		2	11	103rd N. Y. Infantry, 2nd N. C. Vols., (Confederate).	Col. Egloffstein, F; Col. Robinson, C.	4	2	9	7	2						Federal
	Occupation of Decatur, Ala., by Federal Forces.																	
	Reconnoissances on the Corinth, Miss., and Purdy, Tenn., Roads.			45		Thielemann's Cavalry	Maj. Thielemann, F											
	Pursuit of the Confederate Forces, New Mexico. (13th–22d.)																	
	Skirmish	Montavallo, Mo.				2 Companies 1st Iowa Cavalry.												
Apr. 14	Skirmish	Pollocksville, N. C.				(Organizations not Recorded).												
	Skirmish	Diamond Grove, Mo.				6th Kansas Cavalry.												
	Bombardment of Fort Pillow, Tenn., by Federal Navy.																	
	Skirmish	Walkersville, Mo.				2nd Missouri Militia Cavalry.												
Apr. 15	Skirmish	Peralta, New Mexico.				(Organizations not Specified).	Col. Canby, F.	1	6	3	3	50				2		Federal
	Skirmish	Picacho Pass, Arizona.				1st California Cavalry.												
	Skirmish	Pea Ridge, Tenn.				(Organizations not recorded.)												
Apr. 16	Occupation of Tuscumbia, Ala., by Federal Forces.																	
	Skirmish	Lee's Mills, Va.	1 hour			3rd, 4th and 6th Vt. Vols., 3rd N. Y. Battery and Battery of 5th U. S. Artillery.	Brig.-Gen. W. F. Smith, F.	35		121				9				Conf'd.

CHRONOLOGICAL LIST OF EVENTS (1860-1865).—Continued.

DATE.	EVENT	LOCATION	DURATION	FORCE		COMPOSITION OF FORCE.	COMMANDERS.	KILLED.		WOUNDED		PRISONERS TAKEN BY		MISSING.		Guns Capt'd	Small Arms Capt'd	ADVANTAGE.
				F.	C.			F.	C.	F.	C.	F.	C.	F.	C.			
1862																		
Apr. 16	Skirmish	SAVANNAH, TENN.			Pkts.	Federal Cavalry			5		63							Federal.
	Skirmish	WILMINGTON, GA.		200		8th Mich. Vols. and Battery R. I. Artillery.	Lieut. Wilson, F.	13		16								Federal.
Apr. 17	Capture of Federal Refugees	WOODSON'S GAP, TENN.			120	4th Tennessee Cavalry (Confederate)	Capt. Ashby, C.	30		80			473					Confd.
	Skirmish	MONTEREY, TENN.				(Organizations not recorded.)												
	Skirmish	HOLLY RIVER, W. VA.				10th West Virginia Volunteers												
Apr. 18	(18th-28th.) Bombardment and Capture of Fts. Jackson and St. Philip, La.					First of Federal War Vessels	Admiral Farragut, F.											
	Skirmish and Occupation of	FALMOUTH, W. VA.				2nd New York Cavalry	Gen. Augur, F.	5		15								Federal.
	Engagement	EDISTO ISLAND, S. C.				Federal Steamer *Crusader* and 3rd N. H., and 55th Pennsylvania Volunteers	Lieut.-Com. Rhind, F.			3								Confd.
Apr. 19	Engagement	SOUTH MILLS, N. C.		2000		51st Penn., 6th N. H., 9th and 89th N. Y. Vols., 21st Mass.	Brig.-Gen. Reno, F.; Col. Wright, C.	12	K & W 60	48	10	3	12	13				Federal.
	Skirmish	TRENT ROAD, N. C.				(Organizations not recorded).												
	Skirmish	TALBOT'S FERRY, ARK.				4th Ohio Cavalry.												
Apr. 22	Capture of Federal Launches in Aransas Bay, Texas.																	
Apr. 23	Skirmish	BRIDGEPORT, ALA.				(Organizations not recorded.)												
	Engagement	GRASSLICK, W. VA.				3rd Maryland and Potomac Home Guards	Col. Downey, F.	3				5						Federal.
Apr. 24	Skirmish	TUSCUMBIA, ALA.				(Organizations not recorded.)												
	Skirmish	LICK CREEK, TENN.				(Organizations not recorded.)												
	Skirmish	SHELBYVILLE ROAD, TENN.				(Organizations not recorded.)												
	Skirmish	CORINTH ROAD, MISS.				(Organizations not recorded.)												
	Action	FORT MACON, N. C.				Federal Gunboats *Daylight, State of Georgia, Chippewa, Barque, Gemsbok* and Gen. Parke's Division.	Gen. Burnside, F.; Com. Lockwood, F.	1	8	2	20							Federal.
Apr. 25	Surrender of	NEW ORLEANS, LA.				Federal Naval Forces	Admiral Farragut, F.	1		4								Federal.
	Affair at	SOCORRO, NEW MEXICO				(Organizations not recorded.)												
	Skirmish	TUSCUMBIA, ALA.				(Organizations not recorded.)												
	Skirmish	CORINTH ROAD, MISS.				(Organizations not recorded.)												
Apr. 26	Redoubt before	YORKTOWN, VA.			2 Co's	3 Companies 1st Massachusetts Volunteers	Lieut.-Col. Wells, F.	4		13								Federal.
	Skirmish	ATKIN'S MILL, TENN.			4 Co's Plts.	2d Michigan Regiment	Maj. Shaw, F.			1								Federal.
	Reconnoissance to	LICK CREEK, TENN.				Troops commanded by Brig.-Gen. A. J. Smith												
	(26th-29th.) Scout on	FORKED DEER RIVER, TENN.			9	(Organizations not recorded).	Capt. Ballentine, C.											
	Fight with Indians	NEOSHO, MO.		140	600	1st Missouri Cavalry	Maj. Hubbard, F.		30			62						Federal.
	Skirmish	TURNBACK CREEK, MO.				5th Kansas Cavalry.												
Apr. 27	Skirmish	PEA RIDGE, TENN.				Cavalry	L.-Col. McCullough, F.		3			1						Federal.
	Abandonment of Ft. Quitman, La., by the Confederate Forces																	
	Recapture of Forts Livingston, Pike and Wood, La., by Federal Forces.																	
	Skirmish	BRIDGEPORT, ALA.				(Organizations not recorded.)												
	Skirmish	HAUGHTON'S MILL, N. C.		110	30	103rd New York Volunteers	Col. Egloffstein, F.	1	3	7	8	3						Federal.
Apr. 28	Surrender of Forts Jackson and St. Philip, La.						Brig.-Gen. Phelps, F.		11		30							Federal.
	Skirmish	MONTEREY, TENN.		5 Co's	150	2nd Iowa Cavalry			5			10						Federal.
	Skirmish	BOLIVAR, ALA.																
	Skirmish	PAINT ROCK BRIDGE, ALA.		22	250	10th Wisconsin Volunteers	Serg't. Nelson, F.; Serg't Makimson, F.		6	6								Federal.
	Brig.-Gen. Forney, C. S. A., assigned to command of the Department of Alabama and West Florida.																	
	(28th, 29th.) Expedition to	PURDY, TENN.				(Organizations not recorded.)												
Apr. 29	Skirmish	BATCHELDER'S CREEK, N. C.			70	Pickets Confederate Cavalry		1						2				Federal.
	Action	WEST BRIDGE, ALA. (Bridgeport)	2 hours	1000	600	3rd Division, Army of the Ohio	Brig.-Gen. Mitchel, F.		K & W 72			350				2		Federal.
	Skirmish	MONTEREY, TENN.				Federal Troops	Maj.-Gen. Stanley, F.; Col. Elliott, F.; Maj. Love, F.	1		4		20						Federal.
	Raid on the Mobile and Ohio Railroad near Bethel Station, Tenn.																	
	Advance upon and Siege of Corinth, and pursuit of the Confederate Forces to Guntown, Miss.					Major-Gen. Halleck's Army.												
	Reconnoissance and Skirmish	CUMBERLAND GAP, TENN.					Brig.-Gen. Carter, F.			4								Federal.
Apr. 30	Reorganization of the Armies of the Department of the Mississippi. Major-Generals Thomas, Pope and McClernand, respectively, assigned to command of the right wing, left wing and reserve; Major-General Buell retaining command of the Army of the Ohio, and Major-General Grant assigned as second in command over all.																	
May 1	Occupation of New Orleans by the Federal Forces	NEW ORLEANS, LA.				21st Ind., 30th and 31st Mass., 4th Wis., 6th Mich., 9th and 12th Conn., 5th and 6th Mass. Batteries, 2nd Vt. Cavalry	Maj.-Gen. Butler, F.											Federal.
	Skirmish	PULASKI, TENN.				Gen. Mitchel's Wagon Train	Col. Morgan, C.						270					Confd.
	(1st, 2d.) Operations in the vicinity of Athens, Mooresville, Limestone Bridge and Elk River, Ala.																	
	Skirmish	CLARK'S HOLLOW, W. VA.				Company C, 23rd Ohio Volunteers	Capt. Stiles, F.	1	16	17	67							Federal.
May 2	Skirmish	DEEP GULLY, N. C.			30	Pickets Confederate Infantry		1		1								Confd.
	(2d-6th.) Expedition from Trenton to Paris and Dresden, Tenn., and Skirmish near Lockridge's Mill			125	1280		Col. Claiburne, C.	4		6			71					Confd.
May 3	Evacuation of Yorktown by Confederates.																	
	Reconnoissance and Skirmish	FARMINGTON, MISS.			4500	10th, 16th, 22nd, 27th, 41st and 42nd Ill., 10th and 16th Mich. Vols., Yate's Ill. Sharpshooters, 2nd Mich. Cav., and Battery C, 1st Ill. Artillery	Cols. Morgan and Cumming, F.	2	40	10	100	15						Federal.
	Destruction of Bridges on Lookout Creek, Ga.																	
	Skirmish	WATKIN'S FERRY, GA.				(Organizations not recorded.)												
	Reconnoissance to the Memphis and Charleston Railroad.																	
	Martial Law proclaimed in Southwest Virginia.																	
May 4	Raid on Mobile and Ohio Railroad near Bethel, and Skirmish near Purdy, Tenn.																	
	Skirmish	PULASKI, TENN.				(Organizations not recorded).												

CHRONOLOGICAL LIST OF EVENTS (1860-1865).—Continued.

DATE.	EVENT.	LOCATION.	DURATION.	FORCE. F	FORCE. C	COMPOSITION OF FORCE.	COMMANDERS.	KILLED. F	KILLED. C	WOUNDED. F	WOUNDED. C	PRISONERS TAKEN BY F	PRISONERS TAKEN BY C	MISSING. F	MISSING. C	[illegible]	[illegible]	ADVANTAGE.
1862 May 4	Skirmish	Farmington Heights, Miss.	1 hour	3 Co's	300	3rd Mich. Cavalry	Lieut.-Col. Minty, F.			1								Federal.
	Skirmish	Lebing, Mo				5th Missouri Militia Cavalry, 24th Missouri Volunteers												
	Skirmish	Cheesecake Church, Va.				3rd Penn. and 1st and 6th U. S. Cavalry.												
May 5	Action	Williamsburg, Va.				3rd and 4th Corps, Army of the Potomac	M. Gen McClellan F; Gen. J. E. Johnston, C	456	167	1400	755			372	400			Federal
	Action	Lebanon, Tenn.	1½ hours	600	800	Detachments 7th Penn. Cav., 1st, 4th and 5th Ky. Cav.	Brig. Gen. Dumont, F; Cols. Morgan & Wood, C	6		25		150					16	Federal.
	Skirmish	Dresden, Ky.		1 Co.		5th Iowa Cavalry	Jeff Thompson, C.											Conf'd.
May 6	Reconnoissance and Skirmish from Newmarket to	Harrisonburg, Va.			200	Detachment 5th New York Cavalry		1	10			6	1					Federal
	Occupation of Williamsburg, Va., by the Federal Forces.																	
May 7	Skirmish	Purdy, Tenn.				(Organizations not recorded.)												
	Reconnoissance to Mulberry Point, James River.																	
	(7th, 8th.) Expedition from Roanoke Island towards Gatesville, N. C.					"C" Co., 9th N. Y. Volunteers, Confederate Cavalry	Capt. Parisen, F; Capt. Woodward, C. S. N.		1									
	Engagement between Franklin's Division and Army of Peninsula	West Point, Va.				16th, 31st, 32nd N. Y., 95th and 93th Penn. 5th Maine Vols., 1st Mass. and Battery D, 2nd U. S. Artillery	Gen. Franklin, F.; B. Gen. Whiting, C	47	6	18	82		46	28				Federal.
	Major-Gen. Braxton Bragg assumes command of the Confederate Army of the Mississippi.																	
	Action	Somerville Heights, Va.	1 hour			13th Indiana Volunteers	Col. Foster, F.	Cap't 29				7						Conf'd.
May 8	Skirmish	Glendale, Miss.				7th Illinois Cavalry	Lieut.-Col. Minty, F; Maj. Applington, F	1		1								Conf'd.
	Skirmish	Athens, Ala.				(Organizations not recorded).												
	Naval Demonstration upon Sewell's Point, Va.																	
	Action	McDowell, Va.	8 hours		14,000	25th, 32nd, 75th and 82nd Ohio, 5th W. Va. Vols., 1st W. Va. and 1st Conn. Cav., 1st Ind. Battery	Brig.-Gen Milroy, F; Gen. Jackson, C.											Conf'd.
	Reconnoissance towards Corinth, Miss.					2nd Brigade, 1st Division, Gen. Buell's Army		9		6								
	Major-Gen. Loring, C. S. A., assigned to command of the Army of Southwest Virginia.																	
May 9	Skirmish	Washington, N. C.			100	Company A, 24th Massachusetts	Capt. Walker, C.		6									Federal.
	(9th–12th.) Evacuation of Pensacola, Fla., by the Confederates and Occupation by Federal Forces.																	
	Skirmish	Slatersville, Va.				6th U. S. Cav., 98th Penn., 2nd R. I. Vols.		4	10	3	14	2						Federal.
	Skirmish	Elk River, Tenn.	10 minutes	350	480	1st Kentucky Cavalry and Texan Rangers (Conf'd.)	L.-Col. Woodward, C.		6		7		17					Conf'd.
	Engagement	Farmington, Miss.	3 hours		15,000	2 Brigades of the Army of the Mississippi	Cols. Morgan and Cumming, F	10		148				13				Conf'd.
	Skirmish	Elkton Station, Ala.	½ hour	49	600	Company E, 37th Indiana Regiment	Capt. Connet, F.; Col. Woodward, C	5	13	1			42					Conf'd.
	Skirmish	Corinth, Miss.				Federal Cavalry in advance of McCook's Division	Col. Innes, F.											Conf'd.
May 10	Skirmish	Lamb's Ferry, Ala.				(Organizations not recorded).												
	Reconnoissance on the Alabama Road and toward Sharp's Mill, Miss.																	
	Naval Engagement at Plum Point, near Fort Pillow, Tenn.	Plum Point, Tenn.				Federal Gunboats, *Cincinnati* and *Mound City*.	Capt. C. H. Davis, U. S. N.; Capt. Montgomery, C. S. N.		2		1							Federal.
	Occupation of	Portsmouth and Norfolk, Va.		5000		10th, 20th and 99th N. Y., 1st Del., 58th Penn., 20th Ind. and 16th Mass. Vols., Battery D, 1st U. S. Art., 1st N. Y. Mounted Rifles	Gen. Wool, F.									200		Federal.
	Skirmish	Farmington, Miss.																
May 11	Skirmish	Pulaski, Tenn.				Organizations not recorded)												
	Affair at	Cave City, Ky.				(Train captured.)	Col. Morgan, C.						8					Conf'd.
	Skirmish	Bloomfield, Mo		8 Sqd.		1st Wisconsin Cavalry	Col. Phelan, C.		1		11							Federal.
May 12	Skirmish	Farmington, Miss.		1 Co.	Plts.	2 - Mich. Regiment	Capt. Latimer, F.						1					Conf'd.
May 13	Skirmish	Baltimore Cross Roads, Va.				(Organizations not recorded).												
	Martial Law proclaimed in Charleston, S. C.																	
	Occupation of Rogersville, Ala., by Federal Forces				800	1st Wisconsin and 38th Indiana Vols. and Cavalry	Col. Starkweather, F.					4						
	(13th, 14th.) Occupation of Rogersville, Ala., and Skirmish at Lamb's Ferry, Ala.																	
	Surrender of Natchez, Miss., to Federal Fleet.																	
	Skirmish	Barry, W. Va.			Guer.	Brig.-Gen. B. F. Kelley's Command	Brig.-Gen. Kelley, F.											Federal.
	Occupation of Suffolk, Va., by Federal Forces.																	
	Skirmish	Monterey, Tenn.			Pkt-	Portion of Brig.-Gen. M. L. Smith's Brigade	Brig.-Gen. Smith, F.	2	8		3	8						Federal.
	Raid on the Memphis and Charleston Railroad near Corinth, Miss.																	
May 14	Skirmish	Fayetteville, Tenn.				Organizations not recorded).												
	Raid on the Mobile and Ohio Railroad.																	
	Skirmish on Memphis and Charleston Railroad near Corinth, Miss.																	
May 15	Skirmish	Butler, Mo				1st Iowa Cavalry.												
	Skirmishes, (15th–16th)	Trenton Bridge, N. C.; Young's Cross Roads, N. C.; Pollocksville, N. C.				17th, 25th and 27th Mass. Vols., Battery B, 3rd N. Y. Art., 2 troops N. Y. Cavalry	Col. Amory, F.		6	4	4	2		2				Federal
	Skirmish	Chalk Bluffs, Mo				1st Wisconsin Cavalry.												
	Naval Demonstration upon	Galveston, Texas																
	Engagement	Fort Darling, Va.	4 hours			Federal Steamers *Galena, Port Royal, Naugatuck, Monitor, Aroostook*	Com. W. Smith, U. S. N.	12		13								Conf'd.
	Skirmish	Linden, Va.		17	300	One Company Pennsylvania Volunteers		1					14					Conf'd.
	Engagement	Princeton, W. Va.				Kanawha Division	B.-Gen. J. D. Cox, F; —— Marshall, C.	30		20								Conf'd.
	Reconnoissance toward Memphis and Charleston Railroad and Skirmish.																	
	Skirmish	Batesville, Ark.				Detachment 3rd Ill. Cavalry	Lieut. Smith, F.					8						Federal.
May 17	Engagement	Russell's House, Miss.				Gen. M. L. Smith's Brigade of the 5th Div., Army of the Tennessee		41										Federal

CHRONOLOGICAL LIST OF EVENTS (1860-1865).—Continued.

Date	Event	Location	Duration	Force F.	Force C.	Composition of Force	Commanders	Killed F.	Killed C.	Wounded F.	Wounded C.	Prisoners Taken by F.	Prisoners Taken by C.	Missing F.	Missing C.	Guns Taken	[illegible]	Advantage
1862 May 17	Major-Gen. McDowell ordered to move upon Richmond in co-operation with Major-Gen. McClellan.																	
	Expedition up the Pamunkey River, Va.			140		Detachment 8th and 17th Inf. and Detachment Sturgis Rifles and 5th Artillery	Maj. Willard, F.; Gen. Cox, F.											
May 18	Engagement	Princeton, Va.				Federal Troops	Humphrey Marshall, C	80		70								Conf'd.
	Brig.-Gen. Fitz John Porter, U.S.A., assumes command of Fifth Army Corps (reorganized).																	
	Major-Gen. Franklin, U.S.A. assumes command of Sixth Army Corps.																	
	Reconnoissance toward Old Church, Va. (18th, 19th.)						Capt. Forsyth, F.											
May 19	Skirmish	City Point, Va.				Co. I, 24th Georgia Infantry, (Confederate)	Capt. Willis, C	6					9					Conf'd.
	(19th-23d.) Expedition down the Mississippi to Fort Pillow, Tenn.			2300		34th and 47th Ind., Detachment 54th Ill., 2nd Ill. Cavalry, 2nd Illinois Artillery	Brig.-Gen. Quinby, F.											
	Engagement	Searcy Landing, Ark.		150	600	Detachments 4th Mo. Cav., 3rd and 17th Mo. Vols., Battery B, 1st Mo. Light Artillery	Cols. Coleman and Hides, C.		150									Federal.
	Skirmish	Haines Mill, Va.				(Organizations not recorded.)												
	Skirmish	Clinton, N. C.			Pkts.	(Organizations not recorded)		5	9			9						Federal.
	Reconnoissance and Skirmish	Farmington, Miss.				2d Battalion 2d Mich. Regiment	Maj. Moyer, F.		3	2								Federal.
May 20	Occupation of Tucson, Arizona, by Federal Forces.																	
	Skirmishes	Elk River, Tenn.				(Organizations not recorded.)												
	Operations about Bottom's Bridge, Va.					Federal Troops	Brig.-Gen. Keyes, F		13	2				1				Federal.
May 21	Advance across Bottom's Bridge, Va.																	
	Skirmish	Strasburg, Va		150		5th New York Cavalry, Ashby's Cavalry (Conf'd)	Brig.-Gen. Hatch		6			8						Federal.
	Affair at	Paraje, New Mexico		43	110	3d U. S. Cavalry	Capt. Tilford											Federal
	Engagement	Phillip's Valley, Miss.				2nd Division Army of the Tennessee	Brig.-Gen. T. A. Davis, F			3								Federal.
	Reconnoissance and Skirmish	Widow Serratt's, Corinth, Miss.	2 hours			Colonel Sedgwick's Brigade and Battery of Artillery	Col. Sedgwick, F	3		23								
May 22	Skirmish	Trenton Cross Roads, N. C.				Co. I, 17th Mass.		3		8								Federal.
	Reconnoissance to New Castle and Hanovertown Ferries, Va.					6th Penn. Cavalry	Col. Rush, F.				17							
	Capture of Confederate Pickets, near Battery Island, S. C., by Federal Reconnoitering Party																	
	Skirmish	Florida, Mo.				Detachment 3rd Iowa Cavalry.												
	Attack on Federal Pickets	Farmington, Miss.		1 Co.		2d Mich. Regiment	Lieut. Caldwell, F.			1								Federal.
May 23	Affair near	Fort Craig, New Mexico	3 hours	40	200	3rd United States Cavalry	Capt. Tilford, F.			3								Conf'd.
	Engagement	Front Royal, Va.				1st Maryland Vols., Detachment 29th Penn., Captain Mapes' Pioneers and 5th N. Y. Cavalry, 1st Penn. Artillery	Col. Kenly, F.	32		122								Conf'd.
	Skirmish	Lewisburg, Va.			3000	36th and 44th Ohio Vols. and 2nd W. Va. Cavalry	Col. Crook, F; Col. Heath, C.	14	38	40	68	100	5			4		Federal.
	Skirmish	Mechanicsville, Va.				4th Michigan	Col. Woodbury, F.	10	60			30						Federal.
	Skirmish	Buckton Station, Va.				3rd Wisconsin and 27th Indiana Volunteers												
	Reconnoissance and Skirmish	Hogan's, Va.	4 hours			—— Regiment and a Squadron 2d Cavalry	Col. Woodbury, F	2		6	17	22						Conf'd.
	Reconnoissance to Burnsville and Iuka, Miss. (22d, 23d.)																	
	Reconnoissance from Bottom's Bridge towards Richmond, Va.																	
	Reconnoissance from Bottom's Bridge to the Turkey Island Creek Bridge, Va.																	
May 24	Reconnoissance toward Hanover Court House, Va.			125			Col. Rush, F.											
	McDowell's orders to move upon Richmond suspended.																	
	Engagement	Ellison's Mills, Va.				Gen. Stoneman's Brigade, Gen. Davidson's Brigade		2		1								Federal.
	Skirmish and Occupation of	Winchester, Tenn.		300	Cav.	9th Brigade, 3d Division, Army the of the Ohio	Col. Lytle, F.											Federal.
	Skirmish (see Hogan's, Va.)	New Bridge, Va.				4th Michigan Volunteers	Col. Woodbury, F.											
	Skirmish	Corinth, Miss.			Brig	4 Confederate Regiments, Reconnoitering Party		many		4		6						Federal.
	Engagement	Cold Harbor, Va.		5 Cos.		4 Michigan Regiments	—— Bowen, F.	10	60		15	37						Federal.
	Reconnoissance	Seven Pines, Va.				Part of 1st Brigade, 4th Corps	Gen. Naglee, F.	1		1								
	Skirmish	Mechanicsville, Va.			1500	Brig.-Gen. Davidson's Brigade and Batteries	Brig.-Gen. Davidson, F	2		11		3						Federal.
May 25	Engagement	Winchester, Va.	5 hours	5000	15,000	2nd Mass., 29th Penn., 27th Ind., 3rd Wis., 28th N. Y., 5th Conn., 46th Penn., Battery M, 1st N. Y. A., 1st Vt., 1st Mich. and 5th N. Y. Cavalry	Gen. Banks, F.; Gen. Jackson, C.	38		155				711				Federal.
	Expedition from Bottom's Bridge to James River, Va. (25th, 26th.)						Lieut. F. C. Davis, F.											
	Reconnoissance	Vicksburg, Miss.				Federal Gunboat *Kennebec*	Capt. Russell, U.S.N.	1		1								
May 26	Reconnoissance toward Hanover Court House, Va.					1st U. S. Cavalry and McClellan Dragoons	Lieut.-Col. Grier, F.											
	Skirmish	Big Indian Creek, Mo.				(Organizations not recorded.)												
	Skirmish	Grand Gulf, Miss				Small party Federals, Confederate Cavalry	Lieut. DeKay, F.	1										Conf'd.
	Texas enlisted in Confederate Trans-Mississippi Department.																	
May 27	Skirmish	Searcy, Ark		6	40	1st Missouri Cavalry		2	1									Federal.
	Skirmish	Slash Church, Va.				(Organizations not recorded.)												
	Skirmish	Bridge Creek, Miss.	½ hour			Part of 2nd Division, Gen. Buell's Army	Gen. Johnson, F.		2									Federal.
	Skirmish	White Oaks, Va.				(Organizations not recorded.)												
	Engagement. (27th-29th.)	Hanover Court House, Va.				Portion of Gen. Fitz John Porter's Corps	Gen. F. J. Porter, F	62	200	223		500		70				Federal.
	Skirmish	Osceola, Mo.				1st Iowa Cavalry												
	Skirmishes	In Front of Corinth, Miss.				Portions of the Army of the Ohio	Gens. Thomas, Buell and Pope, F.	K&W 25	80									Federal.
	Skirmish	Cache River Bridge, Ark.		1 Cos		9th Illinois Cavalry	Lt.-Col. Sickles, F.; Capt. Blakemore, F		1			1						Federal.
	Virginia Central Railroad Bridge destroyed by Federal Forces.																	
	Destruction of Confederate Supplies at Ashland, Va.																	
May 28	Skirmish	Seven Pines, Va.		Pkts.	200	Federal Troops	Maj. Kelly, F.	2		2								Federal.
	Skirmish	Pocotaligo, S. C.	2 hours		800	50th Penn., 79th N.Y. 8th Mich. Vols. and 1st Mass. Cav.	Col. Christ, F.											Federal.
	Skirmish	Whitesburg, Ala.				(Organizations not recorded.)												
	Occupation of Ashland, Va., by Federal Forces.																	

CHRONOLOGICAL LIST OF EVENTS (1860-1865).—Continued.

DATE	EVENT	LOCATION.	DURATION	FORCE. F.	FORCE. C.	COMPOSITION OF FORCE.	COMMANDERS.	KILLED F.	KILLED C.	WOUNDED F.	WOUNDED C.	PRISONERS TAKEN OF F.	PRISONERS TAKEN OF C.	MISSING F.	MISSING C.	GUNS TAKEN	STANDS OF COLORS TAKEN	ADVANTAGE.
1862 May 29	Skirmishes in front of	CORINTH, MISS.				Portions of the Army of the Ohio	Maj.-Gen. Buell and Pope											
	Richmond and Fredericksburg Railroad Bridge, Va., destroyed.																	
	Skirmish	BOONEVILLE, MISS.			250	2nd Iowa and 2nd Michigan	Col. Elliott, F		1				9			3		Federal
May 30	Skirmish	FAIR OAKS, VA.				100th N. Y. Regiments and Pickets	2d Lieut. Allis, F		6									Federal.
	Skirmish	TRANTER'S CREEK, N. C.		15	15	3rd New York Cavalry			3	1								Conf'd.
	Skirmish	ZUNI, VA.				(Organizations not recorded).												
	Capture of	BOONEVILLE, MISS.				2nd Iowa and 2nd Michigan Cavalry	Col. Elliott, F					700				3		Federal
	Destruction of Cypress Creek and Tuscumbia Bridges, Miss.																	
	Corinth, Miss., evacuated by Confederates, occupied by Federal Forces																	
	Martial Law proclaimed in Texas.																	
	Occupation of Front Royal, Va., by Federal Forces	FRONT ROYAL, VA.		4 Cos		1st Rhode Island Cavalry and Federal Brigade		8		5		156		1				Federal
May 31	Battle. (May 31st, June 1st)	SEVEN PINES AND FAIR OAKS, VA.	11 hours.	30000	35000	2nd, 3rd and 4th Corps Army of the Potomac, Army of Richmond, (Confederate)	Maj.-Gen. McClellan, F. Gen. J. E. Johnston, C.	790	K&W 4,230	3594				617				Federal
	Skirmish	TUSCUMBIA CREEK, MISS.				Company 7th Illinois Cavalry	Maj. Rawalt, F	1		6								Conf'd.
	Skirmish	NEOSHO, MO.		250	500	10th Ill. Cavalry and 14th Mo. Militia Cavalry	Capt. Richardson, F; Maj. Wright and Capt. Coffey, C.	2		3								Conf'd.
	Skirmish	GREENVILLE ROAD, N. C.		15		3rd New York Cavalry	Lieut. Allis, F		8	1	6	9						Federal.
June 1	General R. E. Lee, C. S. A., assumes command of the Army of Northern Virginia.																	
	The Department of Virginia included in Major-Gen. McClellan's command; Major-Gen. Wool assigned to Middle Department, and Major-General Dix to command at Fort Monroe, Va.																	
	(1st, 2d.) Reconnoissance beyond Seven Pines, Va.					2nd Michigan Infantry	Maj. Dillman, F.											
June 2	Skirmish	TRANTER'S CREEK, N. C.		7	Inf.	Mix's New York Cavalry							3					Conf'd.
	Affair near	RIENZI, MISS.		30	Inf.	42d Illinois Regiment							20					Conf'd.
	Expedition to Wormley's Ferry, Pamunkey River, Va.						Capt. Kautz, F.											
	(3d-5th.) Evacuation of Fort Pillow, Tenn., by Confederates and occupation by Federal Forces.																	
	Skirmish	LEGARE'S POINT, S. C.				28th Massachusetts and 100th Pennsylvania Volunteers												
	Skirmish	BLACKLAND, MISS.			100	1st Ohio Cavalry	Lieut. Col. Smith, F.					1						Federal.
	Reconnoissance toward Baldwyn and Carrollsville, Miss.																	
	(3d-7th.) Reconnoissance to the James River to communicate with the Federal Fleet.						Maj. Myer, F											
	North Carolina, west of the Blue Ridge, embraced in the Confederate Department of East Tennessee.																	
	Skirmishes	OSBORN'S AND WOLF'S CREEKS, MISS.				Colonel Elliott's Brig. and Detachment Powell's Battery	Col. Elliott, F	3	K&W 30	8				3				Conf'd.
June 4	Skirmish	SWEEDEN'S COVE, TENN.				5th Ky. Cav., 7th Penn. Cav. and 78th Penn. Vols., 1st Ohio Battery	Brig.-Gen. Negley, F. Gen. Adams, C.	2	20	7	20	12						Federal.
	Skirmish	WOODVILLE, ALA.				(Organizations not recorded.)												
	Skirmishes. (4th, 5th.)	HUNTSVILLE, ALA.				(Organizations not recorded.)												
June 5	Action	TRANTER'S CREEK, N. C.	45 minutes	404	520	24th Mass., Co. I, 3rd N. Y. Cav., Det. Marine Art.	Lt.-Col. Osborn, F; Col. Singeltary, C	6	5	6								Federal.
	Attack on Federal Scouts	PACTOLUS ROAD, N. C.				24th Mass. Regt., Confederate Inf. Regt.		7										Conf'd.
	Skirmish	NEW BRIDGE, VA.				1st Maryland Light Artillery	Capt. Snow, F.		3									Federal.
June 6	Naval Engagement off Memphis, Tenn., and occupation of that city by Federal Forces		1½ hours.			U. S. S. *Queen* and *Monarch*, Gunboats *Benton*, *Louisville* and *Carondelet*, *Cairo* and *St. Louis*	Brig.-Gen. Strong, F; Flag Off. Davis, F.		100			4						
	Skirmish	TOMPKINSVILLE, KY.		60	180	9th Pennsylvania Cavalry	Cpt. McCullough, F; Lieut. Longsdorf, F	1		4								Federal.
	Skirmish	HARRISONBURG, VA.				1st N. J. Cav., 1st Penn. Rifles, 60th Ohio and 8th West Virginia Volunteers	Col. Wyndham, F; Gen. Bayard, F.	K&W 90										1 Con., 2 Fed.
	Reconnoissance from Booneville toward Baldwyn, Miss., and Skirmish						Col. Sheridan, F			1								
June 7	Reconnoissance on the East bank of the Chickahominy, Va.					3 Companies 4th New Jersey Volunteers	Lt.-Col. Hatch, F.											
	Skirmish	READYVILLE, TENN.				3rd Tennessee Cavalry, (Confederate).	Col. Starnes, C.	8					68					Conf'd.
	Capture of	JACKSON, TENN.				30th Illinois and 78th Ohio Regiments	Cols. Dennis and Leggett, F.											Federal.
	(7th, 8th.) Attack on	CHATTANOOGA, TENN.	5 hours.			Portion of Gen. Negley's command	Col. Hambright, F.		K&W 100			18						Federal.
	Reconnoissance on the New Market Road, Va.					85th and 92nd N. Y. Vols. and Co. of Cavalry	Capt. Oary, F											
June 8	Engagement	CROSS KEYS, VA.	5 hours.	9000	6000	8th, 39th, 41st, 45th, 54th and 58th N. Y., 2nd, 3rd, 5th and 8th W. Va., 25th, 32nd, 55th, 60th, 73rd, 75th and 82nd Ohio, 1st and 27th Penn. Vols. and 1st Ohio Battery	Gen. Fremont, F. Gen. Jackson, C.	155		500								Federal
	Reconnoissance on	JAMES ISLAND, S. C.				3 Federal Gunboats and Federal Troops	Col. Morrow, F.	3		7								
	Department of the Mississippi extended (in Orders) to embrace all of Kentucky and Tennessee.																	
	Martial Law proclaimed in Arizona.																	
	Skirmish	FAIR OAKS, VA.				(Organizations not recorded.)												
June 9	Reconnoissance	BALDWYN, MISS.				2nd Iowa and 2nd Michigan Cavalry	Col. P. H. Sheridan, F											
	Engagement	PORT REPUBLIC, VA.				5th, 7th, 29th and 66th Ohio, 84th and 110th Penn., 7th Ind. and 1st W. Va. Vols., Battery E, 4th U. S. A. and A and L, 1st Ohio Artillery	Gen. Shields, F. Gen. Jackson, C.	67		361				574				Conf'd.
	Brig.-Gen. Berney reassumes command of his Brigade (acquitted by C. M.)																	

CHRONOLOGICAL LIST OF EVENTS (1860–1865).—Continued.

DATE.	EVENT.	LOCATION.	DURATION.	FORCE. F.	FORCE. C.	COMPOSITION OF FORCE.	COMMANDERS.	KILLED. F.	KILLED. C.	WOUNDED. F.	WOUNDED. C.	PRISONERS TAKEN BY F.	PRISONERS TAKEN BY C.	MISSING. F.	MISSING. C.	GUNS TAKEN.	STANDS OF COLORS.	ADVANTAGE.
1862																		
June 10	Skirmish	James Island, S. C.	3 hours			Federal Troops.		3	17	13	30	6						Federal.
	Skirmish	Winchester, Tenn.				(Organizations not recorded).												
	Skirmish	Wilson's Gap, Tenn.; Roger's Gap, Tenn.				42nd Ohio Volunteers.	Lieut.-Col. Pardee, F.											Federal.
June 11	Skirmishes. (11th–12th).	Big Creek Gap, Tenn.				3rd, 5th and 6th Tennessee Volunteers.	Brig.-Gen. Spears, F.		3			3						Federal.
	Re-enforcements sent from Army of Northern Virginia to the Valley District.																	
	Skirmish	Montgomery, Ky.			Guer.	Capt. Blood's Mounted Provost Guards and 13th Ind. Bat.	Capt. Nickle, F.	2				23						Federal.
June 12	Skirmish	Waddell Farm, Ark.				Detachment 9th Ill. Cav., Hooker's Co. Confederates.	Col. Brackett, F.		K&W 28	12		1						Federal.
	Occupation of Mount Jackson, Va., by Federal Forces.						Gen. Fremont, F.											
	(12th–13th.) McCall's Division re-enforces the Army of the Potomac, Va.																	
June 13	(13th–15th.) Stuart's Raid: Including Skirmishes at Hawe's Shop, Old Church and Garlick's Landing.					Confederate Cavalry.	Brig.-Gen. Stuart, C.						174					Conf'd.
	Skirmish	James Island, S. C.				(Organizations not recorded.)		3	19	19	6							Federal.
	Skirmish	Old Church, Va.				5th United States Cavalry.	Capt. Royall, F.	4		10								Conf'd.
June 14	Confederates fire into a Railroad Train.							4		8								
June 15	Action	Big Creek Gap, Tenn.				3rd, 4th and 6th Tennessee Volunteers.	Col. Houk, F.											Federal.
	Reconnoissance to vicinity of New Market, Va.																	
	Skirmish	Seven Pines, Va.				73rd N. Y. Infantry.	Maj. Moriarty, F.	1		7				1				Conf'd.
	Parley between Brig.-Gen. Howell Cobb, C.S.A., and Colonel Key, U.S.A.																	
June 16	Action	Secessionville, S. C.		3337		46th, 47th and 79th N. Y., 3rd R. I., 3rd N. H., 45th, 97th and 100th Penn., 6th and 7th Conn., 8th Mich., 28th Mass. Vols., 1st N. Y. Engineers, 1st Conn., Batteries E, 3rd U. S. A., and I, 3rd R. I. Art. and Co. H, 1st Mass. Cavalry.	B.-Gen. Wright, F.; Col. Lamar, C.	85	48	472	106			128				Conf'd.
June 17	Skirmish	Warrensburg, Mo.				7th Missouri Militia Cavalry.												
	General Jackson's command moves from vicinity of Staunton and Weyer's Cave, Va., for the Peninsula.																	
	Engagement and Occupation of Fort.	St. Charles, Ark.				U. S. Gunboats *Lexington*, *Mound City*, *Conestoga* and *St. Louis*, 43rd and 46th Indiana Vols.	Flag Off. Davis, F.; Col. Fitch, F.	Acdt 125		Acdt 25								Federal.
June 18	Skirmish	Nine Mile Road, Va.				2nd and 3rd South Carolina (Confederates)	Cols. Kennedy and Nance, C.				10				1			Federal.
	Skirmish	Smithville, Ark.				(Organizations not stated).	Maj. Zeley, F.	2		4	4	10						Federal.
	Skirmish	Wilson's Gap, Tenn.				(Organizations not recorded.)												
	Cumberland Gap, Tenn., occupied by Federal Forces.					3rd, 5th and 6th Tenn. Vols. and Gen. Carter's Brigade.	Gen. DeCourcy, F.											
	Skirmish	Fair Oaks, Va.				16th Mass. Vols. and Capt. Bramhall's Battery.	Col. Wyman, F.	16	20	24				16				Federal.
	Brig.-Gen. Hébert, C.S.A., assumes command of the District of Texas.																	
	Skirmish	Tallahatchie, Fla.				(Organizations not recorded.)												
June 19	Skirmish	Charles City Road, Va.	1 hour		800	20th Indiana Infantry.	Capts. Bell and Dick, F.			8								Federal.
June 20	Artillery Affair near	New Bridge, Va.				Battery B, 1st N. Y. Light Artillery, and Battery I, 5th U. S. Artillery.	Capt. Voegelee, F.; Capt. S. Weed, F.		2	1	4							Conf'd.
	Affair at	Gill's Bluff, Va.				(Organizations not recorded.)												
June 21	Engagement	Battle Creek, Tenn.				42nd and 33rd Ohio, 10th Wis., 24th Ill. Vols., 4th Ohio and 4th Ky. Cav. and Edgarton's Battery.	Col. Sill, F.			4				3				Federal.
	Skirmish	Fair Oaks Station, Va.		Pkts.		(Organizations not recorded)		2		7								Federal.
	Engagement	Simon's Bluff, S. C.				U. S. Gunboats *Crusader* and *Planter*, and Co. 51st Pennsylvania Volunteers.	Lieut. Rhind, U.S.A.											Federal.
	Confederate Department of North Carolina extended to the South bank of the James River.																	
June 22	(22d, 23d.) Reconnoissance to the left of White Oak Swamp, Va.					Federal Troops.	Col. Gregg, F.						1					
	Reconnoissance and Skirmish	Raceland, La. (Algiers).			Guer.	8th Vermont Volunteers.		3		8								Conf'd.
	Reconnoissance into Gloucester and Mathews Counties, Va.					3rd Battalion 5th Pennsylvania Cavalry.	Colonel Campbell, F.											
June 23	Operations about the New Kent Court House, Va.					11th Pennsylvania Cavalry.	Capt. Ward, F.											
	Skirmish	Raytown, Mo.				7th Missouri Cavalry.												
	Martial Law proclaimed in the Cities of Norfolk and Portsmouth, Va.																	
June 24	Reconnoissance from Washington to Tranter's Creek, N. C.			Pkts.		3rd New York Cavalry.	Capt. Jocknick, F.											
	Skirmish	Mechanicsville, Va.				Portion of the Army of the Potomac.												
June 25	Battle	Oak Grove, Va.	7 hours		5000	3rd and 4th Maine, 2nd N. H., 1st, 7th, 10th, 11th, 16th and 19th Mass., 2nd R. I., 1st, 2nd, 20th, 37th, 40th, 70th, 71st, 72nd, 73rd, 74th, 87th, 101st N. Y., 2nd Battery, N. J. Art., 5th and 7th N. J., 26th, 63rd, 105th Penn., 2nd, 3rd and 5th Mich., 20th Indiana and 4th U. S. Artillery.	M.-Gen. Hooker, F.; Brig.-Gen. Wright, C.	59	69	362	222			19	11			Federal.
										1								
	(June 25th–July 1st.) "The Seven Days' Battles."			[illegible]	[illegible]	Army of the Potomac; Army of Northern Virginia (Confederate).	Maj.-Gen. McClellan, F.; Gen. R. E. Lee, C.	1734	3286	8062	15,909			6053	946			
	Skirmish	Ashland, Va.				(Organizations not recorded).												
	Skirmish	Germantown, Tenn.				56th Ohio Volunteers.												
	Skirmish	Little Red River, Ark.				4th Iowa Cavalry.												
	Formation of the Army of Virginia from Forces under Major-Generals Fremont, Banks, and McDowell, and command assigned to Major-Gen. Pope, U. S. A.																	

CHRONOLOGICAL LIST OF EVENTS (1860-1865).—Continued.

DATE.	EVENT.	LOCATION.	DURATION.	FORCE. F.	FORCE. C.	COMPOSITION OF FORCE.	COMMANDERS.	KILLED. F.	KILLED. C.	WOUNDED. F.	WOUNDED. C.	PRISONERS TAKEN BY F.	PRISONERS TAKEN BY C.	MISSING. F.	MISSING. C.	[illegible]	[illegible]	ADVANTAGE.
1862 June 26	Engagement	Vicksburg, Miss.	8 hours			Federal Mortar Fleet	Com. Porter											Conf'd.
	Gen. Stoneman's Operations, including Destruction of Stores at White House Landing, Va. (26th–July 2d.)																	
	Skirmish	Atlee's Station, Va.																
	Skirmish	Hanover Court House, Va.			Cav. & Art.	8th Illinois Cavalry	Col. Farnsworth, F.											Conf'd.
	Skirmish	Meadow Bridge, Va.																
	Battle	Mechanicsville, Va.	8 hours	5000	12000	Mass. Light Art., 3rd Battery, 9th and 22nd Mass., 13th, 14th and 25th N. Y., 4th Penn. Cav., Penn. Light Art., Penn. Reserves, 62nd Penn., Brady's Sharpshooters, 1st and 4th Mich., 8th Ill. Cav., 1st U. S. Sharpshooters, 3rd and 5th U. S. Art. (C, K, L and M)	Maj.-Gen. McClellan, F.; M.-Gen. R. E. Lee, C.; M.-Gen. Jackson, C.	49		207				105				Federal.
	Expedition to Appomattox River, Va.					9 Federal Gunboats	Capt. Rogers, U. S. A.											
	Engagement	Point of Rocks, Va.				(Organizations not recorded.)												
	Skirmishes. (26th–27th.)	Hundley's Corner, Va.				(Organizations not recorded.)												
June 27	General Jackson re-enforces the Army of Northern Virginia.																	
	Major-Gen. Fremont, U. S. A., relieved from command by Brig.-Gen Rufus King.																	
	Skirmish	Williamsbridge, La.				21st Indiana Volunteers	Lieut.-Col. Keith, F.	2	4	4		11						Federal.
	Battle. (27th, 28th.)	Gaines's Mill, Va.	4 hours	33000	36000	5th Corps, Army of the Potomac, re-enforced by Meagher's and French's Brig., 1st Div., 2nd Corps	Maj.-Gen. McClellan, F.; Maj.-Gens. Jackson and Lee, C.	894	589	3107	2671			2836	24			Conf'd.
	Skirmish	Waddell's Farm, Ark.				Detachment 3rd Iowa Cavalry.												
	Action	Garnett's Farm, Va.			Art.	Artillery of Brig. Gen. Smith's Division	Brig. Gen. Smith, F.; Gen. Hancock, F.											Federal.
	Skirmish	Fair Oaks, Va.				(Organizations not recorded.)												
June 28	Skirmish	Village Creek, Ark.				9th Illinois Cavalry	Col. Brackett	2		31								Conf'd.
	(28th–July 4th.) Expeditions from Fort Monroe, Va., to open communication with Army of the Potomac						Capt. J. C. Lee, F.						8					
	Action	Garnett's and Golding's Mills, Va.				33rd and 49th N.Y. Vols. and 3rd N. Y. Battery	Brig.-Gen. Smith and Capt. Mott, F.		K & W 150			20						Federal.
	Battle	Chickahominy, Va.				Federal Troops	Gen. Toombs, C.											
	Skirmish	Dispatch Station, Va.				Companies I and K 8th Ill. Cav.; Cav. and Art. (Conf'd.)	Capt. Farnsworth, F.											Conf'd.
June 29	Engagement	Allen's Farm, Va.	3 hours			Richardson's and Sedgwick's Div. of the 2nd Corps, Army of the Potomac	Brig.-Gen. Sumner, F.											Federal.
	Skirmish	James River Road, Va.			Cav.	Federal Cavalry	Brig.-Gen. Couch, F.		K. W. & P. 80									Federal
	Skirmish	Williamsburg Road, Va.				(Organizations not recorded.)	Gens. Sumner and Franklin, F.											Conf'd.
	Battle	Savage's Station, Va.			2250	2nd and 6th Corps, Army of the Potomac.												
	Reconnoissance and Skirmish	Jordan's Ford, Va.		Pkts.		Brig.-Gen. Kearny's Brigade.												
June 30	Engagement	Glendale, or White Oak Swamp Bridge, Va.	6 hours			2nd, 3rd, 4th, 5th, 6th and McCall's Div. of the 1st Corps, Army of the Potomac	Maj. Gen. Sumner, F.; Maj.-Gen. Hooker, F.; Gens. Longstreet and Hill, C.											Federal.
	Skirmish	New Market Road, Va.			Cav.	Troops of Gen. Couch's Division	Col. Tompkins, F.	1	K. W. & P. 80	8		4						Federal.
	Action	Brackett's, Va.				Battery K, 4th U. S. Artillery	Lieut. Seeley, F.											Federal.
	Engagement	Turkey Bridge, Va.				Portion of Gen. Fitz-John Porter's Brigade	Col. Warren, F.											Federal.
	Skirmish	New Kent Court House, Va.				(Organizations not recorded.)												
	Skirmish	Jones's Bridge, Va.																
July 1	Battle	Malvern Hill, Va.	12 hours		28000	2nd, 3rd, 4th, 5th and 6th Corps, Army of the Potomac	Maj.-Gen. McClellan, F.; M.-Gen. Jackson, C.		377		1745				89			Federal.
	Skirmish	Morning Sun, Tenn		G'ard	Cav.	37th Ohio Volunteers												Federal.
	Action	Booneville, Miss.	7 hours		4700	2nd Iowa and 2nd Michigan Cavalry.	Col. Sheridan, F.	K & W 41	65									Federal.
	Skirmish	Russellville, Tenn.				1st Ohio Cavalry.												
July 2	Skirmish	New Kent Court House, Va.				(Organizations not recorded.)												
	Skirmishes	Malvern Hill, Va.				Federal Cavalry	Lieut. Col. Martin, C.											Conf'd.
July 3	Affair near	Haxall's Landing, Va.				14th Ind., 7th W. Va., 4th and 8th Ohio Volunteers.												
	Reconnoissance from Harrison's Landing, on Charles City Road, Va.						Capt. Reno, F.											
	(3d–4th.) Skirmishes	Herring Creek, Va.				4th and 8th Ohio, 14th Ind., 7th Va., Tibball's Battery	Brig.-Gen. Kimball, F.	2		17								Federal.
	Skirmish	Grand Haze, Ark.			6000	13th Illinois Cavalry.												
July 4	Attack on United States vessels near Velasco, Texas.																	
	Reconnoissance from Harrison's Landing, Va.					8th Illinois Cavalry	Lt.-Col. Gamble, F.											
	Skirmish	Westover, Va.				Skirmishers of Gen. Ewell's Division (Confederate)	Maj.-Gen. Ewell, C.											Conf'd.
July 5	(5th–6th.) Operations against Federal Shipping, James River, Va.						Col. S. D. Lee, C.											
	Skirmish	Sperryville, Va.				1st Maine Cavalry.												
July 6	Maj.-Gen. Burnside sails with re-enforcements for Army of the Potomac, leaving Brig.-Gen. Foster in command of the Dep't. of N. Carolina.																	
	Skirmish	Grand Prairie, Ark.			Cav.	24th Indiana Volunteers	Col. Spicely, F.											Federal.
July 7	(7th–9th.) Reconnoissance from Yorktown, Va.			200		5th Pennsylvania Cavalry	Maj. Wilson, F.						10					
	(7th–17th.) Operations in	Aransas Bay, Texas																
	Action	Bayou Cache, Ark.		600	2000	11th Wis., 33rd Ill., 8th Ind. Vols., 1st Mo. Light Art., 1st Ind., 5th and 13th Ill. Cav.	Col. Hovey, F.; Gen. Albert Rust, C.	7	110	57								Federal.
July 8	Reconnoissance to Waterloo, Va.					1st Maine Cavalry.												
	Skirmish	Black River, Mo.				5th Kansas Cavalry.												
	Skirmish	Lotspeach Farm, Mo.		1 Co.		1st Iowa Cavalry.												
	President Lincoln reviews the Army of the Potomac.																	
July 9	Skirmish	Clinton, Mo.				(Organizations not recorded.)												
	Engagement	Aberdeen, Ark.				24th, 34th, 43rd and 46th Indiana Volunteers.												

CHRONOLOGICAL LIST OF EVENTS (1860-1865).—Continued.

DATE	EVENT	LOCATION	DURATION	FORCE F	FORCE C	COMPOSITION OF FORCE.	COMMANDERS.	KILLED F.	KILLED C.	WOUNDED F.	WOUNDED C.	PRISONERS TAKEN BY F.	PRISONERS TAKEN BY C.	MISSING F.	MISSING C.	GUNS TAKEN	STANDS OF ARMS TAKEN	ADVANTAGE
1862 July 9	Skirmish	TOMPKINSVILLE, KY.		250	1500	3rd Pennsylvania Cavalry	Maj. Jordan, F.; —— Morgan, C.	4		6			19					Conf'd.
	Reconnoissance on the Long Bridge Road, Va.					Federal Troops	Gen. Davidson, F.											
	Capture of	HAMILTON, N. C.				Federal Gunboats *Perry*, *Ceres* and *Shawsheen*, and 9th New York Volunteers	Capt. Hammell, F.	2		10								Federal.
July 10	Reconnoissance from Harrison's Landing toward White Oak Swamp, Va., and Skirmish.																	
	Skirmish	SCATTERVILLE, ARK.			80	Detachment 1st Wisconsin Cavalry	Capt. Allen, C.											——
July 11	Reconnoissance from Harrison's Landing beyond Charles City Court House, Va.					Federal Troops	Col. Childs, F.		1			8						
	Skirmish	WILLIAMSBURG, VA.		Phia.	Phia.	(Organizations not recorded.)			2			7						Federal.
	Skirmish	PLEASANT HILL, MO.		1 Co.	Guer.	1st Iowa Cavalry and Missouri Militia			11									Federal.
	Skirmish	NEW HOPE, KY.			Cav	33rd Ohio Volunteers	Lieut. Col. Moore, F.											Federal.
July 12	Skirmish and Capture of Lebanon, Ky., by Confederate Forces	LEBANON, KY.				Lebanon Home Guards and 28th Ky. Vols.	Col. Johnson, F.; —— Morgan, C.											Conf'd.
	Engagement	CULPEPER, VA.			Cav.	1st Md., 1st Vt., 1st W. Va. and 5th N. Y. Cav.	Gen. Hatch, F.		1		5	11						Federal.
July 13	Engagement, and Capture of Murfreesboro', Tenn., by Conf'd. Forces	MURFREESBORO', TENN.				9th Mich. and 3rd Penn. Vols., 4th Ky. and 7th Penn. Cav. and 1st Ky. Battery	B.-Gen. Forrest, C.	38		63				800				Conf'd.
	Skirmish	FAIRFAX, VA.				1st Maryland Cavalry	Maj. Deems, F.											Federal.
July 14	Skirmish	BATESVILLE, ARK.				4th Iowa Cavalry.												
July 15	Skirmish	APACHE PASS, ARIZ.				2nd California Cavalry.												
	Attempt to destroy the Confederate ram *Arkansas*	VICKSBURG, MISS.	2½ hours			Federal Steamers *Carondelet*, *Queen of the West*, *Tyler* and *Essex*, and 4th Wisconsin Volunteers	Flag Officers Farragut and Davis and Commander Porter, F.	9		19								Conf'd.
	Skirmish	FAYETTEVILLE, ARK.		600	1600	Federal Troops	Maj. Miller, F.											Federal.
	Skirmish	DECATUR, TENN.				Detachment 1st Iowa Cavalry.												
July 16	Reconnoissance from Westover on the Richmond Road, Va.			2 Sqd.		5th United States Cavalry	Capt. Harrison, F.											
July 17	"Morgan's Raid"—Capture of	CYNTHIANA, KY.	2½ hours	340	2200	18th Ky. Vols., Cynthiana, Newport, Cincinnati, and Bracken Co. Home Guards and 7th Ky. Cav.	Lt.-Col. Landram, F.; —— Morgan, C.	17	24	34	78							Conf'd.
	Major-Gen. D. H. Hill, C. S. A., assigned to command of the Department of North Carolina.																	
July 18	Skirmish	MEMPHIS, MO.		400	800	2nd Mo. Cav. and 9th and 11th Mo. State Militia	Maj. Clopper, F.; —— Porter and Dunn, C.	k. w. & m. 83	23									Federal
July 20	Skirmish	ORANGE COURT HOUSE, VA.				Federal Troops	Col. Brodhead, F.											Federal.
	Skirmish	PITTMAN'S FERRY, ARK.				13th Illinois Cavalry.												
	Cavalry Raid upon Virginia Central Railroad at Beaver Dam Creek.																	
	Skirmish	TURKEY ISLAND BRIDGE, VA.		Squ.	Phia.	8th Pennsylvania Cavalry	Capt. P. Keenan, F.											
July 21	Skirmish and capture of Picket at	NASHVILLE, TENN.		Phia.	Guer.	2nd Kentucky Volunteers												Conf'd.
July 22	Major-Gen. Sherman, U. S. A., assumed command at Memphis, Tenn.																	
	Major-Gen. Dix, U. S. A., assumes command of the Seventh Army Corps, Department of Virginia																	
	Major-Gen. Burnside assumes command of the Ninth Army Corps, Va.																	
	Affair near	WESTOVER, VA.			5	Federal Cavalry	Capt. Taylor, F.			1								Federal.
	(22d–30th). Scout in King William, King and Queen, and Gloucester Counties, Va.				90	3rd, 4th, 5th and 9th Virginia Cavalry (Confederate)	Lieut. Robins, C.											
July 23	Maj. Gen. Halleck assumes command of the Armies of the United States																	
	Skirmish	FLORIDA, MO.		2 Co's.	300	3rd Iowa Cavalry	Maj. Caldwell, F.; —— Porter, C.	k. & w. 26										Conf'd.
	Skirmish	NORTH ANNA RIVER, VA.				2nd New York and 3rd Indiana Cavalry	Col. Kilpatrick, F.											Federal.
	Skirmish	COLUMBUS, MO.				7th Missouri Cavalry.												
July 24	Skirmish	COLDWATER, MISS.				(Organizations not stated.)												
	Skirmish	BOTT'S FARM, MO.				3rd Iowa Cavalry.												
	(24th–28th), Expeditions from New Berne, N. C., to Trenton and Pollocksville, etc., N. C.					17th, 25th and 27th Mass., 5 companies of Cav. and Battery of Artillery	Brig.-Gen. Foster, F.											
	Skirmish	TRINITY, ALA.				Company E, 31st Ohio Volunteers	Capt. Harman, F.		10		30							Federal.
	Skirmish, (24th–25th)	SANTA FE, MO.				3rd Iowa Cavalry.												
July 25	Engagement and Skirmishes	BIG PINEY, MO.		100	60	3 Companies 3rd Mo. Cav. and Battery L, 2nd Mo. Artillery	Capt. Bradway, F.; Col. Coleman, C.		8		13	17						Federal.
	Skirmish	ORANGE COURT HOUSE, VA.				Reconnoitering Party of Federal Troops	Gen. Gibbon, F.		5									Federal.
	Skirmish	BROWNSVILLE, TENN.				Federal Cavalry	Maj. Wallace, F.; Capt. Faulkner, C.											——
	Reconnoitering Expeditions from General Gibbon's Division.																	
	Skirmish and capture of Federal Troops	COURTLAND BRIDGE, ALA.				2 Companies Ky. Vols. and 2 Companies 1st Iowa Cav.	Capt. Davidson, F.					2 Cos.						Conf'd.
July 26	Skirmish	MILL CREEK, N. C.				(Organizations not recorded.)												
	(26th–29th) Reconnoissance from Newport, N. C., to Young's Cross Roads, N. C., and Skirmish on 27th.				300	9th N. J. Vols., 3rd N. Y. Cav. and Section of Rocket Battery	Col. Heckman, F.		6			3						Federal.
	Skirmish	PATTEN, MO.		1 Co.	200	Missouri Militia			k. & w. 25	8								Federal.
	Skirmish	GREENVILLE, MO.				3rd and 12th Missouri Militia Cavalry	Capt. Bradway, F.; Col. Coleman, C.		5		12							Federal.
	Skirmish	BUCKHANNON, W. VA.				(Organizations not recorded).												
July 27	Skirmish	BROWN SPRINGS, MO.				2nd Iowa Cavalry.												
	Naval Expedition up the Ogeechee River, Ga.					Federal Gunboats *Paul Jones*, *Unadilla*, *Huron* and *Madgie*												
July 28	Engagement	BAYOU BERNARD, I. T.				1st, 2nd and 3rd Kansas Indian Home Guards and 1st Kansas Battery	Col. Phillips, F.; Col. Taylor, C.		125									Federal
	Expedition from Batchelder's Creek, N. C., on Neuse River Road			105		Companies D, G and H 27th Mass., Co. C, N. Y. Art. and Co. G, N. Y. Cav.	Capt. Sanford, F.		2			10						

CHRONOLOGICAL LIST OF EVENTS (1860-1865).—Continued.

Date	Event	Location	Duration	Force F.	Force C.	Composition of Force	Commanders	Killed F.	Killed C.	Wounded F.	Wounded C.	Prisoners taken by F.	Prisoners taken by C.	Missing F.	Missing C.	Guns taken	Stands of arms taken	Advantage
1862 July 26	Engagement	Moore's Mills, Mo.	2 hours	650	900	3rd Iowa Cav., 2nd Mo. Cav., 9th Mo. Vols. and 3rd Ind. Battery	Col. Guitar, F.; Porter and Cobb, C.		K&W 75			1						Federal
	Reconnoissance from Harrison's Landing to St. Mary's Church, Va.						Capt. Duncan, F.											
July 29	Skirmish	Arrow Rock, Mo.		120	180	2 Companies 13th Missouri Volunteers	Capt. Whybark, F.; Maj. Tenley, C.		10									Federal.
	Skirmish	Mount Sterling, Ky.			240	18th Kentucky and Home Guards	Capt. J. J. Evans and Maj. Bracht, F.		K&W 75									Federal.
	Skirmish and capture of	Russellville, Ky.			Guer.	Russellville Home Guards and 70th Indiana Volunteers	Col. Gano, C.			2								Conf'd.
	Skirmish	Brownsville, Tenn.		1 Co.	80	13th Illinois Cavalry	Capt. Dollins, F.	4	4	6	6	11						Federal.
July 30	Reconnoissance from Harrison's Landing to Jones Ford, Chickahominy River					Federal Gunboat Fleet.												
	Skirmish	Paris, Ky.				9th Pennsylvania Cavalry	Lieut.-Col. James, F.; —— Thompson, C.		27			29						Federal.
July 31	(31st–Aug. 1st). Attack on Federal Camps and Shipping, between Shirley and Harrison's Landing, Va.	Harrison's Landing, Va.				Forces under Maj.-Gen. McClellan		10	1	12	9							Conf'd.
Aug. 1	Skirmish	Newark, Mo.	9 hours	1 Co.	Guer.	73 Men 11th Missouri State Militia	Capt. Lair, F.; Capt. Porter, C.										100	Conf'd.
	Skirmishes	Orange Court House, Va.				Reconnoitering Party of Federal Troops	Gen. Bayard, F.											Federal.
Aug. 2	Skirmish	Ozark, Mo.		75	125	14th Missouri Militia	Capt. Birch, F.											Federal.
	Skirmish	Austin, Miss.				8th Indiana Volunteers.												
	(2d–8th). Reconnoissance from Harrison's Landing and re-occupation of Malvern Hill, Va., by Federal Forces.																	
	Skirmish	Orange Court House, Va.				5th New York Cavalry and 1st Vermont Cavalry	Gen. Crawford, F.	4		12								Federal.
	Skirmish	Clear Creek, Mo.		4 Co's		1st Iowa Cavalry.												
	Skirmish	Coahoma Co., Miss.				11th Wisconsin Volunteers.												
Aug. 3	Reconnoissance on South Side of James River, Va., and Skirmish at Sycamore Church, Va.	Sycamore Church, Va.				Federal Troops	Col. Averell, F.				6	2						Conf'd.
	Skirmish	Chariton Bridge, Mo.				6th Missouri Cavalry.												
	General McClellan ordered to withdraw his forces to Aquia Creek, Va.																	
	Skirmish	Jonesboro, Ark.				1st Wisconsin Cavalry.												
	Skirmish	L'Anguille Ferry, Ark.				1st Wisconsin Cavalry.												
Aug. 4	(4th–5th). Reconnoissance from Coggin's Point beyond Sycamore Church, Va.					5th U. S. and 3rd Penn. Cavalry	Capt. Wilkins, F.											
	Skirmish	Sparta, Tenn.	1 hour	170	700	Detachments 4th Kentucky and 7th Indiana Cavalry	Col. Wynkoop, F.		30	1	10	1		1				Conf'd.
	Skirmish	White River, Mo.			Guer.	Party Federal Troops	Capt. Birch, F.; Col. Lawther, C.		8		7							Federal.
	Order issued for draft of 300,000 Federal Militia.																	
Aug. 5	Engagement	Baton Rouge, La.	4 hours	2500	5000	14th Maine, 6th Mich., 7th Vt., 21st Ind., 30th Mass., 9th Conn., 4th Wis., 2nd, 4th and 6th Mass. Batt., U. S. Gunboats	Com. Porter, U.S.N., B.-Gen. Williams, F.; Gen. Breckinridge, C.											Federal.
	Skirmish	White Oak Swamp Bridge, Va.			30	3rd Pennsylvania Cav. and 5th U. S. Cav.	Lieut. Byrnes, F.		3			22						Federal.
	Engagement	Malvern Hill, Va.				Portion of Hooker's Div., 3rd Corps and Richardson's Div., 2nd Corps and Cav. Army of the Potomac	Gen. Hooker, F.; Brig.-Gen. Hampton, C.	3		11		100						Federal.
Aug. 6	Skirmish	Montevallo, Mo.			Guer.	3rd Wisconsin Cavalry	Maj. Montgomery, F.											Federal.
	Skirmish	Beech Creek, W. Va.				4th West Virginia Volunteers.												
	Engagement	Kirksville, Mo.		1000	Guer.	Missouri Militia	Col. McNeill, F.; —— Porter, C.											Federal.
	Skirmish	Malvern Hill, Va.			Pkts.	Portion of Gen. Hooker's Division	Brig.-Gen. Evans, C.						4					Conf'd.
	Skirmish	Mataponi, Va.				Portion of King's Division	Col. Cutler, F.											Federal.
	Engagement	Tazewell, Tenn.	4 hours			16th and 42nd Ohio, 14th and 22nd Ky. Vols. and 4th Wis. Battery	Col. DeCourcey, F.; —— Stephenson, C.	3	100	15			50					Federal.
Aug. 7	Engagement	Fort Fillmore, New Mexico				California Troops	Gen. Canby, F.; Col. Sibley, C.		1									Federal.
	Skirmish	Trenton, Tenn.			Cav.	2nd Illinois Cavalry	Capt. Faulkner, C.		30		20							Federal.
	Skirmish	Dodd County, Mo.			Guer.	Federal Troops	Maj. Montgomery, F.; —— Coffin, C.		11		4	17						Federal.
Aug. 8	Skirmish	Panther Creek, Mo.				1st Missouri Militia Cavalry.												
Aug. 9	Engagement	Cedar Mountain, Va.	3 hours			2nd and 3rd Corps, Army of Virginia	Maj.-Gens. Banks and McDowell, F.; Gen. Jackson, C.	450	K W & M 1307	660			29	290				Federal.
	Skirmish	Stockton, Mo.				Missouri State Militia	Col. McNeill, F.; —— Porter, C.											Federal.
Aug. 10	Occupation of Bayou Sara, La., by Federal Forces																	
	Affair on the Nueces River, near Fort Clark, Texas					Texas Loyalists.												
	Skirmish	Bensville, Mo.			Guer.	Missouri State Cavalry	Col. Sweet, F.; Capt. Cobb, C.											Federal.
Aug. 11	Skirmish	Grand River, Mo.				9th Missouri Militia and Detachments	Col. Guitar, F.; Col. Poindexter, C.		K&W 100			200					150	Federal.
	Skirmish	Kinderhook, Tenn.		108	176	Detachments of 3rd Ky. and 1st Tenn. Cavalry	Col. McGowan, F.; Maj. Anderson, C.		7			27						Federal.
	Skirmish	Helena, Ark.			Cav.	3rd Wisconsin Cavalry												Federal.
	Affair at	Velasco, Texas.																
	Skirmishes	Williamsport, Tenn.			Guer.	Troops of Brig.-Gen. Negley's Command	Maj. Kennedy, F.											Federal.
	Skirmish	Tabbsville, Ark.				1st Missouri and 3rd Wisconsin Cavalry												
	Skirmish	Independence, Mo.			3500	7th Missouri Militia Cavalry	Col. Buell, F.; Col. Hughes, C.	26		30								Conf'd.

CHRONOLOGICAL LIST OF EVENTS (1860-1865).—Continued.

DATE.	EVENT	LOCATION.	DURATION.	FORCE		COMPOSITION OF FORCE.	COMMANDERS.	KILLED.		WOUNDED.		PRISONERS TAKEN BY		MISSING.		GUNS TAKEN.	STAND OF ARMS TAKEN.	ADVANTAGE.
				F	C			F	C	F	C	F.	C	F	C			
1862																		
Aug. 11	Capture of	SALISBURY, TENN.			Guer	11th Illinois Cavalry						1						Federal.
Aug. 12	Capture of the *Breaker* and destruction of the *Hannah* in Corpus Christi Bay, Texas																	
	Capture of Post at Gallatin, Tenn., by Confederates	GALLATIN, TENN.			Guer	2nd Ind., 4th and 5th Ky. and 6th Penn. Cav.	Col. Morgan, C		6									Conf'd.
Aug. 13	Skirmish	YELLOW CREEK, MO.				Federal Troops, Poindexter's Guerrillas, (Confederates)	Col. Guitar, F.					60						Federal
	Occupation of Gallatin, Tenn., by Federal Forces	GALLATIN, TENN.				69th Ohio and 11th Michigan Volunteers	Col. Miller, F.											
	Battle	CLARENDON, ARK.				Brig.-Gen. Hovey's Division, 13th Corps	Brig.-Gen. Hovey, F.; —— Hindman, C.	7				200						Federal.
Aug. 14	Skirmish	HELENA, ARK.		Scts	Guer	Federal Troops												Federal.
	(14th-15th). Reconnoissance from Newport, N. C., to Swansborough.					24th Mass. Marine Battery and U. S. Gunboats, Wilson and *Ellis*, Squadron of Cavalry and 100 Inf.	Gen. Stevenson, F.; Col. Heckman, F.											
	(14th-16th). Third and Fifth Army Corps move from Harrison's Landing for Aquia Creek, Va.																	
	(14th-18th). Operations of the Cavalry, covering the rear of the Army of the Potomac, from Harrison's Landing to Williamsburg, Va.																	
Aug. 15		MERRIWEATHER'S FERRY, TENN.		1 Co.	Guer	2nd Illinois Cavalry	Col. Harris, F.; Capt. Bluffield, C.		20			9						Federal.
Aug. 16	Capture of	HOPKINSVILLE, KY.			Guer		Col. Johnson, C.											Conf'd.
	(16th-18th). Bombardment of	CORPUS CHRISTI, TEXAS.				4 Federal Gunboats and Marines	Capt. Kittredge, F.; Major Hobby, C.		1									Conf'd.
	Engagement	LONE JACK, MO.	4 hours	900	3000	Missouri Militia Cavalry	Maj. Foster, F.; Col. Coffee, C.	60	k&w 110	100								Conf'd.
Aug. 17	Reconnoissance, toward Forge Bridge, Va.	FORGE BRIDGE, VA.			12	Jeff Davis Legion (Confederate)	Lieut. Waring, C.											
Aug. 18	Capture of Confederate Steamer *Fair Play*, near Millikens Bend, La.					58th and 70th Ohio Volunteers.												
	Massacre by Indians	HEBWOOD, MINN.		1 Co		5th Minnesota Volunteers		100										
	U. S. Steamers *Skylark and Sallie* burned by Guerillas at Duck Creek, Tenn.																	
Aug. 19	Skirmish	RIENZI, MISS				(Organizations not recorded.)												
	Surrender of Post at Clarksville, Tenn., to Confederates			183	800	71st Ohio Volunteers.	Col. Mason, F.; Col. Woodward, C.											Conf'd.
	Attack on Confederate Camp	WHITE OAK RIDGE, KY.				2nd Illinois Cavalry	Capt. Moore, F.		1	2		19					100	Federal.
	Major-Gen. H. G. Wright, U. S. A., assigned to command of Department of the Ohio.																	
Aug. 20	Engagement	BRANDY STATION, VA		R Gd		Cavalry of the Army of Virginia												Federal
	Skirmish	EDGEFIELD JUNCTION, TENN.			Guer	Detachments 50th Indiana Volunteers	Col. Morgan, C.		7		20							Federal.
	The Fifth Army Corps embarked at Newport News, Va.																	
	Skirmish	UNION MILLS, MO.			Guer	1st Missouri and 13th Illinois Cavalry	Maj. Price, F	4	1	3		4						Federal.
	(20th-22d). Fight with Indians at	FORT RIDGELY, MINN				Companies B and C, 5th Minn. Vols. and Renville Rangers.	Lieut. Sheehan, F.	3		10								Federal
	Texas and Arizona embraced in Trans Mississippi Department.																	
Aug. 21	The Third Army Corps sail from Yorktown, Va.																	
	Engagement	GALLATIN, TENN.			800	3 Regiments and Detachments 2nd Ind., 4th and 5th Ky. and 7th Penn. Cavalry.	B. Gen Johnson, F.; Col. Morgan, C.	30		30			75					Conf'd.
	Skirmish	KELLEY'S FORD, VA.				Cavalry of the Army of Virginia, and Artillery.	Gen. Reno, F.											Federal.
	Skirmish	PINCKNEY ISLAND, S. C.		Pkts		(Organizations not recorded)		3		3			82					Conf'd.
	Gens. Hunter and Phelps, U. S. A., "outlawed" by Jefferson Davis.																	
Aug. 22	Skirmish. (Attack on Federal Train)	COURTLAND, TENN			Guer	Detachment 42nd Illinois Volunteers			8	2				2				Conf'd.
	Skirmishes	CRAB ORCHARD, KY.			Cav.	9th Pennsylvania Cavalry	Gen. G. C. Smith, F.; Col Scott, C.											Federal.
	Raid on	CATLETT'S STATION, VA.			Cav.	Purnell Legion Maryland and 1st Pennsylvania Rifles.												Conf'd.
Aug. 23	Engagement	BIG HILL, KY.				7th Kentucky Cavalry and 3rd Tennessee Volunteers	Col. Metcalf, F.	10	25	40								Conf'd.
	The Sixth Army Corps embarked at Fort Monroe, Va.																	
	Skirmishes, (23d-25th), at	WATERLOO BRIDGE, LEE SPRINGS, FREEMAN'S FORD, AND SULPHUR SPRINGS, VA.				Army of Virginia	Maj.-Gen Pope, F.											
Aug. 24	Skirmish	DALLAS, MO		4 Co's	Guer	12th Missouri State Militia Cavalry	Maj. Lazear, F.; Col. Jeffries, C.											Federal.
	Engagement	CANE CREEK ON LAMAR, KANSAS	2 hours		Guer	Detachments 2nd and 6th Kansas	Maj. Campbell, F.; —— Quantrell, C.	3		21								——
Aug. 25	Attack on	FORT DONELSON, TENN.	1 hour	155	785	71st Ohio Volunteers and 5th Iowa Cavalry	Maj. Hart, F.; Col. Lowe, F.; Col. Woodward, C.		k&w 30									Federal.
	Skirmish	BLOOMFIELD, MO.		180	250	13th Illinois Cavalry	Maj. Lippert, F.; Col. Hicks, C.		20									Federal.
	Indian Fight. (25th-26th)	NEW ULM, MINN				(Organizations not recorded).	Capt. Flandrau, F.	10		80								Federal.
Aug. 26	The Second Army Corps left Fort Monroe.																	
	Engagement	CUMBERLAND IRON WORKS, TENN.		130	500	71st Ohio Volunteers and 5th Iowa Cavalry	Col. Lowe, F	2		10								Federal.
	Skirmish	MADISONVILLE, KY.			Guer	Cavalry	Lieut.-Col. Porter, F											Federal.
	Skirmish	RIENZI AND KOSSUTH, MISS.				2nd Iowa and 7th Kansas Cavalry.												
	Skirmish	HARRODSBURG, AND DANVILLE, KY.				Home Guards		1	8	2	12	30						Federal.
Aug. 27	Engagement	BULL RUN BRIDGE, VA. (Manassas)			Cav. 2000	11th and 12th Ohio and 1st, 2nd, 3rd and 4th New Jersey Volunteers	—— Fitz Hugh Lee, C											Conf'd.
	Battle	KETTLE RUN, VA.				Major-Gen. Hooker's Division, 3rd Corps, Army of the Potomac.	Gen. Hooker, F.; Gen. Ewell, C.		k&w 300									Federal

CHRONOLOGICAL LIST OF EVENTS (1860–1865).—Continued.

Date	Event	Location	Duration	Force F.	Force C.	Composition of Force	Commanders	Killed F.	Killed C.	Wounded F.	Wounded C.	Prisoners Taken F.	Prisoners Taken C.	Missing F.	Missing C.	[illegible]	[illegible]	Advantage
1862 Aug. 27	Evacuation of Battle Creek, Ala., by Federal Forces.																	
	Skirmish	Fort McCook, Ala.				33rd Ohio Volunteers and Detachment of Cavalry.	Col. Mundy, F. / Gen. Forrest, C.											
Aug. 28	Engagement	Readyville, Tenn.			Cav.	23rd Kentucky Infantry												Federal.
	Occupation of Hernando, Mo., by Federal Forces.																	
	Skirmish	Howard Co., Mo.				4th Missouri Militia Cavalry												
	Destruction of City Point, James River, Va., by Federal Gunboats under Commodore Wilkes.																	
	Skirmish	Shady Springs, Va.		20	75	2nd West Virginia Cavalry	Lieut. Montgomery, F.					5						Federal.
Aug. 29	(28th–29th.) Engagements	Groveton and Gainesville, Va.	11½ hours			1st and 3rd Corps, Army of Va., Hooker's and Kearney's Div. of 3rd Corps and Reynolds Div. of 1st Corps and 9th Corps, Army of the Potomac	Maj. Gens. Pope, Sigel, McDowell, Hooker, Kearney, Reno and King, F. / Gens. Jackson and Longstreet, C.	K&W 7000	K. W & M. 7000									Federal.
	Reconnoissance from St. Charles Court House, La., to Bonnet Carre.																	
	Skirmish	Manchester, Tenn.			Ca	2 Cos. of 18th Ohio and one Company 9th Mich. Vols.												Federal.
Aug. 30	Battle	Bull Run, Va. (2nd.)	6 hours			1st and 3rd Corps, Army of Va., Hooker's and Kearney's Div., 3rd Corps, Porter's 5th Corps and Reynolds Div., 1st Corps and 9th Corps, Army of Pot.	Maj.-Gens. Pope, Sigel, McDowell and Reno, F. / Gens. Lee, Jackson and Longstreet, C.	800	K, W & M. 3700	4000				3000				Conf'd.
	Engagement	Bolivar, Tenn.	7 hours		6000	2nd and 11th Ill. Cav., 9th Ind. Art. and 20th and 78th Ohio Vols.	Col. Leggett, F. / Gen. Armstrong, C.	6	..	15				64				Federal.
	Engagement	McMinnville (or Little Pond), Tenn.	10 minutes		1300	20th Ohio, 17th and 38th Ind. Vols. and 8th Ind. Battery	Col. Fyffe, F. / Gen. Forrest, C.		1		20			1500				Federal.
	Engagements	Richmond, Ky.		-	16,000	6th and 7th Ky. Cav., 95th Ohio, 18th Ky., 12th, 16th, 55th, 66th, 69th and 71st Ind. Vols. and Batteries D and G, Mich. Art.	Gen. Manson, F. / Gen. Kirby Smith, C.	200	250	700	500			4000				Conf'd.
Aug. 31	Evacuation of Huntsville, Ala., by Federal Forces under General Buell.																	
	Evacuation of Fredericksburgh, Va., by the Federal Army under General Burnside.																	
	Skirmish	Weston, W. Va.		3 Cos.		9th West Virginia Volunteers.												
	Skirmish	Medon, Tenn.			1500	45th Illinois and 7th Missouri Volunteers	Maj. Oliver, F.											Federal.
	Engagement	Stevenson, Ala.	4 hours	1200	900	(Federal organizations not recorded)	Col. McKinstry, C.				2							Conf'd.
	Skirmish	Yate's Ford, Ky.				94th Ohio Volunteers.												
Sept. 1	Engagement	Chantilly, Va.	1 hour			McDowell's Corps Army of Va., Hooker's and Kearney's Divisions, 3rd Corps Army of the Potomac and Reno's Corps.	Gen. Pope, F. / Gen. Jackson, C.	K&W 1800	K&W 800									Federal.
	Engagement	Britton's Lane, Tenn.	4 hours	800	5000	20th and 30th Ill. Vols., Battery A, 2nd Ill. Art., 4th Ill. Cav. and Foster's Co. of Ohio Cav.	Col. Dennis, F. / Gen. Armstrong, C.	5	179	53	231							Federal.
	Occupation of Lexington, Ky., by Confederate Forces.																	
Sept. 2	Reconnoissance to	Vienna, Va.				1st Minnesota Volunteers.												
	Skirmish	Morgansville, Ky.			Guer	Federal Troops	Col. Shackleford, F. / Col. Johnson, C.											Federal.
	Occupation of Versailles, Ky., by Confederate Cavalry.																	
	Indian Fight. (2d–3d)	Birch Coolie, Minn. (Action.)																
	Skirmish	Plymouth, N. C.	1 hour	800	1400	Co. F, 9th N. Y. and 1st N. C. Volunteers	Or.-Ser. Green, F. / Col. Garrett, C.		30			40						Federal.
Sept. 3	Fight with Indians. (3d–4th)	Hutchinson, Minn.	3 hours															Federal.
	Fight with Indians. (3d–6th)	Fort Abercrombie, Dakota				Federal Troops.												
	Evacuation of Winchester, Va., by Federal Forces.																	
	Skirmish	Slaughtersville, Ky.			Guer	Cavalry	Lieut.-Col. Foster, F.		3		2	25						Federal.
	Engagement	Geiger's Lake, Ky.	3 hours		600	8th Kentucky Cavalry	Col. Shackelford, F. / Col. Johnson, C.											Federal.
Sept. 4	Skirmish	Big Creek Gap, Tenn.				Detachment 6th Tennessee Volunteers												Federal.
	Occupation of Ravenswood, Va., by Confederate Troops.																	
	Skirmish	South Mills, Va.			113	Detachment New York Mounted Rifles	Maj. Wheeler, F.					118						Federal
	Major Gen. McClellan, U. S. A., assumes command at Washington.																	
	Evacuation of Frederick City, Md., by Federal Forces.																	
Sept. 5	Capture of Poolesville, Md., by Confederate Forces.																	
	Capture of Pikeville, Va., by Confederate Cavalry.																	
Sept. 6	Attack on Fort Abercrombie by Indians	Fort Abercrombie, Dakota			300	Federal Troops		1		3								Federal.
	Attack on Washington, N. C., by Confederates	Washington, N. C.	3 hours			1st N. C. and 24th Mass. Vols. and 3rd N. Y. Cav., and Gunboat *Picket*		K&W 8	33	36	100	50						Federal.
	Engagement	Cacapon Bridge, Va.				1st New York Cavalry	Col. McReynolds, F. / Col. Imboden, C.											Federal.
	Engagement	Martinsburg, Va.		Outp	400	Federal Troops	Gen. White, F.	2		10		50						Federal.
	Occupation of Frederick, Md., by Confederate Army under General Lee.																	
	Skirmish	La Grange, Ark.				1st Missouri Cavalry.												
	Engagement	Chapmansville, Va.		40	800	4th Virginia Regiment	Maj. Hall, F. / Col. Stratton, C.	1		1								Federal.
Sept. 7	Capture of Shepherdsville, Ky., by Federal Troops.																	
	Re capture of	Clarksville, Tenn.				11th Ill., 13th Wis. and 71st Ohio Vols., 5th Iowa Cav. and 2 Batteries	Col. Lowe, F.											
Sept. 8	Occupation of Poolesville, Md., by Federal Troops.				Cavl.	3rd Indiana and 8th Illinois Cavalry	Maj. Chapman, F.	1	8	7								Federal.
	Occupation of Boyd's Station, Ky., by Confederate Troops.				Cavl.													
	Engagement	Des Allemands, La.			500	31st Indiana and 4th Wisconsin Volunteers			5			25						Federal.
Sept. 9	Skirmish	Columbia, Tenn.				42nd Illinois Volunteers	Col. Farnsworth, F.		5	1		15						Federal
	Skirmish	Nolansville, Md.				3rd Indiana and 8th Illinois Cavalry.												
	Skirmish	Big Creek, Mo.			Guer	Federal Cavalry	Col. Burris, F. / —— Quantrell, C.											Federal.

CHRONOLOGICAL LIST OF EVENTS (1860-1865).—Continued.

DATE	EVENT	LOCATION	DURATION	FORCE F.	FORCE C.	COMPOSITION OF FORCE	COMMANDERS	KILLED F.	KILLED C.	WOUNDED F.	WOUNDED C.	PRISONERS TAKEN BY F.	PRISONERS TAKEN BY C.	MISSING F.	MISSING C.	[illegible]	[illegible]	ADVANTAGE
1862																		
Sept. 9	Occupation of Middletown, Md., by Confederate Troops.																	
	Engagement	Williamsburg, Va.	½ hour		Cav. & Art.	8th Pennsylvania Cavalry	Col. Campbell, F.; Col. Shingler, C.		9				50					Conf'd.
Sept. 10	Engagement	Cold Water, Miss.		370	1000	Federal Cavalry	Col. Grierson, F.		4		70							Federal.
	Skirmish	Sugar Loaf Mountain, Md.			C & A	6th United States Cavalry	Capt. Saunders, F.											Conf'd.
	Engagement	Fayetteville, W. Va.		1200	5000	34th and 37th Ohio and 4th West Virginia Volunteers	Col. Siber, F.; Gen. Loring, C.	18		90				86				Conf'd.
Sept. 11	Evacuation of Frederick, Md., by Confederate Army under General Lee.																	
	Occupation of Newmarket, Md., by Federal Forces.																	
	Evacuation of Gauley, Va., by Federal Forces.																	
	Occupation of Westminster, Md., by Confederate Forces under Colonel Rosser.																	
	Occupation of Maysville, Ky., by Confederate Forces under Brig.-Gen. Gano.																	
	Engagement	Cotton Hill, W. Va.				34th and 37th Ohio and 4th West Virginia Volunteers.												
	(11th–13th) Capture of Bloomfield, Mo., by Confederates		2 hours	1300	Guer.	Battery E, 2nd Mo. Art., 13th Ill. Vols., 1st Wis. Cav. and Mo. Militia												Conf'd.
Sept. 12	(12th–15th). Engagement	Harper's Ferry, Va.				12th N. Y. State Militia, 39th, 111th, 115th, 125th and 126th N. Y., 32nd, 60th and 87th Ohio, 9th Vt., 65th Ill., 1st and 3rd Md., 15th Ind. Vols., Battery 5th N. Y. A., 3 Batteries, 9th N. Y. A., 12th Ill. and 1st Md. Cav.	Brig.-Gen. White, F.; Col. Miles, F.; Gen. A. P. Hill, C.	80	K & W 1500	120				[illegible]		47	[illegible]	Conf'd.
	Occupation of Frankfort, Ky., by Confederate Forces.																	
	Engagement and Destruction of	Charlestown, W. Va.				34th Ohio and 4th West Virginia Volunteers	Col. Lightbourn, F.											Federal
	Skirmish	Frederick, Md.		Ad. G.	R. Gd.	Advance of the Army of the Potomac	Gen. Burnside, F.											
	Re-capture of Bloomfield, Mo., by Federal Troops under Colonel Boyd.																	
Sept. 13	(13th–14th). Operations at	Flour Bluffs, Texas.																
	Skirmish	Newtonia, Mo.				3rd and 6th Missouri Militia Cavalry.												
Sept. 14	Evacuation of Maysville, Ky., by Confederates, and occupation by Federal Forces						Col. Norton, F.											
	Surrender of Fort at Bacon Creek, Ky., by Federal Troops						Col. Morrison, C.						20			50		Conf'd.
	Battle	Turner's and Crampton's Gaps, South Mountain, Md.				1st, 6th and 9th Corps, Army of the Potomac	Maj.-Gens. Hooker, Franklin and Reno, F.; Gen. R. E. Lee, C.	443	500	1806	2343	1500		76				Federal.
	Occupation of Ponchatoula, La., by Federal Forces					12th Maine, 26th Mass. and 13th Conn. Vols.	Maj. Strong, F.											
	(14th–16th). Engagement	Munfordsville, Ky.	7 hours	2122		18th U. S. Inf., 28th and 33d Ky., 17th, 50th, 60th, 67th, 68th, 74th, 78th and 89th Ind. Vols. and Battery 13th Ind. Art. and Louisville Guards	Col. Wilder, F.; Gen. Duncan, C.	K & W 50	K & W 714					3566				Federal.
Sept. 15	Engagement	Shelburne, Mo.	2 hours		Guer.	Missouri Militia	Col. McNeill, F.; —— Porter, C.		9									Federal.
	Skirmish	Boonsboro, Md.				Cavalry, Army of the Potomac.												
	Surrender of Harper's Ferry, Va., to Confederate Forces under General Jackson.																	
Sept. 16	Battle	Antietam, Md. (Sharpsburg)				1st, 2nd, 5th, 6th, 9th and 12th Corps, Couch's Div., 4th Corps and Pleasonton's Cavalry Division, Army of the Potomac	M.-Gen. McClellan, F.; Gen. Lee, C.	2010	3000	9416		[illegible]		1043			[illegible]	Federal.
Sept. 17	Skirmish	Durhamville, Tenn.		150		Detachment 52nd Indiana Volunteers	Lieut. Griffin, F.; L.-Col. Faulkner, C.	2	8	10	20			1				Federal.
	Engagement	Florence, Ky.		53	101	Detachment 10th Kentucky Cavalry	Maj. Foley, F.	1	5	1	7							Federal.
	Reconnoissance and Engagement	Goose Creek, Va. and Leesburg Road, Va.			Inf.	Kilpatrick's Cavalry Brigade	Col. Kilpatrick, F.											Federal.
	Surrender of Munfordsville, Ky., by Federal Forces under Colonel Dunham.																	
	Engagement	Falmouth, Ky.		10	24	Kentucky Home Guards	Col. Berry, F.		2	1	4	1						Federal
	Evacuation of Cumberland Gap by Federal Forces under General Morgan.																	
Sept. 18	Brig.-Gen. Carleton, U. S. A., supersedes Brig.-Gen. Canby in command of the Department of New Mexico.																	
Sept. 19	Skirmish	Hickory Grove, Mo.				4th Kansas Cavalry.												
	Battle	Iuka, Miss.	2 hours			Stanley and Hamilton's Divisions, Missouri Cavalry	Gen. Rosecrans, F.; Gen. Price, C.	144	K & W 1200	598		1000		40				Federal
	(19th–20th). Skirmish	Owensboro, Ky.			Guer.	14th Ky. Cav. and Spencer's (Ind.) Co. Home Guards	Col. Netter, F.; L.-Col. Wood, F.	3		18								1 Con. 3 Fed.
Sept. 20	Skirmish	Blackford's Ford, Va.		1711		Griffin's and Barnes' Brigades, 5th Corps	Col. Barnes, F.	92		131				103				Conf'd.
	Engagement	Shirley's Ford, Mo.			600	2nd Kansas and 3rd Indiana Home Guards	Col. Ritchie, F.		K & W 60									Federal.
	Skirmish	Helena, Ark.				4th Iowa Cavalry.												
	Occupation and Evacuation of Williamsport, Md., by Confederate Forces.					Couch's Division, Army of the Potomac.												
	Engagement	Prentis and Bolivar, Miss.	½ hour		Guer.	Federal Ram *Queen of the West*, with Transports, and 33rd Illinois Regiment	L.-Col. Lippincott, F.	8		[illegible]								
Sept. 21	Capture of Cassville, Mo., by Federal Troops					1st Arkansas Cavalry	Capt. Gilstrap, F.					10						Federal

CHRONOLOGICAL LIST OF EVENTS (1860-1865).—Continued.

DATE	EVENT	LOCATION	DURATION	FORCE F.	FORCE C.	COMPOSITION OF FORCE	COMMANDERS	Killed F	Killed C.	Wounded F	Wounded C	Prisoners Taken by F	Prisoners Taken by C	Missing F.	Missing C.	[illegible]	[illegible]	ADVANTAGE
1862																		
Sept. 21	Occupation of Munfordsville, Ky., by Federal Forces	Munfordsville, Ky.				Federal Cavalry	Col. McCook, F.; Maj. Foster, F.	2										Federal.
	Attack on Shepherdsville, Ky., by Confederate Troops	Shepherdsville, Ky.			Cav.	Colonel Granger's Command	Col. Granger, F.		6			29						Federal.
Sept. 22	Skirmish	Ashby's Gap, Va.				2nd Pennsylvania and 1st West Virginia Cavalry	Col. Price, F.; Lt.-Col. Green, C.											Federal.
	Skirmish	Sturgeon, Mo.			Guer.	Major Hunt's Command	Maj. Hunt, F.; Cpt. Cunningham, C.											Federal
	Emancipation Proclamation issued by President Lincoln.																	
Sept. 23	Engagement	Wood Lake, Minn.	2 hours		Sx. In. 300	3rd, 5th and 7th Minn. Vols. and Renville Guards	Col. Sibley, F	4	30	30								Federal.
	Skirmish	Wolf Creek Bridge, Miss.				77th Ohio Volunteers												
	Attack on	Sutton, Va.			100	10th West Virginia Regiment	Maj. Withers, F.											1 Fed. 2 Con.
Sept. 24	General Beauregard, C. S. A., assumes command of the Department of South Carolina and Georgia.																	
Sept. 25	Capture of Sabine Pass, Texas, by Federal Steamer *Kensington*.						Act. Mas. Crocker.											
Sept. 26	Skirmish	Warrenton Junction, Va.		125	400	Cavalry	Col. McLean, F.											Federal.
	Skirmish	Cambridge, Mo.				9th Missouri Militia Cavalry.												
Sept. 27	Capture of	Augusta, Ky.			Guer.	Gunboat *Belfast*, Kentucky Home Guards	Col. Bradford, F.; Capt. Duke, C.	K&W 12	K&W 75									Conf'd.
	Attack on Confederate Camp at	Buffalo, W. Va.			Cav.	34th Ohio Regiment	Col. Toland, F.; —— Jenkins, C.		7			9						Federal.
Sept. 28	Engagement	Blackwater, Va.		8 Cos.	Inf.	1st New York Mounted Rifles	Col. Dodge, F.											Federal.
	Reconnoissance from Centreville to	Warrenton, Va.				Brigade of Cavalry	Lieut.-Col. Karge					1620						
Sept. 29	Brig.-Gen. Gillmore, U. S. A., assigned to command of the District of Western Virginia.																	
	Skirmish	Sharpsburg, Mo.				(Organizations not recorded).												Federal.
Sept. 30	Battle	Newtonia, Mo.		4000	...	1st Brig. Army of Kan. and 4th Brig. Mo. State Militia	B.-Gen. Salomon; Cols. Cooper and Shelby, C.	K&W 50					115					Conf'd
	Engagement	Russellville, Ky.			850	Federal Troops	Col. Harrison, F.		35			10						Federal.
	Occupation of Greyson, Ky., by Confederate Troops.																	
Oct. 1	Engagement	Floyd's Fork, Ky.			Cav.	4th Ind. Cavalry, 34th Ill. 77th Penn. Volunteers	Col. Kirk, F.											Federal.
	Engagement	Gallatin, Tenn.			Guer.	1st Tennessee Cavalry	Col. Stokes, F.; Col. Bennett, C.		40			30						Federal.
	Skirmish	Shepherdstown and Martinsburg, Va.				8th Ill., 8th Penn. and 3rd Ind. Cav. and Pennington's Battery	Gen. Pleasanton, F.; Gen. Hampton, C.		60	12		10	8					Federal.
	Evacuation of Shelbyville, Ky., by Confederate Troops.																	
Oct. 2	Skirmishes	Baldwin, Miss.				Cavalry of the Army of the Mississippi.												
	Skirmish	Olive Hill, Ky.			1,000	Carter Co. Home Guards	—— Morgan, C.											Federal.
	Skirmishes	Mount Washington, Ky.				Advance of the Army of the Ohio	Gen. Buell, F.; Gen. Kirby Smith, C.											—
Oct. 3	(3d–4th). Battle	Corinth, Miss.	(Actual.) 18 hours	20,000	38,000	McKean's, Davies', Hamilton's and Stanley's Div., Army of the Mississippi	M.-Gen. Rosecrans, F.; Gen. Van Dorn, C.	315	1423	1812	5692	2248			232	2	3300	Federal.
	Reconnoissance to	Franklin, Va.	6 hours		9000	Federal Gunboats *Commodore Perry*, *Hunchback* and *Whitehead*	Gen. Spear, F.; Cpt. Flusser, U.S.N.	K&W 10										—
	Occupation of Fortifications on	St. John's Bluff, Fla.		1500		Nine Gunboats	Gen. Brannan, F.									9		Federal.
Oct. 4	Engagement	Bardstown, Ky.		Adv. G.	R'gd	Advance of the Army of the Ohio	Maj. Foster, F.; Gen. Polk, C.											Conf'd.
	Engagement	Paw Paw, Va.		1 Co.		54th Pennsylvania Regiment												Conf'd.
	Capture of Confederate Camp at	Paw Paw, Va.				Cavalry	Col. McReynolds, F.											Federal.
Oct. 5	Engagement	Big Hatchie River, Miss. (Metamora)	7 hours			Hurlbut's and Ord's Divisions, Army of the Mississippi. (Confederate Forces in retreat)	Maj.-Gen. Ord, F.; Gen. Price, C.	K&W 500				400				8		Federal.
	Engagement	Glasgow, Ky.				20th Kentucky Volunteers	Col. Bruce, F.											Federal.
	Occupation of Jacksonville, Fla., by Federal Forces.																	
	Skirmish	Madisonville, Ky.				4th Indiana Cavalry.												
Oct. 6	Skirmish	Charleston, Va.				6th United States Cavalry	Col. Robertson, F.											Federal.
	Skirmish	Liberty and Sibley's Landing, Mo.			Cav.	5th Missouri Militia Cavalry	Col. Quantrel, C.											Federal.
		Springfield to near Texas, Ky.				Advance of 3rd Corps, Army of the Ohio												
Oct. 7	Battle	La Vergne, Tenn.	½ hour	2500		Palmer's Brigade	Gen. Palmer, F.; Gen. Anderson, C.	5	K&W 80	9		175			4	8		Federal.
	Evacuation of Lexington, Ky., by Confederate Forces.																	
Oct. 8	Battle	Perryville, Ky.	4½ hours	14,000	...	1st and 3rd Corps, Army of the Ohio	Maj.-Gen. Buell, McCook and Gilbert, F.; Gen. Bragg, C.	916	K&W 2500	2943	W&M 4500				489			Federal.
Oct. 9	Skirmish	Aldie, Va.				Detachment of Cavalry						40						Federal.
	Engagement	Lawrenceburg, Ky.	5 hours	3000	3000	15th and 19th U. S. Inf., 1st and 49th Ohio Vols., Battery H, 5th U. S. A. and 9th Ky. Cavalry	Col. Parrott, F.; Gen. Kirby Smith, C.	6	13	18								Federal.
Oct. 10	Capture of	Harrodsburg, Ky.			1600	Federal Troops	Lieut.-Col. Boyle, F.					1600						Federal.
	Fight on Upper Missouri River between a party of Sioux and a party of Miners																	
Oct. 11	Engagement	La Grange, Ark.				Detachment 4th Iowa Cavalry. (Texan Rangers)	Maj. Rector, F.; Lt.-Col. Giddings, C.	8		9		0						Federal.
	Attack on Federal Gunboat	Cape Fear River, N. C.			Bat'y	Federal Gunboat, *Maratanza*		2		5								Conf'd.
	Skirmish	Mouth of Monocacy, Md.				3rd and 4th Maine Volunteers.												
	Engagement	Cacapon Bridge, Va.		300		Federal Cavalry	Col. McReynolds, F.; Col. Imboden, C.											Federal.
	Reconnoissance in vicinity of	Paris, Va.					Gen. Stahel, F.					150						

CHRONOLOGICAL LIST OF EVENTS (1860-1865).—Continued.

Date	Event	Location	Duration	Force F	Force C	Composition of Force	Commanders	Killed F	Killed C	Wounded F	Wounded C	Prisoners Taken by F	Prisoners Taken by C	Missing F	Missing C	Guns Lost	Stands of Arms	Advantage
1862																		
Oct. 14	Skirmish	Stanford, Ky.			8 Gs	Advance of the Army of the Ohio	Gen. Buell, F.; Gen. Bragg, C.					14						Federal.
	Skirmish	Hazel Bottom, Mo.				(Organizations not recorded.)												
Oct. 15	Naval Expedition and Destruction of Apalachicola	Apalachicola River, Fla.				Armed Boats of Blockading Fleet												Federal.
	Skirmish	Carsville, Va.		1 Co.	Guer	7th Pennsylvania Cavalry	Lieut. Williams, F.											Conf'd.
Oct. 16	Reconnoissance and Occupation of Charleston, Va., by Federal Troops				Batt	Army of the Potomac	Gen. Hancock, F.	1		8		9						
Oct. 17	Engagement	Lexington, Ky.		350	Cav 3000	Detachments, 3rd and 4th Ohio Cavalry	Maj. Seidel, F.; Gen. Morgan, C.	4		24								Conf'd.
	Engagement	Thoroughfare Gap, Va.			200	Detachment Cavalry	Gen. Stahel, F.	3				100	23				27	1 Con. 2 Fed.
Oct. 18	Attack on Pickets	Helena, Ark.		Pkts.	Guer	Detachment 43rd Indiana Volunteers		1										Conf'd.
	Skirmish	Haymarket, Va.		22	700	Detachment 6th Ohio Cavalry							23					Conf'd.
	Skirmish	Lexington, Ky.			Cav.	4th Ohio Cavalry	Capt. Bobey, F.; Gen. Morgan, C.											Conf'd.
Oct. 19	Reconnoissance between Centreville and Leesburgh, Va.																	
	Occupation of Commerce, Tenn., by Confederate Cavalry under Colonel Jeffries.											60						
Oct. 20	Skirmish	Auxvois River, Tenn.			Guer	10th Missouri Militia Cavalry	Maj. Woodson, F.											Federal.
	Skirmish	Nashville, Tenn.			Cav.	Federal Troops	Col. Miller, F.; Gen. Forrest, C.											Federal
	Skirmish	Marshfield, Mo.			200	10th Illinois Cavalry	Lieut. Col. Stuart, F.					27						Federal
Oct. 21	Reconnoissance near	Lovettsville, Va.				Detachment of General Geary's Brigade	Gen. Geary, F.					75						
	Skirmish	Woodville, Tenn.			Guer	2nd Illinois Cavalry	Maj. Mudd, F.; —— Haywood, C.					40						Federal.
	Fight	Fort Cobb, Indian Territory			Ind's	Loyal Indians	Col. Leeper, C.		1									Federal.
Oct. 22	Engagement	Old Fort Wayne, Ark.	1 hour		5000	1st Division, Army of the Frontier	Brig.-Gen. Blunt, F.	5	50	8						4		Federal
	Skirmish	Van Buren, Ark.			450	Federal Cavalry	Maj. Lazear, F.; Col. Boone, C.											Federal.
	Reconnoissance near	Hedgesville, Va.		2 Sq.		4th Pennsylvania Cavalry	Capt. Duncan, F.					19						
	Battle	Pocotaligo, S. C.	6 hours	3200		47th, 55th and 76th Penn., 46th N. Y., 6th and 7th Conn., 3rd and 4th N. H., 3rd R. I. Vols., 1st N. Y. Engineers, 1st Mass. Cavalry, Batteries D and M, 1st, and E, 3rd U. S. Artillery	Gen. Brannan, F.; Gen. Beauregard, C.	30	20	180	60							Conf'd.
Oct. 23	Skirmish	Big Hill Road, Ky.		500	Cav.	Cavalry	Col. McCook, F.		4									Federal.
	Skirmish	Waverly, Tenn.	1 hour	200	Guer	83rd Illinois Volunteers	Maj. Blott, F.	1	K&W 40	5		30						Federal
	Skirmish	Bullet Depot, Tenn.			Guer	Reconnoitring Party	Col. D. Stuart, F.		8									Federal.
Oct. 24	Engagement	Manassas Junction, Va.		90	150	(Organizations not recorded)							17					Conf'd
	Scout near	Catlett's Station, Va.			Guer	Detachment 3rd West Virginia Cavalry	Capt. Conger, F.					2						Federal.
	Skirmish	Grand Prairie, Mo.			Guer	2 Battalions, Missouri Militia Cavalry	Maj. White, F.		8	3	20							Federal.
	Skirmish	Blackwater, Va.				1st N. Y. Mounted Rifles, 39th Ill., 62nd Ohio Vols.	Brig.-Gen. Ferry, F.	1	6									Federal.
	Skirmish	Morgantown, Ky.			Guer	(Organizations not recorded)	Col. Morgan, C.					16						Federal.
Oct. 25	Major-Gen. Rosecrans, U. S. A., assigned to command of Department of Kentucky, vice Buell, relieved.																	
	General C. S. Hamilton, U. S. A., assigned to command at Corinth, Miss., vice Rosecrans.																	
	Attack on Foraging Party at	Helena, Ark.			Guer	Detachment 43rd Indiana Regiment		3		2								Conf'd.
Oct. 26	Surrender of Indianola, Texas, to Federal Gunboats *Clifton* and *Westfield*.																	
	Destruction of St. Mary's, Ga., by Federal Forces.																	
Oct. 27	Engagement	Putnam's Ferry, Mo.			1300	23rd Iowa and 24th and 25th Mo. Vols., 1st Mo. Militia and 12th Missouri Cavalry	Col. Lewis, F.					40						Federal.
	Skirmish	Labadieville, La.				8th N. H., 12th and 13th Conn. and 75th N. Y. Vols., 1st La. Cavalry and 1st Maine Battery	Brig.-Gen. Weitzel, F.; Col. McPheeters, C.	18	6	74	15	268				1		Federal.
Oct. 28	Engagement	Cross Hollows, Ark.	1 hour	Cav. 1000	Guer	One Division of the Army of the Frontier	Brig.-Gen. Herron, F.; Col. Craven, C.		8									Federal
	Expedition to	Clarkson, Mo.			Guer	Detachment, Federal Troops	Capt. Rodgers, F.; Col. Clark, C.		12			45					70	Federal
	Skirmish	Williamsburg, Ky.				7th Kentucky Volunteers												
Oct. 29	Skirmish	Butler and Osage, Mo.			Guer	1st Kan. Colored Troops (79th U. S. C. Troops)	Col. Seaman, F.; —— Cockrell, C.	8	K&W 30	10								Federal.
	Skirmish	Petersburg, Va.			Cav.	Reconnoitring Force	Lieut. Col. Lewick, F.					16						Federal
	Reconnoissance from Purcellville to Aldie, Va., under Major Keenan, U. S. A.																	
Oct. 30	Skirmish	Thoroughfare Gap, Va.				Cavalry	Col. Wyndam, F.											Federal.
	Major-Gen. Rosecrans, U. S. A., assumes command of Department of the Ohio.																	
Oct. 31	Skirmish	Aldie, Va.			Cav.	1st N. J. and 2nd N. Y. Cav. of Gen. Bayard's Brig., Army of the Potomac	Gen. Stuart, C.											Federal
	Bombardment of	Franklin, Va.		3 Bat		(Organizations not given)												Federal.
Nov. 1	(1st-2d). Skirmishes	Philomont, Va.				Cavalry of the Army of the Potomac	Gen. Pleasonton, F.; Gen. Stuart, C.											Federal.
	Expedition up the Pungo Creek, N. C.					Federal Steamer *Northerner*, Gunboat *States of the North*, Detachment 3rd N. Y. Cavalry	Maj. Garrard, F.					25						
	Bombardment of	Lavacca, Texas				Federal Gunboats *Clifton* and *Westfield*.												
Nov. 2	Occupation by Federal Forces	Snicker's Gap, Va.				Batteries of the Second Corps, Army of the Potomac	Gen. McClellan, F.					10						Federal.
	(2d-3d). Skirmishes	Bloomfield and Union, Va.				Cavalry advance of the Army of the Potomac.												
	Expedition to	Pittman's Ferry, Mo.					Col. Dewey, F.					13						
	Skirmish	Upperville, Va.				Cavalry advance of the Army of the Potomac.												

CHRONOLOGICAL LIST OF EVENTS (1860-1865).—Continued.

Date	Event	Location	Duration	Force F.	Force C.	Composition of Force	Commanders	Killed F.	Killed C.	Wounded F.	Wounded C.	Prisoners taken by F.	Prisoners taken by C.	Missing F.	Missing C.	Guns [illegible]	Stands of Arms [illegible]	Advantage
1862																		
Nov. 3	Engagement	Bayou Teche, La.	3 hours		3500	Federal Gunboats *Kinsman*, *Estrella*, *St. Mary*, *Calhoun* and *Diana* and 21st Ind. Vols.		1		5								Federal.
		Rawle's Mills, N. C.				24th and 44th Mass., and 9th N. J. Vols. and N. Y. and Maine Batteries.		1										Federal.
	Attack on Federal Escort	Harrisonville, Mo.		28	300	5th and 6th Missouri Cavalry	Lieut. Newby, F. / —— Quantrel, C.	8		4		5						1st Conf. 2d Fed.
	Bombardment of Tampa, Fla., by Federal Forces.																	
	Occupation of Piedmont, Va., by Federal Cavalry.																	
Nov. 4	Occupation of La Grange, Miss., by a portion of General Grant's Army.																	
Nov. 5	Capture of	Lamar, Mo.		80	Guer	8th Missouri and 6th Missouri Militia Cavalry	Maj. Braden, F. / —— Quantrel, C.											Conf'd.
	Engagement	Manassas Gap, Va.				Federal Cavalry Brigade	Gen. Averill, F.											
	Skirmish	Barbee's Cross Roads and Chester Gap, Va.				Federal Cavalry Brigade	Gen. Pleasonton, F. / Gen. Stuart, C.	1		5		16						Federal
	General Burnside, U. S. A. assigned to command of the Army of the Potomac, vice McClellan.																	
	Occupation of Salem, Va., by Federal Cavalry.																	
	Engagement	New Baltimore, Salem and Thoroughfare Gap, Va.			Cav. & Art.	Federal Cavalry Brigade	Col. Wyndham, F.											Federal.
	Skirmish	Greenville Road, Ky.			Guer	8th Kentucky Cavalry	Maj. Holloway, F. / Col. Fowler, C.		8									Federal.
	Battle	Nashville, Tenn.			3300	16th and 51st Ill., 69th Ohio 14th Mich. and 78th Penn. Vols., 4th Tenn. and 7th Penn. Cav.	Bg.-Gen. Negley, F. / —— Forrest and Morgan, C.	5		10		23						Federal.
Nov. 6	Skirmish	Leatherwood, Ky.			Guer	Captain Ambrose Powell's command	Capt. Powell, F.		7									Federal.
	Skirmish	Garrettsburg, Ky.				8th Kentucky Cavalry.	Gen. Reynolds, F.					7						
	Occupation of Warrenton, Va., by Federal Troops.																	
Nov. 7	Engagement	Big Beaver Creek, Mo.	5 hours	4 Cos	1300	10th Illinois and 2 Companies Missouri Militia	Capt. Burstow, F. / Col. Green, C.						4 Co.					Conf'd.
	Skirmish	Rheas Mills, Ark.				3rd Arkansas Indian Home Guards.	Capt. Perkins, F.		6	1								Federal.
	Skirmish	Mamaka, Ark.				3rd and 4th Iowa and 9th Illinois Cavalry												Federal.
Nov. 8	Engagement	Rappahannock Bridge, Va.				Cavalry Brigade, Army of the Potomac	Gen. Bayard, F.					13						Federal.
	Reconnoissance near	Hudsonville, Miss.		1600		7th Kansas and 2nd Iowa Cavalry	Col. Lee, F.		16			135						
	Evacuation of Holly Spring, Miss., by Confederate Forces.																	
Nov. 9	Reconnoissance to	Fredericksburg, Va.		160		1st Indiana Cavalry	Capt. Dahlgren, F.	1	2			29		4				Federal.
	Skirmish	Baxter Mountain, Mo.				(Organizations not recorded.)												
	Skirmish	Moorefield, Va.				1st N. Y., Ringgold and Washington Cav. and 23rd Ill. Vols.	Brig.-Gen. Kelley, F.			4		50						Federal.
	Skirmish	Perry County, Ky			Guer	14th Kentucky Cavalry	Capt. Morgan, F.		5									Federal.
	Bombardment of	St. Mary's, Fla.				Federal Gunboat *Mohawk*.												
Nov. 10	Expedition through S. W. Kentucky.			400		Federal Troops	Col. Foster, F.					7						Federal
	Skirmish	Warrenton, Va.			Cav.	Federal Cavalry	Lieut. Ash, F.											
	Reconnoissance into	Greenbrier County, Va.				Federal Troops	Capt. Gillmore, F.											
	General Burnside, U. S. A., assumes command of the Army of the Potomac.																	
Nov. 11	Engagement	Bachelor's Creek, N. C. (Newbern)		Pkts.		(Organizations not stated.)												Conf'd.
	Skirmish	Huntsville, Tenn.			Guer	Tennessee Home Guards.	Capt. Duncan, F.		4									Federal.
	Skirmish	Lebanon, Tenn.			Cav.	1st Kentucky and 4th Michigan Cavalry	Capts. Kennett and Wolford, F. / —— Morgan, C.		7			125						Federal.
Nov. 12	Engagement	Lamar and Holly Springs, Miss.			Cav.	2nd Ill., 3rd Mich., 2nd Iowa and 7th Kansas Cavalry	Maj. Mudd, F. / Col. Lee, F.		4									Federal.
	General Hooker, U. S. A., assumed command of the Fifth Corps, Army of the Potomac.																	
Nov. 13	Expedition to the Doboy River, Ga., under Lieutenant Col. Beard.																	
	Attack on Confederate Camp at	Calhoun, Ky.		400	Guer	Federal Troops	Col. Shanks, F.											Federal.
Nov. 14	Re-organization of the Army of the Potomac, by General Burnside.																	
Nov. 15	Engagement	Fayetteville and White Sulphur Springs, Va.	1 hour			1st and 2nd Brig., Sturgis' Div., 9th Corps and Cav., Army of the Potomac	Gen. Sturgis, F.	1		8								Federal.
Nov. 16	Skirmish	Nashville, Tenn.			Cav.	Advance of General Hill's Brigade.												
Nov. 17	Skirmish	Gloucester, Va.			Cav.	104th Pennsylvania Volunteers. (Outpost Picket Guard.)		1		8			2					Conf'd.
	Evacuation of Warrenton, Va., by General Burnside's Army.																	
Nov. 18	Engagement	Cove Creek, N. C.				3rd New York Cavalry	Lieut.-Col. Mix, F.											Federal.
	Skirmish	Rural Hills, Tenn.			Cav.	9th Kentucky Cavalry	Col. Hawkins, F.		16									Federal.
	Occupation of Falmouth, Va., by Advance Column of Army of the Potomac under General Sumner.																	
Nov. 19	Raid by Federal Troops at	Blackwater, Va.				New York Mounted Rifles	Col. Dodge, F.											Federal.
	Skirmish	Wallace's Creek, Ky.			Guer	Harlan County State Guards												Federal.
Nov. 20	Raid on Federal Pickets	Bull Run Bridge, Va.			Cav.	Federal Troops							4					Conf'd.
	Occupation of Warrenton and Leesburgh, Va., by Confederate Cavalry.																	
Nov. 21	Skirmish	Bayou Bontouca, La.	½ hour		150	31st Massachusetts Volunteers	Capt. Darling, F. / Capt. Evans, C.		4	1								Federal.
	Occupation of Salem, Va., by Confederate Forces.																	
Nov. 22	Skirmish	Winchester, Va.				Detachment 1st New York Cavalry	Capt. Harkins, F.		4									Federal.
	Expedition into Mathew Co., Va., by Forces under Commander Parker and Brig.-General Naglee.																	
Nov. 24	Attack on Federal Supply Train at	Beaver Creek, Mo.		50	Guer	3rd Missouri Cavalry and 21st Iowa Volunteers		5	5	12	11							Conf'd.
Nov. 25	Engagement	Zuni, Va.		3 Bat.		Mounted Rifles	Col. Dodge, F.			1								Federal.

CHRONOLOGICAL LIST OF EVENTS (1860-1865).—Continued.

DATE.	EVENT.	LOCATION.	DURATION.	FORCE F.	FORCE C.	COMPOSITION OF FORCE.	COMMANDERS.	KILLED F.	KILLED C.	WOUNDED F.	WOUNDED C.	PRISONERS TAKEN BY F.	PRISONERS TAKEN BY C.	MISSING F.	MISSING C.	[illegible]	[illegible]	ADVANTAGE.
1862.																		
Nov. 25	Skirmish	Camp Babcock, Ark.				3rd Kansas Indian Home Guards.												
	Skirmish	Crawford County, Mo.				Missouri Enrolled Militia	Capt. Bowen, F.		2									Federal.
	Capture of Henderson, Tenn., by Confederate Cavalry.																	
Nov. 26	Engagement	Cold Knob Mountain, Va.			Cav.	2nd West Virginia Cavalry	Col. Paxton, F.					100						Federal.
	Attack on Confederate Camp at	Summerville, Miss.				7th Illinois Cavalry						29						Federal.
	Reconnoissance from Harper's Ferry to Berryville, Va., by Federal Force under General Geary.																	
Nov. 27	Expedition from Helena, Ark., into the State of Mississippi by Federal Forces under Brig.-Gen. Washburne.																	
	Evacuation of Rienzi, Miss., by Federal Forces.																	
	Skirmish	Carthage, Ark.				2nd Kansas Cavalry.	Col. Dodge, F.											
	Skirmish	Scrougesville, Tenn.				5th Brig. Sill's Div., Army of the Ohio	Gen. Wheeler, C.			10								Federal.
Nov. 28	Expedition from Helena, Ark., to Delta, Tenn., by Federal Cavalry under General Hovey.																	
	Engagement	Cane Hill, Boston Mountains and Boonsboro, Ark.				1st Division, Army of the Frontier	Gen. Blunt, F. / Gen. Marmaduke, C.	4	75	30								Federal.
	Engagement	Little Bear Creek, Ala.				Portion of the 2nd Division, 16th Corps.												
	Skirmish	Hartwood Church, Va.		Pkts.	Cav.	3rd Pennsylvania Cavalry		4		9								Conf'd.
	Skirmish	Cold Water River, Miss.				1st Indiana Cavalry												
Nov. 29	(28th–30th). Skirmishes	Waterford and Lumkin's Mills, Miss.				Advance Cavalry of General Grant's Army	Col. Lee, F.		6									Federal.
	Skirmish	Berlin, Md.			Cav.	Maryland Home Guards	Capt. Means, F. / —— White, C.		2									Federal.
Nov. 30	Reconnoissance to	Snicker's Ferry and Berryville, Va.				1st Cavalry Brigade, Stahl's Division	Gen. Stahl, F.		43			40						Federal.
	Skirmish	Abbeville, Miss.				Reconnoitering force	Col. Lee, F.											Federal.
	Expedition to	Yellville, Ark.				1st Iowa, 10th Illinois and 2nd Wisconsin Regiment	Col. Wickersham, F.										600	
	Skirmish	Charlestown and Berryville, Va.				2nd Division 12th Corps	Gen. Slocum, F. / —— White, Henderson & Baylor, C.		5		18							Federal.
Dec. 1	Skirmish	Horse Creek, Mo.			Guer.	Detachment 4th Missouri Cavalry	Maj. Kelly, F.					5						Federal.
	Capture of Warrenton, Va., by Federal Troops					Detachment 3rd Virginia Cavalry	Capt. Cruger, F.					1						
Dec. 2	Evacuation of Abbeville, Miss., by Confederates, and Occupation by General Grant's Federal Cavalry.																	
	Skirmish	Franklin, Va.			Cav. & Art.	11th Pennsylvania Cavalry	Col. Spear, F.					20				2	85	Federal.
	Attack on Federal Troops at	King George Court House, Va.		80	Cav.	8th Pennsylvania Cavalry	Capt. Wilson, F.											Conf'd.
	Reconnoissance from Bolivar Heights, Va., to Charlestown, etc., by Federal Forces under General Geary	Charlestown, Va.				Federal Forces	Gen. Geary, F.		K&W 70			145						
	Skirmish	Ozark, Mo.		150		3rd and 9th Missouri Cavalry	Col. Glover, F.		4			2						Federal.
Dec. 3	Skirmish	Oakland, Miss.				1st Indiana Cavalry.												
	Skirmishes	Oxford, Miss.				2nd Cavalry Brigade	Col. Hatch, F.	K&W 20				92						Federal.
	Occupation of	Princeton, Ky.				91st Indiana Infantry and 13th Kentucky Cavalry	Maj. Henry, F.											
Dec. 4	Skirmish	Tuscumbia, Ala.										70						Federal.
	Skirmish	Whitman's Shoals, Ky.				39th Kentucky Volunteers.												
	Engagement	Water Valley, Miss.				1st and 2nd Cavalry Brigades	Cols. Hatch and Lee, F.					300						Federal.
	Engagement	Port Royal, Va.	3 hours.			6 Federal Gunboats and Confederate Batteries.												
Dec. 5	Engagement	Coffeeville, Miss.	2 hours.	2000	Inf. 5000	1st, 2nd and 3rd Cav. Brigades, Gen. Grant's Army	Cols. Hatch, Lee and Mizner, F.	K&W 100										Conf'd.
	Attack on Federal Troops at	Helena, Ark.			300	30th Iowa and 29th Wisconsin Volunteers			8			80						Federal.
	Skirmish	Reed's Mountains, Ark.				2nd Kansas Cavalry.												
Dec. 6	Attack on Federal Forage Train near	Lebanon, Tenn.				93rd Ohio Volunteers	Col. C. Anderson, F.	1		3								Federal.
Dec. 7	Battle	Prairie Grove, Ark.			35,000	1st, 2nd and 3rd Divisions, Army of the Frontier	Brig.-Gens. Blunt and Herron, F. / Gen. C. Hindman, C.	495	K&W & M 1500	600				183				Federal.
	Battle	Hartsville, Tenn.			4000	106th and 108th Ohio, 104th Ill. Vols., 2nd Ind. and 11th Ky. Cav. and 13th Ind. Battery	Col. Moore, F. / Gen. Morgan, C.	35	K&W 149	100				1800				Conf'd.
Dec. 9	Skirmish	Bean's Station, Tenn.				(Organizations not recorded.)												
	Attack on Federal Forage Train Escort	Dobbin's Ferry, (La Vergne), Tenn.				35th Ind., 51st Ohio, 8th and 21st Ky. Vols. and 7th Ind. Battery		9		30			5	1				Federal.
	Skirmish	Brentsville, Tenn.			400	25th Ill., 8th Kan. and 81st Ind. Vols. and 8th Wis. Battery	Col. Martin, F.											Federal.
Dec. 10	Engagement	Port Royal, Va.	3 hours.			8 Federal Gunboats and Confederate Batteries		1		3								Federal.
	Capture of Plymouth, N. C., by Confederate Forces																	
Dec. 11	Expedition from Newberne, N. C., under Major-Gen. Foster, U. S. A.																	
	Bombardment of Fredericksburg, Va., by Fed. Forces under Gen. Burnside.																	
Dec. 12	Skirmish	Little Bear Creek, Ala.				Federal Troops	Col. Sweeney, F.											
	Reconnoissance to	Zuni, Va.	3½ hours.	Art.	Art.	Federal Brigade	Gen. Terry, F.											
	Skirmish	Corinth, Miss.				Federal Troops	Col. Sweeney, F. / Col. Roddy, C.	1	11		30	40	?					Federal.
	Skirmish	Trenton, N. C.				3rd New York Cavalry	Capt. Hall, F.					18						Federal.
	Descent upon	Franklin, Tenn.				Stanley's Cav. Div., Army of the Cumberland	Brig.-Gen. Stanley, F.	1	5		10	12						Federal.
	(12th–18th). Expedition to	Goldsboro, N. C.				Wessell's Brig. of Peck's Div., 1st, 2nd and 3rd Brigs., 1st Div., Dept. of N. C.	Gen. Foster, F.	90	K&W 739	478				9		12		Federal.
Dec. 13	Battle	Fredericksburg, Va.				1st, 2nd, 3rd, 5th, 6th and 9th Corps, Army of the Pot.	Gen. Burnside, F. / Gen. Lee, C.	1819	K&W 1800	9600			2078					Conf'd.
	Engagement	South-West Creek, N. C.			400	9th N. J. and 85th Penn. Vols., 3rd N. Y. Cav. and 3rd N. Y. Art.	Gen. Wessells, F.									1		Federal.

CHRONOLOGICAL LIST OF EVENTS (1860-1865).—Continued.

Date.	Event.	Location.	Duration.	Force F	Force C	Composition of Force.	Commanders.	Killed F	Killed C	Wounded F	Wounded C	Prisoners Taken by F	Prisoners Taken by C	Missing F	Missing C	[illegible]	[illegible]	Advantage.
1862																		
Dec. 13	Skirmish	Tuscumbia Creek, Ala.				Federal Troops (2 Regiments Inf., 1 company Cav.)		4		11		70						Federal.
Dec. 14	Battle and Capture of Kingston, N. C., by Federal Troops	Kingston, N. C.				Wessell's Brig. of Peck's Div. and 1st, 2nd and 3rd Brigs., 1st Div., Dept. of N. C	Gen. Foster, F.; Gen. Evans, C.	90	71	478	268	400				13		Federal.
	Wagon-Train captured by Mexicans near	Fort Brown Road, Texas.				Troops not given.												
	Skirmish	Wichman's Shoals, Ky.		200	800	Federal Troops.	Capt. Thornberry, F.										700	Conf'd.
Dec. 15	General Butler superseded by General Banks in command of the Army of the Gulf.																	
Dec. 16	Major-Gen. Banks, U. S. A., assumes command of the Department of the Gulf																	
	Artillery Fight	Whitehall, N. C.	1 hour			9th N. J., 17th, 23rd, 24th and 45th Mass. Vols., 3rd N. Y. Cav. and 3rd and 23rd N. Y. Batteries	Gen. Foster, F.; Gen. Evans, C.											Federal.
	Surprise of Confederates at	New Haven, Ky			1200	Detachment Wolford's Cavalry	Capt. Adams, F.					1200						Federal.
	Army of the Potomac withdraws from Fredericksburgh, Va.																	
Dec. 17	Engagement	Goldsboro, N. C.	1 hour			9th N. J., 3rd, 17th, 25th, 27th and 43rd Mass. Vols., 3rd N. Y. Cav. and 3rd and 23rd N. Y. Batteries	Gen. Foster, F.; Gen. Evans, C.											Federal.
	Occupation of Baton Rouge, La., by Federals under General Banks.																	
Dec. 18	Engagement and Occupation by Confederate Forces, of	Lexington, Ky.	3 hours			11th Ill. and 5th Ohio, 1st and 2nd Tenn. Cavalry	Col. Ingersoll, F.; Gen. Forrest, C.	40								2		Conf'd.
	Engagement	Jackson, Tenn.				11th Ill. and 5th Ohio Cav., 43rd and 61st Ill. Vols.												
Dec. 19	Engagement	Occoquan, Va.				Wagon Train Guard of the 12th Army Corps	Col. Rush, F.											Federal.
Dec. 20	Occupation of Holly Springs, Miss., by Confederate Forces	Holly Springs, Miss.				2nd Illinois Cavalry.	Col. Murphy, F.; Gen. Van Dorn, C	K. W. & M. 1000										Conf'd.
	Capture by Confederate Forces of	Trenton and Humboldt, Tenn.				Detachment 7th Tenn. Cav., 122nd Ill. Vols. and Convalescents captured by Forrest	Col. Fry, F.; Gen. Forrest, C.	1	17		80							Federal!
	Skirmish	Halltown, Va.			Guer	Federal Cavalry	Capt. Vernon, F					5						Federal.
Dec. 21	Engagement	Davis Mill, Miss.	8½ hours	250	Cav. 5000	25th Indiana Volunteers and 5th Ohio Cavalry	Col. Morgan, F.; Gen. Van Dorn, C		2	8	30	20					100	Federal.
	Skirmish	Nashville, Tenn.			Rec'g Party	Troops of General Van Cleve's Division												Federal.
	Resignations of Secretaries Seward and Chase proffered, but not accepted by the President.																	
	Attack by Confederate Forces on	Isle of Wight, Court House, Va.				Detachment 2nd New York Mounted Rifles	Lieut.-Col. Onderdonk, F.; Gen. Pryor, C.		2									Conf'd.
Dec. 22	Major-Gen. Schenck, U. S. A., assumes command of the Middle Department and Eighth Army Corps.																	
Dec. 23	Occupation of Winchester, Va., by Federal Forces.																	
Dec. 24	Skirmish	Middleburg, Miss.		115		12th Michigan Volunteers.												
	Skirmish	Glasgow, Ky. (Munfordsville).		5 Cos	Adv. G'rd.	2nd Michigan Cavalry	Capt. Dickey, F.; Gen. Morgan, C.	1	8	1			23					Conf'd.
	Skirmish	Joiners Bridge, Va			Cav. & Inf.	Detachment 11th Pennsylvania Cavalry						4						Federal.
Dec. 25	Attack on Confederates near	Bear Wallow, Ky		2 Bat	R. G'd	12th Kentucky Cavalry	Col. Shanks, F.; Gen. Morgan, C.		1		9	10						Federal.
	Skirmish	Green's Chapel, Ky (Munfordsville)			Adv. G'rd.	Detachment 4th and 5th Indiana Cavalry	Col. Gray, F.; Gen. Morgan, C.		9		22	5						Federal.
	Skirmish	Bacon Creek, Ky		1 Co	Adv. G'rd.	2d Michigan Regiment	Capt. Dickey, F.; Gen. Morgan, C.						23					Conf'd.
Dec. 26	Scout and Skirmish	Powell County, Ky.		160	Guer.	14th Kentucky Cavalry	Maj. Stevens, F.					10						Federal.
	Engagement	Nolensville, Tenn.				2nd Brigade, 1st Division, McCook's Corps.												
Dec. 27	Capture of Elizabethtown, Ky., by Confederate Forces	Elizabethtown, Ky.				9th Illinois Volunteers	Lieut.-Col. H. S. Smith, F.; Gen. Morgan, C.						500					Conf'd.
	Engagement	Dumfries, Va.	6 hours		3500	5th, 7th and 66th Ohio Vols., 6th Maine Battery, 12th Ill. and 1st Maryland Cavalry	Col. Candy, F.; Gens. Morgan and Fitz-Hugh Lee, C.	3	25	8	40		80					Federal.
	Attack on Confederate Forces at	Vicksburg, Miss.																
Dec. 28	Engagement	Chickasaw Bayou, Miss.				6th Indiana Cavalry												Federal
	Capture by Federal Forces under General Blunt, of	Van Buren, Ark.																
	Engagement	Moldraugh's Hill, Ky.	10 hours		Cav.	71st Indiana Regiment	Gen. Morgan, C.											Conf'd.
	Skirmish	Suffolk, Va.			Cav.	Reconnoitring Force	Brig.-Gen. Gibbs, F.											Federal
	Engagement	Dripping Springs, Ark.				Army of the Frontier.												
	Skirmish	Elkhorn, Ky.		250	350	8th and 10th Kentucky Cavalry	Maj. Foley, F.		30		170	51						Federal.
	Skirmish	Occoquan, Va.				2nd and 17th Pennsylvania Cavalry.												
	Skirmish	Clinton, La			Cav.	Federal Cavalry		1										Conf'd.
Dec. 29	(28th-29th). Battle	Chickasaw Bayou, Miss. (Vicksburg)				Four Divisions, Army of the Tennessee	Gen. Sherman, F.; Gen. Johnston, C.	191	K. & W. 207	982				750				Conf'd.
	Skirmish	Stewart Creek, Tenn.				3rd Kentucky Regiment.												
Dec. 30	Engagement	Wautauga Bridge and Carter's Station, Tenn.				7th Ohio and 9th Pennsylvania Cavalry.												
	Battle	Parker's Cross Roads, Tenn.				18th, 106th, 119th and 122nd Ill., 27th, 39th and 63rd Ohio, 50th Ind., 39th Iowa, 7th Tenn. Vols. and 7th Wisconsin Battery	Gen. Sullivan, F.; Gen. Forrest, C.	K. & W. 200			W. 400					6		Federal.
		Jefferson, Tenn.				2nd Brigade, 1st Division, Thomas' Corps.												
Dec. 31	(31st—Jan. 2d, '63). Battle	Stone's River, Tenn. (Murfreesboro)	20 hours			3 Corps, Army of the Cumberland	Maj.-Gen. Rosecrans, F.; Gen. Bragg, C.	1533	K. W. & M. 25 000	7245				2800				?

CHRONOLOGICAL LIST OF EVENTS (1860-1865).—Continued.

Date	Event	Location	Duration	Force F	Force C	Composition of Force	Commanders	Killed F	Killed C	Wounded F	Wounded C	Prisoners Taken by F	Prisoners Taken by C	Missing F	Missing C	Guns Capt.	Stands of Arms	Advantage
1863																		
Jan. 1	Capture of	Galveston, Texas	4½ hours	300		Federal Gunboats *Westfield*, *Harriet Lane*, *Owasco*, *Sachem*, *Clifton* and *Corypheus* and 3 Companies 42nd Massachusetts Volunteers	Com. Renshaw, F; Gen. Magruder, C						600					Conf'd.
	Skirmish	Stewart's Creek, Tenn.				3rd Ohio Cavalry and 10th Ohio Volunteers.												
	Skirmish	La Vergne, Tenn.				1st Michigan Engineers and Mechanics.												
	Emancipation Proclamation issued by President Lincoln.																	
Jan. 2	(Dec. 31st–Jan. 3d.) Battle	Stone River, Tenn. (Murfreesboro')		43,400	60,000	Army of the Cumberland	Gen. Rosecrans, F; Gen. Bragg, C	1533	K&W 9000	7245			2800		1000			Federal.
	Skirmishes	Vicksburgh, Tenn.				(Organizations not recorded)												Federal
	Raid by Confederates	Dumfries, Va.			Cav		Major Herring, C											Conf'd.
Jan. 3	Attack on Confederate Camp	La Grange, Ark.			Cav	Portion of General Washburne's Cavalry Regiment	Gen. Washburne, F.		K&W 10			12						Federal.
	Attack by Confederate Troops	Moorefield, W. Va.	Sev'l h'rs.			116th Ohio Volunteers	Gen. Jones, C						65				65	Federal.
Jan. 4	Proclamation issued by General Hurlbut, U. S. A., commanding District of Tennessee, against encouragement of Guerillas.																	
	Proclamation issued by General Magruder, C.S.A., declaring the Harbor of Galveston, Texas, "open for trade to all friendly nations."																	
Jan. 5	Skirmish	Middletown, Tenn.				Cavalry of the Army of the Cumberland.												
	Raid by Confederates	Hardy County, W. Va.			Rgrs.	Troops not specified	Capt. McNeill, C	1					33					Conf'd.
	Troops in the Department of the Gulf constituted the 19th Army Corps (from Dec. 14th, 1862), under command of Major-General Banks U. S. A.																	
	Attack on Confederates	Kinston, N. C.		AdvG	Pkts.	General Foster's Forces												Federal.
Jan. 6	Order issued by General Rosecrans denying parole to captured Confederate Officers, consequent on the publication of a similar order by Jefferson Davis)																	
Jan. 7	(7th–8th). Engagement	Springfield, Mo.	10 hours.	800	4000	Missouri Militia, Convalescents and Citizens	B. Gen. Brown, F; Col. Crabb, F.; Gen. Marmaduke, C	14		144				4				Federal.
	Reconnoissance from Winchester to Woodstock, Va., by party of 1st N. Y. Cavalry under Lieutenant Col. Von Schickfoss.																	
Jan. 8	Raid on Confederates	Ripley, Tenn.			Cav	2nd Illinois Cavalry	Capt. Moore, F.; Lt.-Col. Dawson, C.		8	3	20	46						Federal.
	General Mansfield Lovell, C. S. A., dismissed for incapacity.																	
Jan. 9	The Army of the Cumberland divided into 3 Army Corps, Fourteenth, Twentieth and Twenty-first, commanded by Maj.-Gens. Thomas, McCook, and Crittenden respectively.																	
Jan. 10	Skirmish	Catlett's Station, Va.			Cav	Federal Cavalry	Col. Schimmelfennig, F; —— Hampton, C											
	Proclamation issued by Governor Letcher of Virginia, calling out Militia of Counties bordering on North Carolina line, for Confederate service.																	
Jan. 11	Engagement	Off Coast of Texas	20 minutes			Federal Steamers *Hatteras* and *The Alabama*	Lieut. H. G. Blake, U.S.N.; Capt. Semmes, C	2		5				6				Conf'd.
	Capture of	Fort Hindman, Ark.	3½ hours			13th and 15th Corps, Army of the Mississippi and Gunboats of Mississippi Squadron	Maj.-Gen. McClernand, F; R. Adm. Porter, F; Gen. Churchill, C	129	550	831		5000		17		17	3000	Federal.
	Battle	Hartsville, Mo. (Wood's Fork)	2 hours		6000	21st Iowa and 99th Ill. Vols., 3rd Iowa and 3rd Mo. Cav. and Battery L, 2nd Mo. Artillery	Gen. Warren, F; Col. Merrill, F; Gen. Marmaduke, C	7	K&W 150	61		150	3	2				Federal.
Jan. 12	Skirmish	Lick Creek, Ark.				2nd Wisconsin Cavalry.												
	Raid	Holly Springs, Miss.			Guer													
Jan. 13	Surrender of Federal Gunboat *Major Slidell*, commanded by Lieut. Van Dorn, to Confederate Guerillas, on Cumberland River, Tenn.																	
Jan. 14	Engagement	Bayou Teche, La.	Sev'l h'rs.			8th Vt., 16th and 75th N. Y., 12th Conn., 6th Mich., 31st Ind. Vols., 1st La. Cav., 4th and 6th Mass. and 1st Maine Batteries and Gunboats *Calhoun*, *Diana*, *Kinsman* and *Estrella*	Com. Buchanan, F; Gen. Weitzel, F.; Col. Gray, C	7		27		40						Federal.
	The Federal Steamer *Forest Queen* captured and burned by Guerillas at Commerce, Miss.																	
	The Federal Gunboat *Queen of the West* captured by Confederates on Red River																	
Jan. 15	Attack on Federal Troops	Helena and Clarendon Road, Ark.				2nd Wisconsin Cavalry			K&W 7				17					Conf'd.
	Mound City, Arkansas, burned by Federal Troops.																	
Jan. 16	Naval Expedition	Duval's Bluff, Ark.				Federal Gunboat *De Kalb* and 24th Indiana Volunteers	Lt. John G. Walker, U.S.N.; Gen. Gorman, F.					7				2	200	Federal.
	Wreck of the Transport *Planter*, with Federal Troops, near Stranger's Key, Bahama.																	
Jan. 17	Skirmish	Pollocksville and N. E. River, N. C.				3rd New York Cavalry												Federal.
	Occupation of Des Arc, Ark., by Federal Forces.																	
Jan. 19	Reconnoissance	Burnt Ordinary, Va.		19	Cav. 75	5th Pennsylvania Cavalry	Lieut. Vezin, F.											Federal
Jan. 20	Governor Andrew of Massachusetts authorized to raise Volunteers, including "persons of African Origin."																	
Jan. 21	The Federal Man-of-War *Morning Light* captured by Confederate steamers in the Sabine Pass, Texas.																	
	Scout	Columbia, Mo.				Detachment 61st Missouri Volunteers				2		6						Federal.
	Raid by Confederates	Murfreesboro', Tenn.			Cav. 100	Federal Troops	Lieut.-Col. Hutcheson, C											Conf'd.
	General Fitz-John-Porter, U. S. A., dismissed.																	

CHRONOLOGICAL LIST OF EVENTS (1860-1865).—Continued.

Date	Event	Location	Duration	Force F.	Force C.	Composition of Force	Commanders	Killed F.	Killed C.	Wounded F.	Wounded C.	Prisoners Taken by F.	Prisoners Taken by C.	Missing F.	Missing C.	[illegible]	[illegible]	Advantage
1863																		
Jan. 23	Attack on Federals	Fish Springs, Tenn		70	Cav.	Loyalists"	—Taylor, F.; Col. Folk, C.	4										Conf'd.
	Destruction and Evacuation of Arkansas Post, Ark., by Federal Forces																	
Jan. 24	Brig.-General Donelson, C. S. A., appointed to command of Department of East Tennessee, vice General Kirby Smith.																	
	Skirmish	Woodbury, Tenn			2 Bgs	2nd Division Crittenden's Corps	Gen. Palmer, F.	2	35	9		100						Federal.
Jan. 25	Attack on Federal Guard	Murfreesboro', Tenn			Cav.	Re-enforcement, 10th Michigan Volunteers							50					Conf'd.
Jan. 26	Skirmish	Township, Fla				33rd Federal Colored Troops												
	Indian Fight. (29th)	Bear River, Wash. Territory	4 hours	300		4 Cos. 2nd Cal. Cav. and 1 Co. 3rd Cal. Vols.	Col. Connor, F.	14	Ind. 220	49								Federal.
	Scout	Morrisville, Va.		21	Inf.	Federal Cavalry		1		1								Conf'd.
	Maj.-Gen. Hooker, U. S. A., assumed command of the Army of the Potomac.																	
Jan. 27	Skirmish	Plaquemine Bayou, La.				1st Louisiana Cavalry	Capt. Williamson, F.											Federal.
	Raid on Confederates	Bloomfield, Mo.			Guer.	Detachment 68th Missouri Militia	Col. J. Lindsay, F.					62					100	Federal.
	Bombardment of	Fort McAllister, Ga.				Iron Clad Monitor *Montauk*, 3 Gunboats and a Mortar Schooner	Capt. Worden, F.											
Jan. 28	Scout	Van Buren, Mo.		130		Detachments 1st Arkansas Cav. and 10th Ill. Cav.	Lieut.-Col. Stewart, F.		2			200						Federal.
Jan. 29	Skirmish	Pinos Altos, Arizona Territory				1 Company 1st California Volunteers	Col. West, F.; Capt. Dawson, C.		k & p 34									Federal
Jan. 30	Attack on Confederates	Dyersburg, Tenn. (Trenton)			Guer.	22nd Ohio Volunteers												
	Engagement	Suffolk, Va. ([illegible] and Kelly's Store)	3 hours			Portion of Major-General Peck's Forces	B.-Gen. Corcoran, F.; Col. Spear, F.; Gen. Pryor, C.	24	k & w 50	80								Federal.
Jan. 31	Engagement	Rover, Tenn.				4th Ohio Cavalry	—Kennett, F.; —Wheeler, C.		12			300						Federal.
	Raid on Confederate Camp	Middleton, Tenn			Cav.	2nd and 3rd Tennessee Cavalry	Col. Stokes, F.; Maj. Douglass, C.					100						Federal.
	Attack on Federal Vessels	Off Charleston Bar, S. C.				Federal Steamers *Mercedita, Keystone State, Augusta, Quaker City, Housatonic* and *Memphis*	R.-Adm. Du Pont, F.; Flag-Off. Ingraham, C.	24		23								Conf'd.
	Occupation of Shelbyville, Tenn., by Federal Troops under General Jeff. C. Davis.																	
Feb. 1	Bombardment of	Fort McAllister, Ga.				Federal Navy	Maj. J. B. Gallie, C.		1									
	Occupation of Franklin, Tenn., by Federal Forces					Troops not specified	Col. R. Johnson, F.; Gen. Forrest, C.	1				3						Federal.
	Attack on Federal Troops	Island No. 10				Federal Transport												Federal.
	Raid	Warrenton, Va.				1st and 5th Virginia Cavalry	Col. Percy Wyndham, F.											Federal.
Feb. 3	Reconnoissance to Liberty, Auburn and Lebanon, Tennessee, by Federal Troops under General J. J. Reynolds.																	
	Engagement	Mingo Swamp, Mo.			Guer.	12th Missouri Militia	Maj. Reeder, F.; Cap. McGee, C.		9		20							Federal.
	Engagement	Fort Donelson, Tenn. (Cumberland Iron Works)	5 hours	600		83rd Ill. Vols., 2nd Ill. Art. and a Battery 5th Iowa Cav.	Col. Harding, F.; Gen'ls. Wheeler and Forrest, C.	16	150	60	400	100						Federal.
	Skirmish	Independence, Mo.				5th Missouri Militia Cavalry.												
Feb. 4	Raid on Confederates	Batesville, Ark			Cav.	Brigade of Cavalry	Col. G. E. Waring, Jr., F.; —Marmaduke, C.		k & w 20									Federal.
	Skirmish	Lake Providence, N. C.				Federal Troops												Federal
Feb. 5	Scout	Bear Creek, Mo.			Guer.	40th Missouri Enrolled Militia	Capt. Rainey, F.		7									Federal.
	Attack on Federal Troops	Wiggington's Mills, Va.			Cav.	Federal Cavalry				1								Federal.
Feb. 9	Raid	Middleburg, Va				Detachment 5th New York Cavalry	Capt. Penfield, F.					8						Federal.
	Attack by Confederates	Milwood, Va.		3 Cos.	Cav.	1st New York Cavalry	Capt. Jones, F.; Lieut. Laverty, F.		1	1		1						Federal.
Feb. 7	Engagement	Williamsburg, Va.		Sqd.	Guer.	5th Pennsylvania Cavalry	Lieut.-Col. Lewis, F.	22					5	13				Conf'd.
	Capture of the Guerilla leader, Dawson, near Dyersburg, Tenn., by detachment of Federal Troops under Colonel Wood.																	
Feb. 8	Engagement	Independence, Mo.	½ hour	50	Guer.	5th Missouri Militia Cavalry	Lieut. Colvin, F.		8		2							Federal.
	Occupation of Lebanon, Tenn., by Federal Forces					(Organizations not recorded)						600						Federal.
Feb. 9	Skirmish	Summerville, Va			Cav.	Federal Cavalry	Major Knox, F.											Federal.
Feb. 10	Skirmish	Old River, Lake Providence, La		100	250	Detachments 1st Kan., 17th and 95th Ill., 16th Wis. Vols. and 3rd La. Cav.	Capt. Tucker, F.	1	4	7	7	26						Federal.
	Skirmish	Gloucester Point, Va.				(Organizations not recorded.)												
	Indian Fight and Capture of	Wachita Indian Agency, Texas				Loyal Delawares and Shawnees		Ind. 4				Ind. 100						Federal.
	Skirmish	Bone Yard, Tenn				18th Missouri Volunteers.												
Feb. 13	Attack on Federal Troops	Smithfield, Va.		12	Cav.	12th Pennsylvania Cavalry	Lieut. Taylor, C.	1		3		7	4					11 Con. 12 Fed.
	Skirmish	Bolivar, Tenn.			Cav.	Federal Cavalry			4			5						Federal.
Feb. 14	Skirmish	Brentsville, Va.				1st Michigan Cavalry.												
	Attack on Federal Steamer	Gordon's Landing, La				Federal Ram, *Queen of the West*, abandoned.		k & w 15										Conf'd.
	Attack on Federal Troops	Annandale, Va.				5th Michigan Cavalry.												
Feb. 15	Engagement	Cainsville, Tenn.			Cav. Guer.	123rd Ill. Vols. and 1 Company of 5th Tenn. Cav.	Col. Monroe, F.		20	3		6					200	Federal.
	Attack on Federal Wagon-train	Nolensville, Tenn.		14	135	Detachment 2nd Minnesota Volunteers	Sergt. Holmes, F.		8		20	4						Federal.
	Skirmish	Arkadelphia, Ark.	4 hours			Captain Brown's command	Capt. Brown, F.	2	14	12	12							Federal.
Feb. 16	Capture of Federal Forage-train	Near Romney, Va				Detachments 116th and 122nd Ohio Volunteers												Conf'd.
Feb. 17	The Federal Steamer *Hercules* burned by Guerillas near Memphis, Tenn.																	

CHRONOLOGICAL LIST OF EVENTS (1860-1865).—Continued.

Date	Event	Location	Duration	Force F	Force C	Composition of Force	Commanders	Killed F.	Killed C.	Wounded F.	Wounded C.	Prisoners Taken F.	Prisoners Taken C.	Missing F.	Missing C.	Guns Capt.	Stands of Arms taken	Advantage
1863																		
Feb. 19	Skirmish	Milton, Tenn.				2nd Michigan and 3rd Ohio Cavalry												
	Siege of Vicksburg, commenced by Federal Mortar-boats.																	
	Capture and Destruction of Clifton, Tenn., by Detachment 3d Mich. Cavalry.																	
Feb. 19	Skirmish	Spring River, Mo.		1 Co.		9th Kansas Regiment.												
	Reconnaissance	Cold Water, Miss.			Cav. 200	Federal Cavalry	Lieut.-Col. Wood, F.		9			15						Federal.
	Destruction of Hopefield, Ark., by Federal Force.																	
Feb. 20	Skirmish	Yazoo Pass, Miss.			Cav. 60	5th Illinois Cavalry			6	5		20						Federal.
Feb. 21	Skirmish	Prairie Station, Miss.				2nd Iowa Cavalry.												
	Reconnoissance and Engagement	Rappahannock River, Va. (Fort Lowry)	1 hour		Batt	Federal Gunboats *Freeborn* and *Dragon*	Lt.-Com. Magaw, F.			3								Federal.
	Skirmish	Greenville, Ky.			Guer	Detachment 9th Kentucky Cavalry						4						Federal.
Feb. 22	Scout	Tuscumbia, Ala.				Cavalry Brigade	Col. F. M. Cornyn, F.											Federal.
Feb. 23	Engagement	Deer Creek, Miss.				General Burbridge's Division of the 13th Corps	Gen. Burbridge, F.; Gen. Ferguson, C.											
	Skirmish	Athens, Ky.			Guer	(Organizations not recorded)					1							Federal.
Feb. 24	Engagement	Mississippi River, below Vicksburg	1½ hours			Federal Steamer *Indianola*. (4 Conf. steamers.)	Lieut.-Com. Brown, U. S. N.	1	35	1				7				Conf'd.
	Capture of the Steamer *Hetty Gilmore*, at Woodbury, Tenn., by Confederates under W. C. P. Breckenridge.																	
Feb. 25	Attack on Federal Cavalry	Hartwood Church, Va.			Cav.	Brig.-Gen. Averill's Cavalry Brigade	B.-Gen. Averill, F.; —— Stuart, C.		2									Federal.
	Expedition of Federal Troops under General Ross, up the Yazoo Pass.																	
Feb. 26	Skirmishes	Strasburg Road, Va.			1-80 2 —	13th Pennsylvania and 1st New York Cavalry			K&W 212									Conf'd.
Feb. 27	Skirmish	Newbern, N. C.			Inf. Scts	Detachment 3rd New York Cavalry	Capt. Jacobs, F.		3	1		48						Federal.
	Resignation of General Cochrane, U. S. A., Army of the Potomac.																	
Feb. 28	Destruction of armed Confederate Steamer *Nashville* by Federal Gunboat *Montauk*.						Capt. Worden, U. S. N.											
Mch. 1	Engagement	Bradyville, Tenn.	20 minutes		Guer	1st Tennessee and 3rd and 4th Ohio Cavalry	Gen. Stanley, F.; Col. Duke, C.	2	6	6	20	100						Federal.
	Scout	Bloomfield, Mo.			Guer	Federal Troops	Adjutant Prole, F.		1			21						Federal.
	Skirmish	Aldie, Va.		50		1st Vermont Cavalry	Capts. Ward and Huntoon, F.											Conf'd.
Mch. 2	Engagement	Eagleville, Tenn.			Cav.	13th, 16th, 18th and 19th United States Infantry	Col. Shepherd, F.											Federal.
	Cavalry Fight	Petersburg, Tenn.		200		1st Tennessee Cavalry	Lt. Col. Brownlow, F.		12		20							Federal.
	Skirmish	Aldie, Va.		1 Co.	Cav.	Federal Cavalry	Capt. Schutze, F.					30						Federal.
Mch. 3	Bombardment	Fort McAllister, Ga. (Genesis Point)	8 hours			Federal Gunboats *Passaic*, *Patapsco*, *Montauk*, *Nahant* and 3 Mortar Schooners	Capt. Drayton, U. S. N.											Conf'd.
	Skirmish	Owen's Valley, La.				2nd California Cavalry.												
Mch. 4	Skirmish	Skeet (or Swans' Headquarters) N. C.		Scts.	Guer	3rd New York Cavalry	Capt. Richardson, F.	3	28	15								Federal.
	(4th-5th). Engagement	Thompson's Station, Tenn. (Springhill or Unionville)	4 hours		30600	33rd and 85th Ind., 22nd Wis., 19th Mich. and 124th Ohio Vols., 18th Ohio Battery and 2nd Mich., 9th Penn. and 4th Ky. Cav.	Col. Coburn, F.; Gen. Van Dorn, C.	100	150	300	450		1200					Conf'd.
	Skirmish	Harpeth River, Tenn. (Chapel Hill)			Cav.	1st East Tennessee Cavalry	Majors Burkhart and Macy, F.; Col. Rogers, C.		12			72						Federal.
Mch. 6	Order issued by General Hunter, Department of the South, drafting negroes for garrison duty																	
Mch. 8	Mosby's Raid	Fairfax Court House, Va.		30	Guer	Federal Troops	Brig.-Gen. Stoughton, F.; Capt. Mosby, C.						81					Conf'd.
	Capture of Confederate Cavalry	Trent Road, Newbern, N. C.				43rd Massachusetts Regiment	Col. Holbrook, F.											Federal.
Mch. 9	Skirmish	Bolivar, Tenn.			Guer	(Troops not specified)						18						Federal.
	Skirmish	Franklin, Tenn.				124th Ohio Volunteers.												
	Reconnoissance of Federal Troops under Colonel Chickering from Baton Rouge, La.																	
Mch. 10	Attack on Confederate Camp	Covington, Tenn.			Guer. 400	4th and 7th Illinois Cavalry	Col. Grierson, F.; Col. Richardson, C.		25									Federal.
	Capture of Confederate Troops	Rutherford's Creek, Tenn.				4th Cavalry Brigade	Col. Minty, F.											
	Capture of Jacksonville, Fla., by Federal Colored Troops					1st South Carolina Regiment	Col. Higginson, F.											
Mch. 11	Skirmish	Paris, Ky.			Guer	Federal Wagon Train Guard												Federal.
Mch. 13	(13th-April 5th). Bombardment	Fort Greenwood, Miss.			4000	Federal Gunboats *Chillicothe* and *De Kalb* and troops of the 13th and 17th Corps	Gen. Ross, F.; Gen. Tilghman, C.											Conf'd.
	Skirmish	Berwick City, La.				160th New York Volunteers												Federal.
	Raid by Confederates	Spanish Wells, S. C.			70	Signal party	Lieut. Fenoor, F.						9					Conf'd.
Mch. 14	Bombardment	Port Hudson, La.			Batt	Federal Fleet and Troops	Adm. Farragut, F.; Maj.-Gen. Banks, F.											Conf'd.
	Bombardment	Newbern, N. C.	4 hours	450		92nd New York Volunteers and Gunboats	Col. Anderson, F.; Gen. Pettigrew, C.		15	8	30							Federal.
Mch. 16	(16th-22d). Expedition	Steele's Bayou, Miss.				2nd Division, 15th Corps and Federal Navy	Gen. Sherman, F.; Adm. Porter, F.											
Mch. 17	Attack on Confederate Breastworks	Blackwater, Va.	1 hour			11th Pennsylvania Cavalry	Col. Spear, F.	1		10								Conf'd.
	Cavalry Engagement	Kelly's Ford, Va.	4 hours		Cav.	1st and 5th U. S., 3rd, 4th and 16th Penn., 1st R. I., 6th Ohio, 4th N. Y. Cav. and 6th N. Y. Battery	Gen. Averill, F.; Gen. Fitz Hugh Lee, C.	9		85		60	40					Conf'd.
Mch. 18	Running Fight	Brashear City, La.			Cav.	1st Louisiana Cavalry	Capt. Perkins, F.		10		20							1st Fed.
Mch. 19	Skirmish	Duck River, Tenn.				(Organizations not recorded.)												2d Conf.
Mch. 20	Battle	Vaught's Hill, Tenn.		1323		105th Ohio, 101st Ind., 80th and 123rd Ill. Vols., 1st Tenn. Cavalry and 6th Ind. Battery	Col. Hall, F.; Genls. Wheeler and Morgan, C.	7	K&W 300	33		20						Federal.

CHRONOLOGICAL LIST OF EVENTS (1860-1865).—Continued.

Date	Event	Location	Duration	Force F	Force C	Composition of Force	Commanders	Killed F.	Killed C.	Wounded F	Wounded C.	Prisoners taken by F.	Prisoners taken by C	Missing F	Missing C.	Guns taken	Stands of arms taken	Advantage
1863																		
Mch. 21	Skirmish	Salem Pike, Tenn.				3rd Tennessee Cavalry.												
	Engagement	Cottage Grove, Tenn	2 hours.		Guer	Federal Garrison.												Federal.
	Engagement	Deer Creek, Miss	Sev'l hours			2nd Division, 15th Corps	Gens. Stuart and Sherman, F.											Federal.
Mch. 22	Skirmish	Blue Springs, Mo		50	Guer	1st and 5th Missouri Militia Cavalry	Quantrell, C.	9						5				Conf'd.
	Capture of Mount Sterling, Ky., by Confederate Cavalry.	Mount Sterling, Ky.				10th Kentucky Cavalry	Capt. Radcliff, F; Col. Cluke, C.											Conf'd.
Mch. 24	Capture of Ponchatoula, La., by Federal Troops	Ponchatoula, La				165th and 177th N. Y., 6th Conn., 14th and 24th Maine and 6th Mich. Vols	Col. Clark, F.		4	9	10	12						Federal.
	Engagement	Danville, Ky.				1st Ky. and 2nd Tenn. Cav., 18th and 22nd Mich. Vols. and 1st Ind. Battery.												
Mch. 25	Capture of Brentwood, Tenn., by Confederate Troops	Brentwood, Tenn.		500 / 545	3000	Detachments 22nd Wis. and 9th Mich. Vols.	Col. Bloodgood, F; Gen. G. C. Smith, F					47						1 Con. 2 Fed.
	Skirmishes	Franklin and Little Harpeth, Tenn.				4th and 6th Ky., 9th Penn. and 2nd Mich. Cav.												
Mch. 26	General Burnside, U. S. A., assumes command of the Department of the Ohio																	
Mch. 27	Destruction of Jacksonville, Fla., by Federal Forces under General Rust.																	
	Engagement	Warrenton, Miss.			Batts.	Federal Steamer *Hartford*	Adm. Farragut, F.											Federal.
Mch. 28	Occupation of Cole's Island, S. C. by Federal Troops					100th New York Volunteers	Col. Dandy, F.											
	Engagement	Pattersonville, La				Federal Gunboat *Diana* with detachments 12th Conn. and 160th N. Y. Vols												
	Skirmish	Hurricane Bridge, W. Va.		1 Co.		13th West Virginia Volunteers.												
	Skirmish	Amite River, La				14th and 24th Maine Volunteers.												
Mch. 29	Attack on Federal Camp	Somerville, Tenn.			Guer	Detachment 6th Illinois Cavalry	Col. Loomis, F; Col. Richardson, C	K&W 40										Federal.
	Expedition	Jacksonville, Fla. (Baldwin)				8th Maine and 6th Conn. Vols. and 2nd U. S. Colored Troops, (1st S. C.).												
	Attack on Federal Pickets	Williamsburg, Va			Cav.	5th Pennsylvania Cavalry	Lieut. Wingel, F.	2		6			8					Conf'd.
Mch. 30	Skirmish	Tahlequah, I. T.				3rd Kansas Indian Home Guards.												
	Massacre on Steamer *Sam Gaty*	Sibley's Landing, Mo				Civilians, Missouri Militia and Contrabands.												
	Skirmish	The Island, Mo.				3rd Wisconsin Cavalry.												
	Battle	Dutton's Hills, Ky. (Somerset)	5 hours	1200		1st Ky. and 7th Ohio Cav. and 44th and 45th Ohio Mounted Volunteers and Artillery	B.-Gen. Gillmore, F.; Gen. Pegram, C.	6	K&W 200	25			30					Federal.
	Capture of Point Pleasant, W. Va., by Confederate Troops	Point Pleasant, W. Va.	4 hours.	1 Co.	Guer.	13th West Virginia Volunteers	Capt. Carter, F.; Col. Jenkins, C.	2	20	1	20	27	13					Federal.
	Occupation of Richmond, La., (Roundaway Bayou), by Federal Force		2 hours.		Cav.	69th Ind. Vols. and detachment 2nd Illinois Cavalry	Gen. McClernand, F.											
	(30th–April 4th). Attack on Washington, N. C., (Rodman's Point), by Confederate Forces	Washington, N. C.		2000		Federal Troops and Gunboat *Commodore Hull*	Maj.-Gen. Foster, F; Gens. Hill and Pettigrew, C.											Federal.
Mch. 31	Major-Gen. Herron, U. S. A., assigned to command of Army of the Frontier.																	
	Proclamation issued by President Lincoln forbidding commercial intercourse between citizens of loyal and disloyal States.																	
Apr. 1	Engagement	Grand Gulf, Miss.			Batts	Federal Gunboats *Hartford*, *Switzerland* and *Albatross*	Adm. Farragut, F.											Federal.
	Skirmish	Chalk Bluff, Ark		1 Co.		2nd Missouri Militia Cavalry.												
	Confederate Raid	Broad Run, Va.			Cav.	Detachments 1st Vt. and 5th N. Y. Cavalry	Capt. Mosby, C			2								Conf'd.
Apr. 2	Attack on Confederates	Jackson County, Mo.			Guer.	6th Kansas Cavalry	Major Hanson, F.		17									Federal.
	Skirmish	Little Rock Road, Ark		1 Co.		5th Kansas Cavalry												
	(2d-3d.) Skirmish	Woodbury, Tenn.			Cav., etc.	3rd and 4th Ohio Cavalry	Gens. Crufts and Hazen, F.		K&W 12	1		30						Federal.
	Riot at Richmond, Va., (suppressed by Militia).																	
	Engagement	Snow Hill, Tenn				2nd and 4th Ohio Cavalry	Gen. Stanley, F.	1	K&W 50	2		60						Federal.
Apr. 4	Attack on Confederate Battery	Rodman's Point, N. C.		200		Federal Infantry	Gen. Potter, F.	K&W 5										Conf'd.
	Return of Federal Troops from Scout in	Carroll County, Ark				1st Arkansas Cavalry	Capt. Worthington, F		22	1		7						
	Skirmish	Madison, Ark.				3rd Iowa Cavalry.												
	Destruction of Palmyra, Tenn., by Gunboat *Lexington*, under Lieut. L. Fitch, U. S. N.																	
Apr. 5	(5th-10th). Expedition	Black Bayou, Miss.				Division of 15th Corps	Maj.-Gen. Steele, F.											Federal.
	Bombardment	Hill's Point, N. C.	2 hours.		Batts	Federal Gunboats												Conf'd.
Apr. 6	Raid on Confederate Camp	Green Hill, Tenn.		350		Federal Cavalry	Gen. Mitchell, F.		5	1		16						Federal.
	Capture of Federal Steamer *Fox* (Whittemore), at Pass a L'Outre, Mississippi, by Confederate Troops.																	
	Expedition of Federal Gunboats *Hartford*, *Switzerland* and *Albatross* to Bayou Sara on the Mississippi.																	
Apr. 7	Bombardment	Fort Sumter, S. C.	2 hours.			South Atlantic Squadron *Keokuk*, *Weehawken*, *Passaic*, *Montauk*, *Patapsco*, *New Ironsides*, *Catskill*, *Nantucket* and *Nahant*	Adm. Du Pont, F			19								Conf'd.
	Reconnaissance on Amite River, La., and loss of the Federal Gunboat *Barataria*.																	
	Reconnaissance of Federal Troops under Colonel Grimshaw into Gloucester Co., Va.																	
Apr. 8	Engagement	St. Francis County, Mo.				Detachment of Cavalry and 1 company 4th Iowa Cavalry	Major Winslow, F.											
	Engagement	Broad River, S. C.				3rd Rhode Island Artillery on Gunboat *Washington*.												
	Reconnaissance up Broad River, S. C., and destruction of the Federal Gunboat *George Washington* by Confederate Troops							2		6								Conf'd.

CHRONOLOGICAL LIST OF EVENTS (1860-1865).—Continued.

DATE.	EVENT	LOCATION	DURATION	FORCE F.	FORCE C.	COMPOSITION OF FORCE.	COMMANDERS	KILLED F.	KILLED C.	WOUNDED F.	WOUNDED C.	PRISONERS TAKEN BY F.	PRISONERS TAKEN BY C.	MISSING F.	MISSING C.	Guns taken.	Stands of Arms taken.	ADVANTAGE.
1863																		
Apr. 9	Expedition to	East Pascagoula, Miss.		180	Cav. etc.	74th U. S. Colored Troops (2nd Louisiana).	Col. Daniels, F.		20									Federal.
	Skirmish	Blount's Mills, N. C.	1 hour			3rd and 17th Mass., 1st R. I. and 3rd N. Y. Artillery	Capt. Pond, F.			10								Conf'd.
Apr. 10	Skirmish	Waverley, Tenn.		1 Co.	1 Co.	5th Iowa Cavalry	Maj. Blondin, C.					21						Federal.
	Confederate Attack	Franklin and Harpeth River, Tenn.	4½ hours			40th Ohio Regt. and portion of Granger's Cav. Division.	Gen. Granger, F. Gen. Van Dorn, C.	100	k & w 300			70						Federal.
	Skirmish	Antioch Station, Tenn.				Detachment 10th Michigan Volunteers.												
	Raid on Confederate Troops	Germantown, Ky.				Federal Cavalry	Lieut. Rickertson, F. —— Caldwell, C.		1		3							Federal.
Apr. 11	Attack on Federal Camp	Whittaker's Mills, Va.				5th Penn. Cav., 50th Va. Regiment. (Confederate)	Col. Tabb, C.	5			3		10					Conf'd.
	Skirmish	Blackwater, Va.		Pkts.		Federal Troops												Federal.
	Expedition of Federal Troops under Colonel Streight into Alabama and Georgia																	
Apr. 12	(12th–14th). Skirmishes	Irish Bend, La. Bisland, La.				Grover's Division, 19th Corps. Emory's and Weitzel's Divisions, 19th Corps.												
	(12th–May 4th). Siege	Suffolk, Va.				Troops of Department of Virginia and North Carolina	Maj.-Gen. Peck, F.											
	Reconnoissance from	Gloucester Point, Va.		180	Cav. 20	Federal Infantry	Lieut.-Col. Tevis, F. Col. Goodwin, C.					2						Federal.
Apr. 13	Skirmish	Suffolk, Va.				Detachment of Federal Troops	Col. Spear, F.											Conf'd.
	(13th–14th) Attack on Confederate Works	Bayou Teche, La.	Sev'l hours			Federal Forces	Genls. Banks and Emory, F.	350										Federal.
Apr. 14	Engagement	West Branch and Nansemond, Va.	4 hours		Batt.	Federal Gunboats *Commodore Barney, West End, Mount Washington*, and *Stepping Stones*	Lieut. Cushing, U.S.N.	5		7								Federal.
	Destruction of the Confederate Gunboats *Diana, Hart*, and *Queen of the West.*																	
	Attack on Federal Gunboat *West End*, near Suffolk, Va., by Confederate Battery	Suffolk, Va.			Batt.	Federal Gunboat *West End*		k & w 7										Conf'd.
Apr. 15	Siege of Washington, N. C., raised by Confederates.																	
	Fight with Indians	Spanish Fork Cañon, Utah Territory			200	2nd California Cavalry	Col. Evans, F.	1	30	2								Federal.
	Engagement	Pikeville, Ky.		200		39th Kentucky Mounted Infantry	Col. Dills, F.					73						Federal.
	Skirmish	Dunbar's Plantation, La.				2nd Illinois Cavalry.												
	Occupation of Franklin, La., by Federal Forces under General Banks.																	
Apr. 16	Running of Batteries, Vicksburg, Miss., by Federal Vessels	Vicksburg, Miss.				Ironclads and Transports of Commodore Porter's Fleet and General Grant's Army.	Commodore Porter, F.											Federal.
	Fight with Indians	Medalia, Minn.		18	Inds.	7th Minn. Volunteers		1		2								
Apr. 17	Skirmish	South Quay, Va.				Detachments 99th and 130th New York Volunteers		2		3								Federal.
	Skirmish	Bear Creek, Cherokee Station, and Lundy's Lane, Ala.				10th Missouri and 7th Kansas Cavalry	Gen. Dodge, F.	1										Federal.
	Engagement	Bayou Vermillion, La.				Division of the 19th Corps	Brig.-Gen. Grover, F.											Federal.
	(17th–May 2d). Expedition from	La Grange, Tenn. to Baton Rouge, La.				6th and 7th Ill. and 2nd Iowa Cavalry	Col. Grierson, F.											Federal.
Apr. 18	Engagement	Hernando, Miss.				2nd Brigade Cav. Div. and Inf. and Art. from the 16th Corps.	Gen. Smith, F.											
	Reconnoissance	Sabine Pass, Texas				Crews of the Gunboats *Cayuga* and *New London*		1		5			8					Conf'd.
	Attack on Federal Troops	Fayetteville, Ark.	4 hours			1st Arkansas Volunteers and 1st Arkansas Cavalry	Col. Harrison, F. Brig.-Gen. Cabell, C.	4	20	26	50	50	16	25			100	Federal.
	Skirmish	Battery Huger, Va. (Hill's Point)				Detachment 89th N. Y. and 8th Conn. Vols.												
Apr. 19	Skirmish	New Albany, Miss.				7th Illinois Cavalry.												
	Engagement	Coldwater, Miss.				2nd Brig., Cav. Div. and Inf. and Artillery from the 16th Corps	Col. Bryant, F.	10	20	20	40							Federal.
Apr. 20	Skirmish	Celina, Ky.				5th Indiana Cavalry												Federal.
	Engagement	Patterson, Mo.		400		3rd Missouri Militia Cavalry	Col. Smart, F.	k & w 50										Conf'd.
	(20th–?). Occupation of McMinnville, Tenn., by Federal Forces					1st Brigade of Cavalry, Army of the Cumberland	Col. Minty, F.											
	Capture of	Bute La Rose, La.				Federal Gunboats *Estrella, Clifton, Arizona* and *Calhoun*	Capt. Cook, U. S. N.	1										Federal.
Apr. 21	(21st–22d). Skirmish	Palo Alto, Miss.				2nd Iowa Cavalry.												
	Capture of Confederate Cavalry	Berryville, Va.				1st New York Cavalry and 2nd Virginia Infantry	Lieuts. Powell and Wykoff, F. Capt. Laypole, C.					8						Federal.
Apr. 22	Confederate Raid	Tompkinsville, Ky.				(Organizations not recorded)		5										Conf'd.
	Skirmish	Strasburg Road, Va.			300	3rd West Virginia Cavalry	Major McGee, F.	1	6	1	9	25						Federal.
	Occupation of McMinnville, Tenn., by Federal Forces.																	
Apr. 23	Engagement	Chuckatuck, Va.			Cav. 40	Crew of the Federal Gunboat *Commodore Barney*	Lieut. Cushing, U. S. N.	1	2									Federal.
Apr. 24	Skirmish	Webber Falls, Ark.				Federal Troops	Col. Phillips, F.											Federal.
	Occupation of Tuscumbia, Ala., by Federal Forces					2nd Division, 16th Corps	Gen. Dodge, F. Col. Chalmers, C.											Federal.
	Attack on Federal Outpost	Beverly, W. Va.	4 hours	1000		5th West Virginia Cavalry	Col. Latham, F. —— Imboden and Jackson, C.											Conf'd.
	Skirmish	White Water, Mo.				1st Wisconsin Cavalry.												
Apr. 25	Engagement	Little Rock Landing, (Duck River Shoal), Tenn.			Batt.	Ellet's Miss. Ram Fleet, Gunboat *Lexington* and ram *Monarch*	Lieut. Com. Fitch, U. S. N. Gen. Ellet, F.	2	k & w 25	1								Federal.
	Engagement	Greenland Gap, W. Va.	1¾ hours			Detachments 23rd Ill. and 14th W. Va. Vols.	Col. Wallace, F. Gen. W. E. Jones, C.	2		4								Federal.
Apr. 26	Attack by Confederates on the town of	Cape Girardeau, Mo.				1st Wis. and 2nd Mo. Militia Cav., 32nd Iowa Vols. and Batteries D and L, 1st Mo. Artillery	Gen. McNeil, F. Gen. Marmaduke, C.		1									Federal.

CHRONOLOGICAL LIST OF EVENTS (1860-1865).—Continued.

DATE.	EVENT.	LOCATION.	DURATION.	FORCE F.	FORCE C.	COMPOSITION OF FORCE.	COMMANDER.	KILLED F.	KILLED C.	WOUNDED F.	WOUNDED C.	PRISONERS TAKEN BY F.	PRISONERS TAKEN BY C.	MISSING F.	MISSING C.	GUNS TAKEN.	STANDS OF ARMS TAKEN.	ADVANTAGE.
1863																		
Apr. 26	Capture of Confederate Troops	Franklin, Tenn.				Federal Cavalry	Col. Watkins, F.											Federal.
	(26th–May 3d). Raid from	Tuscumbia, Ala., to Rome, Ga. (Day's Gap, Black Warrior Creek and Blount's Farm)				3rd Ohio, 51st and 73rd Indiana Vols., 80th Ill. Mounted Inf. and 2 Cos. 1st Ala. Cav.	Col. Streight, F.											
	(27th–May 7th.) Stoneman's Raid through	Virginia		5000		Cavalry Corps, Army of the Potomac	Maj.-Gen. Stoneman, F.	2		W & M 98		200						
Apr. 29	Skirmish	Rowe's Ford, Ky. (Weaver's Store)		60	Pkts.	1st Kentucky Cavalry	Capt. Alexander, F.					4						Federal.
	Engagement	Dover Road, N. C.				Troops of the District of North Carolina	Brig.-Gen. Palmer, F.											
	Engagement	Town Creek, Ala.				Portion of the 16th Corps	Maj.-Gen. Dodge, F.											
	Skirmish	Union Church, Miss.				6th Illinois Cavalry.												
Apr. 29	Skirmish	Castor River and Bloomfield, Mo.				1st Wisconsin Cavalry.												
	Capture of Fairmount, W. Va., by Confederate Forces	Fairmount, W. Va.		800	4000	Detachments 106th N. Y., 6th W. Va. and Va. Militia	Capt. Chamberlain, F. / Gen. W. E. Jones, C.	1	K & W 90	4								Conf'd.
	Attack by Federal Gunboats	Grand Gulf, Miss.	3 hours		Batt.	Federal Gunboats *Louisville, Carondelet, Mound City, Pittsburg, Tuscumbia, Benton* and *Lafayette*	Adm. Porter, F.	21										Conf'd.
	(29th–30th). Engagement	Fitzhugh's Crossing, Va.				1st Corps, Army of the Potomac.												
Apr. 30	Reconnoissance and Skirmish	Spottsylvania Court House, Va.			Cav.	Detachment 6th New York Cavalry	Lt.-Col. McVicar, F. / Gen. Fitz-Hugh Lee, C.	K W & P 32										Conf'd.
	Skirmish	Snyder's Bluff, Miss.				Portions of the 13th Corps.												
	(30th–May 1st). Skirmishes	Chalk Bluff and St. Francis River, Mo.				3rd Mo. and 1st Iowa Cav., 2nd Mo. Militia and Battery E, 1st Mo. Light Artillery.												
	(30th–May 1st). Skirmishes	Day's Gap, Sand Mountain and Black Warrior Creek, Ala.				Federal Troops	Col. Streight, F. / Gen. Forrest, C.											Conf'd.
May 1	Battle	Port Gibson, Miss. (Thompson's Hill and Magnolia Hills)	12 hours		11,000	13th Corps, 3rd Division, 17th Corps, Gen. Grant's Com.	Maj.-Gen. Grant, F. / Maj.-Gen. McClernand, F. / Maj.-Gen. Bowen, C.	130	K & W 1000	718		500		5			4	Federal.
	(1st–4th). Battle	Chancellorsville, Va. (including Fredericksburg, Salem Heights, and Marye's Heights)		130,000	62,000	1st, 2nd, 3rd, 5th, 6th, 11th, 12th Corps, Army of the Potomac	M.-Gen. Hooker, F. / M.-Gen. Sedgwick, F. / Gen. Lee, C.	K & W 18,000	K & W 18,000			5000	17,000					Conf'd.
	Skirmish	La Grange, Ark.			Cav.	Detachment 3rd Iowa Cavalry	Capt. D. Huff, F.	K, W & M 41										Conf'd.
	Engagement	Monticello, Ky.		5000		2nd Tenn., 1st Ky., 2nd and 7th Ohio Cav., 45th Ohio and 112th Ill. Mounted Infantry	Gen. Carter, F. / Col. Morrison, C.											Federal.
	Skirmish	South Quay Bridge, Va.	2 hours			Detachment 99th New York Volunteers	Lieut.-Col. Mixon, F.	K & W 41										Federal.
	Skirmish	Tickfaw River, Miss.				7th Illinois Cavalry.												
	Skirmish	Rapidan Station, Va.				Averill's Cavalry Division, Army of the Potomac.												
	Skirmish	Louisa Court House, Va.				3 Companies 1st Maine Cavalry, Detachment of Stoneman's Raiding Forces												
May 2	Engagement	Nansemond River, Va.		Art.	Art.	Federal Troops and Gunboat	Gen. Getty, F.	K & W 41										Federal.
May 3	Skirmishes	Blount's Farm, Ala.				51st and 73rd Ind. and 80th Ill. Vols., 3rd Ohio Mounted Infantry and 1st Alabama Cavalry	Col. Streight, F. / Gen. Forrest, C.	12		69								Conf'd.
	Skirmish	Warrenton Junction, Va.			Guer. 300	1st W. Va. and 5th N. Y. Cavalry	Col. De Forest, F. / Gen. Mosby, C.	1		16		23						Federal.
	Grand Gulf, Miss., occupied by Federal Forces under Admiral Porter.																	
	Skirmish	Forty Hills, Miss. (Hankinson's Ferry)				7th Division, 17th Corps, General Grant's Command.												
May 4	Skirmish	Shannon Hill, Va.				5th New York Cavalry.												
	Skirmish	Tunstall Station, Va.				12th Illinois Cavalry.												
	(Siege raised)	Suffolk, Va.				Troops of Department of Virginia and North Carolina.												
May 5	Occupation of Fort de Russey, Red River, by Federal Forces under Admiral Porter.																	
	Expedition of Federal Troops (3d N. Y. Cavalry) to Pettie's Mills, N. C., and capture of a Company of Confederates	Pettie's Mills, N. C.				3d N. Y. Cavalry						1 Co.						Federal.
May 6	Engagement	Tupelo, Miss.	½ hour			10th Missouri and 7th Kansas Cavalry	Col. Cornyn, F. / Gen. Ruggles, C.					90						Federal.
	Occupation of Alexandria, Miss., by Federal Forces under Admiral Porter.																	
	The Army of the Potomac, under Major-General Hooker, U. S. A., withdrawn from Fredericksburg to the north bank of the Rappahannock River	Fredericksburg, Va.				Army of the Potomac	Maj.-Gen. Hooker, F.											
May 7	Reconnoissance of Federal Troops from West Point, to White House, Va.																	
May 8	Commencement of Attack on Confederate Batteries	Port Hudson, Miss.			Batts.	Federal Gunboats and Mortar Schooners.												
	General Van Dorn, C. S. A., shot by Dr. Peters of Maury County, Tenn.																	
May 9	Scout near	Stone River, Tenn.				2nd Indiana Cavalry	Col. McCook, F.					8						Federal.
May 10	Engagement	Civique's Ferry, La.				14th and 24th Maine, 177th N. Y. Vols. and 21st N. Y. Battery.												
	General T. J. Jackson, C. S. A., ("Stonewall") died at Guinness Station, Va.																	
May 11	Engagement	Horse Shoe Bend, Ky. (Greasy Creek)	7 hours		Cav.	Detachment Federal Troops	Col. R. T. Jacobs, F. / Gen. Morgan, C.	K & W 25	K & W 109									Conf'd.
	Skirmish	Mount Vernon, Ark.				5th Kansas and 5th Illinois Cavalry	Col. Powell Clayton, F.											
	Occupation and Destruction of Crystal Springs, Miss., by Federal Cav.																	

CHRONOLOGICAL LIST OF EVENTS (1860-1865).—Continued.

DATE.	EVENT.	LOCATION.	DURATION.	FORCE. F	FORCE. C.	COMPOSITION OF FORCE.	COMMANDERS.	KILLED. F.	KILLED. C.	WOUNDED. F	WOUNDED. C.	PRISONERS TAKEN BY F.	PRISONERS TAKEN BY C.	MISSING. F.	MISSING. C.	Guns Lost.	Stands of Arms Lost.	ADVANTAGE.
1863 May 12	Raid on Confederate Troops	LINDEN, TENN		65	120	1st Western Tennessee Cavalry	Col. Breckinridge, F		3			47						Federal.
	Skirmish	FOURTEEN MILE CREEK, MISS.				13th and 15th Corps, General Grant's Command		4		24				5				Federal.
	Engagement	RAYMOND, MISS.	3 hours			17th Corps, General Grant's Command	Gen. McPherson, F. Gen. Gregg, C.	51	75	181	236	186		23				Federal.
May 13	Capture of Yazoo City, Miss., by Federal Gunboats under Lieut Walker, U. S. N.																	
	Skirmish	CALL'S FERRY, MISS.				2nd Illinois Cavalry.												
	Skirmish	PONTCHATOULA, LA.			Guer & I'ds	Colonel Davis's Command	Col. Davis, F.					Ind. 17						Federal.
	Attack on train by Confederate Troops	SOUTH UNION, KY.			Guer.	Federal Guard												Federal.
May 14	Capture of	JACKSON, MISS.	3 hours			15th and 17th Corps, General Grant's Command	Gen. Crocker and Sherman, F. Gen. J. E. Johnston, C.	40	k&w 400	240				6	6			Federal.
	Scout to	WARRENTON JUNCTION, VA.			Cav	(Organizations not specified)				8								Federal.
May 15	Expedition and Engagement	CAMP MOORE, LA.				Federal Troops	Col. Davis, F.											Federal.
	(15th–16th) Expedition and Skirmishes	CARRSVILLE and SUFFOLK, VA. (Holland House)				Federal Troops	Brig.-Gen. Foster, F.											—
	Capture of a Company Federal Cavalry by Confederates at Charlestown, Va., (re-captured on 16th).																	
May 16	Skirmish	CARTHAGE, MO.				7th Missouri Militia Cavalry.												
	Recapture of Federal Cavalry	PIEDMONT STATION, VA.				West Virginia and Pennsylvania Cavalry	Capt. Vitt, F.	2	2			40						Federal.
	Federal Cavalry Charge	CRIPPLE CREEK, VA. (Bradyville)		85	85	Detachment 5th Tennessee Cavalry	Gen. Palmer, F. Lt.-Col. Thompson, C.					18						Federal.
	Engagement	CHAMPION HILLS, MISS. (Baker's Creek and Edward's Station)	6½ hours		25,000	Hovey's Division, 13th Corps and 17th Corps, Grant's Command	Gen. Grant, F. Gen. Hovey, F. Gen. Pemberton, C.	426	k&w 3000	1842		3000		180		29		Federal.
	Attack on Confederate Troops	BERRY'S FERRY, VA.		16	22	Detachment 1st New York Cavalry	Lieut. Vermillion, F		2		5	10						Federal.
May 17	Engagement	BIG BLACK RIVER, MISS	1 hour			Carr's and Osterhaus's Divisions, 13th Corps, Grant's Army	Gen. Grant, F., Gen. McClernand, F., Gen. Pemberton, C.	29		242		1800		9		18		Federal.
	(17th–20th). Skirmish	FAYETTEVILLE, VA.		Pkts.		12th and 91st Ohio Vols. and 2nd W. Va. Cavalry	Capt. Wilson, F.	K, W & M. 17										Federal.
	Evacuation of Jackson, Miss., by Federal Forces under General Grant																	
May 18	Attack on Federal Troops	SHERWOOD, MO.		54	Guer. 206	Detachments 2nd Kansas Artillery and 1st Kansas (20th U. S. Colored Troops) Volunteers	Maj. Ward, F. Col. Livingston, C	17		18			4					Conf'd.
	Attack on the Transport *Crescent City*	ISLAND NO. 82, MISS.				3rd Iowa Volunteers.												
	Occupation of Haine's Bluff, Yazoo River, by Federal Forces under Admiral Porter.																	
	Two parties of Federal Troops fire into each other by mistake	CARRSVILLE, VA.				170th New York Volunteers		3		4								
	Siege. (18th–July 4th). 1st Assault, 19th; 2d Assault, 22d; surrender, July 4th)	VICKSBURG, MISS.				13th, 15th and 17th Corps, Grant's command and Mississippi Fleet, 3 Divisions, 16th Corps, 2 Divisions, 9th Corps and Division from Department of the Missouri.	Gen. Grant, F. Admiral Porter, F. Gen. Pemberton, C.	545	k, w & m. 3277	3688				303				Federal.
May 19	Skirmish	WINCHESTER, VA.				Detachment of Cavalry, Milroy's command	Gen. Milroy, F.		6			7						Federal.
	Capture by Confederate Guerillas of	RICHMOND, MO.				25th Missouri Volunteers		3										Conf'd.
May 20	Engagement	FORT GIBSON and FORT BLOUNT, IND. TERR.				6th Kan. and 3rd Wis. Cav. and 1st, 2nd and 3rd Kan. Indian Home Guards	Col. Phillips, F.	23		13								Federal.
	(Second assault on Fortifications)	VICKSBURG, MISS				Army of the Tennessee	Gen. Grant, F.											
	(20th–26th)	FREDERICKSBURG, VA.				8th Illinois Cavalry	Lt.-Col. Clendenin, F.											
May 21	Attack on Confederate Camp	MIDDLETON, TENN.				4th Mich., 3rd Ind., 7th Penn., 3rd and 4th Ohio, 4th U. S. Cav. and 39th Indiana Mounted Inf.	Gen. Stanley, F.			8		90						Federal.
		PLAINS STORE, LA.				1st Division, Augur's 19th Corps.												
	Vicksburg, Miss., completely invested by Fed. Forces under Gen. Grant																	
May 22	Reconnoissance	GUM SWAMP, N. C.				158th Penn. and 5th, 25th, 27th and 46th Mass. Vols. and Bogg's Battery	Col. J. R. Jones, F.	1				165						1 Con 2 Fed
	Skirmish	MIDDLETON, TENN.			Scts. 18	Detachments 103rd Illinois and 1 company Unionists	Capt. Street, C.					11						Federal.
	General assault	VICKSBURG MISS.	9 hours	30,000	25,000	Army of the Tennessee	Gen. Grant, F. Adm. Porter, F.											Conf'd.
May 23		BATCHELOR'S CREEK, N. C.				58th Pennsylvania and 46th Massachusetts Volunteers.												
	Engagement.	BEAVER DAM LAKE, MISS				Miss. Marine Brig. of Cav. and Inf.	Brig. Gen Ellet F											Federal.
	Destruction of Austin, Miss., Federal Forces. (24th–?)																	
May 24	General Schofield, U. S. A., assumed command of the Department of the West, vice General Curtis.																	
May 25	Skirmish	FISHING CREEK, KY.				(Organizations not recorded)												Federal.
	Skirmish	POLK'S PLANTATION, ARK.				3rd Iowa and 5th Kan. Cav.												
	Skirmish	FRANKLIN, LA				41st Mass. Vols. and other Regiments	Col. Chickering, F.											
	Attack on Confederate Troops	SENATOBIA, MISS.				3rd Illinois Cavalry	Col. McCrellis, F.		6		8							Federal
May 27	Skirmish	LAKE PROVIDENCE, LA.				47th United States Colored Troops.												
	Siege (27th–July 9th)	PORT HUDSON, LA.	8 hours		Batt	16 Divisions, 19th Corps, Maj.-Gen. Bank's Army of the Gulf and Federal Fleet	Adm Farragut, F. Gen. Banks, F. Gen. Gardner, C.	600	k, w & m 7208	2500								Conf'd.
	Engagement	FLORENCE, ALA.				Brigade of Cavalry	Col. Cornyn, F.											

CHRONOLOGICAL LIST OF EVENTS (1860-1865).—Continued.

Date	Event	Location	Duration	Force F.	Force C.	Composition of Force	Commanders	Killed F.	Killed C.	Wounded F.	Wounded C.	Prisoners Taken by F.	Prisoners Taken by C.	Missing F.	Missing C.	Guns taken	Stands of arms taken	Advantage
1863																		
May 28	Engagement	Stony Creek, Mo. (Little Black River)	½ hour			13th Illinois Cavalry	Major Lippert, F.	K.W. & M. 50										Conf'd.
May 29	Engagement	Mechanicsville, Miss.				Portion of the 17th Corps	Maj.-Gen. Blair, F.											
	Skirmish	Thoroughfare Gap, Va.			Cav. Scts.	Detachment 1st Vermont Cavalry			1		2	1	1					Federal.
May 30	Skirmish	Greenwich, Va.			100	1st Vermont, 5th New York and 7th Michigan Cavalry	Lt.-Col. Preston, F.; —— Mosby, C.											Federal.
	Attack on Confederate Camp	Carthage, Tenn.				Detachment 26th Ohio Regiment						23						Federal.
	Capture of Tappahannock, Va., by four Federal Gunboats.																	
May 31	Reconnoissance of Federal Cavalry from Somerset to Monticello, Ky.								16									Federal.
	Destruction of the Federal Gunboat *Alert*, in Navy Yard, Norfolk, Va.																	
	Engagement	Rocheport, Mo.			Guer.	1st Mo. Enrolled Militia and 9th Mo. Militia Cavalry		10										Conf'd.
June 1	Expedition of Federal Troops under Colonel Montgomery, up the Combahee River, S. C.																	
	Engagement	Clinton, La.				Federal Troops	Col. Grierson, F.		K.&W. 21									—
June 2	Evacuation of West Point, Va., by Federal Troops																	
June 3	Destruction of Ashepoo, S. C., by Federal Forces under Colonel Montgomery	Ashepoo, S. C.																
June 4	Engagement	Clinton, La.				Federal Cavalry	Col. Grierson, F.											
	Engagement	Mechanicsburg and Sartoria, Miss.	½ hour		2000	3rd Illinois Cavalry and 5th Wisconsin Volunteers	Gen. Kimball, F.; Gen. Wirt Adams, C.	1		17		10						Federal
	Scout	Frying Pan, Va.		Rear Guard	100	Detachment 5th Michigan Cavalry	Colonel Gray, F.	3				1						Federal.
	Attack on Federal Garrison	Franklin, Tenn.				35th Ind. Vols., 4th, 6th and 7th Ky., 9th Penn., and 2nd Mich. Cavalry	Col. Baird, F.; Gen. Forrest, C.											Federal.
	Skirmish	Bluffton, S. C.				(Troops not specified.)												
	Destruction of Simmsport, La., by Federal Ram *Switzerland*, commanded by Lieut.-Col. Ellet	Simmsport, La.																
June 5	Engagement	Franklin's Crossing, Va.				26th N. J. and 5th Vt. Vols., 15th and 50th N. Y. Engineers and 6th Corps												
	Reconnoissance across the Rappahannock at Deep Run, by the 2d Division, 6th Army Corps, under General Howe							6		35		3						
June 6	(4th–7). Attack on Federal Cavalry	Murfreesboro', Tenn.		Pkts.	Cav.	2nd and 8th (?) Indiana Cavalry	Col. Harrison, F.; Gen. Wheeler, C.											Federal.
	Destruction of Shawneetown, Kan., by Confederate Bushwhackers	Shawneetown, Ks.				(Organizations not recorded)	—— Gordon and Yeager, C.	4										Conf'd.
	Attack on Federal Wagon-Train	Berryville, Va.			100	Detachment 67th Pennsylvania Volunteers		1										Conf'd.
	(6th–8th). Battle	Milliken's Bend, La. (Ashland)	(Actual) 24 hours	1400	2700	5th U. S. Colored Heavy Art., 9th La., 40th U. S. Colored Troops, 11th La., 51st U.S. Colored Troops, 1st Miss. and 23rd Iowa Vols., Gunboats *Choctaw* and *Lexington*	B.-Gen. Dennis, F.; Gen. Kirby Smith, C.	154	200	223	W.&M. 500			115				Federal.
June 7	Railroad Bridge at Brentwood, Tenn., burned by Confederate Guerillas	Brentwood, Tenn.																
June 9	Organization of Military Districts of "The Frontier" and "The Border," under General Blunt and Brig.-Gen. Ewing.																	
	Organization of Military Departments of the Monongahela and the Susquehanna, under Major-Generals Brooks and Couch.																	
	Engagement	Fort Lyons, Va.				3rd New York Artillery.												
	Engagement	Monticello and Rocky Gap, Ky.			Cav.	2nd and 7th Ohio and 1st Ky. Cav., 45th Ohio and 2nd Tenn. Mounted Infantry	Cols. Carter and Kautz, F.; —— Pegram, C.											Federal.
	Engagement	Beverly Ford and Brandy Station, Va.			Cav. 12000	2nd, 3rd and 7th Wis., 2nd and 33rd Mass., 6th Me., 86th and 104th N. Y. Vols., 1st, 2nd, 5th and 6th U. S., 2nd, 6th, 8th, 9th and 10th N. Y., 1st Md., 8th Ill., 3rd Ind., 1st, N. J., 1st, 6th and 17th Penn., 1st Me., and 3rd W. Va. Cav.	Gens. Pleasanton, Buford and Gregg, F.; Gen. Stuart, C.	K.W. & M. 500	K.W. & M. 750									—
	Attack on Federal Cavalry	Triune, Tenn.				Federal Cavalry Division	Gen. Mitchell, F.; Gen. Forrest, C.	K.W. & P. 100										Federal.
June 10	Skirmish	Lake Providence, La.				(Organizations not recorded.)												
June 11	Port Hudson, La., completely invested by Federal Troops under General Banks.																	
	Destruction of Darien, Ga., by Federal Troops under Colonel Montgomery	Darien, Ga.																
	Attack by Confederate Cavalry	Triune, Tenn.				Federal Troops	Gen. Forrest, C.	6	21		10	60						Federal.
	Attack on Federal Cavalry	Slate Creek, near Mt. Sterling, Ky.	3 hours		300	1st Tennessee and 14th Kentucky Cavalry	—— Everett, F.											Conf'd.
	Capture of Federal Cavalry	Port Hudson, La.		5 Cos.		14th New York Cavalry	Maj. Mulvey, F.; Col. Logan, C.						5 Cos.					Conf'd.
	Organization of Reserve Corps, under Maj.-Gen. Granger, U. S. A.																	
	Attack on Federal Cavalry	Seneca, Md.		1 Co.	Cav. 250	6th Michigan Cavalry		4	2	1								Conf'd.
	Skirmish	Middleton, Va.			Cav. 400	13th Penn. Cav., 87th Penn. Vols. and Battery L, 5th Artillery	Col. Shaw, F.		8			37						Federal.
*5	Attack on Federal Forces	Berryville, Va.		8000		1st Brigade, Milroy's Division	Col. McReynolds, F.; Gen. Rhodes, C.											Conf'd.
	Reconnoissance of Federal Troops under General Corcoran, from Suffolk, Va., to the Blackwater.																	
	Brig.-General Gillmore assumes command of the Department of the South, vice Maj.-Gen. Hunter relieved.																	

CHRONOLOGICAL LIST OF EVENTS (1860-1865).—Continued.

DATE.	EVENT.	LOCATION.	DURATION.	FORCE. F	FORCE. C	COMPOSITION OF FORCE.	COMMANDERS.	KILLED. F	KILLED. C	WOUNDED. F	WOUNDED. C	PRISONERS TAKEN BY F	PRISONERS TAKEN BY C	MISSING. F	MISSING. C	GUNS LOST.	STANDS OF ARMS TAKEN.	ADVANTAGE.
1863																		
June 13	(13th–15th). Battle	WINCHESTER, VA.		7000	18,000	2nd, 67th and 87th Penn., 18th Conn., 12th W. Va., 110th, 116th, 122nd and 123rd Ohio, 3rd, 5th and 6th Md., 12th and 13th Penn., 1st N. Y., and 1st and 3rd W. Va. Cav., Bat. L, 5th U. S. Art., 1st W. Va. Bat., Balt. Bat. and 1 Co. 14th Mass Heavy Art., of the 2nd Div., 8th Corps	Gen. Milroy, F.; Gen. Ewell, C.	K, W & M & T's M. 3000	850							29	3000	1. Fed. 2. Con.
	Attack on Confederate Troops	WILSON'S CREEK, KY.		Guer.		Kentucky Provost Guard	Capt. Haro, F.; —— Bine, C.		4			5						Federal.
	Destruction of Eunice, Ala., by Federal Gunboat *Marmora*.																	
June 14	Occupation of Martinsburg, Va., by Confederate Forces					106th N. Y. and 126th Ohio Vols. and W. Va. Bat., 3rd Brigade, 2nd Div., 8th Corps	B.-Gen. Tyler, F.; Gen. Rodes, C.		1		2		150					Conf'd.
	(Second assault on Fortifications).	PORT HUDSON, LA.				Army of the Gulf	Gen. Banks, F.; Gen. Gardner, C.											Conf'd.
	Occupation of Hagerstown, Md., by Confederate Troops.																	
June 16	Attack on Confederate Forces	RICHMOND, MISS.			4000	Gen. Mower's Brg. and Ellet's Miss. Marine Brig.	Bg.-Gen. Ellet, F.; M.-Gn. Walker, C.											Federal.
	Occupation of New-Kent Court House, Richmond, Va., by Federal Troops under General Keyes.																	
	Chambersburg, Pa., sacked by Confederate Cavalry under General Jenkins	CHAMBERSBURG, PA.					Gen. Jenkins, C.											Conf'd.
June 16	Engagement	TRIPLETT'S BRIDGE, KY.			Cav.	10th and 14th Ky. and 7th and 9th Mich. Cav., 16th Mich. Vols. and 11th Mich. Battery	Col. De Courcey, F.; —— Pate Everett, C.	1		3		100						Federal.
	Skirmish	JORNADA DEL MUERTO, N. M.		1 Co.		1st New Mexico Cavalry.												
	Occupation of Littlestown, Pa., by Confederate Cavalry.																	
	Harper's Ferry, Va., invested by Confederate Troops.																	
	Engagement	FLEMING COUNTY, KY.				18th Michigan Volunteers		15		30								Federal.
June 17	Skirmish	ORLEANS, IND.	1 hour	100	Guer.	Home Guards				3			12					Conf'd.
	Engagement	ALDIE, VA.	3 hours			2nd and 4th N. Y., 6th Ohio, 1st Mass., 1st Me. and 1st R. I. Cav.	Gn. Kilpatrick, F.; Gen. Stuart, C.					100						Federal.
	Attack on Federal Troops	WESTPORT, MO.		70	Guer.	6th Kansas Volunteers	Capt. Fletcher, F.	10		W & M 17								Conf'd.
	Capture of the *Atlanta* by the Federal Ironclads *Weehawken* and *Nahant*.	WARSAW SOUND, GA.				Federal Ironclads	Comm. Downes, U. S. N.; Cpt. Rodgers, U. S. N.; Capt. Webb, C. S. N.		1		16							Federal.
June 18	Confederate Raid	PLACQUEMINE, LA.			Cav. 300	(Organizations not recorded)	Col. Phillips, C.											
	Occupation of Middleburg and Philomont, Va., by Federal Cavalry.																	
	Engagement	ROCKY CROSSING, MISS.		600	2500	10th Ill. Mounted Infantry, 5th Ohio Cavalry and Detachment 10th Missouri	Lt. Col. Phillips, F.; Gen. Ruggles, C.	7	35	28	100	30						Federal.
	Evacuation of Chambersburg, Pa., by Confederate Forces.																	
June 19	Skirmish	BUCK ISLAND near LEAVENWORTH, IND.				Home Guards	Major Glendenin, F.											
	Skirmishes	MIDDLEBURG, VA.	8 hours			1st Me., 2nd, 4th and 10th N. Y., 4th and 16th Penn. and 6th Ohio Cav.	Gen. Gregg, F.; Gen. Kilpatrick, F.	K & W 50	K & W 30			40						Federal.
	Evacuation of Boonsboro, Md., by Confederate Forces.																	
June 20	Engagement	JACKSON'S CROSS ROADS, LA.				Detachs. 6th and 7th Ill. and 2nd R. I. Cav., 52nd Mass. Volunteers and Section of Artillery												Federal.
	Skirmish	GREENCASTLE, PENN.			Cav.	1st New York Cavalry						20						Federal.
	Skirmish	WARM SPRINGS, FORT MCRAE, N. M.				Detachment 1st New Mexico Cavalry.												
	Fight with Indians	PAWNEE RESERVATION		1 Co.		2nd Nebraska Cavalry.												
	Engagement. (18th–?) and Capture of Federal Troops	FERNANDO, MISS.		400	2000	5th Ohio, 2nd Ill. and 1st Mo. Cavalry	Maj. Henry, F.; Gen. Chambers, C.											Conf'd.
	Occupation of Frederick, Md., by Confederate Forces under General Stuart.																	
	(20th–21st. Engagement	LA FOURCHE CROSSING, (or Thibodeaux)			5000	Detachment 23rd Conn., 176th N. Y., 26th, 42nd and 47th Mass. and 21st Ind. Vols.		8	60	10	240	70						Federal.
June 21	Attack on Confederate Cavalry	UPPERVILLE, VA. (Middleburg)				Cavalry Corps, Army of the Potomac	M.-Gen. Pleasanton, F.; Gen. Stuart, C.	10	K & W 110	100		60				2		Federal.
	Skirmish	LOW CREEK, W. VA.				(Organizations not recorded)												
June 22	Skirmish	HILL'S PLANTATION, MISS.				Portions of 3 Companies, 4th Iowa Cavalry.												
	Attack on Federal Vessels	CYPRESS BEND, MISS.				Federal Gunboats and Steamers												Federal.
June 23	Occupation of Chambersburg, Pa., by Confederate Troops under Gen. Rodes.																	
	(20th–?). Engagement and Capture of Brashear City La., by Confederate Forces	BRASHEAR CITY, LA.				Detachment 176th and 114th N. Y., 23rd Conn., 42nd Mass. and 21st Ind. Volunteers	Gens. Green and Morton, C.						1633			16	7,000	Conf'd.
	(23d–30th.) Campaign from Murfreesboro' to Tullahoma, Tenn., (including Middleton, Hoover's Gap, Beech Grove or Liberty, and Guy's Gap	MURFREESBORO' to TULLAHOMA, TENN.				14th, 20th and 21st Corps, Reserve and Cav. Corps, Army of the Cumberland	M.-Gen. Rosecrans, F.											
	The Federal Gunboat *Sumter* sunk off Cape Henry.																	
June 24	Evacuation of Shippensburg, Pa., by Federal, and Occupation by Confederate Forces	SHIPPENSBURG, PA.																
	Engagement	MIDDLETON, TENN. (Shelbyville)				1st Cav. Div., Army of the Cumberland	Gen. Mitchell, F.; Gen. Wheeler, C.	6	K & W 200	20		829				8		Federal.
	Engagement	HOOVER'S GAP, TENN.				17th and 72nd Ind., 123rd and 98th Ill. Mounted Infantry and 18th Ind. Battery	Col. Wilder, F.; Gen. Bates, C.	K & W 61	100		500							Federal.

CHRONOLOGICAL LIST OF EVENTS (1860-1865).—Continued.

DATE	EVENT.	LOCATION.	DURATION.	FORCE. F.	FORCE. C.	COMPOSITION OF FORCE.	COMMANDERS.	KILLED. F.	KILLED. C.	WOUNDED. F.	WOUNDED. C.	PRISONERS TAKEN BY F.	PRISONERS TAKEN BY C.	MISSING. F.	MISSING. C.	Guns taken	Stands of arms	ADVANTAGE.
1863 June 24	Occupation of McConnellsburg, Pa., by Confederate Forces.					12th Pennsylvania Cavalry.												Conf'd.
	Department of West Virginia constituted, under Brig.-Gen. B. F. Kelley, U. S. A.																	
	Skirmish.	CHAKAFOOLA STATION, LA.		5 Cos		9th Connecticut Volunteers.												
June 25	Skirmish.	BEECH GROVE, TENN.			Inf.	20th Corps, Army of the Cumberland.	Col. Wilder, F.	40										Federal.
	Siege of Vicksburg.	FORT HILL, VICKSBURG, MISS.				General McPherson's Corps.	Gen. McPherson, F.	40		250								Federal.
	Engagement.	LIBERTY GAP, TENN.				Federal Troops.	Gens. Willich, Wilder and Carter, F.; Gen. Cleburn, C.	40		100								Federal.
June 26	(26th-?). Engagement.	SOUTH ANNA, VA.				11th Penn. Cav., 2nd Mass., and 12th Ill. Vols.	Col. Spear, F.	8		8		111						Federal.
	Engagement.	BALTIMORE CROSS ROADS, VA.				4th Corps.	Maj.-Gen. Keyes, F.											
	Evacuation of McConnellsburg, Pa., by Confederate Troops under General Stuart.																	
	Occupation of Frederick, Md., by Federal Cavalry.																	
June 27	Engagement.	FAIRFAX, VA.		1 Sqd	Cav	11th New York Cavalry.	Maj. Remington, F.							80				Conf'd.
	Skirmish.	WALNUT BOTTOM ROAD, PA.				Detachment Pennsylvania Militia.	Capt. Murray, F.			1			10					Conf'd.
	Skirmish.	BEAVER CREEK, KY.				39th Kentucky Volunteers.												
	Occupation of Shelbyville by Federal Forces.	GUY'S GAP AND SHELBYVILLE, TENN.				Cav. Div., and Major-Gen. Granger's Infantry Division, Army of the Cumberland.	Gen. Rosecrans, F.; Gen. Bragg, C.	85		463		1634		13				Federal.
	Evacuation of Carlisle, Pa., by Federal, and occupation by Confederate Forces.	CARLISLE, PA.																
	Occupation of Manchester, Tenn., by Fed. Forces under Gen. Reynolds.																	
June 28	Attack on Federal Forces.	DONALDSONVILLE, LA.				28th Me. Vols. and Convalescents, assisted by Gunboats.	Ad. Farragut, F.; Gen. Green, C.											1 Con. 2 Fed.
	Skirmish.	WRIGHTSVILLE, PA.				Pennsylvania Troops.	Col. Frick, F.											Conf'd.
	Part of Siege of Vicksburg.	FORT HILL, VICKSBURG, MISS.																
	Skirmish.	OYSTER POINT, PA.				71st N. Y. Militia and Miller's Philadelphia Battery.												Conf'd.
	Major-General Meade, U. S. A., assumes command of the Army of the Potomac.																	
	Surrender of Mechanicsburg, Pa., to Confederate Forces.	MECHANICSBURG, PA.																
	Engagement.	HOVER, TENN.	2 hours.			Division, Army of the Cumberland.	Gen. Mitchell, F.			7								Federal.
June 29	Engagement.	MCCONNELLSBURG, PA.		60	Cav. 100	1st New York Cavalry.	Capt. Jones, F.		2	1		95						Federal.
	Engagement.	WESTMINSTER, MD.	20 minutes	95	Cav.	Detachment 1st Delaware Cavalry.	Maj. Knight, F.	2	8	7	15			89				Conf'd.
	Skirmish.	LAKE PROVIDENCE, LA.				(Organizations not recorded.)												
	Evacuation of Wrightsville, Pa., by Confederate Forces.																	
	Columbia, Pa., placed under Martial Law.																	
	Occupation of Hanover and York, Pa., by Federal Forces.																	
June 30	Engagement.	SPORTING HILL, PA.				22nd and 37th N. Y. Militia and Landis's Battery.	Col. Roome, F.		18		20							Federal.
	Engagement.	HANOVER, PA.				3rd Div., Cav. Corps, Army of the Potomac.	Gens. Pleasanton, Custer and Kilpatrick, F.; Gen. Stuart, C.		16		40							Federal.
	Engagement.	BAYOU TENSAS, LA.				Mississippi Brigade of Infantry and Cavalry.	Col. Ellet, F.											
	Baltimore, Md., placed under Martial Law by General Schenck.																	
July 1	Occupation of Tullahoma, Tenn., by Federal Forces.					Advance of Major-Gen. Rosecrans's Army.										8		Federal.
	(1st-3d). Battle.	GETTYSBURG, PA.	Actual 21 hours	70,000 to 80,000	70,000 to 80,000	1st, 2nd, 3rd, 5th, 6th, 11th and 12th Corps, and Cavalry Corps, Army of the Potomac.	M.-Gen. Meade, F.; Gen. Reynolds, F.; Gens. Longstreet and Hill, C.	2834	K. W. & P. [illegible]	[illegible]				6643				Federal.
	(1st-3d). Engagement.	BLACK RIVER, MISS.				Portion of the 17th Corps.												
	(1st-3d). Engagement.	CABIN CREEK, IND. TERRITORY.				3rd Wis., 6th and 9th Kan., 2nd Colorado Cav., 1st Kan. (79th U. S. Colored Troops and 3rd Kansas Indian Home Guards.	Col. Williams, F.; Col. Watie, C.	8	40	15		6						Federal.
	(1st-26th). Morgan's Raid into Kentucky, Ohio and Indiana.																	
	Engagement.	BALTIMORE CROSS ROADS, VA.				Portion of the 4th Corps.	M.-Gen. Keyes, F.; Gen. Getty, F.	5		8								Conf'd.
July 2	Engagement.	ELK RIVER, TENN.				Cavalry, Army of the Cumberland.												
	Expedition of Federal Troops from Newbern, N. C., under General Foster.																	
	Skirmish.	BOTTOM'S BRIDGE, VA.				5th Pennsylvania Cavalry.		3				20						Federal.
	Attack on Federal Troops.	BEVERLY, VA.			1700	10th W. Va. Vols. and Battery G, W. Va. Artillery and 1 Company Cavalry.	Col. Harris, F.; Gen. W. Jackson, C.											Federal.
	(Morgan's Raid).	MARROWBONE, KY. (Burkesville).				1st and 9th Ky. Cav. and 24th Ind. Battery.												
	Evacuation of Suffolk, Va., by Federal Forces.																	
	Skirmish.	SPRINGFIELD LANDING, LA.				2nd Rhode Island Cavalry.												
July 3	Engagement.	FAIRFIELD, PA.			Cav.	6th U. S. Cavalry.	Maj. S. H. Starr, F.; Gens. Robinson and Jones, C.											
	(Morgan's Raid).	COLUMBIA, KY.				1st Ky. and 2nd Ohio Cav. and 45th Ohio Mounted Volunteers.												
July 4	Engagement.	UNIVERSITY PLACE, TENN.			Cav.	9th Kentucky Cavalry.		K. & W. 12	K. & W. 40									Federal.
	(Morgan's Raid).	GREEN RIVER BRIDGE, KY. (Tebb's Bend).	3½ hours.	5 Cos		25th Michigan Volunteers.	Col. Moore, F.; Gen. Morgan, C.	6	50	23	200							Federal.
	(4th-5th). Battle.	BOLTON and BIRDSONG FERRY, BIG BLACK RIVER, MISS.			Rear G'rd.	Federal Troops.	M.-Gen. Sherman, F.; —— Joe Johnson, C.					2000						Federal.

CHRONOLOGICAL LIST OF EVENTS (1860-1865).—Continued.

DATE.	EVENT.	LOCATION.	DURATION.	FORCE.		COMPOSITION OF FORCE.	COMMANDERS.	KILLED.		WOUNDED.		PRISONERS TAKEN BY.		MISSING.		GUNS TAKEN.	STANDS OF ARMS TAKEN.	ADVANTAGE.
				F.	C.			F.	C.	F.	C.	F.	C.	F.	C.			
1863																		
July 4	Surrender. (See May 18th.)	VICKSBURG, MISS.				Federal Army under Gen. Grant.	Gen. Grant, F. / Gen. Pemberton, C.										1	Federal.
	Battle	HELENA, ARK.	9½ hours.		9000	One Div., 16th Corps and Gunboat *Tyler*	M.-Gen. Prentiss, F. / Gens. Marmaduke, Price and Holmes, C.	K&W 830	K&W 1300			1900						Federal.
	Capture of Confederate Train, and Engagement	MONTEREY GAP and SMITHSBURG, MD.				3rd Cavalry Division, Army of the Potomac.	Gen Kilpatrick, F. / Gen. Stuart, C.				200	1700						Federal.
July 5	Engagement.	FAIRFIELD, PA.				Cavalry, Army of the Potomac.												
	Attack on Federal Troops.	LEBANON, KY.	7 hours.	400	Cav. 4000	20th Kentucky Volunteers.	Col. Hanson, F. / Gen. Morgan, C.						300					Conf'd.
July 6	Expedition.	POUND GAP, TENN.				13th Kentucky and 1st Ohio Cavalry	Maj. Brown, F.	1	30	14	30	123						—
	Engagement.	QUAKER BRIDGE, N. C. (Comfort).				9th N. J., 17th, 23rd and 27th Mass., 81st and 158th N. Y. Vols. and Belger's and Angel's Battery	Gen. Heckman, F.											Federal.
	(6th–7). Reconnoissance and Capture of Confederate Troops.	HAGERSTOWN, MD.		1 Co.	1 Co.	Gen. Stahel's Cavalry.	Col. Wynkoop, F.					1Co.						Federal.
	Battle.	WILLIAMSPORT, MD.			Cav.	3rd Cavalry Division, Army of the Potomac.												
	Skirmish	JONES' FORD, BLACK RIVER, MISS.				5th Iowa and 48th Ill. Volunteers												
July 7	(7th–9th). Skirmish.	IUKA, MISS.				10th Missouri and 7th Kansas Cavalry.												
	Reconnoissance.	BOONSBORO', MD.				6th Regular Cavalry.	Capt. G. Challant, F.	6										
	Indian Fight	GRAND PASS, FORT HALLECK, IND. TERR.	3 hours.		Ute Inds.	9th Kansas Volunteers.	Lieuts. Brundler and Williams, F.	1	31		80							Federal.
	Indian Fight	REDWOOD CREEK, CAL.		1 Co		1st Battery, California Mountaineers.												
	Attack by Confederates.	CONVALESCENT CORRAL near CORINTH, MISS.		1 Co.	Cav. 11Cos	39th Iowa Volunteers.	Capt. Loomis, F. / Col. Roddy, C.		2	1			21					Conf'd.
	Skirmish.	HARPER'S FERRY BRIDGE, VA.				Potomac Home Brigade and 1st Mass. Heavy Art.												
July 8	Engagement	BOONSBORO', MD.				Federal Cavalry.	Gen. Buford, F. / Gen. Stuart, C.											Federal.
	(Morgan's Raid).	BRANDENBURG, KY.				Indiana Home Guards.	Gen. Morgan, C.	2					45					Conf'd.
July 9	Surrender	PORT HUDSON, LA.				Army of the Gulf.	Gen. Banks, F. / Gen. Gardner, C.					5000				46	5000	Federal.
	(Morgan's Raid).	CORYDON, MD.	4 hours.			Indiana Home Guards.	Col. Timberley, F. / Gen. Morgan, C.		3		7		200					Conf'd.
	(9th–16th). Siege.	JACKSON, MISS. (Rienzi Bolton Depot, Canton and Clinton).				9th, 13th, 15th and portion of 16th Corps.	Gen. Grant, F.											
July 10	(10th–Sept. 6th).	FORT WAGNER, S. C.				Troops of the Dept. of the South and Fed. Navy	M.-Gen. Gillmore, F. / Adm. Dahlgren, F.											
	Salem, Ind., sacked by Confederate Cavalry under General Morgan.	SALEM, IND.																
	Assault	FORT WAGNER, S. C.	3 hours.			7th Conn., 76th Penn., 9th Me., 3rd N. H., 48th and 100th N. Y. Volunteers	M.-Gen. Gillmore, F. / B.-Gen. Strong, F.											Conf'd.
	Skirmish.	UNION CITY, TENN.				4th Missouri Cavalry.												
	Louisville, Ky., placed under Martial Law.																	
	Skirmish.	BIG CREEK, ARK.				(Organizations not recorded.)												
July 11	Engagement	HAGERSTOWN, MD.			Cav.	Cavalry, Army of the Potomac												Federal.
	Lieut. Sanborn, 1st Regt. of Colored Volunteers, killed at Norfolk, Va., by Dr. Wright.																	
	Destruction of Jefferson Railroad Depot and Bridge, Vienna, Indiana, by Confederate Cavalry under General Morgan.	VIENNA, IND.				Confederate Cavalry	Gen. Morgan, C.											Conf'd.
July 12	Occupation by Federal Forces of	FUNKSTOWN and HAGERSTOWN, MD.				Inf., Cav. and Art. of Army of the Potomac.												
	(Morgan's Raid).	VERNON, IND.		1200		Indiana Minute Men	Col. Lowe, F. / Gen. Morgan, C.											Conf'd.
	Skirmish.	ASHBY GAP, VA.				2nd Massachusetts Cavalry.												
	Occupation of Natchez, Miss., by Federal Troops under General Grant																	
July 13	Capture by Federal Forces of	YAZOO CITY, MISS.		5000		Maj.-Gen. Herron's Division and 3 Gunboats.	M.-Gen. Herron, F. / Admiral Porter, F. / L.-Com. Walker, F.					500				6		Federal.
	Skirmish	JACKSON, TENN.				3rd Mich., 3rd Iowa, 1st Tenn. Cav. and 9th Ill. Cavalry.	Col. Hatch, F.	K&W 13	K&W 175									Federal.
	Occupation of Fort Powhatan, Va., by Federal Fleet and Admiral Lee																	
	Engagement.	DONALDSONVILLE, LA.				Portions of Weitzel's and Grover's Divisions of the 19th Corps.	B.-Gen. Dudley, F. / Col. Morgan, F.	K&W 450								2		Conf'd.
	Bombardment.	WILLIAMSTON, ON THE ROANOKE.				4 Federal Gunboats.	Capt. Flusser, U.S.N.											Federal.
	Draft Riots.	NEW YORK CITY, N. Y.																
July 14	Occupation of Falling Waters, Md., by Federal Troops.					3rd Cavalry Division, Army of the Potomac.	Gen. Kilpatrick, C.	10	K&W 400	25		60				2		Federal.
	(Parties of Federals firing into each other). (Morgan's Raid).	LAWRENCEBURG, O.				105th Indiana Minute Men.												
	Skirmish.	ELK RIVER, TENN.				Advance of the 14th Corps, Army of the Cumberland.	M.-Gn. Thomas, F. / Gen. Buckner, C.											Federal.
July 14	Skirmish.	SHADY SPRING, W. VA.				2nd West Virginia Cavalry.												
	Skirmish.	BOLIVAR'S HEIGHTS, VA.				1st Connecticut Cavalry.												
July 15		PULASKI, ALA.				3rd Ohio and 5th Tennessee Cavalry.												
	Engagement	HALLTOWN, VA.				16th Pennsylvania and 1st Maine Cavalry.						100						Federal.
July 16	Attack on Federal Troops. Evacuation of Jackson, Miss., by Confederate Forces.	JACKSON, MISS.	½ hour		S. C. Trps.	Federal Troops.	Gen. Parke, F.	K, W & M 1000	300	W&P 400								Federal.
	Engagement	SHEPPARDSTOWN, VA.		800		1st, 4th and 16th Penn., 1st Me. and 10th N. Y. Cav.	Col. Gregg, F.	K, W & M 150	K, W & M 75									Conf'd.

CHRONOLOGICAL LIST OF EVENTS (1860-1865).—Continued.

DATE.	EVENT.	LOCATION.	DURATION.	FORCE. F.	FORCE. C.	COMPOSITION OF FORCE.	COMMANDERS.	KILLED. F.	KILLED. C.	WOUNDED. F.	WOUNDED. C.	PRISONERS TAKEN BY F.	PRISONERS TAKEN BY C.	MISSING. F.	MISSING. C.	GUNS TAKEN.	STANDS OF ARMS TAKEN.	ADVANTAGE.
1863. July 16	Attack on Federal Troops	SECESSIONVILLE, S. C.				Brig.-Gen. Terry's Brigade	Brig.-Gen. Terry, F.											Federal.
	Maj.-Gen. Foster, U. S. A., assigned to command of the Department of Virginia, vice Maj.-Gen. Dix, assigned to command of Eastern Department.																	
July 17	Battle	HONEY SPRINGS, ELK CREEK, IND. TERR.	5 hours	250		2nd, 6th and 9th Kan. Cav., 2nd and 3rd Kan. Batteries and 2nd and 3rd Kan. Indian Home Guards	Gen. Blunt, F. / Gen. Cooper, C.	17	180	36	40	60				1	200	Federal.
	Occupation of Huntsville, Ala., by Federal Troops under Maj.-Gen. Stanley.											200						
	Occupation of Corinth, Miss., by advance of Federal Forces under Gen. Hurlbut.																	
July 18	Expedition of Federal Troops under Brig.-Gen. Potter, from Newbern into North Carolina	NEWBERN, N. C.				Federal Troops	Brig.-Gen. Potter, F											
	Action	YATES POINT ON THE POTOMAC			Trps.	Federal Gunboats *Jacob Bell*, *Resolute* and *Teaser* and Mortar-boat *Dan Smith* and Federal Troops												Federal.
		BRANDON, MISS.				Portions of Gen. Sherman's Troops.												
	Indian Fight	RIO HONDO, NEW MEXICO		1 Co.		1st New Mexico Cavalry.												
	(Second assault)	FORT WAGNER, S. C.				54th Mass. (Colored), 6th Conn., 48th and 100th N. Y., 3rd and 7th N. H., 76th Penn., 9th Me., 62nd and 67th Ohio Volunteers	Gen. Gillmore, F. / Gen. Strong, F. / Gen. Beauregard, C.	K. W. & M. 700	500		331							Conf'd.
	Capture and Destruction by Federal Forces of	WYTHEVILLE, W. VA.				34th Ohio Vols. and 1st and 2nd W. Va. Cav.	Col. Toland, F. / Maj. Bowyer, C.	17	15	K. & W. 61		125						Federal.
	Engagement	CANTON, MISS.		2000	5000	2nd Wis., 5th Ill., 3rd and 4th Iowa Cav., 76th Ohio, 25th and 31st Iowa and 3rd, 10th and 17th Mo. Vols. and a Battery of Artillery	Col. Bussey, F. / Col. Wood, F. / Gen. Jackson, C.	K. & W. 20				72						Federal.
	Raid. (18th-21st)	TAR RIVER and ROCKY MOUNT, N. C.				3rd and 12th N. Y. and 1st N. C. Battery	Brig.-Gen. Potter, F	K. W. & M. 25										
July 19	(Capture of Morgan's Raiders)	BUFFINGTON ISLAND, O. (St. George's Creek)				1st, 3rd, 8th, 9th, 11th and 12th Ky., 8th, 9th and 12th Mich., 2nd and 7th Ohio and 5th Ind. Cav., 45th Ohio and 2nd Tenn. Mounted Infantry, Militia and Federal Gunboats	Gen. Shackleford, F. / Col. R. Morgan, C.	K. & W. 30	K. & W. 200			200						Federal.
July 21	Engagement	MANASSAS GAP, VA.				1st, 2nd and 5th U. S. Cavalry, Advance Cavalry, Army of the Potomac.												
	(21st-22d). Engagement	CHESTER GAP, VA.				8th N. Y., 3rd Ind., 12th Ill., Advance Cav., Army of the Potomac.												
July 22	Skirmish	CONCHA'S SPRINGS, NEW MEXICO		1 Co.		New Mexico Cavalry.												
July 23	(24th-5). Engagement	WAPPING HEIGHTS, VA. (Manassas Gap)				3rd Corps, Army of the Potomac	Gen. Spinola, F. / Maj.-Gen. French, F. / Gen. Wright, C.	30		80								Federal.
July 24	Fight with Sioux Indians	BIG MOUND, DAKOTA TERRITORY			1000	1st Minn. Cavalry, 3rd Minn. Battery, 6th, 7th and 10th Minn. Volunteers	Lt. Col. Marshall, F. / Maj. Bradley, F.		35									Federal.
	Attack on Confederate Cavalry	WASHINGTON, OHIO			Guer	Federal Troops	Maj. Krouse, F. / Gen. Morgan, C.											Federal.
	Occupation of Brashear City, La., by Federal Forces.																	
July 25	Capture of Confederate Steamers *Merrimac* and *Lizzie*, by Federal Gunboat *Iroquois*	WILMINGTON, N. C.				Federal Gunboat *Iroquois*												Federal.
July 26	(Surrender of John Morgan, and remainder of his forces)	NEW LISBON, O.			400	Portion of Brig.-Gen. Shackleford's Cavalry	Brig.-Gen. Shackleford, F. / Gen. Morgan, C.					400						Federal.
	Fight with Sioux Indians	DEAD BUFFALO LAKE, DAKOTA TERRITORY				1st Minn. Cavalry, 3rd Minn. Battery, 6th, 7th and 10th Minn. Volunteers.												
	Skirmish	PATTACASSEY CREEK (Mount Tabor Church), N. C.				Troops of the District of North Carolina.												
	Destruction of Smyrna, Fla., by Federal Gunboats and Steamers.																	
July 28	Skirmish	LEXINGTON, TENN.				Federal Forces	Col. Hurst, F. / Col. Campbell, C.					30						Federal.
	Skirmish	MARSHALL, MO.				4th Missouri Militia Cavalry.												
	Attack on Federal Troops	RICHMOND and LEXINGTON, KY.				(Organizations not recorded.)	Col. Sanders, F.											Conf'd.
	Lexington, Ky., placed under Martial Law																	
	Skirmish	COLDWATER, MISS.				Illinois Troops.												
	Fight with Sioux Indians	STONY LAKE, DAKOTA TERRITORY				1st Minn. Cavalry, 3rd Minn. Battery, 6th, 7th and 10th Minn. Volunteers.												
	Skirmish	ST. CATHERINE'S CREEK, MISS.				Detachment 72nd Illinois Volunteers.												
July 29	Attack on Federal Troops	PARIS, KY.	3 hours		2000	(Troops not specified.)	Gen. Pegram, C.											Federal.
	Skirmish	NATCHEZ, MISS.				72nd Illinois Regiment	Capt. James, F. / Gen. Logan, C.					80						Federal.
July 30	Skirmish	IRVINE, ESTILL COUNTY, KY.		2 Sqds.		14th Kentucky Cavalry	Col. Lilly, F. / Col. Scott, C.	4	7	15	16	75	10					Federal
	Attack on Confederate Troops	SALINE COUNTY, MO.		75	63	1st and 4th Missouri Enrolled Militia	Capt. Cannon, F. / Capt. Blunt, C.	2		1								Conf'd.
	Fight with Indians	MISSOURI RIVER, DAKOTA TERRITORY				1st Minn. Cavalry, 3rd Minn. Battery, 6th Minn. Vols.												
July 31	Capture of Stanford, Ky., by Confederates, and re-capture by Federal Cavalry	STANFORD, KY.																
	Capture of the Confederate Steamer *Kate*, by the Federal Gunboat *Iroquois*	CHARLESTON, S. C.				Federal Steamer *Iroquois*												Federal.
	Kentucky placed under Martial Law, by order of General Burnside, U. S. A.																	
Aug. 1	Engagement	RAPPAHANNOCK STATION, VA.			Cav. & Inf.	1st Division of Cavalry	Brig.-Gen. Buford, F	16		124								1 Con. 3 Fed.
Aug.	Capture of 300 Confederates by 4 Cos. of "Lost Children" (N. Y. Volunteers), near Folly Island, Charleston Harbor, S. C.	FOLLY ISLAND, S. C.				N. Y. Volunteers						500						Federal

CHRONOLOGICAL LIST OF EVENTS (1860-1865).—Continued.

DATE.	EVENT.	LOCATION.	DURATION.	FORCE. F.	FORCE. C.	COMPOSITION OF FORCE.	COMMANDERS.	KILLED. F	KILLED. C	WOUNDED. F	WOUNDED. C	PRISONERS TAKEN BY F	PRISONERS TAKEN BY C	MISSING. F	MISSING. C	GUNS TAKEN	STANDS OF ARMS TAKEN	ADVANTAGE.
1863																		
Aug. 3	Engagement	Jackson, La				73rd, 75th and 78th U. S. Colored Troops.												
Aug. 4	Skirmish	Rappahannock Station, Va		Pkts.	Cav.	Federal Cavalry	Gen. Buford, F.	1		2								Federal.
Aug. 5	Attack on Federal Gunboats	Dutch Gap, James River, Va				Federal Gunboats *Commodore Barney* and *Cohasset*	Maj.-Gen. Foster, F.	3										Conf'd.
	Skirmish	Brandy Station, Va				Federal Troops	Gen. Merritt, F.; Col. Davis, F.	1	2	2	1							Federal.
Aug. 6	Disturbance	Visalia, Tulare County, Cal.			Cvls.	Federal Troops		1										
Aug. 7	Skirmish	Waterford, Va				Detachment 1st Conn. and 6th Mich. Cavalry.												
	Skirmish	New Madrid, Mo.		1 Co.		24th Missouri Volunteers.												
Aug. 9	Impressment of one-fifth able-bodied Slaves (to be paid $25 monthly), in S. E. and S. W. Georgia, for erection of fortifications, by order of Brig.-Gen. Mercer.																	
Aug. 9	Engagement	Sparta, Tenn				Cavalry of the Army of the Cumberland.												
	Reconnoissance of Federal Troops from Natchez to Woodville, Miss., under Major Warden	Natchez to Woodville, Miss.				Federal Troops	Maj. Warden, F.											
Aug. 10	Organization of Camps for "freed people of color out of employment at Military Posts within his command," by order of Maj.-Gen. Grant.																	
Aug. 13	Engagement	Granada, Miss				3rd, 4th, 9th and 11th Ill., 3rd Mich. and 2nd Iowa Cav. and 9th Ill. Volunteers.												
	Attack on Federal Camp	Pineville, Mo.				6th Missouri Militia Cavalry	Col. Catherwood, F.; Col. Coffee, C.		K & W 30									Federal
	Reconnoissance by Federal Gunboats, from Clarendon up the White River, Ark., under Captain Bache, U. S. N.																	
	Expedition of Federal Troops under Lieut.-Col. Phillips, from La Grange, Tenn., to Central Mississippi.																	
Aug. 14	Action	West Point, White House, Ark.				Federal Gunboats *Lexington*, *Cricket* and *Mariner* and 32nd Iowa Volunteers.												
	Raid on Telegraph Station, Poolesville, Md., by Confederate Troops.																	
Aug. 15	Citizens in Department of the Cumberland held responsible for Guerilla operations, by order of Maj.-Gen. Rosecrans.																	
Aug. 16	Capture of the Confederate Steamer *Cronstadt* by Federal Gunboat *Rhode Island*, near Abaco	Abaco, N. C.				Federal Gunboat *Rhode Island*.												
	Evacuation of Bridgeport, Ala., by Confederate Forces.																	
Aug. 17	Bombardment of Fort Sumter, commenced by Siege and Naval Shore Batteries, and Federal Monitor Fleet	Fort Sumter, S. C.					Gen. Gillmore, F.; Adm. Dahlgren, F.											
Aug. 18	Skirmish	Pocahontas, Ark.			71	Detachment of Federal Engineers	Lieut. Bross, F.; Col. Street, C.					4						Federal.
	Attack on Federal Cavalry	Pasquotank, N. C.			Guer	1st N. Y. Mounted Rifles and 11th Penn. Cav.	B.-Gen. Onderdonk, F	2	80									Federal.
	Skirmish	Pueblo, Colorado, New Mexico		2 Cos		1st New Mexico Cavalry												
Aug. 21	Massacre by Guerillas (Town sacked and burned)	Lawrence, Kan					—— Quantrell, C.	205	40									Conf'd.
		Coldwater, Miss.				3rd and 4th Iowa and 5th Illinois Cavalry.												
	Bombardment of Chattanooga, Tenn., by Federal Forces		7 hours			Artillery of Major-General Rosecran's Army	Col. Wilder, F.			1								Federal.
	Maj.-Gen. Gillmore, U. S. A., demands the surrender of Fort Sumter.																	
Aug. 22	Fort Sumter reduced to a ruin by Federal Forces. (Not captured.)	Fort Sumter, S. C.																
	Reconnoissance of Federal Cavalry, under Captain Gerry, from Martinsburg to Leetown, Va.																	
	Capture of Federal Gunboats *Satellite* and *Reliance* by Confederate Troops under Lieut.-Commander Wood, C. S. N.	Rappahannock River				Federal Gunboats *Satellite* and *Reliance*	Lt.-Com. Wood, C.											Conf'd.
	Riot at Danville, Illinois	Danville, Ill.																
Aug. 23	Bombardment of Fort Fisher, Wilmington, N. C., by Federal Frigate *Minnesota*	Fort Fisher, N. C.																
Aug. 24	Skirmish	Coyle's Tavern Va.		23	Guer	2nd Mass. Cavalry	Col. Lowell, F.; —— Mosby, C.	2	2	8	4		9					Federal.
	Engagement	King George County, Va.			Cav.	3rd Div. Cav. Corps, Army of the Potomac												
	Descent of Federal Cavalry on	Pocahontas, Ark.			Cav.	Missouri Cavalry	Col. Woodson, F.; Capt. Gentry, F.		4		3	50						Federal.
Aug. 25	Skirmish	Waynesville Mo.				Detachment 5th Missouri Militia Cavalry												
	(25th-30th). Raid	Hardy to Pocahontas County, W. Va.				Federal Cavalry	Gen. Averill, F.	K, W & M 100				80						
	(25th-28th). Evacuation of Brownsville, Ark., by Confederate Forces			5000		Davidson's Cav. Div., Dep't of Missouri (Advance Guard)	Gen. Davidson, F											Federal.
Aug. 26	Engagement	Perryville, Ark.				6th Mo. Militia, 3rd Wis., and 2nd Kansas Cav. and 2nd Ind. Battery	Gen. Barbridge, C.; —— Cabell, C.											Federal.
	Engagement	Rocky Gap, Va. (White Sulphur Springs)	Actual, 12 hours			2nd and 3rd W. Va. and 14th Penn. Cav. and 3rd and 8th W. Va. Volunteers	B.-Gen. Averill, F; Maj.-Gen. Jones, C; Col. Patton, C.	K W & M 200	K & W 200				160			1		Conf'd.
	Capture of Confederate Rifle Pickets	Vinegar Hill, S. C.				Federal Troops	Maj.-Gen. Gillmore, F	10		17								Federal.
Aug. 27	Skirmish	Vicksburg, Miss				5th Heavy Artillery (U. S. Colored Troops.)												
	Skirmish	Clark's Neck, Ky.				20th Kentucky Volunteers.												
	Battle	Bayou Metea, Ark.			Inf. & Cav.	Davidson's Cav. Div., Department of the Missouri	Col. Glover, F.	K & W 43										Federal.
	Engagement	Hanover, Ala				Detachment Col. Wilder's Cavalry			3			1						Federal.
Aug. 29	Skirmish	Bottom's Bridge, Va. (Dry Creek)			Inf. & Cav.	1st N. Y. Mounted Rifles and 5th Penn. Cavalry	Gen. Wistar, F.; Col. Onderdonk, F.; Lieut.-Col. Lewis, F	1	4	1		5						Federal.
Aug. 31	Engagement	Austin, Ark.				Davidson's Cav. Div., Department of the Missouri.												
	Confederate Transport *Sumter* sunk in Charleston Harbor by the guns of Fort Moultrie.																	
Sept. 1	Capture of Fort Smith, Ark., by Federal Forces under General Blunt.																	
	Engagement	Bayou Metea, Ark.				Rice's Division, Department of Kansas.												
	Skirmish	Barbee's Cross Roads, Va		47	Guer	Detachment 6th Ohio Cavalry	Maj. Cryor, F.	3		4			24					Conf'd.

CHRONOLOGICAL LIST OF EVENTS (1860-1865).—Continued in Volume II., Page 395.

Date.	Event.	Location.	Duration.	Force F.	Force C.	Composition of Force.	Commanders.	Killed F.	Killed C.	Wounded F.	Wounded C.	Prisoners Taken by F.	Prisoners Taken by C.	Missing F.	Missing C.	Guns Captured.	Stands of Arms.	Advantage.
1863																		
Sept. 1	Engagement	Devil's Back Bone, Ark. (Fort Smith and Cotton Gap)				1st Ark Vols., 6th Mo. Militia, 2nd Kansas Cav. and 2nd Ind. Battery	Col. Cloud, F.; —— Cabell, C.	2	25	12	40							Federal.
	Engagement	Charleston Harbor, S. C.			Forts	Federal Ironclads				1								
Sept. 2	Occupation of Kingston, Tenn., by Federal Forces under Gen Minty.																	
	Destruction of Federal Gunboats *Satellite* and *Reliance*, by Federal Troops under Gen. Kilpatrick at Port Conway, Va.																	
Sept. 3	(3d-5th). Fight with Indians	White Stone Hill, Dakota Territory		600		2nd Neb., 6th Iowa and 1 Company 7th Iowa Cav.	Brig.-Gen. Sully, F.	20	300	3[illegible]		200						Federal.
Sept. 4	Occupation of Knoxville, Tenn., by Federal Forces under General Burnside.																	
	Bread Riot in Mobile, Alabama.																	
Sept. 5	Engagement	Limestone Station, Tenn.		5 Cos		100th Ohio Volunteers	Lt.-Col. Haynes, F.; Col. Haynes, C.	12	6	20	30		300					Conf'd.
	Engagement	Moorefield, W. Va.		3 Cos.	Cav	1st West Virginia Volunteers	Maj. Stephens, F.; Capt. McNeil, C.											Conf'd.
	Bombardment of Forts Wagner and Gregg, Charleston Harbor					Federal Fleet and Batteries	Adm. Dahlgren, F.; Gen. Gillmore, F.											—
Sept. 6	Engagement	Brandy Station, Va.			Cav	Cavalry, Army of the Potomac	Gen. Custer, F.; Gen. Stuart, C.			1						2		Federal.
	(7th?) Evacuation of Forts Wagner and Gregg, Charleston Harbor, by Confederate Forces											75				21		Federal.
Sept. 7	Bombardment	Fort Moultrie, S. C.				Federal Vessels *Ironsides* and Monitors *Nahant*, *Montauk*, *Patapsco* and *Lehigh*												—
	Skirmish	Bear Skin Lake, Mo.				2nd Missouri Cavalry.												
	Engagement	Ashley's Mills, Ark.				Davidson's Cav. Div., Department of Missouri.												
	Reconnoissance and Skirmish	Atchafalaya River, La.			Pkt.	2nd Brig., 2nd Div., 13th Corps	Maj. Montgomery, F.	1		8								Conf'd.
Sept. 8	Skirmish	Baton Rouge, La.				4th Wisconsin Cavalry												
	Night Attack on Fort Sumter, S. C., by Federal Forces	Fort Sumter, S. C.		413		Federal Marines and Sailors	Com. Stevens, U. S. N.	3				114						Conf'd.
	Evacuation of Chattanooga, Tenn., by Confederate Forces																	
	Attack on Federal Troops	Bath, Va.			200	Detachment 7?th Penn. Cavalry												Federal.
	Capture of Federal Gunboats *Clifton* and *Sachem*	Sabine Pass, La.				Federal Navy, escort to the 19th Corps	Maj.-Gen. Franklin, F.											Conf'd.
Sept. 9	Surrender by Confederate Forces of	Cumberland Gap, Tenn.				Cavalry Division and Army of the Ohio	Gen. Burnside, F.; Gen. Frazer, C.					2000				14		Federal.
	Engagement	Telford, Tenn.	2 hours.	5 Cos	1800	100th Ohio Regiment	Lt.-Col. Hays, F.; —— Jackson, C.	K., W. & P., 300										Conf'd.
	Skirmish	Webber's Falls, Indian Territory				2nd Colorado Cavalry												Federal.
	Attack on Confederate Troops	Dardenelle, Ark.			1000	2nd Kansas Cavalry and 2nd Indiana Battery	Col. Cloud, F.											
	Occupations of Chattanooga, Tenn., by Federal Forces.																	
Sept. 10	Engagement	Graysville, Ga.				Cavalry, Army of the Cumberland.												
	Capture by Federal Forces of	Little Rock, Ark.				Troops of the Department of Arkansas and Cav. Div. of the Department of the Missouri	Gen. Davidson, F.; Gen. Steele, F.; Gen. Price, C.									0		Federal.
	Skirmish	Brimstone Creek, Tenn.			Guer	11th Kentucky Mounted Volunteers	Col. Love, F.; Col. Hamilton, C.				7	2						Federal.
Sept. 11	Engagement	Ringgold, Ga.				Advance of the 21st Corps, Army of the Cumberland	Col. Wilder, F.; Gen. Van Cleve, F.		4	3			18					Federal.
	Skirmishes	Dug Alpine and Stevens's Gap, Ga. (Davis' Cross Roads)				Advance of the Army of the Cumberland.												
	Skirmish	Moorefield, W. Va.				(Troops not mentioned.)												
	Skirmish	Waldron, Ark.				14th Kansas Cavalry.												
Sept. 12	Engagement	Sterling's Plantation, La.				Battery E, 1st Missouri Artillery.												
	Attack on Federal Troops	Texas County, Mo.		1 Co.	Guer. 300	5th Missouri Militia Cavalry	Capt. Whybark, F.		20	3								Federal.
	Engagement	Grant's Pass, Mobile, Ala.			B-at & Frt.	Federal Steamer *Genesee* and Gunboats *Calhoun* and *Jackson*												Federal.
	Engagement	Paris, Tenn.			Guer 110	Detachment of Mo. Cav. and 1 Company Ky. Inf.			6		31	83						Conf'd.
	Cavalry Fight	Culpeper Court House, Va.	4 hours.		Cav.	1st, 2nd and 3rd Div., Cav. Corps, Army of the Potomac	Gen. Kilpatrick, F.; Gen. Lomax, C.; Col. Beale, C.	8		40		40						Federal.
	Engagement	Lett's Tan Yard, Ga.				Wilder's Brigade of Mounted Infantry.												
	Attack on Federal Troops	Salem, Mo.			400	Federal Troops			20									Federal
Sept. 14	(14th-16th). Skirmishes	Brownsville, Ark.				5th Kansas Cavalry.												Federal.
	Skirmishes near	Racoon Ford, Va.			Cav.	Cavalry Corps, Army of the Potomac	Gen. Pleasanton, F.; —Coffee and Brown, C.											Federal.
	(15th-?). Attack on Confederate Troops	Seneca Station, Ind. Territory	2 hours.	800		1st Arkansas Volunteers			5									Federal.
	Skirmishes	Vidalia, La.		30	250	Detachment 30th Missouri Volunteers	Col. Madison, C.	2	6	4	11	2						Federal.
	Engagement	Rapidan Station, Va.		3 Sqd.		1st Maryland Cavalry		1		8		2		3				Federal.
Sept. 16	Engagement	Hendricks, Miss.				10th Missouri Cavalry.												
	Skirmish	Smithfield, Va.	2 hours.	100		Detachment 1st N. Y. and 12th Penn. Cavalry	Capt. Jones, F.; Capt. Bailey, F.; Lieut. Irwin, F.			2		10						Federal
	Proclamation issued by President Lincoln suspending the writ of *Habeas Corpus* in certain cases.																	
Sept. 16	Skirmish	White Plains, Va.				Federal Troops												Federal.
	Confederate Forces attempt to cross the Rapidan River, Va.																	
Sept. 17	Seizure of Steamer *Marcella* by Confederate Guerrillas near Dover Landing, Mo.	Dover Landing, Mo.						8										Conf'd.
Sept. 18	Attack on Federal Troops	Fort Donelson, Tenn.			Guer	83rd Illinois Regiment	—— Gen. Hinson, C.	2										Federal.
Sept. 19	Reconnoissance	Racoon Ford, Va.				1st Cavalry Division, Army of the Potomac.												
	(19th-20th). Battle	Chickamauga, Ga.	Actual 16 hours.	45,000	70,000	14th, 20th, 21st and Reserve Corps, Army of the Cumberland	M.-Gen. Rosecrans, F.; Gen. Bragg, C.	1644	[illegible]	9262				4945		36	8150	Conf'd.

www.ingramcontent.com/pod-product-compliance
Lightning Source LLC
Chambersburg PA
CBHW022058300426
44117CB00007B/502
* 9 7 8 3 3 3 7 1 3 5 5 1 5 *